AMERICAN NATIONAL SECURITY

American National Security

POLICY AND PROCESS

—

Revised Edition

—

AMOS A. JORDAN
WILLIAM J. TAYLOR, JR.

THE JOHNS HOPKINS UNIVERSITY PRESS
Baltimore and London

To ANNE ARMSTRONG, chairman of the CSIS Advisory Board and vice chairman of its executive board.

Her service as chairman of the President's Foreign Intelligence Advisory Board and, earlier, as counselor to the president and as ambassador to the Court of St. James are but highlights in a life dedicated to American values and to the national security policies that sustain them.

Originally published, hardcover and paperback, 1981
Revised edition, paperback, 1984

The Johns Hopkins University Press, Baltimore, Maryland 21218
The Johns Hopkins Press Ltd., London

Library of Congress Cataloging in Publication Data

Jordan, Amos A.
American national security.

Includes bibliographical references and index.
1. United States—National security.   I. Taylor, William J. (William Jesse),
1933—   II. Title.
UA23.J66 1984   355'.033073   83-49194
ISBN 0-8018-3214-4 (pbk.)

CONTENTS

FOREWORD

It is a personal pleasure to be allowed to comment on the revised edition of this textbook on national security policy by an old friend, Amos A. Jordan, and Dr. William J. Taylor, Jr. Their work is a timely reappraisal of the meaning of national security and its requirements for safeguarding our country in the international environment foreseen for the remainder of the century.

The timeliness of the book arises from the growing national concern over the state of our security stimulated by evidence of increasing Soviet military strength and willingness to use it to advance an expansive foreign policy in Africa, Southeast Asia, and the Middle East. The situation is made more ominous by concurrent evidence of our own impotence in dealing with events inimical to American policy in these same regions. Happily, our government is giving signs of intention to redress this imbalance in relative strength by a substantial program to rebuild and improve our military forces despite an unfavorable economic situation at home that discourages any such new undertakings. As this matter is likely to become a national issue, it behooves all citizens to acquire a clear understanding of what our security entails and how we can assure it against the most probable and most dangerous threats that may arise.

Despite the abundance of literature on the subject, I know of no agreed definition of national security. One would expect to find it in the National Security Act of 1947 which, with its amendment, provides the statutory foundation for our military establishment—but not so. The best it offers is an intimation of the scope of national security found in the statement that the function of the National Security Council is "to advise the President with respect to the integration of domestic, foreign and military policies relating to the national security." To the authors of the act, national security had become far more than the protection of our shores and skies from an armed enemy, and the responsibility for it was no longer a monopoly of the military—if it ever had been.

Dr. Jordan and his colleagues give us an explicit definition, entirely in accord with the broad concept that underlies the National Security Act. National security, in their view, is not only the protection of our people and territory from physical assault but also the protection by a variety of means of vital economic and political interests, the loss of which would threaten the vitality and fundamental values of the state. Under this definition, the OPEC oil weapon becomes quite properly as much a matter of concern of national security as the Warsaw Pact forces facing our troops in Western Europe.

To achieve national security of this breadth, the drafters of security policy must first determine the national valuables requiring protection and then identify the threats thereto that have both the greatest damage potential and the highest probability of occurrence. As the richest nation in the world, we have many valuables to safeguard—at home our people, our political institutions, the national economy, and vast reserves of human and natural resources. Abroad, we must be ready to protect thousands of nationals, allies, scores of public and private investments, military forces, bases, and markets. There are also intangible national interests to protect such as the principles of the Bill of Rights and of the United Nations charter, our treaty engagements, a favorable balance of power, freedom of the seas, and our international reputation. The assured security of such a variety of assets and interests is costly not only because of their number and geographical dispersion but also, in many cases, because of their exposure to the hostile actions of unfriendly foreign governments or the consequences of destructive environmental forces.

The exposure to danger of such interests is in many cases the result of physical proximity to the Soviet Union—for example, our interests in Western Europe, the Middle East and Northeastern Asia. In a different way, our economy is exposed to danger as the result of its dependence on imports. To maintain an adequate level of productivity, the economy must have uninterrupted access to raw materials, located mostly in four regions: Latin America, the Middle East, parts of Africa, and the Southwest Pacific. Continuity of trade with these regions will be affected by the consequences of the excessive population growth that plagues the producer countries—scarcities of land, food, water, energy, capital, and foreign exchange. Such conditions induce political instability ranging in form from frequent changes of government to revolution, civil war, and chaos.

With such a future in prospect, our leaders are justified in assuming that the greatest dangers to our valuables will come from three sources: the malevolence of the Soviet Union, the consequences of our dependence on imports, and the turbulent conditions in many regions of the Third World. An adequate security policy must provide the means, military and nonmilitary, to forestall the most likely and dangerous threats that may arise from these sources.

The authors of this text describe at length the many agencies and procedures involved in producing such a policy. Numerous difficulties will always intervene to prevent or delay its formulation. In the light of experience, at least two major obstacles are sure to arise—inadequacy in political guidance as to the likely course of future national policy, and disagreement over the priorities in resources and effort to be accorded the principal threats.

No solution has yet been found for the chronic dearth of political guidance that impedes security planning. Although a president from time to time will give a broad indication of the goals of future foreign policy and of some of the obstacles that he expects to encounter, such guidance is rarely sufficiently specific or timely to meet the needs of effective security planning. We have had a recent example of what may happen when a change in foreign policy exceeds the supportive capabilities of existing military policy.

The Carter Doctrine, enunciated in January 1980, is an example of what can happen when a change in foreign policy exceeds the supportive capabilities of existing military policy. Although our armed forces had long been aware of the increasing importance of Mideast oil to the United States and its allies, they were unprepared for President Carter's order to be ready henceforth to defend the entire Persian Gulf region against any attempt by the Soviets or any other party to gain or exercise control over it. The new mission suddenly assigned to this distant, vaguely defined area a strategic importance comparable to that of Western Europe, and, in so doing, it added a responsibility beyond the means provided the armed forces under current military policy. In short, our foreign policy has adopted an objective out of range of military support—a dangerous imprudence of a kind that, often in past history, has exacted a heavy price from the offending nation.

Even with the best of political guidance, security planners would still face the difficulty of distributing available financial and human resources wisely to meet the competitive needs of several threats at the same time. Ever since the advent of nuclear weapons, this kind of conflict has arisen between the policy planners who would give first priority to the needs of the strategic forces and those who favor the claims of conventional (nonnuclear) forces. On the one hand, the argument has been that a strategic war with the Soviets is by far the most dangerous threat since it might well result in the complete destruction of our country. Hence, an ability to deter or win such a war quickly should be the number one objective of military policy and enjoy an unqualified first priority in the allocation of resources.

The opposing argument is that, although the vast destructive potential of nuclear war is undeniable, that very fact makes its occurrence highly unlikely because of the enormous risks run by both sides. In such a war, there could be no victory if the term denotes, as it should, a situation more favorable to the victor than the one prior to the resort to arms.

In contrast, the argument proceeds, we shall always need conventional forces to deal with numerous but unpredictable minor conflicts and to reinforce foreign policy by a visible strength in being. Our newly acquired dependence on foreign imports creates new tasks for such forces in assuring access to essential markets and keeping open the sea and air lanes. Because of the high probability of such conflicts, we must have ample ready forces of the right kind to deal with them.

The dilemma posed in this debate is whether to favor the most destructive but least probable threat or the most probable threat with a variable damage potential ranging from minor to very great. In the past, the partisans of the strategic forces usually have prevailed, but the growth in importance of the economic factor in international relations may now force greater attention toward the needs of the conventional forces.

The authors have treated thoroughly many of the foregoing points. From their description of policy-making, one is bound to be impressed with the importance of blending effectively the input of many elements of the executive branch in conjunction with parallel activities by key congressional committees. Despite the integrative role performed by the National Security Council, the government still displays great ineptitude in formulating and carrying out multidepartmental programs—witness the prolonged frustration in achieving a national energy program.

In focusing attention on the intricacies of the national security process, let us never lose sight of the predominant role of the president, who is alone responsible for the goals, means, and outcome of all national policy. The complicated procedure described in this text has a single purpose—to assist the president to choose the right goals, adopt the best alternative course of action, achieve the specified aims, and verify the effective execution of his decisions. The national security process can do no more than bring its product to the threshold of the Oval Office where the president takes over and his personal methods replace those of the bureaucracy. While the latter can assist him by orderly staff work and to some extent lighten his burden, in the end he will conduct his business in his own way.

As the authors point out, the inner working of the White House varies with the personality and work habits of its occupant. The duty of his immediate staff is to present to the president the external input, preferably in an orderly way but always in a way compatible with his own work style. Some presidents prefer to acquire information by reading, some by listening, some by a combination of both. All whom I have observed have, without exception, wanted the unadulterated truth—no matter how unpleasant—from their staffs, and have never tolerated "yes men" for long. One quickly concludes that character is by far the most important attribute for occupants of key White House positions, beginning but not ending with the president. As in most endeavors of moment, the human factor in the national security process far transcends in importance all matters of form, organization, or procedure.

In the 1980s, our leaders responsible for national policy-making will be confronted to an increasing degree by the complexities arising from military imbalance, economic interdependence, and the expansive foreign policy of the Soviet Union. The challenges to these leaders in formulating and executing an adequate national security will be formidable. Understanding those challenges and the problems and prospects they create in an increasingly dangerous world is a responsibility of all Americans. This textbook is a useful contribution toward that understanding.

Maxwell D. Taylor

PREFACE

The genesis of this book was the idea from Dr. Frank N. Trager, who observed in 1972 that there was a crying need for a college textbook on U.S. national security. His forecast was that, after the trauma of Vietnam was behind us, there would be renewed interest among the nation's faculties and youth in the study of national and international security. He has, of course, been proven correct. He suggested to two of his friends on the West Point faculty, Amos A. Jordon and William J. Taylor, Jr., that they undertake the task of writing a text. At the time, there were many books on particular aspects of U.S. defense policy and several edited compendia of articles. By their very nature, however, none of them could serve adequately the needs of students at most colleges and universities to gain a basic understanding of the policies and processes involved in American national security. By the end of the decade, nothing had been published that changed the early estimate of the situation.

In 1972 the principal authors completed a detailed outline of 160 pages and drafted the first few chapters. Thereafter, major changes in assignments and responsibilities denied these two the long periods of consistent research and careful attention that a sound textbook requires. Over the intervening years, as the project's completion was delayed, a number of people listed as "Associates" in the first edition contributed significantly to research and writing, as chapters were drafted and redrafted to serve as material for the instruction of West Point cadets and also to capture changes in the international system and the development of new dimensions in national and international security.

Finally, in 1980 the principal authors carved out the major block of time needed for a complete rewriting and updating of the first edition manuscript. This effort was assisted by several in the Department of Social Sciences, U.S. Military Academy, who read, critiqued, and worked in last-minute reserarch. Their contributions are acknowledged in that edition. The penultimate draft was critiqued carefully and most helpfully by one of America's leading soldier-statesmen, General Maxwell D. Taylor, to whom we are deeply indebted for writing the foreword. Various chapters were reviewed and critiqued by several distinguished scholars and practitioners—George Carver, Chester Crocker, William T. R. Fox, Lieutenant General Robert G. Gard, Jr.,

Alexander Haig, Ralph Nurnberger, James Schlesinger, Lieutenant General DeWitt C. Smith, and Admiral Stansfield Turner, among others.

The first edition was a huge success. Feedback to the authors and to the Johns Hopkins University Press was most positive; so were the published reviews of the book.

As we approached this second edition, we solicited written comments from many professors who had used the book in the classroom. We asked for appraisals of strengths and weaknesses and sought guidance on additions or deletions to our coverage. In general, the response indicated that we should stay with our basic approach, updating only as necessary. We have followed that advice.

This second edition has been prepared at the Georgetown University Center for Strategic and International Studies in Washington, D.C., where the coauthors are president and chief executive officer, and chief operating officer, respectively. We are especially indebted to two of our associates at CSIS, George Sinks and John Henshaw, who worked with us many extra hours on this revision. For their unique insights in examining regional chapters, we owe our thanks to Fred Axelgard (Middle East), Robert Downen (Asia), Georges Fauriol (Latin America), and Helen Kitchen (Africa). Lieutenant Colonel Richard H. Sinnreich, CSIS army fellow; Richard Wilcox, CSIS fellow from the U.S. Arms Control and Disarmament Agency; and Reginald J. Brown, CSIS senior associate, were most helpful in providing insights for updating chapters in their areas of expertise.

Finally, we want to acknowledge once again the inspiration and support of Polly Jordan and Louise Taylor, who have shared our dedication to education in the field of national security affairs.

ABBREVIATIONS

ABM	antiballistic missile
ALBM	air-launched ballistic missile
ALCM	air-launched cruise missile
ANZUS	Australia, New Zealand, U.S. (treaty)
ASAT	antisatellite
ASEAN	Association of Southeast Asian Nations
AVF	all-volunteer force
BMD	ballistic missile defense
BNW	battlefield nuclear weapons
C^3	command, control, and communications
CD	civil defense
CENTO	Central Treaty Organization
CIA	Central Intelligence Agency
DCI	Director of Central Intelligence
DIA	Defense Intelligence Agency
DOD	Department of Defense
D.P.R.K.	Democratic People's Republic of Korea (North Korea)
D.R.V.	Democratic Republic of Vietnam (North Vietnam)
EEC	European Economic Community
FBS	forward-based systems
FY	fiscal year
FYDP	Five-Year Defense Program
GAO	Government Accounting Office
GNP	gross national product
HUMINT	human intelligence
ICBM	intercontinental ballistic missile
IG	Interdepartmental Group
INF	intermediate nuclear forces
IRBM	intermediate-range ballistic missile
IRG	Interdepartmental Region Group
JCS	Joint Chiefs of Staff
JFM	Joint Force Memorandum
JSOP	Joint Strategic Objectives Plan

LDC	less developed country
LTB	Limited Test Ban (treaty)
MAD	mutual assured destruction
MARV	multiple-aimed reentry vehicle
MBFR	mutual and balanced force reduction
MFN	most favored nation
MIRV	multiple, independently targetable reentry vehicle
MRBM	medium-range ballistic missile
MRV	multiple reentry vehicle
NATO	North Atlantic Treaty Organization
NORAD	North American Air Defense Command
NPT	Non-Proliferation Treaty
NSA	National Security Agency
NSC	National Security Council
NVA	North Vietnamese army
OAS	Organization of American States
OAU	Organization of African Unity
OECD	Organization of Economic Cooperation and Development
OMB	Office of Management and Budget
ONUC	Organization des Nations Unies dans le Congo (UN Organization in the Congo)
OPEC	Organization of Petroleum Exporting Countries
OSD	Office of the Secretary of Defense
PD	Presidential Directive
PGMs	precision-guided munitions
PPBS	Planning, Programming, Budgeting System
PRC	Policy Review Committee
P.R.C.	People's Republic of China
R&D	research and development
R.O.K.	Republic of Korea (South Korea)
R.V.N.	Republic of Vietnam (South Vietnam)
SAC	Strategic Air Command
SALT	Strategic Arms Limitation Talks
SEATO	Southeast Asia Treaty Organization
SCC	Special Coordination Committee
SIG	Senior Interdepartmental Group
UMT	universal military training
UNFICYP	United Nations Force in Cyprus
WWMCCS	World-Wide Military Command and Control System

NATIONAL SECURITY POLICY:
WHAT IS IT AND HOW HAVE AMERICANS
APPROACHED IT?

The capabilities that together serve as the foundation for a nation's security are always relative to the capabilities of other nations. Thus, an understanding of the elements of national security should begin with an examination of the international context within which a nation's security must be shaped. This setting determines the security problems and prospects that face the nation and also limits the choices available. A small, self-sufficient island-nation faces problems different from those of a landlocked, underdeveloped but re-sourceful nation bordered by both enemies and friends. The internal structure of a nation must also be considered because, for some countries, principal threats may be almost totally internal as different ethnic, cultural, religious, or political groups fight for control of the government. In Part 1 we examine the overall setting within which U.S. national security exists.

U.S. national security policies have been focused upon security within an international system that can be characterized as loosely ordered anarchy.

1

Despite attempts to bring some greater semblance of order to the system, individual nation-states remain the sovereign actors. Each nation pursues its own interests, which may at times conflict with the national interests of another state. While such conflicts need not lead to violence, all too often they do, and Chapter 3 describes and analyzes the ways the United States has tradition-ally dealt with national security challenges. The necessity of dealing with external threats (as opposed to internal ones) has been the dominant preoc-cupation in U.S. national security, but elements of the domestic situation have helped form a distinctly "American" approach to dealing with foreign threats.

Conflict and violence among nations is hardly a new phenomenon, but the means for violent conflict have taken a quantum jump in the twentieth century. The acquisition of nuclear weapons has given individual nations the ability to destroy major parts of the world in a matter of hours. America's brief monopoly on these weapons of destruction produced hope that war could be prevented by mere threat of their use. These hopes, like the American nuclear monopoly, were short-lived. Rather than preclude any resort to force in the settling of conflicts, nuclear weapons may actually have loosened controls on lower levels of violence and created a danger of escalation to nuclear warfare. In the last two chapters of Part 1, we examine the role of force in the nuclear age, America's attempts to deal with perceived threats, and the continued use of force to resolve international conflicts.

1

NATIONAL SECURITY:
THE INTERNATIONAL SETTING

National security, a term that has come into broad usage only since World War II, means widely differing things to different people. Clearly, it signifies protection of the nation's people and territories against physical assault and, in that narrow sense, is roughly equivalent to the traditionally used term, *defense*. National security, however, has a more extensive meaning than protection from physical harm; it also implies protection, through a variety of means, of vital economic and political interests, the loss of which could threaten fundamental values and the vitality of the state.

Helmut Schmidt, former chancellor of the Federal Republic of Germany, expressed one element of this broader meaning of national security in noting that the past few years—which have included the oil crisis, monetary instability, worldwide inflation and unemployment, and other ills—have revealed, in his terms, a new "economic dimension" of national security. "By this," he said, "I mean the necessity to safeguard free trade access to energy supplies and to raw materials, and the need for a monetary system which will help us to reach those targets."[1] The chancellor stressed that this new dimension was an addition to, not a replacement for, the more traditional elements of security such as military balances and arms control.

Broadening the concept of security to include key international economic factors, as Chancellor Schmidt has done, is now widely accepted. Indeed, foreign policy and national security are now seen to broadly overlap. A generation ago this was not the case; one might then have depicted the relationship between foreign policy and national security policy as two slightly overlapping, but largely tangential, spheres (fig. 1.1, left). One sphere was concerned generally with international political, economic, scientific, cultural, and legal relationships, and the other sphere focused primarily on specific features of military policy and the domestic politics of defense forces and budgets. The area of overlap between the two resided largely in alliance

3

FIG. 1.1

politics and coercive diplomacy. Since World War II—especially during the period toward the end of the Cold War and the beginning of détente—the two spheres of foreign policy and national security have drawn closer together (fig. 1.1, right), as strategic arms limitation talks began, political measures to contain East-West competition were launched, and international trade and finance and multinational business became increasingly "linked" with international politics. The suddenness with which the 1973 oil embargo impelled "interdependence" into the consciousness of political leaders and academicians alike has further pushed together the spheres of foreign policy and national security policy.

As noted, there also are important domestic aspects of national security policy, such as defense budgets and personnel policies. Domestic support, political and psychological as well as material, is the bedrock on which any national security policy is built. It is easy to drift from that self-evident statement, however, into a view that dissent from a whole variety of policies poses a threat to national security and hence must be suppressed. One of President Nixon's difficulties with the Congress and the nation at large was precisely his tendency to use the concept of national security too broadly, invoking it as a cloak to cover various unwise or even illegal actions.

Despite such unwarranted domestic extensions of the term, national security does have important domestic elements. These will be focused upon primarily in Part 2, which examines the process and actors involved in national security decision-making. In the remainder of this chapter and the rest of Part 1, we will deal essentially with the international dimensions of national security policy.

Theory and International Politics. If theory were money, political scientists would be the wealthiest people on earth—and not among the *nouveau riche.* Theorizing about politics and power has abounded ever since the first person found reality too complex to grasp in its entirety and experience too limited to explain everything that happened. Members of every society from the hollows of caves to the halls of the White House have had to act upon occasion with a sinking feeling of uncertainty as to where chosen courses of action will lead. Yet they must act on that most basic of theories, namely, that effects do have causes and that changing the latter will necessarily modify the former.

It is from this starting point that empirical theory has grown to its present immense proportions in all fields, national security policy included.

The number of political theories dealing with national security and international politics is so large that it is essential to divide them into broad categories. Stanley Hoffmann suggests a dichotomous arrangement between *systems theory* and *philosophical history*.[2] In the former classification he places theories that are suggested by regularities and patterns in international relations which lead inductively to testable generalizations. This category of theory, closely attuned to empirical methods seeking to identify relationships between causes and effects, is also variously known as the *empirical* or *behavioral* approach.

In philosophical history, Professor Hoffmann places the "grand design" thinkers who, in seeking to unify large masses of historical data, have identified a principal cause or causes of international behavior. This group tends toward greater use of deductive reasoning, and it should come as no surprise that it includes the major ideologues of past and present. This category of theory is also known as the *classical* or *traditional* school.

The third group of growing influence, not identified by Professor Hoffmann, is in the minds of its adherents a synthesis of the best of both. In this company, called the *post-behavioralist* or *contemporary* school, are found those theorists who feel that the wisdom of the traditionalists is often basically valid, though incomplete and needing refinement. To rectify these shortcomings they turn to the methodology of the empirical school, employing its statistical formulations to verify and complete the work of earlier thinkers. In doing so, the post-behavioralists hope to discover both new applications and undetected limitations of established theory.

The most successful theories, measured in terms of acceptability and endurance, are those that best reflect reality. But since reality is different in the faces it presents to people in various times and places, it is no surprise that different theories have coexisted over the years. Furthermore, theories tend to be expressed in broad terms subject to wide interpretation, allowing for applications of a given theory in widely differing ways, some never imagined by the originator.*

Theories centered on power—its acquisition, management, use, and balance—have a particularly wide following. Among proponents of various schools, the late Hans Morgenthau, the primary apostle of the "power approach" to politics, is generally considered a traditionalist.[3] Yet Morton Kaplan, a noted behavioralist, also uses power as the basis for his various systems models, which identify the configurations that the distribution of power can produce in the international system.[4]

Other schools dealing with the general field evade simple classification.

---

*This is not to imply that theorists deliberately seek the safety of rhetorical ambiguity but rather to point up the limitations of language itself and the limitations of authors in using it. Words not only mean different things to different people but also change usage and meaning over time.

There are *man-milieu* theories, which exalt the role of environment in international relations; there are also theories broadly labeled as realist, utopianist, economic, integrationist, decision-making, bargaining, gaming—and more.[5] The breadth of political reality is more than enough to furnish endless speculative frontiers.

Thus it is essential to simplify, to bring the bewildering into comprehensible pieces. This is the first purpose of theory. It is not enough, however, merely to simplify, for people engaged in politics, academia, and business demand more in order to achieve their purposes. As a second goal, then, theory must also help explain reality, demonstrating and clarifying the relationships that occur regularly enough to be identified as norms. This leads to the third and final purpose of theory, namely, to predict.[6]

It becomes clear, then, that the use of theory is fundamental to the subject of national security policy for two reasons. First, students and citizens need help in understanding; there is more happening in one minute in the world than can be grasped directly by anyone in a lifetime. Second, political leaders and elites must comprehend the reality in which they function; they, too, whether they realize it or not, rely upon theory to provide the basis upon which to act. The leaders are handicapped, in one sense, beyond the public or the academic analysts, for they must act within the limits set by their tenure in office, by their security in positions of power, and by events generated by others throughout the international system. Theory in their hands becomes the basis for the reality in which all of us live.

One can easily see how the theories of Locke and Jefferson have consequences for hundreds of millions of people, effects that are vastly different from those that flow from the theories of Marx and Lenin. The potential results are even more awesome when societies guided by such widely differing theories find themselves technically competent to destroy the planet they share.

The Practice of Theory. None of the many international relations or national security theories thus far developed has seen totally consistent application. Moreover, experience dictates continuous revision and refinement of preconceived ideas, as circumstances arise that defy full understanding under existing theories. This experience then becomes the grist for new theory, as well as a critique of the old. Thus, reality and theory are in constant flux and interaction.

The generation that grew up shortly after World War II developed in an international system described by Western analysts as principally *bipolar*. That is to say, the political world was widely seen, and by some still is seen, as divided for all practical purposes into two opposing camps, each camp centered upon one of the superpowers. This simplistic view had great attraction as long as both the United States and Soviet Union were perceived as being unchallengeable, except by each other—with virtually all other major and minor nation-states compelled to seek the protection of one of the giants against the designs of the other.

Reality, however, never was that simple. A considerable number of states, a group that grew over time, chose to go their own way as the "nonaligned" movement. The Soviet camp, where Russia's allies were getting "protective custody" as well as "protection," was never quite so solid as Secretary of State John Foster Dulles, for one, saw it to be.[7] Neither was the Western camp so solid as the exponents of the bipolar theory indicated. Dissent among even our principal European allies existed from the early postwar days. The French were adamantly opposed, first, to the formation of the Federal Republic of Germany and, later, to its rearmament. Britain, which never really recovered from the losses of World War I and the Great Depression, was often unable or unwilling after World War II to support American initiatives outside Europe if they detracted from efforts to hold the crumbling British Empire together.

The "orderliness" suggested by the bipolar theory could have been achieved only through virtual subjugation of all other states by the respective superpowers. But great as their strength has been in some respects, neither has possessed sufficient power to achieve and maintain over time such control—and the United States has been unwilling to use, unrestrainedly, its power for such an end. The result has been that some autonomy always existed for the lesser states, and for the Western allies a great deal.

During the latter 1940s and the 1950s, Yugoslavia and the People's Republic of China demonstrated by their breakaway actions the limits of Soviet power. With this cracking of the Soviet monolith, the further development of the nonaligned states, and the growth of economic strength and political self-confidence among U.S. allies, the bipolar era gradually faded during the course of the latter 1950s and the 1960s.

If changing circumstances have outdated and exposed the imprecision of the bipolar theory, what has replaced it? Some theorists have suggested that the international system has returned to the earlier *balance of power* system wherein not two, but several, great powers compete for the realization of their respective goals. In this pattern, the several major actors, generally three to five, depending upon which theorist is consulted, vie back and forth, forming and reforming alliances to protect themselves against the hegemony of any one or group of the others. Historically, to make such a system work, there has had to be an exceptionally flexible major party willing to shift sides as necessary in order to preserve the balance. The "theory" springs straight from the experience of eighteenth- and nineteenth-century Europe in which England played the swing role. As a political system, the balance of power arrangement broke down in the early twentieth century when England abandoned the balancing role and Europe moved toward bipolarity between the Entente and Triple Alliance powers.

The balance of power design never was truly a world system, since it was largely played out in Europe by what were the major powers of the time. For a number of reasons, it is inapplicable to the modern world. Henry Kissinger has suggested that a contemporary version would include five members, the United States, the U.S.S.R., Japan, Western Europe, and China, but he has neglected the fact that there is as yet no Western Europe in a political or security sense; moreover, his formulation ignores the pervasiveness of ideologies in the current scene, which interfere with the free movement of potential balancers.[8] Also, the technology of modern weapons of mass destruction allows some states, specifically the United States and the U.S.S.R., to deter attack upon themselves with or without allies.

The evident inapplicability of earlier theories has caused some analysts to speculate that the political world of today is neither bipolar nor balance of power in character but is instead "multipolar."[9] According to this view, several states are so powerful that they can largely assure their own survival and independence without the aid of allies and are checked in their adventurism only by caution engendered by the presence of other great or superpowers with whom they must avoid general war or risk utter destruction.

All these various views of the world rely upon some estimation of the distribution of power among the several major political actors of the world. Each view has insights to offer, to a point; each misleads when its proponents attempt universal application. The reality is that the varying levels of autonomy among states, their unequal abilities to influence events around them, and the different and changing priorities of the larger powers dictate that many members of the international community must find their own formulas for survival. This means that, in some regions of the world, reality more closely approximates the balance of power design, such as in Africa. In other places, bipolarity fits better. Central Europe is one such bipolar region, albeit much looser on the Western side than on the Eastern. In the case of a few states, for example, India, Japan, and China, multipolarity is approximated, for on some issues and in some ways they stand apart from most others and can be checked in their policies only by a select few. Finally, there are some situations or cases in which none of the three "power models" helps explain reality.

The Meaning of National Power. A considerable part of the disagreement among analysts of the international scene rests upon the absence of a universally accepted definition of power and the means by which to calculate it. This lack stems in large part from the fact that *power is dynamic.* New instruments of power have appeared continuously over the centuries, and new applications of old forms are always being found. Even the seemingly most backward societies can achieve surprising results under the guidance of strong political leadership, willing and able to engender sacrifice and a sense of purpose among its people. The rapid conquest of the Near East, North Africa, and part of Europe by the relatively few adherents of Islam in the seventh and eighth centuries is a classic case. Thus, too, the Soviet Union was able to rebound within a few years from its near destruction at the hands of Hitler to become the most formidable military and political opponent of the United States. Similarly, West Germany and Japan were resurrected from the ashes of defeat—in Germany's case twice in thirty years—to acquire major economic and political status.

What then is power? In the simplest terms, it is the ability to get others to do something they would not do of their own volition. All too often there is a tendency to think of power solely in coercive terms. Certainly, the ability to inflict physical violence upon an adversary represents an important type of power, but it should be recognized as just one of several and not necessarily the most appropriate or sensible form in many situations. Persuasion, based on common interests and values, and bargaining ability rooted in the possession of some desirable attribute or commodity (oil, perhaps?) and threats are also important forms of power.

Power can be viewed and appraised in several ways. Since it is based upon capabilities, power has certain objective characteristics. But *it also has a highly subjective element*, for the reputation for having and being willing to use power is sufficient to achieve results in many cases, without actually applying it. Hobbes rightly wrote, "Power is what people think it is until tested."

Power is also essentially relative in character, for its utility depends in part on comparing it with whatever opposes it;[10] when this comparison is made explicit, the resulting calculus is often called *net power*. Further, *power is highly situational*; what may generate power in one set of circumstances may not in another. Such intangibles as the political and technical skills of the key actors, national will and solidarity on the issue, the nature of the issue in question, and the purposes being sought, all condition the power a state can bring into play in a given situation.

If power is dynamic, subjective, relative, and situational, as well as objective in character, can it usefully be defined at all? Despite the caveats and difficulties, the answer is "yes." Particularly if we focus on its objective characteristics (which are, more accurately, measures of "strength" and may or may not yield influence, as already noted) and qualify it appropriately for time and circumstances, we can say at least a few things useful about power.

In *Foundations of National Power*, Harold and Margaret Sprout provided an early approximation of the answer to the question, What is national power?[11] They suggested a crude equation thus: power is equal to human resources, plus physical habitat, plus foodstuffs and raw materials, plus tools and skills, plus organization, plus morale and political behavior, plus external conditions and circumstances.

In a subsequent article for the *Journal of Conflict Resolution*, Clifford German added his own arithmetical refinements to the Sprout theory.[12] He suggested that the factors should be weighted—admittedly in arbitrary fashion—before summing. His components of national power were land area, population, national economy, and military power; however, he weighted each of these so as to take into account qualitative factors. Thus, he adjusted actual land area in order to account for population density and for communications facilities; raw population was compressed, then stretched, to take into account age distribution, morale, productivity, and so on. To these square miles and square heads was added a third figure—largely constructed out of industrial production data on steel, coal, oil, and the like—to account for economic strength. If the nation acquired nuclear weapons, everything up to this point was doubled. Finally, a multiple of the country's military personnel was added and a grand total obtained.

Recently, a similar, but more sophisticated, approach to "world power assessment" by Ray Cline has used essentially the same quantitative factors as Sprout and German, weighted and manipulated more ingeniously.[13] Cline's approach has improved upon the earlier efforts by multiplying the sum of various quantitative measures by a qualitatively defined factor compounded of "strategic purpose" and "national will." The resulting product, "perceived power," has again been expressed as a number—apparently hard and suitable for comparative use but in reality as ambiguous and subjective as the numerous judgments that went into its compilation.

As a final example of this approach, the Communist formulation of power, associated with *the doctrine of the "correlation of forces,"* deserves special attention. This Leninist concept contains the notion that a nation's "force" consists not only of its political, economic, and military strengths but also of the cohesion and loyalty of its people and the will and strategic vision of its leaders. *In contrast to the other formulations we have examined, this one is intended to have direct operational consequences; a true Marxist-Leninist is obliged to try to exploit every favorable balance or "correlation of forces."*

It is apparent from all the foregoing formulas that assessing national power is an art, not a science, and that any specific assessment will be open to a variety of challenges. National security analysts in and out of public office are inescapably faced with the task of identifying a moving and ill-defined target and of counting that which has often yet to be accurately measured. Still, policy-makers in Washington and the rest of the world must act, however scant and unreliable their information may be.

Practical Assessments of Power. When decision-makers actually set out to assess power they invariably do so in specific contexts; that is, they engage not in some general, theoretical exercise but in a specific, situational analysis: *who* is involved, over *what issue, where, why,* and *when.*

Taking each of these questions in turn, the *who* element is crucial. Not only are not all states equal in the quantity of resources over which they exercise dominion, but the quality of resources also differs among societies, even if the nations are roughly equal on the basis of quantitative data. This is where the intangibles mentioned earlier hold sway. Health, education, motivation, and other factors all confound attempts to establish reliable equivalency ratios across national boundaries. Hence, Nazi Germany, while occupying most of the European Continent and assaulting the British at home and in North Africa, still came close to crushing the Soviet Union. In fact, the Russian themselves had been set reeling by the "weak" Finns only a few years earlier. Even today, Israel manages to more than hold its own against adversaries many times its size. The conclusion is that while no government can make something from nothing, clearly some can and do make much more with equal or lesser amounts of similar resources.

Making the most of available resources entails having organizational and managerial talents that enhance efficient operation, technical and scientific skills that maximize the use of resources and generate substitutes for resources in short supply and, perhaps most important, leadership that is able to call up and orchestrate the other elements by instilling in its people the willingness to struggle and carry on, even in the face of imminent disaster.

This leads to the second element of situational analysis, namely, the *issue*. Its significance lies largely in the support or lack thereof given to national leaders over a particular matter. All governments depend upon at least the passive support of their citizens in order to function, and none can expect to endure once it has lost that minimum loyalty embodied in the term *legitimacy*. As long as a government satisfies the minimum expectations of the politically active or potentially active members of its society, there is little chance of internal upheaval.[14]

Mobilizing resources to apply to national security tasks requires more than passive support, however; it invariably necessitates some degree of sacrifice and active involvement. For some issues, such support may be difficult to muster; others have almost an electrifying effect upon a nation's consciousness, eliciting enormous willingness to sacrifice. The attack of Pearl Harbor in 1941 had such an effect upon the American people. The morass of Vietnam elicited no such support, even at the outset, and gradually generated quite the opposite. Between these extremes of support and dissent lie most national security policy issues faced by decision-makers. Under such circumstances, the leaders must themselves build support for those tasks they believe important—or resign themselves to impotence.

The third situational feature of power to be examined is geographic, *where*. All states are capable of making some sort of "splash" somewhere in the pool of world politics, normally in their own immediate areas. Some countries, of course, make a more pronounced splash than others and, through ripples moving outward from the center, make their presence felt throughout a larger portion of the pool. No matter how large a given "splash" may be, its effects tend to dissipate with distance from the source. This latter phenomenon can be termed *the limited projectability of power*. The ability to apply resources at a distance sufficient to overcome resistance generated by those closer to the conflict area has always characterized great powers; it continues to provide a useful test by which to appraise claimants to that status. The states wealthiest in terms of the currency of power not only make the largest waves but are able to make them felt at great distances, regardless of countercurrents generated in opposition. Thus, certain actors and groups of national actors can be placed, *at specific points in time*, in a rough rank order of influence ability, or power. (The phenomenon of proxy states, which will be discussed in Chapter 2, complicates the issue, but we shall ignore that for now.)

This introduces the final situational feature of power, namely, *time*. The interplay of leaders' ambitions and creativity, changes in resource base, the momentum of technology, and the public response to challenge all work to effect a redistribution of global power over the years. Empires acquired to the great satisfaction of their builders have overtaxed the abilities of their leaders to maintain them, resulting not only in the loss of domain but in the collapse of the founding unit as well. Both ancient and modern empires illustrate this phenomenon. Similarly, the piecemeal application of resources to what appears at each step a short-term goal may ultimately produce a long-term drain that adversely affects areas of national life not originally thought vulnerable by the planners. The effects of the Vietnam experience on the American economy, morale, and national will are indicative. Seldom, if ever, in history—short of military catastrophe—has a power shift occurred more rapidly and decisively than in the decade after 1965, during which the United States slipped from world predominance to shaky parity with the Soviet Union.

Application of Power. Power for its own sake can be likened to money in the hands of a miser; it may delight its owner but is of little consequence to the world since it is applied to no useful purpose.[15] The American experience between the two world wars in many ways resembles such a situation. In profound isolation, the United States forfeited the initiative in world affairs to other states, principally to the traditional European powers and Japan. The reputation of the United States as a significant military power, established in the Spanish-American and First World War, plus the geographic advantage of the oceans served to protect the nation and its interests during this period. But reputation is a fleeting thing, especially for great powers that are identified in their own time with the existing world order. Steamship and bomber technology partially overcame the barrier of the oceans, while a foreign policy of isolationism eroded the American military reputation. Pearl Harbor and four very expensive years of war were the result of ignoring the uses of power.

All international actors, be they states, alliances, international organizations, or any of several other types of institutions that transcend national boundaries, have control over certain resources that provide them a power base. The power available to each participant will be applied by each in its own way to advance or maintain its purposes and goals; and, in the absence of a universal willingness to compromise on all issues, conflict between and among these actors is inevitable. Thus power and the will to use it become the prerequisite for success, even survival. This is the essence of power politics.

The purpose of power is to overcome resistance in an effort to bring about a new or preferred order of things. When the resistance is generated by other human beings, the purpose of power is to persuade those others to accept the designs or preferences in question or to destroy their ability to offer continued resistance. Reserving to themselves the right to judge what type of application is appropriate in each case, national decision-makers use the power at their disposal in order to achieve the national (or personal) goals they have chosen to pursue. Depending upon the importance attached to the goal, the capabilities available to the respective protagonists, the skills they possess in applying those capabilities, the vulnerabilities each has in other areas upon which the opposition may capitalize, and the history of conflict behavior between them, the techniques of persuasion take either of two principal forms: rewards or punishments.

Rewards themselves are of two types: the presentation of some positive benefit in exchange for the desired reaction or the willingness to forego some negative behavior in exchange for compliance. Threats in this context are considered part of the reward approach to persuasion for the simple reason that unless and until the threatening actor delivers on its threat, no actual harm has occurred. Either type of reward will work as long as all parties concerned feel they are getting something worthy of the exchange or are minimizing their losses in a situation where all the alternatives appear worse.

History is replete with examples of both types of rewards, and both are demonstrated by contemporary events. The 1978 treaty between the United States and Panama over the canal, for example, shows elements of both.

Negative rewards, as already suggested, are the threat or promise not to take away or withhold something of recognized value. By contrast, when nations in a dispute decide to carry out a threat, or initiate negative action without prior threat, they are seeking to persuade through punishment or coercion. Clearly, such persuasion works only if the actor being punished can avert its predicament by compliance. Therefore, the threatened punishment and timing and point of application must be chosen carefully in order to achieve the desired effect. To punish indiscriminately not only squanders resources, driving up costs, but also may be counterproductive in that it antagonizes and sharpens resistance by forcing a change in the perception of stakes.

Of the several schools of theory mentioned earlier, that which calls itself the realist school is more concerned in its central assumptions with the nature and use of power than the others. It is an old and traditional line of thought which boasts many notable contributors: Machiavelli, Hamilton, Napoleon, Bismarck, Lenin, Morgenthau, and Kissinger, among others. Interestingly enough, many of these theorists were also holders of considerable power in their own day. What ties them together, across time and distance, are shared perceptions of the role of power in politics. From their thoughts and behavior the following "realpolitik" postulates can be drawn.

1. Power is amoral, lacking in distinction between right and wrong. It can serve good or bad ends. Each actor, insofar as it is able, sits as judge in its own case.

2. The overriding common goal of all nations is self-preservation. All other goals and ambitions are contingent upon survival.
3. Each actor is ultimately responsible for its own survival. Pledges, promises, and good will notwithstanding, no actor can surrender its fate to another and remain even a theoretical equal.
4. Applied power (or the evident ability and willingness to apply power) is the chief determinant in relations among nations. Unwillingness to act invites others to take command of a situation.[16]

Naturally, if one accepts these precepts as true, one becomes predisposed to act in certain ways: first, because it is assumed to be the correct way to behave and, second, because it is expected that other actors will behave that way. Charity or readiness to come more than half way, the realists contend with a good amount of historical support, will always be construed as weakness to be exploited by those ready and able to do so.

Alternative Approaches to National Security. Since power is widely distributed among the world's many actors and is of limited projectability, none of the participants is entirely self-sufficient; none is perfectly capable of fully satisfying its national security needs. Therefore, at one time or another, all have found it necessary to resort to one of several devices or approaches to compensate for national inadequacies. Principal among these are collective security, alliances and coalitions, and international law.

Collective Security. Collective security arrangements on a global basis, as embodied in the League of Nations and the United Nations, advance the hope that peace can be preserved if all states are prepared to unite in opposition to aggression. Under such an approach, an attack upon one member is taken as an attack upon all, with the expectation that such a united opposition would deter any would-be aggressor. In order for the concept to work, however, this design must have the unconditional support of all or virtually all the major power holders in the system and this, in turn, is contingent upon their satisfaction with the status quo—or their agreement on its replacement. This never has been, nor is it now, the case. The result is that collective security in any universal sense does not now exist, nor does it seem likely to come to exist, given the sovereign state system and the inequalities within it. This does not mean, however, that all attempts at security cooperation are doomed at their inception; what it does mean is that the dreams of some have outpaced the ability or willingness to sacrifice necessary to achieve those goals.

As interdependence takes shape in its multiple political, economic, and other forms, national leaders are increasingly recognizing that closer cooperation is mandatory for both the economic welfare and national security of their polities. Industrialized nations recognize their dependence upon the raw materials of the developing nations; for their part, developing nations recognize the need to import the technologies of the developed nations. All nations recognize the importance of a stable international monetary system, which depends in large part upon multilateral cooperation and restraint. International sharing of the resources of the high seas and multilateral efforts to meet worldwide environmental pollution have also become important targets. These mutual interests not only hold the promise of adding significantly to international political stability but also of reinforcing the bases for collective security. Both interdependence and collective security are discussed in some detail in subsequent chapters.

Alliances and Coalitions. Because global approaches have thus far failed to find the universal consensus needed to support them, most states have found it necessary to seek the help and cooperation of one or a few other actors in satisfying their security needs. The principal reason is, of course, that the cooperative approach is a practical, useful one. Alliances and coalitions come to exist for very specific and defined purposes, which permit their few members to pursue a wide variety of other interests without disturbing the basis for the arrangement. Thus, strains between the participants are less likely to occur than in a collective security pact, where all are supposedly allied in the preservation of an order that inevitably favors some more than others. Chapter 21 examines the topic of alliances in detail.

International Law. This third major approach to coping with national security problems is often dismissed as being without real effect in regulating the affairs of nations. This erroneous view can be attributed in part to a failure to understand the development and purpose of law. Law exists not only to improve the distribution of justice but also to make life predictable by providing all who live under the law with a code of expectations regarding the behavior of others in the system. In more developed societies, if that code is violated, the wronged party can seek redress through authorities whose chief function is to enforce the rules. This is *mature* law.

There is another type, called *primitive* law, which derives its name from primitive societies that have not yet developed centralized administrative procedures including law enforcement structures. Within such a system, the members accept certain practices as customary among themselves and thereby achieve the benefit of predictability. Certain things are done under certain circumstances because they have always been done that way, or because they were agreed upon in advance by the parties concerned. In the event, however, that the custom is broken or the agreement ignored by a member of such a society, the aggrieved party has no police officer or court upon which to call for satisfaction. The only recourse is self-help—to enforce the rule oneself, to seek the help of others in doing so, or to gain compensation or revenge by reneging in some other area involving the wrongdoer.[17]

The outline of primitive law describes the level of development of international law, which is also unenforceable and made up of both *customary and treaty* elements. *The former are those norms of behavior that have general acceptance* among most states, while *the latter establish specific obligations and responsibilities* between and among those governments that agree to be bound by them. In neither case is the commitment inflexible, and states continue to violate both types as suits their needs. The decision to do so, however, is made with care, since the violator may find itself called upon to enforce its choice over the objections of others, which returns us to the topic of power.

The student of national security affairs must recognize these central distinctions between national law in developed societies and international law if he or she is to avoid the error of assuming pure anarchy in world affairs. International law has an important effect upon global politics because it provides the framework for most of the political traffic among states. The secret of its usefulness is not in forming rules that cannot be enforced but in achieving a consensus among states to observe certain practices because to do so is in their overall best interests.

All three of these approaches—collective security, alliances, and law—have been tried by states at one time or another to meet their perceived security needs or as means to advance national goals. Each approach can count both successes and failures in avoiding armed conflict. One principal reason for this mixed record is that it is not generally peace but security that governments pursue in the conduct of their affairs—security to assure survival and to realize the betterment of the societies they represent.

Change and Challenge. This brings us to the final theme of this introduction: major trends and issues that dominate the contemporary international political scene and powerfully influence the quest for national security. Some of these themes—nationalism, ideology, and inequality—have been around a long time. Other trends, such as interdependence, are new or are new presentations of older concerns that have been magnified or accelerated by technology and rapid growth. We have grouped these trends into four "revolutions," both for the changes they have already occasioned and for the potential they have to affect further massive change.

Human Revolution. Largely as a result of the breakup of colonial empires and of increased communications after World War II, a human revolution has taken shape in the mobilization of hitherto passive masses, particularly in Asian and African states.[18] "Nationalism" in these countries was initially the political expression of an intense anticolonialism, which sought to rejuvenate traditional values and cultures suppressed by colonial powers. It also was, in some instances, the expression of an identity that came to being as an outgrowth of colonialism wherein the administration of the conqueror provided the first semblance of unity for diverse peoples. A major consequence of anticolonial nationalism was to shift the focus of the masses from traditional loyalties involving family, tribe, and village to national government and to create expectations about that government.

Newly mobilized publics expect to share quickly the benefits so long enjoyed by their colonial masters. A new nation's government is therefore confronted with rather extreme alternatives: (1) quickly close the gap between expectations and reality, (2) find a scapegoat for the gap, or (3) violently suppress dissent. Often elements of all three are employed simultaneously.

Meeting expectations through economic development programs is fraught with many economic and political difficulties. Yet failure to close the expectation-reality gap or to provide hope that it will soon close can threaten the fledgling government with a new revolution or coup d'etat. In an attempt to buy time or to assert control over additional resources, the new elites may choose the scapegoat route.

Scapegoats may be domestic or foreign, but it is not uncommon to find both being utilized. The Nazi regime did quite well with antisemitism at home and international communism abroad in explaining away the plight of the German people prior to 1939. Stalin was plagued by capitalists, saboteurs, and counterrevolutionaries in need of shooting, and Idi Amin was surrounded by white, Asian, and tribal traitors who failed to appreciate all he did for Uganda. But whichever scapegoat is used, the primary preoccupation is to satisfy popular expectations and quell dissent. The principal focus is inward.[19]

The forceful suppression of dissent as well as the use of the more subtle techniques of censorship and propagandizing have become standard practices in many states, old and newly emerging. Overburdened with massive social problems and hindered in finding remedies by insufficient managerial and material resources, new rulers are often tempted to resort to coercion with a fine disregard for those "human rights" that helped fire the nationalist revolutions. Repression requires organized force in the form of armies and auxiliaries. That same military structure also provides defense against regional enemies and serves as an important national symbol for a regime still struggling to establish its identity and legitimacy. For all these reasons, the newly emerged states have shown an enormous appetite for weapons.[20] For their own purposes, ranging from political competition to balance-of-payments problems, the industrial suppliers have been prepared to feed that hunger. The result is that the world has never been so well armed as it is today.

Nor is the human revolution played out. As the population of the planet continues to climb, expectations seem to grow even faster; as material resources become more strained and costly, the legitimacy of even longstanding regimes will be tested. Disadvantaged elements in mature states also are increasingly demanding a larger share of resources and more voice in their distribution. Inability of governments to cope and violent fragmentation may be the waves of the future.[21] The quality of political leadership will be the deciding factor.

Ideological Revolution. Ideological cleavages between societies die hard.

In the case of East-West confrontation, the intensity had, however, somewhat abated in the 1960s and 1970s from the level of the late 1940s and the 1950s As nuclear arsenals grew, and particularly after the Cuban Missile Crisis of 1962, leaders in both the United States and the Soviet Union saw catastrophic dangers in the deterioration of ideological competition into military confrontation. Moreover, it became apparent to all in the 1960s that ideological allies could disagree in terms of the traditional political concerns of national governments. Thus, China, in conflict with Russia over mutual borders and over leadership of the Third World, could refer to the "revisionism" of the Soviet "paper tiger," and the Soviets could refer to China's "irresponsible" conduct in foreign affairs. By the same process, France could withdraw from NATO military coordination, asserting that the only meaningful defense was truly national defense. As a related point, both the Soviet Union and the United States learned that the claims of ideological allies often raised unwanted responsibilities and sometimes generated greater costs than benefits. Finally, both the Soviet Union and the United States became increasingly aware of the advantages of cooperation in various fields. The Soviet Union needed the technology and agricultural surplus of the West and appeared to be willing to make limited political gestures for them. The United States, caught between the tremendous cost of high military preparedness and expensive domestic programs, sought East-West detente as a means of reducing both the dangers of military confrontation and large military expenditures.

The significance of the muting of East-West ideolgical differences was not that the danger of nuclear war between the Soviet Union and the United States has disappeared or will disappear but that divergent philosophies need not themselves drive the two societies toward conflict. Most knowledgeable observers in the West accept this idea. Whether the Soviet leaders have fully accepted this line of reasoning is a key question.

Further tempering the East-West cleavage has been the birth of what one might call "functional ideologies," which are shared by increasing numbers of people around the world and which respect no state boundaries—though they are clearly more important in the West than in the East. Functional ideologies are founded in the widespread perception of common problems facing all people, regardless of nationality. Examples of such mass perceptions that tended to have the driving force of ideology from the late 1960s on are the antiwar movements in most of the Western democracies and the environmentalist movement to bridle national and international pollution.

The foregoing observations do not lead to the conclusion that political ideology is dead as a divisive force in international politics among the industrialized states of the East and West. Even during the heyday of detente in the 1970s, the Soviet leaders continued to proclaim the irreconcilability of the communist and capitalist camps. On the Western side, by the end of the 1970s, many had come to perceive that the East had exploited detente in Africa, the Middle East, and elsewhere at the expense of Western interests. Indeed, Ronald Reagan made this exploitation and traditional American suspicion of "godless communism" central themes in his successful bid for the presidency in 1980. This hard line about the evils of the East continued on into the 1980s.

In addition to this resurgence of East-West tension are the ideological cleavages between the less-developed "have not" nations of the Southern Hemisphere and the industrialized "have" countries of the Northern Hemisphere. While there has been no common ideology with sufficient force to unite the nations of the South, most of them share a common background and hatred of colonial exploitation of human and material resources. By and large, these states are major suppliers of resources vital to production in the industrialized nations of the North and, therefore, theoretically have a power base from which to press demands. The successes of OPEC with oil and Brazil with coffee have inspired other attempts at cartelizing resources for the purpose of gaining economic and political advantage—thus far unsuccessfully. The purpose of the international commodity organizations that have been formed has been, for the most part, to facilitate the exchange of technical and scientific data, the expansion of trade, and most recently production and pricing arrangements. This development may yet give new economic power to producers ("scarcity politics") but that remains to be seen. However, this new threat to industrial consumers has to a degree been offset by the current tendency for such associations to include both producers as reliable sources of materials and consumers as reliable markets for resource exports.[22]

Technological Revolution. Technological development carries with it forces for both international stability and instability. Which impact occurs at any point in time will depend upon the ability of people to assimilate the products of technology and to adjust to the changes it generates. Assimilation has been increasingly difficult, for the rate of technological development staggers the imagination. One astute observer at the beginning of the 1970s noted the astonishing pace of change, as follows:

In the brief lifetime of protesting youth today, we have had four major epochs—the atomic age, the computer age, the space age, and the bioengineering age, or DNA age. Each of them is as significant as the Bronze Age, the Iron Age, the Renaissance, or the Industrial Revolution, and all have been telescoped into the postwar years.[23]

The communications and transportation revolutions have made it possible to contact any part of the world in minutes and to travel to any part of the world in hours. The arena of diplomacy has quickly and dramatically been collapsed. Political decisions may be communicated instantaneously from heads of state to resident ambassadors (reducing their discretion), as well as between heads of state.

Political differences among states can be sharpened more quickly; so, too, can mutual interests. Yet, the ability to communicate decisions more quickly tends to reduce the time available for making decisions. "Muddling through," or letting difficult situations resolve themselves over time, becomes a less and less viable course.

Communications and transportation also have impacted significantly upon political mobilization of the masses. Increased contacts with the developed nations, through the news media and the travels of businessmen, have helped shape the expectations of the masses in the developing nations while, at the same time, the populations of the developed nations have become more aware of the directions of their governments' public policies at home and abroad—including their policies toward the developing nations. The communications revolution has also provided more sophisticated techniques for propaganda and psychological warfare.

In the short space of thirty years technology has yielded the nuclear means of destroying in a matter of hours civilizations that have evolved from the beginning of time. Yet nuclear energy may hold the solution to one of industrial society's most critical problems—finding alternatives to the dwindling supplies of fossil fuels, energy sources that increasingly pollute the world environment. The danger of proliferation of nuclear weapons compounds the problem of finding ways to use the power of the atom constructively. It is largely the realization of this dilemma that has led the superpowers to a degree of cooperation in seeking means of controlling nuclear arms between themselves and of preventing the spread of nuclear weapons to others.

The total impact of the post-World War II technological revolution cannot yet be assessed, but it is clear that the revolution has both simplified and complicated international politics. Technology creates an awareness of existing problems and leads to a complex of new problems, but it also provides capabilities to solve many of these problems. It can both exacerbate and ameliorate the problems of international cooperation. Thus, the technology that produced intercontinental missile delivery systems also provided the scientific underpinning of space exploration, which served into the 1970s primarily as an arena of peaceful competition and cooperation between the United States and the Soviet Union.

The impact of technology has put social institutions everywhere in a state of flux. Part of the American experience with the technological revolution was summarized in 1973 by an American scholar.

Fewer decisions of social policy seemed to be Whether or Not, as more became decisions of How-Fast-and-When. Was it possible even to slow the pace, to hold back the momentum—of packaging, of automobile production, of communications, of image-making, of university expansion, of highway construction, of population growth?

This new climate of negative decision, this new unfreedom of omnipotence was confirmed by forces outside the industrial machinery. For the atomic bomb along with space adventure and a thousand lesser daily demonstrations—the automobile and the airplane, radio and television, computer technology and automation, or the myriad products of Research and Development—were showing that the "advance" of science and technology, whether guided or vagrant, would control the daily lives of Americans. Not legislation or the wisdom of statesmen but something else determined the future. And of all things on earth the growth of knowledge remained still the most spontaneous and unpredictable.[24]

The real challenge of technology for the international political system is not more technological progress but finding politically compatible means of harnessing technological progress to serve the common interest of humanity.

Institutional Revolution. By definition, "international politics" refers to the political relations among "nations" (or synonymously, "nation-states" or "states"). In describing the contemporary setting of international politics, we have referred primarily to the principal actors, i.e., states, in the international system. Yet since World War II there have appeared so many new "actors" to be taken into consideration in the political system that one can refer to an "institutional revolution." These other actors are international organizations and transnational organizations.

International organizations can be categorized as *universal* or *regional*. Universal international organizations are described by the nature of the matters falling within their purview.[25] Those organizations with general competence to consider all aspects of the international system have been few, i.e., the League of Nations and the UN. Those with competence to deal with specific functions are many, represented by the fourteen so-called specialized agencies (e.g., the Universal Postal Union, the International Monetary Fund, and International Civil Aviation Organization), which have emerged as the international community's functional response to the new social, technical, economic, and humanitarian requirements of modern interrelated societies.

Regional international organizations have grown as a response to communities of interest smaller than the scope of any world community of interest. Regional actors can be categorized as general or specialized. Two regional organizations with general competence to consider a broad range of matters are the Organization of American States and the Organization of African Unity. Specialized regional organizations have a narrower focus on economic, social, or technical matters. Examples are the Organization of Economic Cooperation and Development, made up of nineteen European states plus Australia, New Zealand, Canada, the United States, and Japan. Another is the Council for Mutual Economic Assistance, consisting of the Soviet Union, Vietnam, Cuba, Mongolia, and the communist states of Eastern Europe.

International organizations had their greatest growth at the end of World War II, but they continue to proliferate. Their founding was and is based upon agreement among sovereign national actors, arising from shared or traded interests. This base constitutes an inherent limitation on the effectiveness of both general and specialized international organizations, especially the former. With rare exceptions, nation-states will not yet diminish their sovereignty by relinquishing decisions on important national interests to any "higher" authority.

A relatively new addition to the international system is the *transnational* organization. It is, in both organization and function, very different from international organizations. Several important contrasts distinguish the two systems.

- International organizations are based upon shared interests among nations; a transnational organization has its own interests in many nations, which may or may not be closely related to particular national interests.
- Nations operate in international organizations; transnational organizations operate within nations.
- International organizations recognize explicitly the principle of nationality; transnational organizations seek to ignore it.
- International organizations are internationally managed; transnational organizations may be managed nationally, internationally, privately, or governmentally.[26]

Examples of transnational organizations are the Universal Postal Union, the Chase Manhattan Bank, the Ford Foundation, the General Motors Corporation, the International Television Satellite Corporation, and the Catholic Church. These organizations are transnational in the sense that each is centrally directed organization with large-scale operations in the territory of two or more nation-states.

Transnationalism could become highly significant for world politics in the future as both nationalism and internationalism encounter barriers. True, nationalism has shaped world order as we now know it, but interdependence is undercutting that base. Internationalism, after World War II, was seen by the framers of the UN charter as the great hope for a future peaceful world order; but the charter contains the limitation of dependence on consensus among sovereign nation-states with their own particular interests. Transnationalism on the other hand is based upon the interest of the transnational organization, which are the same in any nation-state where the organization conducts its operations. It is conceivable that within various fields transnational organizations could grow so large and so important to the economies of nation-states that many states will acquire a major interest in the preservation and prosperity of the organization. Technology has provided the communications and transportation capability for transnational organizations to treat markets and production across national boundaries as if they were parts of a whole.

DISCUSSION QUESTIONS

1. What technological changes have "politicized" vast numbers of human beings in the last century?

2. What historical and geographical factors, unique to the United States, have contributed to its political development and to its image in international politics?

3. What factors contributed to the change from a bipolar to a multipolar international system? Is a multipolar international system more stable than one that is bipolar?

4. What is national power? Why are the United States and the Soviet Union referred to as "superpowers"? What are the indicators of "great power" status? Can you quantify national power? How?

5. Is it correct to say that a nation is a "great power" on one issue but not with respect to another issue? Why? Can you give illustrations?

6. What factors determine or influence the effective use of a nation's national power? What contributes to the effective use of power?

7. What is an alliance? To what alliances is the United States tied today? Why do nations align?

8. What is the role of international law in enhancing national security? How does international law differ from national law? Who makes international laws? Give examples of international laws.

9. What impact has the human revolution, ideological revolution, technological revolution, and institutional revolution made on the international system? What are the indicators of each revolution?

10. What is "balance of power" politics? Can you provide examples of balance of power in action?

11. Does the emergence of economic interdependence indicate a probable shift to greater efforts toward collective security or does it signify increased efforts toward individual national security?

RECOMMENDED READING

Boorstin, Daniel J. *The Americans: The Democratic Experience*. New York: Random House, 1973.

Cline, Ray S. *World Power Trends and United States Foreign Policy for the 1980s*. Boulder, Colo.: Western Press, 1980.

Dougherty, James E., and Pfaltzgraff, Robert L., Jr. *Contending Theories of International Relations*. Philadelphia: J. B. Lippincott, 1971.

Dulles, John Foster, *War or Peace*. New York: Macmillan, 1950.

Gulick, Edward V. *Europe's Classical Balance of Power*. New York: W. W. Norton, 1955.

Jervis, Robert. *Perception and Misperception in International Politics*. Princeton: Princeton University Press, 1976.

Kissinger, Henry A. *American Foreign Policy*. 3d ed. New York: W. W. Norton, 1977.

Knorr, Klaus. *Military Power and Potential*. Lexington, Mass.: D. C. Heath, 1970.

Morgenthau, Hans J. *Politics among Nations*. 5th ed. New York: Alfred A. Knopf, 1973.

Rosenau, James N., ed. *International Politics and Foreign Policy*. New York: Free Press, 1969.

Sprout, Harold, and Sprout, Margaret. *Foundations of National Power*. 2d ed. New York: D. Van Nostrand, 1951.

2

MILITARY POWER
AND THE ROLE OF FORCE IN
THE NUCLEAR AGE

Chapter 1 portrayed international politics in large part as a struggle for power to protect or advance national interests and ideologies. National power was viewed as the general capability of a state to influence the behavior of others. Among the traditional elements of national power—geography, natural resources, industrial capacity, population, military strength, national character, and political cohesion—military strength was cited as the most obvious, yet one of the most difficult to estimate.

Military strength has as its rationale the contribution to a state's national security and the attainment of national foreign policy objectives. Accordingly, every sovereign polity has sought such strength. Indeed, until Japan chose to be the exception to the general rule by minimizing its military forces after World War II, the significance of a nation on the world scene had tended to be correlated directly with its armed strength.

No "great power" in the present or past has failed to maintain a large military establishment and those states which aspire to great power status allocate a large portion of their resources to developing an impressive military machine.

Yet this link between armed forces and state purposes is not the only explanation for building military forces. A military establishment has always been one of the trappings of "sovereignty," and heads of state feel compelled to maintain one as a status symbol. For some of the smaller developing nations, maintenance of a military establishment to influence external political relations appears to be purely a case of irrational allocation of scarce resources that could otherwise be devoted to internal development. In other less developed countries, however, the military has been instrumental in preserving internal political order and in fostering economic development.[2] Though in-

24

teresting and not to be underestimated, these latter purposes—status, policing, and economic ends—are peripheral to our enquiry, namely, to elucidate the appropriate role of military force in national security in the nuclear age.

The Nature of Military Power. As suggested in Chapter 1, it is a fundamental error to refer to military power in the abstract. To observe that the United States is one of the two most militarily powerful nations in the world means that, contrasted with every other nation except the Soviet Union, the United States has the strongest military forces. Even given that additional precision, however, the statement tends to mislead; there are specific objectives, in certain situations, at certain times and places, that the United States might be powerless to achieve, despite its possession of great military strength.

As is the case with the abstraction *national power*, the term *military power* has little significance until it is understood in a specific context and is filtered through precise analysis. There are two quite different ways to assess the military problem posed by an adversary: analyze the adversary's capabilities or its intentions. The latter course is often taken by those who believe that potential adversaries "have no aggressive intentions," or who have strong reasons for wishing to cut defense budgets and forces. Certainly, if there are but a few, relatively minor, differences of interests with a potential opponent, intentions analysis is an enticing (though dangerous) way to proceed. A more cautious (and more expensive) way is to consider what the other side is capable of doing. There are two reasons for this. First, intentions can change for the worse for a variety of reasons and in a relatively short time. Second, an adversary may change its intentions for the worse if it senses opportunities opened up by our side's having underestimated it—i.e., having taken the easier, cheaper road of assessing its intentions.

Both civilian and military agencies within the National Security Council structure are continually involved in military capability analysis and in providing the supporting data and estimates on the military forces of other states. But a military capability analysis, like a theater ticket, is useful at one time and at one place only. This is so because, as in the case of national power discussed in Chapter 1, the factors involved are *dynamic*—susceptible to constant, and sometimes dramatic, change. Further, factors are *situational*, varying not only with the given time period but also with the particularities of situation and geography. Finally, all factors considered in capability analysis are *relative* to other states' capacities to employ military means directed to the same objective or related objectives.

A classic example of the dynamic, situational, and relative nature of military capability is found in the Korean War. At the outbreak of that war in the summer of 1950, the United States enjoyed a virtual monopoly of nuclear weapons. One would think that American military capability was almost unlimited. If two atomic bombs dropped on Hiroshima and Nagasaki could end World War II with such finality, why not a repeat performance in Korea? First, the two cases were drastically different; by 1945 the United States had defeated all other enemies except Japan. In 1950, however, the Soviet Union was becoming an increasingly threatening cold war enemy. It maintained powerful conventional forces and had its own fledgling atomic force. In fact, the U.S. chiefs of staff felt that the Korean War might well be a Soviet diversion and that America needed to save its small arsenal of nuclear weapons for the main Soviet attack in Europe. Second, nuclear weapons were not particularly appropriate for the Korean War where the targets were bridges and troop concentrations rather than cities like Nagasaki. Third, America's allies especially the British, and substantial numbers of Americans as well were strongly opposed to the use of nuclear weapons.[3] Obviously, the United States did not have in 1950 the same freedom to use nuclear weapons that it had had in 1945; military capability had changed significantly because the overall situation had changed fundamentally.

Capability analysis is complex, requiring multivariate analysis. However, the following factors, illustrated at a high level of generalization, must normally be considered.

1. *Force size*—How large are the relevant military establishments in terms of forces-in-being and trained reserves? How many people under arms are at the disposal of the various services (e.g., army, navy, air force, marines), and in how many active and reserve units are they deployed?
2. *Weapons systems*—How many weapons systems of what types are at the disposal of the opposing forces? What is the potential of these weapons in terms of range, accuracy, lethality, survivability, and reliability?
3. *Mobility*—What are the locations of units and weapons systems? How quickly and by what means could they be moved to strategically and tactically important locations?
4. *Logistics (supply)*—Given the fact that military units can carry only so much equipment with them and must be resupplied if they are to remain in action for more than a few days, how efficient are systems of resupply?
5. *Strategic and tactical doctrines*—What is the quality of the doctrines of force deployment and military engagement that fundamentally control the employment of military units?
6. *Training*—What is the level of training of both forces-in-being and reserve units? How proficient are soldiers in employing their weapons under varying conditions?
7. *Military leadership*—How effective are the military and noncommissioned officers in the chain of command through which orders are issued and carried out?
8. *Morale*—A function of many variables and absolutely vital to success in combat, what are the levels of unit morale? Especially important for the armed forces of democratic nations, what would be the level of popular support for the employment of force in various contexts?
9. *Industry*—What is the industrial capacity of a given nation to produce military equipment of the types and in the amounts likely to be required

for sustained, longterm combat? How quickly can the nation switch from production of civilian goods to war materiel?

10. *Technology*—What is the level of technological capability of existing weapons systems and command, control, and communications (C^3) systems? What is the status of technology of weapons and C^3 systems at various stages of progress in a nation's military research, development, test and evaluation processes?

11. *Popular will*—How prepared would the population be to sustain the domestic deprivations (conscription, rationing of various types, etc.) that would result from sustained, large-scale wartime activities?

12. *Alliances*—What is the status of alliances which can change opposing force ratios significantly? What is the quality of alliance commitments under various conditions in terms of military units, weapons systems, bases, and supplies likely to be made available?

13. *National leadership*—What are the levels of resolve and skill of a nation's leaders in conducting a conventional war effort against the backdrop of nuclear deterrence?

"Answers" to such questions establish the factors to be weighed and blended to produce a judgment of military capability. The analysis process is and must be continuous, for there is insufficient time available in crisis situations to gather anew all the data required for analysis.

No single judgment resulting from analyses such as just outlined can be made of how much "capability" a state needs except, obviously the amount adequate to meet the anticipated requirements of specific policy objectives. The more useful product of such an analysis is a series of cost/risk calculations, which can then form the basis for decisions about the preparation and uses of the military instrument. Most major policy choices confronting decision-makers involve certain "costs"—material and nonmaterial, domestic and international—arising from the impacts of those choices. "Risk," in terms of the probabilities of success or failure, is also inherent in major policy decisions. Military capability analysis aids the policymaker in judging what costs and risks are acceptable relative to the values of the objective sought. The more

Hagar the Horrible

Copyright 1981 King Features Syndicate, Inc.

important the objective, the higher the costs and risks the policymaker will be willing to judge "acceptable."

Uses of Military Force in the Nuclear Age. Assuming that conflict will continue to mark international life, a vital question for national security policy is, What are the most suitable means for pursuing or controlling conflict and how should those means be used? The military instrument is only one such means—albeit the most potentially violent and conclusive of all.

Historically, military force has been employed for both the aggrandizement of interests and the defense of interests, although the distinction between the two has sometimes been more rhetorical than real. The nation-state system as we know it is postulated on the ultimate right and capacity of states to resort to military force.

The legitimacy of force as an instrument of foreign policy, although often denounced by philosophers, historians, and reformers, has rarely been questioned by those responsible for foreign policy decisions of their nations.[4]

Military force has, historically, been also a technique for the resolution of disputes. Given the possibilities of conflict escalation, the range of situations in which disputes can be rationally resolved by the use of military force has been narrowed by the technology of the nuclear age.

What, then, can be said about the range of contemporary uses of military force? One can envision seven categories of "use," none of which are mutually exclusive. First, both nuclear and conventional military force can be employed in a *deterrent role*. Deterrence is not an invention of the nuclear era. The objective of deterrence has always been to prevent others from initiating an action that threatens a particular interest. Most people would agree that strategic deterrence functions at the nuclear level by threatening retaliation so severe as to discourage any rational government leadership from initiating a large-scale nuclear attack. According to some analysts, although far less probable, strategic nuclear weapons serve to deter conventional attack also by convincing an adversary that the costs and risks of potential escalation attendant to an attack would be higher than the objective is worth. The same contention is sometimes advanced for tactical nuclear weapons.

Second, military force can be employed in a *compellent* role, i.e., to compel an adversary to stop a course of action already undertaken.[5] The means of compulsion is the direct application of military force. The objective of compulsion is to hurt the adversary to the degree that it determines that further pursuit of its course of action would incur increasing costs incommensurate with any possible gain. If the application of force is tuned too finely, however, as was apparently the case with the gradual application of U.S. force in Vietnam, then the adversary may be able to take countermeasures that will mitigate the harm and avert compulsion.

Third, military force can be employed in an *acquisitive* role to seize territory or resources of others for exploitation or to use them for bargaining purposes.

In view of the escalatory dangers, great powers may choose not to use their own forces but to employ the conventional military forces of a proxy in an acquisitive role, pursuing interests related to those of proxy states. (Of course, proxies can be used in a number of these military roles.)

Fourth, military force can be employed for *intervention* by one state in the internal affairs of another when a change in the other state's government or policy is deemed threatening to important national interests. The intervention might have as its purpose to stabilize a preferred regime against rebels or insurgents or to overthrow a hostile regime.

Fifth, military force can be used in a *counterintervention role*, to prevent success of another state's intervention considered contrary to important interests.

Sixth, military force may be employed by small groups of states in *collective actions* under authority granted by the United Nations or regional international organizations.

Finally, military force always serves as a *backdrop for diplomacy*. Louis XIV called military force "the last argument of kings" and so inscribed his cannons. The situations in which military force remains a final arbiter have been somewhat circumscribed in the nuclear era, at least in relations among nuclear powers and their allies. Accordingly, the employment of "gunboat diplomacy," the diplomatic use of force as a coercive instrument, has dwindled in frequency. Still, the opposing potentials of military force do serve to limit and regulate claims among states with competing interests.[6]

Constraints on the Military Instrument. The threat of resort to military force appears to have diminished in some ways in international politics. Some analysts would argue, for example, that, except for deterrence and prestige value, nuclear weapons are and should be unusable for and largely inapplicable to diplomacy.[7] Thus, a threat by the United States to use nuclear weapons against a small, developing nation that expropriated U.S. property would not, it is held, be received as credible. Similarly, *as long as both superpowers have massive nuclear forces and their national wills and alliance structures remain strong*, a military threat by either nation against an ally of the other would tend to be noncredible. The threat of escalation and of consequent mutual annihilation suggests that, under such circumstances, neither superpower could employ nuclear weapons to achieve policy objectives other than deterrence. (Whether the Soviets might credibly threaten nations not allied to the U.S. with nuclear destruction is another matter; superpower nuclear self-restraint became the pattern in an era of U.S. strategic superiority. Whether the U.S.S.R. will continue to be restrained in an era of strategic parity or even Soviet advantage is a central concern.)

Constraints on the use of nonnuclear military forces may also be growing. The use of military force historically has been a "prerogative power," reserved for the decisions of sovereigns. Beginning with the rise of European mass nationalist movements in the Napoleonic era, however, the power bases of heads of state have rested increasingly upon the support of the populace from which come the personnel and resources of mass warfare. Prior to the nineteenth century, battlefields were usually relatively restricted, for the most part touching only the lives of those directly involved in combat. The virtually total wars of the nineteenth and twentieth centuries—i.e. the Napoleonic wars, the American Civil War, and the two world wars—changed this situation, bringing the carnage and anguish of war into the lives and homes of whole populations.

The communications and information revolutions have increasingly led to widespread revulsion (in democracies, at least) of the use of military force as a diplomatic tool. World opinion (or, more accurately, the opinion of the Western great powers) has begun to articulate its abhorrence of unrestricted warfare, codifying "laws of war" and turning to definitions of "just war," which had long been the province of theologians and philosophers. The League of Nations and United Nations both attempted to frame distinctions between legitimate and illegitimate uses of military force. Although problems of agreed definition still plague international law, "aggression" is outlawed and the use of military force for defense against aggression is "just."

Behind the development of international law on the use of military force has been an uneven and still weak—but growing—international moral consensus against any international violence. The impact of such a consensus, and the world opinion that reflects it, upon the governments and foreign policies of nation-states has long been a controversial issue among students of international politics. Certainly, there is no unitary "world opinion" in the abstract, but there may be a near consensus of opinion among world leaders on specific international issues. As a matter of simple prudence in statecraft, policymakers must calculate the breadth, strengths, and likely consequences of such opinion when making cost/risk assessments of possible courses of military action.

In day-to-day diplomacy, an international consensus against an act of military aggression usually tends to represent more sound than fury. However, the longer-term impacts may be quite different:

> If a state flagrantly flouts an internationally sanctioned restraint on military aggression, it may, in the event of success, gain the object of aggression and in addition perhaps inspire increased respect for its military prowess; but it may also tarnish its non-military reputation and provoke attitudes of suspicion and hostility that, over the longer run if not immediately, will become organized politically, and perhaps militarily as well. This amounts to saying that the respect a nation enjoys—respect for acting properly, with sensitivity to internationally widespread moral standards, and with sobriety and restraint in resorting to military power—is a precious asset in foreign affairs. It is an asset that assists in holding and gaining allies, and generally in promoting a favorable reception for its diplomatic initiatives.[8]

One might argue that the widely respected status of West Germany and Japan by the late 1970s disproves the thesis of adverse long-term effects of aggression. Yet it should be recalled that West Germany and Japan are watched especially carefully by neighboring states; that Japan has rejected all but self-defense forces since World War II, and that neither state now has—nor is likely to acquire—a military nuclear capability at its discretion.[9]

Although international opinion clearly does not deter invariably the use of military force, as the Soviet invasion of Afghanistan showed, there is another route through which world opinion can have significant impact upon a state's choices on the use of military force. The communications revolution has made it possible, especially in the case of the democracies, for world opinion to impact upon the domestic opinion of a state contemplating or taking military action. What world opinion cannot accomplish by direct impact upon the head of a democratic state it may be able to effect indirectly by influencing public attitudes and national legislatures. Foreign opposition and criticism, for instance, had considerable impact upon American public attitudes during the U.S. involvement in Vietnam from 1965 to 1975. In turn, domestic public concern regarding "unrestricted" use of military force in that conflict resulted in the War Powers Act passed by the American Congress in 1973. To the extent that opinion can thus influence decisions about the resort to military force, a new and complicating phenomenon has emerged in international politics.[10] This phenomenon, it should be noted, has little counterpart in strongly authoritarian states; Soviet military adventures in Africa and the Middle East in the late 1970s and the Chinese and Vietnamese attacks in the same period upon their neighbors do not seem to have encountered such indirect checks.

In addition to fear of escalation and public opinion, there is another important constraint on the role of military force in diplomacy, namely, the high monetary costs associated with the military instrument. This problem is especially difficult for the more industrialized nations with advanced weapons. Technological sophistication has driven up the costs of weapons systems enormously. Costs associated with personnel requirements have also skyrocketed in the industrial democracies. The defense budget for the United States was $122.7 billion for fiscal year 1980, approximately 5 percent of the American gross national product (GNP), but larger than the total GNPs of Greece, Norway, Turkey, and Portugal combined. Although difficult to measure and equate with U.S. figures, Soviet defense expenditures increased rapidly in real terms during the 1960s and 1970s, probably by more than 3 percent annually (measured by the cost of duplicating the effort in the U.S. economy). By the end of the 1970s, the Soviet defense effort exceeded that of the United States by 25 to 45 percent, depending on the type of comparison involved.[11] (There was little evidence, however, that Soviet public opinion was beginning to be a brake on these large sums.) Maintenance of a large military establishment and especially its use in war involve not only domestic expenditures but also payment for military-related goods and services to other countries. The costs of maintaining overseas forces have risen dramatically and, despite "Buy America" campaigns, "tied foreign aid" (recipient must expend in the country which provides the aid), restrictions on capital exports, defense "offset payments" by allies, and other measures, U.S. payments deficits became a problem in the late 1960s and 1970s. Deficits generated by the military have added to the strains on the dollar and hence have contributed to exchange rate instability and attendant political animosities.[12]

Widespread focus on the high costs of the military instrument is relatively new. This focus is related in part to the broader, gradual orientation of the industrialized democracies toward the welfare-state psychology,[13] although U.S. public sentiment had begun to swing back from butter and toward guns by the end of the 1970s. But the strength of this sentiment in the face of increasing deficits is unclear. Cuts will likely come from both social and military spending.

The differences in the intensity and rate at which welfare state psychology is translated into domestic priorities in the Western democracies in contrast to the communist countries could present a danger for the West. One-sided reductions in defense spending for forces-in-being and for military research and development, especially if coupled with popular rejection of the social value of military service, could place the democracies at a decided, perhaps fatal, disadvantage. Unilateral pressures in the West to cut forces could not only weaken the democracies but also scuttle any prospect for arms control arrangements aimed at mutual reductions, which would preserve the key military balances in the world. By the end of the 1970s, however, there were increasing indications that the earlier pressures to cut defense had eased in the West and that many Americans, at least, were prepared to support larger military forces and more activist defense policies.[14]

Types of Military Force Employment. Analyses of military doctrine and strategy have proliferated since World War II. Many factors account for the rapid growth of literature on the employment of military force: the cold war's focus on the military threat of communism; widespread psychic involvement in the balance of terror; lack of faith in the UN capability to prevent wars; concern over the extent to which military preparedness establishes claims on scarce national resources; continued development of the welfare ethic; the rise of pacifism; and the information revolution. There is no easy route to comprehension of this plethora of conceptual treatments of the roles of military force. However, as a preliminary categorization of the types of military force employment, we can speak of deterrence, nuclear war, general conventional war, guerrilla (or unconventional) war, and political bargaining.

Deterrence. Deterrence has a number of definitions. As used here, it means the ability "to hinder or prevent action by fear of consequences, or by difficulty, risk, unpleasantness, etc."[15] Deterrence is, therefore, at base a psychological phenomenon; its object is to master the expectations and fears of one's actual or potential opponents. Yet deterrence must rest on *hard capability*—the clear, demonstrable ability to do what is threatened if the necessity arises. Deterrence also rests on will, namely, the threatener's will to carry out the threat. Further, the success of a deterrent strategy

depends on the deterrer's ability to convince his adversary that an attempt to gain his objective would cost more than it is worth, and that the cost to the deterrer of applying the deterrent would be less than conceding the objective.[16]

Deterrence assumes a rational, informed opponent. An irrational (or ill-informed) opponent who will accept destruction or disproportionate loss as a consequence of a selected course of action cannot be deterred. Accidents, by definition consciously unintended, cannot be "deterred." The deterrent roles of any weapons systems must always be considered in relation to the states, alliances, or groups that are to be deterred and what action is to be deterred. For example, a threat of massive nuclear retaliation could hardly deter a terrorist group from planting bombs on aircraft. On the other hand, the Soviet Union probably cannot be deterred from interventions in Central Europe by conventional force deployment divorced from the strong possibility of North Atlantic Treaty Organization (NATO) nuclear escalation.

Strategic nuclear deterrence rests on the concept of "assured destruction" of the adversary, preventing that adversary from launching its strategic nuclear weapons for fear of an unacceptable level of devastation in return through nuclear retaliation. For this type of deterrence, the United States employs three strategic nuclear deterrent systems, i.e., the Triad of intercontinental ballistic missiles (ICBMs), ballistic missile submarines, and bomber aircraft.

Tactical nuclear deterrence is theoretically possible as well. There are two quite different ways in which the deployment of tactical nuclear weapons could deter aggressors from the use of either conventional or tactical nuclear forces. First, such deployments could help convince the aggressor that its battlefield costs would be too high. This approach assumes that tactical nuclear weapons could be used effectively. Second, the aggressor would have to calculate that *any* nuclear weapon use will likely escalate to strategic nuclear war. This second approach to deterrence is the converse of the first in that it denies the "tactical" utility of low-yield nuclear weapons for battlefield fighting.[17] By the early 1980s this second approach could be vitiated if the Western allies were to deploy the enhanced radiation devices, or "neutron bombs," which they have developed; for these weapons inflict casualties in a relatively restricted area without great property damage and thus are more persuasive battlefield weapons. Theoretically, these weapons could induce Soviet leaders to believe more in NATO resolve to defend with tactical nuclear devices and thus lead to greater deterrence.

Conventional (nonnuclear) force deterrence is possible between nonnuclear states where one state or alliance of states holds "sufficient" military capability to convince would-be attackers that costs and risks would be greater than benefits. Conventional force deployments may also serve in the spectrum of capabilities required for deterrence between nuclear powers by providing "flexible response" (the ability to respond appropriately at subnuclear as well as nuclear levels). For example, as an alternative to early use of nuclear weapons and the attendant dangers, NATO strategy since 1967 has been designed to " . . . convince the Soviets that the alliance would respond to any attack but that its response might initially be conventional, reserving the right to use nuclear weapons."[18]

How well and when deterrence works in specific situations is difficult to assess. In fact, *successful* deterrence is virtually impossible to identify; so much depends on how one evaluates adversary intentions. Assessments can easily take the form of post hoc conclusions based on single-factor analysis.* Additionally, it should be noted that military force designed to deter military action does not necessarily deter action in the economic or political fields.[19]

Nuclear War. Nuclear war may be fought because deterrence breaks down and the parties involved believe no other viable option exists but employment of nuclear force. It may also occur by accident or, improbably as it may seem in view of past nuclear stability, by deliberate design. Finally, nuclear war may also arise out of escalation of conventional hostilities between nuclear powers or their allies.

Studies on escalation in warfare invariably draw distinctions among the types and yields of weapons employed and the types of targets attacked. The difference between the use of conventional weapons and the use of nuclear weapons is often referred to as *firebreak*, signifying a highly significant qualitative difference in levels of warfare. Some analysts argue that there is also a significant firebreak separating the use of tactical and strategic nuclear weapons and that tactical nuclear weapons can, as a consequence, be employed in "quasi-conventional" combat without undue risk of escalation to strategic levels. Others even argue that numbers of firebreaks exist at various rungs of a tall ladder of nuclear escalation, suggesting further that "deescalation" is as possible as escalation and that deterrence can work at various rungs in the ladder.[20]

Certainly, it is possible to identify theoretical distinctions among major classes of nuclear warfare.[21]

- *Spasm War*—All-out attacks both on "counterforce" targets (military installations and major force deployments) and on "countervalue" targets (people and industrial centers).
- *Total Counterforce*—All-out nuclear attacks on military installations and major force deployments.
- *Limited Strategic Warfare*—Attacks on selected targets, counterforce or countervalue, for demostration and bargaining advantages.

*Whether or not NATO actually has at its disposal sufficient conventional capability to postpone early use of tactical nuclear weapons is highly debatable. For example, whether or not the Soviet Union has been deterred by NATO from attacking Western Europe depends, in part, on whether or not the Soviets ever intended to attack Europe. See André Beaufre. *Strategy of Action* (New York: Frederick A. Praeger, 1967). p. 12.

● *Tactical Nuclear Warfare*—Selected use of low-yield nuclear weapons on the battlefield or its approaches for tactical military advantages.

However neat these distinctions may be in theory, many analysts suspect that the dividing lines would become blurred quickly in the reactions of military commanders and strategic decision-makers to the first use of nuclear weapons on any scale. (Further attention to these and other distinctions is given in Chapter 11 on "Nuclear Strategies.") In the rapid tempo of crisis situations involving nuclear warfare, neat scenarios are not likely to be played out precisely as planned. Thus, many analysts conclude with Alain C. Enthoven that the use of one nuclear weapon in the field will likely lead to the use of any and all nuclear weapons.[22]

General Conventional War. The two world wars are commonly regarded as general conventional wars in which the resources of coalitions of belligerent nations were mobilized on a massive scale in a war fought for "victory" over the enemy.[23] In both wars one could measure progress toward victory by observing the geographical movement of battlelines established by mass military formations and by destruction or capture of enemy units. Victory was realized by advancing on the enemy's capital and by forcing a capitulation in the form of a formal exchange of signatures on a document of surrender.

It is widely held that the advent of the nuclear balance of terror has precluded general conventional war along the lines of World War II.[24] Of course, general conventional war is still possible among small nonnuclear states fighting for objectives not centrally involving important interests of the nuclear powers. Some theorists would argue that even among the nuclear states conventional war can occur, inasmuch as nuclear deterrence is firm under the doctrine of "mutual assured destruction," whereby the Soviet Union and the United States in effect tacitly agree they cannot protect themselves against each other (see Chapters 10 and 23). Since no rational head of state would invite nuclear self-destruction by first use of strategic nuclear weapons, this argument goes, traditional military strategy and tactics remain applicable even among nuclear opponents. There are practical problems with this thesis, which has never been tested in the nuclear era. Carried to its logical conclusion, it obviates the traditional notion of victory. It is hard to imagine a situation in which a head of state still in possession of an arsenal of strategic nuclear weapons would surrender the nation without any nuclear use. It is noteworthy that Soviet doctrine recognizes no such general conventional war possibility, calling instead for total force application, including chemical as well as nuclear weapons, until victory is achieved.[25]

Limited War. A limited war is one in which at least one side fights with only limited resources for limited objectives. Limited war

reflects an attempt to *affect* the opponent's will, not *crush* it, to make the conditions to be imposed seem more attractive than continued resistance, to strive for specific goals and not for complete annihilation.[26]

While familiar to historians, the concept of limited war thus defined is new to most Americans, for it marks a significant departure from traditional American approaches to war discussed in Chapter 3. Although the Korean conflict (1950–54) was fought as a limited war, it was not the wellspring of limited war doctrines. In fact, Secretary of State Dulles's formulation of "massive retaliation" with nuclear weapons—designed to deter future limited wars such as the Korean War—was still widely viewed as a viable policy in the mid 1950s.[27]

Contemporary limited war doctrines were essentially the product of Western fears of nuclear war growing out of cold war hostilities, Soviet development of a thermonuclear capability in the 1950s, Russian sputniks, bomber and missile "gaps," and the balance of terror. Obviously, alternatives to massive retaliation had to be found when the consequence of nuclear retaliation to nonnuclear threats was the possible destruction of oneself. Moreover, massive retaliation seemed particularly inappropriate to "containing" the threat of communist subversion in the form of so-called wars of national liberation in the Third World.

The most innovative period for limited-war doctrines was from the mid 1950s to the mid 1960s. During those years several distinct scenarios were considered possible by various analysts.

- Limited tactical nuclear war
- Use of conventional forces to enforce "pauses" during crises and to raise the threshold between conventional and nuclear war (thus reinforcing strategic deterrence)
- Combinations of conventional and tactical nuclear forces as reprisals and demonstrations for political bargaining purposes
- Limited conventional force application for the purpose of compulsion
- Counterinsurgency warfare

The American military involvement in Vietnam was influenced in its early years largely by various doctrines of counterinsurgency warfare (see Chapter 13). After the U.S. troop buildup in 1965 these doctrines were supplemented by theories of limited war and controlled escalation in the application of conventional military force. Difficult though they were to identify, important intrinsic U.S. objectives—principally the security of an independent, non-communist government in South Vietnam—were rather clear and limited at the outset. Few could have surmised that, relative to North Vietnam's apparently unlimited objectives in the South, the objectives of the U.S. would come to be perceived by its own people as not "limited" enough—or alternatively, as too limited. Except with hindsight, few could have estimated in advance the intensity of the restraints limiting strategy, tactics, and resources. As limits on U.S. means grew—from mounting casualties, escalating monetary costs, concern about Chinese direct involvement, and international and domestic public sentiment against the war—U.S. objectives became still more limited, settling for the acceptability of any kind of government in South Vietnam as long as it was freely elected and free of North Vietnamese military aggression.

The outcome of the American experience with limited war in Southeast Asia has been stated succinctly. "The war is over, the cost enormous, and the side which the United States backed lost." Perhaps few conclusive lessons concerning the general utility of limited war can be drawn, but it was clear that for Americans the utility of the method was very low indeed. Public disenchantment with and ultimate lack of support for the Vietnam war suggest that the reasons for and types of future U.S. interventions are sharply constrained. However, limited war remains an alternative in U.S. national security policy—albeit an approach fraught with various problems (see Chapter 12).[28]

Guerrilla, or Unconventional, War. The word *guerrilla* comes from the Spanish term "little war." Although on the low end of the spectrum of violence, guerrilla warfare has been a powerful instrument in shaping history. Governments may employ it against their enemies, but populations may use it against their governments as well!

For a further discussion of this subject see Chapter 13.

Political Bargaining. The most common employment of military force in history has been as an instrument of political action. The possibility that force might be employed in a given situation introduces a powerful element into the calculus of diplomacy and has done so since mankind began to record either diplomacy or war. In the New Testament we read, "What king, going to make war against another king, sitteth not down first, and consulteth whether he be able. . . . Or else, while the other is yet a great way off, he sendeth an embassage, and desireth conditions of peace."[29]

Britain's fleet gave the state a powerful voice at virtually every nineteenth-century council table, yet that fleet did not fight a major engagement during the entire century between the battles of Trafalgar and Jutland. Naval forces have been a major diplomatic instrument for the U.S. as well. President Jefferson began the tradition of American "gunboat diplomacy" along the Barbary coast. Theodore Roosevelt polished the instrument and used it broadly during his presidency. Successive presidents have similarly found the presence of a naval squadron a persuasive indicator of American readiness to take action—military in character, if necessary—in troubled situations.

A recent comprehensive analysis of the use of military force as a diplomatic instrument found that, in the period January 1, 1946, to October 31, 1975, there were 215 instances of the use of American forces for political purposes. In 4 out of 5 of the instances the forces were naval.[30] Navies, which have the advantages of mobility and flexibility, also have weaknesses: first, they can be just as easily withdrawn as inserted, giving rise to questions about the constancy of the intentions behind their employment and, second, there are a variety of instances in which a naval force is not readily applicable, even though it may have some symbolic value. During the three decades described above, analysts found that "forces actually emplaced on foreign soil tended to be more frequently associated with positive outcomes than were naval forces . . . the movement of land based forces . . . involves both real economic costs and a certain psychological commitment which is difficult to reverse, at least in the short term."[31]

The U.S. use of military force in diplomacy, ranging from sending fleets to deploying major army units (as occurred in Lebanon in 1958 and in Laos in 1962) to alerting strategic nuclear forces (as in the Yom Kippur War's terminal phases in 1973 when the Soviets threatened intervention) may be on the wane—at least as far as the U.S. is concerned. After reaching a high point in the decade from the middle 1950s to the middle 1960s, the frequency of American use of this tool dropped off sharply. In part, this was undoubtedly due to the U.S. focus on the hostilities in Vietnam after 1965 and to the disillusionment with military power which followed the conclusion of those hostilities; in part, it may also have been that American policy-makers came to believe there was less value in demonstrations and shows of force in the modern era. This perception of lessened value may, in turn, be due to enhanced Soviet ability to "counterdemonstrate" and to increased sophistication of possible targets who discern American reluctance actually to use the force behind the demonstration. Whether either of these conditions will change in the 1980s will depend on a rebuilding of American strength and a recovery of American willingness to use force, as well as on developments in the Soviet Union and elsewhere.

In addition to their role as active instruments of political action, military forces also serve as a backdrop for diplomacy merely by being there and capable of deployment. An arms control negotiator's ability to achieve a satisfactory agreement, for instance, will likely depend significantly on there being suitable forces in the background; so, too, will the ability of a diplomat attempting to persuade an adversary to neutralize an area or issue in contention. Hans Morgenthau has reminded us that military strength is a prime element in prestige, which is itself a political multiplier of power.

Besides the practices of diplomacy, the policy of prestige uses military demonstrations as means to achieve its purpose. Since military strength is the obvious measure of a nation's power, its demonstration serves to impress the others with that nation's power. Military representatives of foreign nations are, for instance, invited to peacetime army and navy maneuvers, not in order to let them in on military secrets, but to impress them and their governments with the military preparedness of the particular nation.[32]

Of course, the uses of armed forces as potential instruments do not solve underlying problems. In the short run they may avert a reverse and temporarily secure an advantage, but they cannot indefinitely substitute for other policy instruments. Summing up the study of the 215 instances already cited, the analysts observed that the demonstrative use of the armed forces for political objectives is a useful step to shore up a situation sufficiently so that more extreme adverse consequences can be avoided, so that domestic and international pressures for more forceful and perhaps counter-productive actions can be avoided, and so that time can be gained for sounder policies that can deal adequately with the realities of the situation to be formulated and implemented.

To reach this conclusion about the *effectiveness* of armed forces as a political instrument is not to reach any judgment about the wisdom of using the armed forces for these purposes. That question is a more difficult one, one which can only be answered in the context of the specific choices—and the various costs and benefits associated with each choice—facing decision-makers at the time.[33]

Military Doctrine in Crisis. Barring the millennium, military forces will continue to be an instrument of sovereign states. The central question for policymakers in the nuclear era remains, How does one manage the employment of military force to achieve national security objectives in the most effective, efficient way? Several distinct problems in military doctrine bear on this question and require solution or at least clarification.

First, a crucial problem remains of resolving the dichotomy between the view, first, that nuclear weapons have abolished all-out war and, second, that such war can occur and be controlled. A difficulty with the former position is that rational calculations conceivably might have ruled out total war between nuclear powers as an instrument of national policy, but such a war could result from miscalculation or accident, to which deterrence is not applicable. Proliferation of nuclear weapons would make the situation worse and the list of nations capable of aquiring nuclear weapons in the not too distant future has grown to more than a dozen today.[34]

Second, the doctrinal problem surrounding the use of tactical nuclear weapons need clarification. Although there may be some deterrent value in maintaining ambiguities and uncertainties between opponents, there appears to be little such value among allies. NATO strategy has long included the use of tactical nuclear weapons, although the conditions and modes in which they might be used have remained vague. Even with precisely defined criteria and scenarios for use, so repugnant has the specter of nuclear weapons employment become that it is difficult to visualize a situation in which an American president would be the first to initiate the use of tactical nuclear weapons. Morever, it is difficult to imagine a nuclear battlefield so controlled that the distinction between tactical and strategic nuclear weapons would hold in the heat and turmoil of conflict. Yet tactical nuclear weapons form an important part of the spectrum of deterrence and ensure that conventional forces and strategic nuclear forces are securely linked or "coupled" in such a way that the adversary cannot hope to prevail at any one level of violence.

Of course, the Europeans are extremely reluctant to visualize their homelands being turned into nuclear battlefields.[35] One can assume, for example, that Germany would strongly oppose the use of tactical nuclear strategy except in the very early stage of Soviet invasion—when the weapons would land on

East European, not German, soil. Thus, the European partners in NATO favor the deployment of tactical nuclear weapons primarily because they believe that either deterrence will be enhanced or war fighting will thereby quickly escalate to the strategic nuclear level involving U.S. and Soviet territory.[36]

A third major problem with the role of military force resides in the ambiguities of limited war. Limits on war's objectives must be related to the nature of the interests to be pursued. Resort to military force in the nuclear era carries with it so many dangers that the interests to be served should be particularly clear, strong, and specific. Although interests are difficult enough to identify, specific objectives in particular circumstances present an even more difficult problem. National interests tend to change slowly; specific objectives are situational. Objectives are shaped both by what is desirable and what is feasible in given situations. Determination of the militarily feasible must be the result of careful capability analysis that determines the limits of resources and adjusts the objectives thereto.

DISCUSSION QUESTIONS

1. Under what conditions would you expect the mass media to be a factor in limiting or expanding the role of the military in conflict resolution?

2. How important is the reality of "assured destruction" if one side in a political conflict does not consider the concept valid?

3. What is "flexible response"? Is conventional (nonnuclear) force a deterrent between nuclear states? Under what conditions?

4. Under what conditions could the use of military force be limited to general conventional war between states possessing a nuclear capability?

5. What makes modern nuclear deterrence different from pre-1945 conventional (nonnuclear) deterrence?

6. What problems for nuclear deterrence does the proliferation of nuclear weapons create?

7. What nonmilitary factors must be considered when estimating a state's "national power"?

8. What are the dangers associated with employing military forces in a "compellent" role? What nonmilitary factors of national power can be employed in a compellent role?

9. What kinds of economic costs are associated with maintaining military power in developing Third World and advanced industrialized nations? Are there economic advantages?

10. Does a credible military force make some nations more sovereign than others? If so, why?

11. What are the realities of military conflict that challenge the concept of *firebreak*?

12. Why are "intentions" a dangerous guide to use when assessing the military problem that an adversary poses?

13. Did the advent of nuclear weapons mark a watershed in the decision-making process used to authorize military force to resolve disputes?

RECOMMENDED READING

Bienen, Henry. *The Military and Modernization*. New York: Aldine Atherton, 1971.

Blechman, Barry M., and Kaplan, Stephen S. *The Use of Armed Forces as a Political Instrument*. Washington, D.C.: Defense Advanced Research Projects Agency, 1976.

Brodie, Bernard. *Strategy in the Missile Age*. Princeton: Princeton University Press, 1959.

Coffey, J. I. *Strategic Power and National Security*. Pittsburgh: University of Pittsburgh Press, 1971.

Freedman, Lawrence D. *The Evolution of Nuclear Strategy*. New York: St. Martin's Press, 1981.

Halperin, Morton H. *Defense Strategies for the Seventies*. Boston: Little, Brown, 1971.

Hoffmann, Stanley. *Gulliver's Troubles, or the Setting of American Foreign Policy*. New York: McGraw-Hill, 1968.

Huntington, Samuel P. *The Common Defense*. New York: Columbia University Press, 1961.

International Institute for Strategic Studies. *The Military Balance, 1982–1983*. London: IISS, 1982.

Kahn, Herman. *On Escalation: Metaphors and Scenarios*. New York: Frederick A. Praeger, 1962.

Knorr, Klaus. *On the Uses of Military Power in the Nuclear Age*. Princeton: Princeton University Press, 1966.

Schelling, Thomas C. *Arms and Influence*. New Haven: Yale University Press, 1966.

Schlesinger, James R., et al. *Defending America*. New York: Basic Books, 1977.

Sokolovskiy, V. D. *Soviet Military Strategy*. New York: Crane, Russak, 1975.

3

TRADITIONAL AMERICAN APPROACHES
TO NATIONAL SECURITY

Generalizations about distinctly American approaches to national security matters should be advanced with the same caution that all large generalizations warrant. For one thing, not all Americans at all times are of the same mind. As much as anything else, democracy is a variety of viewpoints. Americans tend to differ among themselves on policy issues along lines of age groups, sex, region, party, social class, education level, etc. Even during times when the nation has been committed to war, various citizens have been dedicated to pacifism. Invariably, some people have felt that the United States was committed to war for the wrong cause—or for the right cause at the wrong time, or for the right cause at the right time in the wrong place. At times of low defense budgets, some citizens have argued for greater armament; high defense budgets always have their antagonists.

Nevertheless, there are central themes in the American cultural tradition that repeatedly recur, providing patterns of thought and action in national security matters. Short of war, for instance, Americans have traditionally focused much of their energy on the pursuit of private interests, and consequently have viewed national security as secondary, if they thought of it at all. On the other hand, once conscious of a threat, American attitudes have tended to shift quickly and dramatically. Gabriel Almond has suggested that such American attitudes are matters of "mood" and that moods are affected by two variables.

1. Changes in the domestic and foreign political-economic situation involving the presense or absence of threat in varying degrees.
2. The character and predispositions of the population.[1]

It is to this latter variable that we now turn, briefly examining certain tendencies of thought and action arising out of American experience and its historic context. We shall later examine the first variable at length.

Public Opinion and National Security Policy. As in most democracies, American public opinion on the various aspects of national security policy has historically been important. Public opinion, for instance, has always been to some degree a constraint on policy-makers. De Tocqueville, writing in 1835, stressed this situation when he observed that a democratic system of government is by nature incapable of formulating and implementing a coherent foreign policy.

Foreign politics demand scarcely any of those qualities which a democracy possesses; and they require on the contrary, the perfect use of almost all of those faculties in which it is deficient. . . . a democracy is unable to regulate the details of an important undertaking, to persevere in a design, and to work out its execution in the presence of serious obstacles. It cannot combine measures with secrecy, and it will not await their consequences with patience. . . . democracies . . . obey the impulse of passion rather than the suggestions of prudence and . . . abandon a mature design for the gratification of a monetary caprice.[2]

De Tocqueville, along with others who take a so-called realist position, essentially argued that the realm of policy-making should be reserved for a small group of highly educated and competent elites who would discharge their duties secretly, efficiently, and effectively. In this view, there is no room in the policy-making arena for the uninformed and unsophisticated mass public.

Walter Lippmann felt that de Tocqueville's view of the dangers of the public role in national security policy-making became increasingly relevant with the passage of years.

The people have imposed a veto upon the judgments of the informed and responsible officials. They have compelled the governments, which usually knew what would have been wiser, was necessary, or was more expedient, to be too late with too little, or too long with too much, too pacifist in peace and too bellicose in war, too neutralist or appeasing in negotiation or too intransigent. Mass opinion has acquired mounting power in this century. It has shown itself to be a dangerous master of decisions when the stakes are life and death.[3]

De Tocqueville, Lippmann and others, then, have seen the involvement of the American public in foreign affairs as dysfunctional, and some support can be offered for that position.

There are, of course, arguments to be made contrary to the realists and in favor of public involvement in national security and foreign policy decisions. When public opinion impacts upon international problems it has certain strengths. For one thing, public debates tend to clarify major issues. For another, if the public's view impinges on the process, the resulting policy is more likely to be in keeping with current national purposes.[4] Third, if the public's involvement has been steady, there is apt to be more continuing support for the sacrifices for which the policies call.

Clearly, there are many arguments that can be made for greater or lesser public involvement in foreign affairs, and those mentioned above are only representative. The classic liberal argument that grows out of the normative view that citizen opinions *should* influence all affairs—that all policy *should* reflect the beliefs of the people—or at least the majority of the people—could also be offered. On the other hand, realist propositions can be advanced, maintaining that foreign and security policy is so important that it deserves the control of the most educated and informed; that mass opinion is often too slow to crystallize; that public discussion can provide other governments premature information concerning U.S. national security policy.[5]

Whatever the position taken on the desirable depth of public involvement, it is clear that any U.S. security policy requiring national sacrifices must be founded, in large part, upon basic public values. Indeed, inasmuch as values are often imprecise, diverse, and subject to change, part of the job of the policy-maker is to clarify, interpret, synthesize, and articulate them as they bear on foreign and national security issues. Further, the diversity of values impinging upon the process of policy formulation often requires the policy-maker to reconcile competing values in relation to a particular aspect of national security. He or she may have to compromise, accept some values and reject others, or find some other rationalizing device. The necessity of formulating policy on a foundation of implicit or explicit value choices cannot, however, be avoided.[6]

THE PEOPLE TRY TO GET THE WHITE HOUSE VIEWPOINT

Fitzpatrick in the *St. Louis Post-Dispatch*.

One time-tested means of generating consensus is to couch policy in terms that command a broad value base within American society, i.e., in terms describing values so cherished by the polity that they are virtually beyond challenge; or, at least, such that it would appear almost "un-American" to challenge them. This practice is generally recognized by policy-makers as desirable, on occasion politically necessary. Woodrow Wilson's call for morality in international politics and Jimmy Carter's stress on human rights were intended to have just such rallying effect.

During the Truman, Eisenhower, and Kennedy years the executive branch was able to exercise a great deal of influence on public opinion. Public information organizations within the departments and agencies concerned with foreign and national security policies were able to use the media to articulate the administration's viewpoint while sometimes withholding information that would tend to support opposing views. During this period, members of Congress generally deferred to the executive branch, for it was widely believed that Congress lacked the expertise necessary for challenging foreign and national security policy decisions.[7]

Most Americans, of course, look to the president for leadership in foreign affairs, particularly when the issues involve national security. Historically, this has meant that the president has had wide scope for initiative when working in the field of foreign relations. Cognizant of this, Lyndon Johnson told Eric Sevareid, "I can arouse a great mass of people with a very simple kind of appeal. I can wrap the flag around this policy, and use patriotism as a club to silence the critics."[8] However, the link between policy and mass values must be credible.

The Johnson approach appeared to work fairly well until about 1968, by which time the administration's "credibility gap" had grown to serious proportions over the war in Vietnam. By then the news media had begun to focus on the inconsistencies or inadequacies of U.S. policy in Vietnam, giving wide publicity in particular to the February 1968 reexamination of the Gulf of Tonkin incidents by the Senate Committee on Foreign Relations. Those hearings appeared to convince many that the Johnson administration had hoodwinked Congress and, therefore, the American people, into the Gulf of Tonkin Resolution, which had been cited repeatedly by the president as proof of public support for his Vietnam policy.

Certainly, American presidents had been under attack before by the various media, but the 1968 attack was particularly strong; in effect, an American president and his administration, already suspect for news management, were implicitly labelled "frauds"—and only a few months before elections. Something truly serious happened: a major policy, inextricably linking American national security and foreign policy interests, apparently no longer commanded a broad national consensus. In traditional political terms, this was a presidential disaster. On the evening of March 31, 1968, President Johnson announced on TV that he would not run for reelection.

To some, the President's announcement meant recognition that U.S. policy in Vietnam, as articulated and executed by the Johnson administration, had failed. To others, the speech announced "the collapse of the messianic conception of the American role in the world."[9] Whatever conclusions one might draw from that dramatic event, it is clear that the public's role and interest in American national security policy took a dramatic turn in the spring of 1968. Not only was this true in the obvious case of Vietnam but also in other aspects of national security policy.

A change of administrations did not reduce the credibility gap. Indeed, it appeared to many that under President Nixon the link between American values and policy was becoming even more tenuous. The number of antiwar demonstrators and organizations increased, and on October 15, 1969, in various cities throughout the United States, more than one million people demonstrated against the Vietnam War.[10] These demonstrations tended to arouse the fear that continuing the war would rend the fabric of American society.

During the same period, the general American attitude regarding involvement abroad was undergoing fundamental change. The public—or at least a major part of it—was becoming more vocal, critical, and discriminating with respect to foreign commitments; its mood seemed to vacillate between "noninterventionism and selective interventionism."[11]

This change of mood, combined with Watergate and other problems on the domestic front, resulted in growing public and congressional disenchantment with presidential leadership and in erosion of the influence of the office of the presidency in national security affairs.[12] Major legislation, such as the War Powers Act of 1973 and the Budget Reform Act of 1974, shifted the executive-legislative balance away from the executive branch. Growing congressional assertiveness was also manifested in the House passage of a nuclear freeze resolution in early 1983. The impact of these changes is analyzed in Chapters 5 and 6.

Primacy of Domestic Affairs. As noted earlier, until recent decades American concern with distant events and matters of security was extremely limited. Geographic position provides a partial explanation of this lack of interest. Ocean barriers and great distances from likely sources of invasion made physical security a matter to be taken for granted. The fact that British sea power was committed to preserving the status quo in North America for most of the nineteenth century was further reason for complacency over security from foreign threats. Early security interests were essentially domestic—family or community security from hostile Indians, or from British troops supported by other Americans during the Revolution. The War of 1812 was relatively short, and much of the important action was at sea.

Most of the American historical experience occurred during the century of unprecedented and prolonged world peace from the Congress of Vienna in 1815 to the outbreak of World War I in 1914. (For Americans, of course, there was the bloody domestic experience of the Civil War, midway in that period, and there were other conflicts in the world as well; but, relatively speaking, the international scene was unprecedentedly peaceful.) Despite several minor variations, there were no general wars between great powers during the century. One exception was the Crimean War (1853–56), which pitted Russian forces against the allied armies of England, France, Turkey, and Sardinia. There was also a pair of bilateral wars between great powers, namely, the Franco-Prussian (1870–71) and the Russo-Japanese (1904–5) wars. Though few Americans gave much thought to the exceptional nature of this good fortune, the extended period of peace allowed Americans to focus almost exclusively on things close to home—continental expansion and, secondarily, consolidation of American hemispheric interests (for example, those expressed in the Monroe Doctrine).

The idea that the American continent belonged by right to those who could colonize it was typically expressed by the Virginia planter Lewis Burwell, who wrote to the board of trade in London in 1751.

That, notwithstanding the Grants of the kings of England, France or Spain, the Property of these uninhabited parts of the world must be founded upon prior Occupancy according to the Law of Nature; and it is the Seating & Cultivating the soil and not the bare travelling through a territory that constitutes Right; and it will be highly for the interest of the Crown (sic) to encourage the Seating of the Lands (sic) Westward as soon as possible to prevent the French.[13]

The founding fathers conceived the new nation as an expanding empire. Benjamin Franklin advocated westward expansion on the basis that it was necessary for the growing colonial population, which would double itself every quarter century.[14] Thomas Jefferson placed no hemispheric limits to American expansion in writing to James Monroe in 1801.

However our present interests may restrain us within our limits, it is impossible not to look forward to distant times, when our rapid multiplication will expand it beyond those limits, and cover the whole northern if not the southern continent, with people, speaking the same language, governed in similar forms, and by similar laws.[15]

The Louisiana Purchase secured the heartland of the American continent and became the basis of further claims for westward expansion to be pressed against Spain's holdings in Texas and New Mexico. The "All Mexico" movement swept the United States further westward in the 1840s and into the Mexican War of 1846.

America's lack of concern about its security during this period was reflected in the size of the military establishment. The naval fleet was almost nonexistent and regular army strength, with the exception of the Civil War, averaged about 10,000, varying between 8,220 in 1817 and 47,867 in 1898.[16] The principal tasks of the army were to provide security for western settlements and to furnish engineering assistance for railroad expansion.

The Spanish-American War began a period of expansion into the Caribbean and the Pacific and marked a shift in the foreign policy involvement of the United States. The size of the army almost doubled from 1898 to 1901 as the United States, almost without knowing it, emerged from the "Splendid Little War" as a great power with a limited imperialist position in both the Pacific and the Caribbean. However, these holdings were unrelated to the impulse that drew the United States into World War I. Violation of American neutral rights, especially the sinking of the *Lusitania* by German submarines in 1915 and revelation of German plots in Mexico finally ended a great debate over America's involvement in a European war. The United States entered the "War to End All Wars" as an "associated power" of the Allies.

Following World War I, America again tried to turn its back on the world outside the Western Hemisphere, rejecting President Wilson's approach to the League of Nations, pushing for disarmament in the Washington and Geneva Naval Conferences of 1922 and 1927 and renouncing war "as an instrument of national policy" in the Kellogg-Briand Pact of 1928.[17] Americans focused on a return to "normalcy," i.e., getting on with domestic concerns.

The Great Depression in 1929 and the early 1930s insured that public attention would remain riveted on domestic problems. Meanwhile, the United States sought to legislate itself out of foreign political entanglements through the Neutrality Acts of 1935, 1936, and 1937, which barred sales or shipments of munitions to belligerent nations. A popular "lesson" derived from World War I was that the United States had been unwittingly dragged into that war by the deceit and trickery of European diplomats and the "merchants of death" who provided the instruments of war to these diplomats. "Never again!"

Dissociation and Depreciation of Power and Diplomacy. "Normalcy" has traditionally meant more to Americans than merely the primacy of domestic affairs. It has also implied that peace or tranquility in international relations is the normal condition of world order. This is not surprising when we recall that until recently most of the American experience has been peaceful. There is another important reason for the view that order is the norm. The American political heritage has been strongly influenced by the philosophy of the Age of Enlightenment and particularly by the Englishman John Locke, whose basic precepts were known to the founders of the United State and were important in both the American Revolution and in the framing of the Constitution.[18] Locke expounded a natural rights doctrine, which conceived the state of nature as a condition of peace, mutual assistance, and preservation. He posited the ability of humans to arrive at a conception of "the right" through innate humanity, leading to trust in the rationality, even goodness, of humanities. Rational people would not want war and, hence, nations (viewed as the geographic personifications of humans) could and should resolve their differences through discussion and compromise.

Americans tended to ignore the contrary views of an earlier English philosopher, Thomas Hobbes, who wrote in *Leviathan* that in the state of nature a person's life is "solitary, poor, nasty, brutish, and short."[19] How do states naturally behave?

In all times, kings and persons of sovereign authority, because of their independency, are in continued jealousies, and in the state and posture of gladiators; having their weapons pointing, and their eyes fixed on one another; that is, their forts, garrisons, guns upon the frontiers of their kingdoms; and continual spies upon their neighbors; which is a posture of war.[20]

In the traditional American view, diplomacy should represent a process of ironing out differences through discussion, with eventual agreement based on rational accommodation of reasonable interests.[21] Power, in relation to diplomacy, was largely irrelevant, at best, and immoral, at worst. Given the many widely publicized idealistic attempts to eliminate the struggle for power from the international arena,[22] this public perception is hardly surprising.

Diplomacy, however, is also depreciated in many American minds, largely because of diplomats' longstanding reputation in the Western world for deviousness, duplicity, and secrecy. As noted, both during and after Word War I, the opinion was widely held that the secret dealings of European diplomats were largely responsible for that war.[23] Deeply committed to this view, President Wilson was largely instrumental in the development of a new diplomatic procedure for "registering" and publishing treaties. "Open covenants, openly arrived at" became his credo. But the principles of open methods "almost wrecked diplomacy on the shoals of impotence. Taken literally (and it often was), negotiation must then be public."[24] Little wonder that politicians have subsequently laced formal instruments of agreement and their public statements with platitudes, whenever possible, leaving important details to secret exchanges. President Carter's promises to return to open diplomacy proved short-lived as he encountered the realities of power politics. Yet his successor's attempts to back American diplomatic initiatives with military strength, such as the MX missile, received widespread criticism.

Utopianism. The great ideals of Christianity and the philosophy of the Enlightenment imbedded in the Western political heritage have impacted not only upon American values and goals but also on the means Americans typically embrace for attaining national goals. Humanity's presumed innate goodness and natural preference of peace have tended to condition the American approach to issues of national security.

The standards by which Americans have judged the world have been constructed quite naturally out of their own experience. By the turn of the twentieth century, the United States had become not only a great power but also a relatively satiated power enjoying phenomenal economic growth and social harmony. In overall terms, America had become a status quo power, its people essentially satisfied with life as they knew it, holding their condition of peace and harmony at home as the ideal for all rational people everywhere. They believed in the virtues of democracy and took it for granted that the fruits of democracy should represent meaningful goals to all people throughout the world.[25]

Given this experience and the important role of religion in the origins of the republic, it was only natural that the American people early developed a sense of mission that was idealistic, messianic, and hopeful of divine favor for national aspirations.[26] From Cotton Mather (1663–1728) forward, Americans have tended to borrow Biblical metaphor and to view their country "as a city upon a hill," as a beacon for all to see and emulate. While this sense of mission has sometimes served to limit aggressive tendencies, it has also been used, occasionally, to justify expansionism. In the 1840s in an article on the Mexican War, Albert Gallatin provided a classic statement of the prevailing sense of mission.

Your mission is to improve the state of the world, to be the "model republic" to show that men are capable of governing themselves, and that the simple and natural form of government is that which also confers most happiness on all, is productive of the greatest development of the intellectual faculties, above all, that which is attended by the highest standard of private and political virtue and morality.

The sense of mission arose again in the 1880s, this time to check the baser rationales of American imperialism. It held back outright imperialist designs in Hawaii until 1898 and in the Caribbean until its defenders, the old-school Republicans in the Senate and Thomas B. Reed in the House, were overcome by the patriotic fervor of the Spanish-American War in 1898. This messianism reappeared in 1917 as a national sense of responsibility to save democracy in Europe. Woodrow Wilson became its champion in taking the lead after the war in forming the League of Nations. It gave short-lived impetus to the "Good Neighbor Policy" in Latin America in the 1930s and helped give birth to the concept and realization of the United Nations and the Marshall Plan after World War II. Such idealism appeared again as one of the motivating factors for continuing American foreign aid to the less-developed countries throughout the 1950s and 1960s.

Even during the times when the sense of mission was undercut by the forces of imperialism, the leaders of the imperialistic factions clothed their designs in terms of American ideals. They knew that the American self-image was a powerful block to any program expressed in terms of power of materialism.

For most of the twentieth century, many Americans have been preoccupied with a long series of projects for shaping a better international system—after the wars, for returning the world to the natural order of peace and harmony— resting their hopes on various formal legal codes and international institutions. True to tradition, the popular perception of the proper American role in shaping the international order during this period has often been one of leadership by example rather than by major participation in cooperative international projects. Many people have continued to think that the sheer weight of the American example would exert a decisive influence upon the rest of the world.[28] As will be pointed out later, this traditional utopianism has increasingly given way in recent decades to the realization that, while they are vital, ideals and examples are not enough by themselves.

Aversion to Violence. The Judeo-Christian gospel, which has been central in forming American values, teaches "Thou shalt not kill," and the liberal culture of Western civilization has applied that ideal to people in the collective entities called "nations." The Englightenment philosophy of secular perfectionism further strengthened this belief, emphasizing that violence is not only morally wrong but irrational and unnatural. Reflecting these deeply ingrained views, Americans have been unwilling to consider war as anything other than a scourge. It kills, maims, and separates family and friends. Too, war and preparedness for war interrupt the routine cycle of self-directed materialism and prosperity.[29]

In these lights, war and peace are viewed as polar opposites. The resort to war or threats of violence between nations are seen as breaking down the normal, peaceful course of international affairs. With such a set of perceptions, it is not surprising that most Americans have had great difficulty accepting the dictum of Clausewitz: "War is a continuation of policy of other means."[30] Yet war cannot be an instrument, in a typical American view, for it is a pathological aberration.

As a related point, peace has been viewed as the responsibility of civilian policy-makers and diplomats, while war, which should be used only when diplomacy failed, was the province of the military. This dichotomy led to the further notion that the military should have no peacetime function in policy-making. The military function was to be limited to two tasks.

1. To guard the (continental) security of the United States.
2. To fight—and win—a war at the command of the civilian authorities.[31]

Consequently, policies for the raising, deploying, and employing of military forces were generally created in a vacuum. Until American intervention in World War II, such military policies were formulated largley without knowledge of relevant political objectives or consequences, and political decisions were reached without professional military advice about military capabilities.[32]

Traditionally, the American approach to war has leaned on several simple propositions. First, the United States should participate only in a "just war"— a "war fought either in self-defense or in collective defense against an armed attack."[33] The "unjust war" is any war fought for any other reason. Second, as just noted about the reaction to Clausewitz, war should be banished as an instrument of national policy. Third, however, as an instrument of collective defense against armed aggression, war is justified. Among other things, these propositions obviously rule out preventive or preemptive war (to strike an opponent first who clearly is making preparations to attack you).[34] President Truman made the point explicit. "We do not believe in aggressive or preventive war. Such war is the weapon of dictators, not of free democratic societies."[35]

Tied to the traditional devotion to the status quo in the international order, as noted previously, the American aversion to violence has also tended to deny the legitimacy of violent revolution against governments-in-being. Somehow, Americans have been inclined to forget that our own founders were steeped in the Lockean philosophy, which recognized the legitimacy of "the right to rebel" and that the United States was itself born of revolution.

Unwisdom of Standing Military Forces. Given the traditional view, which sees no necessary connection between diplomacy and armed might and which abhors violence, it is not surprising that until recently Americans have only in exceptional periods accorded much importance to the military. The central impulse has not merely been a distrust of large standing armies as a threat to the republic (although this issue has been stressed periodically) but also a blind faith, a view born in the colonial period, that a citizen military force of "unprofessional soldiers" will always be sufficient to defend the nation.

The militia system itself, with its axiom that every man was a trained and ready-armed soldier who would instantly spring to the defense of his country, encouraged the belief—which often proved a dangerous illusion—that the community was always prepared for its peril. In a country inhabited by "Minute Men" why keep a standing army?

The long-standing American myth of a constantly prepared citizenry helps explain why Americans have always been so ready to demobilize their forces. Again, and again, our popular army has laid down its arms with dizzying speed, only to disperse into a precarious peace.[36]

George Washington was aware of the reality, and discussed it in a circular of October 18, 1790.

I am religiously persuaded that the duration of the war, and the greatest part of the Misfortunes, and perplexities we have hitherto experienced, are chiefly to be attributed to temporary enlistments. . . . A moderate, compact force, on a permanent establishment capable of acquiring the discipline essential to military operations, would have been able to make head against the Enemy, without comparison better than the throngs of Militia, which have been at certain periods not in the field, but on their way to, and from the field.[37]

The myth has persisted, however, acquiring reinforcement in the ability of the United States to successfully call its "militia" to arms to fight victorious wars against foreign foes in 1812, 1846, 1898, 1917, and 1941.

Peacetime conscription has always been a notoriously "un-American" idea. It was used late in the Civil War and again in World War I and II. The first peacetime conscription law was passed in September 1940 over substantial congressional opposition and the "Keep America Out of War" movement led by the veteran socialist Norman Thomas. Following World War II, in August 1945, President Truman asked Congress for a peacetime draft for an indefinite period to replace overseas veterans. At that juncture, the issue of peacetime conscription was intimately tied to proposals for Universal Military Training (UMT). In the end, UMT was defeated in Congress, but in June 1948 a two-year peacetime conscription bill was passed and was steadily renewed by Congress each year until 1972.[38] Thus, willingness to support conscripted standing forces in "peacetime" (i.e., absence of "declared" wars) represents only about 7 percent of the American historical experience.

Except in crisis, Americans traditionally have wished that the minimum essential military establishment would "go away" to its posts and camps to do whatever the military has to do—but with minimum diversion of public attention and funds. This wish has been very much a part of American liberal ideology, the dominant corpus of beliefs in the United States. Those who identify with this view tend to argue that the civil-military relationship should be one in which civilians make all but the most narrow, technical decisions, that military spending is essentially nonproductive and, as suggested above, that the citizen-soldier is capable of donning a military uniform and defending the nation during times of crisis.

Once a crisis has passed, as indicated earlier, Americans have traditionally stumbled all over themselves in an attempt to demobilize as soon as possible. The rush to "bring the boys back home" after world War II was a dramatic example of this. A further excellent illustration of this was the deactivation of the Continental Army in 1784.

Resolved, that the commanding officer be and he is hereby directed to discharge the troops now in the service of the United States, except twenty-five privates to guard the stores at Fort Pitt, and fifty-five to guard the stores at West Point and other magazines, with a proportionate number of officers; no officer to remain in service above the rank of captain.[39]

The Crusading Spirit. Since it rejects the notion of war as an extension of politics, the United States cannot logically use the military instrument "to restore a balance of power" or "to protect economic interests abroad," or for any other mundane purpose. Instead, America goes to war in the name of moral principles—"to make the world safe for democracy," or "to end all wars." America gives its sons, daughters, and treasure only when forced and only in righteous indignation or outrage.

Democracy fights in anger—it fights for the very reason that it was forced to go to war. It fights to punish the power that was rash enough and hostile enough to provoke it—to teach that power a lesson it will not forget, to prevent the thing from happening again.[40]

Anger is sometimes further fueled by presumably God-given causes. Outraged by the "sinking of the *Maine*," the United States went to war in 1898 for retaliation but also for the stated purpose of liberating Cuba from Spanish tyranny, annexing the Philippines in the process "to educate the Filipinos, and uplift and civilize them, and by God's grace do the very best we could by them, as our fellowmen for whom Christ also died."[41]

Although aversion to violence has been relatively consistent as one of America's best characteristics, the crusading spirit has itself sometimes been a catalyst toward violence, showing that our worst qualities have sometimes been the other face of our best. Yet Americans do not have a tradition of glorifying violence per se. The problem has always been the relationship of ends to means. A cause noble enough justifies violent means. In fact, the sufficiency of some past causes has been a matter of considerable debate among American historians and philosophers.

The crusading spirit considers war essentially in terms of good versus evil. To engender public support for war—to get the public to sustain the privation thereof—policy-makers are often driven "to draw pictures in black and white, to exaggerate differences with one's adversaries and solidarity with one's friends." [42] This has obvious benefits for the war effort, but the problem is that it is very hard to turn off the public's emotions once they have been aroused. If the president mobilizes support for specific military interventions abroad, for example, he may find later options restricted or foreclosed by the emotional stakes and simplified expectations of the public.

It becomes difficult to fight a war for limited objectives when the process of limitation involves negotiating with the ultimate evil represented by the enemy. "Total victory," or "unconditional surrender," once they have been advocated by policy-makers, tend to become driving goals and progress toward such goals must be demonstrated. But protracted war with limited objectives tends to obscure "victory." Highly competitive by nature, Americans do not relish tie games. [43] They want to win "big"—and early.

Impatience. The crusading spirit is marked by impatience and irritation with time-consuming complexity. Americans believe that, with a little common sense and know-how, things can be done in a hurry. [44] Neither protracted, limited war nor costly, sustained programs for military preparedness fit this temper. The initial public reaction to the need to occupy Germany following World War II was disillusionment; after all, the war was over. Stalemate at Korea's 38th parallel evoked a similar public reaction in the 1950s.

Impatience, as one of several variables of mood, combined with the aversion to violence, is highly likely to produce public outcry for cessation of American involvement in a prolonged conflict demanding self-sacrifice unrelated to any clear vision of overriding national interest. Intensified by one-sided media coverage, such was the case in the Vietnam War from 1966 to 1970.

On the other hand, impatience may mix with the American proclivity for retreat into domestic affairs to yield boredom with or aversion to national security affairs. Thus, although many would agree that the greatest direct military threat to the security of the United States is in the nuclear realm, Americans increasingly have been "forgetting about the unthinkable." [45] Despite occasional peaks of public attention to nuclear-related issues in 1949 (after the first Soviet atomic test), in 1953–54 (after the first Soviet hydrogen tests), in 1958 (crises in Berlin, Lebanon, and Quemoy), and in 1961–63 (crisis in Berlin, the Cuban Missile Crisis, and the nuclear test ban) and in 1981–83 (the deployment of American Pershing missiles in Europe and the nuclear freeze), the American public seemed relatively uninterested in nuclear-related issues.

Civil defense provides an example; the programs emphasized during the late 1950s and during the administration of John F. Kennedy held little interest for Americans by the 1970s. The virtual demise of public interest in civil defense is epitomized by the condition of fallout shelters—empty water barrels and missing or inoperable radiation monitoring equipment.[46] This situation has developed in spite of the fact that numerous careful studies have demonstrated that modest civil defense measures could save literally tens of millions of lives. Though there are several possible explanations for this phenomenon, opinion surveys of the late 1960s shed some light.

While there has not been a significant decline of perception of the threat of nuclear war, there has been a very significant increase in concern about the magnitude and acuteness of national priorites and a relative retrenchment from international concerns and commitments by our people and government.

The declining saliency of civil defense, the general fatigue about war worries, and increased general domestic concerns cause one to doubt that civil defense will become a more acute issue in the 1970s.[47]

Old Traditions and New Realities. The experience of World War II and the birth of the cold war in its aftermath transformed some important aspects of American approaches to national security. Reluctantly at first, Americans came to accept the role of the United States as a world power with worldwide responsibilities. The specter of communism as a challenge to the freedom of peoples everywhere and the advent of Soviet nuclear capability destroyed American's traditional sense of continental security and induced them to look to security matters well beyond their shores.

Traditional faith in the rationality of people was reexpressed through the United Nations. Yet other agreements—military alliances—hedged the bet on a person's rationality as far as communists were concerned. In part, too, American utopianism was revived in the altruism of rebuilding a shattered Europe through the Marshall Plan and in the impulse to share the blessings of economic development worldwide through a massive program of foreign assistance. But, although partially rooted in utopianism and the familiar sense of mission, these initiatives also reflected a pragmatic view that the threat of communism could be stopped on two levels: (1) direct Soviet military threats could be deterred by confronting them with military forces deployed worldwide and backed by strategic nuclear forces; and (2) communist subversion could be stopped through foreign aid designed to "stabilize" allies and less developed nations worldwide. U.S. policy, thus, became one of "containing" communism through military and economic countermeasures.

Not only did the aversion to a peacetime standing army weaken after World War II, as noted earlier, but so did the tendency to isolate the military from decisions about war and peace. General George Marshall began the process during the war when he created the War Department's Special Planning Division (SPD) and charged it with postwar planning. The SPD established direct liaison with the Department of State, the Bureau of the Budget and the War Production Board, and its members made regular appearances before congressional committees to provide information and gain congressional approval of major postwar proposals, e.g., unification of the services and UMT. The National Security Act of 1947 further signaled a conceptual overhaul in the American approach to national security. Military views became an inherent part of overall defense policy and planning. A new organization, the National Security Council, was established by the act to determine at the highest level of government the relationships between national objectives and military policy, in peacetime and in war—and in the zone of ambiguity.

The traditional primacy of domestic affairs remained, but anticommunism and Soviet actions drove Americans to devote a continuing substantial share of the nation's wealth to defense and foreign aid programs. In the aftermath of disillusion over the war in Vietnam and in the light of detente with both major communist powers, many Americans began to think further about the high U.S. profile in world politics and its domestic costs. Defense budgets came under increasing fire and, as part of the rethinking, peacetime conscription was again rejected.

By the latter 1970s, however, the majority of Americans had accepted the main facts of international interdependence and the necessarily important role of the United States as world power. Few Americans doubted the necessity for large and expensive programs for national security, although many were prone to ask, "How much is enough?" There was no real question of a further American retreat into "isolationism." Instead, skeptical about the general utility of military force in the post-Vietnam era, many Americans sought to limit the conditions under which the United States would intervene abroad with U.S. forces.

More than traces of the old traditions in the American approach to national security remained as the United States moved into the 1980s, but the experiences of the previous three decades had forged an awareness of the new realities of the post–World War II era. National security policy-makers had to take into account American traditional values and attitudes, but they could do so with a pragmatism that would have been unthinkable prior to World War II.

DISCUSSION QUESTIONS

1. How would you describe the "American national character"? Would all Americans agree with your description? What influences one's description of "national character"?

2. What is public opinion? How important is it today in national security policy formulation in the United States? How can it be determined? Is public opinion of any importance in the Soviet Union? Why?

3. How does public opinion both enhance and inhibit an effective American national security policy?

4. What is the difference between the Lochean and Hobbesian philosophical views and how have these views impacted on typical American views? How have these views impacted on American national security policy? In your view, which philosophy has dominated American national security policy in the past? In the present?

5. If "war is abhorrent to Americans," how can you explain the fact that the United States has been involved in numerous wars and maintains one of the largest military forces in history?

6. How would you describe the historical role of the military in peacetime national security policy? How has it changed?

7. To what extent do traditional values now constrain American national security decision-makers?

RECOMMENDED READING

Almond, Gabriel A. *The American People and Foreign Policy.* 2d ed. New York: Frederick A. Praeger, 1977.

Booth, Ken, and Wright, Moorhead. *American Thinking about Peace and War: New Essays on American Thought and Attitudes.* New York: Harvester Press, 1978.

Hartmann, Frederick H. *The New Age of American Foreign Policy.* New York: Macmillan, 1970.

Huntington, Samuel P. *The Soldier and the State.* Cambridge, Mass.: Belknap Press, 1957.

Kennan, George F. *American Diplomacy, 1900–1950.* Chicago: University of Chicago Press, 1951.

Levering, Ralph B. *The Public and American Foreign Policy, 1918–1978.* New York: William Morrow, 1978.

Merk, Frederick. *Manifest Destiny and Mission in American History.* New York: Alfred A. Knopf, 1963.

Osgood, Robert E. *Limited War: The Challenge to American Strategy.* Chicago: University of Chicago Press, 1957.

Rainey, René E. *Patterns of American Foreign Policy.* Boston: Allyn & Bacon, 1975.

Schlesinger, Arthur M., Jr. *The Crisis of Confidence.* Boston: Houghton Mifflin, 1969.

Tucker, Robert W. *The Just War: A Study in Contemporary American Doctrine.* 2d ed. Baltimore: Johns Hopkins University Press, 1979.

Walzer, Michael. *Just and Unjust Wars.* New York: Basic Books, 1977.

4

THE EVOLUTION
OF AMERICAN NATIONAL SECURITY
POLICY

National security strategy and military structure are shaped by the inter-actions of a number of influences, many of which defy precise identification. However, there are three principal categories of variables through which the evolution of strategic policy and military structure can be largely traced. They are international political and military developments, domestic priorities, and technological advancements.

International Political and Military Developments. The international environment is an important and constantly changing influence on U.S. policy. U.S. strategy is largely a response to perceived threats to American interests and objectives that exist in the international arena. As Walter Lippmann suggested, a nation is secure to the extent to which it is not in danger of having to sacrifice core values, such as national independence or territorial integrity, if it wishes to avoid war and is able, if challenged, to maintain those values by victory in such a war.[1] The perception of international threats to U.S. core values and interests is thus the base for the formulation and ex-ecution of national security policy.

A major factor in establishing the international environment is the presence or absence of alliances. The defense efforts of friendly and allied states help to define U.S. security problems and to condition the type and size of Amer-ican effort required. American capability to pursue national security objectives is augmented or diminished by both quantitative and qualitative consideration of U.S. alliances vis-à-vis the alliance arrangements of potential opponents. It is also conditioned, of course, by the impact of unaligned nations or other third parties, including international and transnational organizations.

Domestic Politics. A nation's security policy is also heavily influenced by domestic politics. As a minimum, the internal environment determines the amount of effort that a society will devote to foreign and defense policy.[2] In the United States, the impact of domestic politics is seen most heavily in the budgetary process, but it is also felt in such areas as manpower policy (for example, the draft). Manpower strengths, weapon systems, strategic mobility, and other strategic resources available for national security purposes are necessarily defined and tailored by defense budgets. Defense budgets and programs may not determine strategy, but national security options are heavily conditioned by the nature and extent of the resources available. Regardless of the type of regime, domestic goals have a great impact on the development of a nation's security policy and its allocation of resources.

Technological Change. Technology is a major variable in the interaction of influences that determine security policy. What is "possible" in American national security is in considerable part determined by the technological capabilities of both the United States and its adversaries. The impact of technological advances upon traditional security concerns and calculations is enormous. One need only look at the carnage of World War I to see the results of policy not keeping pace with technology. A century of relative peace in Europe had left military strategies largely as they were at the time of the Congress of Vienna, yet there had been a century of unparalleled technological advancement between 1815 and 1914. The military strategies of 1914 simply were not adequate for the proper employment of existing technological capabilities, and the stalemate that developed along the Western front was due in large part to the inability to adapt military strategy and tactics to the new realities of war imposed by those capabilities.

Today, the security of the United States and its allies is based largely on the strength and invulnerability of U.S. strategic nuclear weapons. The extent to which a potential adversary is deterred from threatening the security interests of the United States is shaped in part by the ability to convince an opponent of the U.S. capability and willingness to employ its vast nuclear armory. Rapid technological developments in nuclear capabilities, which could sap that strength or make it vulnerable, can thus be profoundly destabilizing, constituting a major threat to national security.

Strategy and Structure. National security policies or strategies are for the most part "implemented" by military force structures. Since international relations and domestic politics are intertwined, national security policy (which comprises both strategic and structural policies) exists in two worlds; any major decision about it influences and is influenced by both international and domestic politics. Strategic decisions are made largely in response to perceived threats in the international environments; they deal primarily with commitments, deployment and employment of military forces, and the readiness and development of military capabilities. Structural decisions are made most in terms of domestic politics and deal primarily with budget and force decisions on defense personnel, materiel, and organization.[3] The two types of decisions interact at all levels. Strategic decisions "determine" the force structures required to implement them, yet the resources made available through structural decisions limit the extent to which strategic decisions can be made. Indeed, ongoing programs that exist as the result of structural decisions have a dynamic of their own in shaping policy.

CONTAINMENT POLICY: MOBILIZATION OR DETERRENCE STRATEGY?

The United States traditionally has relied on a national security policy of mobilizing to meet threats rather than constantly maintaining adequate forces. America's geographic isolation, both the people and policy-makers believed, would prevent direct attack on the United States, while recognition of impending hostilities abroad would give it sufficient time in a crisis to convert its industrial and manpower potential into operational military strength. Yet the realities of the international arena following World War II seemed to present a threat for which the United States would have to be constantly ready. The security of the United States would depend on its ability to deter war by presenting a posture of military preparedness. The early postwar years were to be marked by a fundamental tension between the old strategy of mobilization and the new strategy of deterrence.

The Return to Normalcy, 1945–46. The end of World War II saw the United States emerge as the most powerful nation on earth. Its homeland was untouched by war, and its enormous industrial potential had produced war materiel not only for its own armies and navies but for those of its allies as well. The collapse of Germany and Japan meant total victory and led to visions of a prolonged period of peace implemented through the collective security machinery of the embryonic United Nations. Technologically, the United States was also in an unchallengeable position. American development of the atomic bomb was probably the most important single event to affect postwar international relations.[4]

With victory came enormous public and congressional pressure for the United States to demobilize its armies and bring the troops home. This pressure led to one of the most rapid demobilizations in history. On V-J Day the army had 8,020,000 soldiers, but by July 1946, less than a year after the end of the war, it was down to less than a quarter of that, to 1,889,690.[5] In the two years from 1945 to 1947, the United States allowed its overall armed forces to decline from a wartime peak of 12 million soldiers to a low of 1.4 million.[6] This massive disarmament occurred despite the fact that the wartime alliance between the United States and the Soviet Union was being replaced by rapidly increasing tension.

American policy-makers, confronted with what they perceived to be aggressive Soviet intentions in Eastern Europe, Greece, Turkey, Iran, and the

Far East, came to agree on the need for a tougher line with the Soviets. In 1947, George Kennan developed and expressed the concept of containment.

> The main element of any United States policy toward the Soviet Union must be that of a long-term, patient but firm and vigilant containment of Russian expansive tendencies.[7]

Acceptance of the policy of containment laid the foundation for the theoretical framework of American strategic policy for the next quarter-century. Opposition to communist expansion became the fundamental principle of American foreign policy. Although there were to be disagreements over the means to achieve this policy, there was little disagreement on the end itself. The United States, public and leaders alike, came to agree upon the policy of containment; that policy led in turn to the development of the strategy of deterrence.

Conflict between the New Strategy and the Old Military Structure. Successful implementation of the policy of containment required ready forces sufficient to deny the Soviets the ability to expand their influence. For this purpose mobilization potential was clearly less useful than forces-in-being. The latter were needed to give American decision-makers the capability to implement their strategy. In December 1947, Secretary of Defense Forrestal listed the "four outstanding military facts of the world" as: (1) the predominance of Russian land power in Europe and Asia, (2) the predominance of American sea power, (3) U.S. exclusive possession of the atomic bomb, and (4) American superior production capacity.[8]

In a sense, the problem confronting President Truman was how to checkmate the first military fact with the latter three. Put differently, the problem for containment was twofold: (1) inadequacy of conventional ground and air units, and (2) doctrinal inadequacy concerning strategic use of a tiny atomic arsenal. The United States could threaten the Soviet homeland with atomic attack if Soviet armies marched into Western Europe, but the atom bomb was of little help in such other defense tasks as preserving the integrity of Iran, deterring attack on Korea, or suppressing guerrillas in Greece.[9] Conventional ground and air power seemed essential for these latter tasks, yet the U.S. force structure was weakest in precisely those respects.

Continued Reliance on Mobilization. Implementing the policy of containment therefore raised the difficult problem of how to deal with narrow domestic political constraints on the size of the military effort. Overriding a presidential veto, Congress passed a general income tax reduction bill in early 1948, thereby limiting the revenue available for domestic and military expenditures. In spite of the president's requests, no substantial tax increases were approved until after the outbreak of the Korean War. Since President Truman was determined to balance the budget, the administration imposed a ceiling on military expenditures consonant with the reduced resources available. To compound the difficulty, the "remainder" approach to defense spending was developed, whereby funds available for security expenditures were calculated by estimating general revenues, subtracting funds earmarked for domestic programs, foreign aid, and interest, and devoting the remainder to defense spending. From fiscal year (FY) 1947 to FY 1950, security expenditures were virtually static at $14.4, $11.7, $12.9, and $13.0 billion, respectively.[10] Domestic political priorites ensured that there would be inadequate monies for the forces-in-being believed needed to contain Soviet power; by default, reliance on mobilization continued.

A second constraint on the successful implementation of the policy of containment was the doctrinal orientation of the military. American military thinking was preoccupied not so much with the development of strategy and forces-in-being to deter or fight limited wars but rather with preparations to mobilize forces to win a major war if one should occur.[11] The army continued to insist that World War III would be similar to the war it had just prosecuted so successfully. In his final report as chief of staff, General Eisenhower urged more extensive preparation for the total mobilization that would be required in the future.[12] "Armed forces and the nature of war, if war comes in the next few years," declared the chief army planner, Brig. Gen. George A. Lincoln, in 1947, "will in general be similar initially to the closing phases of World War II." [13]

Although the air force and the navy felt the weapons of World War II were obsolete and began to push for new strategic systems, in the immediate postwar years the concept of deterrence by forces-in-being had little place in military planning:[14] Effectively, the goals of each of the armed services had been set prior to the end of World War II, and since there was no unified budgetary process each set of goals was based on the parochial conceptions of the roles and missions of the separate services. As Samuel Huntington summarizes, "The two great constraints of effective military planning, the doctrinal heritage from the past and the pressure of domestic needs, combined to produce a serious gap between military policy and foreign policy."[15]

The Truman Doctrine. On March 12, 1947, President Truman appeared before a joint session of Congress and outlined what he felt was the necessary U.S. response to communist pressure in Greece and Turkey. The president maintained, in what came to be known as the Truman Doctrine, that the United States must help other nations to maintain their political institutions and national integrity when threatened by aggressive attempts to overthrow them and to institute totalitarian regimes. This was no more than a frank recognition, Truman declared, that totalitarian systems imposed their will on free people, by direct or indirect aggression, and undermined the foundations of international peace and hence the security of the United States.[16]

The Truman Doctrine represented a marked departure from the U.S. tradition of minimal peacetime involvement in international affairs. The doctrine set forth themes justifying American foreign involvements and initiated military and economic aid programs to nations resisting communist aggression. The justifications it contained for American intervention in foreign lands were used repeatedly by subsequent administrations.[17]

The Marshall Plan. The Marshall Plan, a massive economic aid program launched in 1948 and implemented through the Organization for European Economic Cooperation formed for that purpose, was designed to help restore the war-shattered economies of Europe. American leaders believed that the ability of Europe to resist communist aggression was dependent on its rapid economic recovery.[18] The Marshall Plan, taken in conjunction with the Truman Doctrine, marked the emergence of the United States as a world power bent on establishing stability in the international community and willing to adopt an activist role in seeing that U.S. interests abroad were maintained.

An accumulation of events in 1948 and 1949 solidified the U.S. view of the communist threat. The forced communization of Czechoslovakia and the blockade of surface access routes to West Berlin, both occurring in 1948, intensified Western perceptions of the Soviet Union as an overtly hostile nation. In 1949, two even more dramatic events affected the formulation of U.S. security strategy. In August, the U.S.S.R. exploded its first nuclear device. The U.S. monopoly on atomic weapons had been broken years sooner than anticipated by U.S. planners. In late 1949, the Communist Chinese completed the conquest of the mainland, creating the appearance of a monolithic communist adversary stretching from Central Europe across the length of the Asian continent.

NSC 68 and Its Implications. The disturbing events of 1948–49 highlighted the inadequacies of U.S. military posture. Awareness of these shortcomings

Reprinted by permission of the *Minneapolis Star*.

led to the first serious attempt to reconcile strategy with structure, that is, to balance the strategy of containment with a force capability designed to implement the tenets of the strategy. A joint State-Defense Department committee was instructed "to make an over-all review and reassessment of American foreign and defense policy."[19] The report, delivered to the National Security Council in April 1950 and labeled NSC 68, advocated "an immediate and large scale build up in our military and general strength and that of our allies with the intention of righting the power balance and in hope that through means other than all-out war we could induce a change in the nature of the Soviet system."[20] NSC 68 called for a substantial increase in defense expenditures, warning that the United States must be capable of dealing with piecemeal aggression and subversion, with both limited and all-out war. The problem was how to sell a substantial increase in the defense budget without an imminent threat in an administration committed to a policy of economy and balanced budgets. The problem was solved on June 25, 1950, by the North Korean invasion of South Korea.

War and Rearmament. The invasion of South Korea provided the immediate crisis required to obtain public support for vastly increased defense spending. Expenditures for national security programs rose from $13.0 billion for FY 1950, to $22.3 billion in FY 1951, $44.0 billion in FY 1952, and $50.4 billion in FY 1953.[21]

There were important differences of opinion within informed American circles concerning Soviet intentions in Korea. Some felt that the attack by the Soviets' North Korean satellite was part of a general plan for expansion, while others saw it as a feint designed to divert resources from Western Europe.[22] Whatever the initial view, Communist Chinese entry into the war in late 1950 solidified the perception of an aggressive, monolithic communist threat to the Free World.

The outbreak of the war found the U.S. with an extremely limited conventional capability. The resulting rearmament effort was pulled by three competing, but complementary, purposes: (1) immediate prosecution of the Korean War, (2) creation of a mobilization based for the long term, and (3) development of active forces to balance Soviet strength and to deter further Soviet agression.[23] In short, the war in Korea made rearmament possible, but rearmament was not directed solely at the problem of fighting the war; forces were also being developed for worldwide deterrence purposes. As Huntington describes it, "Competitive and yet equally relevant, mobilization and deterrence marched shoulder to shoulder through the Korean War rearmament effort."[24]

NATO: The Institutionalization of Containment. Soviet pressure on its neighbors to the west and south and the existence of very large Soviet conventional forces, the first of Secretary Forrestal's "four outstanding military facts of the world," caused widespread and increasing concern about the security of Western Europe. As a consequence, for the first time in history, the United States deemed it necessary to enter into peacetime military alliance with foreign states and to deploy its major forces on the territory of its allies in the absence of armed conflict. The North Atlantic Treaty was signed in April 1949. The twelve signatories agreed to keep the peace among themselves and to resist aggression jointly. An attack on one would be considered an attack on all. Europe became America's first line of defense; the North Atlantic Treaty Organization (NATO) was the expression of the American effort to contain communism by military means.

In February 1952, the Lisbon Conference set a 1954 goal of ninety NATO divisions (half active, half reserve) as necessary for conventional defense of Europe. It quickly became obvious that the goal would not be met as European members of NATO, less fearful of Soviet aggression after two years of war in Korea had failed to spread to Europe, began to reduce military budgets, cut terms of service for draftees, and stretch out arms procurements. In December 1952, the North Atlantic Council approved a drastic reduction in Lisbon force goals, and NATO came to rely largely on the tactical and strategic nuclear weapons of the United States to deter Soviet aggression.

Conflicting Priorities. As the Korean War developed into a stalemate, it became evident that the war had not, as some had feared, marked the beginning of a general Soviet assault on the West. With continuing casualties and costs and without a clear perception of an imminent Soviet threat, the American public became increasingly sour on the war in Korea. Public resentment over increasing military spending rose, and by 1952 the Truman administration made a marked shift toward domestic priorities. With the incoming (early 1953) Eisenhower administration's so-called New Look, the basic strategy of the United States explicitly shifted from mobilization to deterrence. By 1954 it was accepted by U.S. policy-makers and public that the international communist threat to American and European security was real and immediate, and that the United States no longer enjoyed the geographic protection that historically had afforded the time required for mobilization of military personnel and other resources. Acceptance of the strategy of deterrence and the necessity for forces-in-being to implement it reflected the acknowledgment of the realities of international and technological affairs.

MASSIVE RETALIATION AND THE NEW LOOK

Domestic Priorities and Strategic Reassessment. President Eisenhower regarded the threat to U.S. security as dual—military and economic. The military threat posed by the communist powers was obvious, but Eisenhower also believed that continued high levels of defense spending by the United States threatened the stability of the economy and was, therefore, also a significant long-term threat. The New Look was an effort to reconcile the conflicting priorities of an economic growth and major military programs. Further, since the dual threat was a continuing one, the proper balance between domestic and military expenditures would have to be maintained for an extended period.

Upon taking office President Eisenhower was determined to reduce military expenditures and balance the federal budget. He had campaigned on a peace and economy platform and was committed to a tax reduction and spending cuts in order to reduce the Truman budget deficit. Proposed cuts in military spending were opposed by the Joint Chiefs of Staff (JCS), who maintained that any reduction in expenditures would endanger national security. An impasse developed between the administration and a JCS committed to a substantial military build-up directed to a future "year of maximum danger" (about 1956–58), the time at which Soviet military capabilities would reach their highest strength relative to those of the West. The old JCS was replaced, and in May 1953 the new Joint Chiefs assumed the task (even before they took office) of wrestling with the difficult problems of strategic reassessment at which their predecessors had balked.

The National Security Council Planning Board, in a study labeled NSC 162, made an effort to define future national security policy in the broadest sense. The paper recommended the continuation of the policy of containment but with greater reliance on nuclear weapons and strategic air power and an expansion of capabilities to defend the continental United States from air attack.

The JCS had also begun its reassessment. The *Sequoia* study (named after the secretary of the navy's yacht, upon which the final decisions had been made) recommended further development of U.S. air defenses and strategic retaliatory forces, withdrawal of some American forces from overseas, creation of the mobile strategic reserve, reliance upon Allied forces for their own local defense buttressed by U.S. air and sea power, and strengthening of U.S. reserve forces.[25]

The Impact of Technology. Technology provided the means by which Eisenhower escaped from the strategy versus structure box. American technological and numerical superiority in nuclear weapons systems provided a strategic option that made possible domestic economic goals. Technology, in the form of strategic air power and tactical nuclear weapons, permitted the blend of seemingly incompatible political goals, i.e., a foreign policy of worldwide containment and a domestic policy focused on driving down military expenditures.

New Look Programs. The Eisenhower New Look strategy made a number of assumptions about the international environment. It assumed that there would be no significant increase in international tensions and no significant change in the relationship between U.S. and Soviet power. Massive retaliation was to be the major deterrent; adversaries were warned that nuclear retaliation would follow aggression.

The programs of the New Look resulted in a further reduction in conventional ground forces and in the expansion of continental air defense capabilities. The key aspect of the New Look was the decision to place very high reliance upon nuclear weapons.[26] Strategic air power became the mainstay of the U.S. deterrent posture, and tactical nuclear weapons were to be used to replace the reduced levels of conventional forces in forward defense areas.

The critical strategic change of the New Look was expressed in Secretary of State Dulles's massive retaliation speech on January 12, 1954, and in the decision by the North Atlantic Council to deploy tactical nuclear weapons in Western Europe and to authorize the NATO authorities to base military planning on the assumption that nuclear weapons would be used in the event of hostilities. Although there were a number of interpretations of just what massive retaliation entailed, Secretary Dulles stated, "There is no local defense which alone will contain the mighty land power of the Communist world. Local defenses must be reinforced by the further deterrent of massive retaliation power."[27] Therefore, Dulles stated, the president had made the basic decision "to depend primarily upon a great capacity to retaliate instantly and by means and at places of our own choosing."[28] In sum, America's military capabilities were to hinge on nuclear weapons to meet even those military contingencies precipitating less than general war.

Extending Containment. Extending the American military alliance system beyond NATO (and the earlier Organization of American States) became an integral part of containment strategy. Prior to the adoption of an explicit strategy of massive retaliation in 1954, the United States had already begun a process of expanding defense commitments worldwide with the goal of containing communism. One principal lesson of the Korean War as perceived by U.S. policy-makers in the 1950s was the judgment that American disengagement and equivocation had tempted the Communists to invade. The conclusion was that America's commitment to defend friendly territories adjacent to communist countries must be made specific, and the most obvious way to do so was through military alliances.

The network of alliances began to form soon after the outbreak of hostilities in Korea. In 1951 the United States negotiated a security treaty with Japan, guaranteeing the defense of Japan and granting the United States land, sea, and air bases on the Japanese home islands. A similar mutual defense treaty was signed with the Philippines as well. Also in 1951 the United States signed with Australia and New Zealand the ANZUS treaty, pledging U.S. support for the security of those two nations. In 1953, following the armistice, Korea and the United States signed a security pact pledging consultation in the event of armed attack and establishing the disposition of land, sea, and air forces in and around the Republic of Korea. In 1954 the United States signed a treaty with Nationalist China which called for joint consultation in the event of danger of armed attack and specified the disposition of American forces on Taiwan and the Pescadores.

The Southeast Asia Treaty Organization (SEATO), of which Australia, France, New Zealand, Pakistan, the Philippines, Thailand, the United Kingdom, and the United States were members, was established in 1954. The SEATO Treaty provided that each member would "act to meet the common danger" in the event of hostilities in the treaty area. In addition to the formal alignment with SEATO, the United States was also sending millions of dollars in military aid to Indochina to help finance the French war with the Viet Minh. In 1954, as the French position in Vietnam became more tenuous, the French government requested the commitment of American troops but was refused by President Eisenhower.

The Central Treaty Organization (CENTO), which the United States supported but did not formally join, was an American and British sponsored alliance to prevent Soviet communism from moving southward; the organization linked Britain, Turkey, Iran, and Pakistan. Additionally, the United States also signed bilateral agreements with Pakistan and Iran.

Given the presumption that American nuclear weapons could and would serve to deter both large and small aggressions, given the policy of a balanced budget and the widespread concern in the United States about communist aggression, it appeared to make sense in the 1950s to strengthen governments on the periphery of the communist bloc by

- Pledging the support of the United States to prevent or stop aggression, especially if communist-inspired
- Providing military assistance to strengthen the defense capabilities of those governments bordering the communist bloc
- Providing economic and/or military assistance to preserve or help create political and economic stability for governments that allied themselves with the anticommunist cause
- Training and supporting foreign troops in their own country as less expensive than maintaining American troops abroad
- Establishing basing rights as the quid pro quo of assistance

The U.S. included the Asian rimlands in its ring of containment and, attempting to preclude another Korea, sought to knit the states of the region into a network of military alliances under American leadership.

The New New Look, 1956. In 1954, when the policy of massive retaliation was established, the United States possessed the ability to destroy the military forces of the U.S.S.R. with little likelihood of serious retaliatory damage in return. By 1956, however, this was no longer clearly so. Major Soviet catchup efforts and technological innovations had led to an arms spiral; the "balance of terror" stemming from mutual vulnerability to nuclear devastation had become a decisive military fact.[29] In short, the rapid growth of Soviet strategic nuclear power had undermined the New Look's two key assumptions: that the earlier ratio of Soviet-to-American nuclear power would not be radically altered and that U.S. nuclear retaliatory forces would deter both large and small aggresssions. It is ironic that in 1954 the Eisenhower administration had placed primary reliance on a strategic policy which, if implemented only two years later, was judged likely to result in serious nuclear destruction to the United States or its allies.

A second major implication of the new balance of terror was that strategic nuclear forces were much less credible in the deterrence of local aggression. Even at the outset the doctrine of massive retaliation had been criticized by such analysts as M.I.T.'s William Kaufmann and Harvard's Henry Kissinger, who argued that the threat of massive nuclear retaliation was not effective in deterring local, ambiguous wars because it was not believable. There exists a threshold of conflict, they argued, below which it is not credible to threaten to use strategic nuclear forces. Given the balance of terror, the insurgencies taking place in developing nations around the world fell below that threshold. Nonstrategic forces would be needed to deal effectively with such relatively low-level conflicts.

The administration began to look for a strategy that permitted greater flexibility. The resulting "New New Look" was an attempt to develop a new approach to deterrence by adjusting existing programs but without increasing military expenditures. The dominant characteristics of the New New Look included: (1) continuing efforts to stabilize military spending; (2) downgrading of mobilization, readiness, and reserve forces; (3) acceptance of strategic retaliatory capability sufficient, but only sufficient, to deter a direct attack on American territory or equally vital interests; and (4) grudging recognition of the need to build and maintain capabilities of limited war.[30] It should be noted that the New New Look purported to provide a credible means of waging limited war, namely, tactical nuclear weapons. Indeed, one of the major distinctions of the new approach was the direct mating of tactical nuclear weapons with the strategy of limited war.[31] Recognizing that massive retaliation was not a credible threat in limited war situations, Secretary Dulles attempted to modify the strategy by linking tactical nuclear weapons and limited war. Writing in the October 1957 *Foreign Affairs*, Secretary Dulles explained that "in the future it may . . . be feasible to place less reliance upon deterrence of vast retaliatory power" because the "nations which are around the Sino-Soviet perimeter can possess an effective defense [through limited nuclear warfare] against fullscale conventional attack. . . ."[32]

New New Look programs were shaped by the twin pressures of Soviet and American technological achievement and an American economy that was plagued by what was, at the time, a unique combination of continuing recession and inflation. Largely as a result of inflation, defense costs were rising. Confronted with a choice between increasing the national debt or reducing military spending, the Eisenhower administration chose the latter. The administration's last years were marked by an effort to limit military expenditures.

Spending in FY 1958 was $39 billion; in FY 1959 and FY 1960, $41.2 billion; and in FY 1961, $43.2 billion. In constant dollar terms, military spending was less in 1960 than it had been in any year since 1951.[33]

The final years of the Eisenhower presidency saw a number of international and technological pressures brought to bear on U.S. national security policy. In August 1957 the Soviets announced the successful test of an intercontinental ballistic missile (ICBM). In October of that year the Soviets launched the first artificial satellite, sputnik, causing an intense reexamination of U.S. strategic programs and demands for increased military expenditures. The Gaither Committee, appointed early in 1957 by President Eisenhower to study a fallout shelter program for the United States, presented its report shortly after the launching of sputnik. Defining its mandate very broadly, the committee recommended a substantial increase in the defense budget, aimed primarily at improving the U.S. strategic posture.[34] Although the committee's recommendations were largely rejected, the discussion of strategic capabilities which it evoked helped provoke the "missile-gap" controversy, which became an issue in the 1960 presidential campaign.

FLEXIBLE RESPONSE, 1960–68

The Necessity for Change. As the new decade began, changes in both the external environment and technology dictated a serious reappraisal of military strategy. The growth of Soviet thermonuclear capabilities cast increasing doubt on the wisdom and credibility of a retaliation threat. The missile-gap controversy raised questions about the adequacy of U.S. nuclear force levels. Western awareness of the increasingly bitter dispute between China and the Soviet Union aggravated the problems of deterrence, for China came to be viewed as a power center and a threat in its own right.

Changes in weapons technology and force structure also made a reexamination of U.S. policy imperative. Overreliance on tactical nuclear weapons, particularly in Europe, was increasingly viewed as dangerous for two reasons. First, in view of the weakened U.S. strategic position, deterrence could well fail; and, if it did, escalation to all-out nuclear war would be hard to check because there is no discernible "firebreak" between tactical and strategic nuclear weapons. Second, should a crisis arise, shortages of conventional forces appeared to place decision-makers in the dilemma of choosing between nuclear retaliation and inaction.

Turbulence in the developing countries of the world also demonstrated the shortcomings of U.S. retaliation strategy. Insurgencies spread in Asia, Africa, and Latin America, dramatically highlighting the inapplicability of nuclear weapons. Communist nations gave their support to "wars of national liberation" and Soviet military and economic assistance was extended to a number of regions. Massive retaliation was inadequate to deal with these complexities, and nuclear technology made general war too costly to both sides. Clearly, a new policy was called for, and the incoming Kennedy administration wasted little time in framing one.

The Search for Options. The search for policy options began at the outset of the Kennedy administration. The budget ceiling approach to defense policy-making was abandoned, and budget constraints on Secretary of Defense Robert McNamara were lifted by the president. The budget ceiling approach had not proven an effective means of rationally structuring the U.S. defense program. In effect, service missions were determined independently, monies were allocated on a "fair shares" basis, and programs were developed with little regard for what the other services were doing. National strategies and priorities were supposedly set forth in an agreed National Security Council document called the Basic National Security Policy (BNSP). However, the BNSP was a vague document that provided little real guidance on how defense dollars should be spent. General Maxwell Taylor summarized the document's weaknesses.

It was so broad in nature and general in language as to provide limited guidance in practical application. In the course of its development, the sharp issues in national defense which confront our leaders have been blurred in conference and in negotiation. The final text thus permits many different interpretations. . . . The Basic National Security Policy document means all things to all people and settles nothing.[35]

Given the vague nature of the guidance that they received, the services had a great deal of latitude to develop their own programs. McNamara, when he came into office, was appalled.

The Army planning, for example, was based, largely, on a long war of attrition, while the Air Force planning was based, largely, on a short war of nuclear bombardment. Consequently, the Army was stating a requirement for stocking months of fighting supplies against the event of a sizeable [*sic*] conventional conflict while the Air Force stock requirements for such a war had to be measured in days, and not very many days at that.[36]

Strategic programs were developed independently by each service. For example, navy briefings to Secretary McNamara in 1961 on the number of Polaris missile submarines required never mentioned the existence of the U.S. Air Force or any of its strategic retaliatory forces. When the air force made analyses of how many Minuteman missiles were required, it assumed that no more Polaris submarines would be authorized than whatever the existing number happened to be.[37]

McNamara was determined to centralize and control the development of U.S. military forces. He received two instructions from the president: "Develop the force structure necessary to our military requirements without regard to arbitrary or predetermined budget ceilings. And secondly, having determined that force structure, procure it at the lowest possible cost."[38]

Before the formal elaboration of a new U.S. strategy, McNamara applied "quick fixes" to the U.S. force structure. He accelerated the procurement schedule for the submarine-launched ballistic missile, the Polaris, doubled the production capacity for Minuteman ICBMs and placed one-half of the bombers of the Strategic Air Command (SAC) on a quick-reaction alert.[39] Improvements began immediately in airlift and sealift capabilities, and the size of the army, Marine Corps, and tactical air forces were expanded.[40] McNamara's purpose was to increase U.S. combat strength measurably and quickly while developing a new policy for the use of U.S. military force.

The Development of Flexible Response. Kennedy and McNamara were determined to tailor U.S. military capabilities to meet any threat with an appropriate force. The strategy of flexible response was developed to give the president the capability to respond effectively with any level of force, nuclear or conventional, to an adversary challenge.

Flexible response within the strategic nuclear posture provided policy-makers a number of options for retaliatory policy. Massive (spasm) retaliation, limited countervalue (i.e., city) attacks, and counterforce strikes theoretically were all feasible war-fighting strategies. The development of submarine-launched ballistic missiles (SLBMs) such as Polaris enabled the U.S. to procure a relatively secure retaliatory force, and antiballistic missile (ABM) defenses were reaching the point of technological feasibility. The Kennedy and, later, Johnson administrations increased the U.S. strategic inventory dramatically and developed a so-called assured destruction capability whereby the United States could inflict "unacceptable damage" on the Soviet Union after absorbing a surprise Soviet first strike.* In fact, the United States developed an overwhelming strategic advantage over the Soviet Union, an imbalance that was not threatened until the end of the decade.

It was in the area of conventional forces that the doctrine of flexible response differed most dramatically from that of massive retaliation. If the United States were to respond with an appropriate level of force to a wide variety of challenges, its conventional forces would most likely be the ones used. Neglected under the policy of massive retaliation, these force capabilities had to be improved and modernized. The army increased from twelve to sixteen divisions, the navy surface fleet was enlarged, and the reserves and National Guard were revitalized. Counterinsurgency forces were enlarged greatly in order to deal with low intensity conflicts. In general, the conventional capabilities of the United States were enlarged and improved to the point where it was asserted (wrongly) that the United States could achieve a "two-and-a-half" war posture, i.e., be capable of fighting simultaneously a large-scale war

---

*What constitutes unacceptable damage to an adversary cannot be measured precisely. However, the current planning figure accepted by U.S. authorities is 25 to 33 percent of Soviet population and about 75 percent of Soviet industrial capacity. This judgment is influenced primarily by the demographics of Soviet population distribution and by the rapidly diminishing marginal returns beyond a certain level of retaliatory attack. For a more complete explanation of assured destruction criteria, see Alain C. Enthoven and K. Wayne Smith, *How Much Is Enough?* (New York: Harper & Row, 1964), p. 207.

in Europe, another sizable conflict somewhere else in the world, and deal with a small-scale local threat as well.

U.S. efforts to introduce flexible response doctrine into NATO strategy initially encountered Allied resistance. Any shift to primary reliance on non-nuclear forces was certain to cause uneasiness among the European members of the alliance, who feared erosion of the nuclear deterrent. Whereas the Eisenhower administration had asserted that such weapons might be used, by the end of the Johnson administration the United States was reluctant even to contemplate the use of nuclear weapons in limited wars.

Conventional Forces and Intervention. Improvements in conventional capabilities were not matched by the development of any clear doctrine governing intervention and the application of force. In his inaugural address John Kennedy had made his famous pledge: "Let every nation know, whether it wishes us well or ill, we shall pay any price, bear any burden, meet any hardship, support any friend or oppose any foe to assure the survival and the success of liberty." Such an open-ended commitment was of course unrealistic, for it did not provide any useful guidance for deciding when the use of force was in the national interest and when it was not. In mid 1965 the United States deployed ground combat troops to the Republic of Vietnam and also intervened in a civil upheaval in the Dominican Republic. As the Vietnam involvement lengthened and deepened, popular dissatisfaction grew, and domestic dissent and economic pressure began to play a significant role in the formulation of U.S. strategy. By FY 1968, defense spending had climbed to $78 billion, $20 billion of which represented the direct cost of the war in Vietnam.[41] The incoming Nixon administration was faced with the prospect of stalemate on the nuclear level and an unpopular, costly war on the conventional level.

REALISTIC DETERRENCE, 1969–76

By 1969 fundamental consensus on the nature of U.S. national security policy had seriously weakened. The prolonged and seemingly unsuccessful U.S. intervention in Vietnam called into question the ability of the United States to deal with insurgencies around the world, and the nature of the strategic balance dictated a reassessment of American defense policy. The policy of containment, practically unchallenged since its inception after World War II, came under increasingly critical scrutiny, for it no longer seemed to reflect a realistic appraisal of the international situation.

Reassessment of the Threat. Changes in both the strategic and conventional environments dictated a reassessment of U.S. military policy. By 1968 the Soviet Union had achieved rough nuclear parity with the United States. Both sides had acquired secure second-strike capabilities, whereby each was capable of inflicting unacceptable damage on its opponent even after an enemy first strike. Since neither side could "win" by striking first there was no pressure in a crisis for the side that might perceive itself to be inferior to launch a preemptive strike. Given the size and nature of their nuclear forces, both the United States and the Soviet Union seemed to realize that it was in their best interests to limit the possibility of confrontation. From such reasoning, *at least on the U.S. side,* came the concept of détente and its associated Strategic Arms Limitation Talks (SALT).

There was also a perceived need for reevaluation of the role of U.S. conventional forces. The war in Vietnam demonstrated the inapplicability of a limited-war doctrine in a revolutionary situation, and public and congressional disenchantment with military and other foreign embroilments dictated a rethinking of where and how U.S. conventional forces might be used. Other constraints also impacted on U.S. military policy. The position of the dollar in the world economy was deteriorating as wartime inflation proceeded. Recognition of the social and economic problems in the United States continued to demand priority for domestic spending. Under these pressures, defense outlays as a percent of GNP fell from 9.4 in FY 1968 to 5.9 in FY 1975. In FY 1964, the last pre-Vietnam War budget, defense spending represented 41.8 percent of the federal budget. Roughly a decade later, for FY 1975, defense expenditures accounted for 27.1 percent of federal outlays.[42] The defense spending decline was not just relative—but also absolute—when measured in constant dollars.

Strategic Sufficiency. Given the Soviet Union's nuclear power and its demonstrated ability and willingness to respond to improvements in American strategic forces, the Nixon administration concluded that nuclear superiority was impossible to maintain.[43] Any attempt to do so would only result in a reescalation of the arms race, with little increase in security for either side. Nevertheless, Nixon was unwilling to allow the Soviet Union to achieve a position of nuclear predominance. Strategic planning for U.S. forces thus focused on a doctrine of "strategic sufficiency." The doctrine of sufficiency, reflecting a recognition that nuclear parity is the best one can achieve, includes a number of precepts.

- *Assured destruction*—To insure the reliability of U.S. forces to inflict unacceptable damage on an opponent, a retaliatory capability was (and is) maintained in three separate and independent offensive systems—land-based ICBMs, SLBMs, and manned bombers—each capable of inflicting unacceptable levels of damage on the enemy through destruction of a major fraction of its population and economy.[44]
- *Flexible nuclear options*—The structuring of U.S. strategic forces is designed to insure that they can respond in a variety of ways to various military contingencies. The development of extremely accurate warheads gives the president the capability for alternative strategic responses. He may choose

a counterforce strike to destroy Soviet land-based missiles or other military targets, large or small, rather than retaliate against population centers. Flexibility of forces and targets allows the president to tailor U.S. strategic response to the nature of the provocation. (On the other hand, opponents of counterforce capabilities argue that the extremely accurate warheads needed for flexible options will be perceived as a first-strike threat to Soviet retaliatory capabilities, thereby destabilizing the nuclear balance.)

- *Crisis stability*—Soviet knowledge that the United States could respond in a variety of ways rather than having to choose between massive retaliation and inaction was expected to stabilize relations by reducing the Soviet Union's willingness to stage a less than all-out attack.[45] Further, large U.S. invulnerable retaliatory capabilities contribute to stability because the Soviets recognize there is no rational advantage to shooting first; accordingly, temptation for a preemptive strike in a crisis is eliminated.

- *Perceived equality*—The final criterion of strategic sufficiency is that a rough balance should exist between the strategic capabilities of the United States and the Soviet Union. The importance of maintaining a balance lies in the perceptions of the superpowers and their allies. If politically attuned people perceive there is an advantage to numerical superiority, then there is. Thus, although numerical comparisons are misleading, a rough balance is necessary in order to prevent coercion or intimidation of the United States or its allies.

Conventional Force Policy. The proliferation of newly independent states during the 1960s and the decline in the cohesiveness of the Western and Communist alliances undermined the traditional vision of bipolar world power. The limited applicability of the use of force, dramatically demonstrated by the inability of American intervention in Indochina to prevent communist dominance, also necessitated a reevaluation of U.S. policy and the implications of U.S. alliance commitments. In 1974 the Nixon administration's appraisal of conventional war policy reaffirmed one traditional commitment and modified another.

The U.S. commitment to NATO was reaffirmed and strengthened following U.S. withdrawal from Vietnam. Although the size of the army was reduced by 50 percent, American NATO forces—which had been stripped of personnel and equipment during the Vietnam War—were strengthened and re-equipped. Additionally, the United States abandoned the so-called two-and-a-half war strategy and began to maintain forces based on a one-and-a-half war strategy, i.e., a large war in Europe or Asia, but not both, and a minor contingency somewhere else. (In reality, the change was not all that dramatic, for, despite declaratory policy, the U.S. had earlier never even approached the kinds and levels of forces needed for two and a half wars.) The NATO commitment became the primary planning contingency for structuring U.S. conventional forces, and the conventional war-fighting capabilities of U.S. NATO forces were improved.

A major reappraisal of U.S. policy was made concerning the feasibility of deterring or fighting local conflicts and insurgencies in developing countries. The resulting policy, known variously as the Guam Doctrine or the Nixon Doctrine, concluded that the United States would no longer automatically intervene against externally supported insurgencies. The Nixon Doctrine could be expressed as three essential principles: self-help, primary regional responsibility, and residual U.S. responsibility.[46]

The principle of self-help dictated that the country being threatened must take responsibility for its own security. In the event of conventional attack, the country under attack must provide the first line of defense. In the case of insurgency, the local government must bear the full load of combat operations. Further, in the case of insurgency, the United States would expect the local government to initiate vigorous programs of economic and political development.[47] Experience had taught that military action alone is generally not capable of dealing successfully with an insurgency but must be accompanied by political and social programs.

Regional responsibility meant that the United States expected neighboring countries to work together to eliminate or deal with the causes of political and social instability. Regional cooperation, it was believed, would enable the countries concerned to better prevent the emergence of insurgency and to develop both politically and economically. If military operations were required to deal with an insurgency and outside forces were needed, the United States expected that they would be provided, at least in part, by the neighbors of the country under attack.[48]

The principle of residual U.S. responsibility indicated that the United States would not conduct programs that the nations should undertake themselves, but would provide military assistance as appropriate. The United States would maintain a minimum presence in friendly, threatened developing areas but would intervene only if vital American interests were threatened. President Ford, and subsequently President Carter, endorsed the policy of stringently limited U.S. involvement as the basis for U.S. action in dealing with insurgencies in the developing nations of the world.

BEYOND CONTAINMENT/DETERRENCE?

As customarily occurs with the advent of a new administration, President Carter initiated a reappraisal of U.S. national security policy when he came to office in January 1977. Such reappraisal was clearly warranted, for much had changed since the last such exercise. The traditional consensus supporting the American policy of containment had been shattered by the U.S. involvement in Vietnam. The failure of U.S. policy there had led critics to question the application of U.S. power anywhere. Further, the steady strengthening of the Soviet Union's strategic retaliatory systems had underscored the momentum of the strategic arms race and the importance, therefore, of moving forward with arms control. The reestablishment of the U.S.-Chinese dialogue in 1972 had reversed a longstanding policy of treating the People's Republic of China (P.R.C.) as a prime danger to U.S. security interests, also contributing to the questioning of traditional American security strategies.

"Détente," whereby relations between the superpowers would ostensibly be marked by a lessening of tension and hostility, even as competition between them continued—which had been a central theme of the Nixon administration's foreign and defense policy—had proven to be a shaky pillar; the U.S.S.R. had interpreted it as mere American acknowledgment of the new power balance and a license to expand its influence and activities in hitherto Western areas of predominant influence.

Although the earlier SALT negotiations (SALT I), culminating in the Strategic Arms Limitation Agreement of 1972 and the Vladivostok Accord of 1974 (also tentatively limiting strategic arms), institutionalized the policy of détente at one level, they seemed only to encourage Soviet expansionism at other levels. Accordingly, the policy of détente—at least as originally conceived—had increasingly become viewed in the United States as ineffective. Although Americans generally recognized the infeasibility of continuing the earlier policy of containment which détente had displaced, they were less than happy with a policy that seemed incapable of checking adventurism in the noncommunist world by the U.S.S.R. and its allies and proxies.

The proliferation of newly independent countries in the preceding three decades and their increasing demands for a more just and equitable international economic and political order had also changed the international security environment. American strategic policy could no longer be based solely on conceptions of East-West rivalry, a competition deemed largely irrelevant by many of the developing areas of the world.

Domestically, the United States had also changed dramatically. Although the national reluctance to become involved in foreign affairs, which faced President Truman in 1945, had largely been replaced by an acceptance of America's role as a world leader, new questions had arisen concerning the nature of U.S. foreign involvements. The wars in Korea and Vietnam seemed to illustrate the reduced utility of military force, feeding renewed skepticism

Copyright 1981 King Features Syndicate, Inc.

about defense spending and worldwide military deployments. The recession of 1974–75 reemphasized domestic priorities and raised further questions about the extent to which resources should be channeled into increasingly expensive defense programs. Candidate Carter emphasized his intent to reduce military spending in favor of domestic programs. Despite the increasing evidence of a continuing, massive Soviet military build-up, there was sufficient uncertainty and dispute about the facts to permit both presidential candidates to downplay the specter of future Soviet pressure and adventurism.

Technology also had, to a large extent, restructured the security environment in which the United States lived. Continued technological advancements such as multiple, independently targetable reentry vehicles (MIRVs), cruise missiles, and antisatellite capabilities threatened to upset perceptions of nuclear stability. Improvements in conventional weapons such as TV-guided bombs and laser-guided artillery shells had enhanced military capabilities with less than fully understood consequences for the stability of conventional force balances. History suggests that, because of their speed and extent, these various technological advances had not been adequately coupled with an appreciation of their strategic and political implications.[49]

In consequence of the dynamic factors cited in the preceding paragraphs and in light of its own comprehensive assessment of the comparative strengths of the United States and the Soviet Union, the Carter administration set forth the main lines of its strategy in a series of announcements and policy initiatives during the course of 1977. It reaffirmed the importance of maintaining a balance in strategic nuclear forces, choosing the label of "essential equivalence." It continued to rely upon the doctrine of "mutually assured destruction" and seemed to back away somewhat from any concept of even limited counterforce capabilities or plans—the so-called limited nuclear options with which the Nixon administration had tinkered. Also in the context of essential equivalence, the new administration picked up the lagging SALT II talks and pressed them vigorously—though initially with little success.

With regard to Europe, the Carter administration underscored the key role of NATO and reaffirmed the existing "forward strategy." Recognizing the mounting Soviet defense build-up in Central Europe, the U.S. persuaded the other NATO governments to increase real defense contributions to the alliance by 3 percent a year. This so-called Long-Range Defense Program was designed both to remedy near-term weaknesses such as inadequate ammunition stocks and to increase the overall readiness of NATO forces over a more extended period.

The overall concept of having forces sufficient simultaneously to fight a major war in Europe and a smaller war elsewhere—the one-and-a-half war strategy of the Nixon administration—was endorsed as the guiding principle behind the size and character of the defense forces. Special attention was focused on the Persian Gulf as the possible site of the one-half war. Although measures to create the kind of force projection capability required for an area such as the Persian Gulf were slow in getting under way, the administration at least staked out a declaratory policy that accorded the region higher and more explicit priority than given it earlier.

In a bid to stabilize the power balance in Asia and to create a more satisfactory framework for U.S.-Soviet relations, the administration proceeded with the normalization of American relations with the People's Republic. Formal recognition of the P.R.C. was accomplished in early 1979, immediately preceding the visit to the United States by Vice Premier Deng Xiaoping. Following up the president's campaign promises, the administration launched a second Asian initiative, aimed more at reducing U.S. commitments than promoting regional stabilization, namely, withdrawal of American ground forces from the Republic of Korea. Congressional opposition, however, forced the administration to reverse its course in the matter.

In terms of overall national security policy, the decade of the 1970s ended on a somewhat surprising note. The Soviet Union's impressive and continuing defense build-up, combined with its gains in a number of regions—generally propelled by Soviet arms and advisers and sometimes by Cuban proxies— had so alarmed large sectors of the public and the Congress that a stronger defense policy and larger spending were being pressed on a reluctant president. In 1981 Ronald Reagan, who had pledged to be firm with the Soviets and increase defense spending, entered the White House. His election was due in part to the public's disenchantment with the Carter defense policy and was followed by substantially higher military appropriations. Disillusionment with détente was manifest; a search for a contemporary equivalent to containment was underway.

DISCUSSION QUESTIONS

1. What international and technological impacts caused the United States to abandon its longstanding reliance on a policy of mobilization? How does a strategy based on deterrence differ from one based on mobilization?

2. What impact did the rapid demobilization of U.S. forces following World War II have on the formulation of American security policy?

3. The policy of containment was based on the perception of an aggressive, monolithic communist bloc of nations. What events of the late 1940s and early 1950s caused the U.S. to so view the nature of the communist threat? What impact did such an assessment have on established U.S. political and military policies?

4. In the early 1960s the United States adopted a strategic policy of "flexible response." What changes in technology and the international environment led to this change?

5. How do domestic considerations make foreign and security policies different than they would be on the basis of international and strategic considerations alone?

6. Has the development of nuclear stability encouraged political multipolarity? If the traditional uses of military power have become less feasible, what new forms of pressure have emerged?

7. Many analysts of national security policy allege that the distribution of nuclear power is at most a minor determinant of the outcome of political disputes. What

impact do nuclear weapons have on the ability of the United States (or the Soviet Union) to influence international affairs? Has nuclear "superiority" ever been a meaningful determinant of the outcome of a dispute in the post–World War II era?

8. How have technological innovations affected the evolution of U.S. security policy since the end of World War II? To what extent can it be said that technology determines strategy?

9. Should technological advances in weapons systems be integrated into the U.S. inventory as rapidly as they become available? Would doing otherwise risk technological obsolescence and military inferiority?

10. Why has the policy of détente with the Soviet Union failed to generate a broad base of domestic support in the United States?

11. How does the doctrine of strategic sufficiency differ from the earlier doctrine of massive retaliation?

12. How has the concept of assured destruction (with its implicit acceptance of nuclear parity) influenced the strategic nuclear posture of the United States?

RECOMMENDED READING

Aliano, Richard. *American Defense Policy from Eisenhower to Kennedy*. Athens: Ohio University Press, 1975.

Enthoven, Alain C., and Smith, K. Wayne. *How Much Is Enough?* New York: Harper & Row, 1971.

Halperin, Morton H. *Defense Strategies for the Seventies*. Boston: Little, Brown, 1971.

Huntington, Samuel P. *The Common Defense*. New York: Columbia University Press, 1961.

Kahan, Jerome. *Security in the Nuclear Age*. Washington, D.C.: Brookings Institution, 1975.

Kaufmann, William W. *The McNamara Strategy*. New York: Harper & Row, 1964.

Kissinger, Henry A. *American Foreign Policy*. 3d ed. New York: W. W. Norton, 1977.

Lippman, Walter. *U. S. Foreign Policy: Shield of the Republic*. Boston: Little, Brown, 1943.

Nash, Henry T. *American Foreign Policy: Response to a Sense of Threat*. Homewood, Ill.: Dorsey Press, 1973.

Quanback, Alton H., and Blechman, Barry M. *Strategic Forces: Issues for the Mid-Seventies*. Washington, D.C.: Brookings Institution, 1973.

Sherry, Michael. *Preparing for the Next War*. New Haven: Yale University Press, 1977.

Taylor, Maxwell D. *The Uncertain Trumpet*. New York: Harper, 1959.

NATIONAL SECURITY POLICY: ACTORS
AND PROCESSES

While nearly all Americans would agree that we must provide for national security, consensus may end at that imprecise point. There is always disagreement over what threats exist, what values and interests should be secured, how much security is "enough," and the optimal means to achieve various levels of security. The disagreement becomes stronger as the practical trade-offs are considered: resources devoted to national security are not available for the achievement of other goals such as tax relief, social welfare, environmental improvement, or public education; youths may have to serve in the army instead of beginning college or civilian work, etc. The differences in perspective within American society are carried over into the governmental structures created to resolve important policy issues. In Part 2 we will examine the people, organizations, and processes that determine our national security goals and how they can best be pursued.

It is tempting to view the president, representative of all the people, commander in chief, and chief diplomat, as the final arbiter and authority on national security policy—but such a view diverges too far from reality. First, the president shares power with Congress, which on many issues has the final say. Second, one person, the president, must rely on many others to acquire the information and expertise necessary to formulate policies. Finally, the president is dependent on others for policy implementation. It should be clear from this that power in national security affairs, as much as in other policy spheres, is shared, both formally and informally.

While the government as a whole and the executive branch in particular may exhibit a greater consensus than the public on which national security goals should be pursued, they often disagree on the priorities among goals and on the means to pursue them. Chapter 5 will discuss the executive branch agencies and their functions in the policy-making process. The role of Congress as a rival to executive branch dominance in national security affairs and as a conduit and molder of public opinion is examined in Chapter 6.

Part of the competition between Congress and the executive branch is over access to information; the role of intelligence in providing this and the difficulties of an intelligence organization in an open society are the subjects of Chapter 7. Since many differences over policy ultimately involve competition for roles and missions and for scarce resources among many agencies and the armed services, we will examine in some detail in Chapters 8 and 9 the roles of the military and the defense budgeting process through which program decisions are shaped. Program decisions give us the capability to implement policy; they also limit policy options.

In Chapter 10 we will attempt to place in perspective the various actors and their goals, pulling the threads together from Chapters 5 through 9 in order to understand the complex processes of national security decision-making.

5

PRESIDENTIAL LEADERSHIP
AND THE EXECUTIVE BRANCH IN
NATIONAL SECURITY

"The direction of war implies the direction of the common strength; and the power of directing and employing the common strength forms a usual and essential part in the definition of the executive authority."[1] With these words, Alexander Hamilton described the crucial role of the president in national security affairs. An appreciation of this vital role was shared by all the founders of the United States, but it was counterbalanced by their determination to avoid investing in the American president the "sole prerogative of making war and peace"[2] exercised by the British monarch. As a result, the Constitution created a system in which the president and the Congress were given complementary, at times naturally conflicting, roles in the national security process.

Under the Constitution, the president is the commander in chief of the army and the navy, but he has nothing to command unless Congress uses the power it possesses to raise and support armies and to support and maintain a navy. In addition, Congress is empowered to make rules for the governance and regulation of those forces. The president has the authority to make treaties and to appoint ambassadors and other public ministers. Each of these actions, however, is subject to the "advice and consent" of the Senate. The president is responsible to insure that the laws are faithfully executed, and he has been vested with the "executive power" to this end. It is Congress, however, that is responsible to "make all laws which shall be necessary and proper for carrying into execution the foregoing powers vested by this Constitution in the Government of the United States." The Constitution has given the president substantial authority and initiative in foreign affairs. However, having given the president important powers to make and execute national security policy, the founders were deliberate in their grant to Congress of the power to declare war. As a consequence of these built-in dynamic tensions, the Constitution has presented to each president and Congress an "invitation to struggle for the privilege of directing American foreign policy."[3]

A History of Increasing Presidential Prerogative. The outlines of the national security process provided by the Constitution were quickly elaborated by the actual conduct of public affairs. In 1793, George Washington asserted the prerogative of the president to act unilaterally in time of foreign crisis by issuing, without congressional consultation, a neutrality proclamation in the renewed Franco-British war.

Succeeding administrations continued to struggle with questions of presidential versus congressional prerogative. In 1812, President Madison was unsuccessful in restraining congressional "war hawks," who helped precipitate war with England. On the other hand, in 1846 it was President Polk who presented Congress with a *fait accompli* by placing American troops along the Rio Grande. The resulting clash of arms quickly led to a declaration of war.

Presidential prerogative in foreign affairs, claimed first by Washington and embellished by his successors, was a generally established concept at the time of the Lincoln administration. Lincoln greatly expanded the potential range of presidential action by invoking the notion of a "war power" as a derivative of the commander in chief clause of the Constitution. The growth of presidential power in the Civil War foreshadowed the relationship between national emergency and executive power. "Time and again, the law of national self-preservation was seen to justify placing extravagant power in the hands of the President."[4]

Prior to World War II, Franklin Roosevelt's carefully orchestrated policy of aiding Britain and her allies once again revealed the power of the president to initiate in national security affairs. Using executive agreements to avoid confronting an uncertain and isolationist Congress, Roosevelt increasingly bound the United States to the Allied cause. With the attack on Pearl Harbor, the power of the executive further expanded to confront the crisis of global war.

With the termination of World War II, the anticipated climate of peace under the aegis of a powerful international organization did not materialize; instead, the postwar years ushered in a period of continuing confrontation—the cold war. An ideological conflict permeated the international environment, a war of nerves stretched particularly taut by the specter of atomic war. In these circumstances, too, crisis spurred the growth of executive prerogatives. President Truman led the United States into the Korean conflict in 1950 under the auspices of the United Nations without even seeking a congressional declaration of war. Similarly, President Kennedy escalated the small (less than 1,000-man) military advisory effort in Vietnam, begun under Eisenhower, into a 16,000-man effort, which included not only advisers but helicopter transportation companies and other logistical elements.

Vietnam: A Turning Point. In the mid 1960s, presidential initiative in foreign affairs again brought the United States into an extended conflict in Asia. This time it was Vietnam; and along with the locale, the rules of the game had changed. The conventional linear warfare of Korea yielded to the amorphous combat of revolutionary warfare. As the war dragged on in Vietnam—and in the living rooms of America, via television—the presidential prerogative in foreign affairs came under vigorous attack. The "imperial president" became the subject of congressional and popular opposition. Congressional opposition culminated in the passage of the War Powers Act, over President Nixon's veto, in July 1973 (see Chapter 6). This measure set a sixty-day limit on the president's power to wage undeclared war.[5]

The War Powers Act confirmed congressional resurgence in the perennial debate about the respective powers of the executive and legislative branches concerning war. It certainly did not, however, signal presidential retirement from the fray. Despite Vietnam and the revolt against the "imperial presidency," the president still must play a crucial role in the national security process. Recent trends have not repealed two hundred years of history nor have they diminished the need for vigorous executive action in national security matters.

The President and National Security. The president as chief of state personifies the United States in its dealings with the world. Through his constitutional powers to appoint and receive ambassadors, the president is placed at the focal point of diplomatic activity. As commander in chief, he is positioned at the apex of a large and elaborate security apparatus. In addition to these constitutional and organizational factors, the congruence of continual crisis and expanded presidential power have operated to build a national contingency system around the president. With the advent of the cold war and, later, the nuclear balance of terror, an atmosphere of constant danger has translated many aspects of this contingency system into standard operating procedures.

Technology, too, has assisted the growth of presidential prerogative. The stakes in crisis management have escalated with the proliferation of nuclear weapons. Questions of peace and war can now relate directly to the survival of the human race. As the stakes of international confrontation have increased, so also has the tempo of communication and response. The national security process has become saturated with information, and it is the executive who largely controls the channels of communication and the organizations capable of assimilating these data. The communication revolution has not only enhanced the executive's ability to receive information, it has also provided him with direct access to operations. No more striking example of this phenomenon exists than President Johnson's personal selection of specific American bombing targets in North Vietnam.

The external environment has thus generated forces encouraging recent presidents to be activists. This, however, should not be construed as implying that until recently the presidency has merely been the benign beneficiary of history. In fact, vigorous presidents have always reached out to grasp the levers of government. Beginning especially with FDR, presidential initiative has grown significantly in generating legislation and promulgating the federal budget. Congress, in this regard, examines presidential initiatives, as much as, or more than, it generates its own.

The president plays multiple roles in the execution of the office. Not only is he chief of state, commander in chief of the armed forces, chief diplomat, principal initiator of legislation, and chief executor of the laws, but he also acts as party leader, national spokesperson, peacekeeper, manager of prosperity, and world leader.[6] None of these roles can neatly be isolated from the other, and the president must satisfy the particular demands of each as he confronts problems of national security. Moreover, in his various roles he must deal with a variety of entities, each with its own interests and viewpoints; these are shown in fig. 5.1.

Despite the complexity of these various responsibilities, three major functions in the conduct of national security can be identified: *resource allocation, policy planning*, and *coordination and monitoring of operations*.[7] The maintenance of national security is expensive, requiring a major commitment of resources each year in the president's budget, the main vehicle through which he communicates his ordering of the nation's priorities in resource use. The Office of Management and Budget (OMB), discussed briefly in subsequent pages, is the principal instrument that the president uses in this allocation function.

Policy planning involves the development of long-range designs, such as the Marshall Plan for the reconstruction of Europe after World War II and NATO, to provide security for the reviving Western European states. It also includes less sweeping and shorter term plans to advance U.S. interests and cope with emerging problems. Inherent in this policy planning function is an intent to shape future events as well as to prepare policy planning for con-

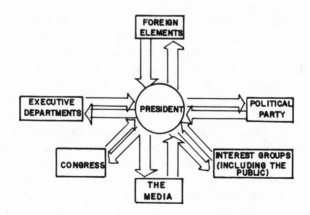

FIG. 5.1

tingencies. Historically, the focus of such planning has shifted among (or been shared by) the Departments of State and Defense and the president's national security assistant, who heads the National Security Council staff.

Coordination of operations requires overseeing the countless day-to-day foreign policy actions of government organizations and officials so that they remain consistent with and advance American policy. The associated monitoring function is designed to provide feedback to the executive branch to insure that appropriate actions are being taken in light of policy guidance and to apprise it of changing conditions, assumptions, or new data. In practice, the president has leaned on the Department of State and/or his national security assistant for the coordination and monitoring task.

The Institutionalized Presidency and National Security Affairs. The complexity, scope, and magnitude of these functions have given rise to the institutionalized presidency. The president, as an individual, has been augmented by staffs acting in his name. This institutionalized presidency, together with certain executive departments, forms the principal means of developing, directing, and coordinating national security. The key elements of this collective executive are: the White House Office, the National Security Council and staff, the State Department, the Department of Defense, the Central Intelligence Agency, and the Office of Management and Budget (see fig. 5.2).

The White House Office. According to George Reedy, former press secretary to Lyndon Johnson, "the life of the White House is the life of a court."[8] Extending the analogy, the White House staff members can be seen as the president's courtiers. They are the personal and political assistants to the president. Without outside constituencies, they owe their status and position wholly to him. Accordingly, the organization and use of the White House staff is the function of a president's personal style.

In recent history, Franklin D. Roosevelt operated probably the most chaotic of staffs, but the chaos was purposeful. "F.D.R. intended his administrative assistants to be eyes and ears and manpower for him, with no fixed contacts, clients, or involvements of their own to interfere when he had to redeploy them."[9] There was overlapping of assignments, lack of coordination, and often frustration on the part of the staff, but these factors served FDR well, presenting him competing sources of information and analysis that enabled him to develop and maintain his personal options. This freewheeling approach was somewhat curtailed by the advent of World War II as sources of information became channeled through secrecy and censorship systems and the focus of efforts turned to the operational concerns of global war.[10]

President Eisenhower was at the opposite extreme. His staff was organized tightly around its chief of staff, initially Sherman Adams. With some exceptions, access to the president was through Adams, who was not reticent to ask if a meeting were really necessary. Responsibilities were clearly defined and there was a military aura of heirarchy, neatness, and order.

THE GOVERNMENT OF THE UNITED STATES

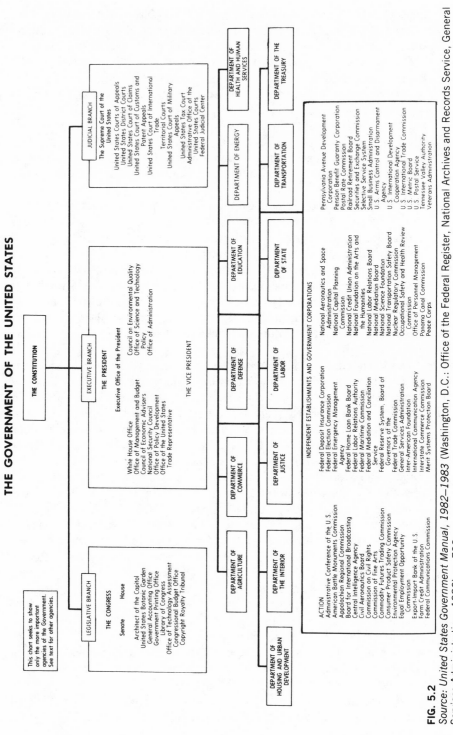

FIG. 5.2

Source: *United States Government Manual, 1982–1983* (Washington, D.C.: Office of the Federal Register, National Archives and Records Service, General Services Administration, 1982), p. 792.

In the 1960s, the Kennedy and Johnson administrations utilized a less formal staffing system, allowing a small staff concerned with national security more direct and frequent access to the president. With Nixon's victory in 1968, the White House staff was again organized along more structured lines. In reaction, the Carter administration returned to a more open and less hierarchical arrangement.

In each of these administrations, from Eisenhower's forward, the position of special assistant to the president for national security affairs was strengthened (starting with Kissinger, "special" was dropped from the title). In each case—and typical of relationships in the White House—the role of the assistant to the president for national security affairs was largely a function of the assistant's personal relationship with the president and how the president wished the office to be discharged. The role has also developed in conjunction with the evolution of the National Security Council staff, which the assistant heads.

Despite the similarities and differences in the functioning of the White House staff under different presidents, there have been some pronounced trends. The most obvious is growth. The entire Hoover presidency was staffed by three secretaries, a military and a naval aide, and twenty clerks. In contrast, the Carter White House contained in excess of five hundred people in 1979—both those "hired" and those "on loan" from other agencies and carried on the agencies' payrolls.[11] The growth in numbers is a symptom, and some would argue a cause, of a centralization of decision-making. In this regard, one should be mindful that centralization can cause a serious cleavage between policy-makers and the instruments of policy. Another aspect of White House staff growth is the tendency for it to shield the president from the outside world. The life of the court can easily become one clouded by perceptions divorced from reality. Finally, as the National Security Council system has evolved and the position of the assistant directing its staff has strengthened, other White House office staffs have played an ever-diminishing role in national security matters.

National Security Council. The formalized coordination and policy planning functions of the presidency in national security matters are located in the National Security Council (NSC), created by the National Security Act of 1947. The NSC inherited many of the functions that had been earlier exercised by cabinet members in the State-War-Navy Coordinating Committee, itself an ad hoc product of World War II operations. As constituted in 1947, the NSC comprises the president, the vice-president, the secretary of state, the secretary of defense, and the director of the Office of Civil and Defense Mobilization (OCDM). The latter office has long since been abolished and its successor organizations are not represented in the NSC, so that there are only four statutory members. The director of the Central Intelligence Agency and the Joint Chiefs of Staff serve as statutory advisers.[12]*

*The functions of the OCDM were absorbed in the late 1960s by director of the Office of Emergency Preparedness until 1974 when the latter office was abolished and its functions passed to several different agencies.

President Truman was instrumental in shaping the NSC to respond directly to the needs of the president rather than merely extending the interagency arrangements of the State-War-Navy Coordinating Committee. "His adroit maneuvers scotched the scheme of those who wanted to assure defense domination of the National Security Council by housing it in the Pentagon . . . and by designating the Secretary of Defense as Chairman in the President's absence."[13] In addition, the legislation that the Truman Administration shepherded through the Congress to become the 1947 National Security Act provided for a separate staff to support the NSC and did not rely, as was previously done, on staff contributed from involved agencies. In this manner, President Truman established the NSC as responsive to the president rather than to competing executive departments.

With the advent of the Eisenhower administration, the NSC system was restructured to reflect both the style of the new president and his view of the world situation.[14] In keeping with his view of the importance of economic health to security, Eisenhower regularly invited his secretary of Treasury and director of the Bureau of the Budget to attend NSC meetings. He attempted to routinize and regularize the decision-making process in line with his experience with military models of decision-making and coordination. He used the NSC apparatus intensively in the belief that "the secret of a sound, satisfactory decision made on an emergency basis has always been that the responsible official has been 'living with the problem' before it becomes acute. Failure to use, on a continuing basis, the NSC, or some similar advisory body, entails losing the capacity to make emergency decisions based on depth of understanding and perspective . . . ."[15]

Two important subelements of the NSC were created by Ike—one at the assistant secretary level (of the departments involved in the NSC) to conduct interagency planning and policy development, namely, the National Security Planning Board (NSPB), and the other at the undersecretary level to oversee and coordinate policy implementation, the Operations Coordinating Board (OCB). While admirably suited to help the president avoid mistakes, these bureaucratic camels were not often the source of innovative, clear-cut recommendations or guidance.

The passing of the torch from the Eisenhower to the Kennedy administration involved a distinct change in presidential outlook and operating style. In regard to the NSC, this was reflected in a dismantling of the NSPB and OCB structure and a move to a more ad hoc system. At the heart of the criticism of the Eisenhower system was the view that it impeded initiative and flexibility by subjecting proposals to overly formalized bureaucratic argument. Regarding the world as inherently dynamic, President Kennedy hoped to shape a national security system capable of coping with rapid change. In lieu of the previous interagency focus, Kennedy built a strong staff in the White House, under his special assistant for national security affairs, to assist him in drawing advice from and coordinating operations of the various agencies involved with national security.

Further, President Kennedy chose to immerse himself in the details of selected aspects of policy much more than his predecessor. The Bay of Pigs fiasco in April 1961, shortly after Kennedy took office, was a lesson he did not soon forget. He had relied on the experts and judgments of the preceding administration and, as he remarked a year and a half later, "The advice of every member of the Executive Branch brought in to advise was unanimous— and the advice was wrong."[16] Partly as a result of the Bay of Pigs, the president relied increasingly on his national security assistant to provide policy options. The full NSC met less frequently and tended to consider long-term questions that had already been extensively explored by ad hoc task forces. These interagency task forces dealt with such specific problems of the early 1960s as Laos, Berlin, and the Nuclear Test Ban Treaty.

Although established to provide a coherent means of coping with the urgency of the atomic age, the formal NSC in practice was not the locus of crisis management. As demonstrated in the Cuban Missile Crisis, Kennedy relied instead on a specially selected "Executive Committee" to bear the burden of deliberation and policy development. Consisting of the president's most trusted advisers and unfettered by the statutory membership requirements of the NSC, it represented a continuation of the ad hoc approach to national security policy-making.

With the assassination of President Kennedy in November 1963, Lyndon Johnson was thrust into the presidency. Although a master of congressional politics, he had but limited experience in international affairs—apart from his knowledge about military affairs as they affected, and were affected by, Congress. This factor, coupled with his desire to bring a sense of continuity to his administration, resulted in few changes to the NSC system as a consequence of the transition. Central coordination and direction continued to be provided by the special assistant for national security affairs.[17]

The emergence of the Vietnam conflict in the mid 1960s became the central drama, if not tragedy, of Johnson's foreign policy. Accepting the existing national security apparatus and, unlike Kennedy, lacking the inclination to go beyond his advisers to key points in the bureaucracy, Johnson narrowed the process of deliberation and decision to a few people. In July 1965, the decision to expand America's hitherto limited commitment reportedly rested on the advice of a handful of people. The NSC and the Congress were consulted only after the decision was made.[18] Other important national security decisions were made at the informal, largely unstructured discussions at the president's periodic "Tuesday lunches"—which generally included the NSC members and invited guests.

In March 1966, the Johnson administration decided to provide more structure to the NSC system. National Security Memorandum 341 established a permanent interdepartmental committee called the Senior Interdepartmental Group (SIG), headed by the Undersecretary of State. Subordinate to the SIG, Interdepartmental Region Groups (IRGs) for each region of the world were created and chaired by regional assistant secretaries of state. In theory, policy planning and coordination of policy decisions would flow through these organizations and up to the NSC. In practice, Vietnam dominated presidential consideration and Johnson was unwilling to employ this new system in dealing with Vietnam. As a consequence, the SIGs and the IRGs found themselves working largely on peripheral issues while crucial decisions concerning Vietnam continued to be resolved by the president and a few advisers.

The Nixon administration departed from the largely ad hoc arrangements of the Kennedy-Johnson years and returned in 1969 to a centralized system more akin to President Eisenhower's but with borrowings from President Johnson. The national security machinery was placed firmly in the White House under the control of the president's security assistant, Dr. Henry Kissinger. Although believing in a comprehensive and formal approach, Dr. Kissinger attempted to avoid the dilution in content and the inflexibility generated by the extended consensus approach of the Eisenhower system. The focus of the new NSC staff effort was not to produce, as in Ike's case, an agreed recommendation for the president but to rigorously develop a set of carefully considered options for presidential choice.

Kissinger adapted the SIG-IRG arrangements of the Johnson administration by assigning issues to Interdepartmental Groups (IGs) similar to the earlier IRGs and chaired, as before, by assistant secretaries of state. The IGs were responsible for studying problems, formulating policy choices, and assessing the merits of various alternatives. A Senior Review Group (SRG) was constituted at the undersecretary level, chaired by Dr. Kissinger, to deal with IG recommendations. By this process, less important or uncontentious issues were decided at subordinate levels rather than being forwarded to the NSC. Although this approach allowed for the inclusion of the views of operating agencies, it lodged control in the White House where the president clearly wanted it.

The Nixon-Kissinger NSC structure was further complicated or "systematized" by the creation of various special groups subordinate to the NSC. For example, major issues centered on the Vietnam War were handled by a Vietnam Special Studies Group, while crisis planning was done by the Washington Special Actions Group (WASAG). This evolution represented a further strengthening of the hand of the assistant for national security affairs and the dominance of the NSC staff over the Department of State. It is noteworthy that, out of office, Dr. Kissinger has decried this trend, recommending that a president should make the secretary of state "his principal adviser and 'use' the national security adviser primarily as a senior administrator and coordinator to make certain that each significant point of view is heard."[19]

In broad outlines President Carter's initial approach was to "streamline" his NSC staff but to entrust it with the same basic functions and powers as the Ford staff. A number of NSC committees of the earlier era (which were really separate entities in name only) were collapsed into three basic committees: the Policy Review Committee (PRC), the Special Coordination Committee (SCC) and the familiar, assistant secretary level IGs. As noted in fig.

5.3, the PRC deals with longer range policy issues and is supported in this by the IGs, while the SCC focuses on short range problems, including crisis actions. As is apparent, the Carter administration's NSC organization and procedures are not much different from those of its predecessors. The primary differences are that the chairpersons of the IGs and PRC vary with the issues under examination and that the PRC and SCC membership explicitly include the secretaries of state and defense (or their deputies), whereas secretarial attendance was a rare event in the predecessor organizations.

The Department of State. The Department of State, since its creation in 1789 under its first secretary, Thomas Jefferson, has been the customary operational arm of the U.S. government in the conduct of foreign affairs. The department performs two basic functions: it represents the interests of the United States and its citizens in relations with foreign countries, and it serves as a principal source of advice to the president on all aspects of foreign affairs—including national security policy (see fig. 5.4).[20]

As a member of the cabinet, the secretary of state is traditionally the president's principal adviser on foreign policy, although this tradition appeared to wane somewhat in the 1960s with the emergence of a succession of powerful presidential assistants for national security affairs. In all cases, the secretary's role is the result of his own talents, the personal relationship between him and the president, and the president's propensity to become directly involved in foreign policy-making. The more a president desires to become involved in foreign policy, the more difficult it is for the secretary of state to take initiatives and conduct his office. Since presidents anticipate their own policy-making tendencies in selecting secretaries, much of the criticism of a "weak" secretary of state should be directed at activist presidents. President Nixon's choice of William Rogers as Secretary of State and his systematic bypassing, even humiliation, of the secretary is an eloquent case in point.[21]

Presidential-secretarial dynamics aside, the secretary of state faces a complex task in managing the internal workings of his bureaucracy. The Department of State is broadly organized along two lines, geographic-regional responsibilities, and functional responsibilities. Special "desks" with the regional bureaus monitor the more detailed actions and interactions of specific countries within the purview of a regional assistant secretary. An alternative view of international dynamics is provided by the functional areas, such as the Bureaus of Intelligence and Research, Economic and Business Affairs, and Politico-Military Affairs. These functional bureaus present analysis that cuts across strictly geographic lines—and sometimes across analyses arising out of the regional desks as well.

The nature and structure of the department presents any secretary of state with a complex managerial and coordination problem. The "desk system" of organization in the department, in which deeply grounded experts on each country or functional problem funnel their analyses and recommendations to the various assistant secretaries, provides the needed expertise, but it also

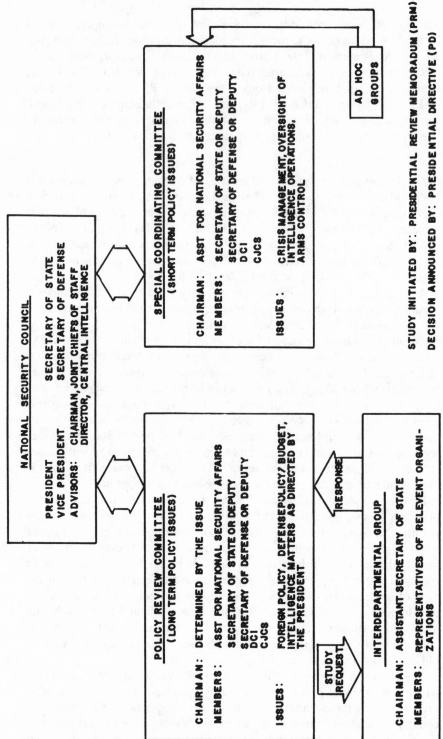

NATIONAL SECURITY COUNCIL

PRESIDENT   SECRETARY OF STATE
VICE PRESIDENT   SECRETARY OF DEFENSE
ADVISORS: CHAIRMAN, JOINT CHIEFS OF STAFF
            DIRECTOR, CENTRAL INTELLIGENCE

SPECIAL COORDINATING COMMITTEE
(SHORT TERM POLICY ISSUES)

CHAIRMAN: ASST FOR NATIONAL SECURITY AFFAIRS
MEMBERS: SECRETARY OF STATE OR DEPUTY
            SECRETARY OF DEFENSE OR DEPUTY
            DCI
            CJCS
ISSUES: CRISIS MANAGEMENT, OVERSIGHT OF
            INTELLIGENCE OPERATIONS,
            ARMS CONTROL

AD HOC
GROUPS

POLICY REVIEW COMMITTEE
(LONG TERM POLICY ISSUES)

CHAIRMAN: DETERMINED BY THE ISSUE
MEMBERS: ASST FOR NATIONAL SECURITY AFFAIRS
            SECRETARY OF STATE OR DEPUTY
            SECRETARY OF DEFENSE OR DEPUTY
            DCI
            CJCS
ISSUES: FOREIGN POLICY, DEFENSE POLICY/ BUDGET,
            INTELLIGENCE MATTERS AS DIRECTED BY
            THE PRESIDENT

STUDY
REQUEST

RESPONSE

INTERDEPARTMENTAL GROUP

CHAIRMAN: ASSISTANT SECRETARY OF STATE
MEMBERS: REPRESENTATIVES OF RELEVENT ORGANI-
            ZATIONS

STUDY INITIATED BY: PRESIDENTIAL REVIEW MEMORADUM (PRM)

DECISION ANNOUNCED BY: PRESIDENTIAL DIRECTIVE (PD)

FIG. 5.3

94

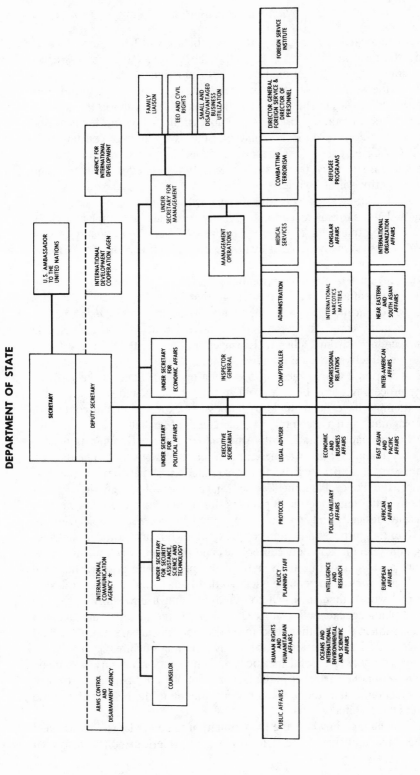

DEPARTMENT OF STATE

DIPLOMATIC, CONSULAR AND OTHER ESTABLISHMENTS AND DELEGATIONS TO INTERNATIONAL ORGANIZATIONS

FIG. 5.4

Source: *United States Government Manual, 1982–1983* (Washington, D.C.: Office of the Federal Register, National Archives and Records Service, General Services Administration, 1982), p. 812.

*The name of the International Communication Agency was officially changed to the United States Information Agency (U.S.I.A.) in August 1982.

95

generates parochial responses to policy problems which, in turn, lead to striking contrasts in the nature of advice the secretary receives—Arabists versus Israeli experts, Soviet analysts versus Chinese analysts, etc. As a consequence, the secretary of state is often forced to sort out contradictory recommendations while shepherding a fragmented organization through the policy process. For those observers of public affairs who long for neat and "efficient" solutions to difficult problems, State is a source of constant frustration. Owing in part to the department's lack of a natural constituency within the United States, this frustration is often translated into vigorous and widespread criticism of its role.[22]

Presidential displeasure with the Department of State seems to be a recurring and nonpartisan reaction. In general, presidential complaints about the State Department have centered around six "faults": (1) quality of staff work in terms of analysis; (2) slowness with which the State Department responds to requests and problems; (3) resistance to change and new approaches; (4) inadequacy in carrying out presidential decisions; (5) failure to lead in foreign affairs; and (6) the feeling that State does not have control of its own department.[23] These misgivings about the State Department—though in many cases exaggerated—have often led activist presidents, and activist secretaries from Dulles to Kissinger, to "go around" the institution and pursue largely individual initiatives in foreign affairs.

The appropriate employment of the Department of State in the national security process has long been a problem for presidents and secretaries. Periodic attempts have been made to harness its expertise in the context of policy planning, such as Secretary of State George Marshall's creation in 1947 of the Policy Planning Staff, with Ambassador George Kennan its head.[24] The Policy Planning Staff was designed in an attempt to focus planning on current issues and to anticipate future contingencies. Yet that staff and its successor, the Policy Planning Council, have invariably fallen short of expectations. Mid- and long-range planning for a complex and untidy world is intrinsically difficult, and it requires exceptionally talented people who are sensitive to the purposes and limits of policy and who can draw clear linkages among policy realms and between policies and programs. Such talents, however, are always in short supply; and, if the people who possess them are kept sufficiently close to genuine issues so that their planning will be relevant to the real world, then they will constantly be drawn into short-range, operational planning and policy advice. In short, if the planners are talented and their subject timely, they tend to be diverted; if they are not, they tend to be ignored. Thus, operational demands ("putting out fires") and the inherent tension between useful specificity and diplomatic generality have made the exercise of policy planning in the Department of State a perennial problem and has tended to shift the locus of policy planning to the NSC staff and the Department of Defense.

There is one area in which the Department of State has largely maintained its hegemony, and that is the daily conduct of American policy in foreign countries. The department's mandate to coordinate all American activities in foreign lands was reaffirmed by President Eisenhower in his (and subsequent presidents') endorsement of the "country team" concept. This approach places the American ambassador in charge of all American programs within the country to which he or she is accredited. (The mandate does not extend to American military forces in the field, though it does apply to military assistance teams and defense attachés.) The country team represents an important attempt to unify the implementation of American national security policy within each foreign country under the direction of the ambassador.[25] Succeeding administrations have continued to endorse this concept, but there is a continual tendency by departments, other than State, to fight it.

The Department of Defense. The Department of Defense (DOD) is the president's principal arm in the execution of national defense policy. Composed of the three military departments—army, navy, and air force—the Joint Chiefs of Staff (JCS) and the associated joint staff, a handful of operational commands (e.g. the Strategic Air Command and the European Command), and numerous defense agencies with responsibility to provide services across the entire department (e.g., the Defense Intelligence Agency and the Defense Communications Agency), the department provides the military instrument essential to credible policies (see fig. 5.5). As originally created in 1947, the position of the secretary of defense was that of a weak coordinator. In the course of a series of defense reorganization acts, the secretary's role has been greatly strengthened and the department centralized in order to improve the efficiency and responsiveness of the military instrument. The essentials of the secretary's role, as they have evolved, have been described as follows.

Foreign policy, military strategy, defense budgets and the choice of major weapons and forces are all closely related matters of basic national security policy and the principal task of the Secretary of Defense is personally to grasp the strategic issues and provide active leadership to develop a defense program that sensibly relates all these factors. In short, his main job is to shape the defense program in the national interest. In particular, it is his job to decide what forces are needed.[26]

During Robert McNamara's tenure as secretary (1961–68), secretarial control was extended throughout DOD by the application of systems analysis techniques to generate and justify military programs. The thrust of McNamara's approach was to steer the nature of debate in DOD on strategy and forces away from the intangibles of military judgment toward quantitative, management-oriented analyses in which civilian officials could dominate. Although the effects of the McNamara revolution have endured in considerable measure, subsequent secretaries have tended to turn more to military professionals in the department for expertise and advice. (The role of the military in national security decision-making is treated at length in Chapter 7.)

The president exercises his constitutional authority as commander in chief

DEPARTMENT OF DEFENSE

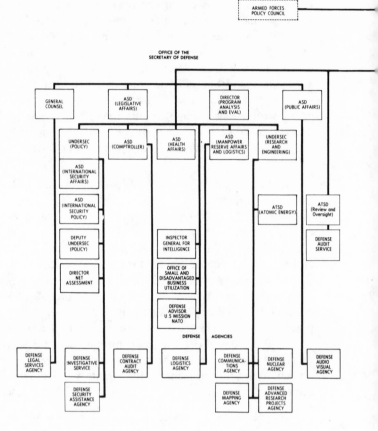

FIG. 5.5
Source: United States Government Manual, 1982–1983 (Washington, D.C.: Office of the Federal Register, National Archives and Records Service, General Services Administration, 1982), p. 801.

of the armed forces directly through the secretary of defense to the commanders of the several unified and specified commands. In effect, the secretary is the deputy commander in chief. In strict legal terms, the JCS is not in the chain of command; in practice, defense secretaries involve the chiefs, drawing on their professional advice on policy and operational means to implement directives from the president. Although the normal flow of advice from the chiefs normally goes up through the secretary of defense, the 1958 Defense Reorganization Act gives the JCS a statutory right to go directly to the president. This "end around" option was designed to assuage those elements who feared that independent military opinion would be stifled by a partisan secretary of defense.[27]

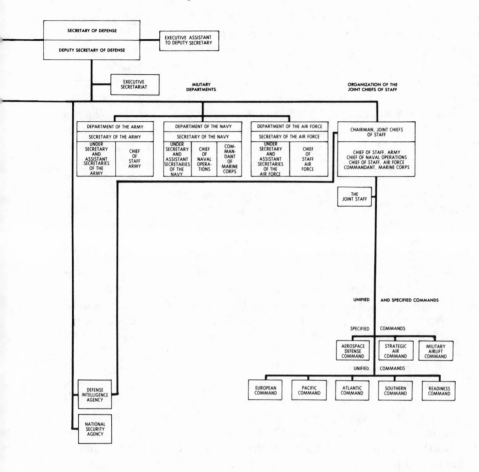

As the "hinge" between the highest civilian authorities and the uniformed military, the members of the JCS have two distinct roles in the DOD. In one, corporately, they are the senior military advisers to the president, the NSC, and the secretary of defense. In the other, individually, they are the chiefs of their respective services. As a corporate body, the JCS includes not only the army and air force chiefs of staff and the chief of naval operations (and the commandant of the Marine Corps on issues that affect the Marine Corps) but also the chairman of the JCS. By longstanding practice, the chairman normally represents the JCS as a whole at meetings of the NSC and in other interagency forums.

The president not only leans on the JCS for military advice and operational plans but also for supporting opinion when he is undertaking politically controversial national security initiatives. Such support by uniformed leaders has often been a key element in developing a popular and congressional consensus. The U.S. political tempest in 1977 and 1978 over ratification of the Panama Canal Treaty was a striking example of the importance to the president of a JCS endorsement—so much so that JCS support of the president led some critics to attack the group's motives. Such critics saw the military's backing of the treaty as a concession to intense presidential pressure rather than a response to strategic considerations.[28] Such complaints recall the remarks of General Ridgway concerning his tour of duty as army chief of staff (1953–55). "The pressure brought upon me to make my military judgment conform to the views of higher authority was sometimes subtly, sometimes crudely applied."[29] Whether or not the Panama debate included such "pressure," it certainly highlighted the president's regard for the concurrence of his senior military advisers in foreign policy initiatives.

In view of the often heated political environment within which the JCS wrestles difficult problems of strategy, policy, and defense programs, it is hardly surprising that the decisions are often marked by "controversy, negotiations, and bargaining among officials and groups with different interests and perspectives."[30] A further discussion of the problems of the JCS recommendation process and interservice rivalry can be found in Chapter 8.

The Central Intelligence Agency. The Central Intelligence Agency (CIA) was established under the National Security Act of 1947 with responsibility for the overall coordination and integration of the intelligence efforts of various governmental groups engaged in national security matters. Its director was named an adviser to the NSC. The CIA inherited many functions of the wartime Office of Strategic Services, in the context of the cold war, including gathering and analyzing information and the conduct of covert operations.

Prior to America's entry into World War II, the gathering of intelligence was not institutionalized in any one agency but was incidental to the activities of several agencies, notably the State Department and the army and navy attachés. The climate of opinion was such that intelligence activities were looked down upon. Henry Stimson, as secretary of state in the Hoover administration, dismissed the "spying" business with the maxim that "gentlemen do not read other gentlemen's mail."[31] However, the ravages of global war and the threat of communism obscured the gentlemanly distinctions of an earlier age. Beginning in 1947, the CIA became a powerful force in the twilight battles of the cold war.

Through the 1950s and 1960s, the CIA played a major role and amassed considerable power within the government. As noted earlier, World War II and the cold war had demonstrated a strong need for a formal intelligence agency. As the dimensions and stakes of the cold war expanded, so did the

CIA. Moreover, the agency enjoyed unusual autonomy. For thirty years, until 1977, the CIA was the only federal agency exempt from openly defending its budget and subjecting its policies and programs to the scrutiny of congressional oversight. Funds for the CIA were disguised in other budgets rendering any outside assessment of program effectiveness impossible.

The CIA's position was also strengthened by its primacy in intelligence gathering and analysis. Information is power, in government as elsewhere. As a result of long-term assignments to specific areas, in contrast to the approach of rotating personnel through differing assignments by other governmental organizations, the CIA's agents in the field, as well as its analysts at home, produced relatively high quality work.[32]

Since its inception, the CIA has been involved in covert operations as well as intelligence production. In Iran in 1953 and in Guatemala, in 1954, for example, CIA-sponsored coups overthrew existing regimes. In the Bay of Pigs in 1961, the CIA was the agent of an unsuccessful attempt to remove Castro from power. Such episodes of clandestine warfare, combined with CIA activity in Chile during the overthrow of Allende and a few instances of improper actions by its personnel at home, convinced some that the CIA's scope and power should be curtailed. Elements in both the Congress and the public were prepared to sacrifice some of the agency's operational effectiveness in order to whittle down its power. The fact that the cold war was presumably replaced by detente and intervention by retrenchment in the early 1970s reinforced this tendency to downgrade and "domesticate" the CIA. (Detailed attention is given to the role of intelligence in Chapter 7.)

Office of Management and Budget. Questions of strategy and national security have their dollars and cents counterparts. With his defense budget, the president structures the priorities of national defense. In the creation of this budget and in the daily oversight of executive operations, the Office of Management and Budget (OMB) plays a crucial role. As Theodore Sorensen remarked, "any President, in short, must always be setting priorities and measuring costs. The official most often likely to loom largest in his thinking when he makes a key decision is not the Secretary of State or the Secretary of Defense but the Director of the Budget."[33]

As presidents have sought to extend their control over an expanding bureaucracy, OMB (and its predecessor, the Bureau of the Budget) has become one of their most effective instruments of influence. OMB personnel establish, under presidential guidance, departmental budget obligations and spending ceilings within which departments must plan. Budgets from the departments, including DOD, are routinely subjected to OMB review prior to presidential approval and submission to Congress to insure that they are in accord with the president's priorities. This process helps restrain the special relationships that tend to proliferate between executive bureaus and congressional committees. In addition, as part of its management responsibilities, OMB exercises a continuing oversight role over ongoing federal programs. This, too, enhances its position within the executive branch.[34]

The Nature of Presidential Power. Central to the Constitution's design was the concept that no institution should hold an unchallenged position of dominance in all aspects of the conduct of public affairs. This constitutional precept and the consequent governmental framework fundamentally shape the president's ability to influence the behavior of institutions, people, and the overall environment of governmental activity. Richard Neustadt has succinctly and insightfully described this system as one "not of separation of powers but of separated institutions sharing powers."[35] The president, as a result, sits in a position where many actors require his help in achieving their objectives. By the same token, the president is also dependent on other actors to accomplish his tasks. In the area of national security policy, this interactive process is clearly illustrated by the dynamic and historic tension between the president and Congress. This crucial dimension of the problem of national security policy leadership is addressed in the next chapter on the role of Congress.

In the context of our system of government, presidential power is then generally the power of persuasion. Teddy Roosevelt called the presidency a "bully pulpit"; his successor FDR said it was a "place of moral leadership." More prosaically, Neustadt notes that presidential power rests in the ability to induce others to "believe that what he [the president] wants of them is what their own appraisal of their own responsibilities requires them to do in their own interests, not his." At the heart of the process of persuasion is bargaining. As Neustadt emphasizes, "power is persuasion and persuasion becomes bargaining."[36]

All too often, the give and take of the bargaining system is obscured by the symbols of power and authority which surround the presidency. The president commands attention in the media by virtue of his office. He enjoys the prestige of being chief of state, as well as the head of government. He has at his disposal a wide spectrum of rewards and a significant number of penalties. These potential points of advantage in the bargaining process should not, however, be confused with presidential power which, at bottom, involves the president's ability to wield these instruments so as to persuade other people that their own purposes are compatible with his and that cooperation with him advances their own interests.

The bargaining advantages accrued by a president come not only from his political acumen and persuasive skills but also from his ability to (1) develop and articulate an overall policy framework and strategy which give coherence to his actions, (2) choose able subordinates and weld them into an effective team, and (3) establish a pattern of successful leadership in important matters which will encourage those who are neutral to cooperate and provide support and those who would oppose or obstruct to await a more favorable time. Establishing a success pattern is, of course, partly a matter of good fortune (but, as Machiavelli has observed, a successful leader grasps good fortune and uses it); it is also a matter of readiness to sort out priorities and make hard decisions—indeed, most presidential decisions should be hard ones simply because the easy ones should be made by subordinates. President Truman needed congressional support for the Marshall Plan. Several factors weakened his hand. As the election of 1948 approached, Truman was viewed as a "caretaker" until a Republican could take office for the first time in sixteen years. In addition, the Congress was Republican and intent on economy in the budget. One element counterbalancing these forces, however, was the prestige and respect Congress and the public had for the secretary of state, George C. Marshall. Of course, Truman's advantage derived from an earlier successful presidential choice—selecting Marshall as secretary of state. Republican Senator Arthur Vandenberg was a key figure whose support was critical to the proposed massive and unprecedented effort. The president courted Senator Vandenberg and acceded to his choice of a particular individual to head the European reconstruction effort, even though the president favored another person. Thus, a brilliantly conceived policy which might have foundered in Congress was greatly strengthened by Truman's yielding his appointment prerogative to Senator Vandenberg.[37]

The only person who truly can view an issue from a presidential perspective is the president; all others' views are colored by their own responsibilities. If he is to protect and advance his power, he cannot squander his time and influence. Since the president is the sole guardian of his power, he must carefully weigh his choices so that they contribute to his influence on issues he deems crucial to the nation and to his administration. He must anticipate major issues early and seek out their crucial elements. When the matter is an important one, he cannot hesitate to invest his reputation and prestige, for they are important elements in the equation of power. Indeed, even the soundest policies and most adroit bargaining can be doomed if the president is suffering from a negative image—as evidenced by President Nixon's inability to lead the nation after the Watergate scandal surfaced.

On the other hand, reputation and prestige have acted as a buffer for many presidents in the face of controversy. The departure in 1959 of General Maxwell Taylor as army chief of staff was widely viewed as a protest against the defense policies of President Eisenhower. (This interpretation was reinforced by the subsequent publication of *The Uncertain Trumpet*, General Taylor's critique of contemporary national security policy.) The political impact of the Taylor action was, however, muted (until the Kennedy administration) in large part by President Eisenhower's personal reputation as a military strategist and by his popularity and prestige both at home and abroad.

Constraints on Presidential Power. The preceding discussion of presidential influence and leadership emphasized some of the counterbalancing forces that are inherent in the system. Although the president sits astride important action channels, his power is constantly challenged and tempered. The dynamic tension between the president and Congress is only the most dramatic of the checks on presidential action. Among the other important countervailing forces are: public opinion, the impact of past policies and programs, and the responsiveness of the executive bureaucracy.

Public Opinion. Effective presidential leadership can tolerate short-term reverses in public acceptance, but, over time, a president must have a favorable popular consensus behind his policies. The demise of LBJ's "Great Society" under the burden of the Vietnam War's unpopularity and the resignation of President Nixon in the wake of Watergate offer two striking examples of this phenomenon.

Since public opinion is a vital factor in maintaining and projecting presidential influence, it is also a subject for presidential attention. In discussing his approach to press relations, President Johnson revealed his view of the nature of the process.

There's only one sure way of getting favorable stories from reporters and that is to keep their daily bread—the information, the stories, the plans, and the details they need for their work—in your own hands, so that you can give it out when and to whom you want. Even then nothing's guaranteed, but at least you've got a chance to bargain.[38]

In addition to underscoring the motif of bargaining as a means of presidential leadership, President Johnson's remarks are suggestive of the complex nature of public opinion formation. Public opinion is seldom a spontaneous expression of the "people's will." It is a reaction to selective information provided by institutions and individuals, often with contradictory purposes. Moreover, the public is frequently highly differentiated. The views of opinion leaders or the "attentive public" are often at variance with those of the mass public. Which "public's" opinion counts will differ with circumstances, but the president cannot long ignore the views of opinion leaders who control the mass media, particularly television, which provides the bulk of political information to the bulk of the people.

In the realm of national security affairs, the president has a substantial, initial advantage in the formation of public opinion. External crises have a cohesive effect on opinion. In addition, the executive frequently dominates the channels of information. As the polls demonstrated in the weeks after Iran seized U.S. diplomats as hostages in late 1979, a president's popularity usually rises immediately after he takes charge in a crisis. The public perceives that based on all available information, the president is taking appropriate action. This is observed even in cases where presidential decisions are later subject to criticism. President Ford's handling of the seizure of the freighter *Mayaguez* by the Cambodians in 1975 won him immediate public approval. Upon close scrutiny, the operation appeared to many as an unnecessary and costly overreaction. By that time, however, it was no longer front page news, and the initial impression remained the critical factor in regard to public opinion.[39]

Events of the past decade or so suggest that the media influence on public opinion has become an increasingly important element in the traditional system of checks and balances constraining public opinion. Adverse opinion becomes really crucial when it is expressed in the electoral process. In spite of growing dissension within the nation, President Johnson "survived" the Vietnam debate until Eugene McCarthy's near victory in the 1968 New Hampshire primary translated opinion into adverse votes. To political leaders, including the president, the electoral process is the most forceful and attention-getting expression of popular opinion.

Public opinion provides a barometer of popular feeling. For a beleaguered president, however, the need is more often for a compass than a barometer. Public opinion polls report general reactions but seldom provide a president with adequate policy directions. Moreover, public opinion generally lags the problem. Roosevelt's struggle to awaken an indifferent or negative America to the dangers prior to World War II is a case in point. Both interpreting public opinion and influencing it have proven to be difficult yet essential presidential arts. This has certainly held true more recently in the public's interest in nuclear policy, as manifested in the nuclear freeze debate. The debate appears to reflect public concern over nuclear issues but provides little in the way of practical or concrete direction.

Past Policies and Programs. As each president assumes office, the rhetoric of autumn campaigning takes on a different perspective in the cold January light. The responsibilities of the presidency, including the continuing programs and initiatives of a previous chief executive, now belong to the new office-holder. An example of this situation is the Bay of Pigs invasion in 1961. President Kennedy "inherited" from President Eisenhower a small army of Cubans poised in Guatemala for a do-or-die strike against the Castro regime. With planning in its final stages and with Eisenhower's previous endorsement, Kennedy pondered the decision to proceed with the assault. Some would have interpreted cancellation as an admission that Castro was too powerful and too popular to be overthrown; others would see cancellation as a sign of presidential weakness and a disavowal of the "free" Cubans.[40] On a practical level, Kennedy was confronted with the problem of disarming and disbanding a sizable and fanatical military force, should he opt for cancellation. He chose to let the Cubans strike but resisted recommendations that earlier planned air support be provided. The results were disastrous. The invaders were routed. Castro's prestige was enhanced, and the image of the United States was tarnished. Kennedy's mishandling of his dubious inheritance was a serious blow to his young administration.

As the foregoing indicates, policy is not created *in vacuo*; rather, each new decision must be made within the context of already existing decisions and commitments. Notable among these accumulations are the budget decisions of previous administrations. This is especially true with regard to the development of weapons, for the military procurement process is characterized by long lead times. A new president is often unable to influence the types and amounts of weapons which are available to conduct military operations and which tend to shape overall strategy during his term of office. President Carter's decision in 1977 to forego production of the B-1 bomber is noteworthy in part because it represented one of the few times a president has rejected an inherited major weapons system after it had completed development and was ready for production. An important element contributing to President Carter's decision was the fact that full scale production had not yet begun. Had Carter approved the B-1, the Air Force would have reached initial operating capability in 1982 rather than 1986, as now planned.

Lack of Bureaucratic Responsiveness. Presidents often find their ability to influence national security policy diminished by their inevitable reliance on the executive bureaucracy for the implementation of policy decisions. During the 1962 Cuban Missile Crisis, for example, President Kennedy was chagrined to learn that Thor and Jupiter intermediate-range missiles located in Turkey had not been removed as he had ordered several months earlier. Undoubtedly, there were many reasons why the presidential directive failed to be implemented; in part, the lapse was due to a lack of enthusiasm for the policy on the part of those who were charged with seeing it through.[41]

The expansion of the executive bureaucracy has been in many respects a two-edged sword. Presidents derive from this expanded bureaucracy greater access to and control over information as well as the ability to develop and analyze a broader range of policy options. However, executive decisions are necessarily implemented through the bureaucracy, and its growth serves to widen the gap between policymaking at the top and implementation at the grassroots level. Within that gap the occasion often arises for presidential decisions to be delayed, amended, or even nullified.

While senior agency officials are generally appointed by the president, the federal bureaucracy is largely staffed at middle and lower levels by career civil servants who may not fully share the president's perspective on national security affairs. Experienced bureaucrats often learn to influence the policymaking process by manipulating the number and range of policy alternatives circulated for consideration, by drafting implementing instructions that blunt the impact of a particular policy, or by delaying the implementation of a policy to the point that it becomes "overtaken by events." Oftentimes, bureaucratic "leaks" develop which alert the media, and thereby the public, to particularly controversial policies under consideration before they can be fully implemented.

One need not always invoke such mischievous motives, however, to explain how the executive bureaucracy may act as a constraint on presidential power. In order to receive the careful analysis and consideration that they deserve, major policy initiatives are circulated, or "staffed," among the various agencies of the bureaucracy with an interest in the ultimate policy outcome. Again due to the increased size of the bureaucracy, this staff coordination can be a time-consuming process. Although clearly possessing the means to bypass much of this process, presidents who attempt to short-circuit the full consideration of policy initiatives do so at the risk of an incomplete or inaccurate understanding of the implications of their action. In short, presidents are often constrained in implementing major policies by the time required to study and analyze, as well as implement, such initiatives.

In many respects, the role of the president in national security policy-making is the most fluid and least predictable of all the major actors in the decision-making process. In both a constitutional and an institutional sense, the president is the focal point of the national security policy process. But more than most participants in that process, the president has wide latitude in defining his own role. Patterns of presidential involvement have varied according to the style and experience of various presidents. Always subject to important constraints, some presidents have chosen to become personally enmeshed in the details of policy-making and implementation. Others have chosen a more passive role while delegating broad responsibilities to their cabinet and other senior officials. Given the nature of presidential authority and power, however, even the most passive chief executives of recent decades have occupied a pivotal position in the national security process.

DISCUSSION QUESTIONS

1. With respect to national security policy-making, how does the Constitution divide responsibility between the president and Congress?

2. How might the War Powers Act of July 1973 shape presidential decision-making on the employment of U.S. military forces?

3. How have changes in technology impacted on the scope of presidential prerogative in determining national security policy?

4. "The role of the National Security Council in the policy formulation process has not been static but has fluctuated, in almost cyclic fashion, according to the style and personal experience of various Presidents." Is this an accurate assessment of the historic function of the NSC?

5. The recent evolution of the national security policy-making process reflects a generally expanding role for the assistant to the president for national security affairs. What factors have contributed to this trend?

6. What factors have tended to blunt the role of the Department of State in the formation of national security policy?

7. What evolutionary changes in the role of the secretary of defense have occurred since 1947?

8. How might each of the key executive branch agencies concerned with national security affairs contribute to the formulation and implementation of a Strategic Arms Limitation Treaty? Which persons or agencies would you expect to be most influential in that process? Why?

9. What is the function of the Office of Management and Budget as it relates to the national security process?

10. What are the domestic constraints on presidential decision-making power? Which constraints, in your judgment, are most important?

11. How does President Ford's handling of the *Mayaguez* crisis reflect both the power of the presidency and constraint on that power?

RECOMMENDED READING

Allison, Graham. *Essence of Decision* Boston: Little, Brown, 1971.

Clark, Keith C., and Legere, Lawrence J., *The President and the Management of National Security*. New York: Frederick A. Praeger, 1969.

Cronin, Thomas E., and Greenberg, Sanford D., eds. *The Presidential Advisory System*. New York: Harper & Row, 1969.

Destler, J. M. *Presidents, Bureaucrats, and Foreign Policy*. Princeton: Princeton University Press, 1972.

Hilsman, Roger. *The Politics of Policy Making in Defense and Foreign Affairs*. New York: Harper & Row, 1971.

Hunter, Robert E. *Presidential Control of Foreign Policy*. New York: Frederick A. Praeger, 1982.

Jordan, Amos A., ed., *Issues of National Security in the Seventies*. New York: Frederick A. Praeger, 1967.

Kissinger, Henry A. *The White House Years*. Boston: Little, Brown, 1979.

Neustadt, Richard E. *Presidential Power*. New York: New American Library, 1960.

Rossiter, Clinton. *The American Presidency*. New York: New American Library, 1960.

Schlesinger, Arthur M., Jr. *The Imperial Presidency*. Boston: Houghton Mifflin, 1973.

Seidman, Harold, *Politics, Position, and Power: The Dynamics of Federal Organization*. New York: Oxford University Press, 1970.

Sorensen, Theodore C. *Decision Making in the White House*. New York: Columbia University Press, 1963.

6

THE IMPACT OF CONGRESS ON
NATIONAL SECURITY POLICY

Historic Alternation of Congressional Activism/Passivity. Few developments in the national security affairs arena have been so significant in the past decade as the increasing assertion by Congress of a strong and continuing role, indeed a full partnership, in the policy process. As noted in Chapter 5, the Constitution presents to the Congress and the president an "invitation to struggle for the privilege of directing foreign policy." In an earlier era, Congress declined the invitation, at least in that part of the foreign policy field known as national security, allowing the president to dominate the process. Since the latter 1960s, Congress has both challenged the president's preeminence across many of the important issues and has also acquired the resources, information, and the legal authority to do so on a comprehensive basis.

The recently asserted claims of Congress are soundly based in the Constitution's deliberate distribution of powers among the three branches of government. The dangers of concentrated power were still fresh in the Constitution's framers' minds from their break with the British crown. "The accumulation of all powers, legislative, executive, and judiciary, in the same hands, whether of one, a few, or many, and whether hereditary, self-appointed, or elective, may justly be pronounced the very definition of tyranny," as Madison put it in Federalist Paper No. 47. Or, as Justice Brandeis expressed it later, the purpose of the constitutional architects was "not to promote efficiency but to preclude the exercise of arbitrary power."[1]

Those selfsame architects were nonetheless conscious of the danger of too much dispersion of power. They had, after all, experienced government by committee during both the Revolutionary War and the Articles of Confederation period and the gross and dangerous inefficiencies to which those eras gave rise. "It is not surprising that an energetic John Adams complained that serving on ninety recorded committees busied him daily from 4:00 a.m. until 10:00 p.m. Within the Congress there developed an unbounded factionalism in which the competition between committees was settled by producing new committees to gain dominance over old ones."[2] (The fact that there are now eighty-three committees and subcommittees in the House of Representatives alone with some claim to jurisdiction in energy matters and that 421 of the 435 House members belong to one or more of these committees suggests that certain lessons have to be relearned periodically.)[3] Reflecting this experience of deliberative dalliance, the Constitution's framers gave certain key powers, namely those clearly requiring central direction, such as treaty-making and commanding the armed forces, to the executive; even so, the wary politicians made the former subject to legislative, i.e. Senate, approval.

The bulk of the enumerated powers relating to national security were reserved for Congress. While there are no explicit "national security" powers in the Constitution, Congress is allocated the power to declare war, raise and support armies and the navy, make rules for the government and regulation of the forces, call the militia, and make all laws which shall be "necessary and proper" for carrying out these functions.[4] Additionally, the advice and consent of the Senate must be obtained for treaties and the appointment of ambassadors, ministers, and other key officers of the government.

As a consequence of this constitutional ambivalence, with some leaning toward congressional preeminence, there have been several periods in American history when Congress has clearly been predominant in national security matters. That the first of these occurred during Madison's presidency is not surprising, for Madison had been the leader of the House of Representatives in the 1790s and an ally of Jefferson in the fight against the executive. "As Corwin notes, their theory was 'that the right to determine the foreign policy of the United States devolves on Congress by virtue of its power to declare war and that the powers of the President in the diplomatic sphere are instrumental only, of no greater range of discretion than the determination of matters of fact.' "[5] Madison was so low-key in his dealings with Congress and the so-called war hawks therein that he permitted the legislators to drag him and the country into war at the end of 1811.

After the Civil War and the strong leadership of Lincoln, Congress again seized the reins, ushering in another generation of what the young scholar Woodrow Wilson called "congressional government." Not until the turn of the century and the deeper involvement in international affairs following the war with Spain did the president, in the person of Theodore Roosevelt, regain the initiative. Roosevelt's technique was to confront Congress with accomplished facts, as in Panama, or in sending the fleet around the world. (Roosevelt noted the following in his autobiography.)

The head of the Senate Committee on Naval Affairs announced that the fleet should not and could not go because Congress would refuse to appropriate the money—he being from an Eastern seaboard State. However, I announced in response that I had enough money to take the fleet around to the Pacific anyhow, that the fleet would certainly go, and that if Congress did not choose to appropriate enough money to get the fleet back, why, it would stay in the Pacific. There was no further difficulty about the money.[6]

President Woodrow Wilson, drawing on his earlier scholarly analysis of the evils of government by committee, also attempted to draw Congress in his wake. As long as World War I was in progress, this approach was reasonably successful, but Wilson's unilateral methods pulled him down in 1918–20 as he attempted to negotiate peace and to bring the United States into the new League of Nations. Senate defeat of the Versailles Treaty, incorporating both peace and the league, ushered in another period of congressional dominance in foreign and national security affairs—one which lasted until world war again forced the nation to close ranks behind the presidency.

The Japanese attack on Pearl Harbor in late 1941 welded Americans together as they had not been since 1918. There was some weakening of this solidarity after the war's end and, in particular, during the Korean War. Essentially, though, from the onset of the cold war in about 1948 until the middle 1960s there was such a strong national consensus on the main lines of national security policy that Congress went more or less quietly along with the executive branch on virtually every major defense issue. Lack of information, perception of danger, complexity of issues, need for solidarity—all were reasons, in addition to public consensus, why the Congress deferred to the executive. In many cases, indeed, it gave the president a blank check in advance in a series of resolutions authorizing him to act unilaterally, namely, on Formosa (1955), Cuba (1962), and the Gulf of Tonkin (1964). By the latter 1960s, however, the public consensus had begun to dissolve under the strains of the Vietnam War, and Congress started the pendulum of executive-legislative powers swinging in the opposite direction—a topic to which we will shortly return.

Structural Explanations of Congressional Role in National Security. Whereas the president can—at least in theory and subject to the constraints cited in Chapter 5—move with dispatch and secrecy in the national security arena, the deliberative processes of Congress are slow and open—or, if not avowedly open, "leaky." Investigations, hearings, debate, resolution of differences between the two houses—all these take time. Hence, in both hot war and cold, the public and the Congress itself traditionally have expected the president to take the lead. The readiness of the public to follow a presidential lead in times of tension or danger was dramatically illustrated in late 1979 as, first, Iranian militants took American diplomats hostage and, second, the Soviet takeover of Afghanistan underscored the possibility of spreading Russian aggression; whereas only 20 percent of the American people approved of President Carter's handling of foreign affairs just before the crises cited, by January 1980, approval had risen to 60 percent.[7]

In part related to its slow and open processes, a second reason for the secondary position of Congress has been the fractionalization of its power and influence. Congress works through committees, and this traditional organization of the legislature powerfully influences its behavior in national security affairs—just as in other realms of foreign and domestic policy. The sheer number of legislators has long necessitated division of Congress into smaller bodies to conduct hearings and debate complex policy issues. Legislation adopted by Congress is not, therefore, primarily the result of discussion by the full body but rather the consequence of tedious committee work. Although the estimated number varies with definitions, by one authoritative count Congress has sixteen Senate and nineteen House committees and literally scores of subcommittees concerned with national security affairs.[8] As a result of this multiplicity, there is no focal point in Congress to bring disparate views together. Each committee tends to have a partial interest and partial view of the broad national security picture. Except implicitly, through the budget, Congress is unable to determine coherent national priorities; the executive has furnished the only focal point in the government. ("Where," columnist George Will has asked, "in any public square in the world have you ever seen a war monument erected to a committee?")

The ways legislators have traditionally tended to define their roles and responsibilities is a third factor in explaining how Congress handles national security. Basically, they have been concerned with subjects that impinge directly on their reelection and on their influence within their respective houses of Congress.[9] In general, members of Congress do not consider questions of military policy in terms of their implications for strategic objectives or goals.[10] Instead, they have focused on constituency-related issues such as spending that aids their districts. Thus, congressional committees considering the annual defense budget have traditionally examined with some care defense *structure*, that is, financial, personnel, materiel, and organizational matters. Yet, while they explore the details of the defense budgets in these areas, they seldom question the *strategy* from which the structural requirements flowed.

Recognizing the importance of committees in the legislative process, congressmen tend to seek membership on committees that offer the most control over policy fields and resources important to their constituents. Because of the seniority system in Congress and one-party dominance in the South for some many decades, an undue proportion of the chairmen of armed services and appropriation committees and subcommittees have been Southerners; it has been observed in this context that had Georgia been an island it would have long since sunk under the weight of the military bases emplaced there. This traditional focus on "delivering the bacon" for the home district has been validated by recent studies showing that constituents do indeed care more about such matters (and about intercession with federal agencies, providing information about federal programs, and similar service functions) than they do about the legislator's classic law-making activities.[11]

Another reason offered in the past to explain congressional roles in national security matters was lack of expertise and access to information. The committee system tended to generate some expertise in the armed services or appropriations committees; members of those committees generally became well versed in some aspect of their committees' work. Yet even those committee members seldom developed a full appreciation of all the full committee's concerns and often did not master national security policy issues under consideration elsewhere in the House or Senate. A given member of Congress might, for example, know a great deal about military personnel expenditures but relatively little about weapons procurement—let alone about strategy, mobilization, economic warfare, or other aspects of national security.

Given the increasing complexity and vast amounts of information relating to any major national security issue, the executive departments that controlled the information producing and intelligence gathering agencies had an advantage over Congress. The executive's affixing a security classification to weapon system capabilities or to strategic intelligence further restricted access to information necessary to formulate and evaluate alternative proposals. (Chapter 8 treats in some detail the topic of congressional access to intelligence.)

Congress could offset executive branch advantages to some extent by using its power to hold hearings and investigations, bringing executive branch witnesses before it to explain policies and programs and to explore various points of view. Such hearings about national security matters often allowed interservice rivalry to surface, giving legislators the opportunity to choose concepts or particular programs that they found personally appealing or in the interest of their constituents. In any case, the hearings showed not only that Congress can use its investigatory powers to acquire information needed to make strategic decisions but also that Congress with its powers of legislation and appropriation could be the place of final decision—even on matters of strategy. We should note, in this context, that congressional decisions, including those on strategic issues, have traditionally been characterized by bargaining that included matters not strictly germane to the strategic question being considered; that is, a senator might trade his or her support on a defense policy matter in exchange for reciprocal support on a water resources project. Not surprisingly then, national security decision-making, as it has occurred in the Congress, both in strategic and structural terms, has been as much political as rational in nature. Only in times of major crisis, and sometimes not even then, have these traditional horsetrading ways been abandoned. (An interesting example of the inapplicability of traditional political compromise methods to national security issues occurred in 1973 when Congress addressed the subject of the bombing of Cambodia. "Doves" said it was wrong and should be terminated at once, while "hawks" insisted it was legitimate and should be continued; they compromised on ending it in forty-five days—apparently adjudging the bombing wrong but continuing it anyway, while vitiating its effect by telling the enemy when it would end!)

Public Opinion. Congress is particularly sensitive to public opinion. The morning paper and the television news, the latest public opinion poll and the hometown press coverage of issues (and of their own activities) are watched extraordinarily closely by legislators, especially by those who must seek public endorsement at the polls every two years. Constituent mail and other communications from important individuals and groups in his or her district or state receive priority attention by an experienced legislator and staff. If, therefore, a strong current of opinion is building "back home," the Congress will respond in Washington.

Ideally, congressional responsiveness to shifting public attitudes will be dampened by the individual legislator's own knowledge and convictions about the nation's security; practically, his or her response to such shifts may well be amplified by reelection calculations. Reflecting on this tendency of Congress to swing with, and often beyond, public moods, Will Rogers is said to have remarked that "if you don't scare Congress, it goes fishing; if you do scare it, it goes crazy." Representative or not, this lack of constancy, what de Tocqueville called the inability of democracies to persist in a design, can prove dangerous under various circumstances.

Ascertaining what public opinion is on a given issue is not, of course, simple or easy. It does not generally arise spontaneously, as the morning mist. The media play a crucial role in generating public opinion, selecting from a glut of facts and ideas just what information to emphasize and deciding what type, amount, and intensity of coverage to give a particular issue. Television has become the principal source of national and international news and opinion for most Americans.

Unfortunately, not many important national security issues lend themselves to the very short, video-drenched treatment typified by the evening news show. The consequence seems to be that while the public at large has more information than ever before, it may not be appreciably better informed about national security matters. Indeed, if there is a systemic press or television bias on some matter, as has been documented on various issues, then the public may actually be less well informed about many key issues than was the case in an earlier era.[12]

Whatever the gauge of public opinion or the authenticity of the claims of those who seek to speak for the public, there is no doubt that, in a democracy such as the United States, popular support is essential if expensive, perhaps risky, national security policies and programs are to be pursued. While both president and Congress subscribe to this observation, the frequency of congressional elections necessarily makes Congress the more sensitive institution. President Johnson's overly confident view that he could manipulate public opinion, as cited in Chapter 5, is not generally found on Capitol Hill.

Return to Congressional Activism. The broad public consensus on national security policy which began with Pearl Harbor melted in the latter 1960s in flames of the Vietnam conflict. Some would date the beginning of the melt somewhat earlier, in 1965, when President Johnson, citing his authority as commander in chief and without congressional consultation, sent an intervention force of 22,000 into the Dominican Republic.[13] Bipartisanship, the notion that party politics should not extend to foreign policy or that "politics ends at the water's edge," is sometimes also listed as a casualty of this period; actually it had been less than robust ever since the 1950s. Whereas bipartisan consensus formally expired in 1979, when the Senate Foreign Relations Com- mittee followed the long-standing practice in other congressional committees by dividing its hitherto unified staff into majority and minority staffs, it had long been more rhetoric than reality. The facts are that politics overleaps water as readily as land and that presidents seek support wherever they can find it.

A President with a large party majority has never been thereby in a strong position to bend Congress to his will on foreign policy; on the contrary, the "great" periods of executive leadership and congressional cooperation have come when the majorities (in terms of party labels) were narrow or nonexistent so that the two branches had to work together . . . it is almost a law of contemporary American politics that a Republican President with a majority is under great pressure from the extreme Right, while a Democratic President is under similar pressure from his liberal constituency. If a President finds—as both Gerald Ford and Jimmy Carter have recently found— that foreign problems rarely yield to extreme approaches, he needs the opposing party to neutralize his own zealots. Although the tradition of bipartisanship grew up in the time of cold war national consensus—and can itself be carried to extremes that stifle needed debate—the pragmatic reasons for cultivating support in foreign policy from both parties are extremely powerful.[14]

With the loss of societal consensus in the latter 1960s came a mounting flood of congressional challenges to executive dominance. It is important to realize that the causes for this return to activism were deep and strong.

Reassertion of congresssional involvement in the many dimensions of Amercian se- curity policy can only be understood in the foregoing context of the breakdown of policy consensus, the erosion of the notion of executive competence, the shock of widespread illegal activities, and the impetus each of these developments gave to the growth of congressional ability independently to create and criticize policy. At the same time, the reassertion must also be viewed in the broader context of constitutional flexibility and the historical pattern of shifting balances between executive and leg- islature.[15]

Congressional challenges to the president on the conflict in Southeast Asia, which had begun when Lyndon Johnson was president, escalated in 1969 when Richard Nixon assumed that office. Under Chairman Fulbright's stim- ulus, the Senate Foreign Relations Committee took the lead. Its new Sub- committee on Security Agreements and Commitments Abroad critically re- viewed worldwide executive agreements and produced a National Commitments Resolution, to the effect that presidential action alone cannot commit the United States to assist a foreign country. Subsequently, in 1972, in the so- called Case Act, the Congress dropped the other shoe, requiring the executive branch to transmit promptly to it the text of any international agreement other than a treaty to which the United States is a party; Congress would then decide whether to withhold funds, or whatever other action seemed appropriate if it did not approve.[16]

The power of the purse strings was also used vigorously by the Congress, from late 1969 on to the final, fateful denial of assistance to the Republic of Vietnam in early 1975, which contributed to the demise of that nation. Repeated substantive amendments to money bills also succeeded in an unprecedented limiting of the commander in chief's role in conducting military operations by U.S. forces in the field. By this new technique of so amending authorization or appropriation bills, the Congress gained the ability to restrict and channel day-to-day operations as well as to guide the grand strategy of the war. (Having succeeded with this technique, Senator Fulbright went on to institute for the first time an authorization bill for the Department of State, so that the same congressional role could be played in diplomacy as well.)[17]

Congressional determination to trim the president's powers and to assert at least a coequal role in national security matters was not limited to the Southeast Asian scene. The antiballistic missile (ABM) fight with the Johnson and Nixon administrations offers another kind of example. The ABM program, which began during the Eisenhower era, was initially propelled by the support of both Congress and the military. It received relatively steady funding and encountered little legislative opposition through 1967, when the Soviet Union announced its deployment of a missile defense system around Moscow. In 1968, however, Secretary of Defense Robert McNamara expressed concern over the effect such an expensive system would have on U.S. defense expenditures and its impact on the existing structure of nuclear deterrence; at the same time congressional defense supporters were prepared to continue backing the proposal. Meanwhile in the Senate, Senators Margaret Chase Smith and Stuart Symington also expressed their doubts about the wisdom of such a costly venture. (This condition of coalitions of like-minded individuals cutting across institutions is common; some members of Congress are usually in the executive branch camp and vice versa.)

The debate that engulfed the ABM program extended for four more years and caused an annual revision of both configuration and intended purpose of the program. While the executive's proposals were never fully rejected and funds were not denied, the congressional challenge did succeed in drastically altering the proposed system, with the president annually adjusting his proposals to minimize the opposition it would face. Incidentally, the debate revealed that in this particular instance a legislator's position on the issue was determined more by ideology than by any other factor; the monetary benefits which would result from passage of the bill did not apparently influence the legislators most apt to benefit.[18]

One further footnote on the ABM debate may be instructive. Congress likes to face issues indirectly and through procedural questions, for such an approach places legislators in a position of expertise and permits them to mask the effect of their votes, if they so choose. As Representative Les Aspin pointed out in an article on defense policy, the 1972 end-the-war vote in the

House of Representatives was on "a motion to instruct conferees to insist on the House version of the Defense Authorization bill in light of the Legislative Reorganization Act of 1970."[19] Similarly, in the case of ABM the most critical votes were on issues of procedure.

An example of another type of congressional initiative that has become common occurred in 1974 when Turkey invaded Cyprus, using American arms. Throughout the subsequent crisis, President Ford continued the policy of arms sales to Turkey, although many members of Congress opposed the policy and to some the sale of arms appeared to violate the military assistance laws. These critics were encouraged when Secretary of State Kissinger, in response to a question by Senator Eagleton, virtually admitted that the sales violated existing laws. Thereupon the Senate passed a sense of the Senate resolution urging termination of the sales.[20]

Fortified with Kissinger's admission and the Senate resolution, both houses then proceeded to pass a bill to compel the president to cease shipments. President Ford twice vetoed such bills until a compromise was reached that permitted arms sales until December 1974. In that bill the Congress directed that no further arms sales to Turkey would be permitted after that date until and unless the president certified to Congress that substantial progress toward agreement had been made regarding Turkish forces in Cyprus.[21] In the summer of 1975, when the president, unable to certify progress, nevertheless again sought to raise the issue, the Congress refused to consider the matter. The resumption of arms sales to Turkey had become not a matter of executive preference within congressional appropriations but an issue of foreign policy and procedure, with Congress establishing the new rules of the game. The fact that a potent Greek-American lobby marshaled the congressional votes is also part of the story, providing a telling example of single-issue politics in the Congress and the country at large.

Another example of the new participatory and activist role of Congress had been the increasing use of "legislative vetoes," which enabled Congress to nullify an action proposed by the executive branch. Presidents contended that such vetoes violated the constitutional separation of powers. Supporters claimed that the vetoes kept the government attuned to public sensitivities. In fact, the legislative veto has since been ruled unconstitutional. However, understanding its application provides useful insight into the increased pressure Congress exerts on national security policy. This pressure is likely to continue, especially in the more traditional forms of authorization and appropriations control.

One of the most significant examples of the use of the legislative veto in national security matters is the Nelson-Bingham Bill. In 1974, Senator Gaylord Nelson of Wisconsin and Representative Jonathan Bingham were able to convince their colleagues to amend the Foreign Assistance Act, so that whenever the U.S. government offers to sell any defense article or service above a certain value, the president, before issuing the letter of offer, must send both houses of Congress a detailed description of the sales terms and the weapons involved. As amended, this act means that all arms sales over $7 million can be blocked by Congress within thirty calendar days should a concurrent "veto" resolution be passed, unless the president certifies an emergency.

During the first five years of the law's operation, no arms sales were actually vetoed by Congress. Still, the law has significantly affected the manner in which the United States now approaches the question of arms sales. The executive branch must develop a detailed defense of each particular sale; Congress then has the role of evaluating each individual sale. This point was underscored during the Senate Foreign Relations Committee's consideration of President Carter's proposed 1978 sale of fighter aircraft to Israel, Egypt, and Saudi Arabia. After submitting these sales to the Congress as a "Middle-East package" with all the provisions of the relevant act attended to, President Carter was forced to write the committee chairman that he understood that each proposed sale must be considered separately and that the package would in fact have to be approved in a series of separate votes. Although the president may have considered the arms proposal a package, the Senate decisively set the rule: the sales were individual.

Another example of the changed role of Congress in national security matters is afforded by the War Powers Act. The hotly contested debates over U.S. policy in Vietnam and over the limits of presidential power culminated in November 1973 in the passage, over President Nixon's veto, of a congressional resolution designed to restrict the president's authority to involve the United States in armed conflict or in situations likely to involve such conflict. The language of the act explicitly requires the president to report to Congress, within forty eight hours of their deployment, any commitment of troops to actual or imminent hostilities or any introduction of troops into the territory, air space, or waters of a foreign nation while they are equipped for combat. The act also requires the president to consult with Congress prior to so acting, though the nature of this consultation is not spelled out.

Further, the act requires the Congress to approve or disapprove the continued use of troops within sixty days of their commitment; if the president certifies that troop safety requires it, this can be stretched to ninety days. If the Congress so chooses, it can by majority vote, not subject to presidential veto, require withdrawal at any time during that period. If Congress fails to authorize within the sixty/ninety days the continued use of the forces, the president must withdraw them.[22]

Although no one can predict whether Congress will be inclined to approve or disapprove various possible uses of force, the very unpredictability under this statute may weaken deterrence. President Nixon's vain veto message put the point thus: the resolution "would seriously undermine this Nation's ability to act decisively and convincingly in times of international crisis. As a result, the confidence of our allies in our ability to assist them could be diminished and the respect of our adversaries for our deterrent posture could decline . . . further increasing the likelihood of miscalculation and war."[23] Proponents of the resolution agree that it will inhibit the executive's willingness to use force but judge that constraint an asset, not a liability. In their view a more measured, careful decision about the use of force—with Congress playing the full role envisaged in the Constitution—is precisely what the resolution is intended to bring about.

The four instances in which the act's provisions have been applied since its passage (transporting refugees from Danang, evacuating Americans and others from Cambodia and, later, from South Vietnam, and retaking the *Mayaguez* and its crew) have been so limited in scope that they give no clue to the act's larger possible consequences.[24] It nevertheless is clear that the check on potential executive branch rashness which the Congress has established has been purchased at a price. If there is a strong underlying policy consensus on the matter about which the use of force is contemplated, the price may turn out to be minimal; if the consensus is weak—either because of paucity of information or of time, or simply because of differences in judgment—then the price could be substantial.

Preparing the Congress for Its New Roles. As the Congress reached out for new roles and a greater share of power in national security matters, it began concurrently to acquire the information and means to underwrite its new activism. In case after case, it mandated that the executive branch evaluate existing programs or study newly identified problems and report these findings with recommendations for legislation to the Congress. By 1972 the requirement to make such reports was contained in 19 percent of all public laws enacted, and 59 percent of all laws required some type of report.[25] In short, through its legislative power the Congress had begun to change the structure and extent of the information flow coming to it from the executive branch. At about the same time, it began to pry away from the executive the ability to acquire data and reports from the intelligence community, as detailed in Chapter 8.

In order further to arm itself with relevant facts and analyses, the Congress created two new organizations, the Congressional Budget Office (1974) and the Office of Technology Assessment (1972), and strengthened two existing ones, the Congressional Research Service and the General Accounting Office (GAO). These institutions, with some four thousand employees, not only conduct studies, surveys, and audits (which include analyses of the efficiency, economy, and quality of various government activities) but also develop, and in some cases calculate the costs of, alternative strategies, programs, and budgets for the Congress. This latter capacity is not yet fully developed, but a solid start has been made.[26]

The increased flow of information resulting from the foregoing initiatives, together with the mounting torrent of information from lobbyists, research organizations, special interest groups, etc., has taxed many legislators' ability to assimilate it. In order to assist in this regard, as well as for other reasons, Congress has vastly increased its staff in recent years. From a total of 500 committee and 2,000 personal staffers in 1947, the number had grown to 3,000 committee and over 10,000 personal staff members by 1979.[27]

This more than five-fold expansion in overall congressionial staff has been fully reflected in the staff time spent on Capitol Hill on national security affairs. It has also had an explosive effect in the executive branch. Table 6.1 suggests the kind of change that occurred in the decade 1964–74—roughly a quadrupling of the detailed oversight and development of tasks for defense by the Congress. The ability of eager congressional aides to informally and personally press the defense establishment for information, or to do so formally over "their" legislator's signature, is limited only by zeal and numbers.

Equally or more startling has been the impact of this dramatic growth of staff on the members of Congress themselves. Not just committee or subcommittee chairmen, but the newest and most junior legislators have sufficient information on which to base judgments. Equally, however, it is true that fewer and fewer of them can assimilate or manage the vast new flow of data which has been added to their traditional concerns. Unable to cope with their workload, in large part because they have all the information and staff resources just cited, members of Congress are increasingly forced to cede power to their staffs, a bureaucracy they created to offset the power of the executive's bureaucracy! "Senators . . . are functioning more and more like the president . . . of a corporation, giving direction to policy and giving staff the responsibility for details."[28]

Side by side with these crosscurrents has been another development that bears importantly on the ability of Congress to fulfill the larger national security affairs role it has demanded, namely, the increasing decentralization of power within Congress. Internal reform, beginning with the 94th Congress, undermined the hierarchy and the seniority system in the House, overthrew certain committee chairmen, and even invaded the jurisdictional lines of committees. Diplomacy by statute was not left to chairmen of standing committees. New members maintained an active caucus and at times built reputations for themselves by ignoring the leadership and having their names attached to amendments that changed foreign policy. Frequently a more junior senator or congressman with the right timing and the right coalition could upstage the leadership. In such a fluid structure new ad hoc coalitions were formed, which happened with the Greek lobby opposing Turkish aid. In an increasingly balkanized Congress, the leadership often became not leaders but followers, who either eventually executed the legislative wishes of the new coalition or, if they opposed them too much, jeopardized their chances of survival.[29]

Decentralization plus increased information encouraged individual legislators to invade hitherto sacrosanct committee preserves. The floor of each house was more frequently the scene of debate over defense bills as legislators were no longer willing to accept the work of the defense committees. For example, twenty-four of eighty-three amendments offered during defense authorization debates in the 1968–71 period were introduced on the Senate floor by senators not involved in committees directly related to security is-

Table 6.1 **Some Measures of Congressional Influence upon Defense Management**

Item	1964	1974
DOD hearing length (words)	3,000,000	12,000,000
Time spent on Hill by principal DOD witnesses (hours)[a]	1,575	7,746
Congressional inquiries to DOD	700,000	1,000,000
Congressional staff committee members dealing with defense	103	275
GAO defense specialists	800	1,350
Line, action, and "special interest" items in budget	312	1,497
Programs and items constrained by conditions/ prohibitions on reprogramming	1,000	5,000

[a] DOD estimates that each hour of principal testimony takes roughly 200 hours of staff time in preparation and follow-up.

sues.[30] Traditionally, of course, Congress quietly ratified the work done in committee.

Also coinciding with decentralization has been the decline of the political party in America generally and in Congress particularly. The majority Democratic party in the latter 1970s was frequently unable to marshall its forces effectively, either to override a Republican president (Ford) or to support a Democratic one (Carter). On such key national security votes as repeal of the Turkish arms embargo and ratification of the Panama Canal Treaty, President Carter was dependent on Republican votes to provide needed majorities for his legislative priorities. One special aspect of the decline of party influence worth noting is the rise of "special interests." Often cutting across the traditional political spectrum, these groups or factions tend to be organized around a single issue or interest—ethnic, economic, or social. Armed with modern communications, computerized mailing lists, and a singleness of purpose that contrasts with the complexity of other, more traditional political groups, these organizations have further fractionalized American politics. Whether the cause be pro-Israel, pro-Greece, antinuclear, or antidraft, the compromises and trade-offs that are the normal stuff of politics and party life are anathema to the special interest lobbies.

The result of the various forces just cited has been a growing inability of Congress to function effectively at a time when it has insisted on at least a coequal role with the executive. Essentially, each of the 535 members is a separate power center with its own imperatives, loyalties, and resources.

Is the Power Pendulum Swinging Back? By the end of the 1970s, many Americans had begun to be concerned about the waning power and influence of the United States in the world. The 1979 seizure of American diplomats by Iranian revolutionaries, sanctioned by Iranian authorities and televised into American homes, brought widespread public reevaluation of the turbulent international arena and the importance of armed strength for dealing

Reprinted by permission from the Chicago Tribune—New York News Syndicate, Inc.

with it. The Soviet invasion of Afghanistan at the end of 1979 powerfully underscored these concerns. As a consequence, the traditional public rallying around a president in time of trouble began with the advent of the 1980s. Sensitive as always to public opinion currents and aware that some of its zeal in correcting executive abuses of the past may have overshot the mark, Congress, too, began to close ranks with the president.

But has the underlying balance of executive-congressional relations been shifted toward the executive by Middle Eastern events or is the apparent change a temporary phenomenon? Certainly, if the international situation continues to deteriorate and the specter of war looms ever larger, the advantages of secrecy, speed, and coherence of policy, which are more characteristic of actions of the executive branch than of Congress, will be needed. Moreover, even if tension relaxes somewhat from the point reached in the early 1980s, it seems clear that East-West cooperation of the 1970s is not likely to reappear soon. Détente may not be dead, but it was dealt a massive blow and the beginnings of Cold War II emerged at the turn of the decade. Under the circumstances likely to prevail, Congress will undoubtedly be prepared to concede to the executive a bit more initiative and freedom of action than it was ready to countenance in the 1970s. Short of massive and continuing reverses abroad, however, there is little prospect that Congress will relinquish the substantial gains it made in that earlier era in prying power away from the president, gains that are imbedded in legislation and institutional adaptation despite the great loss of the legislative veto.

If Congress is not willing to give up the major role of sharing power it carved out in the 1970s, is it prepared to change its internal organization and procedures to enable it to play a fruitful partnership role? Many proposals have been advanced over the years to strengthen the capacity of Congress in national security affairs. As noted, some policies, such as increasing staff and better access to information, have already been effectuated. It is highly doubtful that further staff increases will improve congressional performance;

indeed, many analysts and legislators themselves believe that a trimming of the 1979 number cited above would be beneficial. Senator William Proxmire observed (in August 1979) that "additional staff generates additional bills and work. . . . Senators and staff are stumbling over themselves." From the Republican side of the aisle, Senator Goldwater remarked, "Staff runs Congress. . . . You get off an elevator to vote and you have to beat your way through fifty or sixty [staff members] standing around."[31]

Nor does further information sharing or dissemination gains seem likely to have a salutary effect. Members of Congress may, and undoubtedly many still do, complain that they are inadequately informed about national security matters, particularly in instances where the executive branch has already launched on a course of action. But this problem will not be cured by further data flows, for the difficulty is essentially one of "outsiders" in a policy process ever feeling that they are inadequately abreast of situations. Only if policy formulation is *jointly* conducted will the legislators involved feel confident that they know what they need to know. Unless the constitutional separation of powers is thus diminished, with all the problems inherent in such a unified process, the president will continue to have superior access to information. This is inherently the case, for it is he who controls the bureaucracy that is essential to policy-making and execution; and it is that bureaucracy, by virtue of its responsibilities, that is the primary source of information. It is this perceived lack of input in the national security policy-making process (along with growing public concern) that led to the House passage of the Nuclear Freeze Resolution. This open-ended resolution reflects a congress that is exasperated by its lack of influence on what it perceives as a derailed arms control policy rather than a genuinely useful (or realistic) arms control alternative.

If strengthening the ability of Congress to discharge a coequal role in policy formulation cannot proceed from further increasing staff or enhancing information flow, can it result from institutional reform within the Congress? Would, for example, the creation of a single committee in each house on national security or of a joint national security committee, bringing together the leadership from both houses, significantly improve the situation? If feasible, either of these steps would be a great leap forward in adding coherence to what is currently a badly fragmented process. It is not practical, however, for such committees or committee to be legislative in character, as are the existing armed services, foreign relations, appropriations, and intelligence committees in both houses. For one thing, the workload simply would be unmanageable for such umbrella committee(s) with a legislative function—the existing committees with only a fraction of the scope envisaged are overworked. Moreover, the existing committees would certainly not yield power to an upstart poaching in their terrain or seeking to supercede them. If the umbrella committee or committees were nonlegislative (as is the Joint Economic Committee, for instance), that is, with the power to hold hearings, conduct studies and make recommendations but not to write legislation, then the workload would become manageable and the jurisdictional tangles avoidable. Unfortunately, the results from such a nonlegislative committee, while useful, would likely fall far short of hopes; the existing legislative committees would probably continue with minimum regard for the insights or recommendations of the umbrella group.

Further alignment of committee jurisdictions and certain changes in procedures, such as the holding of joint hearings on issues when jurisdictions overlapped, would be helpful if the Congress is unwilling to create umbrella committees. Some further tailoring and refining of staff roles might also assist. Essentially, however, the search for "structural solutions" to the problem of making Congress a more effective partner in national security policy-making are not likely to resolve the existing difficulties. The tensions between the roles and powers of the two coordinate branches, while reducible, are inherent in the constitutional structure of the United States.

Similarly, the reestablishing of public consensus on the main lines of security strategy and policy is desirable as a means of lessening executive-legislative rivalry and of placing a foundation under the actions of both branches. Unfortunately, however, there are severe limits in an increasingly complex world on the amount of agreement within society that can be expected short of war and perhaps even including war. The willingness of the mass public to defer to elite views, even if the elite is internally agreed, seems destined to diminish as the mass becomes better educated, as has been the case in the nuclear freeze movement. While the extremes of disagreement and fragmentation of American society of the late 1960s and early 1970s may not occur in the 1980s, neither will the relative harmony of the 1950s and early 1960s.

Since neither structural improvements nor consensus revival is likely to settle the problem of appropriate executive-legislative roles, other ways to meet the problem are needed. Congress cannot, by its very nature, provide coherent policy direction on a sustained basis, but is there any way to insure that it will not use its powers to frustrate presidential efforts to that end? One broadly experienced ex-Hill staffer has outlined the nature of the problem.

A foreign and defense policy for a United States heavily influenced by Congress will be even more unpredictable than already is the case. Depending on the issues in question, agreements may be more difficult to make, maintain or dissolve. At any time Congress can attempt to introduce new elements or requirements into a relationship, as it has done with Turkey over Cyprus and with NATO over procurement, or as it could do in the future with Israel concerning her policies towards the occupied territories. . . . The heightening of the unpredictability of American responses inevitably raises the fundamental question of the compatibility of . . . congressional involvement with the requirements of a policy designed to modify and moderate the behaviour of adversaries. If such a policy is to be successful, both rewards and punishments must be available to the Executive and under tight control; availability and precision alike can easily be undermined by independent expressions of congressional will. Indeed, it is impossible to avoid wondering (and worrying) about the compatibility of the new Congress, with its decentralization of authority, its vulnerability to special interests and its tendency to legislate severe but separate norms, with the demands of a world-order policy that could satisfy allies and contain adversaries. Such a policy requires a careful integration of means and ends, a clear sense of priorities and a mixture of flexibility and predictability. . . . Such policies are not the ones most likely to emerge from today's Congress.[32]

In order to reduce the uncertainties just described and to increase the likelihood of coherent national security policy, earlier congressional involvement in policy-making is undoubtedly needed. Such involvement will, itself, produce difficulties and misunderstandings and is certainly not a panacea; yet it is essential if the "new" Congress is to work in tandem with the executive.

Across the board, continual consultation between the two branches is perhaps the most important facet of greater congressional involvement. Though generally given lip service (and sometimes required by legislation), consultation has all too often in the past been *pro forma*. The executive branch has almost invariably minimized congressional consultation because of the difficulties and delays it introduces in the policy process and the possible leaks that might attend continuous consultation on sensitive matters. As a result, "consultation" has largely consisted of informing Congress a few hours before an executive decision is implemented.

Presidents are understandably reluctant to complicate their lives politically by the "shared participation and responsibilities" that the Murphy Commission* called for between Congress and the executive.[33] Even when consultation on an issue has been continuous and detailed over a protracted period, such as on the SALT II Treaty, the result may still be stalemate or defeat of the executive's proposals.

Yet, the two branches must find better ways to work together in the national security arena, where the stakes are so high and history is likely to be so unforgiving. Attitudinal changes are required on both sides. For the part of Congress, it needs to achieve broad agreement within itself that it cannot and should not try to exercise detailed control of policy or military operations— in short, to assume executive functions. For the part of the executive branch, it must accept the reality that the congressional diffidence and passivity of an earlier era will not return and that the executive's personal and institutional working relationships with Capitol Hill must be strengthened through continual consultation and cooperation.

---

*Equally instructive are recent instances in which the "consultation" provisions of the War Powers Act were pointedly ignored by the president. Two examples: (1) Regarding the U.S. show of force in response to the Korean treecutting incident in August 1976, President Ford argued that since U.S. forces were already stationed in Korea, the augmentation of those forces did not trigger the statutory requirements of the act. (2) The hostage rescue attempt in Iran in April 1980 was defined by President Carter as a "humanitarian" mission that fell outside the purview of the act; moreover, the sensitive nature of the mission precluded the possibility of prior consultation.

DISCUSSION QUESTIONS

1. What domestic and international factors contributed to a generally accepted "national consensus" on national security issues prior to the late 1960s?

2. What factors or characteristics of Congress have traditionally inhibited Congress from a more active role in national security policy-making?

3. How does "politics" impact on national security policy-making?

4. What are the constitutional powers of the president and Congress in national security issues?

5. What factors contributed to the loss of a national consensus in the latter 1960s on national security issues?

6. What is the "War Powers Act"? How has it enhanced the role of Congress in national security affairs? Has it inhibited the president in national security policy-making and execution?

7. How has the increase in information available to Congress and a growing staff to assist in analysis impacted on the role of Congress in national security affairs?

8. How might Congress use the Congressional Budget Office and the General Accounting Office to influence national security policy-making?

9. Construct as strong as possible a case for a "Joint Congressional Committee on National Security Affairs" as a means of decisively strengthening the role of Congress in this area. Do you consider the case compelling? Why or why not?

RECOMMENDED READING

Allison, Graham, and Szanton, Peter. *Remaking American Foreign Policy*. New York: Basic Books, 1976.

Bobrow, David B., ed. *Components of Defense*. Chicago: Rand McNally, 1965.

Cutler, Lloyd N. "To Form a Government." *Foreign Affairs* 59, no. 1 (fall 1980).

Fenno, Richard F. *Congressmen in Committees*. Boston: Little, Brown, 1973.

Frye, Alton. *A Responsible Congress*. New York: McGraw-Hill, 1975.

Lawrence, Edward J. "The Changing Role of Congress in Defense Policy-making." *Journal of Conflict Resolution* 20, no. 2 (June 1976): 213–53.

Long, Franklin A., and Rathjens, Goerge W., eds. *Arms, Defense Policy and Arms Control*. New York: W. W. Norton, 1976.

Mayhew, David A. *Congress: The Electoral Connection*. New Haven: Yale University Press, 1974.

Spanier, John, and Uslander, Eric M. *How American Foreign Policy Is Made*. New York: Frederick A. Praeger, 1974.

Stevens, Charles J. "The Use and Control of Executive Agreements." *Orbis* 20 (winter 1977): 905–32.

7

INTELLIGENCE AND NATIONAL
SECURITY

INTELLIGENCE: DEFINITIONS AND CAPABILITIES

Intelligence and Its Role in Policy Formulation. Intelligence in the simplest sense is knowledge about events, trends, and personalities that may affect the observer—or the country, institution, or military service for which the observer works—in some immediate or immediately foreseeable situation. Such information identifies, describes, and defines situations requiring or likely to require decisions.

Intelligence is more, however, than mere description. It is a product "resulting from the collection, collation, evaluation, analysis, integration and interpretation of all collected information."[1] It attempts to envision possible or likely futures by analyzing and synthesizing the flow of current data, providing decision-makers with background projections against which to measure current policy and action alternatives. It may also suggest action alternatives to policy-makers and provide a basis for intelligent choice among them. An example of this direct policy use of an intelligence product is furnished by the request by Secretary Kissinger to the CIA shortly after the 1973 Middle East war "to examine all aspects of possible Sinai withdrawal lines on the basis of political, military, geographic, and ethnic considerations. Eight alternative lines were prepared for the Sinai, a number of which Secretary of State Kissinger used in mediating the negotiations between Egypt and Israel."[2]

Essentially, then, the U.S. intelligence effort is composed of information-gathering and information-analyzing activities in support of the process of policy formulation. Functionally, the activities involve collecting information, processing it, assessing its meaning, relating it to policy issues, and disseminating the resulting intelligence to officials who may use it to form or adjust national security policies.

Though the ability to make informed decisions is especially important in an interdependent and nuclear-armed world, it is not a new concern of national leadership. Intelligence is an inherent function, whether performed well or ill, of every state; the governing authority must provide itself with intelligence in order to be effective and to protect itself. The framers of the Constitution knew about, and valued, the intelligence function of government. They foresaw, in Alexander Hamilton's words, that "accurate and comprehensive knowledge of foreign politics" would inevitably be required in the management of America's external relations.[3] And they knew that the business of *secret* intelligence, managed prudently, would be a useful—and indeed necessary—capability for the infant republic.[4] Two hundred years later, national security policy-makers in the more mature American republic still recognize their reliance on, and indebtedness to, accurate information about the external world.[5] While the best information cannot guarantee sound policy in a complex and dangerous world, policy made without intelligence support, or with inadequate support, can succeed only by accident.

The Policy Implementation or Covert Action Role. The intelligence community also provides policy-makers an "action" capability to assist in some types of policy implementation. Especially during the cold war era, American leadership conceived of and used the intelligence agencies as means of affecting or influencing events abroad in accordance with U.S. foreign policy goals. Among these implementing actions have been such activities as subsidization of foreign newspapers and political parties, arming of guerrilla forces, and logistical or paramilitary support for foreign military organizations or operations. *Covert action,* as this function came to be known, has been the subject of much recent controversy both within and outside of the intelligence community. Any treatment of the community's national security contribution must, therefore, take note of this adjunct capability. It was a significant foreign policy tool in the past, and it could still provide national policy-makers a carefully regulated alternative for carrying out selected policy decisions by means not within the purview or capability of other agencies. There is a danger, however, that unduly focusing on this one aspect of the broader intelligence scene generates control mechanisms and creates a climate, at home and abroad, of opinion prejudicial to the overall intelligence mission. Another danger lies in the fact that "covert action" is a very imprecise, elastic term. It covers everything from having lunch with a foreign journalist to encouraging him or her to write an editorial that may well have been written anyway to running elaborate, large-scale paramilitary operations over a time span measured in years. It is therefore hard to discuss this concept in a rational, meaningful way—especially in a public forum. In any such discussion, strong feelings about certain specific, limited types of covert action almost inevitably spread to, and becloud consideration of, other kinds of activity included under this far-too-encompassing label.

Though clandestine activities abroad have long been a part of statecraft, only recently have the mechanisms by which they are conducted and controlled come under close public scrutiny in America. When Congress created the CIA in 1947 to perform certain intelligence coordination functions, it directed the agency also to undertake "such other functions and duties related to intelligence affecting the national security as the National Security Council may from time to time direct." Since then, NSC directives have given the CIA authority to conduct covert operations abroad consistent with American and military policies.[6] As part of the public and congressional scrutiny of these operations in the 1970–76 period, legislation (principally the Hughes-Ryan Amendment) was enacted in 1974 that required the CIA to report any planned action to the appropriate committees of Congress "in a timely manner." Although such operations survive in theory as an important vehicle for foreign policy implementation in special cases, there is a real question about their practicality under existing constraints (which make virtually impossible the degree of secrecy essential to the successful execution of such operations). Policy-makers still place some value on this capability,* now given the name *special activities*, but its role will likely be minor for at least several years to come.

A Conceptual Look at Players, Products, and Processes. For purposes of their work, intelligence professionals divide the national security establishment into two categories: those who produce information, and those who consume or use it. Producers comprise agencies involved in collecting, analyzing, and disseminating intelligence. The results of their efforts—intelligence products—range from nearly real-time current intelligence reports to longer term, forward-looking National Intelligence Estimates (NIEs), jointly written and fully coordinated by all concerned agencies at the national level. Current intelligence products are normally essentially reportorial in style and often (though not invariably) relatively short on analysis. Documents such as NIEs, on the other hand, are generally wide-ranging, in-depth studies that frequently attempt to project analysis several years into the future.

Consumers of intelligence include the national leadership, their advisers in the policy-making departments/agencies, plus analysts who are (in other capacities) technically part of the intelligence community itself. They "consume" information and analyses as foundations for decision-making or as the bases for decision-making advice. Beyond their role as users of products, however, they also perform an important initiating and directing function in the overall intelligence effort, since it is to meet their needs that the intelligence community exists and continues to operate.

The intelligence community takes its initial bearings and guidance from its mission to support national security decision-making. That responsibility in itself provides continuing direction for the intelligence production effort. In

---

*The CIA operation providing covert aid to antigovernment guerrillas in Nicaragua, which attracted much media attention in 1983 after its disclosure, was a prominent recent example of its exercise.

addition to the overall orientation and momentum imparted by that mission, however, particular policy-making problems generally result in the identification of specialized information needs. These needs, when passed from consumers to producers as tasks, activate a production process that can be conceptualized and described in the four successive stages shown in fig. 7.1.[7]

The first stage begins with announcement of consumers' specific information needs or their continuing interests. Intelligence managers review those statements, and if ongoing production efforts or the existing data base cannot satisfy the requests, the statements are approved as requirements and levied or "tasked" upon agencies having the requisite operational capability. Depending on the original declaration of needs/interests, the requirements may be continuing or long-term, or they may generate only one-time projects.

In the second stage, information is collected. Available techniques of collection include:

- *Gathering of "open" material*—such as news media (including broadcast) reports and popular literature. A very large part of the relevant data on most issues comes from such unglamorous sources.
- *Human espionage*—the cultivation of human sources who have access to the information needed. Though this "HUMINT" technique has been much discussed and dramatized recently, and though it was the preeminent collection technique during much of the cold war, it has been overshadowed in recent years by collection systems that use advanced technologies— particularly the systems mentioned below. It is estimated that HUMINT only receives about one-eighth of all the resources devoted to intelligence collection.[8] However, any statistical ratios—such as the one just cited—can be misleading. Technological collection systems (such as imagery satellites) are unrivalled for generating a solid base of evidentiary data on which to base an assessment of another nation's *capabilities,* particularly in relation to those of one's own country. Even if objectively accurate, X's assessment of Y's capabilities may well *not* be the assessment made by Y's leadership. Nonetheless, whether or not they be objectively accurate, it is the assessment and judgments of Y's leadership (not X's) which will shape Y's policy determinations and decisions. Human sources are the best, often the only, sources that can provide reliable information on what another country's leadership thinks about its capability (relative or absolute) or believes it to be. Furthermore, humans are the best sources of reliable information on the *intentions* of other humans (such as another country's leaders). Consequently, the importance of the critical information gaps that only human sources can really fill is belied by any statistical ratio of the amount of total intelligence resources devoted to human source collection.
- *Signal intelligence*—interception and analysis of electronic communications and other electronic emissions (e.g., missile and satellite telemetry). This "SIGINT" capability requires very large sums of money and manpower

THE INTELLIGENCE PRODUCTION PROCESS A MODEL

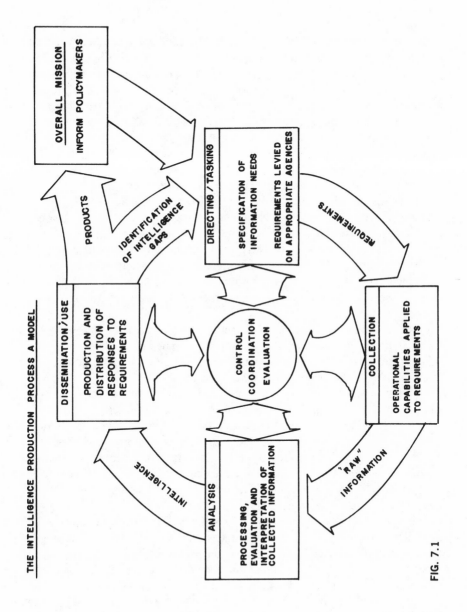

FIG. 7.1

131

resources. The National Security Agency, which is responsible for this means, represents a major resource in the intelligence community.[9]

- *Photographic intelligence*—collection efforts using photography and related imagery-producing techniques from satellites and aircraft (known by the national security establishment as "overhead platforms").

The latter three techniques are often described as complementary sources—complementary in the sense that they facilitate cross-checking of data gained by any one means and also in the sense that each has unique capabilities that remedy the limitations of others. To illustrate: reconnaissance satellite collectors can provide detailed information on observable and countable indicators of military strength or deployment; signal intelligence can provide information on the structure, movements, and planned activities of military units; and human intelligence can help policy-makers understand what kind of adversary opposes them, and what it may be thinking of planning. When fully coordinated, these three collection systems are synergistic.

Impressive as these collection systems may seem, they may not be used at all if information already on hand is sufficient to respond to a given intelligence requirement. Particularly in the case of signal intelligence, the volume of collected information is such that vast quantities are stored immediately after collection, without further processing. Review of that data base may itself yield enough information to satisfy production needs. In such cases, the second stage in the operational model, that is, the collection of fresh "raw" data, will be bypassed.

In the model's third stage, analysts process raw information into intelligence by evaluating it for reliability and interpreting it to determine its meaning and significance. This is the stage in which processing (e.g., translation, photo interpretation, indexing) occurs as well as analysis. It is also the stage that most critics identify as the weakest link in the overall process and one that characteristically receives less than an adequate share of total resources.

In the fourth stage, intelligence products are given to the original requestors and to any other interested agencies. If the original information needs are not thereby satisfied, or if new questions emerge, consumers may generate additional intelligence requirements, activating the production process once again. The process is a continuous one, with many requirements in various phases of the cycle at all times.

The schematic model sketched above, though illustrative, should not be given an overly literal or rigid interpretation. In the real world, things simply are not so tidy. Indeed, real-life intelligence activity involves a degree of human interaction among all who are involved in the total intelligence process that cannot be reduced to a simple schematic diagram. Consumers, to cite but one example, seldom take the time to articulate even their major continuing interests with a precision sufficient to drive the whole collection and analytic phases of the cycle.

THE INTELLIGENCE COMMUNITY

Some knowledgeable observers might contend that the term *intelligence community* overstates the degree of cohesiveness in the American intelligence establishment. The community concept embodies an intent to get disparate entities working together in symbiotic harmony sufficient to meet both national and departmental intelligence needs without excessively duplicated efforts. The four major intelligence entities are the CIA; those of the Department of Defense, including the Defense Intelligence Agency (DIA) and the service intelligence components of the army, navy and air force; the Bureau of Intelligence and Research of the Department of State (engaged solely in analysis); and the National Security Agency (NSA). Although part of the Defense Department, the NSA can be discussed separately both because of its size and primary (national) responsibility in the field of signal intelligence. The CIA, by legislation-enshrined design, is precisely what its name says: "central" in the sense of nondepartmental, and vested with analysis, collection, and other responsibilities.

Diverse and inherently competitive in nature, the community presents a formidable management challenge. It was to meet this challenge that the National Security Act of 1947 established, by statute, the position of director of central intelligence (DCI) and made its incumbent, concurrently, the head of the CIA, which that act also brought into being. (Although the title director of CIA often is and has been used, even on the letterhead of some DCIs, technically there is no such position in the federal government.) The DCI's position has been progressively strengthened in the community since the 1947 act, and the CIA, as an institution, has clearly had a leading role in the intelligence effort. However, recent reorganizations under Presidents Ford and Carter have once again addressed the problem of controlling, managing, and coordinating the community's effort as a whole.

Current Structure and Missions. In the structure (fig. 7.2) established by President Reagan's Executive Order 12333, the National Security Council (NSC) is the highest executive branch entity (other than the president himself) providing direction to the national intelligence effort. The NSC announces national foreign intelligence objectives and priorities, which are then translated into specific guidance for the intelligence community. It reviews all proposals for "special activities," making recommendations on each to the president. It also assesses proposals for sensitive intelligence collection operations and has cognizance of counterintelligence activities (defense against foreign collection efforts). The NSC also—theoretically—evaluates the quality of the intelligence product. Since the NSC does not have an alternative intelligence source, these products are difficult to evaluate qualitatively, often leading to plans based upon misleading estimates of future threats.

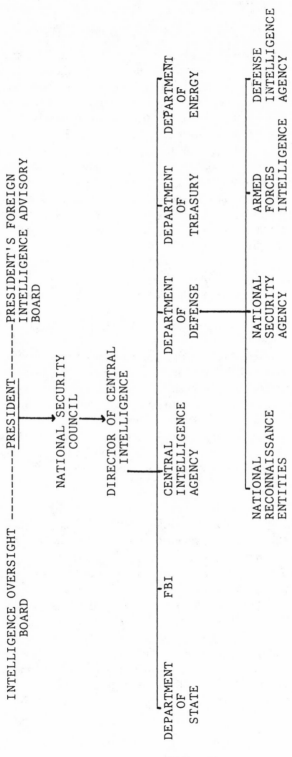

FIG. 7.2
Source: Adapted from U.S. President, Executive Order 12333, "United States Intelligence Activities," *Federal Register* 46, no. 235 (December 8, 1981): 59941.

Below the NSC, the intelligence community is composed of the offices/ agencies that follow.

Director of Central Intelligence. The DCI is appointed by the president (and confirmed by the Senate), acts as his principal adviser on intelligence matters, and holds the position of the U.S. government's senior intelligence officer. As the focal point of management efforts in the community, the DCI's office naturally has far-reaching authority. As with all close presidential advisers, however, the DCI's real influence and effectiveness depends largely upon the working relationship with the president. Frequently, the DCI has not been an intelligence professional but chosen because of the president's special confidence in the candidate.* Every DCI has been faced with the complex managerial problem posed by holding concurrent positions as the head of the entire U.S. intelligence community and the administrative head of the CIA (the only element of that community over which a DCI has personal directive authority). Various DCIs have solved this problem in different ways. During his brief but important tenure as DCI in the spring of 1973, James R. Schlesinger created something called the "Intelligence Community Staff" to assist him in discharging his community responsibilities, particularly those involving community budgets and resource allocation. This staff was retained by Schlesinger's three successors (each of whom has slightly altered its precise structure and functional scope). Schlesinger's immediate successor, William Colby, made the head of the Intelligence Community Staff a "deputy to the director," a practice and bureaucratic nomenclature that both of Colby's successors have retained.

Central Intelligence Agency. The CIA collects information abroad, has "executive agency" responsibility for human source collection, and at its Langley, Virginia, headquarters produces intelligence through participation in the NIE process, through preparation of special research projects and through publication of current intelligence products. It is the only agency within the community authorized to conduct special activities, although the president could direct other agencies to be involved. And, though its operations are conducted mainly outside the United States, it can be involved in counterintelligence activities at home when supporting the FBI, as well as in certain limited domestic activities that support overseas collection operations.

Department of State. Diplomatic reporting is, of course, a valuable information-gathering resource. Representatives of the State Department stationed overseas report to Washington on developments relevant to U.S. foreign policy, including information about foreign political, sociological, economic, and scientific trends or events. For the rest of the community as

---

*Counting the incumbent, there have been eleven directors of central intelligence since the position was established in September 1947. Four have been military officers; seven, civilians. Three of the seven civilians have been professionals in intelligence.

well as for the secretary of state, the department, through its Intelligence and Research bureau, generates intelligence products pertinent to U.S. foreign policy. The secretary of state works closely with the DCI, and the State Department with the CIA, in a continuing endeavor to ensure that intelligence activities are both useful to and cognizant of American foreign policy.

Department of the Treasury. DOT overtly collects and produces intelligence related to U.S. foreign economic policy, and it also is responsible for the Secret Service.

Department of Defense. DOD collects and produces foreign military and military-related intelligence. Its attachés and other military officers abroad are an important source of information feeding into the overall collection effort. DOD agencies normally considered members of the intelligence community include:

- *Defense Intelligence Agency*—DIA, headquartered in the Pentagon, produces military and military-related intelligence for the Defense Department. It also provides military input for national intelligence products (such as the NIEs) and supervises the work of all military attachés abroad.
- *National Security Agency*—The community's signal intelligence operating arm and the largest member of the community, NSA also has a wealth of computer-assisted analytical expertise and a huge data base with which to support the national intelligence effort. From its headquarters at Fort Meade, Maryland, it controls numerous "listening posts" at strategic locations throughout the world. Stations in Iran, Turkey, and Thailand have been highlighted in the past as political events in those countries have interrupted or jeopardized the NSA mission there.
- *Reconnaissance collectors*—Although these assets are under DOD, they serve requirements generated by the entire national security establishment. They include strategic reconnaissance programs—the so-called national technical means of collection—such as those capable of verifying Soviet compliance with treaties that result from strategic arms negotiations.
- *Intelligence and counterintelligence elements of the armed forces*—Each of the services has intelligence and counterintelligence capabilities at both strategic and tactical levels. These serve the information needs of military commanders in a manner analogous to the national intelligence operational model discussed earlier.

Department of Energy. As a minor actor, DOE participates with the State Department in overt collection of information on foreign energy matters, and it also produces such intelligence as the secretary of energy may need to discharge the duties of the office.

Federal Bureau of Investigation. The FBI is mainly a domestic counterintelligence and security agency, operating under the attorney general's supervision. It is included here as a part of the intelligence community because, in addition to its primary domestic mission, the FBI may become involved in counterintelligence activities outside the United States, provided the DCI approves. It may, when requested, also conduct intelligence collection activities *within* the United States, or support such activities by other agencies.

Drug Enforcement Administration. The DEA, also under the supervision of the attorney general, collects and produces intelligence on the foreign and domestic aspects of narcotics trafficking. It may also participate with the State Department in overt collection of general foreign political, economic, and agricultural information relating to its narcotics mission.

Executive Branch Oversight of the Community. In the early and mid 1970s, sensationalized allegations of intelligence community "abuses" generated considerable concern, both within and outside of government. President Ford and, later, President Carter instituted specific "watchdog" procedures to preclude unauthorized activities and clarified intelligence supervisory responsibilities at the national level. An Intelligence Oversight Board (IOB) was created, a three-member panel of private citizens appointed by the president to review and report to him on the intelligence community's internal procedures and operational activities. Where serious questions of legality were involved, the IOB was to report such questionable activities to the attorney general. Within the intelligence community itself, inspectors general and general counsels were specifically made responsible to report to the IOB on all potential breaches of the law by their agencies. The attorney general, in addition to acting upon reports forwarded from the IOB, was charged with establishing or approving operational procedures to ensure that intelligence community activities are conducted in accordance with law. Further, he was to ensure that such procedures protect the constitutional rights of individuals who may be affected. The IOB continues in the Reagan administration, but with a focus on ensuring the legality, rather than the "propriety," of intelligence activities. These formalized executive branch checks are matched by congressional oversight processes, discussed below.

THE INTELLIGENCE PROBLEM: CORRECTING ABUSES

Public Perceptions of Abuses. During the 1970s, American intelligence agencies were subjected to intense public scrutiny in an unprecedented, open debate about their activities. It was exceedingly difficult, however, for most Americans to isolate and analyze pertinent issues with any degree of intellectual balance. The veil of secrecy surrounding intelligence operations, combined with official reticence about them, limited authoritative information to a few partial, often biased descriptions of intelligence community structure, purposes, and activities. Attentive segments of the public had to rely on impressions conveyed by largely unanswered charges in news media coverage.

Spectacular allegations generated limited explanations or denials, and stories improved with every retelling. Reflective and balanced assessment suffered severely at the hands of episodic reporting, and inquiries into intelligence activities were often treated as a kind of exorcism of governmental demons.

In the absence of agreed facts and conclusions, an unsettling public realization grew that America had an important, but as yet undefined, intelligence "problem." Moreover, most of this occurred in the wake of Vietnam and Watergate, when the earlier national security policy consensus had crumbled and Americans were asking themselves hard questions about their government and the nation's ideals, purposes, and directions. Since these public perceptions set the context for official actions taken later to investigate, restructure, and control the intelligence community, it is important to understand the dimensions and general content of the underlying public concern.

Overall, two major themes of criticism appeared: objection to intelligence activities (information-gathering and some aspects of covert action) conducted *within* the United States; and objection to certain activities allegedly conducted, or even contemplated, *abroad.* The word "objection" is used here advisedly, for that was the orientation of many commentators. In a series of "exposés," embittered or disillusioned former intelligence operatives and others sketched sometimes broad and sometimes detailed descriptions of intelligence agency activities and purposes to which they objected.[10] Often these descriptions were cast in terms of indictments, plainly revealing the perspectives of the writers. Apart from the ex-insiders, various outsiders published strident protests based upon officially released government documents that were used to illustrate "runaway official intrusiveness."[11] At other times, serious, professional critiques were offered that may have had more effect within the executive branch and in Congress than in the public debate.[12]

Activities at Home. The attacks on domestic information-gathering focused on the CIA and the FBI, although a precedent had been set several years earlier by criticism and a subsequent curtailment of the army's intelligence role in civil disturbance coverage during the 1960s.* There was particular sensitivity over domestic operations because, unlike most foreign collection situations, the constitutional rights of Americans were directly involved. Examination of FBI operations went beyond the bureau's information collection activities to its now-infamous program of clandestine activity, called COINTELPRO, from "counterintelligence program."† Widespread indignation was

---

*Debates over military surveillance of civilian politics was in part generated by an article written by a former instructor at the army's intelligence school, Christopher H. Pyle, "CONUS Intelligence: The Army Watches Civilian Politics," *Washington Monthly,* January 1970, p. 4. The debate resulted in substantial curtailment of army domestic intelligence activities.

†Although the FBI is a law enforcement and counterintelligence organization, much of its mission depends upon acquisition of information by methods similar to those used in foreign intelligence operations. As its director once noted, "The line between intelligence work and regular criminal investigation is often difficult to describe." Interview with Clarence D. Kelley, *Time,* December 22, 1975, p. 21. The bureau is, in fact, partially a domestic intelligence agency.

aroused and fear was expressed that the FBI might become a political agency instead of a police agency. COINTELPRO was designed to disrupt certain dissident groups—the Communist Party (U.S.A.), the Socialist Workers Party, the Ku Klux Klan, the Black Panthers, and various other extreme left and/or white or black hate groups—and to discredit their leaders. Dating back to the late 1950s, these disruptive activities clearly went beyond the law in many instances and the program was terminated in 1971 by the attorney general.[13]

CIA activities at home were attacked, too, as unwarranted extensions of the agency's *foreign* intelligence charter. Special interest was attracted by allegations of clandestine domestic surveillance operations (including wiretaps, "break-ins," and mail intercepts) whose targets included national political figures, training in clandestine techniques for domestic police officers, and involvement in the academic world through subsidies and research contracts.

While there was no direct challenge to the foreign collection mission itself, there was a drumfire of criticism about supportive activities within the United States which had not been a matter of public knowledge in the past. The public's curiosity was fired, for instance, by charges that CIA programs were

"Father, I cannot tell a lie. The CIA did it."

aimed against innocent foreign students and other visitors to the United States; and that the Agency had programs targeted on Americans traveling abroad.[14] Although the more lurid and exaggerated of these disclosures were later deflated, they helped create a sense that American intelligence itself was on trial.

Activities Abroad. With regard to overseas activities by the intelligence agencies, it was CIA covert action that drew the most criticism. Alleged assassination plots, in particular, were reported as evidence of government betrayal of basic American ideals.[15] Other covert activities abroad were criticized as supportive of repressive, undemocratic regimes or movements. These activities included funding of parties and other groups that were anti-Soviet or had other aims compatible with U.S. governmental interests, propaganda schemes, and support for guerrilla forces opposing foreign governments.[16] While these and other similar activities were particular targets, responsible commentators took pains to note the distinction between such operations and the foreign collection effort; the latter (with its own clandestine methodology) was generally treated as a useful, if overdone, capability.[17]

Outrage in some quarters, particularly among liberal elements, about such domestic and foreign intelligence activities drew strength from initial impressions that the intelligence agencies, especially the CIA, had been operating in large measure on their own.[18] Abuses were thought to have resulted largely from the runaway, uncontrolled initiative of the agencies, many of whose activities were not sufficiently supervised (perhaps were even unknown) at high levels. We will return to these "rogue elephant" charges later.

Modes of Control of Intelligence. The "intelligence problem" is in part an aspect of the larger phenomenon discussed in earlier chapters, namely, the continuing competition between the president and the Congress over national security policy. At the heart of the problem is the question of inherent presidential powers—powers asserted by or assumed to accrue to the president by virtue of his responsibilities rather than by virtue of any explicit constitutional or statutory mandate. Since there is, in fact, no explicit provision in the Constitution for the control of intelligence, authority for it must be inferred from provisions for the national defense and foreign affairs functions that intelligence serves. Inasmuch as the Congress shares power with the president in these latter functions, its claim in the 1970s to comparable authority in the field of intelligence was hard for the executive branch to counter, particularly in the overall political climate then prevailing.

In some respects, as the confrontation between the two branches for policy control took place in the intelligence context, it resembled nothing so much as a siege by the Congress against an increasingly encircled executive. Only under great pressure have presidents permitted entry by others in the intelligence preserve.

Legislative Perspectives and Actions. For the Congress, the intelligence community presents a special opportunity as well as a problem of oversight designed to preclude violations of the law or abuses of individual rights. If congressional participation in foreign policy formulation and control is to be significant, Congress must have access to information. Members of Congress particularly interested in influencing national security have therefore seized the opportunity presented by disputes over the community's actions to gain access to intelligence products. Others have exploited the opportunity to participate in controlling official United States activities abroad—particularly the covert action tool of foreign policy implementation.

Responding to the various currents cited in preceding paragraphs, both the House and the Senate launched investigations in 1975 and 1976. Although the respective committees operated concurrently, the Senate committee (known as the Church Committee after its chairman, Senator Frank Church) took the lead. Its investigatory charter was broad and open-ended, instructing the committee to measure intelligence activities against standards of both legality and propriety. It issued an interim report in November 1975, after the committee had listened to more than one hundred witnesses, and decided that the United States had been implicated in several political assassination plots. While the evidence was admittedly ambiguous in places and fell short of proving that murderous activities had been planned as a matter of national purpose, the committee felt it had nevertheless identified a problem worth addressing immediately: operational authorization procedures within the intelligence community seemed so deliberately compartmented and secretive that a plan to kill a foreign leader could have been generated without explicit presidential approval.

Much of the public debate on this matter, however, missed an important point. The president was deliberately "insulated" from formal involvement in "covert action" decisions; not to keep him ignorant of them—which, in fact, no president ever was—but to "distance" him enough from them so that he could always take and hold the public line that the chief of state was not involved. Most of the rest of the world understood and accepted this posture as being useful, even though it might be widely recognized, in any particular case, as a convenient fiction. (President Eisenhower's public acknowledgement that Gary Powers's U-2 had in fact been overflying the Soviet Union for espionage purposes created such a furor abroad precisely because that was the sort of thing no chief of state ever publicly acknowledges.)

Since the committee was particularly concerned with overly compartmented planning procedures and inadequate approval mechanisms, the interim report argued for clear and open specification of the locus within the executive branch of responsibility for approval of covert action operations. The committee also believed that, as a governing proposition, "traditional American notions of fair play" should control all American activities internationally, even with respect to nations whose ideals, standards, and practices are less than generously disposed toward our own.

The committee's final report echoed that concern for adherence to "fair play" ideals. The committee clearly believed that the looseness of operational rules and discretion had sometimes led to intelligence operations resembling those of our totalitarian competitors. Remedies suggested by the committee included clear legislative delineation of the scope of permissible activities (via a statutory charter for the intelligence community) and better procedures for supervising intelligence agency operations (including more and better congressional oversight).[19]

After completion of those investigations, Congress had before it two self-imposed tasks; to put its oversight machinery in order, and to pass legislative charters announcing authorizations and restrictions for the intelligence community.

To meet the first point, the Senate quickly established an oversight committee: the Select Committee on Intelligence. A companion committee was eventually established in the House of Representatives, but again the Senate committee took the lead. After a year, it issued a brief report confirming the existence of an oversight procedure worked out with the executive and explaining its mechanics.[20] The report also stated the committee's belief that the intelligence agencies were by then well controlled and that national security interests justified retention and exercise of their properly supervised capabilities. The committee also stated its intent to serve congressional and constitutional interests in the following ways.

1. *Obtain information relevant to foreign policy decisions*—The committee was instructed by the Senate to

   provide informed and timely intelligence necessary for the executive and legislative branches to make sound decisions affecting the security and vital interests of the nation.[21]

   This task was clearly intended to diminish that significant information advantage of the executive in foreign affairs which had been recognized early in our constitutional history. Access to intelligence products, then, became a matter of institutional priority, with a view to supporting informed decisions by Congress.

2. *Use of the budget process as a control mechanism*—During the committee's first year, it helped prepare legislation specifically authorizing appropriations for all aspects of intelligence, including a project-by-project review of covert action. This review procedure was a major step beyond the "blind" approvals of the past, when intelligence monies were hidden throughout the budget, and opened the way for far more congressional influence than had been felt before in the intelligence arena.

3. *Control by investigation*—As noted earlier, in its first year, the Senate committee investigated one-hundred allegations of improprieties. The role of Congress as an institutional inquisitor is a well-established one, and the committee cited it as an especially valuable means of discharging congressional oversight responsibilities.

4. *Review of covert operations proposals*—The oversight procedure estab-

lished in conjunction with the executive branch gave the Senate committee what amounted to an approval role in covert action operations. Once the president approves a proposal, the committee is informed. Should the committee feel that pursuit of a covert action would not be in the best interests of the country, its procedures provide for taking the issue to the Senate in closed session. The rules even envisioned disclosure of facts concerning the operation if confrontation over its advisability persisted.

Work on a statutory charter for the intelligence community proved more difficult than the provision of oversight. Congress is, of course, well aware of the advisability of making its intelligence role a matter of law, not of executive condescension or bargaining. To that end, the Senate Intelligence Committee drafted a charter that included a requirement that the DCI serve Congress as well as the president in intelligence production. The proposal also attempted to solidify the operational oversight procedure in statute, establishing specific operational restrictions as a matter of public law.[22]

The Senate committee disagreed over whether the statutory charter should contain any explicit recognition of the president's powers. Although the Ford administration insisted on due recognition to presidential authority, the Carter administration did not.[23] Strong differences in views about the appropriate nature and detailed content of intelligence charters, plus changing perceptions in some quarters about the wisdom of "hobbling" the intelligence community, resulted in protracted delay. Finally, in 1980, a charter emerged from the 96th Congress and was signed into law. Only 750 words long, it reduced the number of committees to which the intelligence community had to report from eight to two, and was widely regarded as a victory for those who opposed intelligence constraints.

But the Carter perspective lives on in other legislation. An early proposal on electronic surveillance—a core issue of presidential prerogative—was signed into law as the Foreign Intelligence Surveillance Act after much work by the Senate Intelligence Committee. It requires judicial warrants for *all* electronic surveillance for foreign intelligence or counterintelligence purposes in the United States when communications of "United States persons" might be intercepted. Not only did the president thereby submit to congressional rule-making in a field long held to be within his protected national security sanctuary, but he also submitted to a system of judicial review of specific operational proposals. President Carter, in his public statement at the signing of the bill, merely observed that the statute introduces clarity where before there was contention.[24]

Legislators, however, were clear that restraining the president and sharing powers are at stake. When President Carter signed the key document setting forth the intelligence community's roles, missions, and restrictions—Executive Order 12036—Senator Bayh framed the remaining issues as follows.

This is the first time in history that the Congress has had this kind of cooperation with the Executive Branch. This is the second step, I would like to remind those who are here, in which you our President have undertaken a landmark initiative. We met in the Rose Garden in the spring where for the first time in history you were willing to waive your inherent authority to get involved in electronic surveillance.

As we move forward with the charters, I think it is important to understand that this is critical.[25]

Judicial Perspectives and Actions. Concern about unilateral presidential power in intelligence matters has found expression not only in the Congress but also in the courts. Judicial decisions have had significant impact upon certain intelligence capabilities long left largely within the province of executive branch discretion. And they continue to influence self-corrective actions undertaken within the community.

Courtroom challenges to domestic and foreign activities of intelligence agencies have been focused on protecting individual rights from unwarranted government intrusion, in particular, on certain investigative activities undertaken in the name of "national security." Under traditionally recognized rules, such activities—for example, wiretapping—were to a large extent exempted from restrictions applicable to the same techniques when used in criminal investigations. Despite challenges, federal courts long adhered to the principle, announced in *Olmstead* v. *United States*,[26] that government wiretapping did not raise constitutional issues. In 1967, two Supreme Court decisions revised that rule, holding that electronic surveillance was a search and seizure within the meaning of the Fourth Amendment and that in criminal proceedings the fruits of domestic electronic surveillance activities would be inadmissible if the probable cause and warrant requirements of the Constitution had not been satisfied.[27] It is significant, however, that these decisions were criminal cases, and two justices took pains to point out in their opinions that national security or intelligence cases might produce different rulings. Subsequently, courts hearing national security cases scrutinized domestic investigative activities closely but still recognized special interests that might justify "intrusive" government action in many national security, or foreign intelligence, cases.[28]

In 1974, intelligence activities conducted abroad were brought to judicial attention in a dispute over alleged invasion of constitutional rights of Americans overseas. In a federal district court ruling, it was stated that electronic surveillance of Americans overseas, if it occurred as there alleged, must be subjected to the domestic rules of the Fourth Amendment, even though the actual surveillance may have been conducted, after U.S. request, by foreign authorities under foreign law.[29] In short, the intelligence community in the course of the 1970s came to face a judiciary that was of the same mind as the legislature—that is, no longer prepared to accept recitation of national security rationales as sufficient to confer absolute protection for the exercise of executive powers either at home or abroad.

Executive Branch Perspectives and Actions. In January 1975, in response to mounting criticism of the CIA, President Ford established a blue ribbon panel headed by Vice President Rockefeller to investigate charges that the agency's activities within the United States had exceeded its statutory authority. The Rockefeller Commission's investigative charter was limited to domestic activities, and legality—not propriety—was the standard against which the commission was to measure those activities.[30] After much study, the commission, ultimately, found the great majority of CIA domestic activities unobjectionable, in essence ratifying the thrust of existing operational rules. It did, however, make specific recommendations in several areas.

The commission urged amendment of the CIA's statutory charter to make it clear that the agency's domestic activities must be related to foreign intelligence. The commission also recommended revitalization of both executive and legislative oversight. In the Congress, the commission recommended establishment of a Joint Committee on Intelligence to supervise the CIA in a disciplined fashion from outside the intelligence community. And within the executive branch, the commission was concerned with checks against misuse of the CIA by the president and others, as well as with clarifying the agency's operational rules.

Executive Order 11905, issued by President Ford in February 1976, was heralded as the executive branch solution to the problems raised by the Congress and the issues in the Rockefeller Commission report, namely, a new charter for the intelligence community that clarified its functions, roles, and restrictions.[31] In a sense, it was exactly as advertised. It listed the intelligence responsibilities of all members of the intelligence community. It forbade involvement in political assassination plots. And it stated clear prohibitions and restrictions applicable to operational activities, especially insofar as those activities might impinge on the constitutional rights of Americans. For those already displeased with the breadth of intelligence actions that were permitted under the law, however, the executive order was a disappointment that led to a redoubling of their efforts to change the applicable law. If the executive would not change the operational boundaries, then efforts would be focused on the charter proposals already in Congress and/or claims in civil lawsuits.

Under President Carter, the executive position regarding the intelligence community was subtly, but significantly, revised. Standards for control of intelligence activities were frequently framed in terms of propriety as well as legality. The president himself gave early guidance to the intelligence community on control standards. He told his director of Central Intelligence that American intelligence activities must be conducted not only in accordance with law, but also in accordance with "American values."[32] Given the new administration's emphasis on human rights in foreign policy, it would indeed have been surprising if there were not similar declarations with respect to behavior of intelligence agencies.

In addition to whatever operational limitations the notion of propriety brought, the Carter administration's view of legality also altered both the structure and process of the intelligence community's effort. In particular,

Executive Order 12036 gave the attorney general an important role in reviewing clandestine operational proposals. If he believes any proposed activities violated the rights of Americans, he could recommend disapproval directly to the president. Some observers considered this the key feature of the executive order.

President Reagan's Executive Order 12333 reflected that administration's concern for reinvigorating intelligence capability to deal with a wide array of national security threats. As key points of contrast with the Carter approach, the role of the attorney general in the intelligence community was appreciably diminished, and, in its own terms, the order's overriding purpose was to *enhance*, not restrain, intelligence activity.

THE CONTINUING PROBLEM OF QUALITY

The quality of the intelligence community's product has been a concern to intelligence professionals and policy-makers alike. President Carter's well-publicized dissatisfaction with intelligence performance before and during the 1978–79 difficulties in Iran, when he and other policy-makers were taken by surprise, is only the most recent manifestation of that concern.

Tasking. One of the more durable problems of quality concerns the policy-makers' own roles in the intelligence process. As noted earlier, the intelligence effort derives both focus and impetus from consumers' declarations of interest. The effort suffers if consumers grow complacent, or if they become too involved in the day-to-day maintenance or defense of policy to generate information requirements. If policy-makers do not periodically seek data and analyses, for example, of Soviet military activities in Cuba, the topic will slide into low-priority status as more pressing matters come to absorb the time and attention of intelligence officials. That just such a process occurred, adding to the flap in late 1979 over Soviet "combat units" in Cuba, is reasonably clear.

Experienced intelligence officials are agreed that one of the most striking and persistent deficiencies affecting intelligence production is the "inadequacy of guidance by policymakers as to their needs."[33] This deficiency is related, in turn, to the difficulties in performing policy planning, discussed in Chapter 5; in both cases, the main problem is officials' reluctance to devote attention on a continuing priority basis to tommorrow's issues as well as to today's.

At this point (as noted earlier), the question of resource allocation comes very much into play. There is an inevitable and continuing "dynamic tension" between the instinctive preferences of intelligence managers and those of policy-level officials, particularly those who set or approve budgets. Intelligence managers would like to keep all bases permanently covered in order to meet any emergent need, interest, or desire of policy-level intelligence consumers. But policy-level officials, especially those with budget and resource management responsibilities, naturally want the weight of effort devoted to their current concerns. However, the redirection and/or retargeting of intelligence efforts is not a simple process. It requires long lead times, often measured in years or even decades, to build a core of analysts trained and experienced in a given, formerly low-priority, area or to develop a reliable pool of human sources with meaningful access to significant information on particular issues.

A more subtle—but nonetheless insidious—problem can arise when consumers *do* energize the production system but primarily to find support for existing or preferred policy. If thus directed, intelligence can become a dangerous instrument. A natural tension between intelligence and policy

should be taken for granted; there would be reason for alarm if it were absent. This is so because if intelligence does its job well, i.e., with as much objectivity as possible, it will present a picture of the external world more intractable and less responsive to our view of our just interests than policy-makers would have it; the latter, and especially political leaders, prefer lesser costs and simpler solutions than generally are possible. A good intelligence organization will frequently be a messenger bearing bad news.[34]

It has been argued both that intelligence and policy should have an arms-length relationship and that they should be closely related. Both arguments are sound; both relationships should hold: there must be both a functional separation—to avoid intelligence's becoming a pliant team player—and continuous two-way dialogue—so that intelligence will know what is needed and policy will be adequately informed.

Policy-makers can, of course, discourage intelligence producers by simply ignoring analyses they do not believe or do not want to believe. Intolerance of, or indifference to, alternative views inevitably reduces the quality of the intelligence product. No one wishes to talk to, or write analyses for, a blank wall. That, in fact, was in part what happened to our intelligence effort in Iran, according to a report compiled by the House Committee on Intelligence.[35]

Inevitably, policy-makers will tend to ignore advice, whatever its source, if it is too fuzzy or delphic to be useful, or if its purveyor has a record of being repeatedly wrong. Alternatively, they will ignore advice if it is internally inconsistent or the key analysts disagree. One way to meet this latter problem was cited for the Commission on the Organization of the Government for the Conduct of Foreign Policy:

It was the intelligence community's judgment, expressed with some dissenting views in National Intelligence Estimates (NIEs), that the Soviets were not testing a MIRV in 1969. Analysts in DOD, with access to the same information, believed that they were. The President's NSC staff could not tell from reading the NIE what the basis for the disagreement was. They were reluctant to choose the DCI's view over that of Pentagon officials simply on the grounds that DOD analysts had a vested interest in believing the worst about the Soviet threat. They wanted to know the basis for the two views.

Dr. Kissinger convened a MIRV panel composed of experts from State, CIA, DIA, and OSD (chosen, incidentally, for their expertise and not for their rank or status). After a series of lengthy meetings and much drafting and redrafting, the MIRV Panel produced an excellent report that precisely and in detail described the evidence, the areas of agreement about its implications, and the points of disagreement. (A similar but much more extensive process took place concerning the U.S. capability to verify arms control agreements.)

What was valuable to policy makers was the thorough and precise analysis that the community in the end provided. Yet, despite the success of this and similar analyses, it always seemed to be unreasonably difficult to get the community to produce them. If the community sets as its objective the production of analysis that is thorough, objective, and well presented, the President and his key aides cannot help but rely on it, ask for more, and invite its purveyors to be close at hand in time of need.[36]

Collection. Quality can also be limited by problems with collection techniques. Reports from human sources are only as reliable and insightful as the sources themselves. Collectors cannot depend on official sources alone; U.S. failure to discern the depth and breadth of popular disaffection with the Shah of Iran in the latter 1970s was apparently due to just such dependence—we did not "stay in" with the "outs." The signal intelligence effort is vulnerable too, for fabricated transmissions and false trails can be broadcast. And overhead reconnaissance, despite remarkable advances in technology, cannot see everything.

Those limitations, and others, can result in collection of too little information or, more likely, of too little information of real value. Equally important, however, inadequately conceived, controlled, and coordinated collection can result in just the opposite: an unmanageable, all-source glut that obscures and defied analysis. Thoughtful members of the intelligence community are particularly concerned about this surfeit and the related problem that "collection tends to guide production."

Analysis. Even when the collection effort is properly focused and well managed and gluts are avoided, analysis remains the most difficult task in the intelligence cycle. The stage in which raw information is assembled, processed, assessed, related, and made understandable is the critical link between the information collector and the decision-maker. The success or failure of particular policy decisions may well depend upon skillful analysis of what the facts in the situation mean or how the other side will react to a U.S. initiative. The analysts' aim cannot be to forecast the future; their data are generally too fragmentary and questionable to make prophecy a sensible enterprise. Rather, they can hope to discern trends, to illuminate the nature of choices facing policy-makers, and to assign probabilities to various possible outcomes.

One of the more intractable problems for the intelligence community to handle internally is institutional bias. It is perhaps understandable that the DIA, as a part of DOD, might tend to view the Soviet defense establishment as highly threatening. Cynics often observe that the intelligence sections of the various armed services are bound to conclude that Soviet tanks, ships, or airplanes are a threat to their respective services, thus lending weight to their parent organizations' budget proposals. Since the CIA ostensibly has no institutional "client" whose interests it might advance, the agency might be presumed to be perfectly objective—serving the national interest even-handedly. Experienced observers have noted, however, that even the CIA has bias problems.

It has been suggested, for instance, that in 1962, CIA analysts believed "that the Soviets would not put missiles into Cuba because such a move would be 'aberrational.' In 1973, most of the intelligence community was disposed to believe that the Arabs were unlikely to resort to war against Israel because to do so would be 'irrational' in light of relative Arab-Israeli military capabilities. The same mechanism operated—the inability to foresee critical events in the face of mounting evidence to the contrary—during the Cyprus crisis in the summer of 1974."[37] That this difficulty is generic and not peculiar to American intelligence is indicated by the fact that Mossad, Israel's CIA and widely acknowledged by professionals to be one of the very best services in the world, misread—until very late in day—Egypt's intentions immediately prior to its surprise attack upon Israel in 1973.

In addition to this general problem of attributing concepts and thought processes to the other side akin to one's own, there is the problem that over time, institutions gradually develop subcultures of their own which their members are loath to challenge or which it never occurs to them to challenge. Thus, during the 1960s it became established wisdom in the CIA, as elsewhere in the government, that the Soviet Union was seeking strategic parity with the United States and that its goal was, therefore, to have as many land-based ICBMs, i.e., 1,000, as the United States. When the U.S.S.R. had already surpassed that number, apparently the analysts simply discounted the evidence, believing that the Soviets were leveling off as the United States had done.[38]

Similarly, and apparently for much the same reasons, the agency developed certain approaches to estimating the production costs and logistical backup for Soviet combat materiel and forces, approaches that it consistently applied in costing Soviet military forces during the 1960s and early 1970s. This method was maintained despite indications that it resulted in understating Soviet defense spending, until defector information overturned the approach in the middle seventies. Similarly, the agency's approach to gauging improvements in Soviet strategic forces resulted in underestimation, until the famous Team A/B exercise of 1976; at that point, the agency's leadership was persuaded to provide the same basic data to two competitive teams of analysts—one of which was largely staffed by nonagency personnel. The nonagency team concluded that the U.S.S.R. was, and for many years had been, doing a great deal more than the agency had believed up to that point; upon cross-checking assumptions, methods and conclusions, senior policy-making officials concluded that the outsiders were a good deal closer to the truth than the insiders were and had been. Such sobering exercises lend weight to the argument against centralizing all collection and analysis activities; a certain amount of competition and duplication can provide a healthy cross-check against blind spots and biases.

INTELLIGENCE FOR THE FUTURE

After the buffetings of the 1970s, the intelligence community entered the decade of the 1980s as a more constrained and carefully supervised entity. Although still lacking a legislative charter by the start of the decade, the community recognized that it essentially had two masters—the legislative branch as well as the executive branch. Covert activities were, for all intents and purposes, a thing of the past, except on very limited and carefully delineated bases.*

At the same time, the challenge to intelligence had never been greater than at the decade's turn. The Soviet's continued surge in military capability and its efforts to convert military strength into political gains in Africa and Asia greatly intensified the need for enhanced U.S. intelligence capability. The growing technical sophistication of the U.S.S.R. military arsenal, including its conventional forces as well as its strategic and tactical nuclear ones, increased the difficulty both of collecting and analyzing data. With regard to the strategic force balance, these technological difficulties were compounded by the loss of U.S. use of critical SIGINT facilities in Iran and Turkey during the late 1970s.

At the same time that the tasks of providing intelligence analyses of traditional subjects were becoming more difficult, new needs were arising. These requirements, many of which surfaced during the 1970s, focused largely on problems arising out of increasing economic interdependence. They included such topics as energy, food, maritime resources, and deep-seabed minerals. Although most of the data concerning such subjects are generally available from open sources and are, in many cases, already collected and analyzed by such agencies as the Departments of Commerce and Agriculture (as well as by private organizations), national security and foreign policy-makers increasingly felt the need to have focused analyses of certain subjects which were pertinent and timely to their needs.

In the face of all these challenges, there was widespread hope both within the intelligence community and among experienced participants and observers of the national security policy-making process that the upheavals of the 1970s in the conduct and control of intelligence would not be repeated in the 1980s.

DISCUSSION QUESTIONS

1. What is "intelligence," and what contributions does the "intelligence community" make to the national security decision-making process?

2. What agencies/organizations compose the American "intelligence community," and what are their roles/missions?

---

*Due primarily to events in Iran and Afghanistan in 1979, both the Congress and the public indicated in 1980 that their sentiment might be shifting toward greater tolerance of covert intelligence activities. The outcry in 1983 against CIA activity in Central America cast some doubt on this trend, however.

3. What information-gathering techniques are used by the intelligence community? What are their respective capabilities and limitations?

4. How is collected information turned into intelligence responsive to the information needs of policy-makers?

5. What issues are raised in America by the intelligence community's information-gathering function and by its "covert action" function?

6. What is your own position on the intelligence community's covert action operations, and should we engage in them? Why or why not? If we should, what constraints should apply to them? What are permissible targets of such operations (e.g., terrorists)?

7. What has been the role of the federal judiciary with respect to intelligence community operations and capabilities?

8. What has been the role of Congress in control or oversight of the intelligence community?

9. How has the executive branch responded to issues raised concerning intelligence operations at home and abroad?

10. What additional or different measure would you recommend for control of intelligence operations or products, or for governmental interaction regarding the intelligence community?

11. Over the years, the news media have provided great amounts of public information concerning intelligence failures. Why is there so little information available on successful intelligence operations?

RECOMMENDED READING

Agee, Philip. *Inside the Company: CIA Diary.* New York: Stonehill, 1975.

Barnds, William J. "Intelligence and Foreign Policy: Dilemmas of Democracy." *Foreign Affairs* 47, no. 2 (January 1969).

Cline, Ray S. "The Future of U.S. Foreign Intelligence Operations." In *The United States in the 1980s*, ed. Peter Duignan and Alvin Rabushka. Stanford: Hoover Institution Press, 1980.

Ellsworth, Robert F. and Adelman, Kenneth L. "Foolish Intelligence." *Foreign Policy*, no. 36 (fall 1979).

Emerson, Thomas. "Control of Government Intelligence Agencies: The American Experience." *Political Science Quarterly* 53 (July-September 1982).

Fain, Tyrus G., ed. *The Intelligence Community.* Public Document Series. New York: R. R. Bowker, 1977.

Oseth, John M. "Regulating U.S. Intelligence Operations, 1974–1982: A Study in Politics of the National Interest." Ph.D. diss., Columbia University, 1983.

Turner, Stansfield, and Thibault, George. "Intelligence: The Right Rules." *Foreign Policy*, no. 48 (fall 1982).

U.S., Congress, Senate, Select Committee to Study Governmental Operations with Respect to Intelligence Activities. *Final Report.* 94th Cong., 2d sess., 1976.

8

THE ROLE OF THE MILITARY IN THE NATIONAL SECURITY POLICY PROCESS

Historic Noninfluence. In only exceptional cases—those directly linked to wartime circumstances—did the military significantly influence the formulation of national policy prior to World War II. General Winfield Scott, commander in Mexico in 1846, established occupation policies as he conquered. Again, during the Civil War, the influence of the commanding general of the army upon the secretary of war, the president, and the Congress was great, especially in the latter years of Grant's ascendancy. Perhaps the most direct instance of military policy-making in that conflict occurred with the reestablishment of state and local governments in the South; the programs instituted by military commanders for such governance were underwritten as national policy by President Lincoln in 1863.

Military influence in policy formulation also was evident during the occupation of the Philippines immediately after the Spanish-American War. During World War I, General Pershing was given wide discretion in dealing directly with Allies and in establishing requirements on the national government at home. Shortly after World War I, both Generals March and Pershing proposed plans to Congress for maintaining an army substantially stronger than the pre–World War I establishment. These plans were at least seriously considered—before being rejected.[1]

The scattered examples above typify the generally accepted rule, prior to World War II, that the military should play a role in the formulation of national security policy only when the duress of war made the armed forces responsible for executing such policy. The general absence of any major threats to the nation's existence, apart from the Civil War, left the military services with only the routine problems of continental defense, internal development (especially of rivers and railroads), protection of trade, contingency

152

planning, and passive support of a largely isolationist foreign policy. Neither the structure of government nor the essentiality of military missions compelled sustained involvement of the military in national policy.

World War II and Its Immediate Aftermath. World War II and the immediate postwar years marked a total break with the past. The imminence of war in the late 1930s had generated new structural arrangements designed to bring military advice into the process of policy formulation. In April 1938 on the suggestion of Secretary of State Cordell Hull and with President Franklin Roosevelt's approval, a Standing Liaison Committee had been established by the State, War, and Navy departments to deal with military and political planning for the Western Hemisphere. The Standing Liaison Committee was discontinued in 1943, having fallen into disuse during the great military operations of World War II. However, the need for interdepartmental coordination of political-military affairs led to the establishment of the State-War-Navy-Coordinating Committee (SWNCC) in late 1944. Consisting of ranking civilian officials from each department and supported by a system of interdepartmental subcommittees, including senior military participants, the SWNCC marked the beginning of institutionalized military influence at the highest levels of national security policy formulation.

In a parallel development—largely to present a more unified American position to the Allies during the war—the uniformed chiefs of the army, navy, and army air forces began to meet with increasing frequency after Pearl Harbor as the Joint Chiefs of Staff (JCS). Although the JCS's authority and responsibilities were never legislatively approved during the war, its position was recognized and, through Admiral Leahy, chief of staff to the president, it maintained direct liaison with President Roosevelt.[2] Admiral King and General Marshall's influence was particularly important concerning strategic operations.

Military influence during the war extended beyond political-military planning for victory over the Axis powers. Give the weakness of the Department of State and its divorcement from day-to-day operations (and the doctrine of "total victory"), the military played the leading role in developing war termination and postwar occupation policies. On a host of issues ranging from zonal boundaries in occupied Germany to postwar policies in the Far East, the military requirements for war termination and logistic support in occupied areas determined broader postwar policies. Indeed, the key political question of whether Berlin was to be taken by the U.S. Army was not decided in Washington but left to the discretion of the military commander in the field.[3] In occupied areas, including Berlin, military government officials made the crucial decisions. The question of the number and ideological composition of the political parties permitted to develop in postwar, Allied-occupied Germany was, for instance, determined by senior War Department officials.[4]*

*The long range strategic planning for the period when normalcy was expected to return (three years) was developed and coordinated by the War Department Special Planning Division.

In part, this imbalance of influence was inevitable, deriving from the necessities of war and the importance of logistic support and security in areas behind the combat line.

Military influence in all areas of national security policy also, however, derived in part from superior organization and resources. Especially effective was the Operations Division (OPD) of the War Department general staff, which formed the core of wartime and immediate postwar political-military planning for the U.S. effort.[5] Also noteworthy was the Civil Affairs Division of the general staff which, by its direct access to theater commanders, insulated many of the policies of military government from State Department influence.[6] Finally, the War Department senior civilians and military leadership played a major role, in large part by default. Secretary of State Hull opted out of political-military planning even before American direct involvement in World War II and during the war devoted a large part of his own and his department's energy and talents to planning the fledgling United Nations Organization.*

When America demobilized after the war, the lessons of political-military coordination were retained. The many joint and interdepartmental committees and advisory groups were first brought into a formalized plan for civil-military coordination in the National Security Act of 1947.[7] In addition to establishing the National Security Council, as discussed briefly in Chapter 6, the act created a "national security establishment," consisting of the three service Departments (army, navy and air force) linked together by a series of joint committees and coordinated by the three services' chiefs, sitting as the JCS. The chiefs were formally recognized and provided with a secretariat and a joint staff. The position of chairman was added to the JCS in 1949. Though given the power to preside and coordinate, he was restricted to only three assistants and was forbidden to appoint a military staff separate from the joint staff, which serves the chiefs as a whole.[8]

The National Security Act was explicitly designed to insure military-civil coordination and balance. In the immediate postwar years, the civilian elements had already begun to reassert their traditional roles in foreign policy. State Department leadership in postwar European recovery, symbolized by the Marshall Plan, and the central role of that department in the overall postwar political and economic structure of planning shifted the initiative in policy-making away from the military establishment. Not only did the military's advantage in organizational terms shrink sharply, but so did its vast resources. Military appropriations dropped sharply and army strength contracted from over eight million personnel on V-J Day to less than two million a year later.[9] At the same time, rapid changes in military technology meant that the vast stores of vehicles and aircraft accumulated during the war already were obsolescent. It remained for events abroad to restore both policy influence and military capabilities to the armed services.

---

*Military officers, however, both active and retired, continued to have a major, if not dominant, influence on the substance of postwar security policy, e.g., Secretary of State George C. Marshall and Gen. Lucius Clay.

The Impact of the Cold War and Korea. By 1949, the Communist victory in China, Soviet initiatives in Greece, the Middle East, Berlin, and Eastern Europe, and the Soviet acquisition of nuclear weapons had prompted a series of Western countermeasures, which together constituted the policy of "containment" discussed in Chapter 4. In turn, recognition of the urgent necessity for allied cooperation led to the provision of large amounts of military assistance by the U.S. to friendly states, a policy confirmed by the Mutual Defense Assistance Act of 1949 spelling out a major, continuing American role in providing materiel and advice to allies.[10] Military influence was also drawn on in constructing the NATO alliance and in securing allied agreement to the rearmament and participation of Germany in the build-up of NATO.[11] Military proconsuls such as Douglas MacArthur in Japan and Lucius Clay in Germany, as well as distinguished World War II leaders such as Marshall, Eisenhower, and Bradley, continued to serve in positions of high responsibility and great influence.

With conversion of mounting cold war into the Korean War in the summer of 1950, a major shift in resources again took place. In a period of four years (1950–54), the national defense share of the Gross National Product rose from 5.2 percent to 13.5 percent expenditures from $13.0 billion in FY 1950 to $50.4 billion in FY 1953.[12] If the hostilities in Korea again expanded the military's role in the formulation and execution of policy, however, they also complicated it. One of the first messages of the Korean War was that the World War II concept of autonomy for the theater commander in the prosecution of war was to be curtailed significantly. General MacArthur's relief for command in the Far East by President Truman was the result of a long series of attempts by MacArthur to shape U.S. policy in his theater independent of events in Europe or of national policy.[13]* In a time of global nuclear superpowers, when expectation of war in Europe was high, the restricted view of a local commander could no longer be followed without regard for worldwide ramifications of local actions. It was a lesson repeated in future deployments of American power.

Restraint on the theater commander did not signal his return to solely military concerns, however. After the accordian-like battles of the first phase of the Korean War gave way to a static war of attrition, the military was given the mission—with appropriate guidance—to conduct diplomatic negotiations for ending the war and to conduct combat operations so as to create conditions favorable for a settlement.[14] Although military planners were accustomed to dealing with broad questions of strategy involving political and military considerations, the new responsibilities for political negotiations, coupled with the limited nature of combat operations in Korea, further deepened military involvement in national policy-making.

---

*Early in the conflict the JCS had been restrained from excessive interference with MacArthur by his great personal prestige and by the tradition of a theater commander's autonomy. By early 1951, however, the JCS had begun to question sharply MacArthur's estimates and objectives. There seems little doubt that the JCS, in fact, was completely supportive of the president's decision.

As the nation moved through the uncharted waters of limited war, military leaders were forced to examine political and military objectives strikingly different from the "unconditional surrender" and "total victory" formulations of World War II. They also had to adjust to fighting a war without total national mobilization. While the doctrines of limited war had to be developed at the cost of considerable casualties and frustration, one result of the learning process was a new pattern of cooperation between the Departments of State and Defense.

During the time that the Korean War focused attention on northeast Asia, events elsewhere were also shaping the military's role in the policy process, both domestic and foreign. Rearmament during the Korean War affected our defense posture worldwide—in Germany as well as Korea. The message conveyed by the initial defeats of the small U.S. units in Korea was that forces that could be mobilized were no substitute for forces-in-being. Reserve forces, even if well trained and equipped, could not be activated and deployed rapidly enough to serve as a deterrent or to provide effective protection should deterrence fail. As detailed in Chapter 4, the "mobilization" approach to defense strategy was replaced after the Korean conflict by the more expensive but less risky concept of deterrence through forces-in-being. Although defense spending declined somewhat under Eisenhower from its Korean War levels, it never again subsided to its "mobilization" nadir of the late 1940s.[15]

Interservice Rivalry and the Continuing Evolution of Military Influence. The enlarged military establishment after Korea and the increased projection of military influence abroad did not reflect a monolithic front of military influence at home. Strong interservice rivalries tended to weaken the military's voice within the national security machine. Paradoxically, these rivalries were generated by attempts to achieve better interservice coordination as well as to reduce defense spending.

Post World War II recognition of the need for better coordination of the services was first manifested in the Legislative Reorganization Act of 1946, which consolidated the old Military Affairs and Naval committees in Congress into the Armed Services Committee. No longer would the services submit separate budgets to Congress. The unified approach to defense budgeting was furthered by the National Security Act of 1947, which gave the newly designated secretary of defense responsibility for supervising the budgeting process. Both actions ensured that the services would compete for slices of the same budgetary pie—a gain for one service would be a loss for another. The results were intense rivalries, command shake-ups, resignations, and a host of strategic disagreements evolving from the fundamental competition for resources—all amplified by the media.

Such rivalry had certain advantages, of course. The conflict of ideas and doctrines provided a form of security from unanimous error in the postwar era. Moreover, potential conflict between civil and military institutions was deflected into competition among military groups. Since the resolution of these basic conflicts required civilian judgment, civil control was enhanced.

Not only were civilian political leaders able to find military support for almost any plausible strategy they might propose, but also they were given a convenient political dodge: interservice rivalry provided "a whipping boy upon whom to blame deficiencies in the military establishment for which (just possibly) they, political leaders, conceivably might be held responsible."[16]

Yet the deficiencies of these rivalries were just as obvious. Cost-effective management of the Department of Defense proved inordinately difficult, with the uniformed services sometimes appealing departmental—or even presidential—decisions to Congressional allies and winning support. The JCS was seldom able to agree upon an overall defense program within budgetary ceilings. Confidence in the efficacy of military judgment, so high in the early years after World War II, tended to be eroded by the spectacle of public disagreement and dissension.* More serious were fears that the defense organization was simply ineffective, relying on logrolling and compromise, with neither effective planning nor real control by anyone.[17]

Continual Defense Department reorganization after 1947 aimed at increasing civilian control over the military while reducing the harmful tendencies to allocate resources and to develop policies on a bargaining for shares-of-the-pie basis. In the 1949 reorganization, the service secretaries were removed from the cabinet, the size of the joint staff was increased, and a chairman was added to the JCS. In 1953, service autonomy was reduced still further by giving the chairman of the JCS responsibility for the joint staff and by increasing the number of assistant secretaries of defense.

Controversy over weapons systems procurement and service mission prompted still further efforts toward centralization of control. In 1958, the National Security Act was again amended to give the secretary of defense greater authority, more influence in strategic planning, and greater control over the JCS. The military departments were further downgraded administratively, and the functions of the services were revised to exclude control over major operational commands such as the Strategic Air Command, the Alaskan Command and the European Command. Under the new provisions, these commands were to be controlled directly by the secretary of defense.

The reforms of the 1950s gave the secretary of defense the legal power to expand greatly his control of the department and the services. The tools of cost-effectiveness accounting and systems analysis developed under Secretary of Defense McNamara in the 1960s made this control a reality. Supported by a host of young, talented, civilian "whiz kids," McNamara used the new techniques to preempt military influence in both procurement and strategy (see Chapter 9). In part, this greater centralization was a logical outcome of

---

*Among the more inflammatory comments noted by one analyst were the following: an army air force general asked, "Why should we have a Navy at all? There are no enemies for it to fight except apparently the Army Air Force"; an air force general called the marines "a small, bitched-up Army talking Navy Lingo," quoted in Huntington, *The Common Defense*, p. 369. Also see Lawrence J. Korb, *The Joint Chiefs of Staff: The First Twenty-five Years* (Bloomington: Indiana University Press, 1976), p. 11.

the development of new budgetary techniques; but more fundamentally, it grew out of the persistent service disagreements, extension of civilian staff, and increased demand for civilian control over the military.

However necessary for both strategic and economic reasons, centralization posed a severe dilemma for the military, and especially for the JCS. Unanimous agreements among the chiefs could usually be obtained only by compromises, which were often unsupportable by systems analysis. Split decisions, however, were even worse—they placed the locus of final decisions on military matters squarely in civilian hands. A fundamental dilemma, it rose from the dual responsibilities of the chiefs described earlier—corporately for defense as a whole and individually for the roles and missions and capabilities of their respective services.

The service loyalties of the individual chiefs as normal human beings were, of course, sometimes a factor in disagreements, but the continued rivalry reflected more fundamental imperatives of the military bureaucracies. Each service chief had a service staff to assist him in running his particular service. As noted earlier, the JCS as a whole was provided with a small joint staff to give assistance in the joint area. Not surprisingly, the advice of the service staffs was heavily colored by their respective service perspectives. In order to overcome service parochialism and provide unified staff work, the 1958 DOD reorganization directed the joint chiefs to concentrate on their joint responsibilities and to delegate running the services to their vice-chiefs. Furthermore, control of the joint staff was transferred from the JCS as a whole to the chairman, and it was increased in size to 400 positions, split evenly among the army, the air force, and the navy and Marines.

In practice, these reforms did not solve the problem. Service members who rotated through the joint staff retained their service orientations. Additionally, every paper prepared by the joint staff had to be cleared by affected service staffs. In fact, each service chief was briefed for his JCS meetings not by the joint staff but by his service staff. Since the issues were often of critical importance to the competing interests of the services, compromise was frequently impossible at the lower working level. Nor could the more senior officers disregard this staffing process without seriously undercutting the authority and trust of their staffs. Not surprisingly, interservice rivalries continued—and still continue—despite logical reasons for ending, or at least attenuating, them.[18]

Military Influence in the Broader Policy-making Arena. Persistent interservice rivalry during the 1950s and 1960s did not prevent significant military roles in the wider policy arena. The increased size of the military after the Korean War left its imprint on the formulation and execution of foreign policy. In the first place, the commitment to relatively larger ready military forces and, after 1961, to forward defense and some form of the strategic doctrine of "flexible response" inevitably gave rise to an important role for military advice. Presidents in crises considered those choices that were available; past budgetary support for military commanders were ready to advise on the execution of those options.

Continuing overseas defense commitments, such as NATO, also greatly furthered military involvement in policy-making. When General Eisenhower, first supreme commander of NATO, reported to Congress on his mission to Europe in 1951, he stated clearly the nature of civil-military relations with regard to NATO.

I spoke in every country to the Prime Minister and foreign minister at their request, and then I talked to the defense ministers and their chiefs of staff. There is no escaping the fact that when you take an area such as is involved in all Western Europe and talk about its defense, you are right in the midst of political questions, economic, industrial, as well as strictly military, and you couldn't possibly divorce your commander from contact with them.[19]

The worldwide alliances developed by Secretary of State John F. Dulles in the 1950s and the extensive military supply and training missions that they generated projected U.S. military presence and influence beyond Western Europe. Associated with this network of bilateral and multilateral alliances were aid funds for "mutual security," to be administered by U.S. military advisory groups. Such military assistance made up more than half of all U.S. foreign aid between 1950 and 1968, with much of the economic aid also justified in terms of "national" security.[20]

Within the country team, as discussed briefly in Chapter 5, the head of the U.S. Military Assistance Advisory Group (MAAG) served as the chief adviser on military affairs for the U.S. ambassador to the particular foreign nation. As such, he was a leading figure in the small group, including the local heads of the Agency for International Development (AID) and the U.S. Information Agency (USIA), who helped formulate and execute U.S. policy abroad. Indeed, the local MAAG chief was often the strongest official in the ambassador's team according to respective local situations and the comparatively large resources that the Defense Department wielded. Not only did military personnel frequently outnumber State Department personnel assigned to a given overseas mission, but many of the competing bureaucracies, such as those of AID and USIA, were weak in the field and in the Washington staffing necessary to support field operations.[21] Too, the extensive field operations of the MAAGs provided timely information and access to important decision-makers—further reasons for deference to military advice and policy influence.

By 1960, a little more than a decade after their inception, there were 61 U.S. MAAGs or comparable advisory missions deployed abroad, comprising 15,000 U.S. and local nationals, with additional thousands of U.S. military and civilian personnel in supporting positions.[22] As discussed in Chapter 2, military forces have often played an important role as instruments of diplomacy. Fleet movements, alerts, and troop dispositions express national concern in conjunction with diplomatic notes, UN statements, and presidential messages. In the 1950s and 1960s, the MAAGs, too, became such instruments—expressions of partial U.S. commitments and possible further U.S. involvement—giving them diplomatic as well as practical military utility.

During the 1960s, military influence on national policy also expanded within the structures that grew up around the National Security Council (NSC). As noted in Chapter 5, a number of new interagency advisory and decision-making committees were created in 1966 to deal with national security. Interdepartmental Regional Groups (IRGs) and the Senior Interdepartmental Group (SIG) included military representatives from the JCS organization on an equal basis with those from the office of the secretary of defense, the Department of State, the CIA, the NSC staff, and other agencies.[23]* As a result of their IRG/SIG participation and vigorous support from above, military officers were often influential in shaping policy in Washington as well as in the field.

The 1960s also saw a limited reemergence of the military elite in personal advisory roles. Given his military experience and prestige, President Eisenhower accepted little military advice. However, during the Kennedy years, retired officers, especially General Maxwell Taylor, who served as the military representative to the president, gained influence. After 1962, when Taylor became chairman of the JCS, he maintained a JCS liaison office in the White House. President Lyndon Johnson also relied on General Taylor, especially with regard to the Vietnam issue. Taylor's successor as chairman, General Earle Wheeler, often met informally with Presidents Johnson and Nixon and reported JCS views to the president independently of Department of Defense views.

During the 1960s, there was concern in many quarters about the extent of military influence on U.S. policies toward Southeast Asia. It is true that, although dreading a land war in Asia, once the military established itself in substantial numbers in Vietnam in the early 1960s it acquired the most extensive information, developed the most comprehensive staffing system, carried most of the burdens of counterinsurgency, and gained a more influential position in policy formulation than competing agencies such as AID or the State Department. Secretary McNamara, so effective in curtailing military influence within DOD, became an early spokesman for military escalation in Vietnam. Secretary of State Dean Rusk let the initiative rest with the Defense Department; he became its quiet supporter.

The final decisions on Vietnam, however, rested with the president. While military information, General Westmoreland's views, and JCS recommendations set the background for these decisions, Lyndon Johnson often overruled his generals, particularly with respect to the heightened intensity and scope of operations that the armed forces felt were needed to terminate hostilities quickly and successfully. That the military significantly influenced

---

*It was during the late 1960s that the Office of the Assistant Secretary of Defense/International Securities Affairs was to reach its zenith of influence.

national policy toward Vietnam throughout the period is incontrovertible; but that military influence was subordinated to civilian views is equally clear.[24]

The Military and Domestic Security. National concern for civil rights, emerging strongly during the latter 1950s, provided yet another political-military role for the services, namely in domestic security. At Little Rock in 1957, the governor of Arkansas mobilized the National Guard to block the desegregation of Central High School. President Eisenhower promptly federalized the guard, using it and regular army units to enforce court-ordered desegregation in the first use of troops for domestic purposes in the South since Reconstruction. Their success established a new pattern of army involvement in law enforcement: the final decision to involve the army would be made at the highest levels of government; commitment of troops would be delayed until all local means of dealing with the problem proved inadequate; local National Guard forces would be federalized and used to assist as soon as practicable; and the channel of authority would extend from the president and attorney general to the executive agent, the secretary of the army, and then to the commander directly involved. In all of this, a request for troops from the governor of the state, as had been customary earlier, was not needed. During the early 1960s, this general pattern of crisis response was repeated in Mississippi (1962) and in Alabama (1965) when local officials defied federal law.

By the mid-1960s, rising frustration in the ghettos of large cities precipitated other kinds of law and order problems. Riots in Watts (1965), Newark, Detroit, and Milwaukee (1967), and Rochester, Baltimore, and Washington (1968) required the National Guard and, in some cases, federal troops to preserve order; numerous lesser disorders also contributed to a rising public outcry against lawlessness. Governmental response to civil disorder was generally predictable; a slow and usually reluctant escalation of forces until order was established. No one professed to want federal troops commited except as the last resort. For mayors and governors, an appeal for federal help was an admission of their inability to govern. Federal officials recognized that to commit army troops would be to assume responsibility for a situation already out of control, fraught with great risks to property, lives, and, some suggested, political reputations.[25*]

Military leaders, though loyal in executing orders, saw these domestic security missions as detracting from their requirement to be ready for possible commitment overseas. Moreover, civil disturbance control required a high state of training of a different variety than normal military missions. Too,

---

*For example, the decision to commit troops in Detroit was delayed over a period of two days while the Republican governor, a potential presidential candidate, negotiated with the Democratic president over the wording of the request for federal troops. For a detailed chronological account of the maneuverings, see Charles P. Stone, "The Lessons of Detroit, Summer 1967," in *Bayonets in the Street*, ed. Robert Higham (Lawrence: University of Kansas Press, 1969), pp. 185–89.

troop commitment to domestic order carried the risk of considerable harm to life and property and associated risks of failure with possible public opposition. Nevertheless, the effectiveness of disciplined, properly trained army units in quelling civil disorders and the inadequacies of local law enforcement made the use of federal troops a feature of the era.

With increased U.S. involvement in Vietnam in the sixties came disturbances of a more focused political nature. The 1967 march on the Pentagon, the attempt to disrupt the Democratic National Convention of 1968 in Chicago, numerous marches on military bases and posts, and finally the dissidents' attempts to close off Washington, D.C., in 1971, left the army with an increasing role in civil disturbance control against an ill-defined but apparently identifiable sector of American youth. Concerned to be prepared to execute this mission, and, by the late 1960s, aware of the lack of coordinated advance information on leaders, issues, and locales of disturbances, the army began to focus part of its intelligence assets on the tasks of identifying ringleaders and plans. Young soldiers were assigned to monitor and infiltrate radical political groups, and many posts developed a network of "coffeehouse informers." An effort was made to coordinate information thus acquired within the army and with other federal agencies. A central data bank started at the U.S. Army Intelligence Center at Fort Holabird, though most of the information for the data bank was gathered from the press and published materials rather than by informers and undercover agents.

As public awareness of these army intelligence activities developed in 1970, there was an outcry against invasion of privacy and free speech. Congressional investigations probed the extent of army involvement in domestic intelligence gathering:[26] Faced with mounting public and media concern, Secretary of Defense Melvin Laird ordered the army to discontinue its collection and dissemination of domestic intelligence. Although the army still retained responsibility for supporting civil disturbance control measures, the restrictions on data collection seemed to indicate that it would remain only in an executory, and not a policy advisory, role. In truth, the army had been pressured to expand its activity into an area peripheral to its main mission of national defense and inimical to its broad tradition of noninvolvement in politics. As the cessation of hostilities in Vietnam reduced domestic disorders in the U.S., the army appeared relieved to settle back into its traditional preparedness concerns, by then in the new environment of the all-volunteer force.

The Military and Congress. Having emerged from the Second World War with high prestige and faced by the developing cold war, the military found Congress generally responsive to its requests. Indeed, Congress was frequently more supportive of the budgetary and weapons procurement views of the military than were secretaries of defense and presidents. Only with the widespread public dissatisfaction during the Vietnam War did the Congress shift from two decades of relatively strong support for the military establishment.

In certain areas of military policy, Congress had remained active and knowledgeable throughout the period of the cold war. Concerned with overall budgets, personnel, and procurement policies, Congress continually exercised its decision-making power in the field of military "structure," exercising considerable influence in questions of the organization of the military establishment, pay scales, conscription, training service discipline, housing, and procurement. Congressional subcommittees developed considerable expertise in many of these issues, and policy initiatives from the executive often were altered substantially.

On strategic matters, however, such as defense policy, weapons system priorities, armed forces deployments, and national strategy, Congress remained generally on the sidelines in the first two decades after the Second World War. In most cases, military programs and policies dealing with these matters were developed largely through the executive's decision-making apparatus. (The rare cases in which executive policy was overruled by the Congress was usually done on the basis of advice from the military!) After Korea, individual service strength ceilings were kept so high, for example, that they tended to provide little restraint on the executive's plans. Reductions of military appropriations were never so great as to jeopardize a strategic program, and in many instances the Congress tried to prevent the administration from curtailing service sizes or activities.*

Congressional hearings and investigations were often forums for the presentation of the viewpoint of the military, as opposed to that of the administration. On at least two occasions—the 1966 move toward the manned bomber and the 1968 decision to end the FB-111 fighter bomber program—Congress sided with the military against Secretary of Defense McNamara. It is important to realize in this context that a military officer has an obligation to present his own professional views to the Congress when asked, not merely to repeat the president or the secretary of defense's view.

Military influence within Congress is often explained in terms of constituency politics—pork barreling—and there is evidence of a strong correlation between the defense-related payroll in a state and congressional voting practices.[27] U.S. Army Corps of Engineers civil works projects are viewed by some observers as critically important tools in maintaining military influence in Congress.[28] Other commonly cited bases for this influence include the significant military resources devoted to lobbying Congress† and the military backgrounds of many Congressional members.‡

---

*For example, between 1950 and 1958, Congress reduced military appropriations requests by about 3 percent, Huntington, *The Common Defense*, p. 134. Examples include the Marine Corps Act of 1952 and persistent congressional efforts in the late 1950s to prevent a reduction in the size of the army.

†Adam Yarmolinsky suggests that visible Pentagon lobbying, budgeted at $3,810,458 in 1967, was ten times more expensive than the largest private lobbying efforts; *The Military Establishment* (New York: Perennial Library, 1973), p. 51.

‡In the 88th Congress, for example, two-thirds of the legislators in both houses were veterans. While military experience does not seem to produce markedly different political attitudes among

In fact, however, other more basic reasons have existed for military influence on Congress. For much of the postwar period, the American people and Congress felt genuinely threatened by hostile forces abroad. The resulting public consensus limited disputes over foreign and strategic policy. The lessons of 1939–41, when Congress approved the draft by only one vote, were not forgotten. Not only was military expertise recognized and respected, but the Congress was loath to assume the burdens of developing military strategy. As suggested in Chapter 6, developing strategy was simply an inappropriate task for Congress in view of its own nature and interests and in light of the assets with which it could work.

As the national consensus on foreign policy broke down during the Vietnam War, however, disenchantment with the military arose in some congressional quarters. Although military spending increased slowly during the Vietnam War, it never reached the 13 percent of GNP achieved during the Korean War. (By 1969, in fact, it was only 8 percent, in contrast to the much higher shares in earlier conflicts.) Yet a majority of the public felt that military spending was too high.[29] Reflecting this shift in public opinion, Congress began to unearth cost overruns and performance shortfalls in military procurement. Elements in Congress fought with the military and the administration over a number of programs, such as the Army's antiballistic missile (ABM) system and the air force's multiple, independently targetable reentry vehicle (MIRV).

Isolated incidents such as the My Lai massacre were painted as typical and magnified by some critics in the Congress in order to cast aspersions on military integrity, while the seemingly interminable war and the unanticipated ferocity of the Tet offensive of 1968 struck at the military's technical competence. Drugs and indiscipline within the forces, subjects that were easily exploited by unfriendly media, added to the tarnish. Although the military retained many of its friends in Congress, lack of public support and occasional but conspicuous lapses in military competence stimulated broadening congressional criticism.

Despite the accusations and the real shortcomings, Congress did not, however, cripple the military by budgetary or force-level restraints. Nor did it mandate the withdrawal of American forces from Europe, despite strong efforts by Senate Majority Leader Mike Mansfield and like-minded colleagues. By 1974, the military as an institution appeared to have weathered the worst criticisms of the Vietnam and early post-Vietnam periods. While some members of Congress continued to attack the military as wasteful and bloated, the grounds for most congressional criticism shifted in the mid seventies from the "failings" of the institution to the nation's security needs, as proposed by military leaders. In this arena—strategy and overall defense

---

national legislators in matters of national policy, Yarmolinsky suggests that it may at least affect their approachability by the military; Ibid, p. 54.

policy as well as weapons selection and procurement and the size and disposition of reserve forces—Congress seems likely to play in the future an even more important role. As the 1980s began, there was clearly a shift toward greater conservatism in public attitudes *and hence in the Congress*, greater public perception of foreign threats to security interests, and increased confidence in the leaders of the military institution relative to the leaders of other American institutions.[30]

The Changing Role of the Joint Chiefs. As suggested in Chapter 5, the JCS plays a crucial role in the national security policy process, for it is the hinge between the most senior civilian leadership and the professional military. As noted, it is charged with providing military advice to the secretary of defense, Congress (as requested), the NSC, and the president. Consequently, the role they play in the policy process can change as the relations among these other actors fluctuate.

During the Eisenhower administration, the JCS was faced with a president determined to balance the budget and restrict military spending. The inability of the chiefs to agree on forces within prescribed budget limits meant that important decisions on the size and organization of forces were left entirely to the president and the secretary of defense. On occasion the chiefs responded to these decisions by criticizing administration policies in front of Congress. While these criticisms greatly irritated President Eisenhower, they had little effect on his policies.[31]

The Kennedy and Johnson administrations were marked by a certain amount of tension between the military and Secretary of Defense McNamara, in large part because of the secretary's management style and his introduction of systems analysis into the decision-making process. His management approach depreciated military advice and favored new quantitative methods rather than traditional threat analysis. Some of the military perceived McNamara's approach as a threat to their very professionalism as well as to their role in the policy process. The result of the secretary's new methods and of the continuing inability of the JCS to overcome service rivalries was that military influence was partially overshadowed by the work of the civilian-dominated Office of Systems Analysis in the Office of the Secretary of Defense.

President Kennedy's view of the JCS was soured at the outset of his administration by the Bay of Pigs fiasco; although the operation was under the aegis of the CIA, not the military, the new president believed the JCS and the other experts had provided him bad advice. He tended to turn henceforth to his brilliant secretary of defense, who was prepared to cudgel the senior military leaders into new modes of analysis and new processes and organizational structures. Initially, President Johnson also relied heavily on the advice of Secretary of Defense McNamara. However, as time passed the military staffs became fully conversant with systems analysis, and McNamara's relationship with the president began to erode as a result of the secretary's increasing disenchantment with the Vietnam War. In effect, the chiefs' influence grew as the president increasingly turned to them for advice.[32]

The chiefs' improved influence within the executive branch continued in the succeeding Nixon and Ford administrations. In particular, Secretary of Defense Laird signaled the reduced role of systems analysis and civilian analysts by leaving the post of assistant secretary for systems analysis vacant for a year.[33] Furthermore, he introduced "participatory management" as his method of dealing with the JCS. Meetings between the JCS and the Secretary of Defense became explicit negotiating sessions in which bargaining and compromise took place. While the chiefs' views often failed to prevail, the JCS at least felt that it had had significant input into the decisions of the executive branch. As noted previously, the 1960s breakdown in the foreign policy consensus resulted in a Congress that, by late in the decade, was often hostile to the military. In that period, the chiefs supported the administration's policy before Congress, not only because they had helped formulate it but because of the low probability of success in making a case before a deeply skeptical Congress in view of their failure with the executive branch.[34]

The relationship between the JCS and the other principal actors in the national security policy process appears to have changed again during the Carter administration. In particular, the chiefs' relative influence in the executive branch and with Congress reversed. In the executive branch, changes in the formal procedures of the defense budget process decreased the impact of the JCS: lack of policy guidance and tight time constraints on the chiefs' review of budget planning documents restricted their role in shaping the budget. Furthermore, the president made key policy decisions, such as the withdrawal of troops from Korea, (since suspended), without real JCS input.[35] By early 1980, the chiefs' concerns about budget adequacy and the diminished impact of their advice thereon resulted in their open and united opposition to the president on military spending levels.[36]

Contrastingly, by the end of the 1970s an increasing awareness of Soviet military potential among influential congressional elements had made Congress more receptive to military advice. The president's decision to cancel the B-1 bomber was sustained by only three votes in Congress; it took a presidential veto to delete a nuclear aircraft carrier from the 1979 budget; and the president's decision not to produce the neutron bomb came under strong congressional fire. Furthermore, prominent members of Congress, such as Senators Sam Nunn and Henry Jackson, made persistent and intensifying demands for increases in defense spending.[37] In sum, when they disagreed with the president and chose to make this known to Congress, the Chiefs got a more receptive hearing of their case than they had during the previous three administrations.

Whatever one's tentative judgment of how the JCS will develop, the Chiefs' future roles will certainly not be static. As long as the JCS remains the primary contact between the military and civilian leadership in national security policy process, its role is bound to fluctuate with changes within that civilian leadership and with the evolution of the military instrument and the purposes to which it is directed.

Future Military Roles. As implied in the foregoing pages, the nature and extent of military influence in the formulation and execution of American foreign and defense policy varies with a number of influences. Among these have been—and will continue to be—the size and nature of the defense establishment, the military's own definition of its appropriate role, the extent of alliance ties and other overseas commitments, organizational structures and political forces in Washington, and the extent of public and congressional support for the military.

Since the end of the Korean War, active duty military forces have tended to hover between 2.0 and 2.5 million men (and, increasingly, women), though during the Korean and Vietnam conflicts force levels reached as high as 3.6 million. Organized reserve and National Guard strengths have tended to be somewhat greater, though by the early 1970s actual force levels—as contrasted to authorized strength—had tended to slip somewhat; by the end of the decade, the reserves of all the services totalled .85 million while the National Guard figure was .44 million. Additionally, it should be noted that approximately 1 to 1.5 million civilians were directly employed by the Department of Defense during most of the period, with anywhere from 1.5 to 5 million working for defense contractors as part of the overall civilian labor force. This latter number declined by about .4 million from its peak in the early post-Vietnam period as a result of the decline in overall defense expenditures.

Although somewhat smaller than in the 1960s, the total of all the foregoing categories, that is, 8 to 9 million people (with perhaps another 3 million dependents) still represents a share of the electorate with a large continuing economic stake in national security policy.[38] If the defense build-up implied by the deteriorating security situation at the close of the 1970s occurs, that total may increase still further. If all of those people were of one mind and tightly organized, the "defense establishment" could indeed wield significant polticial power. That they have not been unified, and hence have not represented a major power bloc regarding defense and foreign policy matters, does not alter the fact that their sheer size provides them the potential to influence public policy in the future. When, in his famous valedictory of 1960, President Eisenhower warned the nation against undue influence by the "military-industrial complex," he undoubtedly had in mind this potential.[39]

Eisenhower's warning was probably intended to apply particularly to the business leaders who direct the major firms supplying defense articles and to the most senior ranks of the professional military. But even if one restricts Eisenhower's meaning, there is room for doubt that the idea of a military-industrial complex reflects reality or has the explanatory power often ascribed to it. Certainly, air force generals and senators from states producing certain aircraft generally have a common interest in promoting airpower. But, placed in the context of overall defense policy and limited budgets and faced with competition not only from navy sea power advocates but also from senators from other states also looking after other aircraft manufacturers, the agreed generalities tend to dissolve into the hubbub of pluralistic politics. Although there appeared to be a surge of prodefense opinion in the nation at the beginning of the 1980s, the sources of its strength were not limited to industrial interests but were spread widely across regional, political, and economic strata.

As has often been observed, the American military itself is far from monolithic in character or in outlook. One of the recurring differences within the profession since World War II has been over its appropriate role in the formulation and execution of national security policy. General Douglas MacArthur expressed one side of the argument in a 1962 address to the cadets at West Point as follows: "Your mission remains fixed, determined, inviolable—it is to win our wars. Everything else in your professional career is but corollary to this vital dedication." He went on to observe that the merits or demerits of our processes of government and of such issues as deficit financing, taxes, and personal liberties are "not for your participation or for military solution."[40]

General Matthew Ridgway, army chief of staff in 1955, had earlier expressed essentially the same traditional, "military purist point of view:

The military advisor should give his competent professional advice based on the military aspects of the programs referred to him, based on his fearless, honest, objective estimate of the national interest, and regardless of administration policy at any particular time. He should confine his advice to the essential military aspects.[41]

The purist case does not deny the complexity of national security issues; they are recognized to be a blend of economic, political, and military components but *as determined by civilian policy-makers*. The professional officer is an expert in the military component. Experience and training prepares her or him to make judgments about how force can be utilized most effectively. In providing advice to policy-makers, therefore, the professional officer should confine himself or herself to the military considerations of a proposed policy. The officer is not competent, nor should he be asked, to provide economic or political judgments or assumptions in offering advice. This was the pre–World War II military's dominant view of its input to the policy process.

The alternate view, the *fusionist* approach, maintained that in the changed circumstances of national security policy in the post–World War II environment, there was no such thing as purely military considerations.[42] In a nuclear world in which the military consumes significant economic resources and in which the use of force may have tremendous political implications, both domestic and international, military decisions have economic and political consequences and vice versa. Therefore, in giving their advice, professional officers should incorporate political and economic considerations along with military factors.

By and large civilian leaders have tended to fusionists; they have not wanted purely military advice. President Eisenhower, for instance, reflecting his experiences both in World War II and in NATO, instructed the Joint Chiefs to consider relevant political and economic factors in formulating their military positions. President Kennedy issued similar instructions. In 1962, also to West Point cadets, President Kennedy further expounded the fusionist thesis when, after stressing their future military command responsibilities he added,

The non-military problems which you will face will also be most demanding—diplomatic, political and economic. You will need to know and understand not only the foreign policy of the United States, but the foreign policy of all countries scattered around the world. You will need to understand the importance of military power and also the limits of military power. You will have an obligation to deter war as well as to fight it.[43]

Robert Lovett, former secretary of war and undersecretary of state, pinned JFK's advice with the additional point of credibility.

The ability of the military expert to give wise advice and to get it listened to by policy-making officials depends in great measure on his possessing knowledge in key non-military fields and in seeing issues in broad perspective. A military career officer must be highly skilled in his own profession, but he cannot afford to become trapped in narrow professionalism.[44]

Not all fusionists were civilians. Indeed, by the 1960s that view of military responsibilities had become influential in the profession. General Maxwell Taylor, chairman of the JCS (and an ambassador as well), was an articulate believer that

Nothing is so likely to repel the civilian decision-makers as a military argument which omits obvious considerations which the President cannot omit. If the Chiefs are concerned only about the record, it may be all very well to try to abstract the military elements of a problem and to deal with them alone; but if they want to persuade a President, they had better look at the totality of his problem and try to give maximum help.[45]

Not only did many military leaders increasingly acknowledge the broader dimensions of their profession, but they also moved to incorporate them into military education and training programs. The new air force academy was launched in 1955 with a broader curriculum than its older army and navy counterparts. In turn, both the latter increased the proportion of nontechnical subjects in their curricula. Graduate schooling programs for promising young and midcareer officers at civilian universities began to flourish in the social sciences as well as the physical sciences and engineering. Senior professional schools, such as the war colleges, added study of the nonmilitary aspects of national security to their programs.[46]

The fusionistic interpretation of the military's policy role has been something of a double-edged sword. Those proponents who encourage military officers to incorporate civilian political perspectives into their policy role argue that such a tailoring of military advice will make it more influential, realistic, and relevant to the civilian authorities who set the nation's strategic goals. In this way, the military will gain increased access to the upper levels of the policy process.

For those who believe that the military has had too restricted a role in the national security policy process and that the conceptional gap between military means and strategic ends has resulted in questionable security goals or confused guidance to military leaders, fusionism is seen as a useful remedy.

An early critic of fusionism, Samuel P. Huntington,[47] warned that if the military "broadened" its professional world view in order to incorporate civilian defined "political realities," it might gain access to the supreme levels of the policy process; but it would no longer speak on strategic matters from a military perspective. Fusionism, he argued, makes the military an excessively civilianized institution that is overly responsive to the political interests (particularly those of a domestic character) of the government's civilian leaders. Given a political culture inimical to traditional military values and a constitutional structure that divides civilian control of the military between executive and legislative authorities, Huntington believes it is inevitable that military and political responsibilities will be hopelessly intertwined in a confusing and debilitating manner.[48]

The country and the national security policy process would be better served, he suggests, by a military that cultivates its autonomous organizational values in a politically neutral, professional institution. Such a military profession would be allowed to separate itself from much of the society it serves and would be concerned primarily with developing and fine tuning its functional expertise as a military instrument of war and deterrence. As such Huntington's analysis is a variation of the "purist" view reinforced by a dose of cultural isolation.

Despite the substantial degree to which senior military officers have embraced the concept of fusionism and adapted their "strategic" advice to the "political realities" defined by civilian authorities, there is little evidence to suggest that the military's influence at the initiating level of the policy process has increased.[49]

In recent years, critics of fusionism have raised a new concern. The political and social principles of fusionism have so permeated the professional values and organizational patterns of the military establishment that now the military's instrumental purposes are in danger of being subordinated to its administrative role in the national security policy process.[50]

Historically, the military's operational functions—its efficiency as an instrument of war and deterrence—have determined its organizational priorities. Concern with such traditional matters as weapons development, the integration of tactics and forces, military logistics, unit morale, and the awful, risk-filled world of the battlefield have dominated the military's traditional character and organizational behavior. This focus on institutional requirements, specialized expertise, and functionally derived values has given the military a "professional ethos."[51]

According to contemporary critics of fusionism, this professional ethos and institutional autonomy has made the military an effective instrument of the policy process. As the military becomes increasingly sensitive to "political necessities" at the instrumental as well as the administrative level of the policy process, a new organizational pattern emerges. The bureaucratic character of the military becomes emphasized. Military officers gradually redefine their policy role and come to see themselves as administrators involved in the management of resources. Ultimately the military's instrumental role in the policy process becomes dominated by its administrative priorities. Five-year budgets, program objective memorandums, personnel management systems keyed to the individual's self-interest, "organizational effectiveness" techniques, negotiated decisions by committee, and quantifiable measures of progress become the driving variables.

Further, the critics say, as fusionism accelerates the convergence of military and civilian values throughout all levels of the policy process, the military instrument increasingly takes on the coloring and operational mode of a large-scale governmental bureaucracy: (1) Its organizational patterns focus on non-traditional forms of manipulation, group consensus, and persuasion; (2) Its organizational skill requirements imitate those of a civil bureaucracy—slots for controllers, procurement specialists, personnel managers, and systems analysts develop; (3) Dominant leadership styles change from the traditional "heroic-Warrior" model to the more secular "managerial-technical" model; (4) The impact of domestic social, political, and economic constraints are routinely included in administrative decisions; (5) The military's senior leaders develop a new "political-bureaucratic" ethos that involves them more actively, but less effectively, in the policy process; and (6) A more extensive involvement of civilian authorities in the establishment and evaluation of the military's requirements and standards—at both the instrumental and administrative level—is accepted.

To critics of fusionism, this "convergence" between the military and its civilian masters has seriously impaired both the national security policy process and the military instrument. The post-1960 pattern of civil-military fusionism, characterized in part by the military officer corps' sublimation of its professional role and institutional autonomy has, it is argued, increased the military's administrative responsiveness to civilian priorities, decreased its instrumental effectiveness, and encouraged severe internal stress within the military organization.

As Edward N. Luttwak, an influential civilian strategist, harshly cautions, it is not the military's purpose to be "administratively efficient."

The conflict between civilian efficiency and military effectiveness runs right down the organization. Conflict is different from civilian activity, and leadership in war is totally different from management. Our people are managers in uniform. Actually, the American armed forces are very efficient; they just aren't very effective.

During the entire conflict [the Vietnam War] the efficiency of the American military organizations was constantly manifested. The efficiency of communications, the efficiency with which firepower was administered, the efficiency of transportation and distribution of medical services; but it was just not an effective war machine. The firepower, so efficiently administered, was not effective because the enemy refused to assemble in conveniently targetable massed formations. Less efficient and less managerial officers would have worked to find a method of war capable of dealing with people who refuse to assemble in conveniently targetable massed formations instead of concentrating on improving the efficiency of their firepower.

The armed forces have deviated from the true study, exercise, and tactics of warfare and become managerial institutions, largely concerned with the management of personnel and equipment, contemptuous of the art of war and indifferent to everything that is of war, like tactics and operations.[52]

While the critics of fusionism overstate their case, they have effectively drawn attention to an important dilemma. The military's political responsiveness to civilian authority and its functional expertise as an instrument of policy are complementary values—yet they are always in tension. Some circumscribed sphere of institutional autonomy within which the military may develop its professional ethos and organizational expertise may be necessary to insure the military's functional effectiveness as an instrument of the national security policy process. What civilian authorities want and value is important; what the objective facts allow is also important.

Morris Janowitz, an early advocate of fusionism, has also suggested its limits. Prior to 1960, many military leaders, remembering the bitter frustrations of Korea, were strongly opposed to any deployment of American ground combat units to the Asian mainland. These military officers, members of the "never again club," initially resisted incremental intervention in Southeast Asia. However, they declared, if the government planned to ignore their advice and decided to commit U.S. forces to Indochina, such a military intervention, if it were to have a minimal chance of success, would require a U.S. ground force of 1,000,000 to 1,200,000 troops. From a military perspective, anything less would not be practicable. Yet, in 1965, those military tary leaders whose attitudes toward a military intervention in Indochina had not changed quietly went along with a national security policy they had excellent reason to believe was militarily unsound. In commenting on their role in this policy decision, Janowitz writes,

It remains to be explained why the U.S. military did not follow its own professional judgment. The appropriate form of dissent would have been a token resignation of the Chief of Staff, particularly the Chief of Staff of the ground forces, when he was assigned a task that he believed could obviously not be achieved with the resources placed at his disposal. The publication of the Pentagon Papers has probably postponed an analysis of the central issue since the answer lies not in examination of specific documents, but in the analysis of the workings of a military bureaucracy which in effect has become "overprofessionalized"—more prepared to follow orders than to exercise independent professional skill and judgment.[53]

If the military continues to follow the precepts of fusionism to the extent that the more traditional standards of military professionalism are subordinated to civilian-defined "political necessities" and bureaucratically derived "administrative priorities," there is a real danger that the military will not adequately fulfill its instrumental role in the policy process. The basic responsibility involved in that role is to relate military means to strategic ends and to indicate when the resources allotted are adequate to achieve the goals established.

The foregoing should not be read as a rejection of the purist viewpoint. Rather, after World War II the profession gradually broadened its self-definition, going beyond the narrow track of the purist (which General MacArthur did *not* at all represent in terms of his own career). Even so, the military's definition of itself necessarily continues to focus—and will undoubtedly do so in the decade ahead—on purely military skills. General Taylor's formulation is instructive.

While unduly narrow professionalism may limit the distance to which an officer may advance in the Armed Forces and thus prevent him from reaching the policymaking strata of government, a military man can never reach these higher positions without a long record of solid performance in those things which some may regard as professional "nuts and bolts." If the leaders of the military profession do not obviously know their own business and demonstrate thorough competence therein, they will not be asked to be present when the critical policy decisions are about to be made. One must be a proved soldier first and then a policy counselor later. The Greeks listened to Ulysses because he had been to the wars and knew what they were, not because he had a Ph.D. from the Ivy League. When the military expert is called to positions of higher responsibility, he is not called as an intellectual dilettante—there are plenty of these available elsewhere—but as someone who really knows by having done in the military service. With such solid credentials, he may then speak, and be assured a hearing on a wide range of subjects extending well beyond the basic content of his profession.[54]

Locating the Military's Role in the Policy Process. The American military's involvement in the national security policy process has, with rare exceptions, been restricted to instrumental and administrative roles. By tradition, functional expertise, and professional inclination, the military had defined itself as a subordinate instrument of the policy process. "Grand strategy"—the first level of the policy process in which fundamental political goals are established—has been largely "off limits" to the military officer. Ironically and perhaps fortuitously, it is a restriction the American military has internalized in both its professional values and organizational purposes.

The military's senior officers, particularly the JCS, are trapped into secondary policy roles by their organizational responsibilities. As leaders and products of complex government institutions that increasingly display the appetites and characteristics of bureaucracies, the JCS has little time and perhaps less inclination to attempt a major role in the formulation of strategic goals. One recent observer has noted, "the present JCS system sacrifices the influence of the uniformed military as a whole in order to protect the interests of the separate military services."[55]

A close review of senior officers' schedules quickly reveals the established priorities. Far more time, energy, staff, and imagination are dedicated to the mundane but essential tasks involved in running the armed services than are committed to the art of strategic thinking and planning. Few military officers think in strategic-political terms; but many have mastered the byzantine intricacies of the planning, programming, and budgeting system that dominates the Pentagon's calendar. America's senior military officers know that in the U.S. government, programs and budgetary decisions tend to determine the military's strategic function, not vice versa.

Some critics of the military believe that this strong orientation to "resource allocation" priorities has had an adverse effect on the military's development because it

has encouraged a mentality characterized by unwarranted confidence in the malleability of war, and by a faith that most, if not all problems of the battlefield are susceptible to technological or administrative solutions. It has fostered an insidious conviction that leadership is little more than a question of good management.[56]

The exclusion from the first or initiating level of the policy process is ironic because the very concept of "grand strategy" has a strong military connotation. In Western culture at least, significant advance in the development of strategic thought is associated with great military names, e.g., Frederick the Great, Napoleon, Clausewitz, Moltke.

In politics, thinking and acting are intimately related. Historically, those military officers who have made the most vital contributions to strategic thinking ususally had a large appetite for utlimate political power—the authority to choose their nation's strategic goals. Or they represented a military elite that was a close partner of an authoritarian ruling class. Deference to civilian authority on the ultimate political issues was not their paramount concern. Perhaps it is because they played such an important role in the formulation of their countrys' security goals that the great military strategists of the past have made such a signal contribution to the development of strategic thought.

It is, however, a price that few democracies are willing to pay. As a result, their military officers are consigned to narrower political functions at the instrumental and administrative levels of the policy process. Thus, the military in the contemporary democracy does not have a major contribution to make on the most critical policy levels—the establishment of strategic goals.

In the United States, the military's leaders are not asked by their political superiors when and where to wage war. They are asked a far more restricted question: How can the military instrument be most effectively used at a particular time for a given strategic purpose? In 1962 President Kennedy did not ask the military's leaders *if* the Soviets should be pressured to remove their missiles from Cuba; he asked them *how* it could be done. During the Vietnam War the JCS was not asked whether the U.S. should intervene on behalf of the South Vietnamese but rather, how the intervention could occur with minimal disruption and maximum effect.

An understanding of the military's role in the national security policy process must therefore begin with this fact clearly in mind—the American military has neither the charter, the inclination, nor the opportunity to play a primary role in the establishment of stragetic ends. Theirs is a secondary but still vital functional responsibility—an instrumental and administrative role. And it can be influential, albeit in an indirect way.

The potential impact of the chiefs' view on the public and the Congress can never be ignored by a president or a secretary of defense. On some issues, such as the amount of defense spending, their opinions may already be discounted; on others like the Vietnam War, their views ultimately become discredited. But the chiefs no doubt retain power to influence national decisions to some degree on some security issues, and to add legitimacy to one view or another.[57]

Restricted to an instrumental role in the policy process, the military officer takes a back seat to the "civilian strategists"—elected and appointed—who makes the key decisions and sets the direction on America's strategic goals. In recent years, a number of officers (e.g., Goodpaster, Haig, and Scowcroft) have served in the White House or on the NSC staff as assistants to key decision-makers. They are the exceptions, however, who were usually selected for their personal qualities as talented, hard-working individuals who could be useful in an unobtrusive way. Only one officer, General Maxwell Taylor, was selected for such a position principally because of his reputation as a strategic thinker.*

Perhaps the quality of America's strategic decisions has been weakened by the absence of an influential and relevant military perspective at the highest levels of the policy process. In some respects it is odd that those most intimate with both the power and limitations of military force are usually consulted only after the strategic issue has been joined and the key decision on strategic ends has been made. One powerful civilian strategist, Henry Kissinger, suggests there is another cogent reason for excluding the military from such a critical role. "The 'agreed' Joint Chiefs of Staff submissions were usually nonaggression treaties among the various services unrelated to a coherent strategy."[58]

No doubt this restriction on the military's policy roles has stunted important aspects of its professional development—the American military does not cultivate strategic thinkers. On the other hand, the very absence from the initiating level in the policy process has also insulated the American military from a dangerous appetite that has destabilized other political systems—a hunger for ultimate political authority, the power to determine the state's priorities and its security goals.

---

*The military establishment has not always welcomed such "tappings" of its sharper officers for temporary duty at the senior levels of the policy process. These officers were never allowed, nor did they seek, to use their influence positions to represent, let alone advance, service or professional interests. Consequently, they did not inject a "military perspective" into the formulation of the national security goals they may have helped formulate.

The size of the American defense establishment in the 1980s and the evolution of the military's definition of its own character, as set forth in preceding paragraphs, suggest that the military will continue to play an important—perhaps even somewhat larger—role in American society in the decade ahead. Of course, if there were a substantial withdrawal of American military power around the world, as might occur for instance if the NATO alliance should crumble, then one might expect a countertrend. As Chapter 23 spells out in some detail, the Western alliance system seems likely to change, perhaps weaken, but it is highly improbable that it will crumble and disappear in the course of the decade. Moreover, unless there is a large retreat of Soviet power from Central Europe and elsewhere, which is highly improbable, the United States will undoubtedly continue to station a sizable portion of its armed forces abroad.

As implied in Chapter 6, the military's congressional support, while it has waxed and waned to some degree over the past thirty years, has tended to be reasonably stable—reflecting as it does American public opinion about the importance of the military's role and the necessity to support large forces in a dangerous world. Unless there is a totally unforeseeable shift in the character of world politics and a consequent change in public and congressional opinion, the 1980s will likely mark at least the degree of support for the military that has been present in the 1960s and 1970s. Indeed, the prospects for such support seemed stronger than at any time since the mid 1960s.

In sum, it is clear that the military will continue to play an important role in American society generally and in the formulation and execution of national security policy specifically. Currents of change in international politics, particularly in East-West relations and within the West, may well create small eddies and turbulence but the 1980s trend on military roles seems reasonably predictable.

DISCUSSION QUESTIONS

1. What was the predominant role of the military leadership in the formulation of security policy prior to World War II? Why?

2. What was the importance of the State-War-Navy Coordinating Committee (SWNCC)?

3. What was the significance of the basic provisions of the National Security Act of 1947? Of its subsequent amendments?

4. What international events in the late 1940s and early 1950s eventually resulted in the greater impact of military advice on security policy formulation?

5. What are the advantages and disadvantages of interservice rivalry?

6. How have the armed services modified their education and training programs to cope with the shifting requirements of participation in political-military planning? Have they been effective?

7. What have been the consequences of increased contralization of decision-making within the Department of Defense?

8. How has the American system of military alliances affected the influence of the military in the formulation and execution of security policy?

9. Does the "blame for the Vietnam fiasco" rest primarily with civilian or military elites?

10. What are the advantages and disadvantages of regular forces being involved in a domestic security role?

11. How effectively has Congress performed its oversight role of the military establishment since World War II?

12. Is "militarization" as alleged by some critics an accurate assessment of American security policy since World War II? Why or why not?

13. Has the overall performance of the military services since World War II warranted the respect and confidence of the American public? Why or why not?

14. What are some reforms which might improve civil-military coordination?

RECOMMENDED READING

Betts, Richard. *Soldiers, Statesman, and Cold War Crisis.* Cambridge, Mass.: Harvard University Press, 1977.

Halberstam, David. *The Best and the Brightest.* New York: Random House, 1972.

Janowitz, Morris. *The Professional Soldier.* New York: Free Press, 1971.

Karsten, Peter, ed. *The Military in America: From the Colonial Period to the Present.* New York: Free Press, 1980.

Millis, Walter. *Arms and the State.* New York: Twentieth Century Fund, 1958.

Ries, John C. *The Management of Defense.* Baltimore: Johns Hopkins Press, 1964.

Russett, Bruce. *What Price Vigilence?* New Haven: Yale University Press, 1970.

Sapin, Burton M., and Snyder, Richard C. *The Role of the Military in American Foreign Policy.* Garden City, N.Y.: Doubleday, 1954.

Schwarz, Urs. *American Strategy. A New Perspective.* New York: Doubleday, 1966.

Smith, Mark D., III, and Johns, Claude J., eds. *American Defense Policy.* Baltimore: Johns Hopkins Press, 1968.

Taylor, Maxwell. *Swords and Plowshares.* New York: W. W. Norton, 1972.

Yarmolinsky, Adam. *The Military Establishment.* New York: Perennial Library, 1973.

9

DEFENSE PLANNING, BUDGETING, AND MANAGEMENT

One central problem of national security strategy is the limitation on the resources that can be allocated to meet security objectives. A nation's resources available—normally categorized by economists as land, labor, and capital—are valued by society because they can be used to produce a variety of outputs of goods and services that the society desires. When part of those resources is transferred to government in order to meet national security objectives, an "opportunity cost" is imposed on society—the lost opportunity of producing other goods and services with those resources to meet private consumption or other social goals. The options open to society broaden over time as total available resources grow and as more efficient technology is developed, but the question of how that expanded output will be shared among competing social claims remains.

The ultimate constraint on security expenditures is most directly related to the potential GNP—the dollar value of all the final goods and services that could be produced in the nation in a given year if all its resources were fully employed. In most years, unemployment will cause actual output to fall below its potential level, but the potential level is useful in national security analysis since all resources could be pressed to maximum use in an emergency. Of course, even in a crisis, the full potential GNP could not be tapped for security objectives, for essential civil consumption and services would have to be provided. Also, the diversion of resources to defense expenditures cannot be accomplished instantaneously or without considerable transitional costs. In a national crisis, security expenditures will be less constrained by the potential GNP than by the resource cost of essential goods and services for nonsecurity purposes and by the short-run costs of diverting production.

Competing claims on the nation's total output are made by individuals for consumption, by firms for investment, and by local, state, and federal governments for a host of public programs—including national security. How

178

should the proportion of total resources directed to national security objectives be determined? In theory, advocates of national security expenditures should demonstrate that the benefits to society of those national security expenditures exceed the benefits society would derive from equal expenditures on other government programs or private consumption and investment. In practice, however, the total federal budget and its division among different agencies are largely determined by prior decisions and external factors with little flexibility in the short run.

Recent history, prior commitments, current political realities, relations with Congress, economic and social events beyond the control of budget makers—all play a role in limiting their ability to change radically the current shape of the budget. What they consider desirable must be tempered by what they consider feasible.[1]

Thus, in practice, the major determinants of the level of national security expenditures tend to be economic and political judgments of the opportunity costs in terms of competing government programs that must be reduced or can be expanded if security expenditures increase or decrease marginally.

While security expenditures are constrained by the limitation on the nation's resources in general, and by interdepartmental competition for those resources allocated to the federal government in particular, ideal security goals are essentially unlimited. Given this condition, one objective of defense policy must be to obtain the most security possible for each dollar of defense expenditure. But even if a system could be designed to achieve the greatest possible efficiency in the defense sector, it would still be impossible to meet all of our ideal national security goals. Resource constraints must translate ideal goals into less than ideal "objectives." National security objectives are therefore not absolutes but are defined by the process of evaluating the options that are available to meet security goals. The realistic options facing society are not bankruptcy in perfect security on the one hand or prosperity with a high risk of national security disaster on the other. Rather, society must confront the far more difficult question of how much expenditure for national security is enough.

As we examine the various approaches that have been used to reconcile security goals and expenditure constraints in the recent past, it will be helpful to focus on three key questions.

1. How is the federal government to determine how much of total government spending to allocate to security expenditures?
2. How should the Department of Defense (DOD) allocate the total amount to be spent on defense to its various subordinate agencies?
3. Perhaps most important of all, are the two preceding questions independent issues to be resolved sequentially, or are they interrelated questions that must be handled jointly and simultaneously?

Evolution of Defense Budgeting, 1947–60. Earlier chapters have traced the major organizational changes within DOD since its birth in the National

Security Act of 1947. Successive amendments and reorganizations in 1949, 1953, and 1958 combined to expand the potential for centralized control in the hands of the secretary of defense at the expense of the individual services, and to enhance the power of the chairman of the JCS. Of course, the actual degree to which power was centralized depended as much on individual personalities and management styles as on formal organization.

Under the 1947 act, DOD—or, more accurately, the National Military Establishment—was to function as a confederation, not a unified department, presided over by a secretary of defense with carefully enumerated statutory powers. Yet the secretary had considerable influence—if he chose to exercise it. His primary source of power was political, derived from his direct link to the president and his influence over promotions and dismissals. In addition, his control of a unified budget applicable to all defense activities and his mandate to provide general direction over all agencies in the defense establishment gave the secretary considerable leverage. Along with the structural reforms of the 1949 amendments, a whole new section of the law (Title IV) was added for the "promotion of economy and efficiency through establishment of uniform budgeting and fiscal procedures and organizations."[2]

The process of centralizing control in the hands of the secretary of defense continued in the reorganizations of 1953 and 1958. As more assistant secretaries of defense were appointed and unified (interservice) commands expanded, the services became subordinate administrative subdivisions of the department; with unified command commanders reporting directly to the secretary of defense through the JCS, the services were no longer operationally independent and indeed found themselves outside the key chain of command. Following the 1958 amendments, the secretary of defense had wide authority to consolidate, transfer, or abolish functions of the services—certainly a far cry from the confederation envisioned in 1947.

While successive defense reorganizations brought the secretary of defense increasing authority, reform of the budgetary process proceeded more slowly and left him with inadequate tools for integrating strategic and budgetary decisions. Any budgetary process assists an organization in performing three essential functions—planning, management, and control. The planning process, which translates the goals of an organization into specific objectives, must provide some mechanism for adjusting objectives and resource allocations to total levels of expenditure. The management function involves the establishment and execution of projects or activities to meet the approved objectives, while the control process monitors the results of various activities measured against the objectives and insures that expenditures fall within specified limits. Although any budgetary process encompasses all three of these functions, any specific system will tend to emphasize particular functions at the central decision-making level.

Of course, centralization is a relative concept, and the operative question concerns the level at which decisions on different issues will be made. A visitor to the Pentagon is overwhelmed by the prospect of monitoring the myriad processes of defense planning, much less coordinating those activities and centralizing decision processes. The building itself, which covers thirty-four acres and provides office space for about thirty thousand persons, cries out for decentralization. Five concentric pentagonal corridors, or "rings," are joined by ten spoke-like main corridors which emanate from a five-acre central court. The structure suggests its content. Independent army, navy and air force staffs garner and analyze data with the full realization that information often means power in institutional battles, while a joint staff drawn from all the services attempts to coordinate interservice planning for the JCS.

Within the joint staff, coordination takes the form of a myriad of pyramiding concurrences as "flimsy paper" first drafts are upgraded in a color-coded process through "buff" and "green" stages. An action officer is assigned to each issue and coordinates the first flimsy draft with other action officers on the joint staff and the services. When differences are resolved at this level, the draft is retyped on buff paper and is then coordinated with the joint staff agencies and more senior officers in the services. Dissenting views by any service, or "purple" comments, are either resolved by a joint staff "planner" (usually a brigadier general) or are attached to the paper. The final staff report becomes a formal JCS green paper, which is presented to the JCS through its operations deputies.

Add to this process a collage of interservice agencies and DOD staffs and it is easy to conjure up a relatively accurate picture of action officers passing in the night, en route to their next concurrence. The point is not that the process is ineffective—indeed, the action officer approach may be a reasonably efficient solution to the coordination problem—but rather that centralizing and enforcing decisions in such a far-flung bureaucracy can be a painful and perhaps empty enterprise. The potential for the services or agencies to abide by the letter rather than the spirit of an unpopular decision is vast. In addition, extracting information from the bureaucracy can be a difficult process even if there is complete cooperation; simply finding the office responsible for monitoring the needed data is hard enough, without then attempting to assemble the information in a desired format.

There can be no definitive answer to the centralization dilemma. A consensus building, decentralized structure is valuable in developing lower level initiative and in generating institutional support for decisions, thereby assuring implementation. On the other hand, a decentralized process is oriented toward the status quo; change, which requires a redistribution of institutional power, is sure to be slow in coming. Within DOD, the management and control functions have traditionally tended to be decentralized, with the individual services establishing and monitoring activities to meet their perceived or assigned objectives. The planning function has been more centralized and has remained the primary concern of the secretary of defense. However, from 1947 to 1960, his ability to control even the planning process was restricted by insufficiently integrated service planning that did not relate operational requirements to budget realities.

In the aftermath of World War II, as national defense expenditures fell from $81.6 billion in 1945 to $13.1 billion in 1950, interservice competition for funds was intense. That competition was heightened by divergent views of the shape of future conflicts. While the army planned to fight future wars on the World War II model, the air force argued that ground force weapons were outmoded and planned for a conflict dominated by strategic air power, and the navy emphasized the need for a new fleet of supercarriers. Despite Secretary Forrestal's attempts to negotiate budget cuts with the JCS, it was impossible to bring their planning into line with new budget realities. Defense expenditure ceilings were independently determined as the residual of gross federal revenues minus required domestic expenditures and foreign aid programs. Hence, arbitrary defense ceilings for the next fiscal year were determined by what was judged to be economic and political feasibility. Plans for meeting security objectives were determined with little regard for budgetary restraints, and budgetary restraints were set with little regard for security objectives. It is not surprising that "Truman's Chiefs were developing plans predicated upon defending at the Rhine, while budgetary constraints did not even allow them to maintain a line of communication in the Mediterranean."[3]

Under President Truman, defense budget requests were scaled down to the budget ceiling by the Bureau of the Budget, and the chiefs were forced to negotiate service cuts or to appeal, often successfully, to Congress for additional funds. It is not surprising that this negotiating process produced budget shares that were approximately equal for each service.

After 1953 the process changed somewhat in form but not in substance. The secretary of defense first established the budget and workforce ceilings for the department, based on economic and political feasibility, and then asked the JCS to allocate that total among the services and to establish force levels. The JCS was required to submit a unanimous recommendation within the ceiling. Through this approach, the secretary of defense could arbitrate service disputes and insure that the financial ceilings were enforced. The JCS was left free to decide the key issues of strategy and force requirements— although, divorced as these issues were from implementing budgetary decisions, their impact was seldom if ever so great in practice as in theory. Each service had its own view of where future battlefields might be and how future wars should be fought. Each had its independent intelligence network and hence, its own threat estimates. Each maintained its own supply system; indeed, by 1960, each had developed its own ballistic missile systems.

Under President Eisenhower, the National Security Council and its staff arms played a significant role in the defense decision process, replacing the Bureau of the Budget as the reviewing agency for defense expenditures. Although the NSC review was effective in limiting the level of defense spending, it was not very effective in controlling the composition of spending. Infrequent NSC statements of Basic National Security Policy provided some guidance for service expenditures, but the policy statements were largely based on institutional tradition and were vague enough to support any one of a number of defense postures.

Attempts were made to integrate service planning through the Joint Strategic Objectives Plan (JSOP), prepared by the joint staff, which contained estimates of the forces needed to carry out national strategy and to meet military objectives. Military requirements therein, however, were based largely on experience and intuitive judgments rarely related to costs; moreover, there was no mechanism to tie force requirements to budgetary ceilings, and as a result, estimated costs of force requirements always greatly exceeded the budget ceiling. For these reasons, the JSOP had little real impact on defense budgeting.[4]

Even after the JSOP was introduced in 1955–56, military planning remained essentially a collage of unilaterally developed service plans. Faced with tight budget ceilings and disagreement over roles and strategy, each service acted quite rationally to preserve its share of the budget. Research and development (R&D), procurement of new weapons systems, and expanding force structures were influential cards in budget negotiations. The services often sacrificed supply inventories and support equipment to obtain them. The "foot in the door" approach to R&D (i.e., beginning major programs with small initial expenditures) was possible for one simple reason: while planning was projected several years into the future, the budget was projected only one year ahead. The services learned quickly that a budget cut might be avoided if they threatened to reduce their most important functions first. As one might suspect from a process requiring the unanimous approval of all the services, service budget shares remained virtually constant from 1954 to 1961. However, the emphasis on strategic defense objectives kept the balance tilted toward the air force, which averaged 47 percent of defense expenditures, while the navy and Marines garnered 29 percent and the army was forced to settle for 24 percent.[5]

Little attempt was made to integrate strategy and budgetary decisions in the planning process. Since requirements were derived without reference to costs, and the budget ceiling was derived without an analysis of requirements, the annual result was a confrontation between large, open-ended requirements and arbitrary budget ceilings. Clearly, requirements had to give, but no basis existed for identifying and cutting those requirements which made the least contribution to security per dollar expended. The wide gap between the demands of the JCS and the budget restrictions imposed by the president put the secretary of defense in an impossible position. Cuts were inevitably arbitrary and resulted in an improperly allocated budget. More security could have been obtained for the ceiling expenditure if requirements had been properly related to costs in the planning phase.

The McNamara Revolution. Like his predecessor Thomas Gates, Robert McNamara viewed his role as a leader in shaping defense policy rather than a reviewer of service plans. Moreover, McNamara arrived at the Pentagon in 1961 with a strong presidential mandate to shift the nation's defense posture from one of massive retaliation to one of more flexible response. The shift required new emphasis on mobile general purpose forces while continuing to emphasize the importance of strategic nuclear delivery systems. The mandate was to be prepared to fight simultaneously major wars in Europe and Asia and a "brush-fire" war anywhere in the world—the two-and-a-half war strategy. To accomplish these more ambitious objectives, something had to give; it was budget constraints. President Kennedy freed Secretary McNamara from specific budgetary ceilings and eliminated any review of the defense budget in the executive branch outside DOD.

Thus, Robert McNamara came into office with strong support and almost unlimited funds, eager to make sweeping changes in the planning and budgeting procedures used by DOD. He was committed to play an active role in shaping defense programs, particularly in determining force and weapon requirements. McNamara agreed with those who argued that the close relationships of foreign policy, military strategy, budget expenditures, and the choice of major weapons and force structures made it imperative that planning be coordinated in each of those areas. Since military experts had been allowed to determine security requirements without any independent review, McNamara reasoned there was a possibility of bias, based on service orientation, institutional pressure, and prior experience. The record of the fifties argued that traditional compromises usually brought pressure for more total spending in order to avoid reductions anywhere, and that such compromises often discriminated against the less traditional elements of the services and against support functions in favor of glamor programs. In his view, the secretary of defense needed to play an active role to insure that all the relevant alternatives were considered, since the individual services might not be able to take the broad perspective needed. Finally, the revolution in technology threatened to render traditional military expertise less relevant in force planning. Since strategic nuclear war had never been fought, analysis would have to replace experience.

McNamara heeded the advice of numerous critics of defense budgeting practices in the 1950s who had observed that national planning required an evaluation of alternate methods of accomplishing security objectives on the basis of the comparative outputs and costs of each alternative.[6] For example, several strategic forces—Minuteman missiles, strategic bombers, Polaris missile submarines—contribute to the objective of deterring nuclear attack by providing a second-strike capability, i.e., the ability to retaliate effectively after an initial attack on the United States. In deciding how much of the defense budget to allocate to each of those strategic forces, the costs and effectiveness of each system should be considered simultaneously. This had been made virtually impossible, however, by the defense budget's arrayal of expenditures in terms of inputs—personnel, maintenance, military construction—used by the services rather than end products or missions. While forces and weapons were normally considered horizontally across services in the planning process, expenditures were portrayed vertically within each service by input category. The integration of military planning (the domain of the JCS) with budgeting (the domain of the civilian secretaries and comptroller organizations) required a link between mission objectives and expenditures.

The solution McNamara adopted was "program budgeting," by which all military forces and weapons systems are grouped into output-oriented programs according to their principal missions, even though missions cut across traditional service boundaries. Contrast the traditional budget categories in table 9.1, which are still used to present the budget to Congress, to the program classifications now used for internal defense planning; clearly, the categories do not correspond. Programs are divided into subprograms (e.g., army forces—divisions, brigades, combat support forces—under the subprogram of General Purpose Forces) and still further into program elements (e.g., army battalions). With expenditure data arrayed in the program format, a decision-maker may readily observe how funds are distributed over objective-related outputs and how those funds are allocated over different forces and weapon systems within each program.

McNamara used the potential of "program" budgeting to establish the preeminence of the Office of the Secretary of Defense (OSD) in the national security policy-making process. The Planning, Programming, Budgeting System (PPBS) he instituted made it possible to link expenditures more closely to the national security objectives to which they were directed, to compare the relative value of various expenditures, and to enforce the resultant decisions on force structure and weapons procurement. The basic document of PPBS was and remains the Five-Year Defense Program (FYDP), which contains an eight-year projection of forces (based on estimates from the JSOP prepared by the JCS) and a five-year projection of costs and personnel requirements divided into mission-oriented programs. By presenting five-year cost projections, the full-cost implications of program decisions are revealed more effectively than they were in former annual projections. The FYDP is

Table 9.1 Traditional Budget Categories and Program Classifications

Traditional Budget Categories	*Program Categories for Defense Planning*
Military Personnel	Strategic Forces
Retired Military Personnel	General Purpose Forces
Operation and Maintenance	Intelligence and Communications
Procurement	Airlift and Sealift
Research, Development, Test and Evaluation	Guard and Reserve Forces
Military Construction	Research and Development
Family Housing	Central Supply and Maintenance
Civil Defense	Training, Medical and Other General
Special Foreign Currency Program	Personnel Activity
	Administration and Associated Activities
	Support of Other Nations

updated annually as part of an iterative planning and programming cycle, as decisions are reached on expenditures within each program. The FYDP plays a central role in linking force and financial planning, providing an official set of planning assumptions, estimating total costs of program packages, and portraying a road map for defense planning over a five-year time span. Estimates expenditures for the next fiscal year from the FYDP become the basis for service and DOD budget requests each fall.

The PPBS described thus far produces an array of force and financial data which facilitates an evaluation of alternative forces and weapons on the basis of their costs and contributions to security objectives. It is perfectly consistent with centralized or decentralized processes for evaluating the alternatives. The key point in understanding the operation of the system from 1961 to 1968 is that McNamara used PPBS to centralize power within OSD. Clearly, such centralization of power would be opposed by the services, but McNamara held strong cards. Most importantly, he had the firm backing of President Kennedy and, subsequently, President Johnson. McNamara's philosophy of management and his personal style argued for his active role in a centralized decision-making process and complemented his willingness to assume the political risks of centralized decisions on policy and the budget. The 1958 amendments to the National Security Act had provided the statutory authority for a strong, activist secretary of defense. The relative inactivity of the NSC machinery under Kennedy and Johnson and Secretary of State Rusk's style provided a low-pressure area for an activist defense leader to exploit. Finally, McNamara's personal analytical skills and those of the civilians working in his office gave him a clear advantage in dealing with the service staffs, other departments, and the Congress.

Charles J. Hitch, McNamara's first comptroller and an early proponent of program budgeting, was charged with producing a budget for fiscal year 1963 formulated in terms of major programs. Hitch was to implement the first FYDP within nine months. In April 1961, he established a small systems analysis section under Alain Enthoven, to give the secretary of defense independent staff assistance in reviewing JCS and service force and weapon proposals, in developing alternative proposals, and in integrating data on requirements, costs, and effectiveness. The systems analysis staff quickly became a focal point of controversy in the McNamara PPBS because it seized the initiative in evaluating competing programs on the basis of statistical analyses of costs and effectiveness. Civilian analysts, often young Ph.D.s with little military experience, dominated the office because Enthoven felt they had a degree of professional and intellectual independence which allowed them to be more objective in evaluating proposals of the different services. As the staff expanded, the status of the office increased and, by 1965, Enthoven had become an assistant secretary of defense for systems analysis.

McNamara used his staff of analysts to define force and weapon issues that required study, to develop alternative proposals for dealing with the issues, to probe the services for relevant data, and to evaluate alternatives. While the secretary's analytical staff and the initiative gained by having the services comment on completed studies provided a strong centralizing influence on the decision process, several other factors worked to McNamara's advantage. Most of the key issues, pertaining to weapons systems and force levels, lent themselves to quantitative analysis, and many concerned nuclear strategy where experience was greatly limited. The historic split among service chiefs within the JCS, which produced the budget battles of the 1950s, persisted into the early 1960s, and the JCS was unable to present a united front to block McNamara's initiatives. JCS planning incorporated in the annual JSOP continued to be unconstrained by any fiscal guidance and continued to call for expenditures vastly in excess of the eventual budget. As a result, JCS planning remained an ineffective counter to McNamara's initiatives, and major resource allocation decisions were deferred until the last weeks of the budget review and then dominated by OSD analysis.

As noted, the essence of the PPBS lay in its division of weapon systems and forces into output related programs, incorporation of cost and force projections for each program in a FYDP, and linking of the planning and budgeting processes. In the abstract, the PPBS provided an improved base of information for analyzing defense decisions and coordinating interrelated activities. In practice, however, it provided a systematic method for focusing attention on key issues, organizing the sequence and participation in the decision process, and recording decisions. As it was applied from 1961 to 1968 under Secretary McNamara, with emphasis on quantitative analysis of alternatives at the initiative of a civilian staff in OSD, PPBS became a powerful tool for centralizing power in the hands of the secretary of defense. Before critiquing the PPBS as it was used under McNamara and tracing developments in the system since 1968, it will be helpful to focus on the techniques of systems analysis which McNamara's staff exploited so effectively.

Systems Analysis. Under Secretary McNamara the systems analysis staff was instrumental in developing the assured destruction strategy for nuclear deterrence, pushing the expansion of army aviation and the airmobile concept, and deciding the fate of numerous weapon systems: the B-70 manned bomber (no), the Skybolt missile (no), the Poseidon missile (yes), the Minuteman III missile (yes), the F-111 fighter (yes), and nuclear naval vessels (no). The forte of the systems analysts was the application of relatively new statistical techniques, often assisted by computer processing of data, to evaluation of the costs and effectiveness of alternative weapons and forces—although most of the systems analysts preferred to explain their approach as applied common sense. Indeed, the basic idea of systems analysis is a straightforward application of the scientific method, although sophisticated techniques of data analysis are often used to evaluate alternatives.

The six-step sequence of systems analysis is similar to that of any logical problem-solving process:

1. Determine the purpose or objective of the system.

2. List the feasible set of alternatives.
3. Evaluate the alternatives on the basis of cost and effectiveness.
4. Develop decision criteria for ranking the alternatives.
5. Check the sensitivity of ranking to assumptions and uncertainties.
6. Iterate the process, exploiting new information and insight.

After the purpose of the system is determined, all of the feasible alternatives that would fulfill the systems' objectives are identified and listed. This is perhaps the most crucial phase of the analysis.

Much of the formal literature on analytical methods—particularly that on operations research—seems to suggest that formulating the problem, gathering data, and making assumptions are uninteresting preliminaries and that the action really starts when the mathematical model begins to calculate the optimum solution. But in most analyses of policy issues, the vast majority of the important effort is devoted to seeking, and then asking the right questions, formulating the problem, gathering relevant data and determining their validity, and deciding on good assumptions. Rather than preliminaries, these items are in fact the heart of good systems analysis.[7]

Next, each of the alternatives is evaluated to determine all of its relevant costs and its effectiveness in meeting the objectives of the system. This process often includes building an analytical model of the system, when real construction and testing of the system are not feasible, in order to evaluate costs and effectiveness over time and to test the implications of risk and uncertainty. The models of cost and effectiveness attempt to represent reality by isolating those factors that are most relevant to the problem under analysis.

After the costs and effectiveness of competing systems are determined, decision criteria are applied to rank the alternatives and aid the decision-maker in selecting the most acceptable alternative. The particular decision rule depends on the nature of the problem but is generally stated as finding the system, or combination of systems, that meets the objective at the least cost. Conversely, an alternate rule is to find the system providing the most effectiveness at a given cost level, a criterion that is applicable when an absolute budget constraint is imposed. The sensitivity of the ultimate system ranking of alternatives to changes in assumptions, or to changes in cost and effectiveness parameters, is evaluated to determine the key assumptions that influenced the ultimate decision. Finally, the whole process is repeated, exploiting the insights into the problem statement and new alteratives gained in the last iteration and refining the estimates of crucial parameters where possible.

A major contribution of this approach to defense issues is the broadening of perspective it requires. Various configurations of individual weapons or forces are viewed as part of a larger "system" for achieving national security objectives. Thus, the first step in analysis is to place a given problem in perspective. What national security objectives are at stake? What alternative approaches could be used to meet those objectives? What are the relevant costs and benefits of a particular method of meeting the objective, and how do they compare with the alternatives? This broad approach requires that the issues and alternatives be defined clearly and makes it possible to demonstrate how disagreements are related to different underlying assumptions. The objective of systems analysis is not to produce "the" answer but to demonstrate how the various answers depend on different assumptions and judgments. Ideally, this approach makes it possible for the high-level decision-maker to evaluate real alternatives and concentrate on the key parameters of a given problem, rather than being limited to a choice between a polished proposal and "straw-man" alternatives.

The "analysis" portion of systems analysis attempts to define issues and alternatives clearly, and to provide the ground rules for constructive and convergent debate. The analytical tools employed vary widely with the specific nature of the problem. Numbers are usually used to replace adjectives for clarity in the analysis, and statistical techniques for evaluating hypotheses are often useful. Utilized properly, however, quantitative analysis should focus, rather than replace, reasoned judgment.

The great debate over the antiballistic missile (ABM) system provides some useful insight into the systems analysis technique. The ABM system clearly falls into the "strategic forces" program, but what particular security objective, does it serve? Prior to 1963, the proposed Nike-Zeus ABM system was designed for area defense and deployment around urban centers. After 1963, its more complex offspring, the Nike-X, added to the long-range Zeus missile a faster, short-range "Sprint" missile for·interception within the atmosphere. The modified system could be used to defend point targets, including the Minuteman missile force, but deployment of the Nike-X was initially rejected based on its alleged vulnerability to a sophisticated Soviet attack that could include decoys, large numbers of warheads, and attacks on vulnerable radar. In 1966, it became clear that the Soviet Union was tipping the strategic balance by deploying an ABM system around Moscow, by developing more sophisticated intercontinental ballistic missiles (ICBMs) with larger warheads which threatened our missile force, and by experimenting with a space bombardment system and a satellite interceptor. Deployment of an ABM system was nevertheless resisted by the administration because the capacity of the contemplated system to handle sophisticated attacks was still in question, and such deployment might be provocative and destabilizing—stimulating further deployment of offensive missiles by the Soviet Union. By 1967, however, the perceived Soviet threat could no longer be ignored, and there was increasing evidence that the People's Republic of China might have a limited ICBM capability sometime in the 1970s.

How should the United States respond? Several alternatives to the ABM were considered. If the objective were defined as protecting our Minuteman force to insure that sufficient missiles would survive to inflict unacceptable damage on an attacking Soviet Union, deployment of the ABM might be justified. On the other hand, the same objective might be reached by "hardening" existing missile sites, that is, by reinforcing the concrete silos to absorb greater overpressure. Other alternatives, such as the dispersal of fixed missile silos and mobile land-based missiles, were also feasible. If the ultimate objective, however, were to deter Soviet attack, perhaps the correct response would not be to build ABMs or improve fixed land-based missiles but to expand the Polaris missile force at sea or to improve the manned-bomber force, or both. After all, the major purpose of the triad deterrent, of maintaining three independent forces—ICBM Minuteman, Polaris submarine-launched ballistic missiles, and the manned-bomber force—was to inflict unacceptable losses on the enemy despite technological breakthroughs in any one area. This "assured destruction" capability was believed essential to deter a first strike by the Soviet Union.

By 1968, three alternative missions for the ABM were being actively considered as part of a deterrence system: (1) defend U.S. cities against a massive, sophisticated attack by the U.S.S.R.; (2) defend U.S. cities against future limited third-power attacks; (3) defend Minuteman ICBMs. Preliminary analysis eliminated the first alternative as infeasible, given the likely Soviet response of expanded offensive deployments. A light deployment to defend the Minuteman force remained a possibility and that option might also provide adequate defense from third-power attacks or accidental Soviet launches. Thus, the first step in systems analysis was to place the ABM issue in perspective and enumerate alternative systems that should be considered.

The second step was to evaluate the full system costs and effectiveness of each alternative. Considering only the hardened silo and ABM alternatives, how did the number of surviving Minuteman missiles vary with different levels of deployment and, hence, costs? To determine the relationship of costs to effectiveness (surviving Minuteman missiles), cost and effectiveness models were needed. Effectiveness was clearly related to assumptions as to (1) the nature of the enemy threat (number of missiles, missile accuracy, warhead number and size, deployment strategy, etc.), and (2) the performance characteristics of the ABM (probability and range of radar detection, probability and range of destroying an incoming missile, deployment strategy, etc.) or the hardened silo (overpressure withstood at varying thicknesses). Costs included future R&D, procurement, installation, and operating costs over the lifetime of the system.

Given the relationship between costs and effectiveness for each system, a decision criterion was needed to rank the alternatives. One such criterion might have been to find the system that assured the survival of a desired number of Minuteman missiles at the least cost. Or, a given budget expenditure might have been stipulated and the systems ranked on the basis of the largest number of surviving missiles for that expenditure. Next the ranking could be tested for its sensitivity to the assumptions or system parameters. Suppose the number of attacking missiles were twice as large as expected, or their accuracy were greater, or procurement costs were understated, or our missile failed if radiation in the atmosphere were too great.

This information was certainly helpful to decision-makers. Indeed, the debate over the proposed deployment of the Sentinel system (the sequel to the Nike-X, which was to be deployed around urban centers) or its modified version, the Safeguard (which was to provide point defense for the Minuteman) centered on estimates of technical performance and cost data. The real issue at stake, however, was the future direction and objective of our nuclear strategy vis-a-vis the Soviet Union and China. Was strategic nuclear superiority essential; would parity suffice; or was an assured destruction capability sufficient? How would the Soviet Union react to ABM deployment—by negotiation or by expansion of its offensive missile force? Mathematical models of costs and effectiveness could not address these bargaining alternatives, but systems analysis could be, and was, used to assist in evaluating feasible and efficient responses. Thus, the 1969 decision to deploy the Safeguard system around Minuteman bases, which passed the Senate by one vote, was based as much on estimates of Soviet response as on systems analysis of the costs and effectiveness of the ABM. Subsequent Strategic Arms Limitation Talks (SALT) blocked further ABM development. In this case, systems analysis helped focus the debate on alternative solutions and correctly emphasized the critical nature of assumptions about Soviet response.

The systems analysis technique for evaluating alternative weapon systems or force postures offers several advantages over traditional techniques of defense analysis. By emphasizing the search for alternative responses, it focuses attention on the need for comparing systems with comparable outputs across service boundaries and helps stress the need for integrated planning. In addition, systems analysis makes the tie between costs and effectiveness explicit, facilitating the integration of budgeting and planning. Risk and uncertainty are examined explicitly, and full system costs and benefits over time are evaluated. The iterative procedure helps illumine the precise nature of the problem at hand and the relevant assumptions and system parameters, providing some assurance that the correct issues are being addressed in the analysis. Perhaps most importantly, the systems analysis approach provides for open, explicit justification of conclusions that may be challenged on the basis of their quality rather than the authority of the advocate.

The use of systems analysis is often confused with a misleading distinction between "rational" and "political" decision processes. PPBS in general and systems analysis in particular are often referred to as "rational" processes stressing objective evidence, presumably devoid of political judgment, and are contrasted with more decentralized "political" bargaining processes stressing subjective evaluations. There is no such thing, however, as a "rational" decision process in that sense—any analysis contains value judgments. The question in any particular case is, What weight is to be given to whose value judgments? One impact of PPBS has clearly been to make conflicts in value judgments more explicit and to permit decision-makers to weigh quantifiable evidence—over which there may also be considerable disagreement—against less quantifiable, often institutional, considerations. The decision on how many missiles to deploy on the Polaris submarine illustrates this trade-off.

Systems analysis suggested that, while any even number of missiles between four and forty-eight was technically feasible, thirty-two launching tubes would be the most cost-effective. However, submarine officer support was essential in gaining congressional approval of the system and implementing the Polaris program. Since the submarine officers had a strong aversion to large submarines, especially large submarines with many six-foot diameter hatches, the ultimate decision was to choose sixteen tubes.[8] To define such a decision as "rational" or "political" would clearly oversimplify the process—it was both.

While the weight applied to judgments from various sources will certainly vary with the individuals operating the system, the systems analysis approach to the evaluation of alternatives does imply some centralization of decision authority, since alternatives could easily cut across institutional boundaries and institutions would tend to take advocacy positions in the analysis. The real impact on the distribution of authority, however, is more apt to be defined by the locus of analytical skill and by the pattern of initiating and responding to the studies within the organization. Under Secretary McNamara, systems analysis became synonymous with centralization due to the initial analytical advantages of his civilian staff, and because his analysts took the initiative in raising issues, drafting studies over the secretary's signature, and requiring prompt service comment before final decisions. That process of centralization produced considerable controversy within and outside the defense establishment—controversy to which we now turn.

Critique of the McNamara PPBS and Evolving Revisions. The overwhelming impact of the PPBS under Secretary McNamara was the concentration of power in the hands of the secretary of defense. Armed with a staff of mostly young civilian analysts—the "whiz kids"—in the systems analysis office, Secretary McNamara used the PPBS to break through traditional service barriers. The rise in power of the OSD and the emphasis on quantifiable cost and effectiveness measures in the planning and budgeting processes were not wholly supported either by the services or by Congress.

The services generally opposed the secretary's reliance on civilian analysts with little or no military experience. It was widely held that attempts to quantify the effectiveness of weapons systems or forces prejudiced decisions against options with nonquantifiable benefits and overweighed quantifiable factors in options where quantification was feasible. Further, many career military officers felt that systems analysis was pushed too far, that insufficient weight was being given to expert intuition and experience, and that too much import was given to abstract mathematical models. In many cases, where effectiveness was hard to quantify, they felt that too great emphasis was placed on system costs, which were consistently underestimated. In short, uniformed officers viewed the civilian analysts as Oscar Wilde viewed the cynic who knew "the price of everything and the value of nothing"—and in the case of the F-111 fighter or the C-5A jet transport, they apparently did not even know the price all that well either.

The centralized approach of McNamara's PPBS also tended to deemphasize the value of bargaining and consensus in gaining the support of the bureaucracy. In an important critique of PPBS, Aaron Wildavsky argued that decision-makers should fragment their areas of concern so that they are not overburdened with details at any one time. This would make it possible to rely on feedback information on whether or not subordinates had unduly been hurt by their actions. He further argued that sequential, nonprogrammatic organization had the advantage of fitting with political reality, since cost-benefit formulas often omitted political costs and benefits. He concluded that a partial adversary system had a better chance than program budgeting to arrive at reasonable decisions that took into account a multiplicity of internal and external political values.[9]

McNamara's approach encountered a mixed reception on Capitol Hill. Legislators were clearly impressed with the detail contained in the secretary's reports and perhaps even more impressed with his knowledge of those details. But frequently they lamented the difficult options with which they were presented. In 1967, at hearings on the PPBS, Senator Karl Mundt revealed his frustration.

We used to face the question, "How much should we spend for a weapons system?" Defense had a united front and asked for a certain amount of money. Now we have to make decisions . . . on which defense system and techniques we should have. . . . It is in the wrong arena at our end of the Avenue, because we are not experts in defense, and we are not economists and the engineers. We are here trying to make overall policy and to do what we can to keep the budget relatively sound. It is very difficult if part of [the] team says you need B-52 bombers, otherwise in the early 70's you will have no bombers at all, and other officials say, "Don't worry about that, just let the B-52 bombers go, and don't put any money in." That shouldn't be the kind of decision we have to make.[10]

Similarly, many critics argued that the secretary was spending too much time on decisions that he should not have made. Centralization through systems analysis, they argued, ran the risk of distorting key issues. True, it did seem that it would be more cost-effective for each service to adopt a standardized belt buckle; but was that issue worthy of the secretary's scarce time and were the potential savings worth the political cost? A small group of analysts could not hope to review all the options available to the secretary. Were they focusing on the right issues? Were they raising and exploring the complete set of feasible alternatives? Many argued that in a centralized decision process subordinates might not reveal all the relevant alternatives as they would in a more decentralized adversary process.

These criticisms have had significant impact on the evolution of PPBS in the post McNamara period. The central concepts of the system have remained, but there has been a clear decentralization in the process of raising issues and analyzing alternatives. The result has been a modified system that provides for an expanded role by the NSC in evaluating security objectives, early fiscal guidance to the services to assist in making their planning more realistic in terms of budget limitations, and a shift in initiative for proposing changes and raising issues for debate away from the systems analysis group within OSD and back toward the services and the JCS.

As noted earlier, under Secretary McNamara operational planning by the JCS had little impact on budget allocations, since planning was unconstrained by realistic budget limitations. Thus, OSD played the dominant role in the process of updating the FYDP and adjusting requests for budget allocations down to a total consistent with federal fiscal policy. Under the PPBS followed since 1968, the FYDP remains the central document, but the process of reviewing alternatives and proposing issues for debate has been decentralized.

The first two volumes of the JCS JSOP, which contain a strategic assessment and force structure requirements, are still drafted each year before any fiscal guidance is considered. However, by the time volume 2 is released each February, the secretary of defense has issued tentative fiscal guidance containing five-year budget planning constraints and a memorandum containing strategic guidance for all defense planning. The tentative fiscal guidance is upgraded to specific budget ceilings for each service as soon as the secretary receives his fiscal guidance from the Office of Management and Budget (OMB). By March, all defense planning is proceeding with a clear understanding of budget limitations for the next fiscal year.

In April, the JCS produces its first budget-constrained planning document, the Joint Force Memorandum (JFM). The JFM spells out force level and support program recommendations consistent with the fiscal guidance, compares the resultant costs with those in the FYDP, assesses the risks inherent in the recommended posture, and highlights issues that remain to be resolved. At the same time, service planning continues to translate broad force structure decisions into more specific program objectives. The resultant Program Objective Memoranda released by each service, beginning in May, for each major mission area and support activity, present the detailed program implications of the JFM and defend deviations from that initial guidance. The net impact of this procedure is to place the initiative in raising issues for further debate with the services and the JCS. Since JCS recommendations are generally consistent with the fiscal guidance, its positions are less vulnerable to last minute budget adjustments.

Just as the role of the JCS has shifted from reaction to OSD initiatives under McNamara to a posture of initiating policy reviews, the function of the systems analysis office has shifted. Instead of distributing finished studies for comment, the systems analysis staff is charged with reviewing service proposals and has the burden of proof in recommending changes to service programs. The name of the office has been changed to Program Analysis and Evaluation (PA&E) to reflect the change in function.

As JCS and service program proposals are reviewed and approved through the summer, the secretary issues Program Decision Memoranda for each budget area. These decisions are incorporated in the FYDP, and the plan's cost and force structure data for the next fiscal year become the basis for service budget proposals submitted to OSD in early fall. Following a joint review of these proposals by OSD and OMB, the consolidated defense budget is reviewed by the president and incorporated in his annual budget submission to Congress early in the new year.

Important to an understanding of the budgetary process within DOD is appreciation for the fact that the process is inherently complex and driven by tight deadlines. It is probably accurate to say that there are relatively few officials within DOD who fully comprehend the entire process in all its intricacy. Those officials who, by virtue of long experience with the annual cycle, understand the process and the techniques by which it can be manipulated find quickly that that understanding often translates into political influence and organizational clout.

PPBS outside DOD and Zero-Base Budgeting. The key elements of the McNamara planning, programming, and budgeting revolution in DOD have remained intact, despite continuing modifications in the terminology used to describe documents, in the precise sequence of guidance and decisions, and in the relative roles of the services and OSD. Indeed, the PPBS process has been so successful in making the interrelationship of objectives and budgetary constraints explicit in a continuous planning sequence that there have been several attempts to implement program budgeting in other government agencies.

In 1965 the Johnson administration mandated that all agencies adopt program budgeting to facilitate the comparison of similar programs within their areas of responsibility. Operating levels for each program were to be projected over future years so that the full costs of current decisions could be reviewed. Analyses in the form of program memoranda were then to be used in evaluating alternate methods of meeting agency objectives. The experiment was short-lived, and by 1971 the program budgeting approach had been discontinued in most agencies.

The failure of PPBS outside DOD may be attributed to a variety of technical factors, such as the expanded need for information and the problems of defining and evaluating program outputs. A principal problem, however, was congressional and agency opposition to a highly centralized budgetary review process. PPBS shifted additional information and analytical capability to OMB and threatened the traditional decentralized political process that dominated the incremental budgeting approach.[11]

A similar fate awaited a creation of the Nixon administration, the Defense Policy Review Committee (DPRC), designed to weigh defense expenditures against other types of government spending and to provide initial fiscal guidance based on a joint consideration of security and economic considerations. The concept behind the DPRC, which was essentially a subcommittee of the

NSC, was eminently sensible: to provide a broad perspective in defining the form and scope of national security expenditures. In practice, however, the DPRC remained a concept rather than a functioning committee. The priority placed on national security expenditures by the president and his reliance on the judgment of the secretary of defense—who was not ready to turn analysis of his department's budget over to an interagency committee—essentially eliminated the role of the DPRC, and, like PPBS outside DOD, it quietly disappeared from the scene.

The lessons of these two experiments are clear. First, the process of clearly defining objectives, establishing priorities, and making budgetary decisions based on analysis of alternatives is very difficult, even within a given government agency. The process has succeeded in DOD only because of an unusually centralized structure, the quantifiable nature of many of its problems, and the continuing commitment of recent secretaries of defense. Second, the process of comparing and allocating resources across agencies is incredibly difficult, and efforts to compare the relationship between costs and benefits of divergent programs have been relatively unsuccessful.

The advent of the Carter administration brought a new emphasis on program budgeting and comparison of programs across agencies. The new vehicle for this process was zero-base budgeting, which emphasizes an annual review of all programs, but the process is similar to that used in program budgeting. As described in an OMB directive of April 1977, zero-base budgeting is a "management process that provides for systematic consideration of all programs and activities in conjunction with the formulation of budget requests and planning."[12] The central feature of this process is that current budget levels are not treated as a base for incremental decisions, but even current levels must be defended in the annual review process. In short, current spending must be linked to current objectives.

Of course, this explicit linkage of budgets to objectives is a major feature of PPBS. Indeed, the five-step process of the zero-base budget procedure identified by OMB closely parallels the PPBS cycle. Those five steps are:

1. Identify explicit organizational objectives or accomplishments expected and specify output services to be provided from a given level of funding.
2. Identify decision units or program packages which contain fairly homogeneous outputs required by the organizational objectives.
3. Prepare decision packages which relate potential outputs to different levels of spending. Such decision packages must include the current level of spending (based on continuing the program at current levels without major policy changes) and the minimum level (below which no constructive contribution to achieving program objectives can be made). Other increments of spending and output levels may be specified as desired. Decision packages correspond to program elements in a program budgeting process.
4. Rank decision packages based on the manager's priorities for the programs under his direction. The minimum level of spending in a given program is always given priority over higher levels.

5. Perform higher level reviews in which priorities are revised and packages are consolidated as desired.

In the PPBS within DOD, the planning and programming steps already relate longterm objectives to desired levels of spending on various output programs over the next five years. The zero-base budget process then serves to fine tune the financial plan required to implement the decisions already contained in the FYDP. Thus, the analysis required to defend the budget in a zero-base review has already been prepared in the earlier phases of the PPBS. The impact of zero-base budgeting on the internal operation of the PPBS is therefore minimal.

In operation during the Carter years, zero-base budgeting failed to alter the way in which defense expenditures were weighed against the programs of other agencies in a meaningful way. The history of program budgeting outside DOD suggested that zero-base budgeting would encounter significant opposition. There were problems with bureaucrats defending threatened programs, in training management for the system, in defining measures of performance, in identifying the right alternatives, and in providing program rankings based on actual priorities rather than shifting priorities to maximize funding. The concept of relating expenditures to outputs in program or decision packages and of providing open analysis of competing alternatives is a sound one, but presidential emphasis has much bureaucratic inertia to overcome if program budgeting is to reemerge under the banner of the zero-base process.

The Outlook for Defense Management. Returning to the three questions posed at the beginning of the chapter, it should now be clear that the allocation of scarce government resources to security expenditures as a whole should closely be related to the allocation of those resources within DOD. Only by determining the maximum increment in security, which may be obtained from a given budget expenditure, and comparing that increment to the additional benefit that might be derived from alternate government expenditures can society choose efficiently between competing social objectives. Such an analysis, however, presupposes that the defense budget has been allocated internally to subordinate agencies to maximize the increment in security. The appropriate level of defense expenditures should therefore be linked to the maximum amount of added security which can be obtained for any given increment in the expenditure level. Hence, the optimal allocation of resources to security objectives and the proper allocation of funds within DOD are interrelated questions that, conceptually at least, should be handled simultaneously rather than sequentially.

Under PPBS DOD has made tremendous strides in relating the internal allocation of budget expenditures to security objectives. The highly centralized process of the McNamara era has been replaced with a more decentralized system of participatory management placing increased weight on institutional costs and service measures of effectiveness. The essential elements, however, of the system of comparing similar outputs across services within a program format and of providing open analysis of the costs and effectiveness of competing weapons or force structures remains.

The ability of the government to decide how much to spend on national security and to evaluate defense versus other types of expenditures, however, has lagged far behind. As noted earlier, program budgeting has been generally unsuccessful outside DOD, and efforts in the early 1970s to coordinate security and economic priorities in a DPRC structure were abandoned. OMB, of course, reviews the budget submissions of DOD, and OMB's budget guidance does provide the initial judgment on the allocation of defense versus other expenditures. That budget guidance, however, has traditionally been strongly influenced by past expenditure patterns and by the interests of the president. Indeed, within the executive branch's review of the DOD budget, the secretary of defense has generally been supported by the president. Even in the unusual case of Secretary Schlesinger's resignation, which was in part over proposed budget cuts in November 1975, virtually all the cuts were restored under his successor, Secretary Rumsfeld. At any rate there is currently little evidence that allocations to defense expenditures are based on explicit analysis of defense programs versus alternate nondefense expenditures.

To suggest that the level of defense expenditures is determined with little reference to competing nondefense programs is not to imply that defense expenditures are unconstrained. Rather, allocations for defense tend to be constrained by past levels of spending, by the desired level of total government spending based on economic conditions, and by changes in national security objectives or perceived threats. Thus, in the early 1970s the reaction to the war in Southeast Asia, concern with inflation, overtures to the People's Republic of China, an apparent era of detente with the Soviet Union, and the prospect of SALT and Mutual and Balanced Force Reduction negotiations all contributed to a period of declining real defense expenditures. In absolute terms, constant dollar outlays from FY 1973 to 1978 remained *below* the pre–Vietnam War level of 1964. In relative terms, defense expenditures fell from over 40 percent of total federal budget outlays in FY 1964 to less than 25 percent in FY 1978.[13] Since the period from 1973 to 1978 was a period of rapidly rising personnel costs, based on the increased wage structure of the volunteer force and growing retirement obligations, tremendous pressure was placed on operational costs, support, and new procurement.

By the late 1970s there were indications that this downward trend would be reversed. While withdrawal from Southeast Asia and the announcement of a phased reduction of U.S. forces in the Republic of Korea temporarily reduced pressure for some expenditure, an increased concern with Soviet defense outlays has replaced the earlier euphoria over detente.[14] This general concern has been translated into plans to upgrade both strategic forces and conventional forces—particularly conventional forces in NATO. In sharp contrast to the period of the early 1970s, defense budget projections for FY 1979 through 1984 call for annual increases of about 10 percent (i.e., for a real increase in expenditures since inflation is projected below 10 percent per year), with an annual growth of almost 20 percent in procurement and 12 percent in R&D. Personnel expenditure increases (with the exception of retirement) on the other hand are projected to increase at a rate less than inflation. Thus the outlook is for a real increase in defense expenditures with a shift in budget composition toward procurement for strategic and general purpose forces.[15] This trend was confirmed after the election of Ronald Reagan in 1980. The defense budgets for FY 1981 and FY 1982 contained significant increases over the level of funds allocated in preceding years.

The 1980–83 period also witnessed the promulgation of highly touted reforms of the defense budgeting process. In the spring of 1981, the deputy secretary of defense, Frank Carlucci, proposed a series of thirty-two management reforms designed to simplify and decentralize the weapons acquisition process. This effort to reduce procurement costs included provisions for multiyear contracting, shorter acquisition times, improvement of the readiness and reliability of weapons systems, and a streamlined procurement process within OSD. The Carlucci Reforms, as these initiatives came to be known, had some initial success, but by mid-1983 it was clear that they had not succeeded in keeping weapons acquisitions costs down permanently. The critical problem stemmed from the reforms' emphasis on decentralized decision-making. One result was a failure to reduce duplication in weapons procurement, and hence acquisition costs, to the extent originally intended. (A complete elimination of duplication would not be possible, or even desirable.) Another problem encountered by the reforms was the difficulty in ensuring that all levels of the defense bureaucracy would live up to the spirit of the changes. Whatever the final judgment on the Carlucci Reforms, experience so far suggests that the mammoth problem of reforming the defense budgeting process will not be solved by one set of changes, however well thought out.

On the larger problem of the relationship between the defense budget and national strategy, there is an inherent dilemma in any reasoned analysis of weapons systems and force levels. Ideally, the decision process of PPBS is designed to translate national security goals into objectives, to define programs that meet those objectives, and to evaluate which weapon systems and force structures accomplish the objectives at least cost in budgetary and political terms. There is, however, an inevitable feedback from forces-in-being which influences the perception of national interest. Having a capability to react to a particular threat makes it more likely that a response will be made and may end to bias the evaluation of national objectives toward commitment of force. In discussing the case of the Fast Deployment Logistics (FDL) ships proposed by Secretary McNamara to provide a rapid response capability, Graham Allison noted that such a capability could increase the probability of force commitment in a crisis. He concluded that "creating some kinds of military capabilities does affect decisions about the use of force, and we must find ways of including this fact in choices about such weapons systems."[16]

Certainly there is a link between the development and the probability of using that capability. For that very reason, it is essential that our national security posture be continually modified in response to shifting security objectives and that defense decision-makers remain alert to institutional pressures that might prevent such adjustments. The PPBS, despite its weaknesses, provides a valuable mechanism for raising those key issues and searching for solutions consistent with budget realities.

DISCUSSION QUESTIONS

1. What are the economic constraints on defense planning and budgeting?
2. How should the proportion of total resources directed to national security objectives be determined?
3. What factors limit the ability of Congress to radically shape the defense budget?
4. How are national security objectives defined?
5. How does the federal government determine how much of its resources to allocate to security?
6. How should DOD allocate its resources?
7. What are the essential functions of DOD?
8. What are the advantages and disadvantages of a centralized system of defense planning and budgeting?
9. What is meant by "the McNamara Revolution"? How was this approach to defense planning and budgeting different from previous arrangements? How did the "PPBS" approve work? What is the "six-step sequence" of systems analysis?
10. What is meant by the statement that "there is no such thing as a 'rational decision' process"? If defense planning and budgeting is not the process of "rational decisions," how would you describe the process?
11. How has defense planning and budgeting changed since the McNamara era?
12. What is "zero-base budgeting"? How does it differ from earlier procedure?

RECOMMENDED READING

Allison, Graham T. "Military Capabilities and American Foreign Policy." *Annals* 407 (March 1973).

Deitchman, Seymour J. *New Technology and Military Power: General Purpose Military Forces for the 1980s and Beyond.* Boulder, Colo.: Westview Press, 1979.

Enthoven, Alain C., and Smith, K. Wayne *How Much Is Enough?* New York: Harper & Row, 1971.

Fallows, James. *National Defense.* New York: Random House, 1981.

Korb, Lawrence J. *The Joint Chiefs of Staff: The First Twenty-five Years.* Bloomington: Indiana University Press, 1976.

Schultze, Charles L.; Fried, Edward R.; Rivlin, Alice M.; and Teeters, Nancy H. *Setting National Priorities: The 1972 Budget.* Washington, D.C.: Brookings Institution, 1971.

Singer, Neil M. *Public Microeconomics.* Boston: Little, Brown, 1976.

Sopolsky, Harvey. *The Polaris System Development.* Cambridge, Mass.: Harvard University Press, 1973.

Taylor, Maxwell D. *The Uncertain Trumpet.* New York: Harper, 1959.

Wildavsky, Aaron. *The Politics of the Budgetary Process.* Boston: Little, Brown, 1964.

10

THE NATIONAL SECURITY
DECISION-MAKING PROCESS:
PUTTING THE PIECES TOGETHER

Policy Rings. National security decision-making is complex and fascinating because of the two worlds it involves. As Samuel Huntington explains:

One [world] is international politics, the world of balance of power, wars and alliances, the subtle and brutal uses of force and diplomacy to influence the behavior of other states. The other world is domestic politics, the world of interest groups, political parties, social classes with their conflicting interests and goals.[1]

National security affairs impact on and are influenced by both worlds, for national security involves the application of the national resources to the international arena in an attempt to make the domestic society more secure.

Previous chapters have discussed the individual roles of the president, the Congress, the military, and the intelligence community in national security affairs. This chapter will address the overall decision-making process and attempt to show how these various roles are combined and how the people and organizations that fulfill them interact.

One way to characterize the national policy-making process is as a series of concentric circles.[2] At the center is the president surrounded by his closest advisers. These are the people who, by virtue of position or personal relationship to the president, are involved in the national security issues that require presidential decision. The inner circle of advisers usually includes the secretaries of state and defense, the assistant for national security affairs, the director of central intelligence and more recently, in the Reagan administration, the vice president. The composition of this "inner circle" will of course depend somewhat upon the issue and the desires of a particular president. Closely associated with this innermost circle are the organizations of the executive office of the president and some members of the White House office. Executives of these organizations, such as the Council of Economic

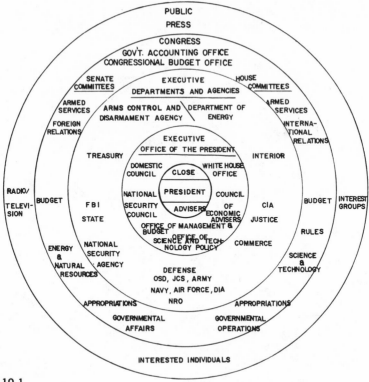

FIG. 10.1
POLICY RINGS

Advisers and the Office of Management and Budget, are members of the president's personal staff and among his most frequent advisers.

Beyond this circle lie the relevant departments of the executive branch and various independent agencies and commissions. Farther still from the center in this particular model is the congressional ring with the organizations of the legislative branch. Beyond them lies the public arena consisting of the media, interest groups, and the general public.

This concept of concentric rings in policy-making obviously focuses upon the president and the executive branch, placing Congress in a very much secondary role. Yet, as explained in preceding chapters, Congress generally plays an important and, in some cases, decisive role in national security affairs. Although it will be useful to pursue the concentric ring analogy for a moment, it should be recognized that in reality Congress occupies a ring in another plane from the executive branch circles.

The boundaries between the policy-making rings should not be viewed as impenetrable barriers. Individuals and even organizations can and do move from one ring to the other depending upon the issue. Most cabinet officers and their deputies and assistants—for example, from the Department of Commerce—are part of the third ring of bureaucracies. When they are invited to participate in the deliberations of the National Security Council (NSC) or its committees, say on a strategic trade issue, they become members of the second ring or even the innermost circle.

There is no one way in which national security decisions are made. Issues range from the relatively mundane, such as how many separate agencies require representation at a foreign embassy, to the more critical, such as the number and type of strategic missiles to be maintained in the U.S. arsenal. There are regularized processes for decision-making, but the issues themselves and the particular ways they arise often dictate the precise method by which they are addressed. Factors such as secrecy, immediacy, political sensitivity, and seriousness of impact tend to place decisions into either the "routine" or "priority" category. Routine decisions generally involve more of the circles of policy-making, while priority decisions, especially those that require great secrecy and quick action, are often made in the inner circle or two circles. An example of the routine would be a proposal for force reductions in the defense budget which is formulated in DOD, debated and reshaped in the inner circle, and sent to Congress where it becomes part of the public arena for discussion. Nixon's opening to China or the *Mayaguez* incident serve as examples of priority decisions in which only a few members of the innermost circle were involved in decision-making.[3]

National Security Council System. The Reagan administration changed some aspects of the NSC system. For example, Vice President Bush was charged with crisis management. However, the basic NSC functions of the Carter administration explained here are likely to remain. As noted in Chapter 5, the NSC is at or near the center of the national security decision-making process within the executive branch and has become the focal point for most important decisions. Which issues are to be placed upon the agenda for full council consideration is a matter tightly controlled by the president, acting with his assistant for national security affairs and perhaps the secretary of state and the secretary of defense.

Before an issue comes to the NSC it will generally have been considered by one of that body's standing subcommittees, namely, the Policy Review Committee (PRC) or the Special Coordination Committee (SCC). If the problem to be dealt with were one of long-term importance such as the desired nature and size of a U.S. military presence in Northeast Asia or in the Middle East, for example, it would be addressed by the PRC. If it were a matter of crisis management, arms control, intelligence operations, or others of a short-term nature, the SCC would be the body to consider it.

In either case, the subcommittee's findings are but recommendations, not decisions. Although the members are cabinet level, or are their deputies, their task is to analyze, recommend, and coordinate, not to decide. If their analysis leads to agreed policy conclusions, their recommendations will go directly to the president. If the members disagree, their analysis and conclusions, including the dissents, will go to the NSC.

Directly supporting the PRC are the Interdepartmental Groups (IGs). They assist the PRC by gathering required information and preparing preliminary or draft reports. Like the parent committee, membership and chairmanship of the IGs vary with the issue and task. Normally, the members are assistant secretaries of the participating agencies or departments.

As noted, crisis situations are usually handled via ad hoc groups established through the SCC machinery. Thus, the Iranian seizure of the American diplomats in Teheran in late 1979 launched an almost daily series of SCC meetings. A well-briefed reporter's authoritative account of how the administration was using the SCC appeared at the time.

Shortly before 9 every morning, the chauffeured black limousines of top officials begin driving through the heavy metal gate from the Ellipse into West Executive Avenue.

The passengers get out by the basement door to the West Wing. Some carry folders of papers, the results of their own staff meetings in departments and agencies around the city, meetings that began before most Washington residents have started work.

The officials hurry inside past guards, turn right, go down a few steps and enter a windowless, wood-paneled Situation Room. Usually a few minutes after the digital clock on the wall has said 9, Brzezinski sits down at one end of the rectangular table and opens the meeting.

Vice President Walter Mondale sits on his right, Secretary of State Cyrus R. Vance on his left, and CIA Director Stansfield Turner faces him at the opposite end of the table. Down the table from Mondale on his side are Defense Secretary Harold Brown and Chairman of the Joint Chiefs of Staff David Jones. By Vance are Attorney General Benjamin R. Civiletti, Treasury Secretary G. William Miller and Energy Secretary Charles Duncan.

A shifting cast of White House officials may be present: Chief of Staff Hamilton Jordan, domestic adviser Stuart Eizenstadt, counsel Lloyd Cutler, special adviser Hedley Donovan and Press Secretary Jody Powell.

The first part of the meeting deals with financial aspects of the crisis, including U.S. banking restrictions on Iran, economic matters, including oil, and legal matters including Iranian students' status here. Then Miller, Duncan and Civiletti leave, and some of the White House people might also depart.

The second part deals with political and military aspects of the crisis.

The officials discuss the latest developments in contacts with Iranian authorities through friendly countries, moves in the United Nations, efforts to obtain support from allies and neutral nations for diplomatic and economic moves, and the changing military dispositions ordered because of the crisis.

The discussion is easy and informal among men who have been working together closely on a number of problems for almost three years. But no problem has demanded the prolonged intensive concentration of this one.

Between the time this administration began and the beginning of the crisis, the SCC had met 40 or 50 times a year. On an average of once a week, it has considered options in arms control negotiations, the Soviet and Cuban build-up in Ethiopia, the Soviet brigade in Cuba, and other problems in the field of foreign policy and national security.

In the six weeks since the embassy in Teheran was taken over, the committee has met about 40 times.

The meetings usually last 60–90 minutes. Then a secretary from Brzezinski's office types up the three pages of minutes. They end with recommendations.

Sometimes Brzezinski goes directly from the meeting to the Oval Office and gives Carter an oral report on the discussions. Sometimes he sends Carter the minutes and talks them over with him later.

On a few occasions, when major recommendations have been involved, the SCC members have gone upstairs to discuss their thinking with Carter. When the president takes charge of the meeting, it turns into a National Security Council session. . . .[4]

As has been the case in preceding administrations, ad hoc study groups are sometimes attached to the NSC staff to analyze particular issues. Such groups may be placed under the directorship of an "outsider" in an attempt to get new insights and to divorce bureaucratic interests from the study. In 1977, Prof. Samuel Huntington, a respected Harvard expert, was designated to chair such a group that conducted an extensive review of U.S.-Soviet competing interests and U.S. military force posture (PRM 10).

Backing up these NSC committees, as well as the council itself, and working under the direction of the assistant for national security affairs is the NSC staff of about thirty to sixty analysts plus clerical support. In the words of its 1980 head, Zbigniew Brzezinski, the staff exists to "assist the President in coordination and implementation of policy, provide a management arm on security questions, and be a think tank for assistance in development of a longer-term perspective on foreign policy".[5] Composed of relatively young analysts with unparalleled access to information, this staff screens, organizes, and often synthesizes most of the information on national security matters which the president sees.

Certain recurring issues, such as defense and intelligence budgets, arms control matters, and alliance relationships are routinely dealt with through the NSC system. Other matters, such as a reappraisal of U.S. policy toward a particular country or the consideration of a one-time issue (e.g., the Panama Canal), are inserted into the policy mill by a special process. This process normally begins with the identification of an issue by any agency in the executive branch. (Theoretically, it could also arise from a congressional initiative.) The agency might be seeking a clarification of policy, a reevaluation of existing policy, or a formulation of policy where none exists. If the policy is interdepartmental in its effects, which national security policy matters almost invariably are, the NSC is the appropriate mechanism to handle it. To introduce it into the NSC system, the agency or department will draft a Presidential Review Memorandum (PRM) and forward it to the NSC staff for consideration. That staff, in turn, reviews the draft and presents it, with recommendations, to the special assistant who discusses it with the president. If the president decides that the issue or policy requires NSC consideration or review, he so directs in a formal PRM.[6]

Of course, the initiative for a PRM need not come from the bottom up; indeed, the president or his assistant for national security affairs will frequently identify an issue for NSC consideration. A PRM requires the agencies and departments that are, or would be, affected by the issue or policy to undertake a study of it and make recommendations for appropriate action. After initial processing by the NSC staff, the PRM is sent to one of the standing IGs or to an ad hoc group created to deal with the particular PRM. The group then has the task of reviewing the responses of the agencies and formulating a draft interagency or interdepartmental response. The group study draft is then sent to the PRC for further debate and consideration and if necessary to the full NSC.[7]

After all this detailed committee and council consideration and debate a decision is made by the president (not the council, which is, again, a recommending body) and then is announced in the form of a Presidential Directive (PD) to the various agencies.[8] The PD prescribes the policies and actions the president wishes implemented and assigns responsibilities and allocates resources accordingly. (It should be noted that, although the foregoing descriptions and labels were those in effect in the 1980 Carter administration, with minor variations they describe the essence of the process which was also followed by the preceding three administrations.)

To give a further hypothetical example of the way the NSC process works, let us assume that the foreign minister of country X in Southeast Asia lets it be known to the American ambassador that, in view of troubled relations with a neighbor strongly supported by the Soviet Union, his country would like to discuss military cooperation, perhaps to include military assistance from the U.S., joint U.S.-X military exercises, and U.S. base rights within X. Passed back through diplomatic channels, undoubtedly with accompanying views from the ambassador, such a message would trigger preliminary discussions among Department of State, Defense, and NSC officials concerned with Southeast Asia, leading to an agreement that the IG for East Asia should examine the matter.

Reprinted by permission of the Chicago Tribune—New York News Syndicate, Inc.

At the subsequent IG meeting will be assistant secretary–level officials from those same agencies, plus a representative from the CIA and perhaps one or two staff officers to back up each principal. The State Department will chair the meeting. From DOD will be the assistant secretary for international security affairs or, more likely, his deputy for East Asia and Pacific affairs, plus a general from the joint staff—perhaps the three-star officer who is director of the joint staff for plans and policy or his deputy. State may well have representatives from its Politico-Military Affairs and Security Assistance offices, as well as the assistant secretary for East Asia and Pacific affairs, who will be chairing the session.

After discussing the elements in the foreign minister's message and their bearing on U.S. interests, the participants turn to the bureaucratic problem: who initiates the draft PRM, what division of labor is called for in the memorandum, and what its general content should be. A joint drafting team from State and DOD is finally decided upon. After several days' or even weeks' work in the various departments and by the drafting team, a draft is developed, circulated for coordination, and forwarded to the assistant to the president for national security.

Meanwhile, the secretary of state will have been informed of this potentially important development (as will the other cabinet level officials) and he may choose to mention it to the president as an information item, noting that a draft PRM is being prepared. The assistant for national security will likely also take the information to the president. The assistant may himself sign the PRM, using the general authority delegated him by the president, or he may get the president's specific approval before signing the PRM.

The PRM, which will be classified at least secret, will go to each of the agencies represented in the IG and, since there will be budgetary implications, will also probably go to OMB. (If so, OMB will ask to be represented in the various study and drafting exercises necessary to respond to the PRM.) Upon receipt of the PRM, which will define rather precisely the nature of the problem to be reviewed and indicate which agency is to take the lead and which may indicate subtasks to be accomplished, each agency will designate appropriate officials to work on the study. At the CIA, the National Intelligence Estimate dealing with X will be reviewed and a special updated and newly focused version of it may be issued. In the Pentagon, the joint staff and International Security Affairs (ISA) will each begin work; they may at various junctures consolidate their efforts or at least coordinate them. The joint staff will be calling on the military services for input as well as undertaking staff work on its own. The air force, for example, will be asked to set forth the type of joint air exercise which would be desirable, the kind of basing arrangement which might be useful, and the type of air force equipment which might be provided in any military assistance program.

In the Department of State (which we will assume is designated the lead agency) not only will the various concerned bureaus begin studying the problem and developing issues, but—at some juncture—the topic of allied involvement will also be addressed. When and how should the Japanese be briefed? What, if anything, should be asked of them? How will the People's Republic of China react? Can it play a constructive role and how should its involvement be managed? What of ASEAN? State will also be responsible for informing the appropriate congressional committees and for maintaining communication with leading members of the Senate and Congress and their key aides as the study proceeds.

Without unduly drawing out this example, we can begin to sense the complexity of the decision process. As the PRM process is completed, the IG, PRC, and perhaps NSC meetings held, the president reaches a decision and issues a PD. The underlying situation in X may change or other complicating factors arise. It is not surprising that the entire decision process generally takes many weeks, often months. Indeed, in a few cases, PRMs finally expire with no PD result. Conversely, there are also PDs issued occasionally without any underlying PRM and study; in such instances, if the PD is a substantive one, either time pressure or familiarity with the issue, or both, induced the president to go directly to PD without the intervening interagency work.

The Bureaucracy. The preceding description of the NSC system as a relatively neat and orderly procedure for national security decision-making is apt to convey an erroneous picture of simplicity where in fact simplicity seldom exists. The NSC serves as a coordinating and advisory body near the center of the policy-making process but beyond it, in the next ring, lie much larger and more complex organizations. This is the ring of the bureaucracy—the so-called permanent government composed largely of career civil servants, Foreign Service officers, and the military who work in the many agencies involved in the daily conduct of national security policy. One need only glance at an organization chart of the State Department's 27,000 personnel or DOD's 950,000 civilian personnel worldwide to realize that the NSC forms only the tip of a huge bureaucratic iceberg.

All of the departments, agencies, and offices in the bureaucratic ring participate to some degree in national security decision-making, for they are the ones conducting the daily business of national security. They develop most of the analyses that go into decision-making and, equally or more importantly, implement the decisions when they are finally made. Most of the input to NSC studies comes from these organizations. It is in this ring that weapons systems are conceived and compared, policy options are formulated, and many of the ordinary or "less important" decisions are made. Much of the budget process described in Chapter 9, for instance, is routinely conducted at this level of the policy process.

For the purposes of studying national security decision-making it is unnecessary to deal with each bureaucracy separately. However, they exhibit important common characteristics. Each of the organizations involved is distinct in that it has a defined mission that contributes to the overall national security goal. These organizational missions are continuing in nature; indeed, the perceived requirement to deal with recurring events or problems is the fundamental reason for establishing bureaucratic organizations.

While distinct, the missions of the organizations are usually stated in rather general or ambiguous terms with considerable latitude for interpretation. The air force, for example, is charged with the mission of "providing an Air Force that is capable, in conjunction with the other armed forces, of preserving the peace and security of the United States." Some organizational missions, such as those of each of the armed services, require development of large capabilities for policy implementation; others, for example, DOD's Office of Program Analysis and Evaluation, require capabilities primarily for research, analysis, evaluation, and planning.*

Once created, organizations tend to take on a life of their own. They develop subunits to carry out portions of the mission, develop standard operating procedures, establish coordinating mechanisms, and recruit and train personnel. The organizations, although usually headed by a presidential political appointee, are staffed with career civil servants and other career personnel—except for the armed forces. As issues appear and disappear and as presidents come and go, these career officials of the organizations do not.[10] They owe their prospects for success and promotion to the organization and develop a sense of loyalty to it.

Typically, career officials are experts in some aspects of their organization's mission and have a relatively narrow organizational outlook, focusing upon the unique importance of their organization to the overall national security mission. In their view national security can be improved primarily through improvements in their organization or agency. The essence of this organizational perspective is captured by Alain Enthoven's description of the "bomber general."

Picture if you will, a man who has spent his entire adult life in the Air Force, flying bombers and leading bomber forces. Bombers are his professional commitment and his expertise. His chances for promotion, public recognition, and success, and those of the officers serving under him, are largely tied to the continued importance of bombers. He believes strongly in what he is doing, that is one of the main reasons he does it well.[11]

Each of the many organizations seeks to be "successful," but success for a government agency is not an easily defined or measured concept. Unlike their business counterparts, government organizations have no product that can be priced and sold for profit on an open market. A dollar measure can be applied to tanks and airplanes and salaries, but not to their final product—national security. Success tends to be measured indirectly, through surrogate means. For example, unable to give a viable definition of "victory" in the traditional sense during the Vietnam War, U.S. government organizations substituted such measures of progress as "body count," weapons captured, tons of bombs dropped, hamlets "secured," etc. We know in retrospect that those numbers were all poor measures of American success. The true measure

---

*Virtually all organizations carry on these latter functions to a degree: the difference between the Navy and PA&E in this respect is one of central mission.

of success was achievement of or failure to meet the national objective—a self-determined government in Vietnam, free from communist coercion.

Another measure of organizational "success" is size; a successful organization is one that is growing, usually in terms of budget and personnel. Organizational growth implies increasing capabilities and greater importance in decision-making and implementation. Morale is tied to these measures of organizational success because career personnel perceive their own chances for influence, promotion, and "success" augmenting as the size of their agency increases.

Organizations seek autonomy; that is, they seek to be as independent as possible from higher authority and safe from threats to their missions and capabilities.

Career officials of an organization believe that they are in a better position than others to determine what capabilities they should have and how they should best fulfill their mission. They attach very high priority to controlling their own resources so that these can be used to support the essence of the organization. They wish to be in a position to spend money allocated to them in the way they choose, to station their manpower as they choose, and to implement policy in their own fashion. They resist efforts by senior officials to get control of their activities.[12]

Organizations pursuing their own interests frequently come into conflict with one another on national security issues. A PRM that directs an overall review of military force posture in Europe could be viewed by the army as a threat to the size of its forces there and by the air force as an opportunity to increase the relative role of air power. The State Department's Bureau of European Affairs may see any force reduction as a threat to good relations with European allies, while the Treasury Department might see a force reduction as a possible means to improve the U.S. balance of payments position vis-à-vis Europe. Each organization's response to a PRM will be designed both to further the national interest and to protect the organization's interests. This quest for security of organizational interests provides a link to the outer rings of the policy-making circles where organizations find support for their positions in the Congress, the media, among interest groups, or in the public at large.

Early in 1978, the navy appeared to be "gearing up" for a battle to protect its organizational interests as the Office of the Secretary of Defense (OSD) decided to deemphasize the navy mission of "power projection" and emphasize the mission of protecting sea lines of communication. This shift in emphasis would imply a reduction in the number of aircraft carriers in the navy. Aircraft carriers, however, are viewed by many naval officers as the "backbone" of the fleet and the essence of the navy.[13] Copies of the secret memoranda dealing with the issue were leaked to the press and Congress became involved in the intra-DOD dispute.[14] The House Armed Services Committee, acting in response to pressure from unhappy navy officials and interest groups (composed largely of retired naval personnel), added to the defense budget funds for a nuclear powered aircraft carrier and a guided missile cruiser. This addition to the budget went against DOD's budget proposal and the intent of OSD's change in emphasis on naval mission.[15] Thus we see the outer rings of the policy-making circles being used to fight a threat to the navy's organizational interests—and perhaps to the national interest as well. (It cannot, of course, be presumed that organizational and national interests are always in opposition.)

The national security decision-making process relies on bureaucracies for such critical tasks as providing information, identifying issues, formulating alternatives, analyzing and evaluating alternatives, making decisions (within certain parameters), and implementing policy. Even when the focus of decision-making is the innermost circle, organizations still provide major inputs and must be relied upon to implement the policy.

Bureaucratic Politics. Thus far the description of national security decision-making has focused upon the NSC system and the bureaucracies operative therein. Decisions are made by people, however, and understanding decision-making necessitates taking account of decision-makers themselves. Bureaucratic politics, as this kind of analysis is named, explains national security decisions as "political resultants,"

resultants in the sense that what happens is not chosen as a solution to a problem but rather results from compromise, conflict, and confusion of officials with diverse interests and unequal influence; political in the sense that the activity from which decisions and actions emerge is best characterized as bargaining along regularized channels among individual members of the government.[16*]

Many individuals who play a role in national security decisions have independent sources of power. As noted earlier the president shares power with Congress and the Supreme Court and, in less formal terms, with his advisers and executive appointees. The secretary of defense, for instance, is an independent power in his own right as the head of a very large organization with a very large budget, the national spokesman on defense issues, and a prominent public figure.[17] He normally enjoys support from some legislators and from interest groups and the public at large.

An individual official's stand on a particular security issue will be determined by many factors, among which are personal analysis of information available, psychological mind-sets or images, organizational interests, the formal position he or she occupies (whether inside or outside government), and personal interests. For critical decisions—those on issues posing the greatest threat to national security—images play a powerful role in determining the stand an individual takes. These images are the consequences of education,

---

*The rational actor and bureaucratic politics models are not mutually exclusive perspectives on the decision process. As noted in Chapter 9, a rational decision process, such as systems analysis, still takes place within a political context. The bureaucratic politics model envisions "players in position" attempting to achieve their goals and interests through political bargaining; each player's goals or objectives, however, may reflect at least an intuitive process of rational analysis.

views of the world, values, past experience, and perceptions of national security interests.[18] President Truman, when informed of the North Korean
invasion of South Korea in 1950, thought of past disastrous experiences with
aggression in Ethiopia, Manchuria, and Austria. The lesson of those experiences seemed to be that aggression must be met with force, and this played
a key part in his decision to respond quickly and with force.[19] Secretary of
State Dean Rusk's various statements during the Vietnam conflict similarly
indicated that pre–World War II experiences shaped his perception of the
national security challenges of the 1960s. Experience deriving from the failure
of military force to achieve "success" in Vietnam powerfully influenced U.S.
policy-makers in the 1970s in their underestimate of the value or potential
of military strength and resolution. In view of Soviet adventurism and mounting Western reverses in the latter 1970s, policy-makers' concepts going into
the 1980s will again be different.

An understanding of the personal images, or *Weltanschauung,* of particular
decision-makers may be sufficient to predict outcomes for particular critical
decisions, but for more routine decisions other factors may dominate a decision-maker's mind. Of course, routine items form the bulk of the national
security decisions. Individuals whose stands on an issue coincide with, and
can be reliably predicted from, their positions within organizations can be
considered "organizational actors," to use Allison's phrase. ("Where you
stand depends on where you sit" is a useful guide.) It is through these actors
that the organizational interests discussed earlier are expressed in the decision-
making and decision-implementing processes.

Influence in decision-making depends on what might be called individual
and position variables. Individual variables include education, the ability to
write, speak, and reason effectively, physical "presence," financial status, and
personal relationships with other key individuals. Position variables include
position within the governmental hierarchy, access to important information,
and command of resources. Robert Kennedy's participation in and influence
on the president's advisory group (Excomm) during the Cuban Missile Crisis
can be attributed not so much to position (attorney general) as to personal
relationship with his brother, the president. Gen. Maxwell Taylor's influence
in a wide range of national security matters during the Kennedy administration
depended largely on his personal attributes. Conversely, the power of the
JCS to influence the SALT debate can generally be attributed not to personal
factors but to the positions of its members. They command information and
resources and are the military advisers to the president, the secretary of
Defense, the National Security Council, and Congress. These multiple roles
give them great influence with many key decision-makers and the legal ability
to appeal to different individuals if their advice is not heeded by one. Henry
Kissinger's influence in the early Nixon administration was a function of both
his personal attributes and his position as assistant for national security affairs.

A key factor in explaining any decision will be the particular individuals
who play a role in the process. To influence a decision an individual must

have access to the decision-making body or decision-making channels. Decision-making channels are usually established in standing operating procedures (SOPs), used by large organizations to regularize the multitude of transactions that occur daily and to routinize or allocate authority for individual decisions on each transaction.

The NSC system specifies the channels for many of the important decisions in national security policy. The PRM process described earlier prescribes the "action channel" for other issues. A PRM is directed to specific departments and agencies, which in turn delegate the study to internal groups or individuals, thus structuring further the decision-making channel. The flow of the PRM up and down the chain, leading to a PD, also gives all members of the IG or PRC direct access to the channel. Individuals sometimes seek to avoid (or to restructure) certain decision-making channels to minimize what they perceive to be adverse impacts; that is, they seek to deny access to their bureaucratic adversaries. The Defense Policy Review Committee (DPRC) of Nixon's NSC serves as an example. The DPRC, chaired by Kissinger, was established to review the annual defense budget and to keep it compatible with foreign policy objectives.[20] The secretary of defense, however, who viewed the DPRC as an encroachment upon his prerogatives by Kissinger, did not cooperate or attend, and the committee quietly expired.

Personal relations among individuals from different agencies can create "informal action channels" that cut across or bypass formal channels or allow an individual access to a decision channel from which he or she might otherwise be excluded. Such relations, which are widespread, are especially important and heavily used when crucial, time-sensitive decisions are being made. Unfortunately, these relations facilitate what is called the "end run," by which an individual bypasses checks in the regular channels and goes directly to the president or other senior officials in hopes of avoiding some perceived disadvantage flowing from the regularized process.

The less time available and the more secrecy and sensitivity involved in a decision the fewer the number of those who have access to the decision-making channel. On one or more of these grounds, some decision-makers will seek to exclude from action channels those whose views might be detrimental to their interests. (Also, they may plead secrecy or sensitivity to hide positions that, if made known publicly, might be unpopular or embarrassing.) Conversely, others with an interest in the outcome of a decision, but excluded from it, may "leak" it to the press, thereby drawing attention to the issue and introducing new or additional pressures on decision-makers.

In a somewhat different and also debatable use of the outer policy-making rings Maj. Gen. John Singlaub, the third-ranking U.S. officer in Korea, predicted to a *Washington Post* reporter in the spring of 1977 that the Carter administration's decision to withdraw U.S. troops from Korea would lead to war. This statement from a responsible military officer attracted much attention in the press, particularly after the president recalled General Singlaub and had him reassigned. The House Armed Services Committee began hearings on the subject, hoping to prove that the Carter decision had overridden the objections of his military advisers. In the face of this opposition and similar objections in the Senate, the administration responded, first with a slowdown and modification of the original withdrawal plan.[21] In 1979, this was followed by a freeze on further withdrawals. Tough congressional opposition to any withdrawal from South Korea remains.

Open disagreement with superiors, in which an official places his or her career on the line, may be disruptive of hierarchical control of the bureaucracy, but it can serve the national interest by providing a means of appeal to upper decision levels or the public on major issues. By contrast, the practice of secretly leaking classified information is disloyal and holds many dangers. Left unchecked, it can, for example, make the keeping of vital secrets impossible and create distrust and paralysis within the decision-making process.[22]

Decision Implementation. Once a decision is made—even by the president of the United States—the decision process does not end. The critical task of implementation remains. A PD may more or less specify policy and actions, but implementation resides in the hands of the organizations of the third ring. Between the president and the final implementers of his decisions lie many levels of hierarchical control. At each level, there is a danger that a policy decision will be misunderstood—inadvertently or advertently. At each level, the individual responsible must understand the decision and then translate it into more specific directives for his or her own subordinates. If one assumes 90 percent accuracy of transmittal at each level and ten levels between the president and the person "in the field," there is only a 35 percent chance that the person in the field will be directed as the president intended.

Neither the president nor his staff has the capacity to specify actions in such detail as to leave no room for manipulation or misunderstanding, nor is great specificity always desirable, since it would waste the expertise in problem solving and implementation that resides at lower levels. As a result, presidents are frequently frustrated by what comes out at the other end of the process. Even that most skillful of presidents, Franklin Roosevelt, remarked:

The Treasury is so large and far-flung and ingrained in its practices that I find it is almost impossible to get the action and results I want—even with Henry [Morgenthau] there. But the Treasury is not to be compared with the State Department. You should go through the experience of trying to get any changes in the thinking, policy, and action of the career diplomats and then you'd know what a real problem was. But the Treasury and the State Department put together are nothing compared with the Na-a-vy. The admirals are really something to cope with—and I should know. To change anything in the Na-a-vy is like punching a feather bed. You punch it with your right and you punch it with your left until you are finally exhausted, and then you find the damn bed just as it was before you started punching.[23]

The cabinet officers and other heads of agencies are appointed by the president, but they are responsible, as well, to Congress, to the staffs, to their "clients," and to themselves. The president appoints them mindful of the constraints of party and, in most cases, the advice and consent of the Senate, hoping that they bring to their positions personal views that are compatible with his own. Over time, however, even compatible heads of agencies tend to view issues from the particular perspectives of the organizations they head and on which their ability to function depends. A president can, of course, remove a recalcitrant agency head from office. But this action tends to reflect unfavorably on the president's initial decision to select the individual, and it also tends to antagonize the supporters of the individual in Congress, among interest groups, and the public. Simultaneous decapitation of several departments, such as President Carter executed in the summer of 1979, is bound to call into question the president's leadership ability, as public and Congressional opinion at the time showed.[24]

Even if the president is ready to fire laggards, he cannot override most objections by fiat. As Richard Neustadt has observed, "Underneath our images of Presidents-in-boots, astride decisions, are the half-observed realities of Presidents-in-sneakers, stirrups in hand, trying to induce particular department heads or Congressmen or Senators, to climb aboard."[25]

Getting the bureaucracy on board in making a decision is not the president's only problem with the exeuctive branch. Because a decision has been reached, it does not necessarily mean that the decision will be finally carried through as the president wishes. As Henry Kissinger has observed, any bureaucracy worth its salt has a considerable capacity to delay, attenuate, and obstruct; even more trying, it can leak confidential information to the press in an effort to reverse or weaken a decision it does not like. This latter difficulty, which has grown to serious proportions in the last decade or so, caused President Johnson to advise Kissinger, "Read the columnists, and if they call a member of your staff thoughtful, dedicated, or any other friendly adjective, fire him immediately. He is your leaker."[26]

"Even when the President does devote his time and effort and the issue is critical, disobedience or mishandling (of a presidential order) can occur."[27] During the Cuban Missile Crisis, President Kennedy allegedly was led to believe that U.S. forces were not in contact with Soviet forces, whereas, in fact, the U.S. Navy was forcing Soviet submarines to the surface in the Caribbean. President Kennedy ordered the navy to move the blockade closer to Cuba; the navy did not initially comply. He ordered the government to avoid provocative intelligence operations during the crisis, yet an American U-2 strayed over the Soviet Union at the peak of the crisis. Air force planes located on bases in the southeastern United States were ordered dispersed; a subsequent aerial photograph flight ordered by the president showed the planes still lined up, wing tip to wing tip.[28]

In order to reduce the probability of faulty implementation, a president must get deeply involved—and early on—in a crisis; he must clearly articulate what he wants done. And he must have a thorough grasp of the capabilities and organizational routines of the participating bureaucratic players. Deep presidential involvement in a particular issue, however, has high opportunity costs. In an environment of cascading deadlines and complex problems, the president seldom has the luxury of detailed involvement, full articulation of his program, or thorough oversight. Should he choose to dedicate himself to a particular policy issue, other programs and policies will not stand still. They too clamor for attention and, lacking presidential direction, they are a potential source of difficulty. President Eisenhower was so absorbed with the Suez Crisis of 1956 that he gave scant attention to the Hungarian Revolution, which exploded almost simultaneously.

Yet the responsibilities of his office are so comprehensive and demanding that the president *must* order his priorities rather than let his attention be diffused. Of course, he must be prepared to refocus his attention and follow through actions as priorities and situations change. It is small wonder that the implementation of a policy is often as difficult and frustrating to a president as the development of that policy in the first place.

Conclusion. Two trends are apparent in surveying national decision-making and the actors and processes therein, namely, increasing centralization and the recently greatly strengthened role of Congress. The trend towards centralized control in the executive branch has been underway continuously since the National Security Act of 1947, reaching something like its present plateau in the mid 1970s. This trend, which has been driven by the increased complexity and dangers of the nuclear age, has been fueled by the communications revolution that has permitted far greater central direction of large organizations than was possible in the past. It has occurred both within the individual departments and agencies in the decision-making process and also in the overall process itself. In this latter context, the increasingly dominant role of the NSC staff and the assistant to the president who heads it may have reached its natural limit. Counterforces grew in the late 1970s as it became apparent that the power available to the assistant to the president as the manager of the NSC system can also be used to take control of it. The Reagan administration sought during its first months in office to cope with this problem by redefining the role of the national security adviser, Richard V. Allen, and by vesting Vice President Bush with new authority and resources for crisis management.

Despite these changes, the precise role of the national security adviser remained in a state of flux. After Allen's resignation in early 1982, President Reagan announced new administrative procedures for the NSC system. These included the establishment of three Senior Interdepartmental Groups (SIGs) for foreign policy, defense, and intelligence. Each SIG, chaired by the appropriate deputy secretary, was to formulate policy objectives, develop policy options, and make policy recommendations for its assigned area. Under the SIGs, Interdepartmental Groups were formed to deal with specific functional and regional issues. This new system faithfully reflected the president's decentralized governing style and provided a potentially larger role for the secretary of state.[29] In 1980, Alexander Haig had sought to expand his role as secretary of state, only to be confronted by a White House staff that saw its own foreign policy role being upstaged. The result was Haig's resignation in 1982. Complicating the operation of the relatively clear, pyramidal NSC structure of the Reagan administration (after the 1982 changes) was the extremely close personal relationship that the new national security adviser, William Clark, enjoyed with the president. The fact that Clark, a newcomer to international affairs, tended to view national security issues in a domestic political perspective only muddied the picture further. By mid-1983, Clark had succeeded in once again expanding the NSC's influence in foreign and defense policy at the expense of the State Department.[30] The *modus operandi* was to avoid publicity, hold issues close to the White House, coordinate approaches to the Congress, and move forward vigorously with the president's programs. One could argue that, under Clark, the NSC has moved closer to what many have suggested is an important goal: defining policy alternatives in ways that reflect the president's broad interests and not those of a particular government department or agency.[31]

The increased power of Congress in national security affairs, one of the most striking developments of the latter 1960s and 1970s, presents an interesting counterpoint. Not only does the congressional role blunt and diffuse the power of the president and his centralized decision-making apparatus, but it also represents a sharp contrast to that power in that the Congress has itself increasingly become decentralized in its decision-making. As party strength has declined and the authority of the committee chairpersons dwindled, single-interest groups have multiplied and individual legislators have become less inclined to follow the leadership of the party and congressional leaders and the president.

The juxtaposition of these two trends poses the unwelcome prospect that in the 1980s the president and the Congress will continue to be at odds and that neither will be prepared to give way, short of major national emergencies.

DISCUSSION QUESTIONS

1. Presidents and high-level appointees come and go, but the career civil servants, the military, and the Foreign Service officers stay. What impact would you expect this to have on national security policy?

2. The NSC staff has been relatively small (30–60 people) and has been composed of many relatively junior people who lack high-level experience in government. What are the good or bad points of this?

3. It is sometimes argued that the constraints imposed upon a president by Congress, by the public, and by a slow-moving bureaucracy virtually preclude anything but incremental changes in national security policy. To what extent is this true? Are large changes in the external (international) environment beyond the capability of the president, or can large changes be made through presidential initiative?

4. If bureaucratic politics characterizes decision-making and is a bargaining process among varying interests, is there anything in the system that insures that appropriate interests have a voice? Who or what determines the weight of the different interests? Does DOD have too much weight in the bargaining?

5. One critique of the "bureaucratic politics" of national security decision-making is that it obscures the power of the president and undermines the assumptions of democratic politics by relieving high officials of responsibility. What positive or beneficial effects may be associated with bureaucratic politics in the national security decision-making process?

6. Democracy is largely defined by the requirement that the ruled be able to hold their rulers accountable for their decisions and actions. Does the existing national security decision-making machinery degrade accountability? Can you suggest ways to alleviate the problem, to the extent that it exists?

7. Congress is formally excluded from the executive branch policy *formulation* process. Would the system work more smoothly if Congress were included earlier in the policy formulation process? Given the inevitable tension between the legislative and executive branches, could such a system be made to work?

8. Can the problem of "leaks" be dealt with without police-state types of controls?

RECOMMENDED READING

Allison, Graham. *The Essence of Decision: Explaining the Cuban Missile Crisis.* Boston: Little, Brown, 1971.

Bernstein, Marver H. *The Job of the Federal Executive.* Washington, D.C.: Brookings Institution, 1958.

Enthoven, Alain C., and Smith, K. Wayne. *How Much Is Enough?* New York: Harper & Row, 1971.

Fallows, James. *National Defense.* New York: Random House, 1981.

Halperin, Morton H. *Bureaucratic Politics and Foreign Policy.* Washington, D.C.: Brookings Institution, 1974.

Hilsman, Roger. *The Politics of Policy Making in Defense and Foreign Affairs.* New York: Harper & Row, 1971.

Hunter, Robert E. *Presidential Control of Foreign Policy: Management or Mishap?* CSIS Washington Papers no. 91. New York: Frederick A. Praeger, 1982.

Huntington, Samuel P. *The Common Defense.* New York: Columbia University Press, 1961.

Nash, Henry T. *American Foreign Policy: Response to a Sense of Threat.* Homewood, Ill.: Dorsey Press, 1973.

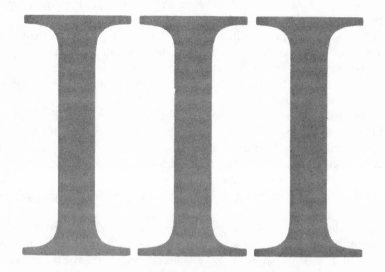

ISSUES OF NATIONAL STRATEGY

Previous chapters have dealt with the setting of national security and the primary actors and processes that determine American responses to perceived threats. In Part 3 we turn our attention to an analytic approach to the strategic problems that confront the United States. Events of the latter 1970s and the early 1980s indicate that problems of strategy and force deployment have not lost their saliency. And, if one believes that the use of force as an instrument of national policy is on the decline, there remains a set of strategic problems that U.S. national security policy must address.

A wonder of the age is that nuclear weapons, originally thought to be the ultimate weapons at the disposal of states, have not been used since 1945. It is perhaps a great (and fortunate) irony that the primary use of nuclear weapons is to prevent or deter adversaries from using them. However, the absence of nuclear weapons use since the attacks on Hiroshima and Nagasaki should not prevent our focus on the possible uses of nuclear weapons and the impact of such perhaps unlikely events. Chapter 11 addresses this topic.

Global war has been prevented since World War II, but limited wars and revolutionary wars of various kinds have not. If these are the more likely contingencies for which we must plan, then an understanding of their nature is critical to the design of viable national security policies. Chapters 12 and 13 provide analytic perspectives for these types of conflict.

In Chapter 14 we turn to a different and increasingly important type of security issue, namely, economics. Over the longer run (and perhaps in some instances the short run as well) nothing will be so important in shaping the international system as the pattern of production and distribution of goods and services. This topic, with special attention to possible energy and raw materials, makes up the bulk of the chapter. A brief examination of economic warfare is also included.

As we study the uses of force, it is wise to bear in mind the impact of technology on strategy. Tactical and strategic doctrine must be related to military capabilities, which are constantly changing in response to rapid advances in technology. This change necessitates an almost continual adaptation of strategy and policy in incorporate our own improvements in technology and to counter those of potential adversaries. This is the subject of Chapter 15.

Each of these strategic problems is treated separately for purposes of study and analysis, but you should keep in mind how inextricably they are linked to one another. Any policy directed toward one influences the others. By the end of Part 3 you should have a good understanding of these linkages.

11

NUCLEAR STRATEGIES

Nuclear strategy encompasses three elements: (1) the strategic *purpose* that the nuclear arsenal is intended to accomplish, (2) the strategic *policies* that are, at least theoretically, designed to accomplish those strategic purposes, and (3) the strategic force design or *programs* to support policies.

Before proceeding further, two pairs of concepts require definition and explanation. Nuclear forces are discussed as being either *counterforce* or *countervalue* and, in another dimension, as being designed for (or trying to achieve) a *disarming first-strike capability* or a *second-strike capability*. Since these pairs of terms are invariably used in discussions of nuclear strategy, it is necessary to understand their meanings.

A counterforce capability implies something about both weapons design and targeting strategy. In terms of the former, counterforce weapons can be relatively small in yield but must be highly accurate.* Accuracy is essential to the targeting strategy of counterforce weapons that aim directly at the enemy's military forces (and especially at *nuclear delivery* forces) as opposed to destroying the adversary's society in a massive way. Counterforce targets include strategic and tactical nuclear forces, command and control centers, airfields, defensive weapon systems, early warning radars, field units and associated equipment, resupply centers, major transportation centers, and so forth.

Countervalue weapons and strategies do not target *primarily* on military installations but rather emphasize destruction of industrial bases and population centers. Phrased differently, countervalue forces attempt to punish by destroying the "value centers" of the enemy society. As is obvious, this kind of targeting strategy is more efficiently served by "area" weapons, implying

---

*One of the most recent examples is the enhanced radiation weapon or "neutron bomb," which has been assailed by the U.S.S.R. as being a counterforce weapon because it limits collateral damage to civilian buildings while aiming at military installations or military troop formations.

larger yield weapons or many warheads; a high degree of accuracy is not so important.

A disarming first-strike capability, as the term is commonly used, is one that can destroy a sufficient portion of the enemy's retaliatory capability (*if* the attacker attains sufficient surprise) to make acceptable the amount of damage the attacker will suffer in retaliation. Having this capability implies having counterforce weapons and targeting strategy as well as a sufficient number of weapons. A second-strike capability is just the converse. It implies that, regardless of the damage that might be inflicted by an enemy's initial strike, the possessor of second-strike capability will have sufficient surviving capability to inflict *unacceptable damage* on the initiator of the conflict. Whereas a disarming first-strike force need not be mobile, sheltered, or concealed, a second-strike force will probably need such defense measures if it is to be exposed to high damage and still survive. These definitions are dynamic and largely dependent on the changing relative strength of two opponents.

Purposes of Nuclear Forces. The most basic purpose of U.S. nuclear forces has been to deter nuclear attack upon America and its allies and friends. Analysis of this task in all its variations is complex and sophisticated; we will explore some of its dimensions in succeeding pages. In addition to deterrence, former Secretary of Defense Harold Brown defined four other objectives.

We must also strive to maintain *stability* in the nuclear balance, both over the long term and in crisis situations. Because nuclear weapons also have political significance, we must maintain actual and perceived *essential equivalence* with Soviet strategic nuclear forces. We also want the structure of our nuclear forces to be such as to facilitate the negotiation of equitable and verifiable *arms control* agreements. Finally, in the event deterrence fails, our forces must be capable . . . of *preventing Soviet Victory* and securing the most favorable possible outcome for U.S. interests.[1] (Emphasis added)

Before returning to the topic of deterrence, we will briefly explore each of these other objectives of nuclear forces. *Essential equivalence* means that U.S. and Soviet strategic nuclear forces have roughly the same capabilities, and that they are recognized as such. Understanding this condition is important, for various political and other advantages would flow to the Soviet Union if other nations perceived that it was able to intimidate or blackmail the United States from a position of nuclear superiority. Such equivalence does not mean that U.S. forces are the "mirror image" of Soviet strategic forces. It does not imply matching capabilities in each type of nuclear weapon; rather, it is aimed at preventing gross disparities between the two sides' strategic forces. Under essential equivalence, one side's advantages are balanced by the other's advantages. Frequently, essential equivalence is defined as a state of general parity between the aggregate capabilities of U.S.-Soviet strategic offensive forces (measured by such static indicators as accuracy, reliability, survivability, command and control, megatonnage, throw weight, reentry vehicles, and strategic nuclear delivery vehicles). For the concept to be of maximum relevance, the parameters of essential equivalence should be expanded to include dynamic elements such as relative war-survival and recovery programs, strategic defensive programs, and strategic doctrines.

Strategic stability in the long-term sense means that the nuclear balance is not so shaky that one side—by a technological breakthrough or by doctrinal change, for example—could threaten the capability of the other's strategic forces to retaliate. *Short-term* or *crisis stability* "means that even in a prolonged and intense confrontation the Soviet Union would have no incentive to inititate an exchange, and also that we would feel ourselves under no pressure to do so."[2] Crisis stability is built by strengthening detection capabilities and command and control arrangements and by reducing vulnerability through hardening, dispersion, mobility, and similar measures.

Since the United States views equitable and verifiable arms control measures as contributors to national security, it seeks to incorporate these characteristics in its nuclear arsenal. The United States has avoided building the number and type of weapons that might be construed as creating a full first-strike counterforce capability.

Strategic Policies. Chapter 2 provides a brief discussion of the general concept of deterrence. Our purpose here is to refine the concept further as it is translated into U.S. strategic policies. Deterrence is both a purpose of the American nuclear arsenal and also the fundamental strategic policy of the United States in that it largely determines the type of force to be sought, how it is to be deployed, and the manner of its employment if necessary.

Deterrence of strikes against one's homeland by the threat of action by retaliatory forces capable of surviving a first strike and delivering an unacceptably damaging blow in return is the starting point for analysis of this policy. Since such deterrence rests upon the threat of retaliation, the threatened reaction must be of such magnitude as to make the objective of the hostile act appear excessively costly. Further, the retaliatory threat must be credible, and must be supported by visible, effective, employable military capabilities.

Minimum or *finite* deterrence is the least demanding type of deterrence policy. In essence, it entails having a relatively small but invulnerable force, which is countervalue-targeted. For this policy a small submarine-launched force may be all that is needed. Parity or superiority in strategic nuclear forces is not necessary. Theoretically, such a small strategic nuclear force, because of its countervalue targeting, *could* provide a sufficient deterrent to general nuclear war while also contributing to a slowing of the arms race. A major weakness of finite deterrence, however, is its inflexibility. It is an all or nothing strategy—and not particularly relevant to the U.S. problem.

Since the viability of minimum deterrence policy depends on the "assured destruction" of countervalue targets, a judgment must be made about the amount of destruction, and of which types of target, to be accomplished.

Such a judgment will, of course, be subjective and dependent in large part on the type of society to be targeted and its ability to withstand stress. As noted in Chapter 4, *unacceptable damage* has been officially defined by the United States, in terms of a U.S.-Soviet nuclear war, as enemy population fatalities of 20 to 25 percent and industrial destruction of 50 to 70 percent.[3] (This is only an educated guess on the part of defense officials. There is not, of course, any conceivably way of predicting precisely the percentage of population and industrial which would have to be destroyed to serve as a deterrent.)

Mutual assured destruction (MAD) is a related concept, resting on the notion that two adversaries each hold the strategic doctrine of assured destruction. The concept implies not only that each side has an assured destruction capability but also that both sides believe in its utility as a strategic doctrine and do not seek to build forces beyond those required for assured destruction.

Currently only the United States and the U.S.S.R. clearly possess sufficient nuclear strength to attain even a minimum deterrent posture. However, other nuclear powers with small strategic forces can be said for two reasons to have an element of minimum deterrence in their policies and forces: first, deterrence is a psychological as well as an objective capability and, second, the dynamics of strategic nuclear forces involve all the nuclear states. Underlying the entire concept of deterrence is the premise that one's opponent will act rationally, and a rational decision-maker does not need too high a probability of sustaining massive damage to make a risk unacceptable. Two direct opponents cannot be considered in a vacuum, even when the two antagonists are the United States and the U.S.S.R.

Deterrence theory can be divided roughly into two schools of thought, although there are many variants of each that make this dual categorization less than tidy.[4] The first school may be labeled *prewar deterrence* and the second, *war-fighting deterrence*. The first school has been officially predominant, both in official and unofficial circles, in the United States since the early or mid 1960s.

As noted in Chapter 4, by 1969 U.S. policy-makers had reached the conclusion that neither could "win" by striking first. The Soviet were believed to have achieved rough nuclear parity, and both sides had acquired secure second-strike capabilities. There appeared to be no rationale for and, given widespread disaffection with U.S. policies in Vietnam, little support for U.S. defense spending increases to achieve nuclear superiority. MAD was, in American eyes, ratified formally in the 1972 SALT I agreement to limit strategic offensive arms and to curtail U.S. and Soviet ballistic missile defense (BMD) systems. Since both sides agreed formally in SALT I not to protect themselves from each other, MAD seemed to be an acceptable nuclear policy to both. It was assumed by Americans that, with no possibility of "winning" in any meaningful sense, stability would prevail at the nuclear strategic level even during crises involving the superpowers.

The second school of thought about strategic policies has the ominous title of war-fighting, but it, too, has the strategic purpose of deterrence. This school is based on the view that the MAD posture based on countervalue targeting present an American president with an "all or nothing" choice. "All" would mean a second strike against Soviet industrial and population centers, inviting certain retaliation in kind by remaining Soviet forces, or mutual suicide. "Nothing" would mean a decision not to retaliate and to negotiate for the best settlement possible—in other words, surrender. According to this view, in order to achieve deterrence the United States should adopt a war-fighting strategic policy grounded on prevailing in war. The proponents of this school have argued that: (1) it is uncertain that Soviet leaders would be deterred from striking first by the threat of a second strike against their population and industrial centers, especially if they thought they had acquired the capability of destroying in a first strike a large part of the U.S. nuclear retaliatory force; (2) the choice of responding to any kind of Soviet first strike by annihilating Soviet cities presents an American president with an option he might fear to take in view of the consequent destruction of U.S. cities; (3) should the Soviets hold or develop a theory of victory in nuclear war, the United States would be unprepared to conduct such a war; and (4) U.S. programs designed to deter against Soviet attack through MAD would not permit America to fight a nuclear war and survive.[5]

Criteria of Strategic Policy Effectiveness. Both schools of thought are founded on the strategic purpose of deterring nuclear attack against the United States; their major disagreements are over the optimal means of achieving that purpose. Both schools agree generally that deterrence requires possession of a credible U.S. second-strike capability.

Nuclear deterrence through a second-strike capability can be said to have eight possible ingredients.[6]

1. Credibility
2. Steady-state peacetime systems
3. Active defense
4. Passive defense
5. Penetration of opponent's active defense
6. Command, control, and communications
7. Penetration of opponent's passive defense
8. Coordinated targeting

Credibility. Credibility rests on clear understanding concerning what one wishes to do and is capable of doing. Although it is possible to argue that one acquires some deterrent value from a reputation for being unpredictable, it is not a position upon which responsible policy-makers can afford to base nuclear strategic policy. Nuclear strategy is developed to protect the most fundamental of interests, namely, the survival of the United States and its allies to whom protection under its nuclear umbrella has been explicitly extended. To deter the Soviets from a nuclear first strike against the continental United States or the homelands of its allies, U.S. policy-makers declare through various media their strategic nuclear policy, specifying U.S. vital interests, in the protection of which America would execute nuclear strikes against the U.S.S.R. Ideally, declaratory policy should delineate the geographical or situational extent of the interests at issue, that is, lines the Soviets cannot cross with impunity.

Readiness of the United States to execute the threatened strikes should be unquestionable. Such readiness is in part a matter of capability, but, equally critical, it is also a matter of will. If Soviet leaders believe their American counterparts have insufficient public support or lack the nerve to deliver on their threatened counteraction, then deterrence will fail.

Declaratory policy based on the will to retaliate is empty unless the United States has the nuclear capability to do what it says. You will recall from Chapter 2 that capability is always relative to that possessed by adversaries and that the analytical net assessment involved is both difficult and subject to error.[7] The elements included in various possible American responses are not, of course, elaborated in declaratory policy. The specifics are contained in a highly classified document known as the Single Intergrated Operational Plan (SIOP). Only a few of the most senior national security decision-makers and high-level Department of Defense civilian and military officials see the SIOP—specifically, those charged with SIOP planning and execution in the event of certain kinds and levels of Soviet aggression.

In short, we can conclude that clearly stated interest, plus will, plus capability equals credibility of commitment. In earlier decades, when U.S. strategic nuclear capabilities clearly exceeded those of the Soviet Union, the credibility of U.S. declaratory policy was presumably high. In an age of perceived nuclear parity or perhaps even Soviet nuclear superiority, U.S. capability may be called into question and the credibility of U.S. declaratory policy thereby severely diminished.

Steady-State Peacetime Systems. Maintenance of strategic nuclear forces involves large sums indeed, although the total amount in the U.S. case has been only a small percentage of the defense budget. The FY 1984 budget request for strategic forces was $28 billion in a total defense budget of $274.1 billion.[8] Aside from expenditures for new strategic weapons there are costs involved in maintaining systems already deployed. Strategic missiles, aircraft, and submarines, just as the family automobile, require periodic maintenance and repair parts, as well as trained operators, mechanics, and other trained technicians. All the equipment and personnel must be at specified levels of readiness all the time and must be tested regularly to insure that those levels are maintained. (Of course, even so, equipment can break down and people can make mistakes, as the accidental explosion at a Titan II missile silo in Arkansas in September 1980 demonstrated.

Funding for all these related programs must be at reasonably stable levels to maintain the high state of readiness required. The U.S. strategic forces budget trend had been declining for several years prior to FY 1979. Since that year, Congress has consistently approved the president's requests for increases in funding for strategic forces. Even so, strategic force spending still accounts for no more than 10 percent of the FY 1984 budget.

Active Defense. Active defense systems are designed, first, to give early warning of a Soviet attack and, second, to provide various capabilities for tracking and destroying delivery vehicles or warheads before they are within range to destroy targets in the United States.

Early warning can be provided in a number of ways. Although the Soviets could be expected to exercise deception to deny information, it might be anticipated that their first launch would take place during a crisis period, when the United States and its allies would be especially alert. Western intelligence would be alert to detect preparations for launch such as unusual communications traffic or military movements. NATO satellite reconnaissance and subsurface ocean sonar arrays at ocean choke points might detect

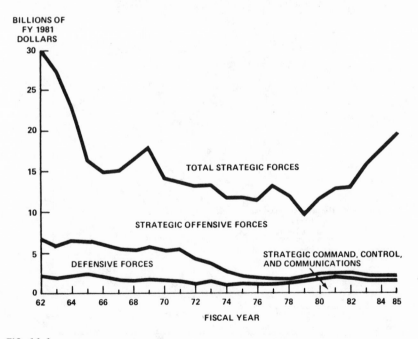

FIG. 11.1
STRATEGIC FORCES BUDGET TREND
Source: U.S., *Department of Defense Annual Report, Fiscal Year 1981* (Washington, D.C.: U.S. Government Printing Office, 1980), p. 71.

unusual activity among Soviet launch systems. The U.S. Ballistic Missile Early Warning System (BMEWS), with stations located in Alaska, Greenland, and England, perimeter acquisition radars (PARS) in North Dakota, and south coast radar warning systems against submarine-launched ballistic missiles (SLBMs) and air-launched ballistic missiles (ALBMs) could all provide confirmation about the character of the attack. Warning would be available also from NORAD (North American Air Defense Command), located inside Cheyenne Mountain in Colorado, as well as from the Distant Early Warning (DEW) radar line with thirty-one stations along the 70th parallel in northern Canada, the Pinetree Line with twenty-four stations in mid Canada, and other phased-array radars based on the east and west coasts of the United States. The United States has also developed, but not yet deployed, over-the-horizon (OTH) radars that can preclude undetected enemy launches from radar "blind

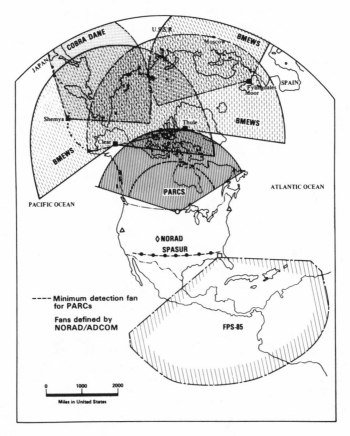

FIG. 11.2
U.S. SLBM WARNING SITES (except satellites)
Source: John M. Collins, *U.S.-Soviet Military Balance: Concepts and Capabilities, 1960–1980* (New York: McGraw-Hill, 1980), p. 160.

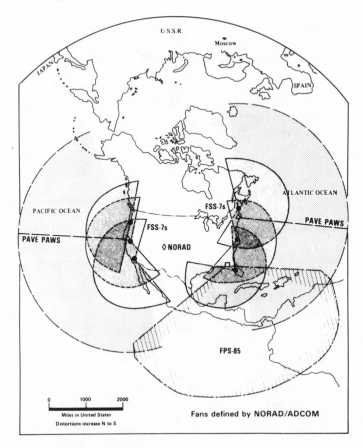

FIG. 11.3
U.S. ICBM WARNING SITES (except satellites)
Source: John M. Collins, *U.S.-Soviet Military Balance: Concepts and Capabilities, 1960–1980* (New York: McGraw-Hill, 1980), p. 161.

spots" resulting from curvature of the earth.[9] Whether all these measures taken together can eliminate surprises is not quite certain; but they must raise overwhelming doubts in Soviet minds about the prospect.

Active defense includes the capability to defeat enemy bombers and missiles in flight. Manned interceptor aircraft, airborne warning and control system (AWACS) aircraft, and surface-to-air missiles can be used against enemy aircraft or air-launched cruise missiles (ALCMs). A ballistic missile defense (BMD) system consisting of radars and antiballistic missiles (ABMs) can be employed against in-flight enemy ballistic missiles. After hotly debating the issue in the latter 1960s (see Chapter 6), the United States initially planned to deploy ABM sites, at various locations around the country to protect its land-based missile sites. The SALT I ABM Treaty limit to two sites resulted in the cancellation of the planned nationwide ABM deployment. Subsequently the U.S. chose not to deploy any ABM sites.

Although the U.S. has no BMD, research and development on the problem continue, and, for reasons to be explained later, there has been a renewed interest in deploying a space- or land-based missile defense system. (In FY 1984, planned funding for development of BMD systems and advanced technology was $709.3 million.[10] Since by far the greatest nuclear threat to the United States is a ballistic missile, it must be noted that the United States has virtually no active defense. As observed in Chapter 16, the Soviet picture is somewhat different.

Passive Defense. Passive defense can take many forms. The most basic of these is to complicate the enemy's targeting by maintaining all three legs of the strategic TRIAD—strategic bombers, ICBMs, and SLBMs. Even though land-based ICBMs are the most vulnerable, merely having them compels the adversary to attack them in a major assault and thereby causes attrition of enemy offensive missiles. For land-based missiles, there are several possible passive defensive measures: missile sites can be "hardened" by reinforced concrete; more extensively, the systems can be installed in bedrock where drilling and construction are much more complicated; missiles can be made mobile by placing them on above-ground or underground motorized road or railway transporters and theoretically, missiles can be placed close together in a "dense pack," whereby an attacker's warheads must be aimed so close together that the detonations from the first to arrive in the target area destroy following missiles (an effect labeled "fratricide").

Passive defense for strategic aircraft carrying nuclear weapons can be achieved by placing them in the air during times of crisis or by increasing the fraction kept at a high level of ground alert. Currently, about 30 percent of U.S. strategic bombers are maintained in the latter category.

Passive defense for nuclear- or diesel-powered submarines armed with nuclear missiles is inherent both in their mobility and in the difficulty of detecting their locations at sea. Approximately one-third of the nuclear submarine force is docked for maintenance, refit, or repair at any given time.[11] Forgoing these routine procedures during a period of crisis and placing more of the force at sea where they cannot be targeted also enhances their security.

A final aspect of passive defense—civil defense (CD)—concerns survival of the American population and its leadership. For many reasons, CD programs were weakened during the latter 1960s and 1970s. There are high costs associated with constructing shelters, prestocking them with provisions that are secure against pilferage and theft, and planning and exercising plans for public communications, warning, and relocation. Cost, however, was not the major consideration. Americans by and large, were not persuaded that CD made sense. When the MAD posture was adopted and BMD deployment discarded, it was concluded that it would be unwise to spend large sums to provide marginal protection for the American population.

For reasons to be discussed later, by 1979 U.S. interest in civil defense renewed. In July of that year, responsibility for U.S. CD programs was shifted by executive order (no. 12148) from the secretary of defense to the director of the Federal Emergency Management Agency (FEMA). This change moved the CD budget from DOD to FEMA. Since 1979 the CD budget has gone from $100 million to $900 million in FY 1982 and back to $560 million for FY 1984. The purpose of CD programs in 1984 is consistent with Secretary of Defense Harold Brown's assessment in his 1981 report to Congress that CD is intended "to enhance, in the event of nuclear war, the survivability of the American people and its leadership, thereby improving the basis for eventual national recovery."[12]

Command, Control, and Communications (C³). At a minimum, the president, charged with the release of strategic nuclear weapons, must be able to communicate his decisions to control the execution and termination of nuclear strikes. He must also have the capability to maintain constant communications with the leadership of potential adversaries. Estimates vary on the time available for the president to make and communicate his decisions for response after a Soviet ballistic missile launch. In the event of a Soviet land-based ICBM launch, the first incoming missiles might arrive on a U.S. target in twenty to thirty minutes. There is the possibility that Washington could be destroyed by Soviet SLBMs with as little as ten to twelve minutes warning.

The United States has developed a World-Wide Military Command and Control System (WWMCCS) to provide the communications required. Despite many news reports of "breakdowns" in the system, informed opinion is that it works well and is improving.[13] WWMCCS includes the National Military Command System (NMCS), consisting of four major subcomponents. The first of these is the National Military Command Center (NMCC) located in the Pentagon. A "soft facility," the center is located above ground. The second, the Alternate Military Command Center is housed within a mountain located a short distance from the nation's capital. A third is the National Emergency Airborne Command Post, comprising four (eventually six) special E-4B variants of the Boeing 747 aircraft, at least one of which is always in flight (commanded by a brigadier general). Additionally, the four principal "unified command" commanders worldwide, i.e., of Strategic Air Command (CINCSAC), European Command (CINCEUR), Atlantic Command (CINC-LANT), and Pacific Command (CINCPAC), have both land-based and airborne command posts capable of communicating with U.S. nuclear forces. Flexibility in the C³ system is provided by several other hard, airborne, satellite, and seaborne telecommunications capabilities.[14] It is to be expected that, were it to attack, the Soviet Union would attempt by all possible means to destroy or jam U.S. C³ capabilities.

"I'd Like To Trade In The Whole Thing For A Guy
With A Horse And A Couple Of Lanterns
In A Church Steeple"

Reprinted from *Herblock's State of the Union* (Simon
& Schuster, 1972), courtesy, Herblock Cartoons.

In a situation of political crisis (except war) in Soviet-American relations, a Soviet nuclear first strike might take many forms, from an unambiguous massive launch of hundreds of land-based missiles on a trajectory toward the continental United States, to a smaller launch, maybe only a few SLBMs from the North Atlantic—perhaps heading toward dispersed targets. In the former case, where there can be little doubt concerning Soviet intentions, the time available for the president to receive notification, possibly to consult advisers and decide, to communicate the decision, and for the U.S. response to be launched, would be less than a half-hour. In the latter case, the president theoretically has twelve minutes or less to determine what the Soviets intend, to decide whether or how the United States should respond, and to give relevant orders.

Although the president's aides always and everywhere have means available for the president to communicate with the major components of the NMCC (which will, in turn, tell the retaliatory forces to go), the decision time is grossly inadequate. There may be a vast range of possible responses, depending on the situation. One assumes that a president would prefer to delay decision until he has all the information available, but *time* is the major constraint. Some strategists have argued that the best solution is to "launch on warning" of a Soviet attack rather than "launch under attack," or wait for the nature of the attack to be clarified as Soviet missiles begin hitting their targets.* Other experts would place greater reliance on the Washington-Moscow telecommunications link (MOLINK), which provides the president with continuous communication with Soviet leaders. Still others advocate a U.S.-U.S.S.R. combined crisis control center. In any case, C^3 is a massive—perhaps unsolvable—problem in maintaining a credible deterrent.

Penetration of Opponent's Active Defenses. U.S. capability to launch missiles and put them on target also depends on a large number of factors. First, the nature of both the Soviet strike and the U.S. response would be critical. If the Soviet strike were a massive launch, targeted against vulnerable U.S. land-based ICBMs and strategic bombers on the ground, and if the U.S. response were slow, a large part of the American retaliatory capability would have been destroyed. On the other hand, if the U.S. retaliatory launch involved large numbers of missiles from dispersed elements of the triad, Soviet detection, tracking, and destruction of U.S. missiles and bombers would be complicated. These Soviet complications can be magnified in a variety of ways. First, if the United States were to acquire an effective antisatellite (ASAT) system, based for example on laser technology, Soviet satellites needed for early warning and tracking might be destroyed or blinded. Second, the United States might use in its retaliatory strike a number of decoy missiles, indistinguishable from nuclear-armed missiles that the Soviets would have to target, thus causing attrition of their limited ABM force. Third, it is possible to release fields of "chaff" or metal particles or other "spoofing" or "stealth" devices to confuse or blind Soviet tracking radars used to guide Soviet ABMs. Fourth, the United States can continue development of multiple reentry vehicles (MRV), the warheads that separate from a single carrier, or bus, and travel independently toward the targets that they are programmed to destroy.

There is a difference in types of missile reentry systems. The older system still deployed on Titan II missiles is the MRV, several of which are released almost simultaneously to descend on the target area in a shotgun pattern. The second, more modern, system is the multiple, independently targetable reentry vehicle (MIRV) deployed on the Minutemen and other newer missiles.

---

*U.S. policy in this respect would be included in the SIOP. Secretary Brown questioned whether or not the United States would launch land-based missiles before Soviet missiles had exploded in the United States. His view was that "it is not our doctrine to do so—neither is it our doctrine that under no circumstances would we ever do so." See "Secretary Brown: 'Launch on Warning or Launch under Attack'?" *Defense/Space Daily*, November 11, 1977, p. 68.

MIRV warheads are carried in a bus which separates from the missile booster, points toward the target area and independently releases each warhead, which descends toward its own separate targets with far greater accuracy than the MRV warhead. In the future, the United States may deploy a multiple aimed reentry vehicle (MARV) with warheads that can be manuevered in flight to avoid the opponent's ABMs and hit the target with great accuracy.

Technology has provided the capability for ever-increasing accuracy in warhead delivery, and accuracy of the warhead is intrinsically more important than its size or yield (expressed in kilotons or megatons). In the past, U.S. warheads have been more accurate than Soviet warheads, whereas Soviet warheads have been larger. The United States has had a lead in the tech-nological capability to place more, smaller, and more accurate warheads on its missiles. The Soviets have enjoyed a lead in numbers of missiles with larger warheads. As the Soviets have acquired greater technological capabilities for accuracy, the importance of both active and passive U.S. defense programs has grown. The need for strategic arms limitations also has increased, for reasons to be discussed in Chapter 23.

Penetration of Opponent's Passive Defense. The Soviets have the same passive defense options as the United States—concerning locations of silos with or without missiles, hardening, mobility, densely packed missiles, or larger numbers of missiles dispersed in a triad. The technological keys to overcome passive defense measures are warhead numbers and on-target accuracy. The major trade-off in counterforce targeting against missiles in silos—or *hard targets* (some counterforce, or military targets such as airfields, supply depots, or troop units are *soft targets*)—has been between warheads with greater explosive power and those with greater accuracy. The measure-ment of accuracy, *circular error probable* (CEP), is a statistical expression denoting where one can expect 50 percent of the weapons to detonate relative to the target. Hard-target kill probability is a statistical function of the number of weapons one is willing to devote to a single target and the accuracy and yield of those weapons. For example:

An improvement in accuracy by a factor of two has the same effect against a hardened target as increasing yield by a factor of eight. . . . However, yield is also important, particularly where there are large differences [as between smaller U.S. warheads and larger Soviet warheads]. The following chart gives some examples of variable com-binations of accuracy, yield and numbers of (reliably arriving) RV's [reentry vehicles] in terms of kill probability against a target hardened to [withstand the blast effects of] 1,000 pounds per square inch, and also demonstrates clearly the difference in hard-target counterforce capability between U.S.-type MIRV's and Soviet-type MIRV's.

Clearly, the difference in detonation in nautical miles from desired ground zero (the center of the target) makes a great difference, as does the number of warheads dedicated to the target. Timing the arrival of the warheads and the distance between them is also of concern in preventing the fratricide effect.

Kill Probability

Yield	0.004 MT		0.15 MT		2 MT	
Number of RVs	1	3	1	3	1	3
0.3nm CEP	0.04	0.08	0.10	0.27	0.45	0.83
0.2nm CEP	0:10	0.25	0.20	0.50	0.73	0.98

MT = megaton or yield equivalent to a million tons of TNT.   nm = nautical miles.[15]

Coordinated Targeting. The import of coordination can be seen in several ways. First, the nature of a target may necessitate programming more than one missile, detonated in a different way (i.e., air burst versus ground burst) and at a different time, in order to destroy it. Post-strike intelligence could show that for a variety of reasons a target had not been destroyed: pre-strike intelligence on the precise location of a target or its hardness may have been wrong; some missiles fired at a target may have been destroyed by ABMs; warheads may simply have malfunctioned or aircraft flying missions to drop nuclear bombs may have been shot down by Soviet interceptor aircraft or ground-based air defense systems.

Lack of coordinated targeting could lead to target survival or produce redundancy or wasteful weapons use—i.e., firing more than the number of weapons required to destroy a single target. The requirement to prevent redundancy also extends to the interaction between strategic and longer-range theater nuclear weapons based in and around Western Europe. Similarly, there is a need for the United States to coordinate targeting of both its strategic and theater nuclear weapons with its allies. In the allied case, however, political realities could outweigh technical requirements.

The foregoing general explanations of the extremely complex functioins to be accomplished in order to have a credible second-strike capability supporting a policy of deterrence should make clear the difficulty of strategic nuclear matters. When one adds to these complexities the competing views of various political, military, scientific, business, religious, and other constituencies both domestic and foreign having interests in America's nuclear strategic posture, it becomes clear why the issues surrounding nuclear strategy have been and will continue in the decade of the 1980s to be debated with great intensity.

U.S. Nuclear Strategies. Military strategy is "the art and science of employing the armed forces of a nation to secure the objectives of national policy by the application of force or the threat of force."[16] Strategic programs combine the people, funds, and military hardware required to implement present and future strategies. Strategy provides the guidance for determining *how* programs must be developed and maintained to achieve national objectives.

Any discussion of U.S. nuclear strategies must begin by recognizing the continuing nature of the U.S. nuclear arsenal and that of the Soviet Union.

U.S. weapons are generally divided into strategic, intermediate, and battle-field categories, despite various difficulties in differentiating the three categories. The primary theater of deployment of Intermediate Nuclear Forces (INF) and Battlefield Nuclear Weapons (BNW) is Europe; their role there lies primarily in "their deterrent value, mainly because they are seen as the link with the strategic nuclear forces.[17] Thus, it is essential that consideration of nuclear strategy include the INF and BNW systems that interface directly with nuclear strategic analysis.

The first issue confronting U.S. policy-makers is whether the current strategic balance and the contemporary international environment require changes in traditional U.S. concepts. Table 11.1 illustrates the disappearance of strategic nuclear superiority that the United States long enjoyed.[18]

The balance of theater nuclear forces in the region of America's most important alliance, NATO Europe, is extraordinarily difficult to evaluate depending upon critical definitions and assumptions about which weapons systems would be used for what purposes and where. An analysis of raw data on the balance of theater nuclear forces which excludes short-range or battlefield delivery systems such as nuclear artillery or surface-to-surface missiles (SSMs) with ranges of less than one hundred miles shows a clear numerical advantage for Warsaw Pact forces. Yet when qualitative indices are applied, as in table 11.2, it is possible to conclude that there is no substantial imbalance in terms of overall system utility. Numbers of systems do not tell the whole story.[19]*

Despite the unsatisfactory status of the total nuclear balance as of 1983, the overall forces of both superpowers are sufficiently large and balanced that neither possesses a true first-strike capability; if the trends of the 1970s and early 1980s persist, however, that will not hold in the future.

That the basic U.S. strategy has been and is second-, *not* first-, strike in character has long been shown by both explicit U.S. statements and U.S. behavior in an earlier period when it had overwhelming strategic superiority, as well as by the concern for survivability which the United States has placed on its strategic forces.[20]

A logical corollary to the obvious inhibition against a first strike would be for nations to renounce completely any recourse to nuclear weapons and dismantle their current inventories. This option is unacceptable to the United States for a number of reasons, which we shall examine in later chapters.

The concept of *limited nuclear options* (LNOs) has been introduced into our strategic vocabulary in an attempt to increase the credibility of our strategic deterrent. Former Defense Secretary Harold Brown, as quoted in the preceding pages, has indicated that we have long had such a capability. Former

---

*It should be noted that NATO figures include a significant number of "U.S. Central Systems" (Poseidon), while the Warsaw Pact totals do not address equivalent Soviet systems.

Table 11.1. U.S. and Soviet Strategic Force Levels

Force	Jan. 1, 1980		Jan. 1, 1981	
	U.S.	U.S.S.R.	U.S.	U.S.S.R.
Offensive				
Operational ICBM launchers[a,b]	1,054	1,398	1,054	1,398
Operational SLBM launchers[a,c]	656	950	576	950
Long-range bombers (TAI)[d]				
Operational[e]	348	156	347	156
Other[f]	225		223	
Force-loading weapons[g]	9,200	6,000	9,000	7,000
Defensive[h]				
Air defense surveillance				
Radars	88	7,000	91	7,000
Interceptors (TAI)	327	2,500	312	2,500
SAM launchers	0	10,000[i]	0	10,000
ABM defense launchers	0	64	0	32

[a] Includes on-line missile launchers as well as those in construction, overhaul, repair, conversion, and modernization.

[b] Does not include test and training launchers or 18 launchers of fractional orbital missiles at Tyura TAM test range.

[c] Includes launchers on all nuclear-powered submarines and, for the Soviets, operational launchers for modern SLBMs on G-class diesel submarines. Excluded are 48 SALT-accountable launchers on 3 Polaris submarines now used as attack submarines.

[d] 1981 figures exclude for the U.S.: 65 FB-111s; for the U.S.S.R.: over 100 Backfires, about 120 Bison tankers, Bear ASW Aircraft, and Bear reconnaissance aircraft.

[e] Includes deployed, strike-configured aircraft only.

[f] Includes, for U.S., B-52s used for miscellaneous purposes and those in reserve, mothballs, or storage, and 4 B-1 prototypes; for the U.S.S.R.: Bears and Bisons used for test, training, and R & D.

[g] Total force loadings reflect those independently-targetable weapons associated with the total operational ICBMs, SLBMs, and long-range bombers.

[h] Excludes radars and launchers at test sites or outside North America.

[i] These launchers accommodate about 12,000 SAM interceptors. Some of the launchers have multiple rails.

Source: U.S., *Department of Defense Annual Report, Fiscal Year 1982* (Washington, D.C.: U.S. Government Printing Office, 1981), p. 53.

Secretary of Defense James R. Schlesinger, the originator of the phrase, explained the reasoning behind this concept when he stated:

The wisdom and credibility of relying simply on the preplanned counter-city strikes of assured destruction are even more in doubt when allies rather than the United States itself face the threat of nuclear war. . . . Since we ourselves find it difficult to believe that we would actually implement . . . assured destruction in response to a limited attack on military targets . . . there can be no certainty that, in a crisis, prospective opponents would be deterred from testing our resolve.[21]

Table 11.2. Long- and Medium-Range Nuclear Systems for the European Theater

Category and Type	Range (km)	Inventory	Available Warheads[a]	Estimated Arriving Warheads[b]
NATO				
Ballistic Missiles				
SLBM				
Polaris A-3	4,600	64	29	21
MSBS M-20	3,000	80	36	26
IRBM				
SSBS S-3	3,000	18	16	8
SRBM				
Pershing 1A	720	180	162	91
Ballistic Missile Subtotal		342	243	146
Land-based Aircraft				
Vulcan B-2	2,800	48	67	16
F-111 E/F	1,900	156	125	45
Mirage IVA	1,600	34	24	6
Buccaneer	950	50	35	8
F-104	800	290	61	6
F-4 (US)	750	252	60	11
F-16 (US)	900	48	12	4
F-16 (Belgium)	900	20	5	2
Jaguar	720	117	47	9
Mirage IIIE	600	30	12	2
Carrier-based Aircraft				
A-6E	1,000	20	16	4
A-7E	900	48	38	6
Super Etendard	560	16	13	3
Aircraft Subtotal		1,301	556	129
NATO Total (less *Poseidon/ Trident*)		1,643	799	275
US Central Systems				
Poseidon C-3 or Trident C4	4,600 or 7,400	(40) —	400	288
NATO Totals (with Poseidon/ Trident)			1,199	563
WARSAW PACT				
Ballistic Missiles				
IRBM				
SS-20	5,600	315	561	404
SS-5 Skean	4,100	16	12	5
MRBM				
SS-4 Sandal	1,900	275	193	63
SRBM				
SS-12 Scaleboard	900	70	56	29
Scud A/B	300	450	360	189
Scud B/C	300	143	114	60

Category and Type	Range (km)	Inventory	Available Warheads[a]	Estimated Arriving Warheads[b]
SS-22	1,000	100	80	51
SS-23	350	10	8	5
SLBM				
SS-N-5 Serb	1,400	57	26	12
Ballistic Missile Subtotals		1,436	1,410	818
Aircraft				
Tu-22M/-26 Backfire B	4,025	100	128	53
Tu-16 Badger	2,800	310	174	46
Tu-22 Blinder	3,100	125	70	22
Su-24 (Su-19) Fencer	1,600	550	176	50
Mig-27 Flagger D	720	550	176	55
Su-17 Fitter C/D	600	688	110	31
Su-7 Fitter A	400	265	37	6
Mig-21 Fishbed J-N	400	100	16	4
Air-delivered Weapon Subtotals		2,688	887	267
Warsaw Pact Total		4,124	2,297	1,085

[a]Available warheads are an estimate, calculated as: Inventory × warheads per system × estimated utilization × estimated serviceability.
[b]Estimated arriving warheads are calculated as: Available warheads × estimated survivability × estimated reliability × estimated penetration.
Source: International Institute for Strategic Studies, *The Military Balance, 1982–1983* (London: IISS, 1982), pp. 136–37.

In analyzing the reasons for and consequences of introducing the LNO concept, we should note that having at least temporarily accepted nuclear "sufficiency" rather than "superiority," having voluntarily abandoned programs for new acquisitions in manned bombers, for a time, and recognizing the competing domestic constituencies that bring pressure against increases in defense spending, U.S. policy-makers have been attempting to extend the credible roles of existing force structures. A result of this extension is the expansion of the U.S. strategic deterrent to conventional war in Europe. The European deployment of the enhanced radiation warhead, known as the "neutron bomb," was originally proposed by the Carter administration as a low-cost solution to the dangerous imbalance of conventional forces between NATO and the Warsaw Pact. That proposal was hastily withdrawn after its somewhat clumsy introduction, as Europeans realized that a low-yield atomic warhead would blur the distinction between conventional and nuclear war. The Europeans felt that such a weapon would increase the likelihood of nuclear use on their territory. The U.S. strategic forces, though formidable, cannot deter other types of conflict. A nuclear warhead is ineffectual against guerrillas, just as a sledgehammer is an unsuitable and somewhat unwieldy tool for swatting flies.

Given these brief perspectives on U.S. strategic purpose and policy, on the strategic functions that programs may be developed to accomplish, and on U.S.-Soviet force comparisons, let us turn to examining some of the alternative concepts involved in fighting a strategic nuclear war.

Strategic Nuclear War. Even though both superpowers might desire to limit war short of direct nuclear attack on each other's homeland, their very possession of strategic weapons poses the risk that such might be used. In the United States, recognition of this risk has spurred periodic analysis of strategies designed to limit even a strategic nuclear war. The LNO concept just mentioned is one consequence of such analysis.

At first glance, *limited strategic war* seems a contradiction in terms. The popular vision of strategic war is one of unrestrained, apocalyptic violence—what Herman Kahn of the Hudson Institute has descriptively called "nuclear spasm."[22] This view of strategic war has been reinforced in the public mind by phrases like "massive retaliation," "full retaliatory response," and "assured destruction," all of which have been employed at one time or another to describe America's deterrent threat.

Some strategists argue, however, that no law of nature requires that strategic war be unlimited. Such a war *might* certainly be one of uncontrolled violence, but it *need* not be. Instead, they suggest it might be possible and even desirable to devise strategies involving the controlled use of strategic nuclear weapons. To the objection that such a deliberate use of massive destruction would be unthinkable, advocates reply that an uncontrolled nuclear war is still more so and that avoidance of an ultimate nuclear catastrophe requires that no possible alternative remain unexplored.

By definition, strategic nuclear war assumes the breach of two critical thresholds: that between conventional and nuclear weapons, and that between attacks on targets outside and within the homelands of the superpowers. Compared with these clear boundaries, other conceivable limiting conditions would be extraordinarily difficult to observe in practice. Belligerents might agree (implicitly or explicitly) to limit the yields of their weapons. They might agree to refrain from using "dirty" weapons—those producing large quantities of radioactive contamination—or they might agree to give sufficient warning of attack to permit the evacuation of civilians from target areas. Most theorizing, however, has been directed to the possible limitation of the number and nature of targets to be attacked.

Problems of Limitation. Controlled war strategies have been assailed by critics on a variety of grounds. Chief among these is the belief that such a war could not in fact be controlled. "It would be a mistake to think that conducting war in the measured cadence of limited reprisal somehow rescues [it] from impetuosity and gives it 'rational' qualities that it would otherwise lack.''[23] Critics contend that such a strategy would require decision-makers on both sides to make unreasonably fine calculations of cost and risk under conditions of nearly unbearable mental and psychological stress. Instead, they argue, misperception by each side of the other's actions, and uncertainty regarding his intentions, would push both sides toward a catastrophic explosion.[24]

Finally, many oppose the effort to develop controlled war strategies, fearing it might increase the likelihood of nuclear war by diminishing its terrors. Such critics contend that the "least worst" consequence of such strategies would be intensification of the arms race, and the worst consequence would be a tendency toward rashness on the part of decision-makers—rashness that might produce the very holocaust that everyone would avoid.[25]

The issue of controlled nuclear war first received wide attention in the mid 1970s, when it became known that the U.S. government was actively exploring *flexible nuclear options*—variously called LNOs or *regional nuclear options* (RNOs). Billed as the "Schlesinger Re-targeting Doctrine" after the then-secretary of defense, this approach became the subject of heated debate, which gradually included issues ranging from arms control to overseas commitments. The debate subsided, overtaken by other national security issues, only to surface again in 1980 in relation to the U.S. *countervailing strategy*. This strategy is based on maintenance of strategic nuclear forces and plans for their use such that any Soviet leader considering aggression against U.S. interests would recognize that no plausible outcome would represent a Soviet success.[26]

Nuclear Strategic Bargaining. Recalling from Chapter 2 that deterrence is essentially a psychological phenomenon involving the attempt to master an opponent's expectations, we should note that in U.S.-Soviet relations deterrence centers on political bargaining at the strategic nuclear level. The process of nuclear strategic bargaining is made up of diverse elements. Articulation of strategic nuclear policies must first take place. U.S. and NATO nuclear programs that support these policies can then be developed. Only then can the various negotiating processes (mutual and balanced force limitation and reduction discussions and dialogues between the top leadership echelons of NATO and the Soviet Union) that may lead to treaties and understandings begin.

The images held by U.S. and Soviet national security decision-makers are critical to the bargaining process, for "mirror-imaging" has seemed to influence both U.S. and Soviet analyses of the nuclear balance. Mirror-imaging can interfere with accurate communication in two ways. First, it implies that your opponent is developing policy for reasons that are the *reverse* (mirror) of your own. For example, the United States knows that it builds nuclear forces only to counter the threat of Soviet forces. Since we have told the Soviets this often enough, we believe they need not feel threatened by any U.S. improvements. But, since they continue to expand and improve their systems, they must be so doing for aggressive purposes; they cannot be expanding because of a U.S. threat. So reflects our mirror—perhaps correctly.

A second communication barrier in mirror-imaging is the assumption that the opponent reflects both your rationality and value system in its decision-making. This assumption can lead to assignment of relative values to negotiating (or crisis) objectives that may have little relation to what the opponent really believes.

A critical problem in nuclear bargaining is to establish the data base from which to bargain. Despite advances in the technology of surveillance and other intelligence-gathering, no nation can be *certain* that it has a complete and accurate inventory of all its opponents' capabilities. Even more critically, possession of capability does not necessarily reveal *intent*, and an opponent's intent is the critical element in bargaining.

One of the paradoxes of strategic nuclear bargaining is that, at least in theory, deterrence may be enhanced by a certain degree of *uncertainty*. That is, if an opponent has some degree of *doubt* as to your exact level of response, it will likely "worst case" its analysis and hesitate to exceed the lowest levels of provocation its analysts estimate. "Mathematically, deterrence should begin to operate when the risk becomes greater than the [potential gain]. . . . Psychologically, however, owing to . . . uncertainty . . . the risk exerts a deterrent effect [earlier]."[27]

Policy analysis in a deterrence situation is a very complex operation. Even considering that the deliberately (or accidentally) irrational element may, as we have seen above, enter the equation, the underlying policy analysis has to be approached on as rational a basis as possible.

One of the most difficult aspects of negotiating strategy is the problem of determining how to terminate any conflict that might occur. Yet, if the conflict does not become total war, negotiation in some form is inevitable. One can alter and modify goals and objectives to fit the possible outcomes as a regular part of negotiating strategy. If, however, a state that attempts a deterrent strategy does not adequately prepare for deterrence failure and the ability to terminate the resulting conflict, its whole policy house is likely to collapse.

Command and control problems complicate planning for war termination. Given the various differences between potential warring powers, one side may control intermediate steps better than the other. Global communications now work in "real time," creating difficulties in two directions: there is less time to explore the implications of offers, and there is almost no time to reflect on intelligence reports in order to verify statements of a "dishonest" opponent.

A further problem for possible war termination stems from the very nature of strategic systems. If one destroys the enemy's command and control facilities, who is left to negotiate termination of the war? Conversely, how quickly and accurately can one accurately assess damage to the opponent in order to determine if the minimum objectives have been accomplished?

Strategic Policy and Program Decisions. On a rational basis, policy decisions should be followed by implementing actions to procure those systems that will support policy. In the real world, as spelled out in Part 2, such is not always the case. Program procurement decisions, despite repeated efforts to centralize, analyze, and modernize the process, remain in large part an internal bureaucratic process subject to the pressures of bureaucratic bargaining.[28] Even in nuclear matters this is the case, as suggested by the air force–navy reversal on the advisability of a counter-city strategy. In the early 1950s, when the air force was arguing for strategic bombers and the navy's only nuclear capabilities were in carrier-based strike aircraft, the air force advocated a strategic counter-city concept while the navy pushed for a more tactical employment of nuclear weapons. By the 1960–63 period, when air force missiles had been improved in accuracy sufficient to hit point targets (at least soft ICBM emplacements) and the navy's Polaris missiles were considered best against area targets, the two services reversed their positions on counter-city strategy.[29]

No matter how rigorously decision-makers try to develop new strategies, they are to a degree bound by the necessity of using military hardware already deployed. The debate over the relative merits of the B-1 bomber and the cruise missile in part reflects this fact. B-1 advocates assert a need for a new manned bomber, capable of penetrating enemy defenses, as an essential portion of the deterrence triad. Opponents of the B-1 argue that new cruise missiles can achieve the same goal using current bomber assets, and that, in any case, new technology for a "stealth" bomber will make the B-1 relatively obsolete not long after it is deployed. The underlying effort on both sides is directed not at examining our strategic policy or developing new policies but at assessing which kind or mix of hardware is the most cost effective.

In assessing program decisions involving nuclear weapons, it is essential to ask if the political implications of a new tool may not be more important than the technical military capabilities. If so, the job of the strategist is even more important, for it is at that level that the military and political implications of policy interact.

Issues in Nuclear Strategy in the 1980s. Perhaps as never before, a vast range of issues has surfaced in the early 1980s centering on nuclear weapons and their uses. These issues reside in the three categories of nuclear strategy with which this chapter began—*strategic purposes, strategic policies,* and *strategic programs.*

Strategic Purpose Issues. There have been two general schools of thought on purpose issues. The first concerns the proposition that the United States should be developing a war-winning strategy, which makes nuclear exchange more likely. The second category centers on the proposition that any use of nuclear weapons would be both horrible and immoral, and that the two superpowers are engaged in a dangerous and costly arms race that is out of control. This view had led to the widespread peace and nuclear freeze movements so prevalent today. However, our focus will remain on strategy.

Strategic Policy Issues. In summer 1980, the NSC reviewed U.S. nuclear strategic policy and incorporated changes in a highly classified document signed on July 27 known as Presidential Directive (PD) 59. Within days major elements of PD 59 had been leaked to the media, and the directive was being referred to in the press and elsewhere as a ''new'' nuclear war strategy designed to deter a Soviet first strike by threatening retaliation at the full range of Soviet war-making capabilities. Evidently, Defense Secretary Brown had intended to unveil PD 59 at a later date as a natural evolution of U.S. nuclear strategy.[30] However, pursued by the press and others in the midst of the 1980 presidential election campaigns, Secretary Brown attempted to explain PD 59 to our NATO allies in an August 8 cable: ''Because some press reports have portrayed this evolutionary development of our doctrine as a major break with past policies, I want to stress . . . that the U.S. has long included in its plans effective and comprehensive coverage of military and control targets.''[31] On August 20, 1980, he elaborated on ''the countervailing strategy'' of PD 59 before a U.S. Naval War College audience. The essential elements of his presentation were:

- Although the details of U.S. nuclear planning must remain secret, the basic premises should be understood clearly by friend and foe alike. This speech is designed to make our strategy clear to the Soviets.
- PD 59 is a refinement or codification of previous statements about U.S. strategic policy.
- Deterrence remains our fundamental strategic objective, but deterrence must restrain a range of threats wider than just massive attacks on the United States.
- Our strategic forces must deter also smaller nuclear attacks on smaller sets of targets in the United States and prevent nuclear coercion of our allies.
- Strategic forces, in conjunction with theater nuclear forces, must contribute to deterrence of conventional aggression.
- Our nuclear forces, plans, and command and control capabilities must convince the Soviets that no kind of aggression that led to the use of nuclear weapons could produce victory, no matter how they define victory.
- The Soviets must know that some intermediate level of aggression by them could be met by ''selective, large, but still less than maximum nuclear attacks'' to exact an unacceptably high price in things they value most— political and military control, and nuclear, conventional, and industrial capability to sustain a war.
- We will retain the capability to attack Soviet cities.
- We have not ignored the problem of terminating a war with the Soviets.
- We have been moving gradually since 1977 to increase the scope, variety, and flexibility of options open to us and to increase the survivability of our command and control should the Soviets choose aggression.[32]

A month later, both Secretary Brown and Secretary of State Muskie appeared at a closed-door session of the Senate Foreign Relations Committee to testify on the reformulation of nuclear strategy. Senator Frank Church later told reporters that both secretaries "emphasized to the committee that neither they, nor President Carter, believe it likely that a nuclear war, once begun, can stay limited. . . . Nor do they believe that there is such a thing as a 'winnable' nuclear exchange between superpowers."[33]

Although cast as "new" by the press, this reformulation of strategy was clearly an evolutionary one.[34] A complex of factors, however, had led national security decision-makers to articulate strategic nuclear policy in a way that would make existing and near-term nuclear strategic programs a more credible deterrent to Soviet nuclear and large-scale conventional aggression. First, it had become increasingly clear over time that by moving quickly to build and deploy nuclear forces to levels permitted under the SALT I Treaty and by moving with unexpected speed to acquire and deploy sophisticated MIRV technology, the Soviet Union had acquired rough parity in nuclear capabilities by the latter 1970s. Second, the Soviets began faster-than-expected deployment in the latter 1970s of more modern theater nuclear forces. Third, as Chapter 23 will discuss, the Soviets proved intransigent on important aspects of SALT II, leading many Americans to conclude that the treaty signed in 1979 by President Brezhnev and President Carter was unfavorable to the United States. Fourth, it became clear that, given Soviet advances in space and nuclear technology, the U.S. land-based missile force was becoming vulnerable.[35] Fifth, large-scale civil defense programs in the U.S.S.R. caused concern. Sixth, Soviet acquisition of important footholds in Angola, Yemen, and Aden and finally, direct aggression in Afghanistan increasingly raised questions about Soviet motives for détente. Seventh, the clear growth of Soviet naval and air capabilities for projection of power, especially in relation to the Persian Gulf and sea lanes for oil shipments to the United States and its allies, became alarming. By the start of the 1980s, many analysts were arguing that the Soviets clearly were seeking a war-winning capability in both nuclear and conventional terms.[36]

The debate over the countervailing strategy had already begun as the new decade opened. Defenders argued that the strategy recognized that the Soviets have been preparing for nuclear war and that the new U.S. strategy marked a progression from the *survivability* required to assure we can launch a second strike to the *endurance* necessary to fight a war that could extend over a period of time and include a series of nuclear exchanges. Some argued that, to acquire the capability to support the strategy, the United States should deploy a BMD system as well as the MX system.[37]

Opponents of the strategy argued that there is only one real issue involved, i.e., if a strategy implicitly assuming that a nuclear war can be controlled and prolonged will improve or erode deterrence. They believe that this strategy, designed to deter a variety of Soviet aggressions, will increase the number of possible conflicts to which U.S. nuclear use is linked and, thus, the probabilities that one of them will escalate to nuclear war. The critics point to Secretary Brown's own statement in September 1980 that limited nuclear exchanges probably cannot be controlled and so would escalate into full-scale nuclear war. The critics also pointed early on in the Reagan administration to such statements as those of former Deputy Defense Secretary Frank Carlucci III about a "nuclear war-fighting" capability, and of former Deputy Undersecretary of Defense Thomas K. Jones that "if there [are] enough shovels to go around, everybody's going to make it [through a nuclear war]."

Finally, critics assert that, in acquiring the weapons systems logically needed to support the countervailing strategy (MX and a BMD system), the United States would destabilize the nuclear balance, signaling to the Soviets that we are acquiring a disarming first-strike capability and accelerating the arms race.[38] The arguments pro and con are not new; most of them were in the headlines during the late 1960s and early 1970s, the period in which the decline of America's relative military strength began.

Debates on U.S. nuclear strategy will assuredly continue in the 1980s, and they will be crucial for the future of U.S. national security. Of the two schools of thought on nuclear strategy mentioned earlier (prewar deterrence and war-fighting deterrence), the second school appeared to be gaining ascendance at the turn of the decade. The countervailing strategy, although evolutionary, appeared to be another step toward the position of the second school, which advocates adoption of a U.S. nuclear war-fighting strategy.

Strategic Program Issues. By 1983, a new public consciousness, inspired by antinuclear weapons and peace movements in Europe and America, had centered on what appeared to many as an inexorable nuclear arms build-up between the Soviet Union and the United States. To an unprecedented degree, Americans were exposed to panels, lectures, and debates on nuclear purpose, policy, and programs in the media, on campuses, and in churches. This new public consciousness was founded in part on a declining national economy coinciding with President Reagan's nuclear weapons modernization programs, which were viewed by some as prohibitively expensive, especially as social spending was reduced. Increasingly, poor and working-class Americans perceived themselves as being forced to pay for the security of the West European and Japanese middle and upper classes. In this context, Congress increasingly scrutinized individual nuclear weapons programs.

The MX missile program became a classic issue. Given increases in Soviet ICBM accuracies, and in the absence of a U.S. BMD, most analysts accepted the proposition that U.S. land-based missiles had become highly vulnerable to a Soviet first strike. Having rejected President Carter's "shell game" scheme to reduce the vulnerability of the MX missile by shuttling 200 of them among 2,400 possible firing positions, the Reagan administration was caught between a perceived imperative to modernize land-based missiles and the lack of a basing mode to significantly reduce their vulnerability. At least thirty possible basing schemes were studied, resulting by 1982 in the "dense pack" concept referred to above. A combination of technological uncertainties aired in the media and the lack of prior consultation by the administration with the Congress made the dense pack scheme appear ludicrous, and the Congress rejected it in December 1982 by blocking MX funds.

By early 1983, it appeared that this major program in the Reagan administration's nuclear force modernization plan had been scuttled in partisan politics battles over nuclear force modernization and the nuclear freeze. The administration moved quickly, however, to form a bipartisan commission whose task was to find a way to create a national consensus. The President's Commission on Strategic Forces (the "Scowcroft Commission," named after its chairman, former National Security Adviser General Brent Scowcroft) included prestigious national security officials, both Republican and Democrat, of previous administrations. The commission members consulted widely on Capitol Hill before producing a proposal with three essential elements.[39] First, reduced numbers of MX missiles would be placed in existing Minuteman silos, some of which would be "hardened." Second, this would be a cost-saving temporary program that would be replaced by a new program founded on small, mobile, single-warhead missiles to be deployed in the 1990s on federal property. The new missile would be largely invulnerable and thus contribute to strategic nuclear stability. Third, the commission called for a new and more flexible approach to arms control negotiations with the U.S.S.R.

Shortly after the Scowcroft Commission report was released to the public, President Reagan endorsed it in totality. Thus, the administration appeared to have the best of all worlds: strategic nuclear modernization would proceed with the MX as the president had insisted, and the new emphasis on arms control would take some of the steam out of the American nuclear freeze movement. The Congress approved a resolution to release $625 million for MX testing and engineering by a vote of 239–186; the Senate followed suit, voting 59–39. Some legislators, especially many Democrats who had opposed the MX, changed their votes as a means of placing more responsibility on the president for serious arms control policies.[40] It appeared a good bet in mid-1983 that the American public and Congress would continue to focus on arms control and nuclear weapons programs, especially as the 1984 elections loomed over the horizon. Probably in anticipation of just that, there were indications that the Reagan administration would seek a new venue to keep the bipartisan momentum going on the MX missile. One of three options was to extend for two years the life of the President's Commission on Strategic Forces.[41]

Debates on U.S. nuclear strategy will assuredly continue in the 1980s, and they will be crucial for the future of U.S. national security. Of the two schools of thought on nuclear strategy mentioned earlier (war-fighting deterrence and prewar deterrence), the former appeared to be gaining ascendancy in the early 1980s. The countervailing strategy, although evolutionary, appears to be another step toward the position of the first school, which advocates adoption of a U.S. nuclear war-fighting strategy.

If the first school continues to prevail, the budgetary costs of ensuring that

U.S. nuclear forces have the numbers, accuracy, reliability, survivability, and flexibility essential to support a credible war-fighting strategy will be high. Developing nuclear programs at costs acceptable to Congress will likely be less difficult than in the 1970s, given an increasingly widespread popular perception of the Soviet threat to U.S. security interests. If, in addition, conventional forces are to receive the continuing budgetary increases needed to maintain well-equipped, high-quality conventional and special operations forces with rapid deployment capabilities, the defense budget will grow still larger, with high opportunity costs for domestic social programs. This risks a taxpayer rebellion. Yet, maintaining a nuclear strategy that deters Soviet nuclear strikes against the United States is the *sine qua non* for America's most fundamental national security objective: survival of the United States.

DISCUSSION QUESTIONS

1. What is the role of images and ideologies in strategic nuclear bargaining?
2. How can nuclear war best be deterred? What are the critical elements of deterrence?
3. How do alliances impact on a bargaining strategy?
4. What are the characteristics of the different nuclear strategies? What strategy (strategies) has (have) been followed by the United States?
5. What is meant by *counterforce? countervalue? first-strike capability? second-strike capability? triad?*
6. What are the difficulties of differentiating strategic nuclear forces from tactical nuclear forces?
7. What is meant by *countervailing strategy?* Is this a new strategy? Why or why not?
8. In strategic force capabilities, is the United States number one or number two? Is this a significant question? Why?
9. Can we determine what strategic concepts guide the development of Soviet strategic forces?
10. What are the two principal schools of thought on nuclear deterrence theory? What are the major differences between them?
11. What are the distinctions between "active" and "passive" defenses against nuclear weapons?
12. Why is warhead accuracy more important than warhead yield?

RECOMMENDED READING

American Academy of Arts and Sciences, *The Nuclear Weapons Freeze and Arms Control.* Cambridge, Mass.: Harvard University Press, 1983.

Beaufre, André. *Introduction to Strategy.* New York: Frederick A. Praeger, 1965.

Coffey, Joseph I. *Strategic Power and National Security.* Pittsburgh: University of Pittsburgh Press, 1971.

Collins, John M. *American and Soviet Military Trends since the Cuban Missile Crisis*. Washington, D.C.: Center for Strategic and International Studies, 1978.

Enthoven, Alain C., and Smith, K. Wayne. *How Much Is Enough?* New York: Harper & Row, 1971.

Freedman, Lawrence D. *The Evolution of Nuclear Strategy*. New York: St. Martin's Press, 1981.

Peckman, Joseph A., ed. *Setting National Priorities: Agenda for the 1980s*. Washington, D.C.: Brookings Institution, 1980.

Quanback, Alton H., and Bleckman, Barry M. *Strategic Forces: Issues for the Mid-Seventies*. Washington, D.C.: Brookings Institution, 1973.

Rose, John P. *The Evolution of U.S. Army Nuclear Doctrine, 1945–1980*. Boulder, Colo.: Westview Press, 1980.

Speed, Roger D. *Strategic Deterrence in the 1980s*. Stanford: Hoover Institution Press, 1979.

U.S., *Department of Defense Annual Report, Fiscal Year 1981*. Washington, D.C.: U.S. Government Printing Office, 1980.

12

LIMITED WAR:

CONVENTIONAL AND NUCLEAR

The world has lived in the shadow of nuclear war for a third of a century. During that time, the number of acknowledged nuclear powers has grown from one to five, all of which have become engaged during the same period in some form of military action. Nevertheless, no nuclear weapon has been fired belligerently since 1945. Instead, the nuclear powers have carefully limited their use of military force, occasionally at a considerable price in military and political frustration.

It might be supposed that such a condition was inevitable. In the face of unlimited risk, extreme prudence seems no more than reasonable. Yet there are objectives for which states would risk physical destruction; at least, there are conditions they would risk war to avert. In 1962 the United States was prepared to risk nuclear war to force the removal of Soviet missiles from Cuba. In 1973 the U.S.S.R. appeared ready to risk war with the United States to prevent military defeat of Egypt by Israel. Apparently, even with nuclear weapons in the background, there *are* interests for which nations will fight despite the risks.

Those risks might be lessened if each side were certain of the other's vital interests. As one observer put it, there are things that

the United States would fight a major war to defend, but . . . these are things the Soviet Union would not fight a major war to obtain. And there are undoubtedly things the Soviet Union would fight a major war to defend, but these are not things the United States would fight a major war to obtain.[1]

That may be putting the case too confidently; still, it is true that clearly vital interests are rarely a matter of dispute. But the interests themselves, unfortunately, are rarely so clear, the less so since states habitually avoid specifying the extent of commitments until challenged.[2]* (Telling the other

*It may also be noted that a state's vital interests are not always known or agreed upon by its governmental decision-makers. This, of course, further compounds the problem.

side what line one is prepared to go to war to defend implies readiness to concede everything up to that line—as the United States learned to its sorrow in Korea in 1950.)

Once hostile actions are underway, even substantial risk cannot by itself guarantee restraint any more than the threat of punishment can by itself deter crime. This is the more true because restraint during war carries with it a number of penalties for the state exercising it. At the very least, such restraint may provoke domestic dissatisfaction with the conduct of the war—the belief that lives and resources are being squandered ineffectively. Obviously, it may also lead to battlefield reverses. Furthermore, restraint or deliberate limitation may appear to strip war of the function of "settling matters once and for all"—a function traditionally attributed to it by most Americans.

Restraint—even restraint induced by fear—is not of course inevitable. It must be generated by the decisions and actions of national leaders. "When the fate of empires is at stake, the convictions of their statesmen are the medium for survival."[3] We have already seen that in the United States once the nation has committed itself to war, self-restraint in the use of force goes against the historical grain.[4] Accordingly, the limitation of war continues to be one of the most intractable of national security policy issues, both intellectually and as a practical matter of policy. Perhaps as a result, America's approach to limitation remains ill defined. Certainly, our most recent experience with limited conflict has produced little consensus about its nature or the requirements for conducting it successfully—and even less consensus about the desirability of engaging in it at all.

LIMITED WAR IN HISTORY

Limited war is hardly novel. Historically, most wars have been limited in one way or another; few have resulted in the utter physical or political demise of a contending state. The total destruction of Carthage occupies a special place in history in large part because it was so unusual an event—to the point where the term *Carthaginian Peace* is frequently used to describe the consequences of total war. In contrast, throughout much Western history at least, the means, scope, objectives, and consequences of war were sharply curtailed by the limited military power of states and by their limited ability to project it beyond their own borders. Together, such constraints tended to restrict both the objectives for which states went to war and their expectations about what might be achieved thereby.

Limitation of Means. The most obvious reason why war was limited was simple insufficiency of means to prosecute it to the utmost. As the destruction of Carthage suggests, it is not strictly true that limited means forbade total war. Even with crude weapons annihilation was possible. But until modern technology began to produce weapons capable of wreaking massive destruction rapidly and at great distances, the prosecution of total war implied an immense expenditure of effort: the raising and equipping of large armies and fleets, their sustenance under difficult conditions and at great distances, and the consequent disruption of normal patterns of agriculture, industry, and commerce. Thus even when simple insufficiency of resources did not impose a physical limit on war, the political and economic difficulties of generating them usually did.

Limitation of Scope. Just as material insufficiency tended to limit the intensity of war, so lack of mobility tended to limit its geographical scope. Once again, the limitation was not rigid, as the exploits of Alexander, Attila, and other famous conquerors attest. The difficulties of transporting and sustaining large bodies of troops far from the homeland nevertheless figured prominently in the strategic calculations of rulers. Conflicts like the Crusades, the American Revolution, or Napoleon's invasion of Russia requiring one side to project its power across very large distances conferred a substantial advantage on the defender—an advantage frequently decisive. Even today, jet aircraft capable of transporting great numbers of personnel and materiel worldwide have not entirely eliminated the logistical difficulties of conducting a larger-scale, lengthy war far from home.

The number of states likely to become involved also limited the scope of war. Most wars centered upon disputed borders, territorial claims, or matters of royal succession and preeminence, and thus tended to concern only the principals. Occasionally, one contender or both would call upon allies for assistance, but even then the number of active belligerents was likely to remain small. Indeed, the record suggests that as the number of participants increased so also did the duration and intensity of the war and the uncertainty of its outcome.[5]

Limitation of Objectives. As suggested, material weakness served to limit war directly, despite the contrary intentions of the embattled states. More often, however, weakness limited war prospectively by influencing strategic calculations of the belligerents, moderating the objectives for which they fought. This interaction of means and objectives was not necessarily explicit; the lucrative target offered by Marco Polo's Cathay could hardly have moved a European monarch, to whom China was as remote as the moon. Even when the means existed, however, the absolute destruction of the adversary was rarely contemplated. Quite aside from the expense of the task, there was usually little to be gained from a policy of annihilation. On the contrary, there was frequently something to be lost, for a defeated state could be exploited and thereby repay the costs of the war with interest.

In any case, even objectives carefully tailored to means did not guarantee the accuracy of the war calculus, as the failure rate of wars of conquest attests. Those leaders concerned with matters of war and diplomacy were accordingly inclined to be fairly conservative in their estimates of attainable objectives. Indeed, it is likely that left to themselves, "professional" politicians would have limited the objectives—and consequences—of war even more severely than was usually the case.

While objectives may be influenced by calculations of relative power, they are not necessarily determined by them. Political pressures on decision-makers also affect objectives. In turn, these pressures are a function of the domestic structures of states. As long as war and diplomacy were the duty and prerogative of aristocratic elites, who enjoyed wide decision latitude and who often had more in common with each other than with their respective populace, war aims were relatively easily limited. Both interest and necessity argued for self-restraint—the first, because no ruler wished to challenge the legitimate basis of the authority by which all ruled; and the second, because ruling elites were frequently reminded of the fragile nature of their domestic support. Such support could easily erode in the wake of successive defeats, with loss of prestige by the ruler and strain on the fabric of society.[6] Assassination or rebellion might be the price of too wasteful an expenditure of the society's resources. It is no coincidence that the two great political convulsions of modern Western history—the French and Russian revolutions—both followed the engagement of these states in unsuccessful, exhausting wars.[7]

MODERN WAR: THE REMOVAL OF PHYSICAL LIMITS

For all the reasons mentioned, most early wars were conducted with limited means in pursuit of limited objectives, and thus produced limited consequences. Such limitation, however, generally constituted a *condition*, not a *policy,* and it frequently reflected, as we have seen, less the preferences of belligerents than their weaknesses. Moreover, the weaknesses were mutual; if the winner's gains were limited, so also were the loser's costs. Modern students of limited war who approvingly quote Clausewitz's injunction that war must be governed by political objectives are apt to forget (as Clausewitz himself did not) that the surest way to achieve war aims is not to nibble at an opponent but to render it incapable of interfering. Most early politicians would have agreed with this view; the problem lay in securing the means to effect it.

By the late eighteenth century, the means were becoming available. The Industrial Revolution made possible a vast increase in the effective means of waging war—at the price, however, of mobilizing the productive, as well as the military, sector of society. The rise of nationalism and the evolution of competing national ideologies provided the incentive for such mobilization, and the nation-in-arms provided the mechanism. Sheer material weakness ceased to be an inevitable governor on the engine of war.

Nor could prudence control belligerence. The very requirement to mobilize public support on a national scale promoted a growing diffusion of political power from aristocratic elites to the middle classes, whose money and members would be required to fight.* Such a shift had been foreshadowed in Great Britain, where the rulers' persistent need to generate war-supporting taxes had led directly to parliamentary checks on royal authority. The result was to limit the freedom of governing elites to frame war aims in accordance with *raisons d'état*. A war demanding the concerted efforts of the entire society could not easily be justified by arguments of diplomatic expedience. Such a war would require universal objectives grounded in high moral purpose— liberty, democracy, universal justice. Inevitably, the opponent in such a contest must be cast in unequivocally hostile terms—a moral leper to be purged from the society of civilized states. Such a characterization invariably made it difficult to end a war by negotiation. Thus, precisely when the removal of physical limits on the use of force made the exercise of prudence essential, development of democratic universalism began to render it impossible.

Finally, in World War I, the link between means and ends came full circle. As the war consumed life and treasure on an unprecedented scale, even the original objectives of the contenders became obscured in the demand for a conclusion capable of justifying the sacrifices already made. Totality of destruction required totality of result. Means had come once again to dominate war—but now, not with the result of limiting it but rather of preventing its limitation short of absolute victory or utter defeat.[8]

THE IMPACT OF NUCLEAR WEAPONS

By the time the United States dropped the first atomic bomb on Hiroshima at the close of World War II, it appeared to many people that total war had become the rule in conflicts rather than the exception. At first nuclear weapons seemed to augur no change in that condition. A future war fought with nuclear weapons would, it was speculated, end as World Wars I and II had ended: with the unconditional surrender of the loser of an essentially military contest. Nuclear weapons might hasten the victory, but initially few observers expected them to transform the process by which victory would be achieved. Even as late as 1955, President Eisenhower could still assert with conviction, "Where these things [tactical nuclear weapons] are used on strictly military targets and for strictly military purposes, I can see no reason why they shouldn't be used as you would a bullet or anything else."[9]

The Korean War seemed to contradict this view of the unconditional utility of nuclear strength. The United States refrained from employing nuclear weapons despite its virtual monopoly. The war offered few lucrative targets, however, and U.S. decision-makers were loath to squander a still-limited

---

*Another sources of diffusion of power from the elites was the institution of bureaucracies to collect the taxes and acquire conscripts. The bureaucracies were in theory responsible to the elites, but were in effect a further dilution of the elite's power. It should also be noted that power was not as much granted by the sovereign to the members of the middle class as it was taken by them. This was especially true in France.

nuclear stockpile on a conflict that many believed to be a Soviet feint. Restraint thus represented no essential contradiction of the general belief in the war-fighting function of the nuclear arsenal. On the contrary, one immediate consequence of U.S. frustration in Korea was renewed insistence in many quarters that the United States must be ready to employ nuclear weapons in any future war.[10]

As nuclear arsenals grew, however, and as increasingly sophisticated means of delivery were developed, more and more analysts began to realize that nuclear weapons were not just "larger bullets." They did not offer simply a quantum jump in the military power of the state that owned them. Instead, they transformed the very relationship of that power to foreign policy—partly because of the immense damage they could do, partly because of the speed with which they could do it, but perhaps most of all because of the *ease* with which they could do it. In the past, international coercion was difficult and time-consuming. Historically, to coerce another state—whether in aggression or in self-defense—a state had first to defeat (or threaten to defeat) its armies. Until then, one could not seriously threaten its civil society. Accordingly, civil damage was incidental to the progress of defeating hostile forces in the field, although in some circumstances it might contribute to that objective by weakening the opponent's industrial base.

Nuclear weapons threatened to stand this relationship on its head. One weapon could destroy a city in the flicker of an eyelash. Highly significant, it could do so without first defeating the opponent's military forces, provided that a few aircraft or missiles could penetrate the enemy defense. In the future, a state might conceivably find itself in total ruins without having lost a single battle—in which case, of course, the traditional notion of victory or defeat would cease to have meaning.[11]

At first, such a prospect seemed tailor-made to the requirements of U.S. security. Caught between what they perceived as a growing threat abroad and economic pressures at home, and enjoying a virtual monopoly of nuclear power, some U.S. policy-makers saw in nuclear weapons the ideal alternative to dangerous military weakness or disastrous inflation. Henceforth, the United States would rely on the ultimate threat of nuclear punishment to deter and, if necessary, defeat Soviet aggression. In Winston Churchill's famous phrase, "Safety would be the sturdy child of terror."

It was not long before the fundamental paradox of such a policy became apparent: nuclear weapons were *too* powerful. To threaten their employment in response to any but the most extreme aggression established an absurd disparity between provocation and response. Worse, a deterrent based on such a threat risked disbelief on the part of the potential aggressor. Thus, sole dependence for deterrence on a threat of nuclear retaliation might well invite aggression.

Not only was nuclear war or the threat thereof a blunt instrument, but it had soon become a dangerous one as well. By the late 1950s, the Soviet Union had achieved its own strategic nuclear capability, and henceforth nuclear war could mean massive mutual destruction. However unhappy the implications, U.S. policy-makers were forced to come to an inescapable conclusion: that far from enshrining total war as the ultimate expression of national will, nuclear arms had instead produced a new incentive to limit—not, as before, because total war was so difficult to wage, but because it had become so easy and so suicidal. (But wars between nonnuclear states can and do proceed on a total basis as in the past with nuclear weapons having little if any influence.)

SOME CURRENT LIMITED WAR ISSUES

Today there is little disagreement among Western strategists that total nuclear war would be an unmitigated catastrophe for both contenders and a large part of the world. Some strategic analysts are not so sure that the Soviet Union's leaders share this view.[12]* Still, one might suppose that agreement on means to avert such a war could be achieved. Agreement on the danger of nuclear war, however, does not automatically imply agreement on how to avoid it. In the end, limitation must occur in the context of actual or imminent conflict, in an atmosphere of uncertainty and danger, and under the pressure of a host of competing objectives and commitments.

As shown in the preceding chapter, the doctrine of "flexible targeting" announced in August 1980 raised once again the issue of limiting a nuclear exchange. When explaining to reporters "the new countervailing nuclear strategy," Secretary of Defense Harold Brown reflected that it is very likely that limited nuclear strikes would get out of control and escalate into full-scale nuclear war.[13] In the next few pages we will examine some of the issues involved in war limitation and the problems this presents for American policy.

Conventional War. An obvious way in which a future war might be limited is by the tacit or explicit agreement of participants to refrain from using nuclear weapons. The very fact that so many years have elapsed without their use provides a powerful impulse to observe such a limitation.

In principle, at least, there is no reason why the United States and its allies could not preserve their national interests by conventional means alone. In Europe alone, the Western allies have both more manpower and a stronger

---

*Soviet military sources refer to the use of nuclear weapons as an integral component of their offensive strategy. One perspective on this is provided by Richard Pipes, "Why the Soviet Union Thinks It Could Fight and Win a Nuclear War," *Commentary* 64, no. 1 (July 1977): 21–34. On the other hand, at least one Soviet military expert, Lt. Gen. Mikhail A. Milshtein, has denied specifically that Soviet leaders consider total nuclear war "winnable." See Anthony Austin, "Moscow Expert Says U.S. Errs on Soviet War Aims," *New York Times*, August 25, 1980, p. A-2. The latter source is in accordance with the public approach of Soviet political leaders who generally refer to the horrors of nuclear war and to the Soviet desire to minimize (or eliminate) the risks of such a war. Soviet doctrinal literature suggests, however, that they at least plan for the possibility of a nuclear exchange during a war. Such ambivalence, it might be noted, is not confined to the U.S.S.R. and constitutes yet another impediment to successful limitation.

industrial base than the Warsaw Pact. In Asia, China's enormous land army constitutes a powerful military resource, but one offset both by the greater technological capabilities of the United States and its allies (especially in air and naval power) and by China's limited ability to project its power beyond its own borders. Moreover, neither the Soviet Union nor China could afford to focus its entire forces against the West, for each must guard against assault by the other.

Notwithstanding these apparent advantages, many strategists believe that the West would be seriously disadvantaged if it were to limit its forces to a conventional response to conventional aggression. This reflects, in part, the West's persistent inability to translate its great military potential into actual military capabilities, and in part, ambivalence and fundamental conflicts of interest among Western states themselves.

Europe. In Western Europe, from Norway around the Mediterranean littoral to Turkey, NATO divisions are outnumbered by Warsaw Pact divisions—more than half of which are Russian—by a ratio of roughly two to three. A relatively high proportion of the pact forces are armored divisions, combining high mobility with heavy firepower. The Warsaw Pact enjoys substantial superiority in tanks and artillery as well. In tactical aircraft—those configured and deployed to support battlefield operations—the pact also claims a wide edge.[14] The pact's relative strength grew significantly in all these respects during the 1970s.

Critics are quick to point out that such statistics are misleading. NATO divisions are considerably larger both in personnel and in firepower than their Warsaw Pact counterparts. Moreover, some analysts doubt the reliability of non-Soviet Warsaw Pact forces, particularly in support of outright aggression. Further, the Warsaw Pact advantage in tanks, some argue, can be offset relatively inexpensively by "emerging technologies" in the areas of target acquisition and deep attack. There are a number of systems that will significantly increase the effectiveness of current NATO firepower. The deep-attack strategy calls for tactical air strikes and sophisticated munitions to disrupt the reinforcing elements of Warsaw Pact forces. Similarly, some analysts discount the tactical aircraft balance for several reasons. Even though NATO has fewer aircraft than the Warsaw Pact, they are generally believed to be qualitatively superior and their pilots better trained. Also, though a large share of pact aircraft are interceptors, whose limited range and payload restrict their ground support capability, most NATO aircraft are multipurpose fighter-bombers, which are equally useful for control of airspace and for close air support of ground forces.[15]

Finally, those who insist that a conventional defense is feasible note that traditionally an attacker requires a two- or three-to-one advantage to defeat a defender, who presumably has the ability to fortify the ground he will defend. The current Warsaw Pact advantage, while significant, is obviously not nearly that great.

Conceding some aspects of the critics' case, we see that it is nevertheless true that the Soviet Union and its allies enjoy certain irreducible advantages in a test of conventional strength in Europe. One is simply geographic: whereas the Soviet Union is a continental power, able to resupply and reinforce its armies by land, the United States must do so across the vast expanse of the Atlantic and in the face of a very considerable Soviet submarine threat. Air transport can only partially alleviate this problem, since airfields and the aircraft themselves would be vulnerable to attack and could not, in any case, move the great tonnage required.

Another advantage accruing to the Warsaw Pact is the fact that the various pact national forces use Soviet-designed weapons and equipment, whereas NATO forces are hampered by a wide variety of weapons and equipment produced competitively by member nations. As a result, many items are not interchangeable or mutually compatible, increasing both the difficulty of co-ordinating the multinational forces and the problems of maintenance and resupply. Some progress has been made recently toward intra-alliance stand-ardization; but it is unlikely that the problem will be solved while arms industries remain symbols of national self-reliance and important economic factors, domestically and in foreign trade, throughout the NATO states.[16]

A third advantage that many analysts ascribe to the Warsaw Pact—perhaps a decisive one—is its presumed ability to choose the time and place of attack. Such an argument, of course, is grounded in the premise that a European war would result from a deliberate act of Soviet aggression. In that case, it is argued, the East would enjoy some measure of surprise, and its forces could easily muster the requisite local three-to-one advantage over a dispersed and unready NATO defense. Eventually, it might be conceded, latent West-ern power could make its weight felt—but in the meantime, politically and militarily vital ground would have been lost. To regain it, NATO would have to go on the offensive in its turn—but without any hope of achieving com-parable surprise.

Critics respond that such a scenario is improbable; an attack on such a scale, they contend, would require extensive preparations that could not be concealed from Allied intelligence. In any case, the attack would most likely follow a period of increasing East-West tension, itself serving to alert NATO. Such warnings, however, have been ignored before. (The United States, for example, ignored continuing significant warnings of Japanese attack prior to Pearl Harbor;[17] more recently, the 1973 Arab-Israeli War demonstrated once again the failure to react to political and military warning signals when to do so would involve heavy economic and political costs.)[18]* Although the United States may be able to act unilaterally in time to fend off disaster, or at least to mitigate damages, it is all too apparent that the burdensome bureaucracy in any alliance command would impose fatal delays on the ability to respond to

---

*Some analysts argue that Secretary of State Kissinger knew of the impending attack but ignored warnings thereof for various reasons. See Ray S. Cline, "Policy without Intelligence," *Foreign Policy*, no. 17 (winter 1974/75), pp. 121–35, and Edward Luttwak and Walter Laqueur, "Kissinger and Yom Kippur War," *Commentary* 58 (September 1974): 33–40.

crises. Moreover, there is disquieting evidence that a major Soviet attack could be launched with less warning time than previously supposed.

All in all, the conventional balance in Europe for the 1980s is precarious. Even so, it is certainly within NATO's power in the decade, given sufficient time and effort, to build forces adequate to defend against Soviet aggression despite the disadvantages mentioned. Potential power can be translated into actual power if the political will exists to do so. Thus far the will has been weak. Notwithstanding NATO's declaratory commitment to forward-deployed conventional defense, at no time since the creation of the Atlantic Alliance have its members been willing to provide the level of forces generally believed necessary for that purpose. Their reluctance stems in part from the severe economic and political costs such a task would entail. Modern conventional forces cost a great deal of money, and Western governments must balance that cost against a host of competing claims for budgetary attention. Of course, Soviet forces are also expensive; but they are far cheaper man-for-man than comparable Western formations. In any case, with greater political latitude than their Western counterparts, Eastern leaders can impose on their societies relatively more severe demands.

Perhaps a more important reason for Western reluctance to increase reliance upon NATO's conventional capability is the fear of the Western European allies that to do so would signify unwillingness to escalate to nuclear war, thereby reducing deterrence against Soviet aggression. The Europeans fear that the United States would almost certainly choose to fight a conventional war in Europe, however protracted, if the means were available, rather than risk a strategic nuclear engagement with the U.S.S.R. Having twice in this century suffered from the devastation of a conventional war, the European members of NATO are understandably reluctant to repeat the experience again. It is immaterial, they add, that the United States might choose not to limit itself to a conventional response in the event of Soviet conventional attack; if the Soviet Union believed the United States would not respond with nuclear weapons, deterrence might fail.

It remains only to note that the entire issue of conventional limitation in Europe has typically been framed against the threat of massive and deliberate Soviet aggression. To many observers on both sides of the Atlantic, such a threat is not very probable. Instead, most analysts believe it much more likely that any European conflict would result from some local crisis, or perhaps from expansion of conflict begun elsewhere. In that event, many of the preceding considerations would be less important, and conventional limitation might then seem desirable to all parties.

Asia. In Europe, the prospects for conventional limitation are heavily influenced by the direct geographical confrontation of two alliances roughly comparable in overall power. In Asia the situation is more complex. Three nuclear powers—the United States, the Soviet Union, and China—and three nonnuclear ones—Japan, North Korea, and South Korea—interact in a highly unstable milieu. Conventional limitation of Asian conflict is accordingly a more complicated matter, and the prospects for limitation depend heavily on the character of a potential conflict, its location, and the major participants. Chapter 17 addresses this topic.

While it is unlikely that a U.S.-Soviet conflict would occur in Asia, except as a part of wider and spreading hostilities, its possibility cannot be discounted. Such a conflict might arise in connection with a confrontation elsewhere, as the result of a Soviet action in the area, or simply as an outgrowth of some local dispute. In any case the prospects for limitation are difficult to forecast. In general, conventional warfare in Asia would seem to favor the West more than in Europe. War in the Pacific area would enhance the relative importance of the powerful U.S. Pacific fleet (especially its aircraft carriers) and the network of advanced U.S. bases. The logistical problem of the U.S.S.R. would be far more acute than in Europe, since it would depend heavily on the limited and vulnerable facilities of the Trans-Siberian rail system. At the same time, because the U.S. Asian allies might be less immediately threatened, there might be less pressure on the United States to escalate quickly to nuclear weapons.

However, precisely because conventional limitation would work to Western advantage, it might be more difficult to achieve. Certainly it is hard to imagine a conventional war in Asia in the event of nuclear war in Europe. Even without that precedent, the U.S.S.R. might well refuse to acknowledge an unfavorable limiting condition. Thus the potential for limitation would depend crucially on the way the conflict arose and the nature of the interests at stake.

Notwithstanding the renewal of diplomatic relations with the United States and even tacit cooperation in checking Soviet designs, the People's Republic of China (P.R.C.) also remains a potential, if not likely, threat to the security interests of the United States and its allies, both because of China's actual and potential power, and because of the apparent aspirations of its leadership to a dominant role in Asian politics. The recent increased cordiality of Sino-American relations in contrast to the cold war period cannot entirely obscure the basic differences between the two systems and the fact that only thirty years have elapsed since American and Chinese forces faced each other in battle. At the same time, U.S. allies—chiefly Japan, Australia, and South Korea—are more cautious than the United States in their evaluations of Chinese objectives.[19]

Still, the prospects for serious conflict with China appear remote in the short- and medium-run. China's military power on land is impressive, but its ability to project that power abroad remains limited. Chinese adventurism is further restrained by continuing Sino-Soviet hostility. For all these reasons, conventional limitation seems entirely possible in the unlikely event of Sino-American conflict, except perhaps on the mainland itself. In the latter case, it is difficult to see how the use of nuclear weapons could be avoided. This is not because conventional success would be impossible but because its price in the face of Chinese manpower superiority would probably be intolerable to Americans while they retained a nuclear near monopoly vis-à-vis China. (When American nuclear superiority weakens seriously, the limiting problem in a war with China will assume somewhat the same aspect it currently bears in relation to the U.S.S.R.)

In any event, the most immediate American security problem in Asia is not the potential for either conventional or nuclear war with a major power, but war involving the two Koreas or revolutionary or interstate conflict in the emerging nations. Because the latter type of conflict has special characteristics, it is treated separately in the next chapter; but we will have a few things to say below about its implications for the limiting problem. Limitation of conflict if North Korea should again attack the South would depend in part on the level and type of Soviet or Chinese involvement. If such involvement were substantial, the problem would become that addressed in preceding paragraphs; if not, then the South should be able to prevail with but limited U.S. force support.

The potential for conventional conflict involving the United States is, of course, not limited to Europe and the Pacific nor to the two major communist powers. Indeed, many analysts consider the Persian Gulf to be the most likely location for future hostilities endangering vital American interests. However, the high probability that such hostilities would involve direct confrontation between the United States and the Soviet Union suggests that in this region, many of the same consideration affecting limitation in Europe would apply. Further analysis of the conflict possibilities in the Persian Gulf can be found in Chapter 18.

Theater Nuclear Weapons. Early in the 1950s, American scientists demonstrated the technical feasibility of producing nuclear weapons with yields of less than one kiloton.[20] This development excited considerable interest in the possible battlefield uses of nuclear weapons—especially on the part of the U.S. Army, which instinctively distrusted claims that air power would be decisive in any future war.[21] When, by 1953, it became clear that NATO would be unable to reach the level of conventional forces believed necessary to repel a Soviet attack on Western Europe, the United States decided to deploy so-called tactical nuclear weapons to fill the gap. The early weapons were crude and cumbersome. The 280 millimeter "Atomic Cannon," for example, was so large that it could travel safely in Europe only on the wider roads. These weapons, however, were merely the forerunners of an arsenal that by now has grown to include many thousands of tactical nuclear weapons of all types. Not to be outdone, the Soviet Union has deployed tactical weapons of its own, including long-range missiles based in the U.S.S.R. and targeted on Western Europe.[22]

Such weapons represent a significant fraction of each side's total nuclear capability. Unfortunately, technology appears to have outrun strategy in this area, for despite their huge inventories, neither the United States nor the U.S.S.R. has articulated a wholly persuasive doctrine for employing such weapons, except in the context of an all-out nuclear war—in which tactical nuclear weapons become largely incidental. In the West, at least, the issue of theater nuclear warfare has been a subject of near continuous debate both within and outside government circles.[23] Not surprisingly, the 1979 NATO decision to modernize its tactical nuclear weapons systems in Europe provoked discussion and public protest, especially in Great Britain and West Germany.

Not the least of the limiting problems posed by theater nuclear weapons is defining what they are. Today's weapons range in yield from the megaton level—far larger than the bombs dropped on Hiroshima and Nagasaki—down to less than one kiloton.* Recent developments in warhead technology have made possible the production of still smaller "mini-nukes," with yields lower than some current conventional weapons.[24] The United States has developed, but not yet deployed, a very low yield type of warhead that produces casualties primarily through enhanced radiation rather than by a blast.

The diversity of types and yields is matched by an equal diversity of delivery means. In NATO, nuclear weapons can be delivered against targets by aircraft of a variety of types, short- and long-range missiles, conventional artillery, or they can be emplaced as mines to produce barriers. Similar capabilities (with the possible exception of artillery) are available to the Soviet Union.

Limiting Theater Nuclear War. Such a diversity of weapons makes it nearly impossible to define—and hence limit—theater nuclear war according to a precise physical distinction, the more so since the U.S.S.R., whose weapons are generally larger than NATO's, acknowledges no such limitation.[25] In fact, neither side has made a serious effort to distinguish between theater and strategic nuclear war on the basis of yield. Instead, efforts to define theater nuclear war have focused on limitations of use and target selection. Thus, the United States has defined theater nuclear weapons as those capable of directly influencing the course of a theater battle. Such a definition is, however, inherently problematic. "Influencing the theater battle" could range from the delivery of nuclear weapons directly against troops in the field to the long-range interdiction of supply lines and communications. Much of Germany, it is worth recalling, was reduced to rubble by Allied bombers in an effort to influence the course of the land battle directly or indirectly.

Clearly, at some point theater nuclear war merges imperceptibly with strategic nuclear war. From the point of view of the United States and the Soviet Union, of course, the borders of the respective homelands represent a highly significant boundary, one that the U.S.S.R. has repeatedly pressed the United

---

*Nuclear weapon yields are expressed in terms of TNT equivalents; thus a megaton weapon has the destructive power of a million tons of TNT; a kiloton weapon has that of a thousand tons of TNT.

States to recognize. Understandably, however, such a distinction does not impress America's European allies, for whom a theater nuclear conflict so defined would be to all intents and purposes strategic.

For that very reason, the problem of limiting theater nuclear war has posed as much of an intra-alliance problem as a U.S.-Soviet one. As far back as the 1950s, NATO studies indicated convincingly that large-scale "battlefield" use of nuclear weapons would leave a considerable portion of Europe in ruins.[26] Since that time, improvements in delivery system accuracy and warhead technology have somewhat reduced the amount of unavoidable "collateral damage" to civilian lives and property. Even so, it is hardly conceivable that highly urbanized European societies could emerge from a theater nuclear conflict of any magnitude without catastrophic damage, especially since Soviet nuclear doctrine continues to emphasize large-scale use of weapons once nuclear hostilities have begun.[27]

All these considerations suggest that the limitation of theater nuclear warfare would be technically difficult to achieve; the psychological difficulties might be greater still. As Thomas Schelling has pointed out, the ability to limit conflict of any kind depends on the existence of a clear demarcation between permissible and prohibited acts.[28] For over a quarter-century, the clearest demarcation has been that of separating nuclear from nonnuclear war. That fact alone—that the initial use of nuclear weapons would rupture a long-standing firebreak—might be the greatest impediment to subsequent limitation efforts. In comparison no subsequent limit would appear so unmistakable. Moreover, the very trauma of crossing the nuclear threshold might so distort both sides' perceptions of the situation as to produce an uncontrolled spiral toward general nuclear war. As we shall see, however, that danger underlies the most persuasive current justification for retaining a theater nuclear capability.

Theater Nuclear Weapons and War-fighting Advantage. Even were it possible to limit the use of nuclear weapons to the battlefield, and even were such limitations tolerable to the European allies (two of whom, it should be noted, possess the independent capability to enlarge such a conflict), it is not clear that the limitation would favor the West. Early arguments by Western strategists claiming that nuclear weapons would favor the defense, and thereby enable NATO to compensate for its conventional deficiencies, have since persuasively been rebutted.[29] Far from reducing the need for forces, the battlefield use of nuclear weapons would greatly increase attrition, enhancing the advantage of the side with the greater and more accessible reserves. Moreover, offensive use of nuclear weapons might enable an attacker to breach a defensive position cheaply, obviating the need to mass for an attack, and thus depriving the defender of both a key defensive advantage and a lucrative target for its own weapons.

The logistical advantage of nuclear use to NATO is also arguable. Nuclear weapons might reduce the need for conventional munitions, but they would make resupply and reinforcement more difficult. The difficulty might well affect NATO more than the Warsaw Pact, for where Soviet supplies can be transported along dispersed and easily concealed land routes, the United States would have to rely on highly vulnerable ports and airfields.

Finally, some analysts have argued that the use of nuclear weapons in a land battle would nullify one of the West's most potent advantages: greater industrial and technological capability. According to this view, theater nuclear warfare tends to favor the side that employs the crudest (that is, the most powerful and least discriminate) weapons. Conventional war, by contrast, puts a premium on technological sophistication—accuracy, reliability, and versatility. Thus, such critics argue, in fighting a theater nuclear war, the West would be playing to the Soviet Union's strongest suit.[30]

Theater Nuclear Weapons and Deterrence. Notwithstanding the difficulties of limiting a theater nuclear war and the uncertain balance of costs and benefits it offers the West, theater nuclear weapons continue to be considered vital to the security of NATO. Today, however, their importance is couched less in terms of war-fighting than in terms of deterrence. NATO planners argue that the very difficulty of limiting theater nuclear war contributes to deterrence by raising the risk for the Soviets that their aggression would initiate, sooner or later and probably sooner, escalation to strategic war. Theater nuclear weapons thus become important chiefly for their ability to "couple" the U.S. strategic deterrent to European security.[31] This function, more than any presumptive battlefield utility, makes the continuing retention of a visible theater nuclear posture essential to the European members of NATO—for whom, as we have already seen, deterrence is far more desirable than defense, however successful the latter might ultimately prove to be. In contrast, the United States is attracted to a theater nuclear capability because it offers at least a way station between conventional and nuclear war. Thus, paradoxically, the United States and its allies support the theater nuclear posture for almost opposite reasons.

Unfortunately, such divergent premises have made it difficult to forge interallied agreement on an operational doctrine for employing theater nuclear weapons should conflict actually erupt. From the U.S. point of view, the longer their use can be delayed, and the more local that use when it occurs, the better the chance that the conflict will be resolved short of a U.S.-Soviet strategic exchange. In contrast, from the European viewpoint, the earlier and more geographically extended the threatened use of theater nuclear weapons, the greater the deterrence; and if deterrence fails, the greater the probability that the conflict will be resolved at the strategic level.*

*The heated debate on the development of the neutron bomb exemplifies the continuing tension between deterrence and war-fighting capability. For a detailed discussion of the history of the neutron bomb and the controversy surrounding it, see S. T. Cohen, *The Neutron Bomb: Political, Technological, and Military Issues* (Cambridge, Mass.: Institute for Foreign Policy Analysis, 1978).

"No-First-Use" and the Conventionalization Debate. During the early 1980s, virtually all of the issues described in the preceding discussions of conventional and theater nuclear conflict for the first time became matters of public controversy, both in the United States and in Europe. In the United States, public interest was aroused in part by the rhetorical belligerence of the Reagan administration, and in part by countervailing pressures in Congress and from antinuclear activists. Perhaps more surprising was the emergence of a broad European antinuclear opposition, which made its first appearance during the "neutron bomb" imbroglio of 1977, but whose attention ultimately focused on NATO's decision to deploy new Pershing II and cruise missiles (see Chapter 23). The breadth of the European antinuclear opposition was significant not simply because it was unprecedented, but also because it produced a peculiar inversion of trans-Atlantic arguments. Thus, the United States, heretofore the increasingly reluctant nuclear guarantor, found itself arguing the need for strategic "coupling" to the Europeans, who were its presumed beneficiaries. On their part, Europeans heretofore suspicious of American efforts to increase reliance on conventional forces found themselves urging conventional alternatives to raise the nuclear threshold. The debate was further complicated by broadly divergent reactions both here and abroad to "no-first-use" proposals, by similar controversy regarding the utility of the new conventional technologies noted earlier, and by active Soviet efforts to exploit the confusion.

At this writing, the debate continues undiminished,* and it is difficult to predict where it will end. It is already clear, however, that in NATO, at least, the issue of limitation as it applies to strategic doctrine and force structure will no longer be the province only of governmental officials and a small, informed elite. Whether the result will be sounder strategic policy or greater NATO disagreement remains to be seen.

The Prospects for Limitation. As this brief review of current limited war issues suggests, conflict limitation has become extraordinarily complex. Unlike limited wars long past, in which restraint was imposed on contenders by their own weakness, limitation in wars involving the major powers henceforth must depend on mutual restraint deliberately self-imposed by contenders because of their own strength. This requirement for conscious self-discipline in the use of force peculiarly complicates contemporary national security policy. In the United States, the need for self-restraint has found doctrinal expression in the flexible response strategy that replaced massive retaliation in the 1960s. Since that time, the United States has been committed to using the minimum of military force commensurate with the provocation and with the mission to be achieved. Unfortunately, there is little

---

*For a more detailed analysis of these issues, see Paul M. Cole and William J. Taylor, Jr., *The Nuclear Freeze Debate: Arms Control Issues for the 1980s* (Boulder, Colo.: Westview Press, 1983); and *The Nuclear Weapons Freeze and Arms Control* (Cambridge, Mass.: Center for Science and International Affairs, Harvard University, 1983).

evidence that the Soviet Union shares the same view. Moreover, the experience of the last decade with efforts at limitation has not been a happy one. As we have seen, the desire for limitation in NATO contends with European insistence on undiminished deterrence, resulting in a continuing doctrinal vacuum. A policy of measured application in Southeast Asia of conventional force in pursuit of expressly limited objectives and under tight political control resulted in a ten-year war that devoured American and Vietnamese lives and resources, produced enormous American domestic upheaval, discredited the United States abroad—and nevertheless resulted in failure.

Such problems have exacerbated disagreement concerning the advisibility of a limited war strategy. Some analysts blame faulty execution of an essentially valid strategic concept; others view U.S. actions during the 1960s and 1970s as a perversion of limited war strategy; some see in the Vietnam experience the predictable failure of unilateral self-restraint and argue for its abandonment altogether once the nation has committed itself to battle.[32]

To a certain extent, of course, such views reflect the interests of those who espouse them. They also indicate, however, that we have not yet fully come to terms with either the limiting problem itself or its implications for U.S. security. Believing the need for limitation to be self-evident, we have assumed that others would share that view; hoping self-restraint would be reciprocated, we have practiced it.

As our examination of current limited war issues has indicated, neither our allies nor our most likely antagonists view the limiting problem as we do. To the former, self-restraint may mean less deterrence. To the latter, it may imply military or political disadvantage. The reciprocation of restraint is therefore by no means assured, but rather, is highly sensitive to the nature of the conflict and the issues at stake, as well as to the skill and strength of the antagonists.

Restraint cannot be guaranteed by the unilateral limitation of political objectives, contrary to what many observers have suggested; for in the absence of any inherent limitation on the means of waging war, the possibility of limitation is determined not only by the objectives each side pursues but also by the consequences each side will tolerate. In a war involving great powers, committed in the full panoply of their prestige, each side may find intolerable the opponent's imposition by force, as well as its objectives. Thus, for example, speaking of American aid to Israel, Secretary of State Henry Kissinger is reported to have told the Egyptians, "Do not deceive yourself, the United States could not—either today or tomorrow—allow Soviet arms to win a big victory, even if it was not decisive, against United States arms. This has nothing to do with Israel or with you."[33] Soviet decision-makers could well hold a similar view; together these convictions illustrate another important prerequisite for limitation: the willingness of both contenders to tolerate an outcome neither had foreseen and in which the objectives of each are achieved imperfectly or not at all.

Many forms of successful limitation presume, paradoxically, a relatively high level of self-interested, implicit cooperation between the belligerents. As a minimum, both sides must be willing to tolerate less-than-satisfactory results while each still has the means to influence them to its own advantage. In an important sense, therefore—in the traditional sense—limited war among great powers must be a war without a winner; for a winner would imply a loser, and a great power cannot afford to lose. Nor, for that matter, is this requirement limited to great powers. Speaking of the Vietnam Peace Agreement, Kissinger noted that it

was always clear that a lasting peace could come about only if neither side sought to achieve everything that it had wanted; indeed, that stability depended on the relative satisfaction and therefore the relative dissatisfaction of all the parties concerned.[34]

Limited war, in short, requires compromise, and compromise presumes the willingness of each contender to accept, in a sense, the other's claim to an interest in the outcome. But when one side rejects that view—when it frames its goals in terms that deny its opponent any standing whatever—limited war is no longer possible in any but the narrowest sense; for then to at least one contender, compromise becomes synonymous with defeat. Such a situation is especially characteristic of revolutionary war, in which for each side the very continued existence of the other is at issue.

Many analysts consider Vietnam to have been essentially a revolutionary war, and they believe that fact helps to explain why a self-consciously limited U.S. strategy nevertheless produced such protracted frustration and ultimate failure. No matter that the United States carefully restrained the application of some aspects of its military power (and it did); to North Vietnam, any U.S. involvement was inherently illegitimate. No matter that the United States claimed to seek only limited objectives (and it did); to the North Vietnamese, the United States had no standing to make any claim, however limited. No matter, finally, that the United States offered to compromise any issue save the political autonomy of South Vietnam (and it did); to the other side, the very existence of such an entity was in dispute.

The strategic failure in Vietnam was perhaps less a failure of self-restraint than a failure to recognize the nature of the conflict in which such a strategy was being pursued. Political expectations based on the premise that the other side would be "reasonable" turned to disillusion when it became clear that North Vietnam had a different view of what "reasonable" meant. Compulsion is easier in theory than in practice against a very determined adversary. In an important sense, the Vietnam conflict was a total war in spite of very considerable American restraint, namely, peace could occur only through the defeat or exhaustion of one side or the other. In that crucial respect, perhaps every revolutionary war is peculiarly total, without regard for the means with which it is conducted.

By itself, therefore, the Vietnam conflict does not justify discarding limitation as an objective policy. It does demonstrate that the desire to limit must not blind the policy-maker to the possibility that an opponent might not share his preference or risk assessment. Early and accurate diagnosis of a serious divergence in risk calculations will be essential if policy is to evade the equally unpleasant extremes of frustration or overcommitment.

If there is an overall lesson to be drawn from the experience of the Vietnam era, it is that the limitation of war is and will likely be excruciatingly difficult. It will require the framing of objectives and the conduct of operations in ways that are, from an American perspective, hard to justify publicly. It will require persistence when the other side appears intransigent, and flexibility when the opponent is willing to negotiate. It will also require the willingness to accept a less-than-preferred outcome—a recognition that the other side may have legitimate claims that must be respected and at least partially conceded.

Finally, the Vietnam experience suggests that, generally speaking, the immediate incentives to escalate will nearly always be more powerful than the incentives to limit, notwithstanding the ultimate risk of overcommitment. This is especially true for a democratic government, whose need to generate and maintain public support may induce its leaders to overvalue the stakes, and in which loss of life and treasure will tend to breed pressure for a result worthy of the sacrifice. Indeed, it is yet to be proven that a democratic state such as the United States can keep the support of its populace in a protracted struggle that drains its blood for limited, perhaps negative, results.

In the future, therefore, more than ever before, a democratic state will go to war at its peril. Its survival will demand of its politicians not merely the wisdom to fight when fighting is necessary and profitable but the courage to refuse when it is not—and the good sense to know the difference.

DISCUSSION QUESTIONS

1. What is an operationally useful definition of *limited war*?

2. Is it possible to establish limits on conflict involving use of nuclear weapons? How can the problem best be approached?

3. In a time of international crisis, would domestic considerations constrain national security decision-makers in establishing limits to conflict?

4. What is the most fundamental requirement for the limiting process to become operative in war?

5. Why can it be said that revolutionary war knows no limits?

6. One of the principal criticisms of strategies calling for less than total nuclear warfare (if, that is, nuclear weapons are to be used at all) is that such strategies make nuclear war more "thinkable" and hence more likely. Does a doctrine of flexible nuclear options make nuclear war more or less possible? Limited or unlimited? Why?

7. What are the major categories in which limits on warfare may be established?

8. Do alliance considerations play an important role in decisions on the limiting process? If so, how?

9. Were the Arab-Israeli wars of 1967 and 1973 limited wars? Explain.

10. Can U.S. policy-makers expect Soviet leaders to cooperate in establishing limits to conflict? In the short-term? Over the long-term?

11. Do limiting considerations come into play in proxy wars? If so, how? Provide a historical example.

12. What limited objectives might underpin any Soviet attack of Western Europe with conventional forces?

RECOMMENDED READING

Blainey, Geoffrey. *The Causes of War*. New York: Free Press, 1973.

Brodie, Bernard. *War and Politics*. New York: Macmillan, 1973.

George, Alexander L., and Smoke, Richard. *Deterrence in American Foreign Policy: Theory and Practice*. New York: Columbia University Press, 1974.

Halperin, Morton H. *Bureaucratic Politics and Foreign Policy*. Washington, D.C.: Brookings Institution, 1974.

Heilbrun, Otto. *Conventional Warfare in the Nuclear Age*. New York: Frederick A. Praeger, 1965.

Huntington, Samuel P. *The Common Defense*. New York: Columbia University Press, 1961.

Kissinger, Henry A. *The White House Years*. New York: Little, Brown, 1979.

———. *A World Restored*. New York: Universal Press, 1964.

Osgood, Robert Endicott. *Limited War: The Challenge to American Strategy*. Chicago: University of Chicago Press, 1957.

Record, Jeffrey, and Anderson, Thomas. *U.S. Nuclear Weapons in Europe*. Washington, D.C.: Brookings Institution, 1974.

Schelling, Thomas C. *A Strategy of Conflict*. New York: Oxford University Press, 1960.

13

LOW-INTENSITY CONFLICT

Briefly defined, low-intensity conflict is the military recourse of nations and organizations to limited force or the threat of force to achieve political objectives without the full-scale commitment of resources and will that characterizes nation-state wars of survival or conquest.[1] This chapter will focus on one variant of low-intensity conflict, revolutionary warfare, a pervasive phenomenon still not well understood in the United States. Despite the seriousness of medium- to high-intensity conventional war, whether in Europe or the Middle East, it is likely that the military challenges of the future will involve low-intensity conflict. The pace and character of these conflicts will differ radically from the conventional ''limited'' wars of the past or the military scenarios envisioned for Europe. The likelihood that any Warsaw Pact attack on NATO would soon lead to escalation to strategic nuclear war should continue to serve as a deterrent to Soviet-conventional aggression in Europe. Moreover, given the future economic difficulties the U.S.S.R. will face in maintaining very high levels of nuclear and conventional forces (see Chapter 16 for a further discussion of this issue), the Soviets are likely to shift to other, low-cost, low-risk operations with potentially high geostrategic payoffs.

Low-intensity conflict and, hence, revolutionary warfare can assume many forms, but three in particular stand out—guerrilla or proxy warfare in the Third World, terrorism, and psychological warfare. From the Soviet perspective these forms of conflict are low cost because the support in most cases is in the form of small political cadres, special intelligence operations, and weapons sales, the latter being an increasingly important source of Soviet hard-currency earnings. Such operations are also low risk since the probabilities of direct conflict between U.S. and Soviet forces are minimal. The geostrategic payoffs are particularly high if the Soviets are able to gain footholds in naval bases located in Third World littoral nations. Soviet presence in these bases gives them the ability to interdict the major sea lanes of communication over which the energy and material resources vital to the security of the world's industrial democracies must be shipped. Already, the U.S.S.R. has acquired base rights

270

in Vietnam (Cam Ranh Bay), South Yemen (Aden), Ethiopia (Assab), Angola (Luanda), and Cuba (Cientuegos) (see Fig. 13.1). Some observers are also concerned that the Soviets may intend to move south from Afghanistan through Baluchistan to acquire a warm-water port on the Indian Ocean—a Soviet goal since the time of the czars. The last general feature of low-intensity conflict is the fact the "enemy" will not likely be the Soviet Union itself, but one of its proxies, or a small band of terrorists owing allegiance to some cause rather than to a nation. Unfortunately, neither the United States nor its allies are prepared pyschologically or materially to meet the low-intensity threat, and it would thus be worthwhile to discuss it in some detail before turning to revolutionary warfare.

The least visible and most insidious form of low-intensity conflict is psychological warfare (PSYWAR). Fighting with words has been a feature of warfare since the Peloponesian Wars of the fifth century B.C., but this form of warfare has experienced a quantum leap in development during the last three decades. Advances in communications technology, the increasing susceptibility of Western governments to pressure from an aroused electorate, and the dangers of a direct confrontation between the superpowers have speeded the evolution of subtle and sophisticated techniques for the accomplishment of political goals without the direct use of force. The Soviet Union, exploiting the openness and ease of communication in Western societies, has become a master at this form of warfare. In 1977, the Soviets succeeded in preventing the deployment and assembly of the neutron bomb in Europe, primarily through a massive propaganda effort in the European print and electronic news media.[2] Their threats in 1983 to retaliate in some unexplained manner if West Germany were to accept U.S. Pershing II missiles represents only the most recent example of a Soviet resort to PYSWAR. Moreover, political trends in Europe (slow but steady disintegration of NATO), and in the Third World (increasing a demographic pressures, deteriorating economies) will present the Soviet Union with even more opportunities for the use of PYSWAR techniques in the future. Growing public disenchantment with certain aspects of military policy in this country may even provide the Soviets with an opportunity to wage PYSWAR directly on the American people. Lest this discussion seem excessively pessimistic, one should add that the United States is just as capable of using PYSWAR techniques in defense of its interests as the Soviets are at using them against those interests. American policy-makers and the public at large must first recognize the existence of PYSWAR as a distinct and legitimate means of attaining political objectives. Concrete steps to improve our PYSWAR capability would include further research into the principles of this phenomenon, better coordination between civilian and military authorities, and a more aggressive broadcasting effort directed at the Soviet Union and its satellites. PYSWAR will be a prominent characteristic of conflict in the next two decades, and it would make sense for the United States to upgrade its capacity both to fight and to counteract this type of war.

The second form of low-intensity conflict is proxy warfare, whereby the

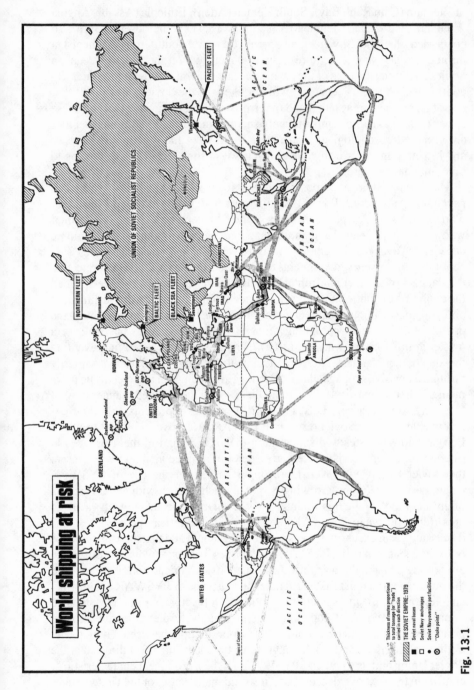

Fig. 13.1

Source: Admiral of the Fleet The Lord Hill-Norton, *World Shipping at Risk: The Looming Threat to the Lifelines*, Conflict Studies No. 111 (London: Institute for the Study of Conflict, 1979), pp. 10–11.

armed forces of one nation serve the political and military interests of another.[3] For a superpower unwilling to confront another superpower directly or to use its own troops in distant and inhospitable lands, proxy war constitutes a perfect tool for the attainment of limited political objectives at low cost. As with PSYWAR, the Soviets have proved to be masters at proxy warfare. Their handling of Cuban troops in Angola and Ethiopia in the middle and late 1970s serves as a textbook example of the use of proxies. The timely transport of Cuban regulars (by both Soviet civilian and military aviation) to Angola in late 1975 was decisive in bringing the Marxist-Leninist Movimento Popular de Libertiacao d'Angola (MPLA) guerrillas to power. Cuba has proved to be the Soviet's most reliable and effective proxy up to this point, but they have also used Libya, South Yemen, and their Eastern European allies as executors for policies in the Third World.

As noted above, proxy warfare offers the Soviets a tool for securing limited political objectives at low risk. Despite the relatively limited character of some of their proxy victories, the long-term effects of this style of warfare are insidious. Using others to do their fighting for them allows the Soviets to profess intentions of peace while continuing to undermine the U.S. strategic position in the Third World.

Dealing with the proxy warfare threat will first require a well-coordinated program to inform American citizens as to the true nature of Soviet proxy activities and the threat they pose to American interests. In containing this type of warfare, the United States has three policy options: deterrence through the judicious granting of economic and military assistance to Third World countries; preemption by active military intervention; or a simple military reaction once the proxy war has begun.[4] Whichever policy response is chosen, U.S. policy-makers should pay heed to the lessons of Vietnam, especially regarding the need for securing public support for military intervention in the Third World.

The third and perhaps the most pyschologically debilitating type of low-intensity conflict is international terrorism. Terrorism, as a psychological form of warfare, presents three main difficulties to the policy-maker. First, the number of terrorists and terrorist acts are totally out of proportion to the potential effect; the attempted assassination of Pope John Paul II in 1982 is a good example. Second, a well-planned and executed terrorist act is almost impossible to detect beforehand and therefore difficult to prevent. Lastly, the rootless, amoral character of many terrorist groups complicates the process of mobilizing the public against them—it is much easier to enlist support for a crusade against a well-defined, omnipresent threat like that from the Soviet Union than against a vague, almost invisible group of poorly armed terrorists. In addition, among the world's industrialized democracies, the number of potential terrorist targets and the means available to publicize terrorist acts will only increase in the future. Nuclear power plants, electricity transformers, water reservoirs, and central computer banks constitute only the most obvious targets for ''high technology terrorism'' of the future.[5] Given further advances in communications technology, a well-staged act of terrorism could easily receive worldwide attention instantaneously, thus adding to the terrorists' victory. Moreover, it is likely that economic and social conditions in the Third World will continue to deteriorate, thus providing fertile ground for the growth of even more terrorist groups. One could argue that the potential of the terrorist threat to disrupt modern societies, combined with the great range of opportunities for action, make this form of low-intensity conflict the most formidable military challenge facing the United States for the rest of this century.

What are some of the implications of low-intensity conflict for U.S. national security policy? First of all, many policy-makers and the public at large are psychologically unprepared to accept any of the forms of low-intensity conflict discussed above as real threats to America's national security. All citizens must supplement their traditional views of conflict with an appreciation for the low-intensity threat. A well-coordinated program of public education on this phenomenon is needed to familiarize the average citizen with the real meaning of low-intensity warfare. Second, the U.S. armed forces (structured principally to fight in Europe) are not configured to deal with unconventional conflict. The large size and weight of many army divisions leaves them ill suited for rapid deployment to a Third World trouble spot. Although the army's small, new "Delta Force" may have enhanced our capability for coping with hostage situations such as the 1979 seizure of the U.S. Embassy in Tehran, U.S. armed forces have not developed the doctrine, tactics, training, or equipment appropriate to meet the range of low-intensity conflict threats of the future.[6] Among the solutions suggested to remedy this situation is a restructuring of army units so as to reduce weight and enhance mobility. Another suggestion calls for transferring the responsibility for the defense of Europe to the Europeans and U.S. Army reserve divisions, freeing active-duty forces to concentrate on Third World threats.[7] Some of these steps sound radical, but there were indications in 1983 that the military was considering several of them.[8] In any event, it is clear that low-intensity conflict constitutes a military challenge that is not yet fully appreciated by many in the U.S. national security policy-making community.

Revolutionary War. Although revolution is an ancient phenomenon, revolutionary war, as distinguished from other forms of political violence, such as the coup d'état, jacquerie, and mass rebellion, is largely a phenomenon of the twentieth century.[9] This is due to the higher frequency of such wars in this century, their broader geographic distribution, and the growth of a body of theory spelling out the nature of revolutionary war and emphasizing it as a path to power. Further, such war may appear new because two of the major world powers, the Soviet Union and the P.R.C., now specifically commend and endorse revolutionary war as a legitimate political act. In the Soviet case, Premier Khrushchev's famous declaration in 1961 that the U.S.S.R. considered it as its duty to support such "wars of naional liberation" formalized what had been Soviet practice since the end of World War II.[10] Indeed, one of the original triggers of the cold war was the Soviet-supported communist insurgency in Greece from 1946 to 1948.

Following the great debate in the United States of the late 1960s and early 1970s over American involvement in Indochina, and the apparent consensus that emerged therefrom that there should be "no more Vietnams," why a section on revolutionary war in a 1980s book on national security issues? The answer is three fold. First, there is no way of assessing how we arrived where we now are without some appreciation of the immediate past—the United States, like many other states, has been involved in several revolutionary wars since 1945. Second, since a number of revolutionary wars continue in various stages throughout much of the developing world, we need to understand this type of conflict in order to understand the contemporary scene. Third, revolutionary war or some variant form of violent political change is likely to continue to be widespread in the foreseeable future.

Some Defining Characteristics of Revolutionary War. *Revolutionary war* is organized violence, largely from within a state, with the political aim of overthrowing a government and restructuring the political, economic, and social order of the state. It is sometimes loosely called *internal war* or *insurgency* but actually is a larger, more precisely focused concept than either of those alternatives. Revolutionary war, in its twentieth-century form, may be distinguished from other forms of conflict by several characteristics. It has an *organized, disciplined leadership*—the general staff of the revolution—usually in the form of an elite party. A charismatic figure frequently has a leadership role, such as did Mao Zedong in China, Ho Chi Minh in Vietnam or Ahmed ben Bella in Algeria; such a figure permits revolutionary movements to manage the divisiveness that generally tends to mark them, particularly in their early stages.

The revolution's leaders follow (or say they follow) and proclaim a *popular ideology that is used to explain the past, present, and future* in ways supportive of the elite's goals. Where possible, the elite attempts to monopolize the appeal of nationalism, anticolonialism, or antiimperialism.

In order to develop, the revolution requires a *sanctuary* to serve as an administrative or logistical base. Such a sanctuary may be outside the national boundary, at least early on, but an internal sanctuary must be created in due course, where the revolutionary leadership has near absolute security. This internal sanctuary also serves to support the claim of the revolutionary movement to legitimacy as an alternative to the regime, as well as to the particular government in power.

A sufficient *mass base* must be built to provide intelligence, material support, recruits, and external legitimacy. It should be noted that if the structure being attacked is sufficiently weak, the revolution may succeed so rapidly that popular support never becomes a true "mass base"; such was the case in Fidel Castro's takeover of Cuba.

Finally, the revolution must have the *military forces* to wage war; these usually will be a mix of local guerrillas, regional militia, and so-called regulars.[11] A measure of popular backing for these forces is essential for their success, crucially so in the early stages when they are most vulnerable to counterintelligence and suppression operations. Mao's dictum that the "people are the water and the guerrillas, the fish" sums up the point.

Revolutionary wars are often further characterized in terms of stages or phases. One may speak of an initial or organizational stage, marked by covert political activity and propaganda. This is accompanied and followed by terrorist activity, designed to paralyze the regime and awe the populace, and by the initiation of guerrilla operations. Then comes a period of stepped-up guerrilla activity and initiation of conventional military activities. Finally, the revolutionary side becomes strong enough to meet and defeat the forces of the regime in major set-piece battles, leading to the defeat or collapse of the regime. Although each stage depends on revolutionary success in prior phases, it is entirely possible that several stages of the war will proceed simultaneously—for example, once the revolutionary forces have initiated conventional military activities, they are likely to continue their organizational, terroristic, and guerrilla activities as well.

Another version of phasing in revolutionary warfare refers to the strategic defensive, stalemate, and strategic offensive. Such characterizations are useful, but they may be misleading in their precision. In most revolutionary wars, there is a blurring of stages as both sides experiment and probe, succeed and fail. From an internal point of view, however, the phase/stage characterizations have great importance because decisions about phases may have significant impact on the strategies and tactics of both the regime and the revolution.[12]

Some analysts characterize revolutionary wars as anticolonial, nationalistic, communist-led or -dominated, and so forth. These, too, may sometimes be useful terms, but they can be misleading. One must be wary of such labels, primarily because of the emotions they evoke. Too often, governments assign labels such as "communist" or "Marxist" to their enemies in order to gain support, both domestic and foreign. Acceptance of such labels can be a semantic trap that obscures the true nature of a revolutionary war.

It cannot be overemphasized that the revolutionaries' aim is to overthrow the old order and to legitimize a new one. The matter in contention is not ultimately one of territorial advantage or destruction of armies but, to use a hackneyed phrase, one of the "hearts and minds" of the people. The revolutionaries' point of strength or vulnerability lies in their popular base—what Clausewitz called their "centre of gravity."

Alexander had his centre of gravity in his Army, as had Gustavus Adolphus, Charles XII, and Frederick the Great, and the career of any one of them would soon have been brought to a close by the destruction of his fighting force: in States torn by internal dissensions, this centre generally lies in the capital; in small States dependent on greater ones, it lies generally in the Army of these allies; in a confederacy, it lies in the unity of interests; in a *national insurrection, in the person of the chief leader, and in public opinion.* Against these points the blow must be directed.[13] (Emphasis added)

Revolutionary War Experience. Social scientists are far from agreed on a comprehensive body of theory on revolutionary war. It understates the case to say that the causes and conduct of revolutionary wars are diverse and particularized. Nevertheless, a brief review of some of the revolutionary war experience since World War II provides several instructive lessons.

Algeria. An outstanding example of a successful anticolonial revolution (1954–62), the Algerian case is a curious one. The revolutionary military forces were suppressed within Algeria, but the colonial power, France, decided that the price of maintaining its rule was too high over the long run and negotiated an agreement of independence *after the suppression.* This offers a useful lesson in the study of execution of revolutionary war, especially an anticolonial one. The political will of the colonial power is of paramount importance; in the Algerian case, the political will of France broke—as it had done earlier in Indochina.

China. It is helpful to the revolutionary party if it can appeal to nationalist sentiment among the people. The Chinese Communist Party (CCP) exploited anti-Japanese and antiforeign sentiments quite successfully, both before and after 1945. With the United States coming to the aid of Chiang Kai-shek's government during and after World War II, the CCP managed to use the United States as a sort of surrogate colonial power upon which to focus antiforeign feelings during the post 1945 civil war. Nevertheless, we should remember that the Chinese revolution was much more than a nationalist struggle against Japanese and Western dominance; it was also a genuine revolution against the Chinese political, economic, and social order. The CCP leadership of the Chinese revolution in its later stages sometimes overshadows the true nature of this cataclysmic event, beginning in 1911 and ending only in 1949–50.[14]

Cuba. The anticolonial element also played an important role in Cuba, another successful revolutionary war since 1945. Sporadic U.S. interference and intervention in Cuba, at least from the time of nominal independence in 1901, and continued U.S. support of dictator-president Fulgencio Batista provided Fidel Castro a useful target during and after the revolution. (Whether or not Cuba, with its extraordinarily heavy economic reliance on the U.S.S.R. and other communist states, truly has attained independence is an open question.) The observation that Castro's successful revolution had anticolonial overtones is not meant to imply that they were a dominant influence. The oppressive, corrupt, and overwhelmingly inept Batista regime was its own worst enemy, and its politically skillful, charismatic opponent was able to rally against it a broad base of rural and urban supporters.

Vietnam. The wars in Indochina after 1946 provide the textbook case of revolutionary war that succeeded despite incredibly difficult obstacles. Frustrated for nearly thirty years by the resistance of internal opponents, aided and encouraged first by France and then by the United States, the Vietnamese revolutionaries finally managed to unify all of Vietnam under their control in 1975. Building on the theories and practice of the Chinese revolutionaries, Ho Chi Minh and his Vietnamese colleagues succeeded—not once, but twice—in revolutionary warfare. From 1946 to 1954 they fought a classical three-phase insurgency against the French colonial forces and their Vietnamese auxiliaries. That war culminated in the partition of Vietnam at the 17th parallel, with Ho in control of the Democratic Republic of Vietnam (D.R.V.) in the north and with Ngo Dinh Diem heading a noncommunist Republic of Vietnam (R.V.N.) in the south. The 1954 arrangements provided for free elections within a year to decide upon reunification of the country. Despite the arrival in the south of nearly a million anticommunist refugees, northerners still outnumbered southerners three to two; besides, as Diem argued later, the northerners would be coerced into 100 percent support of Ho. Accordingly, Diem cancelled the southern reunification vote and proceeded to try to establish a viable republic in the south.

Deprived of their sure victory at the ballot box, Ho and the communists, north and south, launched a second revolutionary struggle—this time against their fellow Vietnamese. From 1956, when they relaunched the struggle, until 1964, when they began moving regular North Vietnamese Army (NVA) units into the south en masse to initiate the conventional warfare stage of the war, the Vietcong (VC, as the southern arm of the D.R.V. was called) assassinated more than twenty-eight thousand R.V.N. officials, teachers, village chiefs, doctors, and other leaders who opposed the campaign of terrorism.[15] Painting Diem as a puppet of the Americans, who were supporting him with arms and a military advisory mission, the VC sought to capitalize on nationalist sentiment as well as to appeal to fear.

By 1965, facing the build-up of VC guerrilla forces and northern regular army troops and suffering from poor leadership, R.V.N. forces were being regularly beaten in the field in company- and battalion-sized battles (involving one to five hundred soldiers on each side); accordingly, the collapse of the South became predictable. At that point (mid 1965) the United States, unwilling to see the whole of Vietnam and perhaps all of Southeast Asia come under communist control, intervened in force, transforming the character of the struggle.

The NVA and VC were overmatched by the American forces, with their overwhelming firepower and helicopter-based mobility; by early early 1966, the North Vietnamese were forced on the defensive. In a series of large unit (battalion- and regimental-sized) battles that year, the NVA suffered heavy losses before withdrawing into secure base areas and cross-border sanctuaries. Mobile, conventional warfare having proven too expensive, Hanoi largely reverted to terrorism and small unit actions. In early 1968, however, the communists made an all-out effort to reverse their declining military fortunes—the famous Tet offensive, into which they threw not only most of their regular forces but also their guerrillas and political infrastructure. Although its immediate aim apparently was to generate popular uprisings and to inflict major, demoralizing defeats upon the South Vietnamese and U.S. forces, the Tet offensive's ultimate target was the enemy's center of gravity, i.e. American public opinion—just as the real objective of the decisive campaign at Dien Bien Phu fourteen years earlier had not been the beleaguered French forces but French public opinion.

The outcome of the Tet offensive was a staggering military defeat for the NVA and VC units and heavy losses in the VC political infrastructure, which had surfaced in order to support the military assaults. Despite these military facts and the lack of mass uprisings in South Vietnam, however, Hanoi won a strategic victory of decisive proportions: American public confidence was shattered by televised accounts of the assault on the American Embassy in Saigon, by screaming newspaper headlines about American and allied defeat, and by panicky reactions of legislative and other public leaders. That collapse of confidence and the consequent swelling U.S. public demand to abandon the Vietnam intervention added a new twist to the tested aphorism that insurgent forces win by not losing—namely, when confronting a democratic society, the insurgents can win by convincing the media, and through it, the enemy public, that defeat is victory.

The post Tet collapse of American will led to accelerated U.S. withdrawal and "Vietnamization" of the war. Once U.S. ground forces were withdrawn, North Vietnam, eager for victory and judging the time again ripe for the mobile, conventional phase, launched a major invasion of the south (1972). The RVN forces, with U.S. air support, defeated that thrust but succumbed to another round of major attacks three years later when U.S. air power had been removed and drastic congressional cuts in military assistance had undercut both morale and material readiness.[16]

Iran. In addition to the revolutionaries' successes of the 1950s, 1960s, and early 1970s just cited, there were three important revolutionary victories at the end of the 1970s, namely, in Iran, Nicaragua, and Rhodesia. The former instance presents such contrasts to the earlier, classic cases of Algeria, China, and Vietnam that some observers might not classify it as a revolutionary war at all. Yet, the Iranian revolution fits the definition given earlier and exhibits (in variant forms) such wars' distinguishing characteristics, namely, disciplined leadership, closed ideology, sanctuary, mass base, and military forces. Several aspects of the Iranian revolution of 1978–79 were new, most strikingly the facts that its ideological force was Islam, rather than the usual anticolonialism or nationalism (although there were important elements of these appeals as well) and that its leadership was clerical rather than secular.

From his sanctuaries—first in Iraq, then in France—the Ayatollah Khomeini rallied a wide coalition of interests opposed to the regime with the call that traditional religious values were being destroyed by the Shah's western-ization program and by his corruption. The coalition included peasants and workers, who were especially disoriented by the process of modernization, together with middle class, merchant, and clerical elements who were victim-ized by governmental repression as well as embittered by far-reaching, hasty, and often ill-managed economic reforms. Drawing on the tradition that the Shia form of Islam, with its uniquely hierarchical structure, has long offered an alternative source of authority to Iran's secular rulers, Khomeini—while still safely in France—stimulated enormous public demonstrations in Teheran and Iran's other major cities, calling for the Shah's overthrow and installation of a new Islamic order.

The mullahs, relatively secure in their mosques and Moslem schools and seminaries from the Shah's secret police, formed the disciplined cadres and agents for the revolution. The Ayatollah and these clerical allies, as well as various leftist factions, had their own military forces—the revolutionary mil-itias—but it was not necessary for them to attempt to proceed through the terrorism-guerrilla-conventional warfare phases of classical revolutionary war in order to defeat the government's armed forces. Rather, the power of the appeal of a new Islamic order, the massive and sustained nature of open public support, the disciplined leadership of the ayatollahs and mullahs, and the charismatic appeal of Khomeini all combined to undermine the Shah's political and military base. The Shah's center of gravity disintegrated like a peasant's house in the all-too-frequent Iranian earthquakes.

Devising a viable, modern Islamic state and successfully integrating Iran's large ethnic minorities (Azerbaijanis, Kurds, Baluchis, Turkomans, and Ar-abs) into it will take many more years and, in all likelihood, considerably more warfare and bloodshed. Nevertheless, and while it takes a somewhat different form, the Iranian revolutionary war of 1978–79 must be adjudged a success.[17]

Nicaragua. The successful insurrection in Nicaragua against the long-stand-ing domination of the Somoza family was the first revolutionary war triumph (1979) in modern times in Latin America. The struggle was marked by serious battles in both urban and rural settings between the Sandinista guerrillas and the National Guard. Widespread popular support for the insurgency tapped opposition from a broad variety of political and economic sources. Not only was there strong rural support for the Sandinistas, but also urban manifes-tations such as strikes and pitched street battles underscored the breadth of determined opposition to the regime. Attempts to settle the affair by media-tion were tried, but the hard core revolutionary elements were determined to carry on to final victory.

Zimbabwe. The revolution in Zimbabwe-Rhodesia, arising out of the dom-ination of a 95 percent black population by a white minority, introduced race as the primary motivation for mass participation in revolutionary war. In this case, stretching through most of the 1970s, the white minority declared uni-lateral independence from the colonial power, Great Britain, and seized total political and economic power in the country. As a result, the efforts of the black political movements—the Zimbabwe African National Union (ZANU) and the Zimbabwe African People's Union (ZAPU)—were directed toward the overthrow of a repressive, racial, ruling elite rather than any particular ideological or colonial element. The resulting struggle earned the support not only of many of the formerly colonial, nonaligned nations, but also of the United States and Great Britain, setting the stage for international efforts to promote a negotiatied settlement of the revolutionary war and elections of a truly representative government.

Great Britain led these efforts despite continuing resistance by the white minority government of Ian Smith. Although the Smith government's forces were uniformly successful on the battlefield, the war dragged on inconclusively as the black guerillas drew on neighboring countries for sanctuary and sup-port—in addition to continued support from the bulk of the Zimbabwean people. Faced by its inability to crush the black revolution, white immigration, economic deterioration, and profound weariness by its own supporters, the Smith regime finally agreed to a negotiated resolution to the war. The patient, persistent, and concerned involvement by Britain with important U.S. support had succeeded—perhaps setting a precedent for political interruption of viol-ence and negotiated solutions to the problems of revolutionary warfare else-where.

The friction between competing ZANU and ZAPU forces since the 1980 elections in Zimbabwe indicates that had the revolutionary war continued, conflict most likely would not have ended with the ejection of the dominating white minority. Rather, factional strife and violence would have persisted, inhibiting the successful political and economic modernization of the country. Zimbabwe became the 153rd member of the UN in August 1980.

Thailand. The foregoing examples of successful revolutions do not exhaust the instructive instances of revolutionary warfare of the recent past or present. Failures also can teach. In Thailand, for example, revolutionary war, despite its persistence, has proven unsuccessful. Thai nationalism, closely identified with Buddhism and the monarchy, has not been captured by the Communist Party of Thailand (CPT). In fact, the latter is dominated by ethnic Chinese, and the CPT has a Chinese identification that it has thus far found difficult to dispel. The CPT has also been unable to generate any genuine anticolonial spirit in Thailand even though one of the major themes of the communist radio station, "Voice of the People of Thailand," is anticolonialism, with the United States cast in the bogus role of colonial power. Nevertheless, a careful observer will see in Thailand the social, political, and economic conditions that could contribute to the success of revolutionary war in the future. The moment of ripeness has yet to arrive, however, and the royal Thai government still has an excellent opportunity of both suppressing the revolution and carrying out the reforms and development that would obviate it.

Malaysia. A revolutionary war broke out in Malaysia even before it was established as an independent state. In West Malaysia (i.e., Peninsular Malaya), the British suppressed the early revolution in a twelve-year campaign from 1948 to 1960. They did so with the support of the Malays, Indians, and most of the ethnic Chinese who live there. Yet the communist-led and -dominated Malayan National Liberation Army (MNLA), now in external sanctuary in the four southern provinces of Thailand, continues to exist. There, the MNLA has succeeded in raising ethnic Malay units in an attempt to overcome its once exclusively Chinese nature. Although weak at present, the MNLA could prove to be a time bomb; much depends upon how successful Malaysian efforts to develop a unified Malaysian nationalism are in the future. In East Malaysia (i.e., Borneo), efforts to organize a revolutionary war have been successful only among ethnic Chinese, and the attempts have degenerated into virtual banditry.

Indonesia. Having attained its independence from the Dutch after a four-year, anticolonial revolutionary war, Indonesia escaped a post independence revolutionary war. A major factor in this escape on the part of the new government was the "united front from above" policy adopted by its opponent, the Communist Party of Indonesia (PKI). This policy, actively pursued since 1952, left the PKI with a large mass base and strong influence at the very top of the government but without the intermediate structure and cadre necessary to carry out revolutionary war. This policy also led the party to attempt a putsch in September 1965, and in the wake of failure the PKI was virtually destroyed. However, the social, political, and economic conditions that favor revolutionary war in Indonesia have yet to be entirely alleviated, and it is at least possible that a revived PKI or some other revolutionary party will rise in the future. If such a party were to derive the right lessons from the experience of the PKI, Indonesia might yet face revolutionary war.

Philippines. A very serious postindependence revolutionary war raged during the period 1948–51 in the Philippines. The Huk (*Hukbalahap,* or People's Liberation Army)* launched a campaign that very nearly brought the Philippine government to its knees, even though conflict was largely restricted to central Luzon. The revolution was suppressed under the Secretary of National Defense Ramon Magsaysay (1950–53), who later became president (1953–57). However, Magsaysay's successors proved unwilling or unable to maintain the momentum he built up, and small-scale revolutionary action has become widespread. The poverty, corruption, and population pressure that

*Originally *Hukbo ng Bayan Laban sa Hapon* (People's Army to Fight the Japanese), it changed in 1948 to *Hukbo ng Magpalayang Bayan* (People's Liberation Army).

provide fertile ground for revolutionary warfare remain, and the Philippines may very well be the scene of a large-scale revolutionary war during the 1980s. The situation is complicated by the presence of a large and defiant Moslem minority in the far south, requiring the government to divert attention and resources from Luzon and the central Philippines.

Korea. During the Korean War (1950–54), the northern Democratic People's Republic of Korea (D.P.R.K.) sent guerrilla forces into the Republic of Korea (R.O.K.). It is not clear whether the D.P.R.K. hoped to generate a revolutionary war in the south or whether the leadership simply hoped to create enough havoc behind the lines to divert major resources and attention from the United Nations Command conventional operations. In any case, although the guerrilla insertions were successful, the overall effort was a total failure. The South Korean population unequivocally rejected the Communist revolution.

Burma. After independence (1948), Burma faced a variety of forms of political violence. The government was plagued by an incipient and persistent threat of revolutionary war, led by the Communist Party of Burma or by separatist movements among the non-Burman ethnic groups. Repeated incursions of so-called Kuomintang military formations. (originally the remnants of nationalist Chinese troops driven from Yunnan province in China in 1949) also threatened the nation's security. The government has managed to confine the major military operations largely to the northeast in recent years. However, the Communist Party of Burma continues its efforts, with some Chinese assistance, to maintain a secure base area along the Sino-Burmese border and to expand its clandestine organization among the majority of Burmans. Since 1953, the prolonged stagnation of the Burmese economy has contributed to the potential for revolutionary war in central Burma, where most Burmans live. The government, however, has thus far proven fairly effective in rooting out covert and clandestine members of revolutionary organizations.

Pakistan. In East Pakistan, a nationalist (Bengali) revolutionary war was underway but was overtaken early in its overt stages (1971) by conventional war between Pakistan and India, leading to the surrender of the Pakistani forces in the east and the independence of the Bengalis in the new state of Bangladesh. It may have been true that the Pakistanis could not have maintained their hold on the rebellious province, even without the Indian invasion, but a full-scale revolutionary war with its attendant tests never developed.

India. The Naxalites (one of the Indian communist parties) made some progress in the depressed rural areas of eastern India until 1970. After that time, the group was split by strong ideological differences, and the government made substantial progress against it in the countryside. Some members of the group remained faithful to their original cause; others turned to urban terror.

The government may not be able indefinitely to contain the further development of revolutionary war, as the preconditions exist in various parts of India. On the other hand, the grinding poverty of much of the Indian populace may help keep revolutionary war from developing an adequate mass base.

Oman. The Sultanate of Oman is the scene of yet another episodic revolutionary war. Operating in the remote and desolate hill country of the western province of Dhofar, the revolutionary forces managed for some time to hold their own in the face of repeated campaigns by the sultan's forces, supported by British and Iranian troops, to root them out. Largely suppressed in 1975–76, the Dhofari revolutionaries have been forced to bide their time. There is, however, deep-rooted resentment of outside rule in this region—a sentiment encouraged by South Yemen. The young sultan is attempting to speed development in order to insulate the people from revolution but has no intention of meeting Dhofari demands. The revolutionary forces have the advantage of a secure sanctuary in South Yemen, from which they may well again launch their struggle inside Oman, perhaps with Cuban or other outside aid.

Palestine. The West Bank of the Jordan River portion of the original British mandate that fell under Jordanian control between 1948 and 1967—Palestine—remains the potential stage for a revolutionary war. The emergence of a successful revolutionary war there has been prevented by a combination of factors: the inability of the various Palestinian refugee groups to agree on a truly unified command structure and strategy; the controls imposed by their hosts on guerrilla groups in the sanctuary states of Lebanon, Syria, and Jordan; the pervasive grip of the Israeli security forces and army; and the willingness of the Israeli government to use whatever force is necessary within the occupied territories and against sanctuaries in neighboring countries. Terrorism and minor guerrilla operations remain the characteristic mode of conflict. The fundamental precondition for any lasting peace settlement in the region is still distant—namely, equitable settlement of the Palestinian issue.

Greece. Greece was the scene of an unsuccessful revolutionary war in the aftermath of World War II. Communist-led guerrillas who had operated behind the German lines during the war contested the restoration of the monarchy. With British and then American support, the Greek government managed to hold on and make some progress in suppression. However, external events had a decisive impact on this war. The revolutionary forces were largely dependent upon the Soviet Union, Albania, and Yugoslavia for sanctuary, training, and equipment. When Yugoslavia, the key country, closed its border with Greece following Tito's break with the U.S.S.R. and the Cominform in 1948, the Greek revolution was suppressed quite rapidly.

Africa. Revolutionary war experience has yielded mixed results in Africa, probably because of the mixed nature of decolonization. The Belgians, British,

French, and, later, Spanish withdrew from their colonies relatively peacefully, and nationalist successor governments were established. Dissident groups and movements in those states have not mounted postindependence revolutionary wars. In the Portugese territories of Guinea-Bissau, Angola, and Mozambique, the political will of the colonial power collapsed before the revolutionary war ran its gamut. However, the struggle of the various revolutionary parties for hegemony continues in Angola.

In the Horn of Africa, a long-standing revolutionary war fought by the Eritreans against Ethiopia was suppressed—and then not decisively—only after Soviet and Cuban assistance to Ethiopia in 1978–79. The other war in the area of the Horn, the fighting between Somalis and Ethiopians over control of the Ogaden, is much more an international struggle over post-imperial boundaries than a revolutionary war.

In Southern Africa, where Europeans or those of largely European descent have established political control, revolutionary war is a continuing factor. The Zimbabwean revolution succeeded in the unusual fashion already cited. In Namibia (South-West Africa), where white settlement and control is of fairly recent origin, a low key revolutionary war is under way, and it appears that majority-rule government will emerge there in due course. In South Africa (Azania) where the ethnic-European population has a much stronger history and tradition, a black revolutionary movement exists only in nascent form. It may be many years before this situation will change markedly, though the installation of black majority governments in Zimbabwe and Namibia may provide sanctuaries for a future black revolutionary movement.

Latin America. Two major waves of attempted revolutionary war have swept through Latin America. The first wave, in the decade of the 1960s, consisted of a series of peasant uprisings and rural guerrilla movements; the failure of this surge was signaled by the 1967 death of Che Guevara, Cuba's foremost exponent and exporter of revolution, who unwisely chose Bolivia as the location from which guerrilla warfare could be best propagated elsewhere in South America. The second wave is attempting to base revolutionary wars on urban insurgency; this effort seems likely to fail also.

Guevara's failure in Bolivia is classic, for it illustrates the difficulties of exporting revolution from one country to another and the need for rebels to analyze the specific realities of the local situation before proceeding to launch a revolutionary war. Guevara's determination that he and his Cuban lieutenants would control the insurgency alienated local political forces whose support was vital to him. Similarly, his choice of thinly populated south-central Bolivia as the theater of operations and his inattention to the makeup of his forces left him without either the rural or urban bases that were essential.[18] Bolivia may yet face revolutionary war, but it will have to have a firmer indigenous base if it is to succeed.

Elsewhere in Latin America, the Peruvian army crushed Hugo Blanco's peasant revolt in the late 1960s. Rebel movements in Colombia and Venezuela were broken up and disintegrated into bandit groups, largely operating in frontier areas. In Guatemala, the army destroyed most guerrilla forces.

Armed guerrilla bands are reported from time to time in the countryside in Mexico, but it is too soon to tell if a serious revolutionary war threat will develop there. The rapid surge of publicly available resources from burgeoning oil production offers both an opportunity and a danger to Mexico's leaders. If the new revenues are used wisely they could ameliorate much of the wretchedness of the Mexican masses; used poorly, the monies could increase inflation, further worsen the already grossly unbalanced distribution of income in the society, exacerbate existing social tensions, and frustrate widespread rising expectations. Skillful handling of the explosive mixture of oil and politics will be essential.

Based on what they believed was to be learned from the disappointing experience of rural-based revolutionary attempts, some Latin American revolutionaries turned to urban insurgency as the basis of revolutionary war. Wealth, power, and population throughout Latin America have been gravitating steadily toward the cities. More than two-thirds of the populations of Argentina, Uruguay, Venezuela, and Chile, for instance, live in towns. In Mexico, Brazil, and Colombia, more than 50 percent do so. Cities are surrounded by vast shantytowns where facilities and services are few and misery is a way of life. Also in the cities are the middle-class intellectuals essential to the general staffs of revolutionary wars.

The earliest of the attempts at urban-based revolutionary war in Latin America, preceding Che Guevara's death by some five years, was in Venezuela. The Venezuelan government, under the skillful leadership of President Betancourt, defeated this potentially successful movement with an astute combination of repression, political development, and effective security forces. In Brazil, the government proceeded more along the strict repression lines of the French "paras" in Algiers but succeeded, like Venezuela, in suppressing revolution.

The most persistent of the urban revolutionary wars in Latin America were those initiated by the Tupamaros (National Liberation Movement) in Uruguay, and the People's Revolutionary Army (ERP) and the Montoneros (Peronist guerrillas) in Argentina. In both countries, however, the armed forces and police finally coordinated their efforts sufficiently to launch major, sustained counterrevolutionary campaigns. They prevailed, though it took a decade to render the urban guerrillas generally ineffective.

In the more developed Latin American states, advocates of revolutionary war continue to look to urban terror as the principal mode of action, despite the reverses just cited. The aim, as stated by Carlos Marighella, the Brazilian guerrilla leader killed in a police ambush in 1969, is to create conditions where "the political situation in the country is transformed into a military situation in which the gorillas [i.e., government forces] appear to be more and more the ones responsible for errors and violence while the problems in the lives of the people become truly catastrophic."[19] As Tom Hayden, one of the founders of the Students for a Democratic Society (SDS) in the United States, put it,

The immediate objective is to provoke government efforts at suppression; the coming of repression will speed up time, making a revolutionary situation more likely. . . . We are creating an America where it is necessary for the government to rule behind barbed wire, for the President to speak only at military bases, and, finally, where it will be necessary for the people to fight back.[20]

Urban-based attempts at revolutionary war tend, however, to disintegrate into pure terror; at least that has been the case in the past. Examples, all from the developed world, may be found in the Weathermen in the United States, the *Front de Libération du Québec* (FLQ) in Canada, and the Irish Republican Army (IRA—both regulars and provisionals) in the two parts of Ireland. While such terrorist operations may appear to offer a distant prospect that genuine revolutionary wars will be generated or accelerated by government responses, the early 1980s is far too soon to so conclude.

Some Lessons from the Cases Cited. We have not attempted the encyclopedic task of looking at all revolutionary movements, only at a few of the more significant revolutionary wars or near wars since 1945. Yet, even from this limited sample it is possible to draw some lessons and principles that will enhance our understanding of the phenomenon and the prospect of its continuance and success. Some of these lessons have already been mentioned, but it may be useful to restate them briefly.

First, though there have been variant patterns, as detailed above, successful revolutionary wars have rested on most or all of the elements listed earlier, namely, disciplined leadership, strong ideology, sanctuaries, mass base, and military forces. Of these factors, leadership and ideology are crucial; given them, the revolution can generally create the other elements. Although anticolonialism furnished the ideological base for most of the successful revolutions for the quarter century after World War II, the virtual elimination of classical colonialism and the revolutionary successes in Iran and Rhodesia, based on religion and race, respectively, suggest that the key ideological element will be different in the 1980s than in most of the postwar era.

Second, it is not necessary for revolutionaries to win a military victory in order to win a revolutionary war—although they have to be able to fight sufficiently to protect their key leaders and cadre and to inflict casualties on the government's forces. The case of Algeria is decisive on this point, as already suggested. (Similarly, in Kenya, the British thoroughly suppressed the Mau Mau, and then turned around and granted independence.) In Angola, Mozambique, and Guinea-Bissau, the revolutionaries succeeded because internal conditions in Portugal forced the colonialists to negotiate—not because of the military situation. In such anticolonial and nationalist tests, revolutionary war becomes predominantly a matter of will and public opinion, as the example of the French in Indochina also attests. The American experience in Vietnam further illustrates the crucial role of public support.

Third, revolutionary movements are notoriously susceptible to fragmentation. Strong, dedicated individuals in revolutionary leadership roles frequently are unable to avoid serious and deep cleavages over ideology, strategy, and tactics. The divisions in the Russian Social Democratic Party prior to 1917 and the growth of factions within the Communist Party of the Soviet Union shortly after the revolution provide an early example of this. The deep fissures within the Palestinian leadership furnish a contemporary example. Splits in revolutionary movements, whatever their origins, weaken the total effort and provide counterrevolutionaries with opportunities to undermine their opponents.

Fourth, many revolutionaries are impatient. Obviously, they would prefer to have the revolution completed so that they could enjoy the fruits that they see as accompanying victory. The path to power through revolutionary war is not an easy one. To choose that route is to condemn oneself to years of difficult, bloody, and dangerous organizational activity and protracted conflict, the end of which is in doubt and the consequences of which may be dire.[21] Willingness to fight for twenty-two years, as was the case with Mao Zedong and the CCP leadership, or to endure the long years of exile, imprisonment, and fighting, as did Ho Chi Minh and much of the leadership of the Indochinese Communist Party, are rare enough. What of the other ranks who see themselves grow old and grey, often deprived of family, without much hope of near success? Many leave the revolution, convinced of its rightness and ultimate success but unwilling to endure. Existing regimes can use this weariness-impotence factor to wear out revolutionary opponents.

Fifth, in the process of revolutionary war, the revolutionaries inevitably make mistakes. Errors may derive from disagreement among members of the leadership group or from impatience, or from other causes, but they provide the regime with opportunities. In retrospect, the 1952 decision of the PKI in Indonesia to adopt a policy of "united front from above" may have been an adroit short-term tactic, but it was a disastrous long-term strategy because it left the party in the aftermath of its coup attempt in 1956 without the hard-core, disciplined cadre so essential to revolutionary war. In other cases, a revolutionary movement may move to the overt action phase prematurely. This would appear to have been the case in Thailand with the CPT in 1965, when a CCP desire to respond to U.S. intervention in Indochina may have influenced the outbreak of violence in northeastern Thailand in August.*

Sixth, in most cases the revolutionaries' struggle is an uphill one; established regimes are supported by inertia, by structures, by habit. Most people, most of the time, accept the legitimacy of an existing regime—even if they are dissatisfied with the way it works. Most states are conceded by their populace to have a monopoly over legitimate forms of violence—defense and the police

---

* This case is not proven.

power. Bureaucracies—civil, police, and military—can often be used by regimes to counter the revolutionary forces soon enough and with enough strength to suppress them. Moreover, in much of the world, people do not really see themselves as a part of a political process—they eke out a living under the current regime and do not see any real alternative.

Seventh, where revolutionary forces are heavily dependent on external support, withdrawal of such support can cause the balance to shift decisively to favor the regime. Although few, examples of this do exist. Once such case is Greece, discussed earlier in this chapter. Another potential case might well have been South Vietnam. During most of the 1960s, U.S. policy was based on an assumption that if the northerners, the D.R.V.N., would withdraw support and direction of the revolutionary war in the south, the revolutionary movement would collapse or be successfully supressed. This assumption was probably true, but it was never tested because the gradual, incremental pressures and penalties that the United States placed on the D.R.V.N. were insufficient to compel it to desist.

Eighth, a threatened regime can often preempt revolution by adopting measures to eliminate the conditions that provide fertile soil in which revolutionary wars are nurtured. This process is under way in many countries. As already noted, President Magsaysay combined the successful use of this approach with skillful military tactics to suppress a serious insurgency in the Philippines in the early 1950s. In contrast, the Shah of Iran attempted too much, too fast and fueled the fires of popular dissent. He embarked on overly ambitious plans of social and economic development, accompanied by a strengthening of both his civil bureaucracy and his security forces, yet failed to build a broad political base and underlying popular consensus—thus providing openings for his revolutionary opponents. Thailand, as we have noted earlier, has contained revolutionary war fairly well and has initiated a number of imaginative plans and programs, although their implementation has been slow.

Ninth, timing and phasing can be crucial. Revolutionary wars represent extremely complex managerial problems. If the revolutionaries take to the streets or hills and jungles prematurely, there is always the chance that the regime will have sufficient time and strength to nip the war in the bud. If they wait too long, the regime may grow stronger and change objective conditions that once contributed to generating support for revolution. In ideological jargon, it is essential that the revolutionary leadership place itself always at the vanguard of revolution. If it ventures ahead of the vanguard, the leadership will fall into adventurism; behind, it will fall into mimicry. In the former case, suppression or liquidation will follow; in the latter, the revolutionary leadership will be swept aside as anachronistic.

Prospects for the 1980s. What, then, of the future of revolutionary war? Certainly, the political and economic demands in many societies will be greater than the governments can meet. In some cases, it is obvious that available resources will not support increased or even present levels of consumption, and the search for alternatives is a long, slow process. Yet population growth and the drive for higher per capita living standards on a world scale indicate that demands for resources will grow rather than stabilize or decline.

Further, the gap in living standards between the advanced, industrialized nations and the less developed or developing nations continues to grow. There is little evidence that the inhabitants of the rich countries will be willing to sacrifice continued growth in their standards of living (to say nothing at all about absolute reductions) to help the poor nations catch up. Not only will this contribute to difficulties in the conduct of international politics, but also it will lead to growing demands on the leaders of the poor nations to produce or face revolutionary wars controlled and directed by alternative leaderships with more utopian designs for the future.* To this prospect must be added the likelihood of the spread of nuclear technology, the Non-Proliferation Treaty and other agreements notwithstanding. Even small-scale nuclear wars would be highly destabilizing.

In the United States, it is safe to say, we have not yet developed the knowledge and techniques that will provide viable intervention strategies in revolutionary war. We know a great deal about, and understand quite well how to conduct, conventional wars. We have developed a considerable body of untested theory about the conduct of nuclear and thermonuclear war. Unfortunately, however, we know too little and understand less about intervening on either side in a revolutionary war. It is popular to dismiss future intervention with the slogan, "no more Vietnams"—forgetting that there are no other Vietnams. There are, however, large parts of the world in which revolutionary war may become endemic. In theory, it would be attractive to recommend nonintervention as a constant operating principle; in practice, it will be difficult to do so if those wars are occurring in areas where we have vital interests.

Policy Implications. The policy implications that flow from the conflict-ridden future outlined above are serious, but they also are mixed. For, as Charles Wolf and Nathan Leites point out, "successful insurgencies are not necessarily detrimental to U.S. interests, nor are successful counter-insurgencies necessarily advantageous."[22] To say that external powers should never intervene in a revolutionary war is as unhelpful as to say that they should intervene in all cases. Indeed, to take the former position is to condemn oneself to unplanned and unprogrammed intervention—the worst kind because the necessary homework will not be done in advance. The latter is equally bankrupt because that is likely to be the outcome—bankruptcy.

This reasoning suggests that each decision to intervene or not in a revolutionary situation or war should be unique, with due regard for the particular

* One is tempted to ask, for example, what could happen if China were frustrated in its drive for modern agriculture, industry, defense, and science and technology by the year 2000.

aspects of the situation at hand at the time. Further, great care should be taken to avoid myth and rigid formulas. The frequently voiced opinion that the fall of Tonkin to the Viet Minh would cause all of Southeast Asia, insular as well as mainland, to come under communist domination was based in great measure on failure to analyze each of the involved countries by itself. By the same token, the faith of the founders of our country that the American revolution would lead the rest of the world to follow in our political footsteps disregarded many particular differences among peoples.

Just as timing is critical for those who would lead revolutionary wars, it is so for those who would intervene. Clearly, if decision-makers decided that a successful revolutionary war in country X would be inimical to their vital national interests, it would be better to intervene early on—preferably before revolutionary violence breaks out. Also importantly, intervention on the side of a revolution must be dependent somewhat on the capability of the revolutionary organization to absorb and employ external resources. Yet, in either case, intervention by an outside power exposes the side on which it intervenes to charges of "selling out" to foreigners. This is especially acute where military intervention is the mode and where troops with white skins show up in brown or black or yellow seas.*

The concept of *vital interest(s)* is crucial in intervention decisions. It is so ambiguous and elusive a concept, however, that politicians and scholars frequently despair over agreeing on a useful definition. At the heart of the idea is maintenance of the physical integrity and sovereignty of the nation and deflection of any threats thereto. This is adequate to explain English resistance to any great power hegemony over the Low Countries—a salient feature of English policy at least from Henry VII through George V.

Definition of vital interest without reference to time and place or the sweeping substitution of ideological slogans for precise interest are typical snares. To a degree, this appears to have happened in the United States with respect to containment. Unfortunately, what was initially a sound doctrine became a widely accepted idea that any status quo was good, any revolution bad. All too often, it was forgotten or ignored that "evil governments may quell virtuous rebellions, and virtuous governments may lose to evil rebellions."[23]

When evaluating vital interest with respect to a specific situation and attempting to assess the desirability of intervention, it is also useful to judge how much in resources a nation is willing to invest for what purpose. If the survival of the state is not at issue, somewhat less than total commitment is probable. If an initial resource input limit is imposed, it may help assure a comprehensive policy review at some later date. In this way, the new look at Indochina that Secretary Acheson desired at the end of 1953 might have been accomplished, even though the secretary left office on January 20, 1953.

---

* It remains to be seen if Soviet interventionists have found a satisfactory solution in the use of darker-skinned Cubans.

Of course, a decision might subsequently be made to escalate the resource allocation for an intervention, but at least it would be done consciously from a certain base.

Modes of intervention may vary widely, but they too must be adapted to specific circumstances to be fully effective. Americans tend to think on a large scale; our background encourages this. Hence, we tend to think of capital, technology, and manpower to be marshaled and maneuvered in mass. If American decision-makers conclude that our vital interest(s) are involved and that intervention, on either side, in a revolutionary war is desirable, we should look at our resource inventory to see if we have what is required and if we are prepared to make the kind of investment required. We may not have appropriate forces; it is popular in some quarters to assume, for example, that forces trained and equipped to fight a conventional war across the North European plain are trained and equipped to fight anything, anywhere. If one is contemplating military intervention in a revolutionary war, this is not likely to be the case.

Revolutionary war, both for the revolutionaries and the regime under assault, is likely to be difficult and bloody, perhaps protracted. It promises to be the same for those who choose to intervene.

DISCUSSION QUESTIONS

1. What will the most likely war of the future look like from the U.S. perspective? What adjustments will the United States have to make in order to cope with low-intensity conflict?

2. If the successful revolutionary wars in the twentieth century have been chiefly anticolonial, will they pass from the scene with dissolution of empires?

3. Does a revolution require a charismatic leader?

4. What are the apparent requirements for a successful revolutionary war?

5. What is the appeal of the concept of urban guerrilla warfare?

6. How would one predict the likelihood of a revolutionary war?

7. What is the meaning of the phrase, "no more Vietnams"?

8. What criteria should be applied in attempting to decide whether or not to intervene in a revolutionary war?

9. If the United States is to plan for possible intervention in revolutionary wars, what kinds of intervention should we foresee?

10. Should the United States maintain military forces for purposes of intervention in revolutionary war? If so, how should these forces be structured, equipped, and trained, and where should they be stationed?

11. What is the relationship (if any) between revolutionary wars and superpower politics?

RECOMMENDED READING

Asprey, Robert B. *War in the Shadows*. 2 vols. Garden City, N.Y.: Doubleday, 1975.

Bell, J. Bowyer. *A Time of Terror: How Democratic Societies Respond to Revolutionary Violence*. New York: Basic Books, 1978.

Davis, Jack. "Political Violence in Latin America." Adelphi Papers, no. 85. London: International Institute for Strategic Studies, February 1972.

Fairbairn, Geoffrey. *Revolutionary Guerrilla Warfare*. Baltimore: Penguin, 1974.

Johnson, Chalmers A. *Peasant Nationalism and Communist Power*. Stanford: Stanford University Press, 1962.

Kupperman, Robert H., and Trent, Darrell M. *Terrorism: Threat, Reality, Response*. Stanford: Hoover Institution Press, 1979.

Laqueur, Walter. *Guerrilla*. Boston: Little, Brown, 1976.

_____. *Terrorism*. Boston: Little, Brown, 1977.

_____, ed. *The Pattern of Soviet Conduct in the Third World*. New York: Frederick A. Praeger, 1983.

Leites, Nathan, and World, Charles, Jr. *Rebellion and Authority*. Chicago: Markham, 1970.

Lewy, Guenther. *America in Vietnam*. New York: Oxford University Press, 1978.

Mao Tse-tung. *Selected Military Writings of Mao Tse-tung*. Peking: Foreign Language Press, 1963.

Moss, Robert. "Urban Guerrilla Warfare." Adelphi Papers, no. 79. London: International Institute for Strategic Studies, 1972.

Taylor, William J., Jr., and Kupperman, Robert, eds. *Strategic Requirements for the Army to the Year 2000*. Lexington, Mass.: Lexington Books, 1984.

14

ECONOMIC CHALLENGES TO NATIONAL SECURITY

Chapter 1 introduced the profound effects on the traditional international political system of the human, ideological, technological, and institutional revolutions since World War II. These revolutionary changes have been accompanied by an unprecedented period of world economic growth, driven in part by dramatic increases in economic interaction among nations. As the economies of the nations of the world have grown more complex, they also have become increasingly interdependent. The United States exported roughly 10 percent of its GNP in 1980, in contrast with less than 5 percent in 1950. From 1965 to 1980, the aggregate exports of the Western European nations increased roughly tenfold; Japan's exports grew more than fifteenfold in that same period.[1] Vital raw materials and food as well as manufactured goods move in international commerce in staggering amounts. Even the Soviet Union, which has long sought to minimize its economic dependence on other nations, is increasingly involved in trade with its satellites and the West.

Moreover, the governments of many countries have assumed in the postwar period much greater responsibility for the economic performance of their societies. Political decision-makers have been answerable for traditional national security policy, but their increasing accountability for economic performance and the new economic interdependence open new relationships between national security problems and economic problems. Decisions made to advance national security objectives may adversely affect the accomplishment of economic goals, for example. Poor economic performance in itself may cause national security problems as unfulfilled expectations lead to political unrest or as budgetary pressures cause defense forces to shrink. The growing interdependence among nations and the deepening involvement of governments in both national security and economic policy complicate the problem of adjusting to rapid change in the international political system.

The annual Defense Department report for FY 1981 concisely expressed the national security interests of the United States in the international economic sphere.

Clearly the independence and territorial integrity of the United States is a necessary condition of security. But it no longer is, if it ever was, a sufficient condition. . . . The particular manner in which our economy has expanded means that we have come to depend to no small degree on imports, exports, and the earnings from overseas investments for our material well-being. In 1978, our imports of goods and services amounted to $229 billion. Exports were $225 billion, or around 10 percent of the Gross National Product. Our direct foreign investments amounted to $168 billion.

With time and a reduction in our standard of living, we could forgo or substitute for much of what we import. But any major interruption of this flow of goods and services could have the most serious near-term effects on the U.S. economy. In no respect is that more evident than in the case of oil. A large-scale disruption in the supply of foreign oil could have as damaging consequences for the United States as the loss of an important military campaign, or indeed a war. Such a disruption could be almost fatal to some of our allies. It is little wonder, in the circumstances, that access to foreign oil—in the Middle East, North and West Africa, the North Sea, Latin America, and Southeast Asia—constitutes a critical condition of U.S. security. More generally, our economic well-being and security depend on expanding world trade, freedom of the arteries of commerce at sea and in the air, and increasingly on the peaceful unhindered uses of space.[2]

In short, increasing international economic exposure of the United States means that national security involves more than safety from military attack. A general condition of international peace, stability, and orderly change is increasingly essential to U.S. national security, as it has long been to Japan and Europe. The DOD report just cited used the example of oil, which is clearly the most dramatic case of our dependence on others for economic security—both because of the importance of oil and because of the vulnerability inherent in over 50 percent of world exports coming from the unstable Persian Gulf region. There are, however, other important, though more prosaic, examples of our dependence. Of the twenty-four major nonfuel minerals needed by an industrial nation (aluminum, copper, iron, manganese, tin, zinc, etc.), the United States is substantially dependent on foreign sources for almost all of them; Japan and the European nations are, again, even more import dependent than are we (fig. 14.1).[3]

While the growth of world trade and interdependence is not new, its tremendous growth rate since World War II and its effects on the economic preeminence of the United States have been significant (table 14.1). At the end of World War II, the United States was the only major industrial nation whose economy had not suffered severe war damage. In 1945, the U.S. economy was relatively self-sufficient and far stronger than that of any other nation or group of nations. As the postwar "economic miracle" unfolded in Japan and Europe, trade among industrialized countries grew rapidly and many large industries, particularly in Western Europe and Japan, became increasingly export-oriented. Many of these foreign industries depended heavily on America as a market for their output. The rapid growth of industrial might in Europe and Japan began to shift the economic power balance away from the U.S. preeminence.

Table 14.1 **World Trade, 1947–81 (in millions of $)**

Year	Exports	Imports
1947	50,299	56,068
1950	50,563	59,476
1955	84,900	89,200
1960	114,700	120,200
1965	167,500	176,100
1970	283,500	297,100
1975	794,900	816,300
1977	1,041,600	1,066,800
1979	1,523,800	1,559,800
1980	1,868,600	1,923,100
1981	1,836,400	1,908,700

Source: International Monetary Fund, *International Financial Statistics* (Washington, D.C.: IMF, 1948–82).

Note: Figures not adjusted for inflation.

The giant American economy did not become substantially dependent upon imports in the early postwar years (table 14.2). Europe, Japan, and the developing world needed American markets for their exports more than we needed the products that those countries produced. Yet, because the stability of allies and trading partners was important to the United States for political and national security reasons, its governmental economic decision-makers had to take increasing account of the impact of U.S. domestic policies on its friends abroad.[4]

In the 1960s and 1970s, the U.S. economy began to develop significant dependence on less developed countries (LDCs) for imports—mainly raw materials, of which oil was the most important. The Arab oil embargo of 1973–74 gave an indication of the degree of dependence of the U.S. economy on petroleum from the Middle East—a lesson underscored in early 1979 by the loss of Iranian exports. Inexpensive oil, largely from the members of the

Table 14.2 **U.S. Trade and the Gross National Product**

Year	GNP (in billions)	Exports	Imports	Exports plus Imports as % of GNP
1946	209.8	11.7	5.0	7.9
1950	286.5	10.2	9.0	6.7
1955	400.0	14.4	11.5	6.4
1960	506.5	19.6	14.7	6.7
1965	691.1	26.4	21.5	6.9
1970	992.7	42.4	39.8	8.2
1975	1,549.2	107.0	98.0	13.2
1980	2,626.1	223.9	249.3	18.0

Source: Adapted from *Economic Report of the President* (Washington, D.C.: U.S. Government Printing Office, February 1982), pp. 233, 346.

U.S. NET IMPORT RELIANCE OF SELECTED MINERALS AND METALS AS A PERCENT OF CONSUMPTION IN 1982

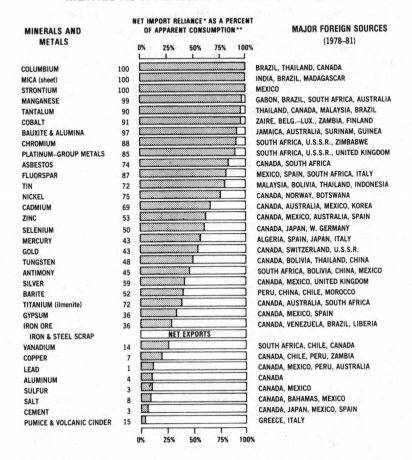

MINERALS AND METALS	NET IMPORT RELIANCE* AS A PERCENT OF APPARENT CONSUMPTION**	MAJOR FOREIGN SOURCES (1978–81)
COLUMBIUM	100	BRAZIL, THAILAND, CANADA
MICA (sheet)	100	INDIA, BRAZIL, MADAGASCAR
STRONTIUM	100	MEXICO
MANGANESE	99	GABON, BRAZIL, SOUTH AFRICA, AUSTRALIA
TANTALUM	90	THAILAND, CANADA, MALAYSIA, BRAZIL
COBALT	91	ZAIRE, BELG.–LUX., ZAMBIA, FINLAND
BAUXITE & ALUMINA	97	JAMAICA, AUSTRALIA, SURINAM, GUINEA
CHROMIUM	88	SOUTH AFRICA, U.S.S.R., ZIMBABWE
PLATINUM–GROUP METALS	85	SOUTH AFRICA, U.S.S.R., UNITED KINGDOM
ASBESTOS	74	CANADA, SOUTH AFRICA
FLUORSPAR	87	MEXICO, SPAIN, SOUTH AFRICA, ITALY
TIN	72	MALAYSIA, BOLIVIA, THAILAND, INDONESIA
NICKEL	75	CANADA, NORWAY, BOTSWANA
CADMIUM	69	CANADA, AUSTRALIA, MEXICO, KOREA
ZINC	53	CANADA, MEXICO, AUSTRALIA, SPAIN
SELENIUM	50	CANADA, JAPAN, W. GERMANY
MERCURY	43	ALGERIA, SPAIN, JAPAN, ITALY
GOLD	43	CANADA, SWITZERLAND, U.S.S.R.
TUNGSTEN	48	CANADA, BOLIVIA, THAILAND, CHINA
ANTIMONY	45	SOUTH AFRICA, BOLIVIA, CHINA, MEXICO
SILVER	59	CANADA, MEXICO, UNITED KINGDOM
BARITE	52	PERU, CHINA, CHILE, MOROCCO
TITANIUM (ilmenite)	72	CANADA, AUSTRALIA, SOUTH AFRICA
GYPSUM	36	CANADA, MEXICO, SPAIN
IRON ORE	36	CANADA, VENEZUELA, BRAZIL, LIBERIA
IRON & STEEL SCRAP	NET EXPORTS	
VANADIUM	14	SOUTH AFRICA, CHILE, CANADA
COPPER	7	CANADA, CHILE, PERU, ZAMBIA
LEAD	1	CANADA, MEXICO, PERU, AUSTRALIA
ALUMINUM	4	CANADA
SULFUR	3	CANADA, MEXICO
SALT	8	CANADA, BAHAMAS, MEXICO
CEMENT	3	CANADA, JAPAN, MEXICO, SPAIN
PUMICE & VOLCANIC CINDER	15	GREECE, ITALY

*NET IMPORT RELIANCE = IMPORTS-EXPORTS
+ ADJUSTMENTS FOR GOV'T AND INDUSTRY
STOCK CHANGES

**APPARENT CONSUMPTION = U.S. PRIMARY
+ SECONDARY PRODUCTION + NET IMPORT
RELIANCE

BUREAU OF MINES, U.S. DEPARTMENT OF THE INTERIOR
(import-export data from Bureau of the Census)

FIG. 14.1

Organization of Petroleum Exporting Countries (OPEC) had, prior to 1973, helped fuel the rapid economic growth of the Western industrial economies. As these developed economies depleted their domestic reserves and increased their rates of energy consumption, the potential economic power of the less developed, but oil rich, nations increased. The steep jumps in the price of OPEC oil in 1973–74 and 1979–80 reflected the shift in economic power away from the industrial nations and toward the oil exporters that had occurred with the exhaustion of U.S. excess capacity in oil.

While this oil-induced shift was highly visible and important, it is quite possible that overall economic growth and expansion of world trade would eventually have transferred economic power from the more mature industrialized nations to faster growing developing nations. What is remarkable is the massive proportion of that shift in economic power and the suddenness with which it occurred—both of which were at least partly the result of faulty American policies. This economic power shift, in turn, upset the traditional balance of political-military influence in the world and posed serious problems for U.S. national security. It is particularly noteworthy that U.S. international preeminence in the 1950s and part of the 1960s rested on simultaneously strong economic, military, and political bases. When both the economic and military legs began to weaken in the latter 1960s and early 1970s, it is not surprising that the whole national security stool became shaky.

This chapter examines international economic interdependence among the nations of the world and the contemporary problems for U.S. national security posed by the vulnerabilities inherent in such increased interdependence. The chapter will first survey the elements of international economics that have increased this interdependence, including international trade and capital flows, the international monetary system, and the adjustment mechanism for balance-of-payments disequilibria. In the latter half of the chapter, we relate these aspects of international economics to current issues that have significance for U.S. national security.

The Elements of Interdependence.

International Trade: Interdependence through Specialization. Before the Industrial Revolution, basically rural countries and perhaps even localities within those countries could be relatively self-sufficient. With industrialization, however, large scale production required land, capital, labor, entrepreneurial talent, and raw materials, which often did not exist in sufficient quantities in one location to allow complete self-sufficiency. Thus, the need for trade arose. Each trading partner could benefit by specializing in the production of those goods in which it enjoyed an advantage and by trading for other goods. Specialization, however, inevitably makes nations more interdependent: when, for example, farmers in Great Britain gave up their crops and herds and went to work in factories producing textiles and machine tools, they had to depend on their American trading partners to produce food to be exchanged for textiles and machine tools. Not only does increased trade among nations extend interdependence at the national level, it also makes individuals within each country more dependent for their livelihoods and living standards upon economic developments abroad.

Trade offsets the risks of increased interdependence by raising real incomes in the countries that participate, because it results in a more efficient use of world resources. "More efficient" means that, with specialization and trade, a given amount of land, labor, and capital will produce more goods and

Reprinted with permission of Ranan R. Lurie from his book, *Lurie's Worlds, 1970–1980*, University Press of Hawaii and King Features Syndicate, Inc.

services than would be possible if the same resources were used without specialization. If each country specializes in the production of goods in which it has comparative advantage and trades for other goods, it will be able to consume more goods and services than if it were to produce every good it used at home.

Comparative advantage theory requires that each country produce the goods that it produces relatively most efficiently, that is, with the smallest input of production resources in comparison with its trading partners, and that it trade for other goods at prices reflecting production costs. Every

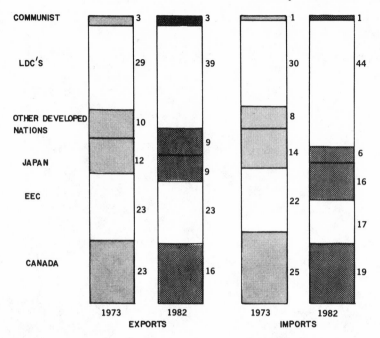

FIG. 14.2
PERCENTAGE OF TOTAL U.S. TRADE BY COUNTRY/GROUP
Sources: International Economic Report of the President, transmitted to the Congress
January 1977, and U.S., President, *Economic Report of the President* (Washington, D.C.:
U.S. Government Printing Office, 1979); Department of Commerce, International Trade
Administration, Office of Trade Information and Analysis.

country will benefit from trade, even *if it can produce every good more
efficiently than any other country.* If it uses its resources in the production of
the goods it makes most efficiently in relation to its trading partners and
exchanges those goods for other things it needs, the country's real income,
that is, the goods and services available to its people, will be increased.
Obviously, increased specialization and trade among nations is one of the
primary means by which economic growth, generally measured as the rate
of increase in the output of goods and services per capita, can occur.

As mentioned above, the post World War II period has been one of
unprecedented economic growth. The total of the GNPs of all the countries
of the world, the gross world product (GWP), has increased more than three
and one-half times in real terms (adjusted for inflation), while world trade
volume (exports), similarly adjusted, has increased more than six times. When
this rate of growth of world trade is compared with the record of the first
forty-five years of this century, in which world export trade volume increased
by only 10 percent, the dramatic developments in postwar international trade
seem the more remarkable.[5]

While most of the nations of the world have increased their participation

Table 14.3 Percentage of Total Trading Partners' Exports Sold to the United States, 1982

Trading Partner	% of Total Exports
Japan	26
Canada	68
EEC	7
Other developed countries	3
LDCs	41

Source: Department of Commerce, International Trade Administration, Office of Trade Administration and Analysis.

in international commerce, the bulk of the postwar increase in world trade has been accounted for by rising trade among the industrialized countries. To the extent it is a function of rising international trade, then, interdependence among nations has grown most among these industrial economies. The depletion of petroleum reserves in developed countries and the rise in world oil use have, however, recently made the industrial powers increasingly dependent on the oil-exporting LDCs.

Fig. 14.2 shows the 1982 breakdown of U.S. international commodity trade by trading partner in comparison with the breakdown in 1973. Note that as recently as 1973, 69 percent of U.S. imports were from other noncommunist developed countries and only 30% from the LDCs. The data for 1982 show that the proportion of U.S. imports from other developed countries has fallen to 58 percent, while 41 percent of our imports are from LDCs. The same kind of shift toward the LDCs has occurred in exports. These quantitative measures, however, mask important developments in the qualitative nature of U.S. imports, particularly with regard to oil imports, for which there may be no viable substitute for some time to come. Needless to say, since nearly 10 percent of our GNP is derived from the international sector, trade has become very important to the health of the U.S. economy.[6]

It is also true that the American market is still an important source of export earnings for U.S. trading partners, particularly for Japan and the LDCs as a group. Table 14.3 shows the percentage of total commodity exports of various nations or groups that were sold in the U.S. market in 1982.

Obviously, policy changes or other economic developments in the United States that tend to restrict imports can have serious consequences for our trading partners. Similarly, if the United States were denied access to goods it imports, American living standards would fall because home-produced import substitutes, if indeed they could be produced, would cost more than the formerly imported goods. Since the maintenance and improvement of living standards have become political imperatives, U.S. policy-makers must always be concerned about developments that hinder or restrict international trade.

International Capital Flows. Capital goods (or capital) are commodities that can be used to produce other goods. They are resources used in the production process, such as machines, buildings, and inventories. *International flow of capital* normally refers to removing money from one country and channelling it into investment in capital goods or financial assets (stocks, bonds, or short- and long-term loans) in another country. These capital flows comprise a second important part of international economic relations. Whereas trade involves movement of commodities, capital flows represent movement of one of the factors of production.[7]

Capital movements increase the resources available for production in a receiving country and expand world output by more efficiently allocating among nations one of the scarce factors of production, namely, capital. The flows accomplish this by moving capital from countries where it is plentiful—and therefore cheap—to those where it is scarce and more expensive.

Capital flows can be categorized in a variety of ways. For simplicity, we begin by distinguishing *public* from *private* capital movements. Public capital flows are those implemented by national governments or international institutions such as the World Bank and the International Monetary Fund (IMF). Since World War II, public flows have been primarily designed to spur economic growth in LDCs through foreign aid or to assist countries in meeting their import bills. As we will see, private capital movements are motivated by the promise of a higher return on investment abroad than in the capital-exporting country.

Many of the world's poorest nations do not offer sufficiently profitable opportunities for private investment, despite the scarcity and consequent expense of capital, due to the woeful state of their economic infrastructure (ports, roads, education, etc.). Development of this infrastructure requires investment in "social overhead capital," the return on which is not easily captured by a private investor. One crucial role of public capital flows, then, is to help a country develop its infrastructure so that it can attract private capital through normal market incentives. There is a growing body of opinion that holds that the United States and the developed world cannot afford to neglect the poverty of the rest of the world, especially in view of the growing trade importance of the LDCs, as shown in figure 14.2.[8] Under these circumstances, foreign aid grants and loans may assume primary importance in the maintenance of U.S. national security.

Private capital movements respond to differences in the available rates of return on investment that can be earned in different countries. Developed countries tend to be relatively capital abundant and may offer, therefore, a poorer return on investment than developing nations, whose capital supply is much smaller. Accordingly, private investment funds, seeking the highest rate of return, tend to flow, due to market forces alone, to the developing nations. These funds serve a vital purpose in the LDCs. Economic growth normally proceeds by continuing capital formation that gives each worker more tools with which to work, raising productivity and real income. Domestic capital formation requires that a portion of a nation's output not be consumed but be saved and invested in capital goods. Many LDC populations exist so close to subsistence level that nearly all available output is needed for consumption. Private capital flows are a way to meet this problem by transferring savings from the developed world to the LDCs, thereby facilitating economic growth.

While private flows are theoretically beneficial to both the investing and receiving nation, it is clear that risks are incurred by both parties. Developed country investors may lose their capital through expropriation or default, and the receiving nation may feel a loss of economic autonomy since the imported capital does not really belong to it and might conceivably be used in ways incompatible with its priorities or values. Clearly then, the developed nations and the LDCs can engage in mutually beneficial investment projects only if they can meet each other's concerns and manage the problems of interdependence which inevitably arise.

Contrary to many Americans' impressions, the U.S. contributed only about 15 percent of world public capital flow in 1981. U.S. foreign aid as a percentage of GNP fell from 1.68% in 1950 to 0.37% in 1980—the lowest percentage among all the developed countries. It is apparent that not only has U.S. public capital flow shrunk as a proportion of all public flows but also that, within overall U.S. capital transfers, private capital flows have become a much larger proportion of the total. The executive branch has pushed for higher public flows, but the political problems of allocating more of the government budget to foreign aid in the face of budget deficits and rising domestic demands for government services at home make real progress in increasing public or official capital flows difficult.

The capital flows discussed so far have been so-called long-term capital flows, that is, investments in financial assets whose duration or maturity is longer than one year. There is, however, another category of investment—short-term capital flows—which serves different purposes and creates another set of problems. Many short-term capital flows reflect the efforts of owners of liquid assets to maximize the return on the funds by shifting them into foreign markets paying higher rates of interest than are available at home. The banking systems of the developed nations are heavily influenced by these short-term capital movements because of their potential volatility and size.

The movement of large sums of short-term funds among countries causes inflows and outflows of bank reserves that form the monetary base in countries with fractional reserve banking systems. This expansion and contraction of the monetary base can quickly affect the money supply that, through its influence on the interest rate structure, is an important determinant of economic activity in developed economies. Since these capital flows are often beyond the control of national economic policy-makers, they can frustrate attempts to use traditional economic policy instruments to influence the domestic economy.

An important development in the international economy which makes

short-term capital flows a problem is the tremendous increase in the number
and size of the various corporations and other organizations that are prepared
to move short-term capital internationally in response to differences in interest
rates and expected currency values among countries. The so-called Eurodollar
market, which deals in bank deposits denominated in American dollars but
placed in banks outside the United States, involves transactions among firms
and individuals of many different countries and therefore entails short-term
capital flows. The Eurodollar market has been a major factor in increasing
the mobility of short-term capital in recent years.

In terms of both trade and long- and short-range capital movements, policy-
makers in today's interdependent world find that they need to coordinate
economic policies with their neighbors if they are to succeed in stabilizing
their domestic economies. Since national circumstances and preferences differ, however, this coordination has not worked well in practice despite the
realization by nearly all nations of the need for increasing it. An interesting
example involves the pleas of the weaker European economies in late 1976 and
again in 1983 for expansive economic policies in the stronger developed
economies (U.S., Japan, West Germany) which would raise demand for the
weaker countries' exports and help them regain noninflationary growth. The
stronger nations, however, showed little interest in risking higher inflation at
home to help their neighbors abroad.[9]

The International Monetary System. In the aftermath of World War II, the
developed nations designed an international monetary system to prevent a
recurrence of some of the more disastrous happenings that marred international monetary relations in the interwar period. The new system, frequently
referred to as the Bretton Woods system, provided for stable exchange rates
and created the IMF, an international organization intended to supervise the
operation of the international monetary system and to assist countries having
balance-of-payments problems by loaning them foreign currency. The overall
system helped create a relatively long period of stable international monetary
relations which, in turn, assisted in the dramatic expansion of international
trade already cited. Exchange rates between currencies were stabilized by
pegging the value of national currencies to gold or to a gold-pegged currency
at predetermined par values. Under the system, countries were obliged to
convert their currencies into gold, at par on demand.

As the system evolved, the U.S. dollar became the key currency to which
other countries tied their currency values, rather than to gold. This development led to increasing use of the dollar, along with gold, as an international
reserve asset. The United States provided liquidity (i.e. increasing dollar
reserves) to the rest of the world by running balance-of-payments deficits,
which were settled by exporting U.S. gold reserves or by generating dollar
claims. As the volume of dollar claims (I.O.U.s) held abroad rose far beyond
the declining value of the U.S. gold reserve, confidence in the dollar began
to weaken; it became obvious during the 1960s that the United States could

not convert all the outstanding claims into gold. It became plain that America could not continue to run substantial deficits without undermining the strength of the dollar and the entire financial system.

By 1971, a continuing deterioration of the U.S. trade balance had created a "dollar crisis," sending a massive outflow of short-term capital from the United States in search of stronger currencies. America finally suspended convertibility of dollars into gold in August 1971, effectively removing the anchor holding exchange rates in a stable pattern and ending the Bretton Woods system. The dollar began to "float," depreciating in value against many major currencies, its value determined by supply and demand in the foreign exchange market.[10]

The resulting floating rate system has both plusses and minuses.[11] It can be argued that floating rates facilitate adjustments of international payments imbalances and, in the short run, insulate countries from economic disturbances generated abroad. On the other hand, the potential extreme volatility of floating rates may be injurious to the expansion of international transactions because of the added risk of exchange rate losses. Moreover, the loss of discipline on national monetary authorities which fixed rates imposed may exacerbate inflation. It is noteworthy that the European Common Market tried, in early 1979, to stabilize a major segment of the world system by creating a European Monetary System (EMS) to operate along with the overall floating rate system.

The EMS established an artificial unit of account, the European Currency Unit (ECU), based on the trade-weighted values of the participating countries, which itself floats but by which terms the individual national currencies are fixed—or, more accurately, float within a very narrow band.[12] Yet despite the EMS and various other efforts to supplement or replace the dollar at the heart of the international monetary system, the dollar is still *the* international currency.

As students of introductory economics know, the primary functions of money are to serve as a medium of exchange and as a store of purchasing power. Economic history abounds with examples of the disruption caused by the loss of the ability of a society's money to serve these functions. The German hyperinflation of the 1920s was an instance in which an economic system's money lost its effectiveness as a medium of exchange because it was not an effective store of purchasing power. If the monetary system fails because money is worthless, trade collapses and living standards plummet. In a sense, then, destruction of the value of the dollar against other currencies would be analogous to hyperinflation at home. World trade would slow dramatically because no acceptable medium of exchange would be available. Given the growing dependence of our living standards on world trade, the stability of the U.S. dollar is, then, of direct concern to U.S. national security. It is also of great concern indirectly, for the vitality of allies and the well-being of the entire international economic system still depend on the health of the dollar.

The Settlement of International Accounts: The Balance of Payments. The functioning of the international monetary system is closely related to the problem of adjusting to imbalances in the international balance of payments. Since there is frequently confusion about the significance of these imbalances, a brief description of the working of the balance of payments may prove helpful. A country's balance of payments measures the flow of transactions between it and the rest of the world. It is essential to realize that the balance of payments, a system of double-entry bookkeeping, must indeed always "balance." If American Widget Corporation sells a widget to France, that transaction results in a credit item in the U.S. balance of payments. When Americans buy Toyota automobiles, a debit item is entered in the U.S. balance. Similarly, capital flows result in debit or credit items; a capital out-flow, such as a loan from a U.S. bank to Zaire, results in a debit item (an import of an I.O.U. from Zaire). A credit item is entered as Zaire makes repayment of the loan, with a reduction of indebtedness as the debit entry.

International payments are divided into several categories. Merchandise trade, service (such as shipping and tourism), income on investments made abroad, and government spending abroad are all included in the *current account*. Capital inflows, whether short- or long-term, public or private, are included in the *capital account*. A final category of international payments—gold and reserve assets movements—must make the debits and credits in the balance of payments equal. If, for example, a country has a deficit on both current and capital accounts, it must pay for these goods, services, and capital flows by making "accommodating" transfers of gold or reserves of foreign currency.

It is possible for a country to run a trade deficit, that is, import more than it exports, but in effect pay for this deficit by a surplus on long-term capital account—i.e., long-term borrowing. In such cases, no accommodating trans-actions are required and the balance of payments is said to be in equilibrium. However, if the long-term capital account surplus is not sufficient to balance the trade deficit and short-term capital flows do not fill the gap, accommo-dating transactions are required. The country must transfer gold abroad or draw down its reserves of foreign currency to "balance" the balance of payments. Accommodating transactions are signs of disequilibrium because they cannot be maintained forever: both the gold stock and foreign currency reserves are finite, and no country can expect foreigners to continue accepting long- or short-term claims. As indicated earlier, the collapse of the Bretton Woods system and the devaluation of the U.S. dollar were largely the result of a prolonged balance-of-payments deficit situation in the United States.

Under floating exchange rates, the problem of disequilibrium can also be solved by changes in the exchange rate. A chronic excess of the value of debit items over the value of credit items for a country will result in excess demand for the currencies of its trading partners in order to pay for the amount that debits exceed credits. This excess demand in the foreign exchange market drives up the price of those foreign currencies or, as we say, depreciates the value of the domestic currency. Real world conditions, however, do not allow exchange rates to move quite so freely in order to correct payment imbalances. Depreciation of a country's currency makes imports more expensive and hence feeds domestic inflation. Appreciation makes a country's exports more expensive abroad, generally lowering demand for them with adverse consequences of employment and profits in export-oriented industries. National decision-makers frequently find it expedient, therefore, to intervene in the foreign exchange market to hold the value of their currency within acceptable limits—resulting in a "dirty float."

It is important, too, to recognize that the workings of the international monetary system imply real changes in incomes and living standards. Political leaders are reluctant to sacrifice living standards at home to restore equilibrium in the international balance of payments. To the extent that the system is effective in making the real economic changes needed to restore exchange equilibrium, the result, as a natural part of the functioning of the world economy, is in unfulfilled expectations and lower profits or fewer jobs in some places. As we have seen, these adverse economic changes can feed quickly into political instability that is of direct national security concern. Italy and Great Britain in the 1970s provide case studies in the political difficulties caused in part by the workings of the international adjustment mechanism. The trauma of a country adjusting its living standard to "live within its means" internationally, raises difficult problems for national security and foreign policy planners.

Another example of the problem of international adjustment is found in the U.S. dependence on foreign sources of crude oil to operate the American economy at its accustomed level—a problem shared by all the industrial democracies. Before the large oil price increases of 1979, the United States was importing about $45 billion worth of oil per year. Given the rough doubling of OPEC prices in 1979 and the relatively small elasticity of demand for oil in the short run, it is not difficult to envision annual U.S. oil imports of $80 or 90 billion in the latter 1980s, as opposed to $4.6 billion in 1972 and $60 billion in 1982. Certainly petroleum imports were the major factor in the huge trade deficits run by the United States in the late 1970s.

Dependence on foreign energy has two important effects on U.S. national security. First, massive dependency undermines the value of the dollar because of the very large import bill just cited; and, second, the U.S. standard of living and defense preparedness are hostage to the continued availability of ample oil supplies from shaky overseas producers. Yet, domestic political pressures have led to energy policies whose purpose was to "protect" Americans from high OPEC oil prices with price controls at home, rather than to policies that encourage conservation and production of alternative domestic sources. By 1980, the political tide had begun to shift with dawning public recognition that the Western world will be highly dependent for its living standards and security upon the continued availability of imported oil well into, and probably throughout, the 1980s. Strong conservation and domestic production measures are likely, therefore, to be maintained in the 1980s, despite the 1982–83 oil price drop of $5 per barrel. Unexpected as it was, the "oil glut" of the early 1980s was a reaction to the speculative excesses of the international oil market following the fall of the Shah and the outbreak of war between Iran and Iraq at the end of the 1970s.

Problems for the 1980s. The economic performance of any nation today depends heavily on world economic developments. Interdependence is real: we are developing a truly global economy. But we have not yet developed international cooperative mechanisms, effective supranational institutions, to help intelligently manage interdependence or to develop sufficient international consensus to guide the resolution of competing national interests.[14] A major threat to U.S. national security lies in this situation—in the increased potential inherent in it for confrontation and conflict over incompatible national economic goals. This theme of possible economic conflict runs through the economic problems discussed below.

Slow Economic Growth in the Developed World: High Unemployment and Inflation. The long postwar economic expansion was dramatically ended by the worldwide recession of 1974–75.[15] As the world slowly recovered from this sharp setback, the worst since the 1930s, developed nations found it difficult to achieve the rates of economic growth of the prerecession years (see table 14.4). As of the early 1980s, the postwar "baby boom" children are still entering the developed countries' labor forces in large numbers, and the slow progress of economic expansion since 1974 has fallen far short of creating openings for all those people desiring work. Combating high inflation rates and their accompanying social stress is essential; yet traditional economic stimulus methods contain the danger of reigniting the double-digit inflation that had been general in the years after 1973–74. Indeed, inflation rates above 10 percent were widely the case among industrial countries by 1980.

Finding they had no mix of domestic policy instruments available which would allow them independently to solve their slow growth and high unemployment problems without excessive danger of renewed inflation, the industrial nations have been searching—unsuccessfully thus far—for cooperative policies. The search will persist, for the political stress produced in the industrial democracies by prolonged economic distress is evident. Although foreign policy and other issues were also involved, electoral outcomes in most of these nations in the early 1980s were powerfully influenced by the twin problems of economic stagnation and inflation.

Meeting the challenges of adequate economic growth and employment has been made vastly more difficult for the developed nations by the necessity, simultaneously, to make large-scale adjustments in the structure of their economies, as a consequence of accelerating technological change and increased competition from such "newly industrialized countries" (NICs) as

Table 14.4 Percentage of Annual Growth (in real GNP per employed person)

Country	1963–72	1973–82
Japan	8.7	2.9
Germany	4.6	2.2
France	4.6	2.3
Italy	5.4	1.3
Canada	2.4	0.2
United Kingdom	3.0	1.2
United States	1.9	0.1

Sources: U.S. President, *Economic Report of the President* (Washington, D.C.: U.S. Government Printing Office, 1980), p. 85; U.S. Department of Commerce, International Trade Administration, Office of Trade Information and Analysis.

Korea, Brazil, and Taiwan. Such structural adjustments as shifting from steel and heavy industrial production into services and "high tech" industries have painful unemployment and other social and political consequences. High rates of inflation and in some cases, political instability have increased uncertainty for business decision-makers contemplating long-term investment projects; moreover, policies designed to reduce inflation have squeezed profits in several nations, and overregulation has widely discouraged investment in many cases. These various disincentives to investment spending are particularly serious in light of the tremendous need for new investment to provide jobs, develop new sources of energy, reallocate resources based on higher energy costs, and reduce pollution.[19]

Thus, economic growth in the developed world will likely be slower in the coming years than might have been expected on historical grounds. The people of the industrial democracies became accustomed to annual rates of GNP growth of 4 percent or more during the quarter century after World War II, providing substantial real increases in standards of living for virtually all segments of the population. The prospect for the 1980s, at least for the early 1980s, is—at most—for half of the historic rates and perhaps for no per capita growth in many cases. Unfulfilled expectations will accompany this painful adjustment and place considerable strain on the political and social systems of the developed countries.[20]

This political and social stress arise from what Daniel Bell calls the "double bind" of the advanced economies: the governments of the developed democracies have become responsible for the simultaneous achievement of inconsistent goals; they are responsible both for aiding capital formation and economic growth and for maintaining high levels of current consumption and spending on social programs.[21] Rapid economic growth in the postwar period enabled progress to be made in both areas, but now slower economic growth intensifies competition among interest groups for society's output. In short, it appears that the advanced economies will have difficulty meeting the expectations of their own populations—let alone helping others. We shall see below that the developing nations have an agenda of their own that will further strain the capacity of the developed economies to deliver all that is expected of them.

Defense expenditures in the developed democracies must compete with the spending for investment and social programs mentioned above. The international economic strains already discussed and the double bind just cited suggest that defense spending will be under continuous pressure. Yet the widely recognized modernization of Warsaw Pact forces oriented toward increased offensive capability demands increased defense efforts throughout the NATO alliance. In Europe, continued concern that increased spending would spur inflation has slowed moves to boost defense spending. In the United States, however, defense spending took a sharp movement upward as the decade of the 1970s ended. The crisis in Iran following the ouster of the Shah, the Soviet intervention in Afghanistan, and the need to augment American military capabilities shown by the SALT II debate made such increased defense spending politically possible. The president's budget for FY 1981 and succeeding years called for increasing outlays for defense by 5 percent in real terms.

Yet, given the serious inflation problem faced by America in the early 1980s and the pressure from competing domestic interests, the United States, too, will have a difficult time freeing the resources required for rebuilding its military capabilities on a sustained basis.

Balance-of-Payments Problems. International balances of payments have generated increasing concern since the early 1970s quadrupling of oil prices and the 1974–75 recession. The U.S. trade deficit in the latter 1970s was huge by any standard, fueled by both oil price increases and greater consumption of oil. After the second oil price shock of 1979–80, and compounded by the high foreign exchange value of the dollar, in 1983 the U.S. deficit broke all previous records. The other OECD nations were by and large in similar straits by the decade's end (see table 14.5). The LDC deficits were even worse, compounded by a growing burden of debt service payments due on loans contracted earlier, largely for oil.

As suggested earlier, the strong efforts to curtail oil imports by the major oil consumers, which were responsible for the "oil glut" of 1982–83, must be maintained. As a result of these measures, world balances of payments require massive adjustment. As shown in table 14.5, the current account surplus of the OPEC oil exporters had dwindled to $2 billion by 1978—an amount that could readily be covered by long-term borrowing on the part of oil importers. (In practice, the importers have generally not borrowed directly from the OPEC nations; rather, the oil exporters have loaned their surpluses to the large private

Table 14.5   Current Account Balances, 1973–83 (in billions of $)

Region	1973	1974	1978	1980	1981	1982	1983[a]
Industrial countries	20.3	−10.8	32.7	−40.1	0.6	−1.2	16
United States	9.1	7.6	−4.0	6.2	9.0	−2.7	−20
OPEC countries	6.7	68.3	2.2	114.3	65.0	−2.2	−27
Other developing countries	−11.3	−37.0	−41.3	−89.0	−107.7	−86.8	−68

[a]Estimate.
Source: IMF World Economic Outlook (Washington, D.C.: International Monetary Fund, 1983), p. 185.

international banks, which have in turn loaned the petroleum importers the dollars they needed—thus "recycling the petrodollars.") The OPEC surplus shot up again in 1980, only to dwindle to a deficit in 1982.

The combination, at the start of the 1980s, of worldwide recession and inflation—in large part caused by the massive oil-induced wealth transfers—resulted in an enormous increase in international debts (see table 14.6). By the end of 1983, these had reached $580 billion, of which $304 billion were owed by Latin American nations—principally, Mexico ($85 billion), Brazil ($90 billion), Argentina ($39 billion), and Venezuela ($35 billion).[22] In view of these unprecedented magnitudes and high rates of interest, many debtor nations, especially among the LDCs, found it impossible to service their debts (i.e., pay back both principal and interest due). Faced with sharply reduced export earnings, they had no recourse—other than default—but to request a combination of rescheduling or stretchout of repayments and fresh loans.

During 1982–83, the international financial system improvised sufficiently to cope with the gross imbalances noted above. Despite recurring fears that one or two major financial institutions would collapse under the strain, triggering a chain reaction in the independent banking system, ad hoc arrangements and corrective measures by debtors held the tottery system together. Whether such would continue to be the case long enough for economic growth and reviving world trade to reduce the pressures, permitting debtors and lenders to work out long-range remedial policies, remained a major uncertainty.[23] Indeed, the widespread growth of protectionist sentiments in the developed nations—including the United States—was by the mid-1980s threatening the revival of world trade, the essential precondition for survival of any sound international financial order.

International Development and the "New International Economic Order." Although existing international economic institutions, which were spawned in the aftermath of World War II, have been largely successful in fostering the economic growth of the more highly developed countries, the LDCs continue to be plagued by a series of factors that inhibit their economic

Table 14.6   The World's Leading Debtors, 1982 (in billions of $)

Country	Total (end of 1982)	Loans from Private Banks	Debt Service Payments Due for 1983	Payment as % of Exports
Brazil	87	67	31	117
Mexico	81	68	43	126
Argentina	43	27	18	153
South Korea	36	21	16	40
Venezuela	35	29	19	101
Israel	27	—	15	126
Poland	26	24	8	94
U.S.S.R.	23	—	12	25
Indonesia	22	10	—	—
Egypt	19	—	6	46
Yugoslavia	19	—	6	41
Chile	18	12	—	—
Philippines	16	11	7	79
East Germany	14	—	6	83
Peru	11	—	4	79
Colombia	10	6	—	—
Rumania	10	—	5	61
Nigeria	10	8	5	28
Thailand	10	8	—	—
Total	517	291	201	

Sources: Adapted from Art Pine, "International Bankers Take Steps to Restore Faith in Their System," *Wall Street Journal*, September 15, 1982, and *Time,* "The Debt-Bomb Threat," January 10, 1983, p. 43.

development. Beginning in the early 1960s, the international community devoted greater attention to the developmental problems of the LDCs but little real success was achieved. The gap between the richest and poorest nations of the world continues to widen. While per capita real income in the developed countries doubled from roughly $2,000 in 1952 to $4,000 in 1972, per capita real income among the LDCs rose only from $175 to $300 during that same twenty-year interval. The poorest two-thirds of the world's population consumes little more than 10 percent of the world's total income.[24]

Underdeveloped countries, with several notable exceptions, are often characterized by political instability and poor administration as well as by severe income inequality, heavy emphasis on agricultural production as a percentage of GNP and, frequently, the existence of a dual economy consisting of a market-oriented industrialized sector alongside a subsistence sector of poor farmers using the crudest technology.[25] LDCs share a number of economic obstacles that prevent or slow the achievement of higher living standards. Many LDCs have very small endowments of the factors of production needed for growth. Often natural resources are scarce or of poor quality, the labor force is poorly nourished, educated and motivated, and savings are inadequate to create the capital needed for growth.[26]

In addition, the economies of many LDCs are inefficiently organized. The governments have neither the knowledge nor the information needed to allocate resources efficiently. They tend to lack either a well developed price system or an informed command structure to provide for optimum use of the resources they do have. As a result, allocational decisions are frequently based on tradition or past practice.[27]

We have already seen that, potentially, international trade can raise incomes in the LDCs by allowing them to specialize in the production of goods in which they have comparative advantage. Likewise, inflows of capital increase the resources available for use in production. While it may be true that economic development is a complex social process that cannot be guaranteed by free trade and movement of capital, it is also clear that there is little hope of success in substantially raising living standards around the world in the absence of trade and capital inflows to LDCs. There is, of course, disagreement about how the benefits of trade and capital mobility have been and are distributed. Generally speaking, the LDCs are dissatisfied with the results achieved and are pressing for changes in the terms upon which the exchange of goods and flow of capital will take place in the coming years.

Understandably, the developed countries have been reluctant to meet the LDC demands for a "New International Economic Order" that would shift the balance of benefits in the world economy toward the developing states. Yet, the agenda of international politics for the rest of this century is bound to include issues involving the relationships between the rich and poor nations of the world. Rising expectations of improved living standards around the world and the failure of strong economic growth to relieve abject poverty in the LDCs have increased the potential for confrontation between the developed and the developing world.

A review of the goals of the LDCs for the coming years demonstrates this potential: substantially faster economic growth, increased transfers of resources from the developed world, and a more favorable distribution of world income.[28] We have stressed that expectations for further economic progress are high in the more developed world; in fact, the frustration of these expectations may well strain the political and social fabric of many countries. If we add the problem of helping the poor countries to avert the same problems, it is difficult to see how expectations all around can be fulfilled. Despite the increased number of international forums dealing with this "North-South" problem, and the seriousness with which both sides have taken the issues, very little substantive progress was made in the decade of the 1970s. As is to be expected in negotiations involving so many independent nations with great disparities among national interests, conflicting and overambitious goals have made agreement on effective programs extraordinarily difficult.[29]

Among the problems for LDCs caused by past international economic interaction has been the evolution of the dual economy mentioned earlier. The developing countries believe that foreign investors have been concerned in too many cases with the rapid extraction of mineral resources and have neglected the development of the rest of the economy. The LDCs therefore propose plans for more "balanced" growth. Additionally, many of the LDC exports are basic commodities, the demand for which varies with the health of their developed country customers. Small changes in demand or supply of these items often cause large fluctuations in their price. For an undeveloped country whose national income is largely dependent on the production of a single raw material, these price shifts can mean dramatic fluctuations in living standards. Accordingly, commodity price stabilization is another LDC goal.

The LDCs also complain that they suffer adverse terms of trade* because their exports are produced under forces of international competition that cause prices frequently to fall below production cost, while their imports of manufactured goods are, on the other hand, produced in oligopolistic conditions in the developed world, with their import prices therefore artificially high. The complaints of the LDCs on this score have some merit and are part of their general dissatisfaction with their share of the economic benefits of world production. As noted above, the developing nations face a massive, related problem in borrowing abroad (and repaying) the large sums needed to finance their trade deficits.

While it is clear that the LDCs will not attain their ambitious goal of accounting for 25 percent of world industrial production by the year 2000 (up from 9 percent in 1972), the important question for U.S. national security is whether they will be satisfied with the concessions they can exact through negotiations or whether their lack of success will lead to frustration and confrontation. To date, negotiations have achieved few of the LDC goals. An eighteen-month search for new trade and financial policies to meet their demands, for example—the Conference on International Economic Cooperation (CIEC)—ended in June 1977 without agreement on any of the major issues.[30]

Economic Leverage and Economic Security. Chancellor Helmut Schmidt, in the speech cited in Chapter 1, spoke of the "new economic dimension of national security"—including therein the "necessity to safeguard free trade access to energy supplies and to raw materials, and the need for a monetary system which will help us to reach these targets." Some of the problems of attaining the international cooperation needed to achieve these aspects of economic security have been discussed in the preceding sections of this chapter. Although intrinsically difficult, these problems in large part deal with distributing the benefits in a positive sum fashion by which all nations stand to share in whatever economic gains may be achieved.

Economic security has, however an obverse face, namely, the use of economic power by one nation explicitly to affect the actions and/or behavior of adversary nations. Here we depart from economics in its usual form as the production and distribution of goods and enter the realm of economics as a

---

*The *terms of trade* is defined as the ratio of import prices to export prices. A deterioration is an increase in this ratio.

political and security instrument. This facet of economic security is commonly referred to as "economic leverage" or "economic warfare." In such a relationship, one country seeks to weaken or strengthen another's capabilities—for instance, through denying it certain kinds of trade. Alternatively, a nation may seek not merely to affect another's strength, but also to manipulate its behavior, for example, by inducing it to change a particular political course by providing or withholding economic benefits. (A milder version of this form of economics as a political instrument is one in which country *A* explicitly develops or exploits existing economic interdependencies with country *B* so as to bind it in cooperative patterns that will help avert or diminish confrontations in other, noneconomic matters. While providing a useful, long-range perspective, this approach proved unsuccessful during the 1970s when Mr. Kissinger was its principal exponent and applied it toward inhibiting Soviet misbehavior.

The instruments of economic leverage most familiar to students of contemporary world politics include foreign aid, credits, embargoes, boycotts, quotas, tariffs, export controls, subsidies, preclusive buying, etc.[31] Their use against adversaries has been common in war and in times of severe international tension. During World War II the United States and its allies used most of the instruments just cited in an orchestrated attack on the viability of the German and Japanese economies. During the Korean War the United States imposed an embargo on all economic relationships with North Korea and the People's Republic of China. A similar course was followed later in the cases of Cuba and North Vietnam. The United Nations declared an embargo on all economic relationships with Rhodesia after the white-controlled government in that nation declared its "Unilateral Declaration of Independence" from the United Kingdom in 1968.

These multiple uses of economic leverage have had varying degrees of success. In no case since World War II do they seem to have been decisive in influencing either capabilities or behavior. In part their mixed record is a result of the difficulties of instituting and maintaining comprehensive economic controls in an era of complex international economic relationships and of varying degrees of intensity of effort by the countries attempting to use such leverage.

In considerable part, too, the apparent weakness of economic instruments in influencing political and security affairs decisively has stemmed from efforts to do too much with too little leverage. Only if a target country has major vulnerabilities and has limited options can a persistent, determined, and coordinated use of economic instruments cause it to change its direction. Indeed, if economic leverage is inadequate for its projected task or is used crudely, it may backfire, as was the case in 1974 when the Congress insisted, via the so-called Jackson-Vanik Amendment, that the Soviet Union permit free emigration of Jews as a condition of its being granted Most Favored Nation (MFN) trade treatment. Prior to that bit of "open diplomacy" the Nixon administration had quietly induced the Soviet leaders to increase Jewish emigration from the U.S.S.R. from a level of about three thousand a month to thirty thousand a month. After the congressional broad-axe action, the Soviet Union renounced the negotiations leading up to the MFN treaty and reduced Jewish emigration to a trickle.[32]

Despite the setback in U.S.-Soviet economic relationships caused by the collapse of the MFN initiative, trade between the two nations prospered under the warming sun of détente in the late 1960s and early 1970s. Partly as a consequence of Soviet eagerness to acquire Western technology to bolster its flagging productivity and partly because the West was prepared to offer the needed credits, trade between the industrial West and the Soviet bloc climbed from $9.1 billion a year in 1965 to $66.6 billion a year in 1978; in the same period U.S.-U.S.S.R. trade went from $115 million per year to $2.6 billion.

The Soviet invasion of Afghanistan in December of 1979 sharply reversed this U.S.-U.S.S.R. trend. In January 1980 President Carter announced a series of economic countermeasures which included suspension of further grain deliveries (of about 17 million tons, worth $3 billion), halt of all high-technology transfers, sharp constraints upon Soviet fishing in U.S. waters, and examination of all existing export licenses in order to screen out anything of possible military value. These measures, plus the symbolic gesture of U.S. withdrawal from the Olympics scheduled to be held in Moscow in the summer of 1980, were intended to demonstrate to the Soviet Union that it could not enjoy business as usual while it engaged in blatant aggression.[33]

In the wake of the Soviet takeover of Afghanistan, Carter also appealed to America's allies and other nations not to undercut these efforts at economic leverage by replacing American exports with their own; rather, he asked that they join the United States in clamping down on economic relations. Yet the sanctions imposed against the U.S.S.R. were not especially effective; certainly the measures did not prompt the Soviets to withdraw from Afghanistan, if that was truly the intended objective. Allied reluctance to support the trade sanctions and adjustments in Soviet trade patterns served to blunt the effectiveness of American economic pressure;[34] President Reagan's lifting of the grain embargo early in his administration epitomized the problem of consistency and constancy in the use of this instrument in peacetime.

Any serious effort to use economic leverage must proceed from a realistic comparison of the objectives being sought, the vulnerability and options of the targeted state, and the strength of the means available to the pressuring state. The economic links between the East and West are many: trade, food, technology, energy, shipping, finance, research and development, etc. In most of these cases the Soviet Union is relatively self-sufficient or has enough reasonably available alternatives to withstand determined pressure from the West. Even in the instance of food, for which it depends heavily on imports in case of crop shortfalls (as has often occurred in recent years), the U.S.S.R. has the means to cope with the damage from a Western embargo. It can squeeze some food from its bloc partners; import from such surplus countries as Argentina, which are unwilling to join an embargo; it can also pay premium prices for foodstuffs handled through complex and concealed multiple-transaction deals. More significantly, since the bulk of its needs are for feed grains for animal use, the U.S.S.R. can feed its cattle more grass, potatoes, or other substitutes, slaughter early, and cull herds as necessary to achieve a supply-demand balance. (It can also, of course, import meat itself.) Thus, while a coordinated Western grain cutoff creates difficulties for the Soviet regime, perhaps extending to short meat rations for an unhappy public, it would not seem likely to cause the leadership to yield to direct pressure. Similarly, denial of Western technology—even in key fields, such as oil drilling and recovery, electronics, and computers—though painful and growth-slowing, is not likely to cause Soviet leaders to desist from pursuing what they view as an important course of action.

Even if the prospects of significantly changing Soviet behavior by available economic leverage are not high, it could nonetheless still be very useful for the West to exercise such leverage. Thus, a sharp reduction of all Western high technology trade would probably slow the overall growth of the Soviet economy appreciably; it should be noted that the U.S.S.R. has emphasized the import of such technology as a means of speeding up lagging productivity. In turn, with slower GNP growth, it should become increasingly painful for Soviet leaders to continue to divert very substantial amounts of resources to armaments, as discussed in Chapter 16. More directly, such a Western clampdown would also stop the leakage from dual civilian-military technology into Soviet military strength. Examples of such leakage are not hard to find; a rather unglamorous instance is instructive.

When Soviet invasion forces rolled into Afghanistan in trucks built at the big new Kama River plant with the aid of U.S. technology and financing, they raised dust in Washington as well as on the road tc Kabul.

Everyone has always assumed it to be U.S. policy not to sell the Russians things that might help them militarily. Quite obviously, that policy has some serious holes in it. Some are even bigger than the one that allowed sophisticated U.S. equipment to go into the production of diesel engines at Kama River and allotted $153,950,000 in Export-Import Bank financing to enable the Russians to buy all that highpriced hardware. . . .

It is most likely the files would show even more serious lapses than the one involving Kama River. Intelligence sources believe that the Soviets could not have installed multiple warheads on their intercontinental missiles as quickly as they have if a U.S. firm had not been permitted to sell them a unique machine that produces high quality miniature ball bearings. Congressional sources, backed by independent intelligence estimates, claim that U.S. technology helped the Russians develop guidance systems and gyroscopes for ICBMs and antisubmarine devices that make U.S. Trident submarines more vulnerable.[35]

If U.S.-U.S.S.R. relations worsen during the 1980s, which had already occurred to a considerable degree by 1984, then a degree of economic warfare between the two nations, with at least some spillover into their respective alliances, seems probable. If the United States is to conduct such a policy successfully, it will have to put its own house in order and provide a strong lead in the allied camp. New information and control systems as well as policies will have to be devised in the United States. In particular, policy coordination among the allies will have to be strengthened. Technically, the cold war mechanism known as COCOM (coordinating committee), through which the industrial democracies have informally coordinated their trade control programs, could be adapted to this purpose. There is serious doubt, however, that America's allies will adequately renovate that mechanism, or take any other measures that will further constrain them in this field. If that proves to be the case, the United States may simply have to settle for a leaky bulwark.

Reflections on the United States in the World Economy. During the nearly three decades of unprecedented world economic growth after World War II, the United States benefited greatly by its leadership of and increasing involvement in the international economy. The price, however, for the gains from this enhanced interdependence has been restriction of its freedom of action in domestic economic policy and in international affairs of all kinds. Over the same period the American economy has gradually lost its preeminence; indeed, in the 1970s, with its large petrodollar deficits and worsening inflation, the American economy in effect became an international disturber of the peace.

The petrodollar imbalances and structural problems cited earlier seem certain in the 1980s to put continuing strain on the international monetary system as a whole as well as on many individual states—including the United States. Similarly, LDC demands for a New International Economic Order will also grow, and there is some prospect that they will become effectively linked to the petrodollar problem. Depending on how this linkage is contrived and on the nature of the response by the industrial democracies, this mix of issues may simply become unmanageable. If, in addition, the United States and the U.S.S.R. become locked in economic warfare, each cudgeling its allies to help, the prospects for economic stability and growth in the 1980s do not appear bright.

Such reflections add urgency to the goal of reviving the American economy, reversing its downward drift in productivity, stanching the petrodollar hemorrhage, and restoring growth. From such a base the United States could again provide the needed leadership, in cooperation with its principal allies among the industrial democracies, to secure and strengthen international trade and to rebuild a sagging international economy.

DISCUSSION QUESTIONS

1. How can economic performance in itself lead to national security problems?
2. Why does U.S. national security now involve more than safety from military attack?
3. Why does specialization raise real income?

4. Why should U.S. national security policy-makers always be concerned about developments that hinder or restrict international trade?

5. How do capital movements expand world output?

6. What circumstances may cause foreign aid and loans to assume great importance in the maintenance of U.S. national security? Why?

7. How can the movement of short-term funds create problems for domestic economic policy-makers?

8. Why does the clear need for internationally coordinated economic policies among at least the industrial democracies not lead to the effective concerting of policies? What are your predictions for the future in this respect?

9. Why is the stability of the dollar of direct concern to U.S. national security?

10. Describe how a country's trade balance can affect the value of its currency and how an imbalance can create political instability.

11. What is the "double bind" of the advanced economies? How does it influence defense spending?

12. Explain the problem of "recycling" OPEC oil profits.

13. What is the "New International Economic Order"? Why does it imply an increased potential for confrontation between the developed and the developing worlds?

14. Why have efforts at economic warfare not been overly successful? Has this been true of U.S. efforts to use trade to influence Soviet actions in Afghanistan?

RECOMMENDED READING

Economic Report of the President. Transmitted to Congress, January 1980. Washington, D.C.: U.S. Government Printing Office, 1980.

Fox, William T. R., ed. *Theoretical Aspects of International Relations.* Notre Dame: University of Notre Dame Press, 1959.

Gilpin, Robert. *U.S. Power and the Multinational Corporation.* New York: Basic Books, 1975.

Keohane, Robert O., ed. *International Organization.* Stanford: Stanford University Center for Research in International Studies, 1975.

———, and Nye, Joseph. *Power and Interdependence.* Boston: Little, Brown, 1977.

Knorr, Klaus, and Trager, Frank N., eds. *Economic Issues and National Security.* Lawrence, Kan.: Regent Press of Kansas, 1977.

Lincoln, G. A., and Associates. *Economics of National Security.* Englewood Cliffs, N.J.: Prentice-Hall, 1954.

Saint Phalle, Thibault de, ed., *The International Financial Crisis: An Opportunity for Constructive Action.* Washington, D.C.: Center for Strategic and International Studies, 1983.

Wu, Yuan-li. "U.S. Foreign Economic Policy: Politico-Economic Linkages." In *The United States in the 1980s.* Edited by Peter Duignan and Alvin Rabushka. Stanford: Hoover Institution Press, 1980.

15

RESEARCH AND DEVELOPMENT

Within the context of national security issues, the topic of research and development (R&D) has two major facets. First, it has the direct impact on national safety of insuring that a potential opponent cannot (or does not) possess weapons or equipment of such markedly advanced design and capability that we have no defense against its military strength. Second, within currently available knowledge, R&D should ensure that we have the "best tool for the job"—that tool or system that will minimize the time and cost of performing any required security task. These goals are not necessarily complementary, which introduces legitimate disputes about how best to balance the various trade-offs between quantity and quality or between sophistication and unit cost. "Superior arms provide real advantages, but at some point greater quantity in deployed lower-quality weapons confers the capability to overwhelm the highest quality defense."[1]

This chapter addresses some of the implications that research and development have for defense strategies and forces and indicates the interrelationship of technology problems to other national security topics, such as the decision-making process.

Meaning of R&D. In the fields of science and technology, definitions are neither uniform nor consistent; nor are they universally accepted. However, some common acceptance of basic terminology is needed for our understanding and discussion.

Science in the most general way is defined as "study dealing with a body of facts or truth systematically arranged" and pursued without regard for its application.[2] *Technology,* by contrast, deals with the applied sciences and engineering. Thus, technology refers to potential applications of knowledge.

In government programs, the distinction between knowledge and application of knowledge is stated in different terms. *Research* or "pure research," is investigation of physical phenomena which may add to our store of knowledge. Any such resulting knowledge may be useful for various purposes, but the rationale for the program is knowledge per se. *Applied research* is an attempt to advance the state of science or technology in a particular field, perhaps, but not necessarily, directed toward certain uses. This often involves the testing of design models or verification of basic theory by constructing laboratory hardware.[3]

Once research has indicated that some scientific principle or new (or improved) design technique is feasible, *development* is undertaken to convert the scientific innovation into an operational element of security policy. If the new development is an entirely new application or requires a completely new system to make it operational, the development stage is usually labeled *weapons systems development*. If the program is smaller or involves only a *part* of a system, it is called *component development*. Because of the complexity of modern weapons systems, this distinction can be somewhat arbitrary.[4]

In a generalized sense, it is fair to say that *research and development* are governmental applications of the general terms *science* and *technology*. Research is concerned with increasing knowledge, and development is concerned with finding ways to apply this knowledge. A final definitional distinction is that between *development* and *production*. Development is concerned with producing a small number of things that contain the proper scientific and engineering qualities to meet a defined need. These "prototypes" are tested and evaluated, to determine how well the product will withstand actual operating conditions. If a decision is made to utilize the product, *production* is the process of actually building the entire quantity to furnish the armed forces with a complete issue of the product.

Technology is a vital component of a nation's security posture. "Any power that lags significantly in military technology, no matter how large its military budget or how efficiently it allocates resources, is likely to be at the mercy of a more progressive enemy."[5] Given the significance of technology, sheer weight of production will likely not compensate for marked technological unpreparedness. Within limits, "in modern war the technological qualities of weapons are clearly more important than the number of battalions and their numerical combat strength."[6]* Thus, technological preparedness is generally a necessary, if not sufficient, condition for having other national security issues to address. Note the qualifications on these statements. While it is unavoidably true that the abstract claim of necessity for "technological sufficiency" is valid, security decisions are not made in the abstract. They are instead made at specific points in time about specific projects, capabilities, and weapons systems.

Thus, in a recent example, there has been debate about whether either or both the B–1 bomber and long-range cruise missile are really sufficient technological advances to warrant their procurement. Advocates of the B–1

*Note that the overriding importance of technology, at least in *all* aspects, is debated later in this chapter. What these questions do imply is the necessity to protect against *marked* technological inferiority.

bomber cite as mandates for its procurement its base for further technological improvements, its ability to maintain survivability of the manned bomber for another decade, and the complicating factor it causes for the defense.

Cruise missile advocates, on the other hand, hold that cruise missiles provide the same capabilities as the B–1 with much less overhead investment. Penetration and terminal accuracy can be achieved with no new base hardware system procurement. The desired complications for the opponent's defense can be achieved both by saturation (made possible by lower unit cost) and the cruise missile's nonballistic trajectory (which confuses antimissile radars).

From a technological standpoint, assuming both types of weapon provide the needed capability, the much higher additional cost of the B–1 is justified by the general advancement in the technological base it creates, versus the exploitation of refinements of current technology via the cruise missile. The purpose here is not to critique a particular decision, but merely to illustrate that such choices are almost constantly facing decision-makers in today's environment.

In considering issues of military R&D, one cannot lose sight of the point that research advances, development programs, and "production runs" all use up resources. Since resources are not unlimited, one must choose which of many competing programs—at various stages—are worthy of the limited amount of resources available. Thus, to optimize national return for expenditures in R&D, nations must carefully develop a *strategy*, or overall coherence, for their technology programs.

Sources and Types of American R&D. Each of the categories of research, development, and production to be conducted in pursuit of national security must be funded and staffed. Sources of support for these activities are scattered, further adding to the problem of coordinating research efforts and insuring that sufficient amounts of effort and resources are allocated to the necessary tasks.

The federal government is the chief source of military-oriented R&D support, requesting some $12.6 billion for R&D in the FY 1979 defense budget.[7] Private industry, for a variety of reasons, also conducts scientific and technological research. While these private sector programs are not necessarily aimed specifically at producing strategic technological advances, the "fact is that many lines of basic research can be regarded as of great strategic importance. . . . No one can predict the ultimate use of any research in any of the pure sciences."[8]

There are important limitations, however, on the subject matter of private sector research. Given the uncertainty of even the existence of positive results—let alone their commercial application—particularly in the basic research fields, it is obvious that the "risk" of financing research programs sometimes exceeds that which the business firm finds prudent.* This leaves

---

*Management economics theory tells the corporation that it ought to see positive returns on research capital within ten years, which leaves industry with a compound trade-off both in terms of the nature and subject matter of research.

the federal budget as the "last resort" source of basic research funds. In addition to the factor of investment risk for industry, some research encounters problems of application, sometimes called the "technology transfer" problem. Discoveries and developments that the Defense Department might find highly useful, such as refinements in technology applicable to nuclear weapons, may simply hold little interest for the commercial industrial sector.

This situation causes the defense, space, and nuclear areas of research and development to be very largely dependent on governmental funding. Moreover, "defense, space, and nuclear R&D is characterized by extremely high costs and high risks, hence only the . . . U.S. and U.S.S.R. have been able to allocate sufficient resources to pursue such programs across the entire spectrum of feasibility."[9] This does not mean that there are no significant programs in nuclear or space technology in other nations; however, the basic research in these fields conducted outside the United States and the Soviet Union is relatively small.

Beyond specific programs in these very high risk fields, private sector research can have considerable impact. Research across a broad spectrum has economic potential in the industrial sector, and firms will not hesitate to push into areas of potential profit advantage. The important qualification is that in most cases they will hesitate to fund programs which have no *foreseeable* profit return. Even here, however, the unit cost of most research is so high that only the largest corporations can fund it. Thus, only the highly industrialized nations can undertake substantial technological exploration.

Because of the differing reasons various agencies and organizations have for supporting research, the problems of maintaining a coherent framework of progress are multiplied. For instance, basic research is "cheap" in relative terms.* As noted above, however, the applications are often so difficult to discover that there is no available return within the time frame relevant to corporate balance sheets. As a result, corporate managers, whose progress and future are measured by those balance sheets, are reluctant to allocate scarce resources to speculative pure research efforts. Consequently, when, in the late 1960s, the federal government downgraded its priority for basic research funds, the result was a general "reduction in basic research and high advanced . . . projects."[10]

In applied research, by contrast, the private and public sectors both contribute heavily.† Here the adage that one will likely not fully anticipate the results of one's own research holds true; many of the advances in military technology were unanticipated effects of other research programs. The United States spends some $30 billion a year on applied research.[11] Even at these

---

*In basic research, the hardware costs are low since no working models on actual scale are required. Laboratory facilities needed are of the general rather than specialized variety, and are more likely to be already available.

†Some 46 percent of total R&D funds, mostly in applied areas, come from the private sector, according to Arthur F. Burns, "The Defense Sector: Its Economic and Social Impact," in *The Military and American Society,* ed. Martin B. Hickman (Beverly Hills, Calif.: Glencoe Press, 1971), p. 61.

high expenditure levels, there are two severe resource limitations: not all potentially fruitful variations of a principle can be explored simultaneously, and any discovery is in danger of being outdated before it can be developed, due to the increasing speed of technological change.* Therefore, there are always troublesome trade-off decisions on whether to delay production of a new design awaiting more refinement or to push into procurement with what may be an inferior model.

Adapting scientific designs into optimum methods of meeting strategic needs is a further challenge. This is the function of the next step in the normal development process—test and evaluation. Test and evaluation (T&E) is the process by which experimental and prototype models of equipment are examined to see how well they actually fulfill the performance needs for which they have been designed and provide guidance for further development.

Devising and producing new defense weapons systems is a complex process. Ideally, it is a rational decision process, initiated by defense planners, taking the following course. A need or required task performance (called a qualitative material requirement, or QMR) is established by force planners.† This request is then sent to the office of the Undersecretary of Defense for Research and Engineering, which surveys all ongoing related research projects to see whether some application of existing basic research efforts could perform the required task. If none are available, and the need has a sufficient priority, a basic research project will be initiated to investigate the potentially feasible approaches for developing the required capability.‡

Once the requisite scientific principles are established, the project moves from research into development. A special task group (known as a *project team*) is organized to design and build (usually in conjunction with a contracting corporation) working models of actual equipment which can perform the required task. These groups are normally at a branch-of-service level, and funds are allocated in the DOD budget. Thus the project manager is responsible both to the particular service and to DOD for the progress and cost of the project.

The final version of the equipment is submitted for test and evaluation. T&E functions are also supervised by DOD, but by a different office than is responsible for development. Finally, if the equipment performs to specified standards under rigorous test conditions, and the task is still needed by the force planners, a decision to procure in quantity will be made. In the case of major systems, a new project manager will establish a task force to supervise the building of the weapons system by the corporation submitting the best bid.

---

*Historically, the United States lead in nuclear fission lasted some six years, despite the best efforts of Soviet science and intelligence. The "lag" in Soviet fusion development was only about two years.
†See also Chapters 8 and 9.
‡If a requirement is specific to a branch of service, normally that service will oversee the research projects. Otherwise the projects will be directly run by DOD.

Overall, this organization and development cycle is designed to translate efficiently requirements into equipment. The difficulties are introduced by the variances of the real world from the idealized model. Some of these variations will be raised later in this chapter.

R&D in the National Security Context. In the present era, technology underlies the entire struggle for national security—at least for the highly industrialized states. Undersecretary of Defense William J. Perry began his program statement to Congress on the FY 1979 R&D budget by quoting Chairman Brezhnev, "The center of gravity in the competition between the two [U.S. and U.S.S.R.] systems is now to be found precisely in [the field of science and technology]. . . ."[12]

Modes of war-fighting and war prevention have become inextricably linked to the sophistication and scientific currency of weapons systems. "We live in an age when a system of international stability could crumble away virtually overnight because of a 'breakthrough' in weapons technology." It is no longer sufficient to be able to out-produce a potential opponent in the last decade's weapons.* "Arms races in the nuclear era differ from those in the gunpowder era in one fundamental way: they are qualitative rather than quantitative."[13] If a major nation does not immediately engage in warfare that tests its current military applications of technology, "war" in a technological sense nonetheless exists.

The level of R&D, to include the establishment and maintenance of a strong technology base and leadership in scientific investigation, is a principal determinant of the future technological capability of a state. This determinant, in turn, becomes an important indicator of the future power of the state. If there is an inadequate base for future advancement and continuing progress in technological fields, the military capability component of national power will erode as technology passes it by. Alternatively, the state will become dependent on importing sophisticated defense systems and thus less free in its policy options.

Once the technological capability to maintain adequately modern weapons has escaped, problems of national security multiply. Not only is a nation confronted by the threat of defeat in an actual war, but it loses some freedom of maneuver in international politics. Dependency on foreign technology introduces new pressure points in a state's interest sphere, and lack of a credible military force may negate the utmost efforts of skilled negotiators. Nations today view the technological potential and capabilities of opponents as a major factor in capability assessments.[14]

Even without reference to either specific research areas or specific applications, the existence of a generic societal orientation toward technology has

---

*However, some strategists do agree that overreliance on more sophisticated weaponry misallocates resources to the point of incapacity to respond effectively to low-level provocations, a point that will be discussed later in this chapter.

some potential advantage. In such cases, there is always a chance for advance from the marriage of available systems, as, for example, the TV-guided "smart bombs." A technologically oriented society will more quickly discover such associations. Also, the broader the general technological base of the society as a whole, the greater the occurrence of "applications associations," some of which may have military utility.

Technology can become a vital component of national security in two distinct fashions. First, a successful technological breakthrough, even if its military significance were indirect, could have a major impact on security. A breakthrough could at the very least increase the burden on opponents to increase expenditures in other areas to compensate for or offset the break-through. For example, U.S. defense leaders have repeatedly defended work on multiple reentry vehicles for ICBMs and development of an advanced manned strategic bomber on the basis that the Soviet Union might score a technological breakthrough in antisubmarine detection and warfare that would invalidate ballistic missile submarines as an effective second-strike force. Less obviously, technology can support national security even if it does not provide sudden major advances. It can (and does) provide refinements and improved production applications of existing technology, which in turn provide im-provements in force effectiveness. One example of this phenomenon is the use of the semiconductor chip, a type of which is so familiar as the core of pocket calculators, in military radios. Not only has performance been en-hanced, but stability under some adverse operating conditons has also been improved.*

A second major component of technology's contribution stems from the uncertainty inherent in newness and change. A sizable R&D program, even if it is unsuccessful in gaining breakthroughs in most of its areas of effort, contributes the possibility of associated successes or surprise advances. This introduces a degree of uncertainty into a potential adversary's calculations, intensifying its sense of risk over particular policy alternatives. A further fear generated by the "unknowable" arising out of possible technological break-throughs is that a breakthrough would make obsolete much of the nation's standing military force. Even if such a breakthrough did not result immediately in military defeat, the cost of rebuilding a security force from the ground up in a very short time period would be prohibitive. (Of course, there is an obverse side to this argument stating that uncertainty breeds caution; in some instances it may impel one's opponent to make extraordinary and destabilizing efforts to reestablish certainty or at least to reduce risks in the new situation.)

---

*As a measure of the complex nature of the interaction of technological factors and the phe-nomenon of unanticipated side effects, this particular "improvement" was not without drawbacks. Recent analysis of previously unappreciated side effects of nuclear explosions has demonstrated that nuclear detonations produce a pulse of electromagnetic energy, which transistorized com-munications equipment is much less able to resist then tube-based electronics. Thus, although the gain in reliability of operation, performance levels and size-weight reduction is significant, it is not an unmixed blessing.

The implications of a true breakthrough pose a dilemma. Given the lengthy lead time from concept to application and the high rate of technological change in the world, planners of the first nation to discover a concept will be reluctant to concede the initiative to the second discoverer, yet they *could* err by "locking themselves in" to the development, procurement, and deployment of a *first-generation* system.* An opponent, in response, could concentrate instead on the development of more advanced *second-generation* applications and, by skillfully collapsing technological stages into each other, could balance the capability with a more advanced system in almost the same time frame. Historically, this case is illustrated by the "missile gap" of 1958–62. The Soviet Union, by launching sputnik, demonstrated the technological capability to build an intercontinental-range ballistic missile. Immediately thereafter, Soviet spokesmen began implying that the Soviets were deploying first-generation ICBMs;[15] in fact, they were not. The United States, uncertain about the truth of Soviet statements, rushed missile programs to completion and deployed first-generation ICBMs to counter the supposed threat.† Both elements, the problem of uncertainty and the fear of technological breakthrough, contributed to the U.S. reactions. In retrospect, the result of this situation was counterproductive for both sides. The Soviet Union suddenly found itself on the inferior side of the strategic balance, faced with a larger U.S. missile force than anticipated. The United States, as a result of its rush to redress, found itself with a costly and obsolete first-generation missile force that had to be phased out and replaced.

International Trends in R&D. The multiplicity of potential areas for research and development leads to a further dilemma in the allocation of resources. "In the past we [the United States] could and did invest in virtually every promising area. . . . Now, we cannot afford to cover all the bets, and we know the competition is strong and productive."[16] National security in the broadest sense is affected by relationships in two distinct arenas—defense posture and economic status in the world. Potential opponents or competitors have varying strengths in these two arenas; U.S. policy-makers have been unwilling to relinquish leadership in either sphere.

In both the U.S. and the U.S.S.R., defense-space-nuclear R&D over the past decade has constituted . . . the major portion of the total R&D effort at the governmental level. . . . The Soviets have concentrated some four-fifths of their program in the defense-space-nuclear area. . . . Thus, though overall Soviet R&D expenditures have not yet reached the U.S. level, spending in this particular area is outpacing that of the U.S. by a considerable margin.[17]

On the other hand, the remainder of the industrialized Western nations,

---

*See also Chapter 4. A first-generation system is the earliest operational prototype.
†The United States, however, concurrently continued work on more adva d technology. This led to an earlier development of second- and third-generation systems, which now constitute most of our current strategic forces.

due in part to their ability to depend for elements of their defense on the United States, have tended to concentrate their research efforts in the commercial sector. Although France, for example, engages in some nuclear and space research, this constitutes less than half its research funding. Japan pursues a "national policy which regards R&D primarily as an instrument of economic growth."[18] Thus, if the United States chooses to concentrate primarily in the defense sector, it endangers its ability to remain competitive with its allies in the international marketplace.*

Examination of trends in U.S. research outlays in light of this problem emphasizes the growing magnitude of the difficulty. Despite the growth of world economic competitiveness, the United States has not devoted additional resources to overall R&D nor to its commercially applicable component. Budgetary constraints, coupled with the high national priority accorded to domestic welfare functions, have severely limited R&D budget allocations, both in defense and nondefense projects.

In contrast to the American trend, the U.S.S.R. is still expanding its overall R&D programs. From 1960 to 1972, it is estimated that "the Soviet effort . . . increased two-and-one-half-fold . . . while the U.S. outlay has doubled. But only a small percentage of Soviet R&D . . . is related to civilian requirements, which indicates a military-space endeavor substantially stronger in the U.S.S.R. than in the U.S."[19] When one considers the significant cutbacks of recent years in the Soviet space programs, the military implications of this overall allocation are even more significant.†

Lack of accurate data on actual Soviet programs and the problem of equating price levels suggests the possibility of even further Soviet advantage. Given the Soviet national priority of technological advance and the relatively high quality of resources and personnel devoted to military-space research, estimated expenditure levels may actually understate the true Soviet resource allocation to these purposes. If so, Soviet programs could well exceed U.S. military-space efforts in absolute terms as well as in relative growth rates. Although Soviet spokesmen emphasize the importance of transferring technological advances into the civilian economic sector, they nonetheless continue developing under defense-run programs.

As noted, Japan and the Western European states have generally relied on U.S. expenditures in the defense-space-nuclear field to reduce the scale of major national efforts on their part. Insofar as this has occurred, the resulting relief from demands on national resources has allowed them to concentrate on economically motivated projects. As the results of their strategy in this regard

---

*Evidence of the impact of this problem can be obtained from comparatively charting commercial sector R&D as a percent of GNP against balance-of-trade figures, although the two may not be causally linked.

†While monetary spending levels, due to problems of translating prices from the controlled economy of the Soviet Union, are not necessarily valid indicators of what one can get from R&D research, the *relative* levels nonetheless accurately indicate national priorities and momentum.

COMPARATIVE U.S. AND SOVIET TECHNOLOGICAL INVESTMENT

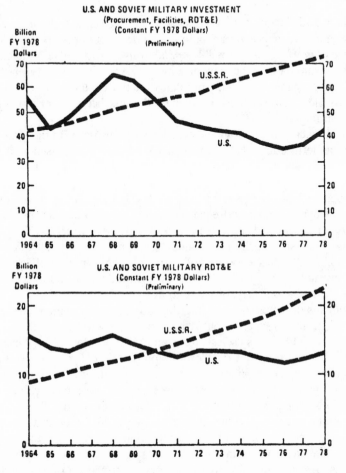

FIG. 15.1
Source: U.S., *Department of Defense Annual Report, Fiscal Year 1978* (Washington, D.C.: U.S. Government Printing Office, 1977), p. 12.

emerge in terms of increased economic competition, the policy implications for U.S.-European and U.S.-Japanese relations become clear. A U.S. review of its technology strategy (the overall planning of technological effort to support national goals and objectives) might well dictate shifts in areas of expenditure. Other Western nations now used to "satelliting" on certain U.S. advances could view such shifts as indicative of changing American interests or priorities in overall foreign policy. In such a case, their responses could, in turn, give rise to collateral strains on the composite of foreign relations between the United States and themselves. In short, the United States could face a problem, given current R&D trends around the world, of having to subordinate technology strategy to foreign policy strategy.

Strategy and Technology. We have already seen how technology is an indicator of future national capability and how it is necessary to differentiate between *knowledge* and possible *applications* of knowledge in defense areas. We have summarized the view of some observers that current trends in R&D may harbor significant policy problems for the United States. Next, we will address the "how" of these problems—the link between technology and security strategy.

The impact of technology on strategy is not restricted to the area of equipment modernization. The very dynamic of technology itself is a factor in strategic equations. To concentrate on applications may be to ignore investigation of new principles which will make current weapons systems obsolete, although such advance is not frequent. "Technology flows on without regard for human intentions, and each technological breakthrough offers the possibility for decisive advantages to the side that first exploits it."[20]* The nature of this dynamism is such that it cannot be controlled unilaterally. For example, if the United States chooses not to pursue development of independently maneuverable reentry vehicles for its missiles, the scientific principles that make such weapons are not going to evaporate.

Elements of technology are interdependent. This statement has two meanings. First, an advance in field *A* may make no sense unless there is also an advance in field *B;* it is useless, for example, to develop a new thermonuclear warhead if one does not develop an appropriate delivery system to employ it. Second, advances in one field frequently suggest associated moves or applications in others; therefore, agreement not to pursue certain areas of research is no guarantee that the technology of the field will remain static.†

Several contemporary "weapons technology" issues illustrate these points. One of the most significant is in laser technology. The U.S. approach to laser application has been primarily one of using it as an adaptation of current systems. As an example, we use lasers to provide terminal guidance for precision-guided munitions (PGMs), which creates the effect of significantly enhancing the utility of the basic munition by virtue of increased accuracy but which does not constitute a "new concept" for the battlefield. Soviet scientists, on the other hand, appear not to be trying to develop laser-designator or laser-optical systems but rather are attempting to create whole new weapons concepts, such as charged-particle beams. The relative long-range utility of the two approaches to the same technology is still open to debate.

*Thus some analysts argue that U.S. efforts to limit the scope of cooperative scientific exchange with the Soviet Union will work to the detriment of the United States. See Mark J. Ablowitz, "Soviet and U.S. Ties in Science," *New York Times,* August 21, 1980, p. A–27.
†For example, an international agreement against chemical and biological warfare experimentation would not preclude the discovery of mutant disease strains in medical research.

U.S. applications are clearly within the present "state of the art" and are not entirely open-ended. Soviet applications are exactly the converse.

As suggested earlier, there has been a major difference in the manner in which the United States and the Soviet Union approach issues of security and technology. While U.S. efforts in technological development have lost influence to the growing priority of welfare and ecology, "Soviet leadership [has] established as a national goal the attainment of world leadership in science and technology."[21] In pursuit of this goal, the Soviets are attempting to marshall their scientific and technological assets and to employ them in a coordinated and rational fashion.* Whether the character of the Soviet economy will permit the U.S.S.R. to attain its world leadership goal remains to be seen.

From the American standpoint, several attempts at creating a national strategy for technology have been tried, with less than total success. Without central management of the entire economy, and lacking the ability to use classified security items in the civilian sector without compromising their security, the United States is less able to rationalize its overall R&D effort than is the Soviet Union. (Because of the rigidity of the compartmentation of the Soviet economy, however, the United States probably realizes a good deal more useful interaction between the two types of R&D than does the U.S.S.R.)

Several governmental offices have attempted or are attempting to organize and coordinate R&D, with varying degrees of success. At the White House level, R&D staffs have been created, dissolved, and created again. The latest version, the Office of Science and Technology Policy, was established in the executive office of the president in 1976 to "serve . . . as a source of scientific, engineering, and technological analysis . . . involved in areas of national concern . . . [and] evaluate the scale, quality, and effectiveness of the Federal effort in science and technology."[22] At the defense level, the undersecretary of Defense for Research and Engineering, and his predecessor, the director of Research and Engineering, has an advocacy function to defend and analyze research proposed by DOD. Unfortunately, the advocacy function on behalf of DOD tends to discredit the office's analysis function in the eyes of Congress. In 1972, Congress itself created the Office of Technology Assessment (OTA) to provide it an independent source of analysis and advice on R&D questions. OTA began its operations in 1974, but it has had only limited success in performing those functions.

The downward drift in national R&D expenditures becomes even more troubling when one considers the problem of lead time in technology. One

*Soviet best efforts may not be too efficient. In defense applications Soviet planners seem far behind the United States in scientific management decision-making, particularly operations research and system analysis methods of determining the most efficient manner of developing, testing, and producing a concept. For a detailed discussion of this problem, see David Holloway, "Technology, Management, and the Soviet Military Establishment," Adelphi Papers, no. 76 (London: International Institute for Strategic Studies, April 1971), pp. 32–35.

area of consistent U.S. concern has been to lower the "lag time" from discovery of a concept to production of an item incorporating the concept. Despite continuing work on this problem, the current average time from concept to design to prototypes is about five to seven years.[23] Thus, even an immediate reorganization and rationalization of overall national effort would not be felt in terms of practical consequences for some time.

Finally, no amount of internal review or rationalization of existing efforts can accomplish the external function of establishing critical national priorities in resource allocation. The most efficient program organizer cannot manage a program without congressional appropriation of R&D money. Good internal organization can increase the efficiency of the budget within limits, but it cannot create an appropriate budget. As indicated above, the trend in budgets since the mid 1960s has been to upgrade spending for domestic welfare programs, partially at the expense of R&D funding. To make matters worse, the research budgets of private corporations tend to reflect economic cycles. In times of narrowing profit margins and heavy inflation, research is primarily directed to finding new or more efficient applications rather than to basic research for new knowledge.

Decision-making in R&D. As indicated previously, decisions about defense R&D would ideally be made on the basis of an optimal way to implement previously determined strategic requirements. However, as implied above, there is a tendency for the reverse to be true, given the speed and complexity of technological advance. Thus one debate in this area is the extent to which R&D should determine strategy, and vice versa.*

Two major observations are often advanced about the technology "tail" wagging the strategy "dog." First, as new weapons systems become available, there is pressure in defense circles to procure and deploy them, which can result in revising strategies in two ways. The structure of forces may be adapted to fit the new weapons, driving the nation toward new strategies even though a coherent strategy for employing the weapon may not have been developed. Also, because the newer weapons are almost invariably more expensive (and more sophisticated), a nation can buy fewer of them, requiring a modification of strategy to match the resulting new force levels.†

The second argument is more complex. Basically, it proposes that *deploying* new and advanced weapons systems may be self-defeating. This does not contradict the argument made earlier that a state must maintain its technological capabilities at the leading edge of scientific knowledge. Once a state discovers a new weapons system, there are internal pressures to procure and

---

*In this sense, Maxwell Taylor's *The Uncertain Trumpet* was a critique of defense policy. Taylor argued that we had structured our whole defense program around nuclear retaliation because nuclear bombs were there and were cheap, rather than analyze possible situations where we might actually be called on to employ military capabilities.

†The closely associated problem of the quantity versus quality dispute in procurement programs will be discussed later in this chapter.

deploy quantities of the weapon.* "The search for *quality*—for the 'techno-logical threshold'—has dominated U.S. force posture for at least a dozen years. . . . The acquisition system provides many incentives for taking this route."[24] To do so, however, may generate a desperate attempt to counter the weapon by the other side, with the net result that both sides expend large sums without a net increase in security for either. Seitz and Nichols have warned about this possibility at the strategic levels.

Simplistic theories about bargaining chips in negotiations, like simplistic notions of military-industrial conspiracies, are not valid. . . . The history of our ABM program and the Soviet reaction to it, . . . as well as . . . our advanced submarine-missile program, . . . suggest that we must be prepared to pursue our own goals in our own interests until we can achieve satisfactory, reciprocal limitations. To the degree that this line of thinking is sound, it means that defense R&D must provide a range of clearly defined options but must *not* be allowed to produce an independent momentum toward procurement of advanced systems that could destabilize past or prospective arms agreements.[25]

At this stage the reader might ask, If deployment of new weapons can be useless as just suggested, but falling behind in military technology can be fatal and, further, if technology cannot be unilaterally controlled, then what options are available? One response is that the United States should awaken to the fact that it is really fighting a "war of technology." It may not wish to procure and deploy each new development, this argument procedes, but it must con-tinue to engage vigorously in R&D to insure that it is *able* quickly to build and deploy superior weapons if the need arises. Framed succinctly:

Technological warfare is the direct and purposeful application of the national tech-nological base . . . to attain strategic and tactical objectives. . . . The aims of this kind of warfare, as of all forms of warfare, are to enforce the national will on enemy powers. . . . The winner of the Technological War can, if he chooses, preserve peace and order, act as a stabilizer of international affairs, and prevent shooting wars. The loser has no choice but to accept the conditions of the victor or to engage in a shooting war which he has already lost.[26]

While those who cite technological war as inescapably decisive overstate their case, viewing technology as a crucial element in power competition—whether or not major procurement follows—makes some sense. The approach suggests a scenario where states conduct "research and development races" rather than traditional "arms races." Advantages to thus viewing the matter could include:

1. A national strategy of technology, to reconcile and rationalize approaches to technological problems.
2. Reduced budget pressure for procurement. Although procurement is not

---

*Sources of this pressure are varied. The industry that has developed the system will press for the large contract for mass production. Both congressional and defense sources will argue that to equip the field army with any but the very latest weapons is to degrade their fighting capability.

the greatest portion of the defense budget, there could be substantial savings in this area.

3. Greater spin-off effects for the rest of society. In such an environment, the only real possibility of advantage would be the scientific breakthrough, which would imply that research be directed into more basic areas. The applications of basic advances are not limited to military fields.

4. An enhanced deterrence effect, since the uncertainty of one side's progress (and laboratories are easier to hide than divisions in the field) would make the other unsure of the safety of any aggressive move.*

Beware, however, of the mirror image of this argument. That is, as a state becomes unsure of its security, at a certain level it may suddenly engage in irrational spasm war, in an attempt to "salvage" some remnant of national existence.

Domestic R&D Issues. Issues of strategy and technology are in one sense conceptual; but research programs do not discover, technology programs do not develop, and procurement programs do not build without budgetary allocation of resources to support them. Many agencies compete for attention in defense budgets, including the armed services, who vie with one another. Within the executive branch, policy planners from DOD, the State Department, and NSC all develop threat estimates and plan defense forces to meet those threats. "The principal determinant of the size and shape of the United States military budget and force structure ought to be the military requirements, nuclear and non-nuclear, of United States foreign policy."[27] Defense planners must compete, however, for the resources to provide these forces, and nondefense agencies do not necessarily share either the view of the threat or the immediacy of the need for resources to counter the threat. Thus, as indicated more fully in Chapter 9, setting national spending priorities within the executive branch of the federal government is a highly competitive process.

The Congress has its own interest bearing on the defense budget and its R&D priorities. "It is particularly difficult for the Congress to achieve either discipline or objectivity on military policy issues because both are so clouded by self-interest."[28] These instances of self-interests may relate to the economic impact of particular defense programs in particular congressional districts, or they may be reflections of military strategy or foreign policy viewpoints held by particular groups of representatives or senators.

Various interest "publics," both organized and unorganized, may lobby for particular programs or overall levels of defense preparedness. Though these groups frequently work through congressional members, they also testify and print publications touting their particular viewpoints. Driven largely by the profit motive, defense industries naturally attempt to influence military budg-

---

*Note that the United States argues for retaining three independent systems in our strategic deterrent (the triad concept) to insure that the Soviet Union remains uncertain about its ability to destroy our retaliatory force.

ets and force structures. Given the sophisticated and expensive nature of military programs, the defense budget may represent a major portion of the entire output of a firm. The difficulties encountered by Lockheed Aircraft in the early 1970s is a well-known case, but it is by no means the only instance of industrial health hinged on defense appropriations.

The composite of these pressures and competing interest groups has frequently been referred to as the "military-industrial complex" (MIC). Such a "complex" is identifiable, though it shifts from year to year and budget area to budget area. Although it is not a sinister conspiracy to usurp the functions of the American government, as some critics charge, its sheer size does make it an influential force in domestic politics. By the late 1970s, employment in defense goods represented about 62 out of every 1,000 workers. As noted by one authority some years ago, "A mere count of the numbers, moreover, does not convey . . . that those involved in the defense effort are, on the average, superior from an economic viewpoint. . . . Two out of five physicists outside of teaching, and three out of five aeronautical engineers were employed on defense goods."[29]*

A related factor in the impact of the MIC is the relative concentration and weight of defense production in various high-technology industries. If defense procurement of underwear is curtailed next year, the looms of the industry certainly will not stop. Even if production is off, there are other types of clothing which could absorb unemployed mill workers, and lateral transfers are possible. The airframe industry, by contrast, is far more dependent on defense. Not only does defense contracting amount to more than 50 percent of total revenue, but the aeronautical skills of the engineering forces employed are not so easily translatable nor readily absorbable in civilian sectors of the economy. Thus considerations such as the maintenance of skilled employment and an industrial base from which to expand should enter into the decision-making process of defense procurement.

It is apparent from the foregoing discussion that technology and force design, as well as threat and strategy issues, enter importantly into the complex business of defense procurement. In particular, R&D considerations are central to decisions on procurement of expensive new advanced weapons systems.

Impact of R&D on Weapons Acquisition. As implied earlier, an argument sometimes lodged against developing new weapons is that such weapons, particularly "glamorous" ones, tend to determine the force structure and mission of the armed forces, rather than the other way around. If we develop and procure a new and very expensive aircraft, the air force may feel obligated to devise a role and mission for it.† Further, budget dollars that are procuring the new weapon system are not procuring old ones. This results in shifting

---

*These numbers include active duty military, which lessens their impact somewhat.

†The corollary is that if we *develop* such a system, the industry, which has set up manufacturing processes and tools to make the prototype, will lobby very strongly for procurement on a larger scale.

military personnel into units using the new weapons, degrading alternate capabilities and limiting the range of mission choices to those appropriate to the new system.

One aspect of this argument is the continued debate over whether one ought to concentrate more on quantity (relatively simple weapons systems) or quality (highly sophisticated weapons systems) in equipping armed forces. Given cost constraints, increasing the sophistication and quality of a given type of weapon system almost invariably entails decreasing the quantity of forces. In this trade-off, the argument for quality has generally been persuasive in the United States.

By and large, the majority of senior officers and R&D officials have argued that neither the threat technology nor the dominant importance of saving American lives permits any compromise with *quality*. . . . [This] approach has enjoyed considerable success on Capitol Hill for the last twenty or thirty years.[30]*

This perspective logically implies that the most advanced system available must be provided.

The counter position is that there is little direct correlation between combat effectiveness and sophistication. First, as a weapons system is made more complex, the maintenance requirements will increase, both qualitatively (it requires a more skilled technician to repair a missile computer than to change the tread on a tank) and quantitatively (there are more things to break down). Reduced skill levels on the part of the armed forces personnel who will be performing this maintenance in an all-volunteer environment may compound this problem.[31] Moreover, the miniaturization of the internal parts of some modern weapons systems may make them too fragile for extended field use. In short, there is a probability that the "sophisticated" system will perform at less than design level when it is actually employed.[32] Given that "our more complex, newer weapons systems have demonstrated little proven relevance to success in combat, but serious deficiencies in reliability and countermeasures-susceptibility, then larger numbers of simpler . . . systems . . . , with fewer demands on supporting troops, are likely to prove more useful.[33]

Defense contracting and budgetary procedures contribute to problems in weapon system acquisition in several ways. Since quantity is a discreetly measurable item, contracts unequivocally specify amounts. Quality is not so easily definable, particularly before the system is actually built. Therefore, contracts allow more leeway in qualitative considerations. A defense contractor who is actually building the prototype thus has much more of a "blank check" in getting the government to subsidize changes in the system if he argues that such changes constitute a qualitative improvement. "Any service which considers developing a cheaper [and simpler] tank, ship, or airplane

---

*A classic example of this trade-off is the historical comparison of the F–86 Sabre Jet and the Russian MIG 15. Not only was the F–86 considerably more expensive on a unit basis, but the armor plate and other pilot survival items degraded its combat performance. We compensated by having better trained pilots, better tactical doctrine, and better survivability.

must face the possibility that it is proposing a decrement to its budget and consequently to its overall manpower, influence, and the like."[34] Thus, to change at all is budgetarily dangerous, and to request change in the direction of less cost is particularly deadly. A much easier strategy is to keep a system that has already been approved and simply modify it to new specifications and roles.* While this strategy has bureaucratic advantages, it tends to generate but marginally useful sophistication at the price of cost overruns.[35]

Results of such ad hoc growth of weapons systems can be damaging in several ways. Not only do maintenance problems increase geometrically, but commanders are very reluctant to train on fragile systems, which results in the soldier-user being unfamiliar with and not confident in the weapon. Also, the size of the maintenance force increases, either drawing personnel strength from the combat units or requiring increases in the overall size of the armed forces.

Further, since there are only limited resources available for the total DOD budget, procurement of more sophisticated (and expensive) weapons can adversely affect combat versatility. As an exaggerated example, consider a total equipment budget of $15 billion for a given fiscal year. If previous budget decisions had already obligated funds for the procurement of a $15 billion super aircraft carrier and associated aircraft, then there could be no other equipment purchased during that entire fiscal year. All other combat equipment requirements would have to come from stocks on hand at the beginning of the year.

The ultimate danger of this process, however, lies in its potential strategic implication. As the budgetary process pushes toward procuring and deploying increasingly sophisticated, specialized, and costly weapons, the combat capabilities of the armed forces become slaves to the weapons they possess. This inevitably leads planners to adopt strategies that utilize these weapons. Ultimately, therefore, this approach does lead to weapons systems dictating strategy, the exact reverse of a rational strategic decision-making process.

Summary. This chapter has introduced some of the issues of research and development which affect national security. In the present era knowledge of advanced science and technology are a component of both present and future military capability. Modern technology is so expensive, however, that it is the almost exclusive realm of the superpowers, and even these giant states must carefully marshal and organize their efforts to maximize returns. Weapons systems, as direct military applications of technology, keep getting more complex and more expensive, without necessarily getting any more reliable or useful. However, no state that wishes to exert international leadership can

---

*The ABM missile system, eventually deployed as the Safeguard, originally began in 1956 as the Nike-Zeus, which was designed as a third-generation air defense missile against aircraft and tactical ballistic missiles. A current (FY 78) example is the AWACS (Airborne Warning Control System) originally designed to provide alternative command and control in strategic exchanges, but not touted for control of the air war in a theater engagement.

afford to forgo the expense of pursuing weapons development, for fear that a true breakthrough by potential opponents will leave its military forces impotent.

DISCUSSION QUESTIONS

1. Why is dependence on imported technology a detriment to national security? Do you see any advantages to such a policy?

2. How has the Japanese and Western European policy of "satelliting" on U.S. technological advances in sophisticated weaponry caused a strain in allied relations? What policy changes would you recommend?

3. Do you think the U.S.S.R. will be successful in realizing its stated goal of world leadership in science and technology? Why or why not?

4. List some of the reasons you think U.S. efforts at creating a national strategy for technology have not been totally successful. What would you do to improve the U.S. program?

5. How can "technological warfare" destabilize existing or prospective arms agreements?

6. How does intraservice rivalry affect the competition for pieces of the R&D budget? Does it affect weapons development?

7. Should defense contracts go to the lowest bidder promising the finest piece of equipment? Explain your answer.

8. How can weapons system procurement drive the strategic decision-making process?

9. Why is it increasingly important that nations develop a strategy, or overall coherence, for their technology programs?

10. Should U.S. policy be to develop quantity (relatively simple weapons systems) or quality (highly sophisticated weapons systems) in equipping its armed forces? Defend your answer.

11. Why has the federal government taken over the responsibility for funding basic research? How can private industry be enticed into spending more money on basic research?

RECOMMENDED READING

Fallows, James. *National Defense*. New York: Random House, 1981.

Gansler, Jacques. *The Defense Industry*. Cambridge, Mass.: MIT Press, 1980.

Head, Richard G., and Rokke, Ervin J. *American Defense Policy*. 3d ed. Baltimore: Johns Hopkins University Press, 1973.

Hickman, Martin B. *The Military and American Society*. Beverly Hills, Calif.: Glencoe Press, 1971.

Lens, Sidney. *The Military-Industrial Complex*. Philadelphia: Pilgrim Press, 1970.

Possony, Stefan J., and Pournelle, J. E. *The Strategy of Technology*. Cambridge, Mass.: Dunellen Press, 1970.

Proxmire, William. *Report from Wasteland.* New York: Frederick A. Praeger, 1970.
Sarkesian, Sam C., ed., *The Military-Industrial Complex: A Reassessment.* Beverly Hills, Calif.: Sage Publications, 1972.
Seitz, Frederick, and Nichols, Rodney W. *Research and Development and the Prospects for International Security.* New York: Crane, Russak, 1973.
Taylor, Maxwell D. *The Uncertain Trumpet.* New York: Harper, 1959.

INTERNATIONAL AND REGIONAL SECURITY
ISSUES

Since 1945 the United States has maintained a global foreign policy. American involvement worldwide has been based on a perception of a global struggle for power and influence with the Soviet Union, a desire for economic well-being through world trade, and a commitment to advancing the principles of freedom. These global concerns and interests are critical elements of our national security, for from them we derive national security objectives, commitments, and programs. The challenge for security planners working with scarce resources lies in being prepared to meet these commitments and in setting priorities for the necessary programs. They must develop plans that provide a basis for force structure and deployments within domestic political and economic constraints and consonant with foreign developments. A sophisticated understanding of the major forces shaping the international system is required if these goals are to be reached.

In Part 4 we focus on this international environment not from a systemic perspective, as in Chapter 1, but from a regional perspective. We will look at five areas in an attempt to identify U.S. interests in and potential threats to them. Our view will encompass the explosive situation in the Middle East, and the only somewhat less violent dynamic evolution of East Asia, Africa, and Latin America. The most obvious and important problem, that posed by the Soviet Union, will be our first concern. A direct clash with the Soviets could result in literal catastrophe on all sides.

16

THE SOVIET UNION

In the preceding chapters we have addressed a range of defense issues involving U.S.-Soviet relations. Here we examine the complex factors which highlight the fundamental importance of Soviet intentions, capabilities, and actions to American national security. This topic is central to the study of American national security policy for a number of reasons. First, for the foreseeable future, the two superpowers alone possess the ability to destroy a significant portion of the globe with nuclear weapons. Thus, even those aspects of their relationship which are strictly bilateral are a matter of broadest international concern. In this sense, the major issues of war and peace in the 1980s will be in large part a subset of U.S.-Soviet relations. Second, since neither can be massively damaged in a conflict without the other's participation, each superpower is always and inevitably the other's principal security concern. Third, in a world where security issues remain largely bipolar, the United States and the Soviet Union are the major actors in the maintenance of global and regional military balances that provide the foundation for other mechanisms of world order, such as diplomacy and international law.[1] As State Department Soviet analyst Marshall Shulman said in congressional testimony, "There is scarcely an aspect of international life that is not affected by this relationship and that would not be made more difficult and more dangerous by a high level of Soviet-American tension and unregulated competition."[2]

Our purpose in this chapter is to survey the relationship between Soviet foreign and military policy and capabilities and United States national security interests. We shall briefly review Soviet policy from 1945 to the present and then examine the contemporary and emerging threat to U.S. interests posed by the Soviet Union. Because our focus is on American national security, many important and interesting aspects of Soviet policy will be beyond our scope, and although brevity also dictates that the domestic determinants of Soviet policy be given less attention than they deserve, the topic is admirably discussed in other analyses.[3]

343

FROM COLD WAR TO DÉTENTE

American-Soviet relations in the period 1945 to 1969 are described by the term *cold war*. This phenomenon may be defined as an era of tension, characterized by intense superpower competition, frequent confrontations, and the virtual absence of cooperative activities.

While hundreds of books have been written on the origins of the cold war, two aspects are worthy of mention here.[4] First, and frequently listed as the chief among all causes, was the set of beliefs, arising out of the Soviet ideology and governmental system, that drastically complicated relations between the U.S.S.R. and the capitalist world. Among these beliefs were, and are, that

1. The ownership of the means of production dictates socioeconomic conditions within a particular country. Domestically, private ownership breeds class struggle. Internationally, this class struggle dictates that conflict will dominate relations between capitalist and socialist states.
2. The United States and Great Britain are implacably hostile to the cause of socialism. Consequently, the World War II alliance between those countries and the U.S.S.R. was only tactical and temporary in nature.
3. History is seen as following a linear course wherein capitalism, through violent revolutions, will eventually give way to socialism. Major wars among capitalist states, like World War II, are regarded as precursors of these revolutions.
4. The relations between socialist and capitalist states are governed by the "correlation of forces," a sophisticated, and somewhat ambiguous, notion of the balance of power, which includes the social, political, and other "subjective" factors, in addition to the economic and military power of the states concerned. To assist "the inevitable march of history," Soviet leaders must exploit the correlation of forces, except where such exploitation would endanger vital interests of the Soviet state.

The net effect of these beliefs was to produce a climate of hostility and confrontation; for, as one of America's foremost Sovietologists, George Kennan, has observed, "It is an undeniable privilege of every man to prove himself right in the thesis that the world is his enemy; for if he reiterates it frequently enough and makes it the background of his conduct he is bound eventually to be right."[5]

A second important origin of the cold war can be subsumed under the heading of "the collision of interests." As stated in Chapter 1, each state, independently or in concert with others, pursues its own national interest within an international system where "self-help" is a nation's principal recourse. The anarchical nature of the international system places a premium on the pursuit of power within the system. Given this fact and the very different values embodied in free societies and authoritarian ones, conflict of some type is the inevitable consequence. Thus, conflict of various kinds between the United States and the Soviet Union has been continuous from 1945 to the present, accentuated by the still largely bipolar nature of the international security affairs and the awesome power of the superpower nuclear arsenals. The first major collision of interests took place over the fate of postwar Germany and Eastern Europe. Stalin wanted to establish a socialist "sphere of influence" in Eastern Europe and ultimately place Germany under Soviet domination. This policy was designed not only to increase the number of nations in the Socialist camp (and thereby validate ideological predictions) but also to provide a "buffer zone" for the territory of the Soviet Union.

The United States was willing to see the establishment of governments friendly to the Soviet Union in Eastern Europe but objected to (and was repulsed by) the forcible imposition of communist regimes throughout Eastern Europe. The survival of a free Germany became a key concern for American leaders, who soon realized that the addition of any significant portion of Western Europe to the newly expanded Soviet bloc would tip the world balance of power, despite the U.S. nuclear monopoly at the time.

While the United States gradually assumed the commitment to keep Western Europe from the fate of Eastern Europe, its policy was initially, in Walter Lippmann's terminology, "insolvent."[6] After World War II, the American drive to disarm its units and "bring the boys home" literally decimated American defenses; overall U.S. forces shrank by 1948 to approximately 10 percent of their 1945 strength (from 12 million to 1.3 million).[7] Furthermore, most U.S. units after the surgery were organized for occupation duty, and nearly all American service members were assigned to ill-equipped, understrength units. At the same time, the Soviet Union maintained about 4.5 million soldiers under arms, nearly all in combat units, the vast bulk of which were deployed in Europe.* The end result of this "position of weakness" was to leave doubt in Stalin's mind as to the strength of the U.S. commitment to Europe. Consequently the United States and its allies were "tested" by the Soviet Union on numerous occasions: in 1946, over the prolonged Soviet occupation of Iran; in 1946–47, over threats to Greece and Turkey; in 1948, by the Soviet coup that installed a Communist government in Czechoslovakia; and in 1948–49, by the blockade of West Berlin by Soviet forces for over a year.

The American response to these crises was incremental, reflecting the slow pace of "lessons learned" by new great powers. In 1947, the United States announced the Truman Doctrine, proclaiming America's intention "to support free people who are resisting attempted subjugation by armed minorities or by outside pressures." Shortly thereafter, George Kennan, then a State Department analyst, published the famous article by "Mr. X" which argued that the United States should aim toward "containment" of the Soviet Union.[8] In response to the Czech coup and the Berlin blockade, eleven Western

---

*The precise extent of Soviet postwar demobilization is still unresolved; that it did not proceed to anything like the American case is, however, clear. See Thomas Wolfe, *Soviet Power and Europe, 1945–1970* (Baltimore: Johns Hopkins Press, 1970), p. 10, n. 6.

European nations and the United States signed the North Atlantic Treaty, a collective self-defense pact, which became the basis for the NATO military alliance. Later, after the rearming of West Germany, the Soviet Union and its Eastern European satellites signed a treaty "On Friendship, Cooperation, and Mutual Aid" in May 1955, which created the Warsaw Treaty Organization.

Even as the United States was adapting to its new role, the international environment produced more changes. First, the Soviet Union exploded its first nuclear bomb in 1949, undercutting the heavy U.S. reliance on nuclear weapons to check Soviet aggression. Also in 1949, the Chinese Communists ejected the Chinese Nationalists, with whom the U.S. was allied, from mainland China. Finally, after a speech by Secretary of State Dean Acheson, in which South Korea was left outside the U.S. security perimeter, Stalin gave his support to the North Korean Communist invasion of South Korea in 1950.* When United Nations forces—led by the United States—made a successful counterattack and entered North Korea, Communist Chinese forces entered the war.

This string of stimuli brought a series of strong U.S. responses. Work began on a thermonuclear bomb, containment was transformed into a global doctrine, and, during the Korean War, NATO forces were strengthened and the groundwork laid for the eventual rearmament of West Germany.

Stalin died just before the end of the Korean War in July 1953. The policy of his successors (for a time, Malenkov, then Khrushchev) showed elements of both change and continuity from Stalin's world view.

The changes in Soviet strategy were significant. First, realizing the awesome effects of nuclear weapons, Malenkov, and later Khrushchev, shelved the rhetoric, perhaps even the idea, of the inevitability of war between capitalist and socialist states. "Peaceful coexistence" between the United States and the U.S.S.R. became a goal, though not the dominant one, of post-Stalinist foreign policy. Second, after 1957, Khrushchev insisted on developing a nuclear-oriented force structure at the expense of (temporarily though it proved) the ground forces and the surface navy. Third, and perhaps most significant from the perspective of the 1980s, in an effort to "embarrass and outflank Western diplomacy," Khrushchev began a major effort to increase Soviet influence with the nonaligned nations of the Third World, many of which were former Western colonies.[9] The doctrine that it was the sacred duty of the Soviet Union to promote and support "wars of national liberation" was enunciated by Khrushchev in January 1961 at the Moscow Conference of Communist Parties.

What is the attitude of Marxists toward such uprisings? A most positive one. These uprisings must not be identified with wars among states. . . . These are uprisings against rotten reactionary regimes, against the colonizers. The Communists fully sup-

*Soviet sources indicated later that Stalin gave his "blessing" to the North Koreans without giving the matter very much serious thought. Nikita Khrushchev, *Khrushchev Remembers*, trans. Strobe Talbott (London: André Deutsch, 1971), pp. 366–73.

port such just wars and march in the front rank with the people waging liberation struggles.*

The most important element of continuity in Soviet policy was the Soviet preoccupation with the settlement of the German question and Western recognition of the status quo in Eastern Europe. Khrushchev twice tried unsuccessfully to push the West into a settlement, using Berlin as the fulcrum for his efforts. It apparently became clear to Khrushchev that to force a favorable solution to the German and East European problem, indeed to pursue its worldwide aims, the U.S.S.R. would have to attain strategic parity with the United States or at least something close to it. To deal with the American president (and to outflank Chairman Mao), the Soviets would have to have the power to directly threaten the United States to the same degree that the United States could threaten the Soviet Union.[10]

In one sense, Khrushchev's problem boiled down to numbers. In 1962 the United States had 720 modern, intercontinental delivery systems. In the most generous estimate, the Soviets had only 260 delivery systems, most of which were of dubious reliability.[11] The immediate question was, Given the Soviets' relatively weak ability to build bombers, how could they redress this imbalance? Khrushchev had two options. He could quickly build vast numbers of primitive, liquid-fueled ICBMs or, as a temporary measure, pending further design advances, he could put some of his plentiful MRBMs within striking range of the United States. The first option would provide an expensive, but not a very effective or timely, solution. The second option, though higher in risk, would be quicker and less expensive.

Khrushchev chose the second option, which led directly to the Cuban Missile Crisis, the most dramatic Soviet defeat in the postwar era. Khrushchev's covert missile build-up was discovered before it was operationally ready, and the Soviets, faced with U.S. nuclear, as well as local conventional, superiority, were forced to back down. While this incident was an essential element in the subsequent dampening of tensions between the superpowers, it also taught the Soviets a hard lesson: the shadow of military power was no substitute for its substance. The Soviet Union concluded that to advance its interests and values against an increasingly strong United States, it would have to improve its military forces significantly.

Soviet determination to correct the problems encountered in the Cuban Missile Crisis was reflected in a statement made by Soviet Deputy Foreign Minister V. V. Kuznetsov to an American official shortly after the crisis: "Never will we be caught like this again."[12]

Khrushchev was replaced in 1964 by the Communist Party Central Committee, whose members had been alienated by his adventuristic foreign policy

---

*President Kennedy thought that Khrushchev's announcement was so significant that he directed that "all the members of his new administration read the speech and consider what it portended." Roger Hilsman, *To Move a Nation* (Garden City, N.Y.: Doubleday, 1967), p. 414.

and his domestic blunders. His successors, Brezhnev and Kosygin, adopted a more moderate tone and businesslike approach to foreign and domestic problems. In retrospect, three factors contributed to the subsequent Soviet successes in the foreign policy realm. First, especially during the decade from 1965 to 1975, the Soviet economy prospered, leaving the Brezhnev regime free to purchase both more "guns" and more "butter."* Thus the military power position of the U.S.S.R. and the domestic standard of living could be simultaneously improved. Second, the United States became increasingly bogged down in Vietnam. Two effects were felt here: (1) the United States curtailed spending for its nuclear force and was also inhibited from improving its NATO forces, especially those in West Germany, and (2) U.S. policy-makers and public alike turned against the notion of military power. Many in the United States (and in the Third World) began to speak of "American imperialism" in the same tone that they once used to discuss the "red menace." A third factor in the Soviet foreign policy successes sprang from the two noted above. Prodded by the findings of the revisionist historians of the cold war, many analysts in the United States began to view the Soviet Union as less fearsome. Herbert Dinerstein wrote in 1970:

The changes in the internal organization of Soviet political life [since Stalin] have tended to make for fewer rather than more initiatives in foreign policy. . . . In retrospect, it now seems that Soviet foreign policy has been more active . . . when the Soviet leaders have been worried about weaknesses in the system of socialist states and within the Soviet Union itself. . . . As we review the events of the last twenty years it no longer seems satisfactory to assume that the Soviet Union will take more risks to improve its political position as its military position *vis-à-vis* the U.S. improved.[13]

In brief, by the latter 1960s, it appeared to many as if the West had exaggerated the Soviet threat to its interests. It now seemed to many quite possible to deal with the Soviets, if we would but try to improve relations. For their own purposes, the Soviets also wished to lessen tensions. The United States, under President Nixon, was making overtures to the People's Republic of China (since the latter 1950s a de facto enemy of the Soviet Union). The Soviets also saw an opportunity to gain from increased trade with the West, especially where high technology items, such as computers, and grain were concerned. Soviet leaders must also have been pleased by the West's recognition of the status of Eastern Germany and Eastern Europe, thanks in part to West Germany's *Ostpolitik*. Increasingly, too, both sides saw the opportunity, indeed, the necessity, to limit strategic arms. Thus, the era of détente (or ''hot peace,'' as one analyst later termed it) was born.[14]

Unfortunately, American optimism of the late 1960s and early 1970s proved

---

*From 1961 to 1970, the Soviet GNP grew at a respectable 5 percent per annum. In the 1970s, it declined to 4 percent and then to 3 percent; in the early 1980s, it was 2 percent or less. Robert Byrnes, ed., *After Brezhnev: Sources of Soviet Conduct in the 1980s* (Bloomington: University of Indiana Press, 1983).

to be unfounded. Indeed, détente was flawed from the beginning. Each side saw the benefits of détente but not the costs that it would entail. For the United States, détente was viewed as a replacement for containment: through the development of a network of policy linkages, the West would somehow enforce discipline on a mellowing Soviet Union. For the United States, as Kissinger said, "Detente [could not] be pursued selectively in one area or toward one group of countries only. For us, detente is indivisible.[15]"

For their part, the Soviets believed détente was merely a consequence of the new correlation of forces, and of American recognition that the Soviet Union was now the "other" superpower. As an element of peaceful coexistence, détente referred *only* to relations between capitalists and socialist states. Brezhnev himself outlined the Soviet definition of détente at the Twenty-fifth Party Congress.

Detente . . . means above all that disputes and conflicts between countries must not be settled by means of war. . . . Detente does not in the slightest abolish . . . the laws of class struggle. No one should expect that in conditions of detente the communists will become reconciled to capitalist exploitation. . . .

We make no secret of the fact that we see detente as a path leading to the creation of more favorable conditions for peaceful communist construction.[16]

In effect, the Soviets were telling the United States that détente *was* divisible. One analyst summed up the true essence of the détente which followed in this manner: "Detente [became] the art of trade-offs between competitors, not an arrangement whereby new friends solemnly swore to end the contest."[17]

The high point of détente occurred in 1972 when the United States and the Soviet Union signed the Strategic Arms Limitation Treaty (SALT I). By 1973, however, it became obvious that the contest had not ended. In October of that year the Soviets threatened the United States with a unilateral intervention in the Arab-Israeli War. Unlike the days of Khrushchev, the Soviet threat was not empty—six airborne divisions stood ready and the Soviet Mediterranean fleet numbered a near record 85 vessels.[18] In response, the United States found it necessary to alert its armed forces throughout the world.

FROM DETENTE TO COLD PEACE

From an American perspective, the Arab-Israeli War damaged, but did not sink, the ship of détente; subsequent Soviet operations in the Third World did. After 1973, with varying degrees of Soviet help, procommunist parties oriented toward Moscow seized power or de facto control in Vietnam, Laos, Angola, Ethiopia, Afghanistan, the People's Democratic Republic of Yemen (South Yemen), and Cambodia. Unlike previous Soviet forays into the Third World, these activities seemed particularly ominous for two reasons. First, the Soviets were no longer content to work through nationalist movements, but rather they began to rely on proclaimed communist or socialist elements.

Secondly, Soviet military moves became increasingly bold. Beginning in 1975, Cuban troops and Soviet arms, advisers, and technicians, became major, direct tools in Africa.[19] In Afghanistan, a Soviet army of about eighty-five thousand troops was sent to preserve the remnants of Marxist power and extend Soviet influence in that country.

The December 1979 Soviet invasion of Afghanistan bears further examination because it represents a new dimension in Soviet policy. The invasion marked the first time since the end of World War II that Soviet ground forces had engaged in combat outside the Warsaw Pact area. No longer limiting its intervention to arms, advisers, and proxies, the Soviet Union became directly involved in a Third World area. Furthermore, the Soviet invasion occurred during a period of unprecedented Soviet military strength, thus adding to Western fears concerning the future course of Soviet foreign policy. Finally, the Soviet invasion again brought into question the value and the future of a superpower détente that became one-sided in practice.

While the outcome of the Soviet invasion of Afghanistan may be in doubt for years, the incursion itself has ominous ramifications. First, the Soviet Union is now in a better position than ever to exploit ethnic rivalries in the area. The Baluchi people, who occupy parts of three countries in the region, are presently receiving aid and advice from Soviet agents. Together with Kurdish separatists and strong leftist elements in Iran, the Baluchis could represent a grave threat to the territorial integrity or the independence of that state. Turbulent Pakistan might represent yet another target. Soviet support for an independent Baluchistan, embracing what is now southwestern Pakistan, could give the Soviet Union access to the Indian Ocean port of Gwadar.[20]

Secondly, the possession of airfields around Afghanistan's Kandahar region puts unrefueled Soviet fighters in range of the critical Strait of Hormuz in the Persian Gulf. Such air support would degrade the advantage that U.S. carriers could give our navy in the event of an Indian Ocean conflict or confrontation. Finally, a strong continuing Soviet presence in Afghanistan could provide a basis for the "Finlandization" of the entire region. Without a strong outside support, the governments in the region could succumb bit by bit to the Soviet mixture of "fear and seduction."[21]

The continuance of Soviet operations in Afghanistan also has ominous implications for the general course of Soviet foreign policy. Earlier operations in Angola and Ethiopia gave Soviet leaders confidence in their logistical capabilities and generalship. Afghanistan provides the Soviet military an opportunity to test equipment (including chemical and biological weapons) and to prove its mettle as a fighting force. Even a limited success in Afghanistan could further increase the Politburo's confidence in the Soviet military establishment, making it more prone to use force to solve future foreign policy problems.[22]

The invasion of Afghanistan has also led to a change in doctrinal emphasis, highlighting the danger of future Soviet military operations. This doctrinal change appears to extend the "protective custody" of the Brezhnev Doctrine (which guarantees the perpetual "socialist" character of Soviet satellites) to all of the proclaimed Marxist states in the Third World, which would include South Yemen, Angola, and Ethiopia, among others. An unsigned, authoritative article in the Soviet weekly *Novoye Vremya* ("New Times") asked:

What is the internationalist solidarity of revolutionaries? Does it consist only of moral and diplomatic support . . . or also of material assistance, including military help? . . . The history of the revolutionary movement confirms the political legitimacy of this form of assistance and support. Such were the cases . . . in Spain in the 1930s, and in China. . . . Today when there exists a system of socialist states, it would be simply ridiculous to question the right to such assistance. . . . To refuse to use the possibilities at the disposal of the socialist countries would signify virtually evading performance of the internationalist duty and returning the world to the times when imperialism could throttle at will any revolutionary movement.[23]

In effect, the Soviets have built a more refined case for using force in areas of the Third World wherever the "correlation of forces" will permit them to do so.[24]

In summary, from the Stalin era to the present, the Soviet Union has proceeded from a regional power, to a power with global pretensions, to a genuine global power at least equal to the United States in virtually every category of military strength. In the course of the 1970s the Soviet Union increasingly tended to rely heavily on its strongest asset, the military establishment. It would be foolish to expect that tendency to disappear in the 1980s.

The Evolving Soviet Threat. The Soviet Union's effort to build its military establishment, capable of conducting warfare in every conceivable manner, has been impressive. A comparison between the Soviet Union under Khrushchev (1964) and the Soviet Union in the post-Brezhnev era is revealing. The trends shown in table 16.1 are even more alarming when one considers that in nearly every category where the Soviets have improved, the United States has made few gains or has even degraded its capabilities.

Many explanations have been developed to account for the continuing Soviet military build-up. Perhaps those explanations that stipulate "defensive" motives contain some truth. In the 1980s it is far more difficult, however, than it was in the 1960s or 1970s to believe that purely defensive aims explain the extraordinary size and continuity of the Soviet effort. In any case, it is clear that the Soviet Union in the 1980s poses a greater military threat to U.S. security interests than ever before. Four major threats will be addressed below: the strategic threat, and the threats to NATO, East Asia, and the Third World. Final notes will address subsidiary threats and Soviet weaknesses.

The Strategic Threat. Every nation's first goal in its foreign policy is to protect its homeland. Under realistic conditions, the only direct, physical

Table 16.1 The Soviet Build-up in Nuclear and Conventional Forces, 1964–80 (in billions of FY 1980 dollars)

Forces	1964	1980
Strategic		
ICBMs	190	1,398
SLBMs	29	950
Bombers	170	156
Total weapons (warheads)	400	6,000
Land		
Tanks	30,000	45,000
Divisions	145	170
Artillery tubes/rocket launchers	11,000	20,000
Tactical air		
Fighter/attack aircraft	3,500	4,500
Naval		
Major surface combatants and amphibious ships	260	360
Other naval vessels	1,440	1,200
Total naval tonnage	2,000,000	2,800,000
Total military manpower	3,400,000	4,400,000
Total defense spending	$105	$175
Military investment (procurement, milcon, R&D)	$49	$80

Source: U.S., *Department of Defense Annual Report, Fiscal Year 1981* (Washington, D.C.: U.S. Government Printing Office, 1980), p. 37.

danger to U.S. territory comes from the Soviet strategic arsenal and vice versa. While overall nuclear "equivalence" will likely hold into the mid 1980s, the enormous momentum of the Soviet build-up may yield some elements of Soviet superiority before too far into the decade. Strategic stability, which has been the pattern during the decades of U.S. preeminence, may disappear along with that superiority.

A number of other, related problems concern U.S. analysts. First, Soviet military doctrine continues to stress not deterrence but rather the maintenance of a damage-limiting war-fighting capability.[25] The implications of this are discussed in Chapter 11. Second, U.S. defense strategy depends on the mutually reinforcing capabilities of our triad, but Soviet advances in missile accuracy, when added to Soviet superiority in total megatonnage, place the future survival of the U.S. land-based ICBMs in jeopardy. These weapons are essential to U.S. defenses because they alone can assuredly knock out Soviet missiles in their silos. Some American analysts believe that the Soviets could use this U.S. vulnerability to establish "escalation dominance" in a war, or that it could be parlayed into a credible nuclear threat in crisis bargaining, in the same way that the Soviets attempted to use the fictitious "missile gap" in 1958 and 1961. Furthermore, even though the United States may begin to field a far more capable missile, namely the MX or Peacekeeper missile, by the end of the 1980s (discussed in Chapter 11), some critics still claim that this will leave a "window of maximum danger" in the mid or latter 1980s.[26]

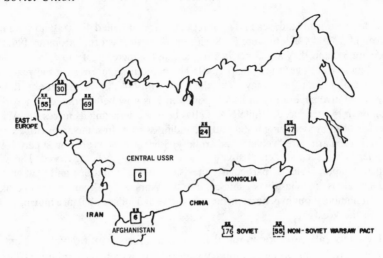

FIG. 16.1
DEPLOYMENT OF SOVIET AND WARSAW PACT GROUND FORCES, 1983
Soviet ground forces are organized into 176 line divisions (excluding 14 artillery divisions), augmented by 55 divisions from other Warsaw Pact countries. The deployment of the pact forces is depicted above. At present, the Soviet Union has about 47 divisions in the eastern U.S.S.R. and Mongolia, primarily to deal with the threat from China. Thirty Soviet divisions are deployed in eastern Europe, backed up by the 55 non-Soviet pact divisions, and approximately 64 more Soviet divisions in the western U.S.S.R. are available for commitment. The other 30 divisions are in central and southern Asia or in the strategic reserve. Under mobilization, another 130 divisions could be deployed. Forces in Afghanistan are estimated at 95,000.

Finally, some analysts, in a variation of the themes noted above, see Soviet superiority in defensive systems—such as air, space, and civil defense—yielding a potential step toward strategic superiority over U.S. forces that have neglected these dimensions.[27]

The Threat to NATO. The independence and prosperity of Western Europe have long been held to be a key to U.S. security. In Europe, the Soviets continue to follow an intricate policy that might be called one of "fear and seduction." On the one hand, the Soviets have fostered good economic relations with Western Europe and have encouraged European initiatives for continental peace and security.[28] The object is to move the increasingly independent Europeans out of the American orbit. On the other hand, the "fear" side of the equation shows the Soviets strengthening their forces in Eastern Europe, modernizing the Warsaw Pact armies, and using coercive naval diplomacy against the Scandinavian countries.

The International Institute for Strategic Studies summed up the deteriorating NATO–Warsaw Pact balance.

The comparisons . . . begin to look rather different from those of a few years ago. The effect of small and slow changes can be marked, and the balance can alter. In

1962 the American land, sea and air forces in Europe totalled 434,000; now the figure is around 300,000. There were 26 Soviet divisions in Eastern Europe in 1967; now there are 31, and they are larger in size (despite the increase of some 25 divisions on the Chinese front over the same period). The numerical pattern over the years so far has been a gradual shift in favour of the East, with NATO relying on offsetting this by a qualitative superiority in its weapons which is now being eroded as new Soviet equipment is introduced. While NATO has been modernizing its forces, the Warsaw Pact has been modernizing faster and expanding as well. In some areas (for example, SAM, certain armoured vehicles and artillery) Soviet weapons are now superior, while in other fields (such as tactical aircraft) the gap in quality is being closed. The advent of new weapons sytems, particularly precision-guided munitions and new anti-tank and air defense missiles, may again cut into the Warsaw Pact's advantage in tank and aircraft numbers, but in general the pattern is one of a military balance moving steadily against the West.[29]

Two general scenarios inimical to U.S. interests could develop. First, the Soviets could achieve clear military superiority, which they might parlay into a decisive military victory, particularly if the war were to remain below the nuclear threshold. This danger is heightened by the development of two powerful Soviet theater weapons, the SS-20 missile and the Backfire bomber, which can strike anywhere in Europe from deep within the Soviet Union; neither is limited under SALT I or SALT II. To offset these weapons, the allies decided in 1979 to deploy new, long-range Pershing II and Cruise missiles while trying to reduce the Soviet threat through negotiations (see Chapter 23).[30] Chemical warfare is a related area of concern for NATO. In the past, the NATO nuclear edge could have deterred the Soviets from using their chemical arsenal during a war. Now, however, parity—or worse—in both the strategic and tactical nuclear realms could enable the Soviets to exploit their one-sided chemical advantage. Two American analysts summed up the NATO–Warsaw Pact chemical balance in this manner:

The Soviets have an impressive capability and appear well trained and ready; . . . the United States and the rest of NATO are neither equipped nor trained to any extent comparable to the Soviet Union for this type of warfare; and . . . the main and significant advantage of chemical warfare emerges in exactly such a condition of asymmetry.[31]

Second, and a more likely scenario, the developments listed above could encourage the "Finlandization" of a Western Europe unsure of American support and unable by itself to balance Soviet military power. Finlandization is a label given to the process whereby the countries of Western Europe, for whatever reason, move away from the alliance with the United States and are transformed into isolated, neutralized states—like Finland—fearful of Soviet military power and hence unable to resist Soviet pressure, especially in the foreign policy realm. The degree to which this describes the Finnish policy situation is arguable, but the metaphor is useful.[32] Finlandization could not only be hastened by a failure in the American commitment, but it could also be spawned by the upswing in Euro-Soviet economic ties or by a European perception that the strategic balance had swung decisively against the United States. The 1981–83 upsurge in European peace movements, which were inevitably directed only against *Western* defense efforts, suggests that the psychological climate for such a weakened, neutralized Europe is developing.

The Soviet Threat in East Asia. The U.S.S.R. is, of course, a major Asian power. On its eastern marches lie a number of states in whose security the United States has a significant stake—Japan, the P.R.C., and the Republic of Korea, for example. Moreover, the Soviet Far Eastern fleet, based in Vladivostok but with ancillary facilities elsewhere in the Soviet maritime provinces and in Kam Ranh Bay in Vietnam, is sufficiently strong and flexible to give the U.S.S.R. the capability to project power throughout the East Asian region. Detailed discussion of the threats to American interests which arise out of these circumstances is discussed in Chapter 17.

The Soviet Threat in the Third World. Since 1964 one of the most notable Soviet military developments has come in the field of power projection forces—the ability to exert military leverage beyond immediately contiguous areas, i.e., in much of the Third World. This problem is intensified by the fact that many key Third World areas, such as the Middle East, are much closer to the Soviet Union than to the United States, and some are subject to direct pressure from nearby Soviet ground forces. The domestic organization of the U.S.S.R. gives its military leaders the logistical advantage of easy access to its considerable civil aviation and merchant marine fleets. Finally, many areas, such as Sub-Saharan Africa, can be crucially influenced by relatively small amounts of Soviet military power or proxy forces.

In the Third World, as in Europe, the United States and the Soviet Union have competing interests. The Soviets are eager to expand their influence in the Third World to further their ideological aspirations, to secure access to raw materials (and deny them to the United States in conflict situations), to develop a base and support structure for their navy, and to expel the United States from its "positions of strength," especially on the Soviet periphery.* Soviet willingness to use arms aid and proxy forces, especially Cubans, in stimulating or capitalizing upon hostilities in the Third World, poses a significant threat.

For the United States, Soviet operations in the Third World represent challenges to its alliances, raw materials lifelines, and markets. Furthermore,

---

*The question of Soviet objectives in the Third World is still a matter of dispute among scholars. For two opposing views, see Walter Hahn and Alvin Cottrell, *Soviet Shadow over Africa* (Washington, D.C.: University of Miami Center for Advanced International Studies, 1977), pp. 1–105, and Robert Legvold, "The Super Rivals: Conflict in the Third World," *Foreign Affairs* 57, no. 4 (spring 1979).

Soviet pressures encourage weaker states to accommodate the U.S.S.R. or to remain neutral on political, economic, or military issues on which their support for the West could be important. The Soviet Union's achievement of strategic parity as well as its vastly increased ability to project military power undoubtedly provide powerful arguments to proponents of accommodation within these nations. In the final analysis, the gravest threat to U.S. interests from Soviet pressure in the Third World may arise from the Soviet Union's increasing confidence in the use of its military power to solve foreign policy problems. An escalating confrontation in the Third World, where neither side believes it can back down, is still a distinct possibility.[33]

Subsidiary Threats. Three subsidiary threats to U.S. interests will be addressed in this section: the naval threat, the intelligence threat, and the additional threat posed by the authoritarian nature of the Soviet regime. While these factors do not constitute separate geographical threats, they compound and, in some cases, magnify the Soviet strategic, theater, and Third World threats.

The most vivid of these threats is that posed by the development of the Soviet navy. To understand the significance of this development, we must consider the missions both the U.S. and Soviet navies would have in a war. On the one hand, the United States would have to exercise sea control to maintain access to its extensive sea lanes of communication as depicted in fig. 16.2. Furthermore, sea control is important to the maintenance of a secure nuclear deterrent by way of our SLBMs. On the other hand, the Soviet Union, by virtue of its land mass, geographical position, and extensive base, needs only to maintain a small navy, capable of protecting its SLBMs and exercising a limited, less rigorous, sea-denial mission. In effect, alliances, geography, and resource base dictate that U.S. naval forces *must* maintain a decided edge over their Soviet counterparts in order to accomplish their more demanding missions.

In recent rears, the U.S. edge in the naval balance has eroded badly. In the past, the United States thoroughly dominated this area through the quality of its ships, its naval aviation support, and the experience of its ships' crews and commanders. Since the mid 1960s, however, spurred by Admiral Sergei Gorshkov,* the Soviets have deployed a combat ready, experienced fleet capable of every relevant naval mission, including force projection in the Third World. While the number of U.S. ships has declined, the Soviets have continued to increase the quantity as well as the overall quality of their naval forces (see table 16.2 for relevant comparisons).

Potentially, the new Soviet "blue water" navy could prevent (or hamper) the United States from reinforcing NATO, securing access to Third World

---

*Admiral Gorshkov is the father of the modern Soviet navy. His published works set down the great-power rationale for the maintenance of global naval capabilities; see his *Morskaya moshch gosudarstva* [Sea power of the state] (Moscow: Voenizdat, 1976).

Selected U.S. Sea Lines of Communication

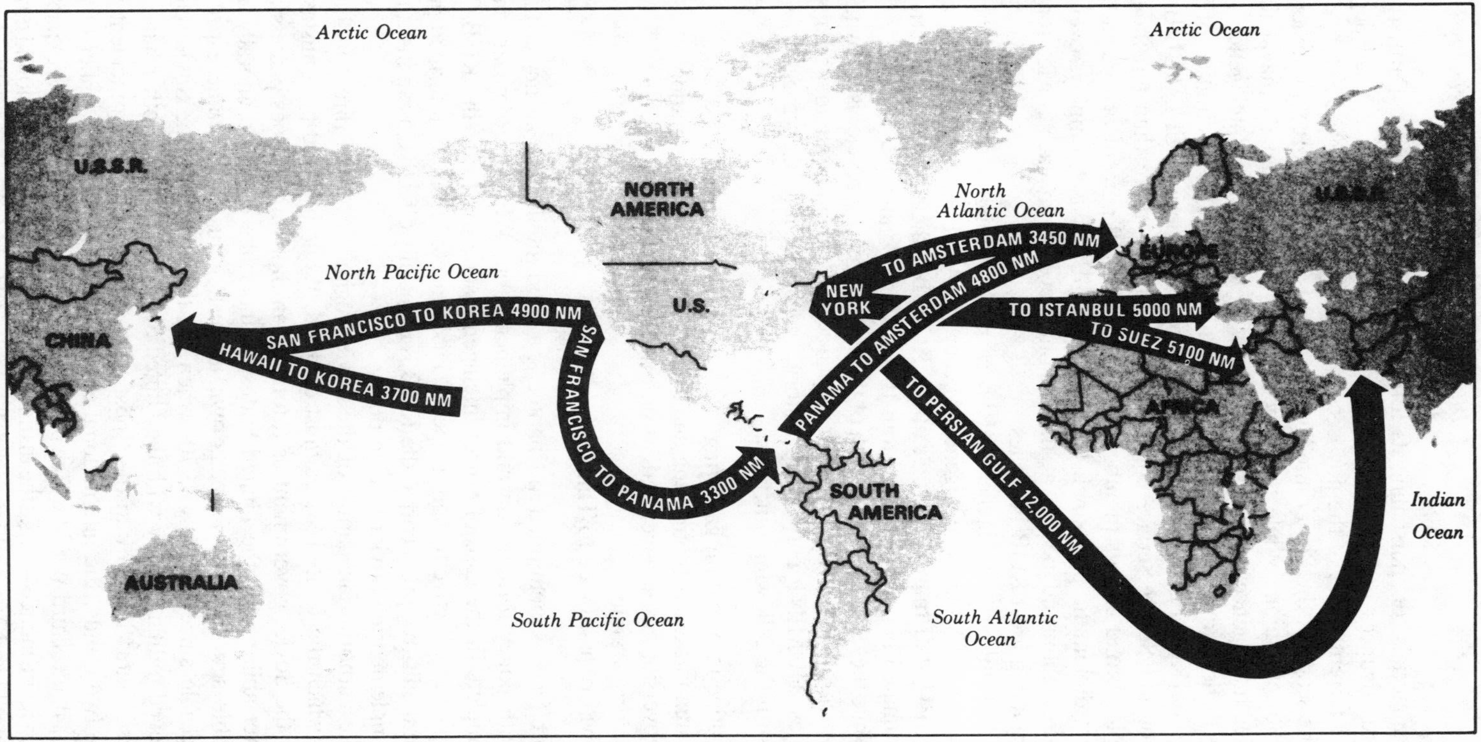

FIG. 16.2
Source: John M. Collins, *U.S.-Soviet Military Balance Concepts and Capabilities, 1960–1980* (New York: McGraw-Hill, 1980), p. 278.

357

raw materials, or marshaling its forces for political purposes. Furthermore, future advances in Soviet antisubmarine warfare capabilities could degrade the deterrent effect of the now secure American SLBM force.[34]

The scope of the Soviet intelligence effort is another "force multiplier" for the Soviet Union. While it is much more "hidden" than the naval threat, Soviet intelligence activities, particularly in the human intelligence (HUMINT) field, dwarf those of the Western nations. The Committee of State Security (KGB) is the Soviet equivalent of the American CIA, FBI, Border Patrol and Secret Service combined. It maintains more than ten thousand people abroad and its members comprise 40 to 60 percent of foreign-based Soviet diplomatic personnel. Overall, the KGB by itself employs over four hundred thousand people at the national level, with each Soviet republic maintaining local KGB branches.

Soviet military intelligence (GRU) carries out roughly the same functions as the U.S. Defense Intelligence Agency (DIA). Even less is known about the GRU staff than about that of the KGB, but their headquarters strength is estimated between two and four thousand personnel.

While the organization of both of these intelligence agencies is known, their activities obviously are a better kept secret.[35] In addition to perhaps the greatest HUMINT network in history, the Soviet intelligence agencies also perform the following functions:

- routine information gathering
- communications monitoring and satellite imagery interpretation
- subversion, espionage, and "disinformation"
- terrorist training[36]
- advisory assistance to Third World allies

In effect, as mentioned in Chapter 7, a good intelligence agency can assist in both policy formulation and implementation. While the data are highly incomplete in the case of Soviet intelligence, one must rate the KGB/GRU complex as effective in both respects. Disconnected from an informed public or an inquisitive press corps, the KGB is especially effective as an instrument for implementing Soviet foreign policy.

The authoritarian nature of the Soviet regime is a final threat multiplier with which the United States must contend. While it would be a mistake to view the Soviet government as a totalitarian monolith, it does possess a far greater ability than the United States to undertake dramatic, morally questionable actions to advance its own interests. This has become especially noticeable since the early 1970s when, on the one hand, the Soviet Union achieved military parity with the United States, and, on the other hand, the United States fell prey to the "post-Vietnam" syndrome. Coincident with these two trends, the international environment produced a number of situations in the Third World which provided easy opportunities for the expansion of Soviet influence—e.g., the disintegration of the Portuguese colonial empire in Angola and Mozambique, the downfall of Haile Selassie in Ethiopia, and

Table 16.2 Naval Combatant Force Level Trends

Active Fleet	1969		1979	
Combatant Classification	U.S.	U.S.S.R.	U.S.	U.S.S.R.
Aircraft Carrier	22	0	13	2
Surface Combatant	279	220	178	269
Submarine	156	354	123	357
Command	2	0	0	0
Patrol Combatant	9	148	3	120
Amphibious Warfare	153	103	63	91
Mine Warfare	74	165	3	165
Auxiliary Ship Classification				
Mobile Logistics	112	56	59	150
Support	119	624	20	610
Total Status	926	1,670	462	1,764

Source: Chief of Naval Operations, *Military Posture and Budget of the United States Navy,* FY 1981, p. 35.

various episodes of unrest in the Persian Gulf/Southwest Asia areas. These situations were tailor-made for an emerging superpower that espoused an ideology based on a ''progressive'' view of change and instability. The advantages accruing to the U.S.S.R. are considerable.

The political strength and activism of the Soviet Union is especially discernible in the broad range of its mutually supportive relations with non-Communist social and political movements in the Third World, a kind of relations in which it clearly surpasses the other superpower. This brings me to what I would consider the greatest Soviet foreign-policy political resource: the Soviet attitude toward change and toward revolutionary and nationalistic aspirations in the non-Communist world. It is an attitude of almost blank underwriting of any and all change and aspiration which in the Soviet opinion undermines the status quo. It makes of the Soviet Union a natural ally of the nations and movements which harbor such ambitions and aspirations, and by itself, especially in the short run, it has cost the Soviet Union very little.[37]

On the other hand, the authoritarian nature of the Soviet regime, favorable (i.e., unstable) external conditions, and Soviet support for such conditions do not necessarily bestow upon the Kremlin any degree of policy wisdom, and, as we shall see, these conditions cannot isolate the Soviet leadership from some debilitating weaknesses.

Constraints on Soviet Policy. Neither global power is omnipotent; certainly, the Soviet Union does not stand ten feet tall on the international stage. The U.S.S.R. is subject not only to applications of countervailing power by the United States and its allies, but also to a variety of constraints imposed by the international system and from within the Soviet Union itself.

Among the most important of these constraints are and will be the sad state of the Soviet economy and the problems the U.S.S.R. will face on the domestic political scene. By the mid 1980s, the Soviet Union will simultaneously undergo an energy shortage, a shortfall in the labor pool, a continuing slump in industrial productivity, and a wide-ranging "generational" leadership succession. Social ills, including alcoholism, corruption, and loss of civic morale, will compound these problems. Food problems, which have proven difficult to manage under the Soviet centralized planning system, will continue to plague the country, depending on weather. While all these difficulties may prove manageable, they are sufficiently serious for the Soviet military posture to merit further attention.

To begin, cheap energy, a rapidly growing workforce, and the exploitation of resources in the developed, European part of the Soviet Union enabled the U.S.S.R. to improve its economic standing and, at the same time, increase its defense outlays during the 1960s and 1970s. In the 1980s the deterioration of these conditions will force the Soviet leadership to make increasingly painful choices.

There is some likelihood that by the latter 1980s the Soviet Union will cease being a net oil exporter and may even become an oil importer. Production may drop from 11.4 million barrels/day (mb/d) in 1978 to about 10 mb/d by the late 1980s.[38] If this occurs, the Soviet Union will lose a major share of its hard currency export earnings. Furthermore, the effects of this decline will be "exported" to Eastern Europe, which in the 1970s obtained three-quarters of its imported oil at bargain rates from the Soviet Union. Growth rates and balances of payments will suffer in both the U.S.S.R. and in Eastern Europe. Economic stress as well as yearnings for national and personal freedom in Eastern Europe will undoubtedly create political problems for the socialist "big brother."

Second, growth in the Soviet workforce will decline from 1.5 million per annum in 1980 to 0.5 million in 1985.[39] No longer will the Soviet Union be able to solve production problems by "throwing people at them." This will exacerbate an already poor aggregate industrial productivity rate and increase the importance of either augmenting investments in capital stocks or procuring high technology capital goods from the West. The labor supply problem will be aggravated by the fact that most of the growth will occur in Moslem areas, where productivity is traditionally low.

Third, the domestic political environment within which these problems will occur will also be troubled. Not only will the agricultural and construction sectors need larger shares of national investment, generating further pressure on politically important consumption, but the Soviet leadership will also be faced with a wide-ranging succession problem. Jockeying new leaders may jeopardize the power required to press the inflexible Soviet economic bureaucracy into new programs or methods. Though it appears unlikely in the near future, there is always a possibility, too, that some of the more dynamic Soviet nationalities (see table 16.3) will seize upon a time of trouble to reach for greater autonomy, leading to large-scale civil unrest and military repression.

It is not clear how Soviet leaders can ameliorate the effects of these various

Table 16.3   The Soviet Conglomerate (total population, 262,436,000, 1979 Census)

Ethnic group	Population	% of Total
Slavs		
Great Russians	137,397,000	52.4
Ukrainians	42,347,000	16.1
Belorussians	9,463,000	3.6
Central Asians		
Kazakhs	6,556,000	2.5
Uzbeks	12,456,000	4.7
Turkmen	2,028,000	0.8
Kirgiz	1,906,000	0.7
Tadzhiks	2,898,000	1.1
Transcaucasians		
Georgians	3,571,000	1.4
Armenians	4,151,000	1.6
Azerbaydzhanis	5,477,000	2.1
Balts		
Estonians	1,020,000	0.4
Latvians	1,439,000	0.5
Lithuanians	2,851,000	1.1
Other		
Moldavians	2,968,000	1.1
Others Over 1 Million		
Tatars	6,317,000	2.4
Germans	1,936,000	0.7
Jews	1,811,000	0.7
Chuvash	1,751,000	0.7
Bashkirs	1,371,000	0.5
Mordvins	1,192,000	0.5
Poles	1,151,000	0.4

Source: U.S., Department of State, Bureau of Public Affairs, Special Report No. 67, 1979.

problems. One option would be for them to cut defense spending (or at least hold it stable) and use the savings (or GNP growth) to finance energy production or capital investment. Along with these measures, the U.S.S.R. could reduce the number of military conscripts or, more likely, reduce their term of service. A second option would entail the Soviet leaders, unable to cope, in effect forcing the Soviet populace to further tighten their belts. Such a course could risk domestic unrest if carried very far. Third, possible only if the Soviet Union is able to resolve its energy and other pressing economic difficulties or acquire sufficient foreign loans, its leaders might continue to pursue an active policy of purchasing capital goods and technology in the West, while maintaining high defense expenditures and an aggressive "forward strategy" in the Third World.

Finally, we must consider a more alarming possibility: faced with economic pessimism, domestic dissatisfaction and short-term military advantages, the

Soviet leadership might be tempted to take bolder Third World initiatives, particularly in the oil-rich Middle East.[40]

In the international environment there are also signs of the superficiality of the Soviet claim of a decisive, favorable shift in the correlation of forces. One sign already mentioned is that the Soviet relationships with the Third World have weakened. Not only have the Islamic nations been alienated by the invasion of Afghanistan, but African leaders have also voiced concern.[41] Second, the Soviet Union has not thus far succeeded in its repeated attempts to parlay its military power or economic arrangements into effective political pressure against Western Europe. Soviet pressure against Europe from 1979 to 1983 to forestall NATO modernization of nuclear weapons also failed, as noted below. In effect, the decline of American influence in Europe has not yet been complemented by a rise in that of the Soviet Union.

The Soviet military build-up in Europe has generated a NATO long-range development program and the 1979 NATO decision to deploy the American Pershing II intermediate-range ballistic missiles and ground-launched cruise missiles. The Warsaw Pact countries cannot long compete with an alarmed NATO whose GNP and population outdistance those of the pact nations by a factor of two or three. Moreover, there are increasing signs of unrest in the European satellites, as the Polish upheaval of 1980-81 dramatically showed.

Continued Soviet improvements in strategic weaponry have sparked renewed U.S. attention to its strategic forces. By the early 1990s, or even late 1980s, with an American lead in guidance system technology and the MX missile, the Soviets could find their own land-based missiles in a vulnerable position. Finally, on the U.S. political scene, awareness of the Soviet threat, which started rising in the latter 1970s, had become sufficiently high by 1984 that both political parties were calling for strong defense and "standing up to the Russians" in a hard-line way.[42]

In summary, one can view the question of "whither the correlation of forces" from two perspectives. In the near term (up to perhaps 1986 or 1987), an observer could cite the growing Soviet military power and its bold policy in the Third World as evidence of a pro-Soviet shift in the hard indicators of the correlation of forces. However, a closer look, particularly if it focuses on the latter 1980s, will show a Soviet Union plagued by a host of foreign and domestic problems, possibly slipping behind its American rival in the strategic realm. A protracted succession struggle could paralyze the Soviet foreign policy-making process. In short, the long-term view from the spires of the Kremlin may in fact be quite gloomy—which may itself be a mixed blessing, for short-term strength and long-term weakness may tempt the Soviet leaders to exploit the West's "window of vulnerability" by the mid 1980s while it lasts.

Implications for U.S. Policy in the Future. It is impossible to develop specific policy options on the basis of a generalized analysis. On the other hand, some observations about the Soviet threat to U.S. interests are in order. First, the

"AT THIS POINT THE ARTIST RAN OUT OF PAINT."

Reprinted with permission of Ranan R. Lurie from his book, *Lurie's World, 1970–1980*, University Press of Hawaii and King Features Syndicate, Inc.

United States (and its allies) will have to maintain their perspective, avoiding the extremes of world view where only the superpowers count or, on the other hand, a world view that focuses unduly on Soviet actions in the Third World. In this latter context the West must remember that, while the Soviets have exploited trouble in the Third World, the root causes of those troubles are economic and social in origin; Western aid can help to alleviate problems that might later prove to be beyond the capability of its military power to resolve. Central America may become a case in point.

Second, the United States received ample notice in the late 1970s that it must continue to maintain key military balances. A world where force is irrelevant to foreign policy influence is not at hand and cannot usefully serve as an inspiration for policy-makers. Since military strength continues to be essential to the functioning of the international system, several measures appear prudent. Among these is the need for the United States to maintain not only an adequate deterrent force, but also its ability to exercise limited nuclear options, "appropriate to the type and scale of a Soviet attack."[43] Important in this regard is the survivability of accurate ICBMs; prompt modernization thus must remain a key policy goal. "Essential equivalence" is indeed essential for U.S. strategic programs. Without it, the United States could be subject to missile-gap style blackmail, and meaningful arms control would become impossible. Neither superpower can negotiate successfully from a position of significant weakness.

Further, the United States should continue to pursue verifiable, genuine strategic arms limitation with the Soviet Union. Although agreements will be hard to achieve, no American president can fail to try; however, arms limitation accords must be free of ambiguity and loopholes. While in general the Soviets have apparently observed the letter of past agreements, they have not hesitated to exploit definitions and procedural matters that were open to question. Furthermore, arms control must be treated as a part of a coherent national security policy, not as a replacement for it.[44]

Next, the United States must maintain its commitment to NATO conventional force development and theater nuclear modernization. The latter is especially important in an era when essential equivalence has eroded the U.S. nuclear edge, decreasing the credibility of the U.S. pledge to use nuclear weapons to defend its allies. Moreover, at a time when America's allies are strengthening their economic ties with the Soviet Union and Eastern Europe, it is important that they do so from a position of military security.

Finally, the Western alliance must find ways to handle four other problems. First, it must resist Soviet incursions into the territorial waters of the Nordic NATO countries and correct gross force imbalances in favor of the U.S.S.R. in that area. Second, NATO must improve the economic standing of Greece, Turkey, and Portugal and thus help keep serious political and economic problems in those countries from damaging the alliance. (Similarly, more must be done to resolve the Cyprus problem and to bring Greece fully back into the NATO fold.) Third, the NATO countries must develop means to deal with Third World insecurity and development problems, if not in the context of the alliance then at least on the basis of coordinated policies designed to share the burden of combating Third World instability. Fourth, the NATO nations and Japan must improve the coordination of economic policies vis-à-vis the U.S.S.R., including strategic exports to the Soviet bloc.

Finally, a comment on the general character of U.S. national security policy and the Soviet Union: in a world of two competitive, relatively equal superpowers there are no easy nor inexpensive policy answers. American policymakers and public alike must recognize that their nation exists in a complicated world, one that requires both competition and cooperation with the other superpower. In the early years of the Reagan Administration, there were signs that this recognition provided the backdrop for U.S. policy. Thus, it was consistent to pursue deployment of middle-range theater nuclear weapons in Western Europe while seeking negotiations with the Soviets on limiting such missiles on both sides in Europe. The policy process involved will be complex and, at times, may appear contradictory to segments of the American public. Over the long run, the public must be both educated and informed of the goals and objectives at issue.

DISCUSSION QUESTIONS

1. Compare Soviet foreign policy under Stalin, Khrushchev, Brezhnev, and Andropov. What elements of continuity and change exist, and what significance does this hold for future Soviet policy?
2. Does Marxist-Leninist ideology lead or follow Soviet foreign policy?
3. Is Soviet foreign policy inherently expansionist or inherently defensive?

4. Soviet nuclear doctrine stresses a war-fighting policy. How is this different from U.S. policy?

5. Could a confrontation like the Cuban Missile Crisis occur in the Persian Gulf area? If so, could you predict its outcome based on "lessons learned" from previous crises?

6. What aspects of national security policy call for cooperation between the U.S. and the Soviet Union?

7. Détente is often said to have marked the end of the cold war. To what extent has the cold war been "born again"?

8. Many defense analysts think that the Soviet Union is attempting to reach "military superiority." In the nuclear age, what constitutes military superiority? What can the Soviet Union do if it succeeds in attaining superiority?

9. What do each of the superpowers see at stake in the Third World?

10. Given the Soviet military build-up since the 1960s, in what areas (policies, types of forces, etc.) should the U.S. respond? If faced with a choice, should the United States concentrate on conventional or nuclear forces?

RECOMMENDED READING

Aspaturian, Vernon. *Process and Power in Soviet Foreign Policy*. Boston: Little, Brown, 1971.

Bialer, Seweryn. *Stalin's Successors*. New York: Cambridge Univ. Press, 1980.

Byrnes, Robert F., ed. *After Brezhnev: Sources of Soviet Conduct in the 1980s*. Bloomington: Indiana University Press, 1983.

Fox, William T. R. *The Superpowers: The United States, Britain, and the Soviet Union—Their Responsibility for Peace*. New York: Harcourt Brace, 1944.

Gati, Charles, ed. *Caging the Bear: Containment and the Cold War*. New York: Bobbs-Merrill, 1974.

Goldman, Marshall I. *U.S.S.R. in Crisis: the Failure of an Economic System*. New York: W. W. Norton, 1983.

Khrushchev, Nikita. *Khrushchev Remembers*. Translated by Strobe Talbott. London: André Deutsch, 1971.

Newhouse, John. *Cold Dawn: The Story of SALT*. New York: Holt, Rinehart & Winston, 1973.

Osgood, Robert E.; Tucker, Robert W.; Dinerstein, Herbert S.; Rourke, Francis E.; Frank, Isaiah; Martin, Laurence W.; and Liska, George. *America and the World: From the Truman Doctrine to Vietnam*. Baltimore: Johns Hopkins Press, 1970.

Schwartz, Morton. *The Foreign Policy of the U.S.S.R.: Domestic Factors*. Encino, Calif.: Dickenson, 1975.

Sivachev, N., and Yakovlev, N. *Russia and the United States*. Chicago: University of Chicago Press, 1979.

Soviet Military Power. 2d ed. Superintendent of Documents, Washington, D.C.: U.S. Government Printing Office, 1983.

Ulam, Adam. *Dangerous Relations: The Soviet Union in World Politics, 1970–1982*. New York: Oxford University Press, 1982.

_____. *Expansion and Coexistence: Soviet Foreign Policy, 1917–1973*. New York: Frederick A. Praeger, 1974.

Wolfe, Thomas. *Soviet Power and Europe, 1945–1970*. Baltimore: John Hopkins Press, 1970.

17

EAST ASIA

The decade of the 1970s witnessed a number of major changes in East Asia* which have modified the major power relationships of earlier decades. These include the emergence of a P.R.C.-Japan-U.S. coalition designed to check Soviet military pressures, the collapse of the Republic of Vietnam (R.V.N.) following withdrawal of U.S. forces and advisers and severe cuts in military aid, and the development of a strong Soviet-Vietnamese alliance in opposition to the P.R.C. The two primary forces behind these changes have been Sino-Soviet rivalry (which may be waning) and Soviet-American competition.

The 1970s marked a sharp break with the past since, for the first time, the two fault lines cited, i.e., the Sino-Soviet and U.S.-Soviet splits, intersected as the U.S. and the P.R.C. normalized relations. Another historic factor came into play. For nearly a century the U.S. had had to choose between supporting either China or Japan in their mutual rivalry; by the early 1980s it was possible for the U.S. to align itself with both. The durability of these realignments, in particular the extent to which East Asian relationships will continue to be polarized around the split separating the U.S.S.R. from the other major regional actors, is a key question for the 1980s.

American Interests in Asia. The principal American interest in East Asia, as in Europe, is that no single nation or coalition of nations should control the resources and people of the region. Accordingly, it has been and continues to be American policy to seek a balance among the major powers in the region. In practice this has meant that the United States should preserve and strengthen the P.R.C. as a counterweight to the Soviet Union. This aim thus requires the United States to conduct its policy in such a fashion as to avoid either Sino-Soviet warfare or reconciliation.

East Asia is used here to refer to Southeast Asia (from Burma eastward, to include the archipelagos of Indonesia and the Philippines), the People's Republic of China, Taiwan, the Koreas, Japan, and the maritime provinces of the U.S.S.R.

366

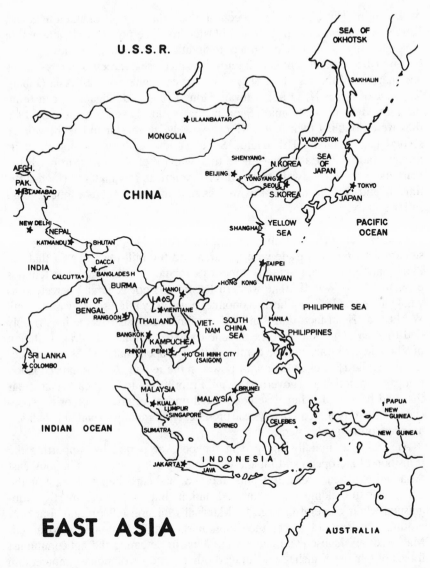

EAST ASIA

FIG. 17.1

A second major interest of the United States in the region is to strengthen Japan's role as a responsible political and economic power in the region, closely allied with the United States and increasingly prepared to share American security responsibilities in and near the Japanese islands.

A third major American interest in the region is to promote regional stability. This in turn entails supporting the Southeast Asian states against Vietnamese expansionism and helping to avert a recurrence of war between the two Koreas, with the concomitant danger that the major powers might be drawn in. The U.S. aim has been, in this context, to strengthen its South Korean ally against the threats and bluster from the north, while attempting diplomatically to place reins on any temptation to initiate hostilities.

A fourth and significant U.S. interest is to increase its access to the resources and markets of the region. The free-market economies of East Asia (Japan, Republic of Korea [R.O.K.], Taiwan, Hong Kong, and Singapore) constitute the most dynamic economic region in the world. Taken together, by 1980 they were doubling their real GNP every twelve years. Japan has the world's second largest GNP. The United States conducts about one-fourth of its foreign trade with East Asia—more than with all of Western Europe. If the markets of the region were to be cut off, American raw material (foodstuffs, timber, and certain minerals) as well as manufactured goods exports would suffer greatly.

Recent History of U.S. Policy toward East Asia. Despite longstanding missionary activities and trade with the area and the pull toward Asia that the Philippine colony represented, America's relations with Asia were tenuous prior to World War II.[1] The western Pacific was not generally perceived as vitally linked to U.S. political, economic, or security interests. It was not until World War II, in fact, that America's national interests became inextricably tied to Asia. The defeat of the Japanese in that conflict, the fragmentation of China in civil war, and the demise of the European nations' Asian colonies left the United States as the major power in the region. American occupation troops remained in and governed Japan. From Korea to Southeast Asia, areas that had been under Japanese control fell under American authority. Associated with this increased physical presence was rapidly expanding political and economic involvement.

America was initially engaged in the postwar period by supporting the transition of European and Japanese colonies to self-government in Southeast Asia and Northeast Asia. In China, the U.S. had early hopes of assisting the Chinese in rebuilding their shattered nation, but these were mostly extinguished when General George C. Marshall's mission (1946), aimed at promoting a settlement between the Communists and the Nationalists, collapsed. Mao Zedong's subsequent success in China in defeating the anticommunist forces of Chiang Kai-shek encouraged others, and revolutionary momentum in the region increased: in the late 1940s Ho Chi Minh launched his Viet Minh forces against the French in Indochina, the Hukbalahap rebellion simmered in the Philippines, and communist-inspired revolts occurred in Indonesia, Malaysia, and Burma. The attack by Communist North Korea—the Democratic People's Republic of Korea (D.P.R.K.)—on South Korea in 1950, causing the U.S. to intervene under UN auspices, was the culmination of this series of political events, behind which most American leaders saw the hand of Moscow—or the joint hands of Moscow and Beijing.

As a result of communist pressure and its own perspective on communism as an inherently expansionist force, America gradually extended its containment policy, which had originated in Europe, into Asia. President Truman's actions to defend South Korea in 1950 and his associated order to move units of the Seventh Fleet in defense of Taiwan were significant not only in Asia but elsewhere, for this was the first time the United States had had to implement containment by committing its own military forces to resist communist aggression and to shore up independent nations.[2]

In this period, it was assumed in the West—particularly in the United States—that the two communist giants, the U.S.S.R. and the P.R.C., constituted a unified, "monolithic" bloc, generally referred to as the Sino-Soviet bloc. American containment policy in Asia was specifically and directly focused on checking the "Sino" element of the bloc—the P.R.C. In the mid 1950s, the United States increased its aid to Chiang Kai-shek on Taiwan and publicly announced assumption of responsibility for helping defend that island. U.S. support of the French in their fight against the Viet Minh in the early 1950s and, after French withdrawal from Vietnam, direct military assistance to South Vietnam (1955 onwards) were also prompted by American preoccupation with containing communism in the region. It was the underlying assumption in Washington that if local communist states emerged throughout Asia, they would be linked ideologically, militarily, and politically with the U.S.S.R. and Communist China. In responding to this perceived threat, as well as to its growing political and economic ties with the region, America found that its interests were being bound ever closer to stability in East Asia— bound, that is, to the political status quo.

In addition to supporting countries battling communism, the United States actively encouraged Asian nations to form regional security pacts including the United States. One of the first of these agreements was the 1951 tripartite security treaty with Australia and New Zealand (ANZUS). The purpose of this treaty was to provide for mutual aid in the event of aggression and to settle disputes by peaceful means.[3] The second major regional security organization was the Southeast Asia Treaty Organization (SEATO), a regional defense organization established in 1954 by the United States, the United Kingdom, Australia, New Zealand, France, Pakistan, the Philippines, and Thailand.[4] SEATO was created as a direct response to the perceived threat of communist expansion in Southeast Asia.

Having consolidated its own revolution, the P.R.C. began playing an increasingly important role in Asia in the 1950s. China became closely linked with Hanoi and openly supported communist insurgents in the Philippines and Indonesia. Initially the P.R.C. publicly criticized many Asian leaders, including Sukarno and Nehru, for being "stooges" of the American imperialists.[5] One of its primary aims was to rid the area of the United States, the only country capable of projecting large-scale military force into the region. For its part, America was prepared to remain in East Asia and to become involved directly in support of other regional states in order to limit P.R.C. expansion.

In the early 1960s the United States continued to be deeply concerned about a perceived Sino-Soviet partnership in Asia—and was slow to recognize that in reality a Sino-Soviet split was occurring. Sino-Soviet rivalry was initially expressed publicly as diverging interpretations of communist doctrine. Thus, attacking the Soviet policy of peaceful coexistence, the P.R.C. maintained that communists ceased to be communists when they no longer made revolution. The Russians affirmed that peaceful coexistence aided revolution because friction within the capitalist countries would increase when external tension was reduced. These and other doctrinal points became entangled with important conflicts between the national interests of the two communist giants—particularly over their disputed borderlands.

Chinese talk of world revolution and emphasis on violence in their diatribes against the Soviet Union only served to strengthen apprehension in the United States about P.R.C. intentions. In fact, in a series of actions between 1955 and 1964, including border skirmishes and its first explosion of an atomic device, the P.R.C. continually reminded American policy-makers of its aggressive potential. With hindsight it is possible to see that the Chinese acted with more restraint than their rhetoric at the time suggested.[6]

In the context of U.S. containment policy in Asia, Vietnam became a central concern. The anticommunist Diem government in the southern part of the country, the R.V.N. (capital in Saigon), was under continual assault, first by guerrilla forces (the Viet Cong—VC) under the direction of Ho Chi Minh's communist government in the north, the Democratic Republic of Vietnam—D.R.V.—(capital in Hanoi), and later by regular forces infiltrated in units up to regimental size from the north.

The United States was faced with the choice of seeing South Vietnam taken over by the communists or of providing military assistance to stave off that outcome. Once committed to aid, American military involvement there escalated from a limited advisory role in 1955–62 to massive combined arms combat operations in 1968–70. Altogether, the American effort was intended to provide the Saigon government the time and opportunity to fend off defeat, establish its authority, and stabilize the countryside politically and economically. It was an ambitious undertaking.

In 1969, ostensibly because the South Vietnamese government forces, freshly trained and supplied, could deal with VC insurgents and incursions by North Vietnamese regulars, the United States announced a policy to "Vietnamize" the war.[7] It is instructive, however, to examine other elements of U.S. domestic and foreign politics which inspired this policy, for it clearly was not an isolated decision.

By 1968, it had become obvious that domestic pressure against U.S. military involvement in Vietnam could neither be ignored nor suppressed. The nation was being ravaged by mass antiwar riots and demonstrations. Many of America's young, caught in the throes of the "Youth Revolution," rejected the war, the government that pursued it, and the public and private institutions that supported it. Government agencies, political parties, and the American public were divided over the ends sought and the means employed in the

"MY COUNTER ATTACK AT PRINCETON SHOULD RELIEVE THE PRESSURE FROM THE IVY LEAGUE ENOUGH TO ALLOW ME TO DEAL SHARPLY WITH THE WEST COAST GUERRILLA ACTIVITY"

By John Fischetti. Copyright Field Enterprises, Inc., courtesy Field Newspaper Syndicate.

Vietnam War. In 1968, President Johnson declined to run for reelection because the American public was so dissatisfied with his inability to end the war and deliver on his promises for a "Great Society" at home. Richard Nixon was elected in 1968 in large part because he had a "secret plan" to end the war.

By the latter 1960s, other forces were also causing Americans to rethink their nation's role in Asia. The reality of the Sino-Soviet dispute had begun to sink in and Washington was faced with the problems and prospects of tripolar, rather than bipolar, politics in East Asia. Another major element in this revised Asian equation was the development of Japan into a major economic power. Previously a passive factor in the area, Japan had become a major political and economic force in Asia and was therefore central to U.S. policy there.

President Nixon's reassessment in 1969 of U.S. responsibilities in Asia, couched in terms of the "Nixon Doctrine," his "Vietnamization" of the war in Southeast Asia, and ultimately his 1972 rapprochement with the P.R.C. were all driven by political reality, both domestic and foreign. The opening provided by the increasingly bitter Sino-Soviet quarrel and the traumatic experience of the Vietnam War provided the catalysts to bring about a redefinition of U.S. policies. This redefinition was based on recognition of the need for the United States to reduce its commitments in Asia and to find ways to share the balance of power tasks it had been largely carrying alone.

Throughout the 1970s America's approach to foreign policy in Asia continued to be based fundamentally on the ideas of the Nixon Doctrine, which called for self-help by others, primarily regional responsibility for security and stability, and only residual responsibility by the United States, who was no longer able or willing to act directly as an international police force in the region. American security assistance would be based henceforth on the willingness and ability of a nation to help itself and on the degree to which others in the region perceived a threat and were willing to assist the nation in question.

Both to facilitate this redirection of policy (and to use Sino-Soviet rivalry as a check on Soviet worldwide ambitions), President Nixon set out to mend relations with America's long time antagonist in the region, the P.R.C. The multipolar relationship that subsequently developed in Asia resulted from a conscious decision to redesign the U.S. policy architecture in Asia.

President Nixon's surprise announcement of Secretary of State Kissinger's visit to the P.R.C. in 1971 was the first of a number of political and economic shocks that signaled the new direction. While it is probably true that this "Nixon shock" and a subsequent visit to the P.R.C. in February 1972 by the president were "not at the expense of [Asian leaders'] nations . . . [and] will be in accordance with their long-range interests,"[8] it is clear that this new policy thrust, made without consulting America's Asian allies, impelled those same allies to move toward greater independence in the conduct of their foreign policies.

The 1973–74 oil crisis resulting from the 1973 Arab-Israeli War also served to reemphasize to Asians the necessity of their taking a more independent economic and political stance. The rapid collapse of South Vietnam in 1975 after the withdrawal of U.S. ground forces and sharp reduction of military assistance to South Vietnam further convinced America's allies in the region of the necessity to discount the power and the promises of the United States. Even though their security treaties with the United States remained in force, most of them began seeking greater flexibility and independence in their foreign policies. Finally, President Carter's 1977 decision to withdraw American ground forces from Korea (a decision later placed in abeyance) created particularly strong concerns in the area about the permanency of U.S. military forces stationed in East Asia.

These changes in the course of the 1970s contributed to undermining the structure that the United States had tried to secure for more than twenty-five years. Also, the presidency, which had enjoyed wide latitude in matters of foreign policy, became all but paralyzed by the domestic politics of Watergate after 1973. In light of all these trends, by the late 1970s American policymakers were busy searching for new options to preserve U.S. national security interests in the area.

The Major East Asian Actors.

Japan. Of the major regional actors, it is clear that in terms of American relationships Japan is special. The roots of this relationship extend back to the enlightened postwar U.S. policies of the 1940s. Despite more than two decades of increasingly close cooperation in the 1950s and 1960s, the various shocks of the 1970s alluded to above caused many Japanese to wonder about their American patron and partner. Japanese political and military leaders were left uncomfortably aware of their dependence for ultimate protection on a distant superpower whose influence in the western Pacific was seen as diminishing. "The important aspect of the change [in relations with the U.S. was] that it [had] been bought at the price of confidence in the United States."[9]

U.S. policy toward Japan at the start of the 1980s had two principal facets: defense and trade.[10] In defense matters, the U.S. position is paramount for the Japanese; they consider a continued strong American role in Asia as essential for the protection of their strategic interests. The security relationship is based on the Treaty of Mutual Cooperation of 1960. As the 1970s ended, the Japanese questioned American guarantees under this treaty as a result of three major developments: first, President Carter's announced intention to withdraw U.S. forces from the Korean Peninsula (a move later suspended); second, the build-up of Soviet forces in the region, accompanied by disclosure of a U.S. strategy to shift naval forces to the European or Middle East theaters in the event of hostilities (a strategy later disavowed);[11] and third, Japan's increasing perception of the vulnerability of her vital sea lines of communication, especially to the oil fields of the Middle East.

The importance of the Japanese-American alliance in contributing to a balance of power in East Asia is central. In Japanese eyes the alliance with the United States not only provides a security umbrella but is also the most important tie it has with the industrial democracies. From the U.S. viewpoint, the alliance buttresses America's basic strategic interest, namely, a continued close alignment of Japan with the United States. More generally, the alliance is a central factor in the power equilibrium in the Pacific.

There has been one major element of disagreement in the security field, namely, the feeling of many Americans that Japan has been "getting a free ride" in defense (which it has translated into a comprehensive economic advantage) and that it ought to be spending more on its own forces.[12] On the other hand, there has been a quite different concern, also widely shared, that Japanese rearmament would be destabilizing in the region, not only because of the fears it would generate on the part of Southeast Asians and Koreans, but also the concerns it would raise in China—and even in the Soviet Union. By the start of the 1980s, the first of these views—namely, that Japan should be spending significantly more on its defense—predominated in the U.S. To an extent, Japan appeared ready to accept this view, for official and public perceptions of national security had shifted substantially in the latter 1970s; and, by 1983, a strong current of support for a greater defense effort had appeared in most quarters of Japanese society.[13] This development was due in part to the continuing Soviet military build-up on the Kurile Islands north of Japan and was accompanied by a more forthright tone on defense matters in the public pronouncements of Japanese leaders.

International trade and finance have also caused friction. The United States is Japan's major trading partner; Japan ranks second for the United States.

Table 17.1 Principal Regional Forces in East Asia

Country/Service	Regular Forces	Reserves	Main Armament	Other
Japan				
(pop. 118,519,000)				
Army	155,000 (13 divs.)	43,000	910 tks. 530 APC	nuclear forces will not be developed
Navy	45,000	600	14 subs. 54 maj. surf ships 110 cbt. acft.	
Air Force	45,000		314 cbt. acft.	
People's Republic of China				
(pop. 1,024,890,000)				
Army	3,150,000 (269 divs.)		11,100 tks. 4,000 APC 15,700 arty.	nuclear forces: 4 ICBM 60 IRBM 50 MRBM
Navy	360,000		103 subs. 34 maj. surf. ships 800 cbt. acft.	
Air Force	490,000		5,300 cbt. acft.	med. bombers: 122
Taiwan				
(pop. 18,200,000)				
Army (incl. Marines)	349,000 (27 divs.)	1,500,000	1,430 tks. 1,250 APL 1,725 arty.	nuclear weapons by the late 1980s cannot be ruled out
Navy	38,000	45,000	2 subs 35 maj. surf. ships	
Air Force	77,000	90,000	484 cbt. acft.	
Vietnam				
(pop. 56,000,000)				
Army	1,000,000 (60 divs.)		2,500 tks. 2,300 AFV 890 arty.	
Navy	4,000		36 maj. surf. ships	
Air Force	25,000		470 cbt. acft.	
North Korea				
(pop. 18,600,000)				
Army	700,000 (40 divs.)	260,000	2,825 tks. 1,140 AFV 4,100 arty.	

Table 17.1 *(cont.)*

Country/Service	Regular Forces	Reserves	Main Armament	Other
Navy	33,000	40,000	19 atk. subs. 55 maj. surf. ships	
Air Force	51,000		700 cbt. acft.	
South Korea (pop. 38,900,000)				
Army	520,000 (24 divs.)	1,100,000	1,000 tks. 850 AFV 2,104 arty.	nuclear weapons by the late 1980s cannot be ruled out
Navy	49,000 (incl. 24,000 Marines)	85,000 (incl 60,000 Marines)	37 maj. surf. ships	
Air Force	32,600	55,000	434 cbt. acft.	
U.S.S.R. (forces directed toward the Far East)				
Army	460,000 (46 divs.)		12,000 tks. 16,000 AFV 7,500 arty.	portions of the strategic nuclear forces and the SS-20 force are also allocated
Navy	12,000	N/A	85 atk. subs. 75 maj. surf. ships 300 cbt. acft.	
Air Force	170,000		4 tac. air armies (approx. 2,000 acft.)	

Sources: International Institute for Strategic Studies, *The Military Balance, 1982–1983* (London: IISS,1982); "The Power Game," in *Asia Yearbook, 1980* (Hong Kong: Far Eastern Economic Review, 1980), pp. 34–58.

Abbreviations not listed below can be found in the list of abbreviations on pp. xv–xvi.

AA = antiaircraft
acft. = aircraft
AFV = armored fighting vehicle
amph. = amphibious
APC = armored personnel carrier
armd. = armored
arty. = artillery
ASW = antisubmarine warfare
ATGW = antitank guided weapons
atk. = attack
bns. = battalions
btrys. = batteries
cbt. = combat
cft. = craft
crvettes = corvettes
destrys. = destroyers

div. = division
frigts. = frigates
hel. = helicopter
hvcrft. = hovercraft
lndg. = landing
mine swprs. = mine sweepers
msl. = missile
prcht. = parachute
ptl. = patrol
regts. = regiments
SAM = surface-to-air missile
sqdn. = squadron
tac. = tactical
tk. = tank
tng. = training
tspt. = transport

Despite these rankings, there is a chronic trade imbalance. As indicated in table 17.2, Japan consistently sells $10–15 billion worth of goods more to the United States than it buys from us. It is estimated that this figure will climb in 1983 to well over $20 billion. This imbalance had led to U.S. pressure on Japan ''voluntarily'' to limit exports and to remove all barriers to imports from the United States. Although Japan has partially accommodated to these pressures, trade policy is likely to be a matter of continuing tension between the two partners. It should also be noted that the United States would like to see Japan use its economic and technical strength to assist the developing nations in the region as well as to increase spending upon its own defense. These issues, too, will remain high on the agenda of U.S.-Japanese relations.

Korea. One major element of Japan's security centers on U.S. policies toward Korea, for Korea has traditionally acted as a bridge between Japan and mainland Asia. When President Carter's plan to withdraw the U.S. Second Infantry Division from Korea was announced in 1977, deep concern was expressed by Japanese leaders as well as by many Korean and U.S. defense analysts.[14] When the plan was devised initially, it rested in part on the judgment that force levels between the northern D.P.R.K. and the southern R.O.K. were roughly in balance, with continuing U.S. air and naval power available to offset any lingering R.O.K. deficiencies. However, based on revised intelligence showing a heavy preponderance of North Korean military forces, the United States announced in 1979 that "any further withdrawal of combat elements from the [Second Infantry] Division will be held in abeyance until 1981."[15]

North Korea is undoubtedly the world's most mobilized nation, with over 750,000 troops serving in its armed forces (from a population of only 19 million) for a compulsory term of five years, starting at age 16. The D.P.R.K. spends 20 to 22 percent of its GNP on its military, in contrast to the usual 2 to 6 percent that most nations spend—South Korea is near the latter figure.[16] The economic strains from this effort are already massive. In some respects, the D.P.R.K.-R.O.K. military balance is a microcosm of the U.S.S.R.-U.S. balance: by extraordinary sacrifices North Korea has acquired a slightly superior military position that it cannot hold if the economically stronger south makes a determined effort to restore the balance. Accordingly, the north has a short-term "window of opportunity" that will likely disappear by the latter 1980s if not exploited.

The Carter decision to withdraw U.S. forces from Korea transcended the purely military equation. Not only are those forces important combat elements, but they also serve as a form of "trip wire," guaranteeing U.S. military involvement were hostilities renewed. As such, the forces are a powerful signal of U.S. military commitment to the defense of an ally. Especially after the debacle in Vietnam, any withdrawal of U.S. forces would be viewed throughout East Asia as a serious weakening of the U.S.-R.O.K. treaty

Table 17.2   U.S.-Japan Trade (in billions of dollars)

Year	U.S. Imports from Japan	U.S. Exports to Japan
1979	26.3	17.6
1980	30.7	20.8
1981	37.6	21.8
1982	37.7	21.0

Source: U.S. Department of Commerce (personal communication).

relationship. Carter's decision to defer the withdrawal helped assure allies throughout the area.

The assassination of South Korean President Park Chung Hee on October 26, 1979, and the subsequent political instability that brought about martial law in May 1980 highlight another dimension of the problem. If the R.O.K. military oligarchy is not prepared to share power and restore some elements of democracy, domestic unrest (which can be exploited by the north) is likely to intensify dangerously at some point in the decade.

The Korean peninsula is very important to U.S. security in part because it is the one place in which there is a distinct possibility of military confrontation among the United States, the P.R.C., and the U.S.S.R. Although there are no Soviet or Chinese military forces in North Korea, these major regional actors compete for influence there and have forces nearby. Although it is probable that, because of the dangers involved, neither the P.R.C. nor the Soviet Union wishes to see the Korean status quo disrupted, the two compete for influence, and neither is likely to press restraint upon its client so strongly as to enhance the position of the other.

China. The rivalry between the P.R.C. and the Soviet Union over influence in the D.P.R.K. is one example of a basic objective of Chinese foreign policy, namely, the containment and, where possible, the undermining of Soviet power and influence in the region. China considers its own security to be threatened by Soviet "hegemony." Because it had long wished to enlist the West to help check this threat, the P.R.C. responded quickly to American overtures for better relations in 1978. Consequently on December 15, 1978, in a joint communiqué, the United States and the P.R.C. announced normalization of relations. From China's viewpoint, it had engineered a new bilateral relationship that would enhance its national security and economy. From the U.S. viewpoint, we had contributed to regional stability and would deal with both communist giants in like manner.[17] In August 1979, Vice President Mondale emphasized in Beijing that Sino-American friendship was not directed against anyone and that the United States neither had nor anticipated a military relationship with the P.R.C.[18] (It should be noted that this statement preceded the Soviet invasion of Afghanistan in December 1979 and the subsequent U.S. announcement in January 1980 that it was prepared to sell "dual technology"—i.e., technology with both civil and military applications—and certain combat support items to the P.R.C.)

Western technology and arms assistance is important to the P.R.C., for it has long neglected its military forces, which are far inferior to the Soviet units poised along the common border. Not only has military modernization consistently been given low priority by China's leaders, but also the "Cultural Revolution," from the mid 1960s to the mid 1970s, virtually halted research and development in this and other fields.

While the United States at the time of normalization with the P.R.C. professed even-handedness in relations with the two major communist powers, it made clear in a variety of ways that it hoped the new relationship would provide a check on Soviet adventures. Whether or not this hope will be realized remains to be seen, but the defense cooperation between the United States and the P.R.C. that would add reality to expectations was slow to develop. Nearly two years after normalization (i.e., by the end of 1980) there had only been some visits and preliminary, general staff talks between the two sides; the United States had merely approved for sale a number of items of interest to the Chinese armed forces, e.g., military vehicles, helicopters, transport planes, flight simulators, radar, aerial cameras, and communications equipment.[19]

China's importance as a trading partner can easily be overstated. U.S. trade with the P.R.C. was only $5.1 billion in 1980—compared with $12.9 billion with Taiwan. Trade with the P.R.C. should grow, for the 1980 U.S.-P.R.C. agreement gave the P.R.C. most favored nation (MFN) tariff status and opened the door for future Export-Import Bank financing for exports to China.[20] Without this financing, U.S. exporters had been at a disadvantage in competing against Japanese and European firms that already have access to official credits. Even with new credits potentially available, U.S. exports to the P.R.C. are likely to grow slowly. If any American entrepreneurs dream of a billion-person market for their products, one may suspect that their vision is at best premature.

In theory, it would be sensible realpolitik to throw the enormous weight of the combined economic resources and technology of Japan and the United States into the modernization and development of an anti-Soviet China. Even if it were in the West's interests, however, China is picking and choosing, playing Tokyo, Bonn, and Washington off against one another. Americans may become sentimental about China, but the Chinese do not get sentimental about trade or power politics.[21]

Trade statistics indicate that the basic P.R.C. policy is one of selectively importing Western technology, especially that which will perform a dual function—that is, support both the technological needs of the civil sector and, where possible, the modernization of defense industries. The presumption in many quarters in the late 1970s that the P.R.C. would try to modernize rapidly its military appeared by the end of 1983 to be off the mark. Modernization of the armed forces, while a important goal, appears not to be the most urgent. In any case, the Chinese have few exportable commodities and little foreign exchange—and are reluctant to go deeply in debt—so their overall purchases will necessarily be limited.

After some hesitation, the P.R.C. seems to have turned its back on the revolutionary excesses of the Cultural Revolution and has started down the path of pragmatic economic development. The post-Mao leadership—in large part rehabilitated moderates, such as Deng Xiaoping, who had been shoved aside during the Cultural Revolution—announced the new course at the Fifth National People's Congress in March 1978. Under the slogan of the "Four Modernizations" (agriculture, industry, science and technology, and defense) Deng and his colleagues

set forth a program of economic and military modernization that implied a significant commitment to acquiring technology and financial credits from Japan and from the capitalist countries of the West. The underlying geopolitical theme of the decisions of the People's Congress was that China must be prepared to meet the challenge of the Soviet Union by transforming a still backward country into a modern industrial power, supported by modern military forces, by the end of the century.[22]

Following these themes and its longstanding "antihegemonic" policy aimed at isolating the U.S.S.R. in Asia, in the late 1970s the P.R.C. moved to strengthen its links with Europe, to pursue normalization with the United States, and to conclude the Sino-Japanese Treaty of Peace and Friendship (August 1978). In part as a riposte, the U.S.S.R. signed a treaty of its own, the Soviet-Vietnamese Treaty of Friendship and Cooperation (November 1978). Reassured by this explicit guarantee of support, Vietnam attacked Kampuchea (Cambodia) the next month—leading to the P.R.C. attack on Vietnam in February 1979 and the short, inconclusive conflict that followed.

Taiwan. The long-awaited normalization of U.S.-P.R.C. relations at the end of 1978 scarcely caused a ripple on Taiwan's political and economic millpond. Although that normalization entailed "ending U.S. recognition of the Republic of China on Taiwan, termination of the U.S.-Taiwan mutual defense treaty [and] withdrawal of the remaining U.S. troops on Taiwan,"[23] even Taiwan's defense position did not seem unduly shaken in the aftermath. This composure was due in part to the U.S. Congress promptly following the termination of the formal treaty with the passage of the Taiwan Relations Act (April 1979), which stipulated that the United States is vitally interested in the continued peace and well-being of the people on Taiwan. The act, which some have viewed as the "functional equivalent" of a treaty, also directed the president to report to Congress on any threat to these interests.

In part, also, Taiwan's security was not immediately threatened by the treaty termination because a P.R.C. assault against the island would be a risky, costly diversion of scarce military materiel and would irreparably damage the valuable P.R.C. relations with Japan and the United States. Nevertheless, Taiwan can be expected to increase its defense efforts, particularly by the acquisition of high performance air defense and ASW (antisubmarine warfare) aircraft.

Taiwan has one of the most dynamic economies in the world, growing at a compounded rate of 8.2 percent over the quarter century from 1952 to 1977.[24] It is the second largest Asian trading partner of the United States, despite its population of only 18 million people. Since Taiwan is heavily dependent on international trade (with over 50 percent of its national product traded), a P.R.C. naval blockade could quickly bring it down. With its overwhelming superiority in attack submarines, Beijing could readily effectuate such a blockade—but, again, at the price of war in the Taiwan Straits and incalcuable damage to the important P.R.C. relations with the industrial democracies.

Vietnam. Emerging victorious and unified in the mid 1970s from the struggle with the United States, Vietnam was a badly battered country. It was widely expected that after political consolidation, the communist leaders would be solely engaged for the next decade or more in rebuilding their shattered economy. Contrary to these expectations, Hanoi had additional priorities, namely, the extension of Vietnamese control over the other two Indochinese states, i.e., Laos and Kampuchea.

Even before the end of the Vietnam War, Hanoi's troops were emplaced in Laos, supporting the communist Pathet Lao. After the American departure from the peninsula, the Vietnamese in effect supplanted their clients, taking over the governmental reins while keeping Lao puppets in apparent authority. In Kampuchea a different approach was necessary. There, the incredible brutality of the communist Khmer Rouge forces had alienated that part of the population that they did not actually kill. (Estimates vary, but it appears that the Khmer Rouge killed, in one way or another, some 2 to 3 million of their fellow citizens, out of a total population of only 6 to 7 million.)[25] It was possible, therefore, for the Vietnamese to invade the country with minimal opposition. They marched in virtually as liberators, resuming their historic thrust toward the rich rice lands of the Khmers, which France had interrupted more than a century before when it colonized all of Indochina.

Whether the decimated, displaced, and famine-haunted Khmers (or Kampucheans) can rid themselves of the Vietnamese occupation troops and their puppet ruler, Heng Sam-rin, is in question. The P.R.C. was and is prepared to help, but the Khmer Rouge is so universally hated that leadership of an anti-Vietnamese resistance movement must be found elsewhere.

In large part "to teach Vietnam a lesson" for its December 1978 invasion of Kampuchea, the P.R.C. invaded Vietnam in February 1979. (Vietnamese mistreatment of more than one hundred thousand of its ethnic Chinese residents who fled the country—along with even larger numbers of refugees of Vietnamese ethnic origin—may also have been a minor cause.) After less than a month of limited fighting and the taking of a provincial capital and some border posts, the P.R.C. forces withdrew, claiming that they had indeed administered a lesson. What the Vietnamese learned is unclear, for they continued their conquest and occupation of Kampuchea with only minor redeployments to meet the Chinese thrust. Additionally, they increased the size of their forces sufficiently to permit them to keep about two hundred fifty thousand regulars in Laos and Kampuchea indefinitely while substantially reinforcing the units along the China border—after the fighting ceased there, that is.

Vietnam has been able to pursue its expansionist course, including its confrontation with the P.R.C., only because of Moscow's backing. Soviet subsidies of an estimated $3 million per day have kept the economy of Vietnam afloat while Vietnamese armies occupied neighboring territories. In return, the U.S.S.R. has apparently been given permission to use, as needed, the great Vietnamese naval and air bases at Cam Ranh and Danang, which the U.S. built during the Vietnamese War. Moscow has other interests in the growth and strengthening of the Vietnamese empire—primarily that it puts pressure on China from the south and provides the basing that greatly strengthens the Soviet navy's position throughout the area.

ASEAN. The Southeast Asian states beyond Indochina, namely, Thailand, Malaysia, Singapore, Indonesia, and the Philippines, formed their own regional organization in 1967—the Association of Southeast Asian Nations (ASEAN). Originally mostly an economic and cultural tool, ASEAN has become an increasingly important political instrument, particularly in the later 1970s. At that time, worried over the American withdrawal from Southeast Asia and the takeover of Vietnam, Laos, and Kampuchea by communist forces, the ASEAN powers launched a series of political and economic cooperation initiatives, at the same time disclaiming any intention of forming a military alliance.

The fears of the ASEAN countries about stability in their region were powerfully underscored in 1978 and 1979 by the Vietnamese invasion of Kampuchea and the installation of a puppet regime there by the invaders. Since the Vietnamese armed forces are substantially superior to those of the ASEAN states, taken singly or together, there has been little the nations could do to confront the threat directly. Instead, they have waged a diplomatic campaign against Vietnam and have encouraged the United States to reassert a stronger role in the region.

Although China, as the foe of Vietnam and the ally of Kampuchea, might also seem to be a logical protector of the ASEAN states' interests, the P.R.C. generally inspires as much fear as it does confidence in the region. Southeast Asian concerns about China arise from the P.R.C. sponsorship and support of local communist insurrections as well as from the 17 or 18 million ethnic Chinese in the area who are potential sympathizers and cooperators with the homeland.

Thailand, which has been faced with a massive influx of Kampuchean refugees fleeing both the civil war and the Vietnamese invaders, is an exception to the foregoing generalizations. It shares a common border with both Kampuchea and Laos, which are occupied by Vietnamese forces, and has been subjected to Vietnamese border incursions in the course of the Kampuchean War. Unable to depend on its ASEAN partners for military help and with the United States unlikely to assist, Thailand has looked to the P.R.C. as the only realistic prospect for assistance. For its part, China has threatened to administer a "second lesson" to Vietnam if it invades Thailand.

In the Philippines, President Marcos's martial law government has been able to place more reliance upon the United States than has Thailand. Although it shares the fears of most of its ASEAN partners about the possibility of future Chinese or Vietnamese adventures in the area, it is much more closely tied to the United States than the other ASEAN nations. Since the United States depends heavily on the use of facilities at Clark Air Base and Subic Naval Base near Manila for its ability to maintain a credible naval presence in the western Pacific and the Indian Ocean, the Philippines enjoys a high priority in American defense plans. Moreover, in view of the normalization of U.S.-P.R.C. relations, Marcos no longer has to be concerned about what used to be China's strong opposition to American use of the air and naval bases in the Philippines.

Wisely, the ASEAN states have consistently placed heavy attention on the political and economic development of their own societies in recent years and have reaped considerable success for their efforts. Each state, however, has economic, ethnic, and other strains that remain to be surmounted. In the Philippines in particular, nagging insurgencies were in progress in the early 1980s. Both the Moslem insurgency in the south, organized by the Moro National Liberation Front, and the Communist New People's Army (NPA), which is now the most active revolutionary group, pose a major threat to the central government. Added to these problems is the prospect of a succession struggle (Marcos is now 65) and the likelihood of an increase in popular dissatisfaction with the Marcos regime. The latter development seemed much more likely after the assassination of a popular opposition leader in 1983. If any major political trouble were to occur, which is not improbable in the 1980s, the American use of the important base facilities at Clark and Subic would almost surely be severely curtailed or eliminated.

Policy Challenges in the 1980s. With the growth of strategic nuclear arsenals in the U.S.S.R., the United States, and the P.R.C., and with the development of U.S. and P.R.C. cooperation to check Soviet military expansions, the entire globe is increasingly becoming one strategic theater. The military balance in East Asia is accordingly influenced by events in places like Poland and Iran as well as by the changing nuclear equation between the United States and the Soviet Union. A crucial question confronting the United States in the decade will be whether to further this trend by drawing closer to China to check Soviet designs in Asia and elsewhere, thus assuring the spillover of dangers and opportunities from East Asia to the rest of the world, or whether to maintain the status quo vis-à-vis the P.R.C. or perhaps move back from it as it tries to manipulate the two superpowers.

For its part, the U.S.S.R. will undoubtedly attempt to break the U.S.-P.R.C.-Japan–Western European community of interests, which its own adventurist policies has generated. Despite the setbacks that its attempt to build an "Asian Collective Security System" encountered in 1978 and 1979 when the P.R.C. was able to strengthen its links with Japan and the United States, the Soviet Union will undoubtedly continue to try to increase its influence in East Asia. Undergirding its efforts to do so will be an increasingly powerful military position in the area.

By 1980 the U.S.S.R. had built a strong and well-equipped force of roughly five hundred thousand troops (forty-six divisions) along China's borders and in Mongolia. These units, equipped with the latest tanks and self-propelled artillery, far outmatch the Chinese defense forces facing them. Soviet air assets in the region are also formidable, including the latest high performance bomber, the Backfire, which has the range to reach all of Japan and China from its central Asian and Far Eastern bases. Equally or more threatening for most of the countries of the region, the Soviet Far Eastern fleet is also a first-class modern force of increasing capability, bolstered by the use of Vietnamese bases. By the end of 1983, this fleet consisted of about 75 major surface combatants, 85 attack submarines, and 300 combat aircraft. A *Kiev* class vessel, the most recent and capable Soviet aircraft carrier, with both VTOL (vertical takeoff and landing) aircraft and ASW helicopters aboard, has been deployed in the region—as have been some of its newest ASW cruisers, destroyers, and frigates. Finally, the U.S.S.R. has not only fixed-site nuclear IRBMs in the region but also a number of the newest intermediate-range SS-20s.

Since the formidable Soviet force in the region, which has been built up over more than fifteen years, vastly exceeds defensive requirements and is still improving qualitatively, it should be clear that the purposes it is designed to serve are not minor or short-range ones. No doubt the U.S.S.R. has expected that by generating a favorable correlation of forces in the region it could exploit political opportunities as they occur, overawe the lesser Asian states as well as the P.R.C. and Japan, and position itself to interdict Western Pacific sea lanes in case of U.S.-Soviet hostilities. Only a substantial, continuing American presence in the area can frustrate these purposes.

A strong American presence would enable some Japanese rearmament, a flow of defense technology (and perhaps some military equipment) to the P.R.C. from the West, a continuing modernization of P.R.C. forces (including nuclear ones), and increased defense cooperation among the United States, Japan, and the P.R.C. to be factors in the balance. Given all these counter-influences, the U.S.S.R. may well decide that adventurism in the region is too dangerous.

Nevertheless, there are substantial dangers of large-scale conflict in the area in the coming decade. These stem mostly from the possibility that a localized conflict on one of the flanks, i.e., in either Korea or Southeast Asia, will spread. Political instability in either North or South Korea could generate local conflict there that would rapidly escalate. Over the longer term, i.e., toward the end of the decade, there is also the possibility of a further complexity, namely, the acquisition of nuclear weapons by the Republic of Korea. A major continuing challenge confronting the United States will be to provide the defense assurances and diplomatic suasion which will convince the South Koreans not to opt for nuclear weapons.

The fishing grounds and offshore oil fields along the Asian littoral will also be potential zones of conflict in the 1980s. The South China Sea is another area of increasing instability and possible resource competition. With all of this flammable material around, it will be surprising if the decade passes without serious conflict in the region.

DISCUSSION QUESTIONS

1. What are the principal goals of the P.R.C.? How would you rank its development goals versus the P.R.C. desire to obtain superpower status?

2. How do you think the P.R.C. views the rest of Asia, and how does the rest of Asia look at the P.R.C.?

3. How would one describe the East Asian system of nations of today? How are power relationships there changing, and how can equilibrium and stability be maintained?

4. What has led to the Sino-Soviet confrontation, how serious is it, and how does it impact on U.S.-P.R.C. relations?

5. Identify the national interests of the United States in Asia. What are the national interests of the P.R.C., and what, if any, mutual interests encourage U.S.-P.R.C. cooperation?

6. What type of role should the United States encourage the P.R.C. to play in Asia? Should the United States encourage the P.R.C. and Japan to work more closely together on various matters, or would a strong Sino-Japanese relationship upset the present equilibrium in Asia?

7. Should the United States be concerned about balancing its P.R.C. and Japanese relations, are they linked, or should the United States be primarily concerned only with bilateral ties and not attempt to balance the two?

8. How do you explain the various Southeast Asian states' fear of the P.R.C.?

9. What position do you think the United States should take on Kampuchea—to support the Sam-rin government or Pol Pot? Why?

10. If the R.O.K. leadership fails to widen its popular base, and public unrest there grows, what should the U.S. attitude be?

RECOMMENDED READING

Backrack, Stanley D. *Committee of One Million.* New York: Columbia University Press, 1976.

Barnett, A. Doak. *China and the Major Powers in East Asia.* Washington, D.C.: Brookings Institution, 1977.

Burt, Richard. "U.S. Strategy Focus Shifting from Europe to Pacific." *New York Times,* May 25, 1980, p. 3.

Clough, Ralph N. *East Asia and U.S. Security.* Washington, D.C.: Brookings Institution, 1975.

Downen, Robert L. *Of Grave Concern: U.S.-Taiwan Relations on the Threshold of the 1980s.* Washington, D.C.: Center for Strategic and International Studies, 1981.

Green, Marshall. "Breakthrough." *New York Times,* April 15, 1972, p. 31.

Holbrooke, Richard C. "Changing Perspectives of U.S. Policy in East Asia." *Department of State Bulletin,* August 1978, pp. 1–5.

Hsiao, Gene, and Witunski, Michael, eds. *Sino-American Normalization and Its Policy Implications.* New York: Frederick A. Praeger, 1983.

McCarroll, Lewis P. *Harry Truman's China Policy.* New York: New Viewpoints, 1976.

Muraoka, Kunio. "Japanese Security and the United States." Adelphi Papers, no. 95. London: International Institute for Strategic Studies, 1973.

U.S. Congress. Senate. Committee on Foreign Relations. *Hearings, U.S. Policy towards China and Taiwan.* 97th Cong., 2d sess. Washington, D.C.: U.S. Government Printing Office, 1982.

Weinstein, Franklin B., ed. *U.S.-Japan Relations and the Security of East Asia: The Next Decade.* Boulder, Colo.: Westview Press, 1978.

Whiting, Allen S. *The Chinese Calculus of Deterrence.* Ann Arbor: University of Michigan Press, 1975.

18

THE MIDDLE EAST

Prior to the 1967 Arab-Israeli War, U.S. interests in the Middle East,* while important, were relatively minor compared with those in Europe and Asia. The positions of Turkey and Iran on the southern border of the Soviet Union gave them a certain strategic value in the context of containment policy, and attempts were made to incorporate them into the network of Western alliances. For essentially moral and domestic political reasons, the United States played an influential role in the creation of Israel in 1947–48, and after 1948 it remained committed to the security and prosperity of the new state. At the same time, largely for trade and balance-of-payment reasons, the U.S. worked to protect and improve the position of American companies developing the oil resources of the Persian Gulf and North Africa. Finally, the U.S. sought to preserve overflight and transit rights through the Middle East to areas of greater strategic importance.[1]

Since the interests of the United States in the area at that time were limited, its direct involvement in Middle Eastern affairs also tended to be limited. Regional crises that threatened to affect U.S. security interests, such as the Soviet occupation of northwestern Iran (1945–47), the Suez War of 1956, and the Cyprus Crisis of 1967, occasionally provoked a vigorous response. For the most part, however, the United States sought to escape becoming entangled in local affairs, avoiding, for example, the role of principal arms supplier to Israel or the Arab states. Generally, American policy-makers evaluated specific events in the Middle East in terms of how they affected U.S. interests elsewhere and reacted to them—or ignored them—accordingly. Little effort

*Middle East is an imprecise term, used to denote the general area of predominantly Moslem culture on the southern and eastern shores of the Mediterranean and on both sides of the Persian (or Arabian) Gulf. The term is used in the chapter to include Egypt, Israel, Jordan, Lebanon, Syria, Turkey, Iraq, Saudi Arabia, Kuwait, Bahrein, Qatar, the United Arab Emirates, Iran, Oman, Yemen Arab Republic, the People's Democratic Republic of Yemen, and Sudan. We do not include the North African states of Libya, Tunisia, Algeria, and Morocco, which are sometimes so listed, nor Afghanistan or Pakistan, which are also sometimes included.

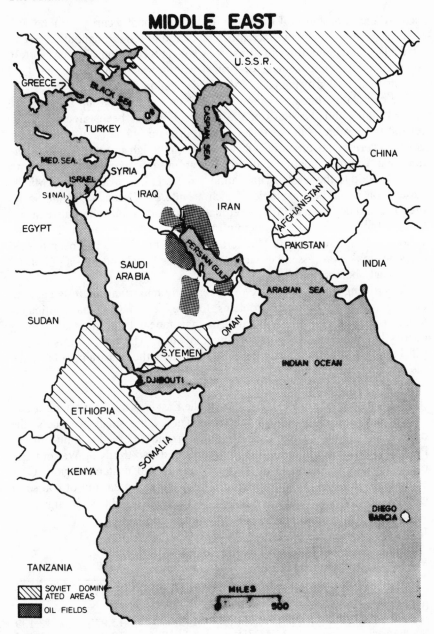

MIDDLE EAST

SOVIET DOMIN-
ATED AREAS

OIL FIELDS

MILES

FIG. 18.1

was expended on dealing with the underlying causes of such events or on developing a comprehensive policy for the region as a whole.

Starting in the mid 1960s, however, a series of political and economic changes in both the Middle East and the rest of the world combined to increase the importance of the region to U.S. national security. Among such changes were the enormous increase in oil consumption throughout the world, particularly in the industrialized nations, Israeli occupation of Arab lands in the 1967 war, announcement of British withdrawal from the Persian Gulf area in 1968, and growing role of the Soviet Union in the area.

The cumulative impact of those changes on the relationship between the United States and the states of the Middle East has been threefold. First, several U.S. interests in the region, which previously had been of only marginal concern to government policy-makers (although not necessarily to the domestic American political and economic groups most concerned with them), were elevated to the level of vital national interests. The availability of Middle Eastern oil is the best example of such an interest. Second, growing Soviet presence and declining British power made it important that alternative means be found to protect these newly important interests in the region. Third, the various U.S. interests in the Middle East, which previously had been treated by policy-makers as essentially separate, such as Israel and Persian Gulf oil, increasingly became intertwined.

The growing interdependence of increasingly important interests has produced some of the thorniest problems, for the United States has continually found itself trying to reconcile interests that appear to be mutually contradictory but that must be pursued simultaneously. The bulk of this chapter will be devoted to examining those interests and the constraints that make the challenge so difficult.

Oil Interests. As table 18.1 shows, the Middle East is by far the most important source of world oil. Although Syria and Turkey are small producers, the overwhelming bulk of the area's production and reserves is found in the Persian Gulf area. Three-fourths of Japan's and two-thirds of Western Europe's oil imports originate in this most unruly and unstable region. Only about one-third of U.S. imports comes from the gulf area, but of course, if gulf oil exports were cut off because of regional hostilities, insurgencies,

Table 18.1 World Oil Production (in thousands of barrels daily)

Region	1982	1979	1978	1977
Middle East	12,780	21,857	21,475	22,434
U.S.S.R., Eastern Europe, and China	14,700	14,364	13,970	13,139
North America	11,750	12,010	12,022	11,406
Africa	4,580	6,704	6,151	6,237
South and Central America	6,490	5,558	4,984	4,632
Far East and Australia	2,730	2,974	2,833	2,799
Western Europe	3,040	2,380	1,798	1,395
Total	56,070	65,847	63,233	62,042

Source: Oil and Gas in 1979, Shell Oil Co., April 1980, and *Statistical Review of World Energy, 1982*, British Petroleum, 1982.

terrorism, or a variety of other reasons, the impact on world energy supplies would be severe, and Japanese and Western Europeans would be competing with Americans for supplies located elsewhere.

Not only is the gulf region overwhelmingly predominant in the world's supply picture at present, it will continue to play this vital role throughout the 1980s (and perhaps even to the end of the century). Roughly two-thirds of the world's proven reserves are found in the area. Moreover, none of the significant producers—Saudi Arabia, Iraq, Kuwait, Iran, and the United Arab Emirates—is a large consumer. Hence, over 90 percent of the oil produced there is available for export. Modestly growing production from Mexico, China, Egypt, the North Sea, and other non–Persian Gulf sources during the 1980s will probably not add much more to world exports than will be needed to meet minimal growth in world consumption, leaving almost unchanged the present massive dependence of the West on gulf supplies.

The West's energy stake in the Middle East provides a new dimension to its geopolitical competition with the Soviet Union. As James Schlesinger has

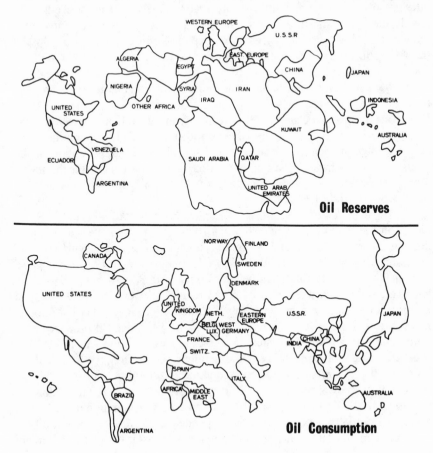

FIG. 18.2

recently written, "This larger dimension places in proper perspective such matters as fuel shortages and economic performance—for it has the power to determine the political destiny of mankind. . . . The underlying implications are stark. Soviet control of the oil tap in the Middle East would mean the end of the world as we have known it since 1945 and of the association of free nations."[2]

American oil companies have been actively involved in the Middle East since 1933, when Standard Oil of California obtained its first concession in Saudi Arabia. By 1966 the United States had invested slightly over $3 billion in oil operations throughout the Middle East and North Africa. That investment was extremely profitable. In 1966 alone, U.S. income from direct investments in oil operations in the Middle East amounted to over $1 billion. Such profits in turn played a major role in maintaining the favorable balance of payments that the United States enjoyed during most of that period.[3] Yet, despite deriving substantial benefits from the revenues obtained from the production and sale of Middle East oil, the U.S. economy made relatively little use of the oil itself. Until the late 1960s, America's energy needs were largely met by domestic oil, gas, and coal production—supplemented to a moderate degree by oil imported from Canada and Latin America. Most of the oil produced by U.S. companies in the Middle East was sold in Western Europe and Japan.

By 1965, however, petroleum consumption was beginning to rise rapidly throughout the world. For example, in the decade between 1964 and 1974, U.S. consumption rose nearly 60 percent—from 10 million barrels per day (mb/d) to 16.2 mb/d. During the same period, Japan's daily consumption rose even more dramatically—from 1.5 mb/d to 5.3 mb/d. Consumption in the industrialized countries of Western Europe also rose steeply.[4] Furthermore, a number of developing countries began to use significant amounts of oil in their efforts to industrialize.

The rapid increase in world oil consumption after 1965 affected U.S. interests in the Middle East in two ways. First, domestic American oil production could not be expanded rapidly enough to keep pace with growing domestic consumption—indeed, U.S. production peaked in 1970 and began a slow decline thereafter until oil began to flow from Alaska in mid 1977 and halted the slide, at least temporarily. The United States resorted increasingly to imported oil to satisfy its growing appetite, moving from 3.4. mb/d of imports in 1970 to 6.2 mb/d in 1973 to 8.2 mb/d in 1978. Since oil production by traditional foreign suppliers such as Venezuela and Canada was limited, an ever larger share of America's exploding imports came from the Middle East. As of 1979, the United States imported about 8.2 mb/d or approximately 43 percent of its daily oil needs, with 25 percent of that total of 8.2 mb/d coming from the Middle East. In the early 1980s, however, consumption in the United States has actually decreased, as has dependence on Middle Eastern oil. In 1982 the United States had cut its imports to 4.9 mb/d, of which 12 percent came from the Middle East.[5]

Although the U.S. economy would not collapse were it to be deprived of imports, it would suffer severe dislocations that could lead to equally severe political and social disorders. As indicated above, key allies such as Japan and the Western European countries are far more dependent on Middle Eastern oil; a serious interruption in their supply of oil would bring their literal economic collapse. Since the economic health and political stability of Western Europe and Japan are vital to U.S. national security, it is crucial to us that they, even more than the United States itself, have access to adequate supplies of Middle East oil.

Second, the rapid increase in world oil consumption after 1965 fundamentally altered the conditions governing the production and distribution of oil. Before then, oil companies had been able to ensure that the supply of oil slightly exceeded demand. The "buyer's market" so created enabled the companies to hold down the price of oil in the consuming countries, thus maximizing sales and profits. The excess productive capacity preserved by the companies also enabled them to cope with temporary disruptions of production, such as Prime Minister Mossadegh's nationalization of the Iranian oil fields in 1951. During the 1950s and early 1960s, the companies sought to preserve their favorable market position by opening up new fields, mostly in the Middle East. By 1970, however, the oil companies were not increasing the supply of oil fast enough to keep up with escalating demand, and competition among consumers for any available oil intensified.

Producing nations gradually realized that the market for oil had become a "seller's market" and took advantage of the new conditions to nationalize the oil business and to raise prices. Between 1968 and 1975, the average price of oil increased from less than $2 per barrel to roughly $11 per barrel.[6]* Most of this increase occurred at the end of 1973 and in early 1974 when prices were quadrupled following an embargo by Arab producers against the United States (and the Netherlands) because of support to Israel during the 1973 Arab-Israeli War. In the United States and other importing nations, such increases led to serious balance-of-payments problems and contributed to inflation. U.S. policy-makers belatedly realized that they had a strong interest in ensuring reliable access to Middle East oil at acceptable prices.

The phenomenal rise in the price of oil after 1968 also had the effect of transferring unprecedented sums of money to the governments of the Middle East oil-producing countries. For example, Saudi Arabian oil revenue rose more than twentyfold from $655 million in 1965 to over $28 billion in 1974. Iranian oil revenue rose from $522 million per year to over $20 billion per year during the same period.[7]† After the second major period of oil price hikes, namely 1979–80, when prices more than doubled again, Middle Eastern

---

*These were average prices for high-quality Persian Gulf oil. Actual prices varied due to sulphur content, specific gravity, and transportation costs.
†Total Middle East oil revenues in 1974 exceeded $84 billion.

surpluses again shot up; Saudi oil revenues in 1980 approached $100 billion. But marked decreases in consumption and the glutted oil market of the early 1980s have led to reduced Saudi revenues as of late.

The United States has an important interest in ensuring that such enormous sums are used constructively, in ways that eventually will bring them back into the world economy in a stabilizing fashion. Were such funds not effectively "recycled," international monetary chaos would ensue.

Even more dangerous to national security than the purely economic dimensions of the West's energy import dependence is the likelihood of interruptions in the flow of oil from such a turbulent area as the Middle East. Whether because of intraregional wars, revolutionary upheavals, embargos, or Soviet intrusions, exports from the area could well be curtailed—conceivably even eliminated—during the course of the 1980s. The loss of nearly 5 mb/d of gulf exports in early 1979, as a consequence of the Iranian revolution, was in considerable part made up after a brief hiatus by other producers expanding their output. Even so, the temporary shortage had a major adverse impact on oil prices, inflation, and international economic and monetary stability.

The Iran-Iraq war that broke out in September 1980 posed a fresh threat to oil supplies, for both sides attacked the other's production and refinery facilities. Despite the consequent loss of about 3 mb/d of exports, oil was initially plentiful, for there was unprecedented stocks on hand throughout the world. Unless the damage proves irreparable or hostilities spread to other producers, these supply interruptions seem manageable.

Another serious interruption of several million barrels a day could not, however, be made up so readily; moreover, there is a possibility that a reduction in supply from the gulf would be on such a large scale that making it up by expansions elsewhere would be physically impossible. The gulf's 12–13 mb/d of exports represent roughly 40 percent of the noncommunist world's total oil consumption and 60 percent of the oil in world trade. Effective closure of the twenty-eight-mile-wide Strait of Hormuz at the gulf's entrance, which might well occur in several contingencies, or even loss of Saudi Arabia's 5 or so mb/d of exports would bring chaos to the economies of Europe and Japan.

The oil supplies of the Middle East would likely be crucial in wartime. Even in peacetime, NATO forces consume close to 1 mb/d of oil products, or about 3 percent of the NATO nations' total economic needs. The wartime figure would likely be at least 2 mb/d, or twice the peacetime rate, for the defense forces themselves, above and beyond what is required for essential civilian purposes. If we assume that, with maximum fuel substitution and conservation efforts, a wartime civilian economy can produce two-thirds of normal peacetime rates of oil use, then about 22 mb/d would be required for this purpose in the alliance as a whole. The total comes to 24 mb/d: roughly three times current U.S. production and about double the present production in all of NATO. The West could not wage war over any substantial period without considerable amounts of imported oil.

Assuring oil supplies of the magnitude needed during a major conventional war of even relatively brief duration is a massive undertaking. Of course, if hostilities were brief enough, the problem could be handled by drawing on stockpiles and reserves—assuming, that is, that they exist in sufficient amounts and that such tempting targets would survive enemy destruction efforts.

In the case of general hostilities in Europe, even assuming that NATO military stocks there survive, it will still be necessary to ship massive amounts of jet fuel, gasoline, and diesel fuel into the area if hostilities extend beyond thirty days or so. Logistics planners estimate, for instance, that over 100 million barrels of petroleum products would have to be moved across the Atlantic in the initial months of a war. Attrition in transatlantic oil convoys is bound to be severe, and thus considerably more than 100 million barrels would have to start the journey.

If a conflict in Europe lasted more than two or three months or if it spread to other theaters, the problem of acquiring and safeguarding the passage of African and Middle Eastern crude and products would become acute. The rapid growth of Soviet naval power makes it questionable if present combined NATO fleets could manage the safeguarding task.

Under wartime conditions would there be adequate petroleum supplies for essential civilian needs? With austerity, its own production, and some continuing access to Western Hemisphere supplies, the U.S. economy could perhaps manage. The Western European allies are in far worse condition. To function effectively, they would need something like 10 mb/d for essential civilian requirements. Yet they now produce only 4 or 5 mb/d—much of which may well be destroyed early in a conflict.[8]

Strategic Interests. Since World War II, the Middle East has been an area of strategic competition between the United States and the Soviet Union, just as it was an area of competition between Britain and Russia during much of the nineteenth century. Traditionally, the primary U.S. strategic goal in the Middle East has been simply to keep the Soviets out. For their part, the Soviet designs upon the Persian Gulf area long predate the predominance of oil in international politics. They were tellingly expressed by Soviet Foreign Minister V. M. Molotov in 1940 at the time of the Ribbentrop-Molotov accord, when the Nazis and the Soviet Union temporarily agreed on their respective shares of the world they planned to dissect. Molotov's statement at the time was that "the area south of Batum and Baku in the general direction of the Persian Gulf is recognized as the center of the aspirations of the Soviet Union."[9] Unsuccessful Russian efforts immediately after World War II to extend their hegemony in that direction by annexing territories in eastern Turkey and western Iran provided one of the opening volleys of the cold war. The rise of oil as the engine of industrialization has merely added an important dimension to this longstanding Russian aspiration for direct access to the warm waters of the Persian Gulf and the Indian Ocean.

American policies in the Middle East have largely responded over time to the perceived Soviet threat. Between 1945 and 1955, the greatest threat seemed to come from direct Soviet military and political pressure on the countries along its southern border. Consequently, both Turkey and Iran were given large amounts of military and economic aid. Turkey was incorporated into NATO in 1952, and in 1955 both Iran and Turkey joined the Baghdad Pact.*

After the Egypt-Czechoslovakia arms deal of 1955 and the Suez Crisis of 1956, another threat came to the fore: internal subversion fomented by the Soviet Union and its "clients" in the region. The United States responded in several ways. It continued to provide aid and pressed for internal reforms that would reduce the appeal of subversive doctrines. As Soviet influence grew in the area, particularly in Egypt, economic assistance was increasingly used in the competition for position. However, the most dramatic response to the perceived threat of Soviet penetration of the area came in 1957 when the United States promulgated the Eisenhower Doctrine.[10] In it the United States pledged that it would come to the aid, with military force if necessary, of any Middle East country threatened by the forces of "international communism." The doctrine served as the basis for committing U.S. troops to Lebanon in 1958 at the request of President Chamoun.

After the 1967 Arab-Israeli War, a further threat came from the massive quantities of conventional weapons, accompanied by Soviet technicians and military personnel, which the U.S.S.R. sent to sympathetic regimes such as Egypt, Syria, and Iraq. The United States responded by building up the military power of its own friends in the region: Israel, Iran and, to a much lesser degree, Saudi Arabia and Jordan.

When Britain announced in 1968 the planned withdrawal of its small but important military forces in the gulf region, it was apparent to all that instability would be the likely result—with a probable strengthening of Soviet influence. Accordingly, the United States—by this time embroiled in Vietnam—sought to bolster the principal friendly states in the area, namely Saudi Arabia and Iran, with the expectation that they would provide a stabilizing influence. This "two pillar policy" was shaky from the start, for the Shah of Iran had his own ideas of reestablishing Persian predominance in the region, and the Saudis, despite their economic and cultural influence, lacked the strength to protect themselves, let alone help protect others. Moreover, as the events a decade later would show, the Iranian pillar, while outwardly sound, was fatally weak at its center and could not bear the policy weight and hopes placed upon it.

The Western desire to contain and minimize Soviet influence in the Middle East has been intensified by the Soviet naval build-up in the Indian Ocean and by the Soviet role in the Horn of Africa. Since approximately 1970, American efforts to limit Soviet influence in the area have been increasingly tempered by reluctance to become involved in a military confrontation as a

---

*The original members of the Baghdad Pact were Turkey, Iran, Pakistan, and Great Britain. Although instrumental in creating the pact, the United States never became a formal member. Iraq withdrew from the pact after the 1958 revolution.

result of conflict in the Middle East. A series of events, starting with the commitment of Soviet pilots and missile troops to Egypt in 1970 after the war of attrition and including President Nixon's global alert on October 25, 1973, apparently convinced both U.S. and Soviet policy-makers that the danger of such a confrontation is very real.[11]

U.S. Interests in Israel. Since 1948, one of the most enduring features of U.S. policy in the Middle East has been a commitment to the security of Israel. This has been true despite periodic contentions between the two nations, such as that which occurred when Israel invaded Egypt in 1956, or when Israel pressed ahead with settlements on the West Bank of the Jordan River after the Camp David peace accords at the end of the 1970s. Israel has been characterized by its supporters as a reliable ally and a democratic bridgehead in an otherwise anti-American, undemocratic region. Alternatively, some have described it as a regional police officer and potential U.S. surrogate that can be used to keep racial, pro-Soviet states, such as Nasser's Egypt had been, in line. Sometimes associated with both these rationales for U.S. policy in the area is the view that, in a Middle East crisis, the United States could use Israeli military facilities if need be. Finally, continued U.S. support for Israel has been justified as essential to maintaining the credibility of U.S. commitments abroad.[12]

While all these points contain elements of truth, the intensity of the American commitment to Israel's security is often more a function of U.S. domestic politics than strategic reasoning. (Only, for example, in a case of U.S.-U.S.S.R. hostilities would Israeli forces and military facilities prove a major regional asset for the West; in other conflict scenarios, U.S. military links with Israel would likely generate far more problems than solutions in this overwhelmingly Moslem region.) Domestic support for Israel exists in two forms. First, and clearly important, is the broad, general sympathy for Israel which characterizes a large portion of the American population. This basic view tends to be shared by both policy-makers and their constituents, and is usually independent of any specific developments in the Middle East—although Israel's 1979–80 policies concerning Palestinians' rights and Jewish settlements in the so-called West Bank area, and the 1982 Israeli invasion of Lebanon clearly eroded that base somewhat.

The second source of U.S. domestic support for Israel is the highly publicized Jewish lobby. The Jewish lobby is a coalition of social, cultural, and political groups which seeks to inform American opinion and influence U.S. policies on subjects of particular interest to the American Jewish community, the most important of which is U.S. support for Israel. Although representing only a tiny portion of the American population, the lobby is highly organized, well financed, and extraordinarily persuasive.[13] (There are other "ethnic" lobbies in Washington as well, such as the Greek lobby that succeeded in cutting off American military aid to Turkey, but these other groups are pale shadows in terms of influence.)

Since 1948, American policies in support of Israel have changed character. Between 1948 and 1966, the United States provided Israel with large amounts of financial and economic aid but relatively little military aid. At the same time, it repeatedly sought to draw Israel and its Arab neighbors into cooperative technical agreements that could serve as a basis for eventual coexistence. In 1966, responding to Israeli fears of increased Soviet arms deliveries to Egypt and Syria, the United States altered its arms supply policy by agreeing to provide Israel with large quantities of modern military equipment. Despite its overwhelming victory in 1967, Israel was incapable of using its military superiority to obtain a secure peace; rather, as the Europeans—who had been its principal suppliers—withdrew support, its demands on the United States for support increased. During the 1973 Arab-Israeli War, Israel received an emergency package of $2 billion worth of U.S. arms, some of which were taken directly from U.S. operational reserves in Germany.[14] Although by 1974 the United States again was using its influence to obtain a mutually acceptable settlement to the Arab-Israeli conflict, it also continued to supply large quantities of military aid to Israel.* (Secretary of State Kissinger's effort to use American arms aid as a bargaining lever with Israel during negotiation of the Sinai peace accords in this period [1974] illustrated both the importance of the instrument and the strength of the Jewish lobby: during the bargaining Israel's supporters obtained the signatures of seventy-four U.S. senators instructing the secretary of state to stand "firmly with Israel in the search for peace in future negotiations, and that this promise is the basis of the current reassessment of U.S. policy in the Middle East.")[15]

Since the 1973 war, a primary Israeli security goal has been to acquire sufficient military resources to conduct a successful, three-week "war of annihilation" against the combined forces of Egypt, Syria, Jordan, Iraq, and Saudi Arabia without having to rely on continuing external (i.e., United States) support. By 1977, U.S. military aid had enabled Israel essentially to achieve that goal. This assurance of supply, combined with Israel's military predominance in the region seriously reduced the possibility of American pressure toward diplomatic flexibility, as did the subsequent removal of Egypt as a possible opponent, and indeed gave Israel the option of redressing any perceived changes in the regional balance of power by launching a "preventive war" without having to worry about short-term U.S. supply pressure or restraint.[16]

The June 1982 Israeli invasion of Lebanon was in part the result of this absence of a basis for American pressure on Israel. Israeli forces invaded southern Lebanon, proceeded to the outskirts of Beirut, and forced the

---

*Part of the Israeli price for cooperating with Secretary Kissinger's step-by-step diplomacy in 1973–74 was a U.S. commitment to substantial increases in arms deliveries. Israeli strategists currently anticipate receiving $2.5 billion worth of U.S. military assistance annually up to approximately 1990. See McLaurin et al., *Foreign Policy Making in the Middle East* (New York: Praeger, 1977), pp. 213–14.

withdrawal of PLO forces from Beirut, all without recourse to outside military support. At the same time, though, controversy over civilian casualties during the invasion and the utilization of U.S. weapons restricted by agreement to defensive purposes only strained U.S.-Israeli relations. It remains to be seen whether the Israeli invasion and sustained occupation of Lebanon leads toward, or away from, the long-term objective of a negotiated peace settlement.

Factors Affecting Regional Stability. The ability of the United States to pursue its interests in the Middle East is affected significantly by a number of factors within the region. Inter-Arab tensions, the persistent Arab-Israeli conflict, the Iranian revolution and the resurgence of Islam—all have greatly complicated U.S. policies for the region. However, such highly visible issues are only part of the problem faced by U.S. policy-makers in the Middle East. Underlying, and to a certain degree causing, such issues is the general political and social instability that characterizes much of the region.

Sources of Instability. Most Middle Eastern states are relatively recent creations, although the peoples living within them may have been there for a very long time. Many of the states were either created or significantly altered in a highly arbitrary fashion by the European powers that dominated the region after World War I.* Furthermore, the political systems set up to govern the new entities often owed more to the values and ideas of the Europeans, or to those of small groups of local "modernizers" who sought to emulate the Europeans, than they did to those of the vast bulk of the people governed by them. Thus, monarchies were established in Egypt and Iraq while Syria was turned into a secular republic. Only in the Arabian Peninsula and, to a much lesser extent, Iran, did traditional political institutions maintain their vitality.

The way most Middle Eastern states were formed created inconsistencies that led to major problems once European control was removed. Borders had generally been drawn to satisfy the interests of the European powers and not according to significant local criteria.† As a result, some ethnic or cultural groups that traditionally conceived of themselves as a community were split among two or more artificial political entities. In other cases, cohesive linguistic or religious minorities were incorporated into states dominated by their

---

*For example, Iraq was formed in 1920 when the former Ottoman provinces of Baghdad, Basra, and Mosul were granted to Great Britain as a League of Nations mandate. It did not become an independent state until 1932. Prior to World War I, Iraq was a geographic term with virtually no political significance.

†Two cases of such arbitrarily drawn boundaries were to become particularly troublesome. First, Ottoman Syria (predominantly Sunni Moslem Arabs) was carved up into the states of Palestine, Transjordan, Syria, and Lebanon, with a sizable part also incorporated into Turkey. Second, the substantial Kurdish community was split up among Iran, Turkey, and Iraq. Kurds thus became a dominated minority in all three states.

traditional antagonists. Bedouin tribesmen and settled farmers with no tradition of cooperation were lumped together in the same state. Trading patterns
and tribal migration routes were disrupted. As a result, the level of national
cohesion and political solidarity in the states of the Middle East tended to be
low. In all parts of the region, the primary focuses of loyalty were the family,
village, and tribe. Beyond that, ties of regionalism, ethnic and cultural solidarity and religion competed vigorously with the new states for popular allegiance.

The problems created by such conflicting loyalties were accentuated by the
growth of intense feelings of nationalism which had spread throughout the
region by the end of World War II. Although virtually all the nationalists
could agree that the corrupt, European-dominated old order had to be destroyed, their conflicting loyalties made it difficult for them to develop alternative systems to replace it. Some nationalists favored creating a state based
on an Islamic revival that eventually would incorporate all Moslems from
West Africa to Indonesia. Others thought in terms of a pan-Arab movement
that would unite all Arabs—Moslem and Christian—into a single state. Still
others sought merely to rejuvenate the existing states on either an Islamic or
a secular basis. No nationalist group was willing to relinquish the power that
it had obtained to other nationalist groups whose ideas differed in any way
from its own.[17]

Such basic disagreement over the legitimate scope, goals, and methods of
political activity had two important effects on the new nationalist regimes.
First, it became virtually impossible for such regimes to create political institutions capable of transferring power or resolving differences over basic
policies. At the same time, such disagreements ensured that the constituency
of each significant version of nationalism reached beyond the boundaries of
any state it happened to control. For example, the Ba'th Party, which ruled
Syria in the mid 1960s, had to cope with a large group of Syrian nationalists
whose primary loyalty was to President Nasser of Egypt; but they also enjoyed
the support of many sympathizers in Iraq, Jordan, and Lebanon. (The generalizations in this entire section apply widely in the Moslem portions of the
region, i.e., to the vast bulk of the area; Israel had a unique origin and has
an entirely different set of internal political dynamics.)

Such conditions contributed to the insecurity of the new nationalist leaders.
The absence of widely accepted political institutions tended to place a premium on conspiratorial methods and violence as ways to obtain political
power. Leaders sought to provide themselves with a measure of security by
forcefully suppressing their opposition while at the same time presenting the
best possible set of nationalist credentials to their people. In practice, that
meant taking a stronger stand in favor of rapid economic development and
against foreign influence, Israel, and the remaining "traditional" regimes in
the region than did any rival. However, any steps taken by a Middle Eastern
leader to increase his domestic legitimacy by such methods automatically

Table 18.2 Principal Regional Forces in the Middle East

Country/Service	Regular Forces	Reserves	Main Armament
Saudi Arabia (pop. 8,100,000)			
Army	35,000	25,500 NG	1600 tks. & AFVs
Navy	2,200	6,500 frntr. guards	9 maj. surf. ships
Air Force	15,000		128 cbt. acft.
Egypt (pop. 42,600,000)			
Army	320,000	300,000	2130 tks. 3100 AFV 1800 arty.
Navy	20,000	15,000	12 atk. subs 27 maj. surf. ships
Air Force	27,000	20,000	429 cbt. acft.
Iran (pop. 39,100,000)			
Army	150,000	400,000	1210 tks. 580 AFV 1200 arty.
Navy	10,000		7 maj. surf. ships
Air Force	35,000		90 cbt. acft.
Iraq (pop. 13,600,000)			
Army	300,000	75,000	2,300 tks. 3,000 AFV 800 arty.
Navy	4,250		8 maj. surf. ships
Air Force	38,000		330 cbt. acft.
Israel (pop. 4,000,000)			
Army	135,000	315,000	3,600 tks. 4,000 AFV 800 arty.
Navy	9,000	1,000	3 atk. subs. 30 maj. surf. ships
Air Force	30,000	7,000	634 cbt. acft.

Table 18.2   *(cont.)*

Country/Service	Regular Forces	Reserves	Main Armament
Jordan (pop. 3,155,000)			
Army	65,000	35,000 (all services)	539 tks. 882 AFV 242 arty.
Navy	300		9 pl. cft.
Air Force	7,500		94 cbt. acft.
Syria (pop. 8,900,000)			
Army	170,000	100,000	3,990 tks. 1,600 AFV 2,600 arty.
Navy	2,500	2,500	20 maj. surf. ships
Air Force	1,500		450 cbt. acft.
North Yemen (pop. 7,200,000)			
Army	30,000	20,000 paramilitary	714 tks. 564 AFV 300 arty.
Navy	550		8 ptl. cft.
Air Force	1,500		450 cbt. acft.
South Yemen (pop. 1,955,000)			
Army	22,000	15,000 paramilitary	474 tks. 320 AFV 310 arty.
Navy	1,000		6 maj. surf ships
Air Force	3,000		114 cbt. acft.

Source: International Institute for Strategic Studies, *The Military Balance, 1982–1983* (London, IISS, 1982). For abbreviations, see table 17.1.

posed a threat to the internal security of his neighbors, who usually were trying to build support in the same way. As a result, minor incidents and differences often took on much greater importance than was warranted. Border clashes and attempts to subvert rival regimes, either through propaganda or the distribution of arms and subsidies to potential dissidents, became common.[18] Hostilities between and among Arab states have been much more frequent, for example, than Arab-Israeli wars since World War II.

Such difficulties were further enhanced by the tensions caused by economic change. After World War II, even the most traditional Middle Eastern governments found it necessary to advocate far-reaching economic development programs, if for no other reason than that of self-defense against nationalist pressure. In countries like Egypt, Iran, and Turkey, such programs involved major land reforms, the development of heavy industry, and the growth of state ownership and bureaucratic controls over the economy. Although such changes may have seemed necessary, they inevitably made heavy demands on the scarce human and natural resources of the countries involved. Previously privileged groups, such as large landowners, naturally resented the reduction in their power which such programs caused. Less privileged groups often were hit hard by increased taxes, scarcities, and heavy inflation that seemed inevitably to accompany the new economic policies. The dissatisfaction created by such a situation could easily be converted into political unrest.*

In the oil producing countries, the problems caused by economic development were somewhat different but no less acute. The vast funds generated by the oil industry enabled them to initiate major economic development programs profoundly destabilizing to the traditional societies and political norms that characterized most of them. Moreover, the shortage of skilled technicians and laborers in the producing countries forced their governments to bring in many foreigners. By the latter 1970s, Americans, Europeans, Egyptians, and Palestinians played key roles in the economies, bureaucracies, and educational systems of the oil producing countries of the Arabian Peninsula. Yemenis, Pakistanis, and Indians made up much of the unskilled labor force. The role of foreigners in Iraq has been far less pervasive but still important. In Iran, the pressure of large numbers of highly visible Westerners was one of the key precipitants of the revival of militant Islam and the destruction of the monarchy.

One of the most profound and persistent of the many regional problems in the Middle East is the Arab-Israeli conflict. The special relationship between the United States and Israel, the universal antipathy of both nationalist and traditionalist Arabs to Zionism, and the high level of militarization which characterizes the conflict all make it worthy of special mention.

The Arab-Israeli conflict has its recent roots in the late nineteenth century, when increasingly large numbers of Jews sought to escape from oppression in Eastern Europe by emigrating to Palestine. In 1917, prominent British

---

*For example, between 1951 and 1958, the Iraqi monarchy devoted most of its development funds to extensive flood control projects. Although such projects were of tremendous long-term benefit to Iraq, the failure of the regime to devote more funds to conspicuous short-term projects such as public housing was an important stimulus behind the 1958 revolution.

Zionists, led by Chaim Weizmann, induced the British foreign secretary, Lord Balfour, to issue an open letter pledging the British government to "view with favor the establishment in Palestine of a national home for the Jewish people."[19] (Further intensive lobbying by the World Zionist Organization obtained the inclusion of the Balfour Declaration in the text of the League of Nations Mandate for Palestine granted to Great Britain in 1920.)

The British government delegated the task of supervising the establishment of the Jewish national home to the World Zionist Organization, which created a number of special agencies to do so.* Between 1922 and 1946, largely as a result of their efforts, the Jewish population of Palestine rose from 84,000, comprising 11 percent of the total population, to 583,000, comprising 31 percent of the total. Jewish landholdings during the same period increased from 2.6 percent to 7 percent of the total area of Palestine, and consisted almost entirely of fertile agricultural land along the coast and in Galilee.[20] Inevitably, in many cases the growth of the Jewish community was achieved at the expense of the Arab population of Palestine—or at least the Arabs intensely believed so.

Arab resentment, combined with a growing awareness of ultimate Jewish political aims, led to a series of bloody riots culminating in the Arab Revolt of 1936. Although the British eventually crushed the revolt, many Jewish settlers were not satisfied with the zeal shown by the British authorities in protecting Jewish interests. By 1938, several clandestine Jewish military groups had been created which conducted terrorist operations against both the Arabs and the British.[21] By 1947, the level of violence had risen to such a degree that Britain decided to give up its mandate and turn the problem over to the UN.

On November 28, 1947, with leadership from the United States, the UN voted to partition Palestine into two states. The projected Jewish state was to contain 55 percent of the total area of Palestine (the population of the Jewish area was 56 percent Jewish and 44 percent Arab) while the projected Arab state occupied 45 percent of the land (of which the population was 98 percent Arab and 2 percent Jewish). After much debate, Jewish leaders, led by David Ben-Gurion, accepted the UN plan and launched a series of military operations designed to consolidate areas placed under Jewish control, while Palestinian leaders rejected the plan and began to attack isolated Jewish settlements.[22] The conflict quickly escalated into a full-scale war, with the

---

*Among them were the Jewish Agency, which organized the recruitment, transportation, and settlement of Jewish immigrants in Palestine; the Jewish National Fund, which purchased and administered the land on which the immigrants settled; and the Histadrut (General Federation of Labor), which constructed housing and public services for the new immigrants and operated a number of factories designed to utilize their skills. See Efraim Torgovnik, "Israel: The Persistent Elite," in *Political Elites and Political Development in the Middle East,* ed. Frank Tachau (Cambridge, Mass.: Schenkman, 1975), pp. 221–29.

armies of five neighboring Arab states intervening haphazardly on the side of the Palestinians while the Israelis obtained sizable quantities of arms and unofficial military assistance from the United States and Europe.[23]* By April 1949, Israel had defeated the combined Arab forces and in the process gained control of a great deal of territory that had not been assigned to it in the original partition plan. Furthermore, over seven hundred thousand Palestinian Arabs had been expelled or fled from their homes and were living as stateless refugees in neighboring Arab countries.

The 1948 Arab-Israeli War was ended by an armistice signed on July 20, 1949. The issues that divided the two groups, however, were by no means resolved by the declaration of Israeli independence or the ending of hostilities. Many Arabs felt that the very existence of Israel was a violation of Arab rights and wanted it destroyed as soon as possible. Other desired to gain revenge for the defeat suffered in 1948. Palestinians in particular wanted to return to the lands that they had left in 1948. Such feelings generated a unremitting hostility toward Israel, leading to continual raids and terrorist attacks on it. In 1964, the Palestine Liberation Organization (PLO) was created and promptly began conducting the same type of terrorist campaign against Israel that the Israelis had conducted against the British and Arabs before 1948.

On the other hand, some Israelis were not satisfied with the amount of territory occupied by Israeli forces in 1948. These ultranationalist and religious party elements desired to extend Jewish control over all of biblical Israel. Other Israelis felt that it was essential to seize and retain additional Arab land in order to settle the new waves of Jewish immigrants which were expected to arrive in due course and to provide space for future defense of urban centers. Consequently, they were unwilling to make territorial or legal concessions to the Arabs—particularly concerning the Palestinians. Israel responded to Arab threats and harassment with punitive raids against neighboring Arab states in the hope that such displays of superior force eventually would compel Arab leaders to accept the presence of Israel on Israeli terms.[24]

As each side sought, and eventually obtained, outside military assistance to strengthen its position, the level of hostilities rose. Major wars were fought in 1956, 1967, 1973, and again in 1982. Although Israel gained a military victory in each war, and greatly augmented its territory in the 1967 conflict, the cost of obtaining such victories rose steadily. Furthermore, the military victories did not ensure Israeli security.

Through the late 1970s and early 1980s, Israel and its front-line Arab

---

*For example, Zionist private arms purchasers were able to provide the Israeli forces with tanks, artillery, and B-17 heavy bombers from the United States as well as Messerschmidt 109K fighters from Czechoslovakia. Furthermore, approximately ten thousand foreign volunteers are estimated to have served in the Haganah in 1948–49. During that period, all Arab and official Israeli arms requests were blocked by an embargo declared by the United States and Britain.

adversaries maintained high military readiness despite severe economic stress.* Serious Islamic-based unrest broke out in Syria early in 1982, and unprecedented fissures in Israeli society resulted from the invasion of Lebanon. Despite the great efforts made, neither party has been able to impose its own version of justice and security on the other. However, both sides continue to maintain large military forces and, with the exception of Egypt, following on President Sadat's peace initiative in November 1977, refuse to compromise on basic issues such as Palestinian rights, West Bank territorial concessions, and recognition of Israel.

Before 1967, the Arab-Israeli conflict had relatively little effect on U.S. interests in the Middle East; Great Britain and, to a lesser degree, France were the principal Western states involved. U.S. policy treated the oil producing countries of the Persian Gulf, the northern tier states (Iran, Iraq, Pakistan, and Turkey), and the nations directly involved in the Arab-Israeli conflict (Israel, Egypt, Syria, and Jordan) as separate areas. Obviously, U.S. support for Israel antagonized the Arab confrontation states. During most of that period, however, the oil producing states felt that the Arab nationalist regimes in Egypt, Syria and, after 1958, Iraq posed dangerous threats to their own security. Thus they were willing to cooperate with the United States despite its support for Israel.

The crushing defeat suffered by the Arabs in 1967 fundamentally changed the political balance in the Arab world. Israeli occupation of Arab lands increased Arab antagonism toward Israel to the point where it increasingly took precedence over internal Arab or nationalist-traditionalist disputes. In their search for support against Israel, nationalist leaders such as President Nasser modified their regional policies so that they no longer threatened the legitimacy of traditional regimes such as Saudi Arabia. The gradual rapprochement between nationalist and traditionalist regimes was demonstrated in early 1973 with the formation of the informal Cairo-Riyadh Axis. The Egyptian-Israeli peace treaty, signed in March 1979 in Washington, D.C., disrupted that axis, with the Saudis joining the other Arabs in opposing Egypt's separate peace with Israel. After a brief period of Arab solidarity under Iraqi leadership, long-standing divisions in the Arab camp resurfaced. Syrian and Libyan support of Iran against Iraq in the Gulf war, contrary to the interests of the Saudis and other Gulf Arabs, highlighted this factionalization.[25]

---

*Inflation in Israel at the end of 1980 was approximately 120 percent annually; J. C. Hurewitz, "The Middle East," *Foreign Affairs* 59, no. 3 (1980):574. Much of the inflation was caused by vast expenditures for defense purposes. See Don Peretz, "The Earthquake: Israel's Ninth Knesset Elections," *Middle East Journal*, no. 31 (summer 1977), p. 8. In January 1978, a major riot broke out in Cairo in which crowds chanted, "Oh hero of the crossing [of the Suez Canal in 1973], give us our breakfast." The riots were caused by the attempts of the Egyptian government to eliminate subsidies that kept the price of food at artificially low levels. President Sadat had to use the army to quell the crowds.

As implied in the preceding paragraph, a sea of change in Arab-Israeli affairs occurred in the late 1970s as a result of Egyptian President Sadat's determination to break Egypt out of the disastrous cycle of wars with Israel. His historic peacemaking journey to Jerusalem in November 1977, followed by the American-engineered Camp David accords between Israel and Egypt in September 1978, transformed the Middle Eastern political and strategic landscape—the Egypt-Israel Peace Treaty of 1979 simply codified this change. In return for restoration of its Sinai territories (captured by Israel in 1967) plus an Israeli promise of autonomy for the predominantly Palestinian West Bank area (also captured in 1967), Egypt shifted from its support of pan-Arab military confrontation to policies toward political accommodation and economic cooperation with Israel.

Despite their unhappiness, the other Arab states, centered on the developing Baghdad-Riyadh Axis, were too weak militarily to challenge the new status quo by force of arms. According to one authority,

After thirty years of unremitting hostility, Israel was fully recognized as a sovereign nation by her largest and most powerful Arab neighbor. But the thorny problem of the Palestinians, which had figured prominently in the lengthy and sometimes acrimonious negotiations between Israel, Egypt and the United States, continued to trouble the region as a whole. There was no indication that any convergence of views on this key question had been reached in the many meetings since President Sadat's visit to Jerusalem in 1977. This failure threatened to reverse the progress made so far, for unless some solution to the Palestinian question could be achieved the region would remain permanently unstable, and the possibility of further fighting would increase.[26]

Iran's Role. Arabs and Iranians have coexisted uneasily within the framework of Islam since the Arab conquest of Iran (formerly Persia) in the seventh century A.D. Whenever subsequent Iranian empires were strong, they dominated Arab inhabited lands on both sides of the Persian Gulf. On the other hand, when such empires were weak, local Arabs quickly threw off Iranian control. It was during such a period of Iranian weakness in the early nineteenth century that Great Britain established its control over the Arab side of the gulf. The series of treaties signed by the British with various Persian Gulf rulers had the effect of "freezing" the transitory political situation which then became into a permanent system guaranteed by British power.

Arab-Iranian tension in recent years stems partly from Arab fears that an increasingly strong Iran will seek to reassert its traditional hegemony over the Persian Gulf. Three factors have combined to intensify such fears during the last decade. First, between 1968 and 1971, Britain abandoned its role as protector of the Arab states in the Persian Gulf. Although Britain's physical presence in the area after World War II was minuscule, it still served as a deterrent to the ambitions of regional powers such as Iran, Iraq, and Egypt. Also, by 1970 Arab leaders were aware of the Shah's concern over the relatively low level of proven oil reserves in Iran. Although the Shah's stated intention to industrialize Iran before the oil ran out was all well and good, Arab leaders were not convinced that he would abstain from using force to gain control of Arab oil once Iranian supplies began to fail.

Perhaps the most important factor behind Arab fears of Iranian ambitions was the rapid growth of Iran's capability to achieve them through the use of force. U.S. military assistance had enabled the Shah to expand and strengthen his armed forces considerably after World War II. Such forces were designed primarily for internal security and to defend against direct Soviet or, later, Iraqi attacks. In the late 1960s, however, the Shah began to purchase large quantities of arms designed to provide Iranian forces with a significant offensive capability. Among such purchases were U.S. destroyers and antisubmarine aircraft, British hovercraft, and several other systems that could only be used in the Persian Gulf or its approaches.* To the Arabs, it seemed that those forces were oriented directly at them. Neighboring Iraq was particularly sensitive.

From the Iranian point of view, such a military build-up was necessary in order to provide security for vital Persian Gulf oil fields and tanker facilities. The Shah had serious doubts about American effectiveness in the area, the internal stability of the Arab states of the Persian Gulf, and those states' ability to defend themselves or to contain subversion. If necessary, he intended to take action himself. Yet Iranian diplomacy went to great lengths to convince Arab rulers that Iran's military power posed no threat to them. Iran signed treaties with several Arab states determining offshore boundaries and oil rights. The border dispute with Iraq was settled peacefully. The Shah gave economic aid to some of the poorer gulf states and proposed other forms of economic and military cooperation. Finally, in 1970, the Shah unilaterally renounced Iran's claim to Bahrain. At the same time, however, he did not hesitate to use force to seize three Arab islands in the Persian Gulf in 1971, or to give substantial military support to the Kurdish rebels in Iraq prior to the 1975 Iraq-Iran agreement.[27]

The Arab states responded to the growth of Iranian power in several ways. Some countries, such as Saudi Arabia and Iraq, replied by seeking foreign assistance in building up their own forces, although they never could hope to match Iranian manpower. Iraq, in particular, built a highly modern force

---

*In 1969, the United States terminated its program of military grants to Iran. All future arms transfers were to be handled on a commercial basis. Ironically, although that action was at least partially intended to limit Iran's acquisition of modern arms, it had the opposite effect. When Iran oil revenues soared after 1973, the Shah was able to embark on a spending spree. See Shahram Chubin and Sepehr Zabih, *The Foreign Relations of Iran* (Berkeley and Los Angeles: University of California Press, 1974), pp. 109–12.

with the latest Soviet equipment. In general, the Arab states were unwilling
to cooperate with Iran in joint military or economic actions despite the benefits
that such actions might provide. The Arab reaction to Iranian intervention
in Oman's Dhofar Rebellion was in many ways characteristic of the uneasy
feelings toward Iran. On the one hand, Arab leaders were happy to see
Iranian troops used to suppress a radical movement threatening them all; on
the other hand, the presence of Iranian troops on Arab soil was an embar-
rassment and a source of dangerous unrest among Arab nationalists.

The Iranian revolution of 1978–79 upset all the old assumptions, both in
Iran and in the region. The Shah's accelerated economic development program, carried out largely along Western lines with a heavy infusion of Western
technicians and values, had proven profoundly destabilizing. Traditionalists,
who felt themselves endangered (the Moslem clergy, landowners, and bazaar
merchants, for example), joined in opposition with the disadvantaged (the
middle classes and the poor, who suffered from the inflation attending compressed modernization), and the displaced (primarily the ex-peasants flocking
to the cities in search of jobs in the mismanaged industrial sector).

The precipitating cause of the Shah's downfall was his attempt to crush
religious opposition to his rule. At least since the start of the sixteenth century,
when Shi'ism was formally adopted as the state religion, Iran's secular rulers
had been uneasy partners with its Islamic leaders. In contrast to the Sunni
sect of Islam, predominant in Saudi Arabia and most of the rest of the Moslem
world, Shi'ism has enough of a hierarchical structure to permit its leaders to

Reprinted with permission of Ranan R. Lurie from his book, *Lurie's Worlds, 1970–1980,*
University Press of Hawaii and King Features Syndicate, Inc.

pose an alternative authority system. Although Iran's rulers have for centuries shared power with religious leaders, the Shah, who was convinced that the mosque stood against his modernization efforts, progressively squeezed down on the clergy in matters of land reform, religious endowments, schools, and so forth. For a variety of reasons, including the mosque's role as the one secure rallying point and meeting place for all the forces opposed to his rule, the Shah found himself confronted with a genuine popular revolution under the banners of resurgent Islam.

Contributing to the Shah's demise was his increasingly repressive and authoritarian rule in the face of a sizable, politicized middle class. Unfortunately for the regime, development success had helped create the very forces that made authoritarianism no longer tenable. Unwilling to share power with the middle class and alienated from traditionalist support, the Shah became increasingly isolated. By and large his answer to demands that he broaden political participation was repression, further intensifying his problem. Corruption, frustrated popular expectations, the Shah's ill health, and American vacillation about supporting a repressive, corrupt regime added to the brew. The result was massive demonstrations and riots in the streets of Teheran and other major cities, culminating in early 1979 in the Shah's flight and the Ayatollah Khomeini's triumphant return from exile in France to establish a "pure Islamic state."[28]

In large measure, the chaos attending the new regime's birth continued in the 1980s. Especially noteworthy in this regard was the disintegration of the once large, well armed, and reasonably well trained Iranian armed forces. Although they had mostly stood aside during the revolutionary upheaval rather than make a widely expected bid for power, the military's senior leaders were executed or retired, or fled into exile. While the lower ranks deserted en masse, revolutionary guards and militia seized the nation's arsenals and distributed their contents. Western technicians, essential to maintaining the advanced weapons systems the Shah had purchased, were pushed out and returned home as quickly as possible. In short, Iran's own defenses became severely weakened; indeed, its ability to hold the country together became highly doubtful.

At the same time, the new government went out of its way to antagonize and humiliate its traditional ally, the United States. The Ayatollah singled out the United States as "Satan"—the source of religious and cultural pollution, the sole reason why its lackey, the Shah, could corrupt and repress the nation, and the font of all evil. Caught up in this ideological crusade and with at least tacit support from the regime, a group of several hundred "students" stormed the U.S. embassy in Teheran in November 1979, taking over fifty American diplomats and marine guards hostage in the process. The United States was able to rally international opinion and law to its side in this flaunting of the ancient right of diplomatic immunity, but the Iranians took no notice. Since its economic leverage (essentially, freezing assets and halting trade) was inadequate and since it was unwilling to use force or agree to Iranian terms for the hostages' release (which included apologies, the return of the Shah, and the billions of dollars the former ruler had purportedly stolen from the Iranian people), the United States was checkmated.

It was into this situation of a gravely weakened Iran at sword's point with its former ally and amidst mounting border incidents that Iraq moved with vigor in the autumn of 1980. Determined to exploit the power vacuum next door, essentially to enforce its version of the border along the Shatt al Arab (the confluence of the Tigris and the Euphrates rivers) and perhaps to pry off additional territory and topple the regime, Iraq denounced the 1975 Iran-Iraq treaty and launched a series of ground and air assaults against Iran in late September. By the end of the month, these assaults had succeeded in penetrating well into Iran, raising the possibility of an Iranian government collapse and fragmentation of the state. The fighting, particularly the exchange of air attacks, also destroyed oil facilities on both sides, resulting in the loss—at least for some time—of about 3.5 mb/d of oil, or roughly 5 to 6 percent of free world supplies. Iraq's surprising inability in 1980–83 to prevail over the weakened forces of Iran both raised doubts about its leadership claims in the Arab world and marked the possibility that the Iraqi-Iranian conflict would become the same kind of running sore as the Arab-Israeli one—except that it would occur in the middle of the world's most important energy region.[29]

Other Regional and Extraregional Developments. Turkey occupies a key position in the Middle East, both geographically and functionally. It is the bridge between Europe and Asia and the barrier between the Soviet Union and the Mediterranean. Simultaneously, it forms the southeastern anchor of NATO and the West's strongest link to the other northern tier states of Iran and Pakistan. As noted earlier, the cold war began with the Soviet Union's demands on the Dardenelles Straits and its effort to annex territory in eastern Turkey.

Yet Turkey has been an uneasy member of the NATO alliance since joining it in 1951, both because of the Turkish exposed flank position and because of the strains within the alliance as a result of continuing Greek-Turkish hostility. The island of Cyprus has long been a particular source of contention as the Turks sought to protect the interests of the Turkish minority there against the Greek majority. In 1967 it required strong American pressure to forestall armed Turkish intervention in Cyprus. By 1974 the situation on the island had deteriorated (as had America's influence in the world) to the point that pressure from the United States was insufficient to stave off any longer a Turkish assault. The ensuing warfare ruptured the NATO southeastern flank as Greece withdrew its forces from the alliance, threatening counter-action, and as the United States ceased all economic and military support for Turkey. American intelligence-gathering facilities, which were important in monitoring Soviet communications and missile tests, were also casualties as the Turks reacted to U.S. pressure by halting all American operations within its borders.

Partly as a consequence of strained relations with the United States and its other Western allies, Turkey also moved in the 1970s to reduce tension between itself and the Soviet Union. Increasing trade and Soviet economic assistance culminated in 1978 in a twenty-year Soviet-Turkish accord on friendly relations and cooperation.[30]

At the same time that Turkey's ties to the West, particularly to the United States, were deteriorating, so was its political and economic health. By the-decade's end, violence generated by both leftist and rightist factions was claiming about one thousand lives a year; inflation was at a 40 percent annual rate, and inability to pay for needed imports, particularly oil, had brought economic life to the point of near collapse. Violence and political and economic troubles continued to mount in 1980, culminating in September in a military takeover of the government. Military coups are familiar phenomena in Turkey, having occurred roughly once a decade as the politicians failed to govern effectively (in 1960 and 1971, for instance, as well as in 1980).

Turkish politics continued to be dominated by the military. However, a measure of stability has been restored to economic life and a new constitution established, pointing to the likelihood that Turkey may soon return to civilian control. Meanwhile, Turkey's relations with NATO, while strained by European opposition to a continued military role in Turkish politics, have veered from the 1970s path of accommodation with the U.S.S.R. Turkish suspicion of Soviet intentions remains with the continued Soviet occupation in Afghanistan. The Turkish government has also agreed to allow modernization and expansion of U.S. military bases near Turkey's eastern border, a possible deterrent to Soviet operations cutting across northwestern Iran toward the Persian Gulf.

Two other major developments affecting the region at the turn of the decade occurred on its flanks: in the Horn of Africa and in Afghanistan, as just cited. In the Horn (comprising Ethiopia, Djibouti, and Somalia) at the close of the 1970s, the Soviet Union had established a position of strength deeply worrisome to both the West and the neighboring states on both sides of the Red Sea. Cuban proxy forces and Soviet arms and advisers helped Ethiopia defeat a Somali-supported revolt in its eastern Ogaden territories (1978) and check the longstanding Eritrean independence movement (1979). Accompanying these African adventures of the Soviet Union and its Cuban proxies were pro-Soviet developments in the two Yemens across the Strait of Bab el Mandeb and Libyan meddling in both Sudan and Chad. Both in Western and Arab capitals, the concern grew that the Soviet Union was engaged in a giant pincers movement directed at Middle Eastern oil resources.

The other arm of the pincers took initial shape in April 1978 when a communist coup in hitherto neutralist, but Soviet-leaning, Afghanistan occurred. Despite significant Soviet assistance and the proximity of Soviet armies, anticommunist Afghans turned on their new Marxist masters in an escalating insurgency. By the autumn of 1979 it had become clear that the Afghan Communist regime could not survive as its army melted away in desertions and its civilian support similarly evaporated. Faced with the choice of seeing a client regime disappear or massively intervening to support it—perhaps seizing the opportunity to position itself more favorably for a subsequent move into the Middle East proper—the Soviet Union chose intervention. In December 1979 it invaded with the first echelons of what quickly became an 80,000-troop intervention force.

Afghan resistance, which had been on the point of bringing down the native communists, further rallied against the Soviet occupiers. Despite massive firepower and the mobility that helicopters and armored vehicles gave the Soviet forces, by mid 1983 they had made little or no progress in subjugating the Afghans. After nearly four years at great costs, they had undermined their own Afghan instruments, deeply frightened other regimes, within the reach of Soviet conventional forces, alarmed the Moslem world, and galvanized the West—particularly the United States—into a series of counteractions.

The Soviet Role in the Middle East. The U.S.S.R. has played a particularly significant role in the Middle East since 1955, when it agreed to supply military equipment to Egypt via Czechoslovakia. Soviet interests in the region have been primarily strategic. The Soviets would like to eliminate U.S. influence throughout the region but, presumably, without risking a superpower confrontation in the process. They want to ensure that the Middle East cannot be used as a staging area for pressure against their own southern borders; at the same time, they must feel that access to the Suez Canal and to facilities in the Indian Ocean increases their ability to exert counterpressures.[31]

The U.S.S.R. has had no compelling economic interests in the Middle East comparable to those of the United States, but that is likely to change. Existing Soviet oil fields are becoming rapidly depleted, and the Soviet government has been unwilling or unable to make the enormous investments necessary to develop new fields, largely in Siberia. Consequently, the U.S.S.R. probably will become a net importer of oil by the mid 1980s; at least it will cease being an exporter to nations outside the Soviet bloc.[32]

Since World War II, Soviet policy in the Middle East has been faced with a dilemma. The U.S.S.R. could seek to use its developing position in the Middle East to subvert the states there and hope to eventually bring local communists to power, or it could support noncommunist regimes, thus enabling them to cooperate effectively with the U.S.S.R. against the United States and its interests. (To their regret, the Soviets found that regimes they helped also tended to use their new strength to crush their domestic communists.)

Since 1955, the U.S.S.R. has generally chosen to support existing Middle Eastern regimes rather than subvert them. Such support has taken two forms. First, the Soviets have provided friendly governments with the military and political support needed to suppress internal unrest and resist external threats.

The classic example of such support occurred after the 1967 Arab-Israeli War when the U.S.S.R. rushed large quantities of arms to Egypt to bolster Nasser's sagging regime.[33]* At the same time, the Soviets have provided technical and financial support for the economic development programs that play such an important role in many Middle Eastern states. Apparently, they believe that such support not only increases the strength of friendly regimes, but that it also generated social changes that will lead to increased Soviet influence in the future.

The U.S.S.R. has achieved occasional successes in the area by following such policies. It has also capitalized on Arab resentment of American support for Israel and has succeeded in part in allaying Arab fears about its intentions by providing counter support. Nevertheless, Soviet influence in the region still is limited by several constraints likely to continue into the future; for example, despite whatever advantages it might derive from a centrally directed economy, the U.S.S.R. has not been able to displace U.S. economic influence in any part of the region. Most Middle Eastern countries still see more economic advantages in dealing with the United States, Western Europe, and Japan than in dealing with the U.S.S.R. Even Iraq, which maintains a variety of close ties with the Soviet Union, has cultivated extensive economic relations with the West.

Middle Eastern leaders also have found that Soviet political and military support, although useful, is of limited effectiveness in dealing with the problems they face. Soviet aid to one country has often triggered even greater U.S. (or Saudi) aid to its rivals. Perhaps more significant, Soviet unwillingness to seek power for local communists has ensured that, regardless of the value of Soviet aid, authority has remained in the hands of local leaders. Such leaders have tended to be concerned primarily with their own or regional problems and have responded to Soviet wishes only when such wishes suited their own purposes.[34] When Arab leaders have deemed Soviet wishes and pressures too oppressive, they have even ejected Soviet advisers, as happened in the case of Egypt.

Perhaps the most important check on the influence of the Soviet Union in the Middle East has been, and continues to be, the fear and distrust it inspires in the region. This aversion is compounded partly by the sheer size of the Soviet Union and its proximity, partly by its antireligious values, and partly by its record in dealing with its southern neighbors—particularly with the Iranians and Turks after World War II and with the Afghans since 1979. As long as there are acceptable counterbalances to the U.S.S.R. available to the region, the Middle Eastern nations will attempt to offset the Soviets there rather than accommodate to them.

From the U.S. point of view, the Soviet role in the Middle East is important in several ways. First, the U.S.S.R. serves as a source of support for Middle

---

*By October 1967, an estimated 80 percent of Egyptian equipment losses in the June war had been replaced.

Eastern nations and groups, such as the PLO, that are dissatisfied with the regional status quo. The availability of such support tends to strengthen the position and resolve of such nations and groups, compelling policy-makers to take their desires into account.* At the same time, Soviet influence places significant constraints on the ability of the United States to press any policy on Middle Eastern nations. Local regimes always have an eager alternative to acceding to such pressure. Finally, the Soviet military presence in and adjacent to the region conditions every nation's calculus of the potential costs and benefits of possible policy options—particularly after Cuban and Soviet actions in the Horn of Africa, Yemen, and Afghanistan.

The Influence of Other States. Western Europe and Japan provide alternative sources of financial, economic, and military support to the Middle East, although their political influence in the region has been limited. The high oil dependence of these nations makes them in turn vulnerable to counterpressures from the region. For example, Japanese willingness to pay virtually any price for Middle East oil greatly strengthened the negotiating position of OPEC in 1973.[35]† Along with the United Kingdom, France has played and will likely continue to play a significant role; it has, for example, provided advanced military equipment to several Arab states when both the United States and the U.S.S.R. were unwilling to do so.‡ However, the importance of the Europeans and Japanese is relatively limited, since none of them has the capability to supply the Middle Eastern states with the range of economic or military support they desire. Sheer size and strength (and, in the Soviet case, proximity as well) ensures that the United States and the U.S.S.R. will continue to be the dominant external powers in the Middle East.

Policy Challenges in the 1980s. The events cited in the preceding pages— the Iranian revolution, troubles in Turkey, fallout from the Camp David accords, Soviet advances in and adjacent to the region, among others—suggest that the Middle East will be turbulent for years to come. While such recent developments provide ample grounds for pessimism, some of them also present opportunities. Seizing those opportunities will require a broader understanding of, and more sustained involvement in, the region by the United States. It will also undoubtedly require more American resources than were available to American policy-makers in the 1970s.

---

*For example, the current Steadfastness Front, which is composed of Libya, the PLO, Syria, and South Yemen, owes much of its stature to the support it gets from the U.S.S.R. Without it, such a loose combination of states could not hope to stand up to a coalition of Egypt and Saudi Arabia.

†Bids reportedly went as high as $22.60 per barrel.

‡Libya has been the primary recipient of French arms since 1967. Of course, France supplied Israel with the bulk of its arms between 1950 and 1965 when both Britain and the United States would not.

Although several of the Middle Eastern nations are oil exporters and capable of providing their own financing, all the nations in the region need American—or at least Western—trade and technology. It is manifestly in U.S. interests to facilitate such flows. In several countries of the area, the United States also needs the flexibility to provide economic aid in appropriate amounts. Although Egypt and Israel have been major recipients of American economic aid in recent years, there have been insufficient overall funds available to provide aid in a number of other instances where it would have been highly useful. American military assistance, too, has tended to focus primarily on Israel and Egypt. Grant military aid, in particular, has been in such short supply that this sometimes irreplaceable instrument—together with associated military assistance advisory groups—has not been available for high priority uses.

In order to seize opportunities to protect its security interests, the United States requires the forces and logistical arrangements to be able to project military power into the region as needed. In his State of the Union address in January 1980, President Carter said, "An attempt by any outside force to gain control of the Persian Gulf region will be regarded as an assault on the vital interests of the United States of America, and such an assault will be repelled by any means necessary, including military force."[36] Unfortunately for the credibility of the Carter Doctrine, even by the end of 1980 the requisite force was not available and in any case could not have been moved to the area. Although plans for a rapid deployment force (RDF) were well advanced and headquarters and command arrangements had been settled by late 1980, the earmarked forces were too small and ill equipped for service in the Middle East; moreover, the airlift, sealift, and other facilities needed to move the RDF were equally unsatisfactory.

It will likely be sometime in the mid 1980s before the RDF provides a substantial intervention capability. In the interim, heavy reliance will have to be placed on sea power, which is itself overextended. Nevertheless, vigorous efforts to create an intervention capability, and clear signals that the United States, having recovered from its post Vietnam shakiness, might use that capability to help stabilize the area, can encourage friends and give adversaries pause.

Given the geography of the region, creating a satisfactory military balance in the Middle East between the Soviet Union and the West is perhaps the most difficult of the defense tasks confronting the United States and its allies. The adverse shift in the correlation of forces in the region at the turn of the decade suggests that this balancing task must be given priority. Doing so is not solely a matter of building American intervention capabilities, but also of inducing Western allies to contribute to the security mission and of convincing states within the region of the wisdom of cooperating with the West rather than accommodating the Soviet Union.

A further major challenge confronting the United States during the decade will be to promote a settlement of the Arab-Israeli conflict acceptable to all the parties. Although the Egyptian-Israeli peace treaty has substantially lessened the near-term danger of an outbreak of war, the persistence of the dispute threatens a longer-term breakdown of peace—including a rejoining of Egypt with the anti-Israeli camp—and provides a primary cause of instability throughout the region.

In the wake of the Iranian revolution and the Iraqi-Iranian war and taking account of the various longstanding inter-Arab quarrels, there is also a need for the United States to help build local balances of power beyond those connected with the Arab-Israeli confrontation. Iraq's claim to leadership of the Arab camp and its predominance in the gulf area could prove especially destabilizing if the lesser gulf states believe that their fate will be at the mercy of Iraqi arms.

The challenge of strengthening vulnerable friendly regimes, particularly Saudi Arabia, which is the key to the energy future, provides another major test of American policy. Turkey needs to be reintegrated into NATO and provided assistance on a substantial scale. A post Khomeini Iran may also be a candidate for American help; certainly it is in the U.S. interests to have a viable Iran again blocking the Soviet path to the south.

Paradoxically, the very complexity of interests limiting the direct use of U.S. military and economic influence in the Middle East contributes to one of the greatest assets that the United States possesses in the region. These varied interests have forced U.S. policy-makers to cultivate good working relations with most states in the region. At the same time, virtually every significant political group in the Middle East has found some area—economic, political, scientific, or military—from which it can derive substantial benefits from maintaining good relations with the United States. Obviously, some groups have found such relationships to be more rewarding, or more necessary, than others. Yet, with the exception of the Ayatollah's Iran, South Yemen (P.D.R.Y.), and some factions within the PLO, none have rejected the United States in the way the various Middle Easterners reject each other. The resulting U.S. ability to exert influence on both sides of most regional disputes is a powerful diplomatic and security asset.

Given such an intricate mix of interests, complications, capabilities, and limitations, U.S. policy-makers will have to balance and advance the various U.S. interests in the region, rather than seek to maximize particular interests. To do so, they must view the region as a whole, not as an agglomeration of units which can be dealt with separately, or even in two distinct subregions—the Persian Gulf and the Arab-Israeli confrontation area.

The conjunction of high stakes in the area, congenital instability, and logistical difficulty make the Middle East the most dangerous area for the United States in the decade of the 1980s, one that will challenge the capacity of the American people and government to the fullest.

In meeting the foregoing list of challenges, the United States still has formidable assets, both in the region and of value to the region. If those assets are used widely, not in an attempt to insure stability—which in the

Middle East is as enduring as a summer snowstorm—but to promote peaceful change, there is hope. The task is more subtle than confronting militant Islam or erecting an anti-Soviet alliance. Meeting such challenges and diverting the forces of disintegration in the area will require a clearheaded concept of what is desirable and possible and a rededication of effort.

DISCUSSION QUESTIONS

1. How have U.S. economic interests in the Middle East changed during the past twenty years?

2. How does the special relationship between the United States and Israel affect U.S. relations with its allies in Europe?

3. What policies could the United States adopt in order to prevent any further large increases in the price of oil? What policies could it adopt to prevent production cutbacks or another oil embargo?

4. How did détente affect the U.S. position in the Middle East? In particular? How has the waning of détente changed matters?

5. Compare the Soviet position in the Middle East with that of the United States. What are its relative strengths? What are its limits and weaknesses?

6. How did the 1967 Arab-Israeli War change the nature of the Arab-Israeli conflict? How did it affect the U.S. role in that conflict?

7. Discuss the advantages and disadvantages for the United States of relying on Israel or Saudi Arabia to further U.S. interests in the Middle East. What advantages or disadvantages would those countries have from such an arrangement?

8. How would Soviet policy in the Middle East likely be affected if it were to become a net importer of oil?

9. Discuss the likely impact on the Middle East of U.S. threats to intervene militarily in the Persian Gulf to gain control of oil resources. Could Israel do so for us?

10. Discuss suggestions that the United States should impose an embargo on food exports to the Persian Gulf in order to compel oil-producing countries to lower the price of oil.

11. Why is the United States so involved in searching for a settlement to the Arab-Israeli conflict? Should it seek to use its influence to impose a settlement on all parties?

RECOMMENDED READING

Anderson, Roy R., et al. *Politics and Change in the Middle East.* Englewood Cliffs, N.J.: Prentice Hall, 1982.

Cottrell, Alvin J., and Burrell, R. M. "Soviet-U.S. Naval Competition in the Indian Ocean." *Orbis* 18 (winter 1975).

Freedman, Robert O. *Soviet Policy toward the Middle East since 1970.* New York: Frederick A. Praeger, 1975.

Jordan, Amos A. "Energy and National Security." *Washington Quarterly* 3, no. 3 (summer 1980):154–63.

Khadduri, Majid. *Political Trends in the Arab World.* Baltimore: Johns Hopkins Press, 1970.

Khouri, Fred J. *The Arab-Israeli Dilemma*. 2d ed. Syracuse: Syracuse University Press, 1976.

Leeden, Michael, and Lewis, William. *Debacle: The American Failure in Iran*. New York: Knopf, 1981.

Quandt, William B. *Decade of Decisions: American Policy toward the Arab-Israeli Conflict, 1967–1976*. Berkeley and Los Angeles: University of California Press, 1977.

Rustow, Dankwart A. *Oil and Turmoil: America faces OPEC and the Middle East*. New York: W. W. Norton, 1982.

Tillman, Seth. *The United States in the Middle East*. Bloomington: University of Indiana Press, 1982.

Whetten, Lawrence L. *The Canal War: Four-Power Conflict in the Middle East*. Cambridge, Mass.: M.I.T. Press, 1974.

Wright, Claudia. "Implications of the Iraq-Iran War." *Foreign Affairs* 59, no. 2 (winter 1980/81).

19

SUB-SAHARAN AFRICA

In recent years U.S. policy in Africa has fluctuated between attempts to help Africans solve Africa's problems, thereby reducing the potential for outside interference, and efforts to counter directly Soviet adventurism. Lacking leverage or suitable instruments, the United States has faced great difficulty in accomplishing its objectives by the first course. The problems inherent in the second approach were reflected at the end of the 1970s in the response by the United States to the May 1978 Shaba Crisis in Zaire and its attempts in 1979 and 1980 to respond to Soviet moves in the Middle East by obtaining access to bases in the Horn of Africa and supporting Morocco with sophisticated arms. In Shaba the United States supported the efforts of its European allies (France and Belgium) to counter the apparently Soviet-backed force in an area rich with important minerals. Because the attackers were former inhabitants of the area with a long history of antigovernment activity on a non-ideological basis, and because there was a demonstrated preoccupation for the safety of Europeans in the region, our efforts were viewed by some Africans as support for a corrupt and bankrupt regime and not a legitimate response in the African context.[1] The decision of the Carter administration in the spring of 1980 to supply sophisticated military equipment to Morocco and to seek access to military facilities in Kenya and Somalia was viewed by many in Africa as a shift away from the earlier Carter policy of seeking local solutions to African problems and as a reintroduction of the cold war into Africa. Although there were also many African supporters of these U.S. actions, both initiatives ran counter to the prevailing attitudes of the majority of African governments.

U.S. Interests in the Region. The strategic interests of the United States in Sub-Saharan Africa* are limited in comparison with its interests in other

---

Sub-Saharan Africa is used herein to denote all of Africa except the North African states of Egypt, Libya, Tunisia, Algeria, and Morocco, which are culturally and economically, as well as geopolitically, apart from their southern neighbors.

areas. Thus a question sometimes arises about whether or not misjudgments in U.S. policy for the area are terribly damaging. Sub-Saharan Africa is not a crossroads of world power or trade, nor a natural place for confrontation between the superpowers. It is underdeveloped for the most part. In the entire region, not a single nation is a significant military threat to the United States or its non-African allies. Only a few African nations possess even significant regional power. Nevertheless, the United States has critical concerns in Africa on several levels.[2]

Strategic Position. The huge African continent sits astride one of the world's key shipping lanes—the route for Middle Eastern oil to Europe and America. This makes its littoral states of geopolitical interest to Western oil importing powers and consequently to their potential Soviet adversary. The East African coastline is similarly important for communications with the Indian Ocean, where superpower rivalry is growing. African ports and bases, particularly those close to the major sources of Middle East oil, are growing in importance.

FIG. 19.1
AFRICA
As reprinted from *Africa Report*.

International Politics. As nearly a third of the world's sovereign nations are on the continent, Africa has contributed to a transformation of the character and scope of international affairs since the mid 1960s. African nations play a large role in seeking change in the international order through increasingly active participation in conferences of nonaligned nations, the UN and its specialized agencies, the North-South dialogues on aid, trade, and investment, and numerous other forums. In many functional areas the United States has an interest in African support—the world environment, the future of the oceans, nuclear nonproliferation, energy, and population growth, for instance.[3]

Economic Interdependence. Africa's role in the world economy is small by U.S., European, or East Asian standards. U.S. trade ($5.34 billion in exports and $13.9 billion in imports in 1982) and direct investment ($5.0 billion in 1981 in the sub-Saharan region, including South Africa) constitute but a tiny proportion of our national product. However, two factors raise the economic importance of Africa well above the basic data cited. First, our European allies, whose health is vital to us, have a much greater stake in the African economies than we do. Relative to GNP, West European interest in trade and investment in Africa is five to ten times that of the United States. Second, all the Western industrialized nations have become dependent on African fuels and nonfuel materials. Nigeria, for example, has become one of the five leading suppliers of U.S. oil imports.[4]

An even more crucial concern than oil from south of the Sahara is long-term Western access to Africa's enormous mineral deposits. In the noncommunist world, Africa yields over half the production of seven crucial minerals—chromium, cobalt, industrial diamonds, germanium, manganese, platinum, and vanadium—and is a major source of several other commodities.[5] Again European dependence considerably exceeds that of the United States, with its sizable strategic stockpiles and its own mineral wealth. The location of most of the mineral deposits in the troubled areas of southern Africa imposes policy constraints on all Western powers.

Unstable Arena for Conflict. The very weaknesses that preclude African states from posing a security threat for the United States invite regional strife and outside intervention. The general instability of African regimes rests upon a host of problems—poverty, tribalism, secessionist and irredentist movements, and inadequate institutionalization, to name a few. Competing with the notion that these are African problems best left to Africans is the fear that Soviet exploitation of such instability has risen to the detriment of U.S. interests in Africa and, more broadly, of U.S. credibility worldwide. On the other hand, there are critics of the "credibility doctrine" who believe that the application of such a doctrine to Africa tempts the United States to react in areas of minimal interest or where other nations dictate the time or interests at stake. Of particular interest in this context is the demonstrated willingness of the Soviet Union (and its Cuban proxies) to intervene militarily in local conflicts such as Angola (1975) and Ethiopia (1977–78) in large numbers and for prolonged periods.

Values at Stake. The growing U.S. interest in Africa is not only material and strategic, it bears strong threads of cultural, political and moral values as well. Fundamental American norms of freedom, justice, and peaceful order create sympathy with African anticolonialism, nationalism, and pan-African solidarity. Other American values—democracy, human rights, free enterprise—encounter fewer parallels in the numerous single party and military regimes of Africa. (It should be noted, however, that in recent years there has been increasing attention to human rights in Africa as evidenced by approval by the Organization of African Unity [OAU] of a proposal to establish a commission to monitor human rights in Africa.) Thus U.S. interests vary with respect to the values that African governments represent.

The issue of majority rule in southern Africa tends to bring these varying values into focus. The size and sensitivity of the American black population and its emergence as a major internal political force since the civil rights struggle give the United States special moral and political interests in southern Africa, although strategic and economic interests accentuated the urgency we attached to finding solutions to the struggle in Zimbabwe (Rhodesia). In that case, the United States acted as an anxious honest broker among the contending parties, a posture that was helpful in obtaining a solution serving as a counter to possible Soviet and Cuban use of force. In Namibia (South-West Africa) the United States took the lead as five Western members of the UN Security Council began a cooperative diplomatic effort in the spring of 1977 to diffuse conflict and find an internationally accepted solution to the problem. It is also true, however, that moral and domestic political factors helped shape U.S. policy in those crises and in our antiapartheid stance vis-à-vis South Africa.

The Historical Context of U.S. Policy. Prior to 1945, the history of Sub-Saharan Africa and its inhabitants usually was addressed as part of the colonial history of the European states. The weakening of colonialism caused by World War II, plus the rapidly changing international power equation, led to most African states achieving independence in the 1960s. The United States for the most part warmly embraced African independence. As France, Belgium, and Britain granted sovereignty to some three dozen nations, the United States offered goodwill and modest amounts of aid and investment. American sympathy for self-rule and hopes for African democracy and development were symbolized best by the creation in 1961 of the Peace Corps. Prior to the genesis of the Peace Corps, however, the Kennedy administration had affirmed the American commitment to contain communist aggression worldwide, particularly in the developing world. Thus U.S. policy for Sub-Saharan

Africa by the early sixties had taken the dual nature it has maintained for two decades—support for socioeconomic development in sovereign states (preferably democratic) linked to the West and opposition to intrusion by communist powers.

In order to understand the 1980s environment of U.S. policy toward this region, it is useful to review its general evolution over the past twenty years. Many factors favored U.S. and Western interests in Africa. Most colonial powers left in their wake a Western-educated elite and a legacy of Western institutions, including ostensibly democratic governments, civil services, and private enterprises. Trade links, almost exclusively Western at the time of independence, were reinforced by special market arrangements such as the French association and British Commonwealth agreements. Europe and America provided African military organization, training, and equipment.

On the other hand, several factors tended to undermine Western success. Colonial rule and, in some instances, the bitterness of the independence struggle brought anti-Western leaders to power in several countries.* Also, the new African states were institutionally weak at their center.† Their largely arbitrary, inherited boundaries contained diverse peoples whose tribal loyalties generally far outweighed any national identity. Many African national leaders found it appropriate, expedient, or essential to articulate anti-Western themes of neocolonialism and neoimperialism to keep attention focused on the "national struggle." This line, plus the poverty of most Sub-Saharan African countries, persuaded responsive audiences that they were continuing victims of capitalist exploitation. Meanwhile, multiparty democracy quickly waned in the face of domestic social heterogeneity, traditional nondemocratic ways, and the weakness of central national institutions.‡ The military coup became a widespread phenomenon, occasionally bringing to power leaders espousing socialist or Marxist doctrines.[6]

The predominant trend in Africa, however, was neither pro-Western nor anti-Western. As diverse as the new states were domestically, a distinctive Africanist style in international affairs emerged, represented most prominently by the OAU. Created in 1963, the OAU came to include all independent African-ruled states and adjacent islands as members (thus excluding South Africa, Namibia and, until 1980, Zimbabwe). Its core principles have been African unity (both internally and internationally), socioeconomic develop-

---

* Seku Toure of Guinea is one example. Only in the late 1970s had Guinea's policy toward the West moderated. In more recent years, the resident hostility to those who supported Portuguese rule and Haile Selassie has resulted in anti-Western rhetoric in Angola, Ethiopia, and Mozambique.

† In his article "Political Modernization: America vs. Europe," Samuel P. Huntington concludes that in contrast to the U.S. pattern of modernizing a new society under an old state structure, the new African regimes are likely to need authoritarian controls to modernize old societies, *World Politics* 28 (April, 1966): 410–14. See also Ruth First, "Political and Social Problems of Development," *Africa South of the Sahara* (London: Europa, 1978), pp. 18–20.

‡In 1983, multiparty polities in sub-Saharan Africa numbered nine—Botswana, Djibouti, Gambia, Madagascar, Mauritius, Nigeria, Senegal, Uganda, and Zimbabwe.

ment, respect for the territorial integrity of all member states, independence from external influence, elimination of all forms of colonialism, and support for the principles of the UN. The OAU has achieved its greatest successes in establishing acceptance of boundaries inherited from the colonial era, moderating several inter-African disputes, and focusing international attention on the struggle for "liberation" of southern Africa.[7]* The theme of nonalignment with the East or the West has come to characterize the OAU despite the proclivities of individual members. African nationalism, with its opposition to all foreign domination, remains the strongest deterrent on the continent to foreign penetration or influence. Awareness of this has generally resulted in U.S. support for the OAU as an institution of African solidarity.

As noted earlier, U.S. policy has alternated between noninvolvement and concern that without a Western presence the U.S.S.R. or P.R.C. might gain influence on the continent. The Eisenhower and Kennedy administrations actively sought to cultivate friendly regimes in Africa by promoting independence and encouraged the installation of Western-oriented governments and continued Western economic ties. When this approach ran afoul of postcolonial turmoil in the Congo (now Zaire), the United States intervened with its Western allies (under UN auspices), in large measure to counter Soviet influence.

For a time during the Kennedy years it appeared that Africa might become a testing place for U.S. intervention against the threat of communist "wars of national liberation"; instead, Vietnam provided that focus. About 1965, as American preoccupation with Southeast Asia grew, American attention to Africa entered a period of "benign neglect." That same year saw whites in southern Rhodesia proclaim UDI—the unilateral declaration of independence—from Britain with the 5 percent minority of whites in total charge.

During the next decade U.S. inaction with respect to Portuguese colonies came to be viewed in Africa as support for that NATO ally's colonial policy.[8] The Nixon administration, persuaded that the Portuguese and local whites would continue in power for some time, attempted to straddle the issue of black-white interests. Rather than actively undermine the status quo, as some would have preferred, the United States was resolutely ambiguous. Meanwhile the Vietnam War dragged painfully on, attracting both African opposition and African fears that America's failure there would undercut its capacity to act as a global power. U.S. support for Israel during 1967 and 1973 alienated several African states with a strong Islamic heritage.

Thus, as the great sweep of independence in Africa approached the borders of Angola, Mozambique, Rhodesia, and Portuguese Guinea, American enthusiasm for change seemed questionable. Moreover, by the late 1960s most anticolonial forces had found that the U.S.S.R. and the P.R.C. were prepared

---

* There are, of course, some notable exceptions to OAU success in these areas. The dispute between Chad and Libya over the latter's occupation of northern Chad, the conflict over the Western Sahara, and Tanzania's military intervention in Uganda to help overthrow Idi Amin provide recent examples of tough issues not resolved by the OAU.

to give them significant backing, particularly in military supplies and training. The United States (and Europe) far exceeded the communist states in establishing trade links and in providing nonmilitary aid, but these positive elements of American policy were partly overshadowed by Vietnam, the Portuguese connection, failure to maintain UN sanctions on Rhodesia,* and perceived indifference to South African apartheid.

The April 1974 coup in Portugal shattered the status quo in southern Africa and the U.S. policy that assumed its continuance for years to come. Over the next nineteen months all five Portuguese African colonies gained independence.† Unprepared for this sudden turn of events, the United States in 1975 nonetheless attempted to influence the outcome in Angola, where three liberation movements contested for power. Despite the administration's efforts, however, American clandestine support for two non-Marxist groups was ended by the U.S. Congress. Meanwhile, the U.S.S.R. transported more than fifteen thousand Cuban troops and Soviet advisers to Angola, enabling a third, Soviet aligned Marxist faction to defeat the two opposing groups and to gain OAU recognition by February 1976.

Angola's civil war and the assumption of power by Marxist regimes in Mozambique (1975) and Ethiopia (1974) signified a new era in Africa. The U.S.S.R. had demonstrated a major strategic logistics capability. Along with its Cuban ally, the Soviet Union had intervened directly and decisively in Africa. The "liberation struggle" had shifted southward, and soon-to-be-independent Zimbabwe was suddenly ringed by black-ruled states willing to tolerate or promote insurgent groups. In the succeeding three years, the guerrilla war intensified to the point where the white-dominated government in Rhodesia had to submit to growing pressure and turn over power to the black majority after British-supervised elections (1980). In April 1977 Lt. Col. Mengistu declared his regime in Ethiopia Marxist, after having seized power following a coup in 1974.[9] In late 1977 and early 1978 a significant infusion of Cuban troops and Soviet materiel and advisers enabled his regime to defeat local guerrillas and Somali forces and drive them from Ethiopia's Ogaden region. In the same period, the Ethiopians temporarily checked the long-standing Eritrean rebellion to a degree unknown before Soviet assistance was provided.

The African Environment of the Early 1980s. As the political, economic, and social improvements that were supposed to accompany independence have not materialized or at least not met inflated expectations, radical solutions now appear to be justified to many Africans. Western models have not, on the whole, suited African political leaders; alternatives have included a mixture of African society, European forms of government, and socialist

* From 1972 to 1977, the Byrd Amendment effectively mandated U.S. importation of Rhodesian chrome.

†The five were Guinea-Bissau (September 1974), Mozambique (June 1975), Cape Verde Islands (July 1975), São Tomé and Príncipe (July 1975), and Angola (November 1975).

patterns. There has been a reliance in Africa on the one-party system, for many African leaders are fearful of organized opposition and/or believe that democratic patterns will lead to parties dividing along tribal or ethnic grounds. The military has played a very large role in these efforts toward centralization, for many Africans seek one form of authoritarian regime or another; the authoritarian state supposedly eradicates corruption and tribalism, builds an identity between the population and the state, and eventually brings about a sense of equality among all members of the nation-state.[10]

Economically, Africa has also been sputtering. While the continent has extensive deposits of minerals, the income from extraction and export of these minerals has not affected the lives of the great majority.[11] Also, the boundaries inherited from the colonial era show little regard for natural economic regions. For most African states, per capita GNP is low and what wealth there is, is concentrated among a small elite. Of the world's twenty-nine least developed countries, eighteen are in Africa. Even by the standards of the underdeveloped world, Africa possesses an extremely low standard of living for the majority.

In addition to the burden of extreme poverty, Africa is heavily dependent on external economic forces over which it has little control. Many African states rely on a single commodity for their export earnings, and price fluctuations of raw materials in the international marketplace have had drastic effects on African economies. Additionally, higher prices of critical imports

Table 19.1   Types of Regimes in Sub-Saharan Africa, 1983

One-Party States (plebicitary or competitive)	Multiparty Polities	Military Regimes
Angola	Botswana	Benin
Cameroon	Djibouti	Burundi
Cape Verde	Gambia	Central African Republic
Comoros	Madagascar	Chad
Gabon	Mauritius	Congo
Guinea	Nigeria	Equatorial Guinea
Guinea-Bissau	Senegal	Ethiopia
Ivory Coast	Uganda	Ghana
Kenya	Zimbabwe	Liberia
Lesotho		Mali
Malawi		Mauritania
Mozambique		Niger
São Tomé & Príncipe		Rwanda
Seychelles		Somalia
Sierra Leone		Sudan
Swaziland		Togo
Tanzania		Upper Volta
Zambia		
Zaire		

Source: African Studies Program, CSIS

such as oil have greatly impeded economic development. Foreign aid is decreasing in real terms, and the general disposition on the part of donors is to concentrate on the states that show some promise. Another handicap is Africa's lack of skilled manpower. Although Africans place a high priority on education, including vocational and management training, foreign enterprises willing to provide training and opportunities for advancement to positions of responsibility are not investing heavily in Africa.

Few African states have moved far in the direction of an industrialized society. Agriculture continues to be the economic mainstay, but it is generally limited to subsistence farming and produces little for national markets. Sporadic efforts to persuade Africans to produce for the urban areas have generally failed because of transportation and marketing problems, the rapid migration of farmers to the cities, and increases in the population. Agricultural growth has also been slowed by *etatist* policies in many countries which have offered few incentives to farmers. Throughout the latter 1970s and into the 1980s, drought across the northern part of sub-Saharan Africa, the so-called Sahel, further intensified rural distress and accelerated migration. While the problems of starvation and civil disorder may be ameliorated in the short run through emerging aid, the long-term consequences of this ongoing natural disaster have implications for the entire region. As one expert has put it, many countries in Africa are "undeveloping" as per capita economic growth rates drop below zero, and over half of the land space of the continent becomes desiccated and unfertile.

Agricultural improvement also faces serious problems in Africa due to communal landholding systems, political indifference, and the difficulty of financing fertilizer and pesticide. In urban areas, hunger and unemployment have not been ameliorated by the reliance of city dwellers on family and tribal support and continuing contact with the villages from whence they came. The sum of all these adverse factors can be seen in the fact that only in Africa has per capita food production fallen in recent years; in the world as a whole it rose almost 2 percent a year over the 1970s while in Africa it fell by 1 percent.[12]

Africa's trade with and investment from the United States and the industrial nations of the West are crucial and expanding, but for some African countries—particularly the poorest and least developed ones—trade and investment have not been enough to overcome the legacy of pervasive poverty. Especially critical are the balance-of-payments problems of these nations. In order to develop, they need credit as well as aid, and with the dramatic rise of oil prices and inflation, many nations have become unable to repay development loans or to get further credit for industrialization. In fact, the trend now is for the developed countries to substitute remission of debt for assistance, without extending further credit, especially to high-risk countries where political instability is commonplace.

Related to the general economic situation are unemployment of uneducated youth, underemployment of the educated, dislocations created by rapid expansion of urban areas, and growing dissatisfaction with rural subsistence life.[13] The cities are likely to continue to be, in many cases increasingly so, disaster areas where the African social system that formerly maintained order has broken down. Actions to ensure the provision of basic food items, housing, and health needs seem beyond the capabilities of many African governments.

Yet despite these problems, Africa has enormous growth potential. Its mineral resources are vast, as shown by table 19.2. Its iron reserves are twice those of the United States and two-thirds those of the U.S.S.R., and its large petroleum reserves have not been totally assessed. There are vast unused areas of arable land, pasture and forests, which with proper techniques could produce virtually every important crop in the world.[14] With the successful completion of the anticolonial drive of the 1970s, the challenge for Africa's leaders in the 1980s is to focus their energies on the mundane tasks of producing more, governing increasingly well, and creating more opportunity for their people.

Intra-African Relations. Often overlooked by Americans and Europeans focused on East-West competition is the broad scope of intra-African affairs. As noted earlier, the OAU provides a semblance of continental unity on various matters. In terms of its goals for African economic development, however, the OAU has had little success. Most intra-African economic activity now takes place under UN auspices in the Economic Commission for Africa (ECA);* through such regional organizations as the Economic Community of West African States (fifteen members), the Common African and Mauritian Organization (ten members), and the Central African Customs and Economic Union (four members); and within a variety of regional and bilateral banking, river, and commodity organizations.[15]

The greatest political success of the OAU has been in presenting a relatively solid diplomatic front regarding southern Africa. OAU pressure has been largely responsible for South Africa's increasing diplomatic isolation and for the international sanctions imposed on Rhodesia after 1965 (porous as those

Table 19.2 South Africa's Mineral Production and Reserves

Mineral	1980 Production	% World	Reserves	% World
Platinum (1,000 tr. oz.)	3,250	48.0	970,000	82.2
Vanadium (1,000 lb. V. Metal)	25,000	31.0	17,200,000	49.4
Manganese (1,000 ST)	5,000	19.8	2,200,000	40.7
Chromium (1,000 ST)	3,450	34.9	2,500,000	67.8
Gold (1,000 tr. oz.)	21,500	56.3	650,000	64.4

Source: U.S. Bureau of Mines.

* The great weakness of African economic agencies is, of course, lack of capital. African states will continue to depend for some time on non-African sources of capital—multinational corporate investment, bilateral aid/loans, multilateral agency loans/grants. Running counter to the trend of greater regional economic cooperation, the East African Community broke up in 1976.

sanctions may have been). In 1976 the OAU came out against recognition of the Bantustans, the black homelands created within South Africa to be given nominal independence. The rest of the international community followed suit.[16]

OAU actions vis-à-vis South Africa have been largely confined to diplomacy. No group of black African states can challenge South Africa's military strength. Furthermore, several southern African nations are too dependent on trade with or through South Africa to afford curtailment of economic relations with the republic. For this and reasons of geographical proximity, initiative for action in southern Africa has passed from the OAU as a whole to its "Liberation Committee," chaired by Tanzania.

In the wake of Zimbabwe's achievement of black majority rule, the focus of intra-African relations has shifted to South Africa, which poses one immediate problem—Namibia—and one longer term issue—majority rule—for the continent.* African nations, led by the so-called Front-line states (Angola, Mozambique, Botswana, Zambia, Tanzania, and now Zimbabwe), have supported the South-West Africa Peoples Organization (SWAPO) since 1966. South Africa tried to impose a policy of separate ethnic development in Namibia but since 1975 has directed its efforts toward Namibian independence under a white-led coalition. SWAPO has benefited from Angolan bases since Angola's independence in 1975 but has also suffered from periodic South African military attacks there.

In 1977, five Western nations (United States, United Kingdom, France, West Germany, and Canada) formed a "Contact Group" to negotiate a UN-sponsored transition to Namibian independence with SWAPO, South Africa, and the Front-line presidents. The South African government response has been an effective delaying strategy. For example, South Africa conducted a Namibian election without SWAPO participation in late 1978, yet simultaneously agreed to eventual UN-supervised independence as demanded by the Contact Group. Also, in June 1980 South Africa launched large-scale military operations in Angola to destroy SWAPO bases while engaging in public diplomacy to obtain UN neutrality, an election, and a cease-fire in the territory.[17]

Although largely isolated diplomatically, South Africa does not confront a serious external threat as did the white regime in Rhodesia. Its black African neighbors are both economically dependent and greatly militarily inferior to Pretoria. Nevertheless, the final outcome of events in Zimbabwe and Namibia could strengthen threats to South African security over the decade of the 1980s. More ominous, however, is the growing internal unrest among blacks within the country. Constituting some 70 percent of the population and an indispensable labor resource, black South Africans can be expected to be

---

* South-West Africa, now Namibia, had been a mandate of South Africa since 1920. Although the UN revoked the mandate in 1966, South Africa has continued to rule over the territory, which encompasses some 800,000 blacks and 100,000 whites.

Table 19.3 Principal Regional Forces in Sub-Saharan Africa

Country/Service	Regular Forces	Reserves	Main Armament	Other
Ethiopia (pop. 30,500,000)				
Army	244,500	20,000 (all services)	830 tks. 710 AFV 700 arty.	Sagger ATGW SA 2/3/7 SAM
Navy	2,500		9 ptl. cft.	
Air Force	3,500		113 cbt. acft.	
Paramilitary	169,000			
Nigeria (pop. 79,000,000)				
Army	125,000		115 tks. 211 AFV 400 arty.	
Navy	4,000		12 maj. surf. ships 8 ptl. cft.	
Air Force	9,000		30 cbt. acft. MIG 21 M	
Somalia (pop. 3,650,000)				
Army	60,000		140 tks. 300 AFV 150 arty.	Milan ATG
Navy	550		2 maj. surf. ships	
Air Force	2,000		55 cbt. acft.	
Paramilitary	29,500			
South Africa (pop. 29,500,000)				
Army	67,500	130,000	96 tks. 3100 AFV 230 arty.	SS-11 ATGW
Navy	5,000	2,000	3 atk. subs. 7 maj. surf. ships	
Air Force	9,000	25,000	211 cbt. acft.	
Paramilitary	90,000			

Table 19.3 *(cont.)*

Country/Service	Regular Forces	Reserves	Main Armament	Other
Tanzania (pop. 19,000,000)				
Army	35,500		96 tks. 70 AFV 290 arty.	SA 3/6/7 SAM
Navy	850		13 ptl. cft.	
Air Force	1,000		29 cbt. acft.	MIG 17/19/21
Paramilitary	50,000			
Zaire (pop. 29,500,000)				
Army	22,000		60 tks. 227 AFV some arty.	
Navy	1,500		39 ptl. cft.	
Air Force	2,500		19 cbt. acft.	

Source: See table 18.2.
For abbreviations, see table 17.1.

increasingly restive in the 1980s. The Soweto riots and subsequent black demonstrations in 1976–77 and 1980 stimulated some minor loosening of apartheid. But the solid National Party electoral victory in 1977 and the government's apparent reluctance to recognize the basic cause of the unrest and the reasons the nonwhite population rejects apartheid suggest that evolution toward a more just society will not be without violence. For the present, at least, the government appears bent on legitimizing "separate development" via creation of a mosaic of nine independent but scrawny homelands in which all blacks will eventually hold citizenship.

A multiracial President's Council, appointed in 1980 to advise on constitutional reform, eventually proposed a framework that would include a tricameral parliament with separate chambers for whites, Coloureds, and Indians; a strong executive presidency; and a division of legislative functions into categories of community concern (one-chamber action) and common concern (three-chamber action). Blacks would be excluded from participation in the "liberalized" central government structure, but Prime Minister Botha announced in April 1983 the formation of a cabinet committee to consider the possibility of a "political dispensation" for urban blacks. As of mid 1983, Parliament was still debating specifics of the new constitution, and plans for white, Coloured, and Indian referendums were moving very slowly.

Although the racial nature of the crises in southern Africa tends to preoccupy the West, the United States and Europe have vital interests at stake in numerous other conflicts in black Africa. Foremost among these in recent years has been the Horn of Africa. In that northeast corner of the continent, strategic to the West for its nearness to Middle Eastern oil, the Ethiopian empire collapsed into anarchy following the deposition of Haile Selassie (1974). While civil wars and famine swept the country, separatist movements made significant gains in Eritrea. Somalia fostered an uprising, then invaded (1977) the Ethiopian province of the Ogaden in pursuit of its long-held irredentist aspirations. As a new Marxist regime emerged in Ethiopia, it requested and received massive Soviet aid and Cuban ground forces. These proved decisive in defeating the Somali forces in 1978, by checking a variety of other rebellions and by furthering Ethiopian control over much of Eritrea.

The conflict in the Horn had four major effects. Within Africa, it renewed the prospect of superpower confrontation on the continent. It also intensified ideological divisions within the OAU. Regionally, it tended to draw conservative Arab regimes closer to the United States as the Somali and Eritrean situations were seen as Arab (and Islamic) causes. Finally, at the superpower level, the United States lost prestige through inaction, while the Soviets again demonstrated, after Angola, a capacity for long distance military intervention and a willingness to change sides to obtain what it perceived as a better bargain (prior to 1977, the Soviets had been the major arms supplier to Somalia).

Three other African conflicts warrant brief mention. The two invasions (1977 and 1978) of Shaba province in Zaire from insurgents based in Angola were followed by a rapprochement between the two countries. On this shaky relationship hangs the continuity of Zairean mineral production and exports. It should also be noted that the Marxist government in Angola has not consolidated its control, and large portions of the countryside are still influenced by antigovernment guerrillas in spite of massive Soviet and Cuban support.

In northwest Africa, Spain's withdrawal from the Western Sahara in 1976 led to armed struggle between Morocco, which initially divided the territory between itself and Mauritania (the latter eventually opting out of the annexation scheme), and the indigenous Polisario movement, stimulated and backed by Algeria. The Western Sahara with its vast store of phosphates may yet become a *casus belli* between Algeria and Morocco, conceivably leading to greater involvement by the superpowers.

Tanzania's ouster of Amin in Uganda may pave the way for reconstruction of the East African Community. Regardless of the popularity of Amin's removal, however, the fact remains that Tanzania set the precedent in independent Africa for military conquest of a neighboring state. Tanzanian involvement, and then withdrawal, from a Uganda torn by continuing ethnic strife could prove costly for both countries.

The Superpowers in Africa. As long as the former colonial powers treated Africa as their sphere of influence, they afforded the United States and the

Soviet Union little opportunity for direct intervention in African affairs. In fact, the only major U.S.-Soviet involvement during the earlier years of African independence was in the Belgian Congo (now Zaire) in the early 1960s, occasioned by the abrupt demise of Belgian colonialism.

For many years, the superpowers' relations with Africa were viewed primarily in terms of the cold war. Each side sought through military assistance and other aid programs to develop a set of allies in the region. For the United States this meant support for friendly governments such as Ethiopia, Tunisia, and Liberia, and indirectly, for Portuguese colonial rule. The Soviets became patrons at various times of Somalia, Guinea, Mali, and others, as well as of many of the revolutionary groups who fought the Belgians and Portuguese, the white Rhodesian regime, and various pro-Western governments. Yet for the most part this competition was never really intense because the United States enjoyed through its NATO allies a far stronger position and because the Soviet Union had but a limited number of tools at its disposal.

The conjunction of a number of factors raised Africa's saliency in the superpower conflict in the 1970s. For the United States, the withdrawal from Vietnam triggered a major questioning of American credibility throughout the world. Contemporaneously, the U.S.S.R. was developing nuclear equivalency with the United States and acquiring major naval forces and intercontinental transport capabilities—in short, a global power projection capacity for the first time. The early 1970s was also the time when OPEC revealed the West's Achilles' heel of energy. The end of Portuguese colonialism and the revolution of Ethiopia thus coincided with a time during which Soviet power vis-à-vis the U.S. seemed on the ascendancy—although the U.S.S.R. suffered one important setback when President Sadat broke Egypt's strong military links with the Soviet Union in 1973.

As the oil routes around Africa grew vital to the United States in the 1970s, as they had been for decades to Europe, the U.S.S.R. began to pose a credible threat to them. And given its support for liberation movements in the past, the U.S.S.R. enjoyed a key advantage over the West with the new governments of Mozambique and Angola. Soviet-Cuban interventions in Angola and the Horn raised concerns in the West and in Africa that the continent would fast become a major arena of East-West conflict.[18]

On assuming office, President Carter inherited the benign neglect policy cited earlier, modified by various ad hoc responses in reaction to the sudden changes described above. During the first years of the Carter administration there were few major substantive changes in U.S. policy, although there was a change of style. The administration developed with the Western powers a plan for UN-supervised Namibian elections in which SWAPO could participate, and cooperated closely with the British in a plan for negotiating a transition to majority rule in Rhodesia. The Carter administration also continued its predecessors' opposition to apartheid in South Africa and urged fuller participation in political life by all South Africans. These responses did not add up to a new policy direction toward Africa; if there was a Carter nuance it was not in substance but in more aggressive application of human rights principles.[19]

As the decade of the 1970s closed, the Carter administration's policy was based on the premise that the best way to deal with the dangers of Soviet intervention in Africa was to eliminate the opportunities for intervention by resolving the problems that create the situations inviting intervention. The basic elements of this approach were to engage in diplomatic activities to help resolve conflicts before outside involvement escalates; to strive for genuine self-determination through diplomatic efforts, rather than seeking to impose American solutions; to support African initiatives to mediate African disputes; to recognize the role of the UN in dealing with African problems; and to seek to minimize American military involvement in African conflicts.[20] Various critics of this approach continued to insist that a more realistic approach would entail strengthening friends and focusing on checking Soviet initiatives.

While not abandoning the long-range goal of bending Africa to its interests, the U.S.S.R. has placed immediate emphasis on short-term political economic and strategic interests. The extension of communism to Africa might well remain an ultimate goal; however, the expansion of Soviet—not communist— influence appears to be the Kremlin's dominant concern as evidenced by Soviet abandonment of one Marxist friend (Somalia) for another (Ethiopia) and support for one of the more moderate elements in the Zimbabwe liberation movement. Soviet objectives in Africa must therefore be viewed in relation to broader Soviet foreign policy goals.[21] Clearly among these objectives are: controling sea lanes around Africa and access to the Persian Gulf in the event of conflict, disrupting Western influence in Africa, promoting dependency on the U.S.S.R. among African states and revolutionary groups, and establishing a strong conventional presence in the Indian Ocean.

In the early 1980s, two major debates in the West center on Soviet activity in Africa. The first poses the question whether the U.S.S.R. is pursuing a long-term strategy aimed at continental hegemony, or merely reacting opportunistically to short-run crises that could increase Soviet influence. Closely related is the question of whether or not Soviet interventionism in Africa matters much. One school has argued that resolving the first question is somewhat inconsequential inasmuch as the same Soviet activity detrimental to the West could occur under either presumption.[22]

Indeed, the second debate obviates the first. Whether or not the Soviets have a long-term strategy is less important than whether their capability for success is high. Those who hold that it is not, generally espouse either a "quagmire theory" (that the Russians will get bogged down and overwhelmed in alien cultures) or an economic determinism theory (that Western butter will triumph over Soviet guns in long-run appeal to African development needs).[23] The opposite view sees potential for lasting Soviet success in the widespread instability of African regimes now that the legitimizing first blush independence has paled. This school also cites the decisiveness of the Soviet-Cuban military interventions in Angola and Ethiopia and the willingness of

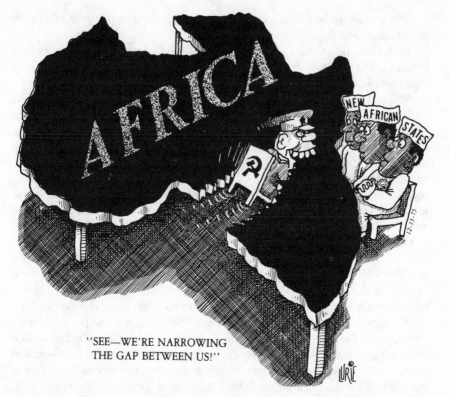

"SEE—WE'RE NARROWING
THE GAP BETWEEN US!"

Reprinted with permission of Ranan R. Lurie from his book, *Lurie's Worlds, 1970–1980,*
University Press of Hawaii and King Features Syndicate, Inc.

the U.S.S.R. to exploit the racial struggle in southern Africa over which
Western ambivalence seems inadequate to many Africans. In addition, the
argument runs, the failure of the West to act to deter Soviet aggression may
encourage further risk-taking by Moscow.[24]

Soviet activity has proven expensive; for example, the decision to arm both
sides in the conflict in the Horn of Africa. The risks may, however, be justified
by the potential gain. The possibility of radical changes in Zimbabwe, despite
the relatively peaceful postindependence period, and eventually in Namibia,
increases the opportunities for Soviet adventurism in South Africa, the most
economically advanced and strategically located country on the continent.[25]

Soviet moves have not gone unnoticed by African leaders, who are concerned about big power involvement; however, they continue to seek Soviet
support for liberation movements as essential in their drive to eliminate the
remaining white-dominated governments in Namibia and South Africa.[26]

The reduced potential for U.S. counter-involvement as a result of post
Vietnam attitudes in the United States increases the likelihood of Soviet
initiatives in Africa. Yet while recognizing that Soviet action in Africa is one
element in the deterioration of U.S.-U.S.S.R. relations, the U.S. government

has yet to gather the will and means to deal with the situation or to prevent future Angolas or Ethiopias. Linking the health of détente with cessation of Soviet activity in Africa has proven fruitless. The Carter administration warned the Soviet Union that there was no legitimate rationale for the maintenance of Cuban and Soviet combat forces in Angola and the Horn of Africa—but to no avail, for U.S. words carry no weight in and of themselves.

African Interests of Other States. Besides the United States and the Soviet Union, countries with major interests in Africa are the West European states, particularly those with previous colonial interests there, the P.R.C. and, most recently, Cuba.

The European relationships are the oldest. Great Britain has strong ties with various parts of East and West Africa, but none so strong as those with southern Africa. Large numbers of English settled in South Africa, and Great Britain is the largest outside investor in the republic. This investment of perhaps $15 billion, the foreign exchange earned from it, and trade with South Africa, place any British government in a difficult position in dealing with strong actions against apartheid.

France is the most deeply involved Western power and a large donor of economic and military aid to Africa, particularly to its former colonies, with which it has maintained strong cultural and economic ties. In addition, France is militarily involved in specific places in Africa to help shore up governments (e.g., Gabon, Djibouti, Senegal) that are strongly tied to the French republic. Among the foreign troop commitments in Africa, French military presence is second only to Cuba's. Despite arms embargoes placed by other nations on South Africa, the French supplied arms to the republic through the mid 1970s and nuclear reactors in the 1980s.

The Belgians, Spanish, and Germans also have economic and political interests in Africa resulting from the colonial era. This tendency to maintain close, sometimes "neocolonial," ties between European and African states is no more dramatically demonstrated than in the case of Portugal. In less than five years after a series of violent "wars of liberation," the Portuguese have already begun to reestablish closer political and economic ties with Angola, Cape Verde, Guinea-Bissau, Mozambique, and São Tomé.[27]

The P.R.C. has become active in Africa as an advocate of armed struggle to achieve independence, but it also counsels on the judicious use of politics to gain advantages. The Chinese have to balance rhetoric with pragmatism, however, because they lack the economic base to compete in Africa with the U.S.S.R. or the West. The P.R.C. has therefore been selective in the use of economic assistance, and the Chinese stress the need for self-reliance. Support for liberation movements has long been central to P.R.C. regional efforts, both as an element of Sino-Soviet revolutionary competition and as a means of cementing relations with African leaders throughout the continent. Long-standing P.R.C. links to those movements were reaffirmed by the establishment of diplomatic relations with Angola in 1983. Material constraints, however, will continue to limit Chinese ability to compete with the Soviets in areas that require significant commitments of resources. On the other hand, Beijing's flexible, undemanding approach on state-to-state relations has in general been an effective response to African nationalism.[28]

Cuba has objectives of its own in Africa, although it is in part acting as a surrogate or proxy there for the Soviet Union. In particular, Castro appears to be seeking to use his African ventures to consolidate his leadership role in the Third World, a goal he has pursued for well over a decade. Cuban involvement in Africa is very large in terms of the proportion of trained personnel it diverts. (Tables 19.4 and 19.5 show the raw data.) Yet it is unlikely that Cuba, which has provided support to African governments and dissident movements since at least 1965, will abandon its objectives in Africa except under great pressure. Since the Soviet Union appears to be subsidizing Cuba sufficiently in economic and military terms, the political, economic, social, and military strains to Cuba of its activity in Africa appear manageable—though cumulatively they may account in part for Havana's internal rumblings and fleeing refugees at the turn of the decade.[29]

Future U.S. Security Issues in Africa. In the 1980s, the United States will face increasingly complex political and economic issues in Africa. Overall one can expect a greater linkage of African problems to the international system as a whole. In a late 1978 survey of forty-nine African countries, Colin Legum characterized ten as being strongly pro-Soviet, seventeen solidly pro-Western, nine usually pro-Western, and thirteen generally neutral.[30] By the early 1980s, however, some of the names and number in the various columns had shifted.

Africans have come to play important roles in international functional issue negotiations such as the Law of the Seas Conference. Rising African trade ties and the Lome Convention link to the European Economic Community will increase Africa's world economic role. African states can be expected to join in Third World efforts to create commodity cartels. In the military sphere, most Sub-Saharan African states will remain weak in absolute numbers of trained personnel and particularly in sophisticated weaponry. Relative to potential external sources of intervention and of military aid the asymmetry will be particularly sharp.

Black and white leaders in southern Africa have set in motion a course of events that could touch off in South Africa the worst civil war in Africa's history, with a high potential for again drawing in all the outside forces that confronted each other in the Angolan conflict in 1976. Also, no one can be overly optimistic concerning the survival of the new government in Zimbabwe or about the chances for a successful transition in Namibia. At stake is not only which black factions will eventually rule in Zimbabwe and Namibia, but whether those areas rich in minerals and agriculture will be socialist, capitalist, Eastern, or Western in orientation.

The South African government appears to have settled on a policy toward the black majority that will significantly modify some of the most resented

Table 19.4 Communist Economic Technicians in Sub-Saharan Africa, 1978[a]

Country	Total	Soviet and Eastern European[b]	Cuban	Chinese
Angola	9,910	1,400	8,500	10
Ethiopia	1,400	650	500	250
Gabon	75	10	—	65
Gambia	75	—	—	75
Ghana	175	95	—	80
Guinea	1,035	700	35	300
Guinea-Bissau	405	265	85	55
Kenya	30	25	—	5
Liberia	210	10	—	200
Madagascar	200	—	—	200
Mali	1,025	475	—	550
Mauritius	15	—	—	15
Mozambique	1,270	750	400	120
Niger	160	10	—	150
Nigeria	1,750	1,625	—	125
Rwanda	60	10	—	50
São Tomé and Principe	260	20	140	100
Senegal	500	100	—	400
Sierra Leone	310	10	—	300
Somalia	3,050	50	—	3,000
Sudan	775	125	—	650
Tanzania	1,365	165	200	1,000
Zambia	5,645	125	20	5,500
Other	7,525	1,020	1,090	5,415
Total	37,225	7,640	18,615	10,970

[a] Number of persons present for a period of 1 month or more during 1978, rounded to the nearest 5.
[b] More than half are Soviets; nearly 1,000 are believed to be East Germans.
Source: Undersecretary for Political Affairs David D. Newsom, U.S., Congress, House, Committee on Foreign Affairs, Subcommittee on Africa, *Statement*, 96th Cong., 1st sess., October 18, 1979 (Washington, D.C.: U.S. Government Printing Office, 1979).

aspects of the apartheid system without weakening the overall structure of white power—the old policy with a face-lift. The question is if neoapartheid or Prime Minister Botha's policy of "adapt or die" is sincere in its efforts to loosen the strictures on the black majority and colored and Asian minorities in the nation.

The South African government consistently restates the principle that there will be no black South African citizen. The new policy accepts the African as an economic necessity, permanently established, with a right to better conditions; however, the mechanisms of enforcement will be maintained.[31] Although South Africa faces a turbulent period, its situation contains hope. Its population is relatively sophisticated, widely urbanized, and deeply involved in an industrialized economy. The ruling white minority, in turn, is

Table 19.5. Communist Military Personnel in Sub-Saharan Africa, 1978[a]

Country	Total	Soviet and Eastern European[b]	Cuban[c]	Chinese
Angola	20,300	1,300	19,000	—
Equatorial Guinea	290	40	150	100
Ethiopia	17,900	1,400	16,500	—
Guinea	330	100	200	30
Guinea-Bissau	205	65	140	—
Mali	195	180	—	15
Mozambique	1,130	230	800	100
Other	1,330	500	485	345
Total	41,680	3,815	37,275	590

[a] Number of persons present for a period of 1 month or more during 1978, rounded to the nearest 5.
[b] Mainly Soviets; among Eastern Europeans, most are believed to be East Germans.
[c] Includes troops.
Source: See table 19.4.

not a colonial class as were the bulk of white Rhodesians, who were there for only several decades. South Africa's whites can trace their roots in Africa to the mid-seventeenth century. As compared with their white counterparts in Zimbabwe, white South Africans see themselves as native Africans, not colonial settlers. It would be wishful thinking to suggest that blacks and whites in South Africa will find a peaceful solution to their national problems in the near future, or that any solutions will come easily. But it would seem equally foolish to say that in the particular conditions existing in South Africa today, a peaceful transition may not occur or that bloody revolution is inevitable.

Although the United States cannot impose solutions upon or dictate terms to any of the parties, and has limited leverage, it is among the few governments in the world that can talk to both white and black Africans frankly and yet with a measure of trust. The United States would lose its ability to be helpful if it were to lose that trust. It is therefore essential that U.S. encouragement of justice for the people of all of Africa be made clear. The alternative to a peaceful solution is escalating violence and greater opportunities for external intervention. The United States will be gauged for many decades by its will-ingness to commit American economic and political power to bringing racial justice to South Africa. Arguments that a transfer of power to the majority would result in black tyranny or that there are other equally oppressive regimes in Africa will in no way lessen African expectations of the United States. Yet the United States must pursue its interests and do so with limited means. We are in no position to dictate or threaten, but we cannot afford to act as though there were no problem.

The ostensible purpose of U.S. policy has been to align Washington with the black majorities that are eventually going to carry the day in Africa. This tactic, it is hoped, will prevent the Soviets from playing on racial fears and prejudices to advance communist penetration of Africa. The policy has not precluded errors in judgment, however, and has occasionally resulted in confusion. For example, the United States initially regarded Prime Minister Smith's internal plan to bring about gradual black majority rule in Rhodesia as a step forward. However, when the plan was rejected as unacceptable by the black Rhodesians waging war from outside and the leadership of neighboring black states, the United States faced a dilemma—half leaning towards a settlement that moved toward democratic rule, and simultaneously standing off for fear of offending the radicals and black Africans.

In an emotionally charged issue, lack of wholesale support for one side is construed as support for the other, and whether U.S. policy-makers agree or not, Africans think that America can do something. If the West is not forthcoming with support for African positions, the Africans will seek, and most likely get, support from communist states. For communist states there is a clear objective, and the costs are not disproportionate to possible advantages.

The southern African confrontation has not as yet affected the vital interests of major powers; nevertheless, the prospects of southern Africa becoming an area for world conflict must be included in any assessment of U.S.-African policy or of Soviet-American relations. Potentially, a "race war" in South Africa could cause domestic American unrest exceeding that of the Vietnam era as black Americans and others who abhor the apartheid policies and practices of the ruling white minority demonstrate either against American involvement supporting the regime or for U.S. support to rebel groups. The questions are whether American economic and security interests will dictate neutrality or intervention or whether concern for human rights and traditional democratic ideals will overcome them—and with what result.

Over the long run, the problems of South Africa notwithstanding, economic development issues ultimately will determine if African leaders can fulfill the aspirations of their people to acquire a degree of stability that will not threaten U.S. interests. What Africa requires above all else is sensible continuing pressure for development. For example, the Sahel region has been a major recipient of international relief assistance, yet the desert is steadily encroaching. In Ethiopia, recurring famines have been more destructive of life than even the archaic civil warfare since 1974. Africa must seek to reverse the economic and ecological decline of the Sahel and lay the foundation for future growth.

As pointed out earlier, Africa is heavily dependent on the future of the world economy. No African nation can plan its future effectively if its income depends on external economic forces over which it has little or no influence. African leaders, in coordination with the industrialized countries, must be prepared to address the crushing balance-of-payment problems and the debt burdens that many poor African nations suffer as a result of rapidly increasing prices for energy and global inflation.

The U.S. economy is not self-sufficient. In the increasing world competition for resources and markets, the United States will become more dependent on Africa. Dependence is a two-way street, though heavily weighted in favor of the Western nations. With few exceptions, Africa needs American capital and technological know-how to fuel its economic development far more than the U.S. relies on African exports.

While the United States supports the authority of the OAU as the arbiter of inter-African disputes, it remains a question whether or not this requires American support for the OAU principle of territorial integrity. The survival of African borders for the past several decades does not mean that they should or will endure. Indeed, the chances that African borders will survive intact over the next two or three decades are remote. The issue of border inviolability therefore may pose a major problem for U.S. policy in the decade ahead—a problem to which there are no simple, universal answers.

The American policy agenda for Africa will be full in the 1980s and the issues will be difficult. For example, African states will likely seek to increase their level of armaments and improve their military capabilities. The United States will continue to face the dilemma of minimizing arms transfers to African states for the sake of stability, while knowing that unilateral restraint risks the defeat of friendly states as well as the loss of influence (as in Ethiopia) and export revenues. Second, particularly if events in southern Africa worsen, the United States will have to have secure special bilateral relationships with major black governments, which will be difficult. In this regard, Kenya, Nigeria, Somalia, Sudan, and Zaire perhaps rank highest in U.S. interests. Third, the continent is flooded with refugees. Social and ethnic divisions within and across African boundaries create external forces posing grave security threats to many nations, e.g., Ugandans exiled in the 1970s and Sudanese sanctuary for Eritrean rebels.

Viable American policies and programs to address these and other African issues in the future will have to reflect thorough understanding of the political, social, and economic dynamics of a very complex continent. They will also have to be predicated on an awareness that Africa must be viewed in a global context, that the Soviets are expanding their role in the continent using primarily military instruments, that African states are tied primarily to the Western economic system but also have very real security problems, that Western responses to African security needs are therefore of great importance, and that the United States must operate in close conjunction with its European, Arab, Asian, and other friends—since our influence and resources are limited as measured against the continent's great needs.

DISCUSSION QUESTIONS

1. To what extent have Soviet successes in Angola and Ethiopia contributed to the deterioration of U.S.-Soviet relations? How do events in the rest of Africa affect this relationship?

2. Will current American policy be responsive to the requirements likely to prevail in Africa in the next five to ten years? Does it adequately take account of the activities of other states that seek to do damage to U.S. interests in Africa?

3. What kind of policies should the United States pursue in those cases where there is a clear violation of the human rights of the inhabitants of a country, but where the leadership or administration of that country is pursuing a dynamic economic policy?

4. A majority of the African states are looking for the United States to assist them as they seek to build modern societies. Will the United States be willing to share its technology with Africa? Will it be ready to help stabilize the basic commodity prices on which many of their economies are based? Will it treat their products fairly in the international marketplace?

5. Can the United States strike a balance between a policy emphasizing human rights and African insistence on noninterference? Should it try?

6. What African forces/factors will likely shape the future of the continent, and how will they impact on U.S.-African relations?

7. Can and will the African military extricate itself from politics?

8. How should the United States approach the Marxist governments in Angola and Mozambique?

9. Will South Africa come to terms with black nationalism? How?

10. How should the issue of apartheid in South Africa be dealt with in U.S. policy on Africa?

RECOMMENDED READING

Albright, David. *The U.S.S.R. and Sub-Saharan Africa in the 1980s.* CSIS Washington Paper no. 101. New York: Frederick A. Praeger, 1983.

Bienen, Henry. *Armies and Parties in Africa.* New York: Africana, 1978.

Busia, Kofi A. *Africa in Search of Identity.* New York: Frederick A. Praeger, 1967.

Gavshon, Arthur. *Crisis in Africa: Battleground of East and West.* New York: Penguin, 1982.

Kitchen, Helen, ed. *AEI Foreign Policy and Defense Review* 1, no. 1 (*Options for U.S. Policy toward Africa*) (1979).

———, ed. *Africa: From Mystery to Maze.* Lexington, Mass.: D. C. Heath, 1976.

Legum, Colin. "The African Crisis." *Foreign Affairs* 57, no. 3 (*America and the World*) (1978): 646–50.

———, ed. *African Contemporary Record: Annual Survey and Documents, 1976–1977.* New York: Africana, 1977.

Nye, Joseph S. "Corruption and Political Development: A Cost-Benefit Analysis." *American Political Science Review* 61, no. 2 (June 1967): 417–27.

Said, Abdul A. *The African Phenomenon.* Boston: Allyn & Bacon, 1968.

Welch, Claude E., ed. *The Soldier and the State in Africa.* Evanston, Ill.: Northwestern University Press, 1970.

Whittaker, Jennifer Seymour, ed. *Africa and the United States: Vital Interests.* New York: New York University Press, 1978.

Young, Crawford. "Zaire: The Unending Crisis." *Foreign Affairs* 57, no. 1 (fall 1978): 169–85.

20

LATIN AMERICA

Relations between the United States and Latin America* have changed dramatically since 1944, when Joseph Stalin's argument may have been taken seriously by many people, including Stalin, that each republic of the Soviet Union should be given membership in the United Nations to balance the votes of Washington's Latin American "provinces." During the past decade or two most Latin American "provinces" have taken great pains to demonstrate that in both domestic and international policy spheres they act independently of Washington. Of course, U.S. power and influence in Latin America were never so strong and all-encompassing as Stalin alleged.

U.S. presence in Latin America during most of this century has varied from pervasive to moderate, depending upon whether one measures it north or south of Panama. North, in the Caribbean basin, a mixture of close military ties, high economic dependence, and the relative smallness of most countries—Mexico excepted—long allowed the United States to do much as it pleased most of the time. On the other hand, even at the height of Yankee influence (and contrary to Stalin), the South American states maintained much greater control over their own situations than did the Latin states further north.

In both South America and the Caribbean basin, feelings about the United States are intense. The Spanish- and English-speaking states of the hemisphere share important cultural values and a common beginning in the revolt against European colonialism, and all pay at least lip service to the ideas of liberty, justice, and social equality. Because of these similarities, some in the Americas long assumed a permanent commonality of interests between the United

* The term *Latin America* is used in this volume to embrace all of the nations south of the Rio Grande River, i.e., Mexico and all its southern neighbors, plus the nations of the Caribbean. *South America* refers to the southern continent of the Western Hemisphere, while *Caribbean basin* refers to the Caribbean states plus Central America and Mexico, i.e., Latin America less South America. In some contexts, the northernmost South American states, that is, Colombia, Venezuela, Guyana, Suriname, and French Guiana, are also counted as part of the basin.

FIG. 20.1
LATIN AMERICA

States and its Latin neighbors. This outlook has been labeled the "Western Hemisphere Idea."[1] For an increasing number of Latin Americans, however, past dominance by the United States and seemingly insoluble present growth and dependency problems have raised questions as to whether their true interests are better served by closer cooperation with Western Europe, Japan, and the less-developed countries of the Middle East, Africa, and Asia, rather than with the United States.

U.S. Interests in Latin America. Since the early nineteenth century, the primary interest of the United States in Latin America has been to have the area be a peaceful, secure southern flank. This objective led directly to President James Monroe's official warning against incursions by the European powers into the Western Hemisphere. "The American continents . . . are henceforth not to be considered as subjects for future colonization by any European power."[2] Monroe went on specifically to warn the "allied powers" that "we should consider any attempt on their part to extend their system to any portion of this hemisphere as dangerous to our peace and safety." His doctrine, it should be noted, had nothing to do with interamerican relations as such, but it contained the seeds of what later grew to be called pan-Americanism.

President Polk, in reaffirming the Monroe Doctrine in 1845, added a corollary forbidding the voluntary transfer of territory by an American state to a European power. Other presidents further spelled out the implications of the doctrine; for instance, Grover Cleveland's secretary of state in 1895 said, "Today the U.S. is practically sovereign on this continent, and its fiat is law upon the subjects to which it confines its interposition." Teddy Roosevelt in 1904 asserted that the doctrine carried "the exercise of an international police power" in the Western Hemisphere—a corollary subsequently used to justify military intervention in the Caribbean basin.

Although many Latin Americans originally welcomed the doctrine (and at the Lima Conference in 1847 in effect endorsed it), disenchantment set in over the decades. By the early twentieth century Latin Americans were unsuccessfully trying to multilateralize the doctrine—an enterprise that President Wilson enthusiastically but unsuccessfully backed. It was not until World War II that the American nations as a whole agreed that an assault by a non-American nation upon the territory or independence of any American state "is an act of aggression against all the other American states."[3]

Ironically, shortly after the basic principles of the Monroe Doctrine were commonly accepted throughout the hemisphere, the Latin American states began to move away from what many of them increasingly viewed as a license for American imperialism in the hemisphere. Despite such Latin American misgivings, the United States has continued to view the doctrine as an integral part of its defense policy and as a signal that it will not tolerate a military threat from the south.[4]

The longstanding lack of a military threat in and from Latin America has facilitated the deployment of U.S. power in other regions. This has been important to the United States, for resources employed in defending against a Western Hemisphere–based opponent would not be available for the defense of Western Europe, Japan, or the Middle East. It is a consequence of this interest that Washington has been adamant that the Soviet Union live up to the 1962 understanding that it not place offensive weapons in Cuba. The high sensitivity of American political leaders in 1979 to the presence of a Soviet brigade in Cuba underscores the point.

Keeping the southern flank secure also explains continuing U.S. efforts to prevent historic rivalries among South American countries from degenerating into armed conflict. War in South America would not only force Washington's attention away from the European and Asian balances; it would also create a situation in which a South American country might seek aid from outside the hemisphere, e.g., from the Soviet Union. Under such circumstances, Moscow might demand and obtain bases on Washington's southern flank. In addition to forcing the United States to develop a southward-facing defense system, such bases would pose an increased threat to the vital 1400-mile-wide South Atlantic Narrows between Natal, Brazil (South America), and Dakar, Senegal (Africa).

Historically, a second major U.S. interest in Latin America has been in the continuing operation and defense of the Panama Canal. To protect the canal, the United States acquired territory and built bases in the 1900–1930 period. The importance of these investments was shown by the great utility of the canal in both World War II and the Korean conflict. However, the wartime role of the canal declined as U.S. carriers in the 1950s became too large for the locks to handle and as the Soviet Union in the middle 1960s deployed nuclear delivery vehicles capable of reaching the vulnerable locks. While still useful in deploying warships prior to general war hostilities and in moving cargo inexpensively between the Atlantic and the Pacific, the Panama Canal is no longer a vital national security consideration—as was confirmed by the Panama Canal Treaty in which Washington (including the Joint Chiefs of Staff) agreed gradually to transfer the canal to Panama between 1979 and 2000.

A third major, continuing U.S. interest in Latin America has been economic: oil, raw materials, markets, and investments. The Latin American regional economy is one of the world's fastest growing: by 1985, it will be about the size Europe's was in 1970. The region already provides about 14 percent of both U.S. exports and imports and has received about 18 percent of U.S. private investment.[5] It is a major supplier of raw materials to the West. During World War II, it was a primary source for the United States of antimony, bauxite, copper, iron, lead, mercury, petroleum, platinum, tungsten, zinc, and a number of lesser minerals. It continues to provide most of these same materials to the industrialized north. In the event of general war, U.S. access to these strategic materials—the supply of which would not be so vulnerable to Soviet interdiction as those in Africa or Asia—might well

2-24-74

"YES! FROM NOW ON WE ARE EQUAL!"

Reprinted with permission of Ranan R. Lurie from his book, *Lurie's Worlds, 1970–1980*, University Press of Hawaii and King Features Syndicate, Inc.

prove vital. This could be particularly important in the case of petroleum, in view of Mexican and Venezuelan potential and Caribbean refinery capacity.

Latin Americans are ambivalent about their economic ties with the United States, yet they need capital, technology, and—in some cases—key skills from the United States. For their part, many U.S. multinational corporations, despite the risks, continue to see Latin America as a potentially profitable region in which to invest. This mutual need and deep-seated distrust that characterize relations between multinational corporations and host Latin American governments can lead to political conflict with international ramifications. The best known recent example occurred in Chile during the early 1970s. At that time, President Salvador Allende nationalized U.S.-owned copper mines several years after the previous government had agreed to joint ownership and operation of the mines. President Allende also seized the U.S.-

owned telephone system as part of his efforts to convert Chile into a socialist economy. The antisocialist coalition against Allende involved opposition political parties, segments of the poor and middle classes, the Argentine and Brazilian militaries, and official agencies of the U.S. government. Communists and leftist radicals accused the latter of having engineered Allende's overthrow, although most evidence suggests that Washington played a relatively minor role.[6] Nevertheless, despite fallout from the Chilean experience, U.S. foreign investment—and the possibility that more will be forthcoming—remains an important factor in keeping Latin American governments more considerate of U.S. interests than they otherwise would be.

Linked to the foregoing interests of the United States is a fourth one of having its southern neighbors, especially those in the Caribbean basin—Mexico, in particular—effectively develop their economies and political structures in ways that benefit their own peoples. Mexico is the focus of this interest as a consequence of

the massive economic, social, and cultural interconnections growing throughout the U.S. Borderlands and extending deep into both countries. The asymmetry of national power and the disparity of socioeconomic conditions between the two bordering nations are among the greatest in the world. . . . Thus, the borderlands could become either the melting pot or the violent cauldron of future U.S.-Mexican relations.[7]

The same reasoning, though with considerably lesser force, applies elsewhere in the Caribbean area.

A fifth prime interest of the United States in Latin America lies in securing the support of the regional states for U.S. foreign and security policies. Despite the recent weakening of the inter-American alliance, other nations—including the U.S.S.R.—continue to weigh this connection in their estimates of U.S. power and purpose. Latin Americans themselves, in spite of their distrust of the United States, hold the belief that the European–North American–Latin American triangle houses a single, although diverse, culture. In view of the growing strains between Europe and North America, on the one hand, and the developing world, on the other, Latin Americans will increasingly be torn between their perceptions of themselves as part of the West or part of the South.

Historical Patterns in Hemispheric Relations: U.S. Hegemony. The Western Hemisphere Idea alluded to above proclaimed that Anglo- and Latin-American interests, while not identical, are in basic harmony. During and immediately after World War II this interpretation seemed reasonable. For the most part, Latin America joined forces with the United States against Nazi Germany—though sometimes reluctantly—and only after the outcome was a foregone conclusion (e.g., Argentina). Even as late as 1969, following a decade of political realignment, as influential an American as Nelson Rockefeller could invoke the "special relationship" assumed by the Western Hemisphere Idea as the basis of Washington's Latin American policy.[8]

Historically, *special relationship* was more descriptive of U.S. ties with the Caribbean basin than with Latin America as a whole. As early as the 1840s, Washington had openly sought to dominate the Caribbean basin. However, England's naval supremacy forced the United States to accept, in principle, joint control over what would be the most important symbol of foreign intrusion into the area—a transisthmian canal. Six decades later, the United States had become a global power and England was preoccupied by the unprecedented growth of German military and industrial might. In search of allies to contain Berlin, London gestured to Washington by withdrawing its fleet from the Caribbean.[9] Soon after the British fleet's departure the United States played a central role in detaching Panama from Colombia. The newly independent Panamanians, apprehensive that Washington's enthusiasm for their independence might fade, accepted President Theodore Roosevelt's terms for constructing a transisthmian canal. Most controversially, Panama ceded to U.S. control "in perpetuity" over the waterway, and over a ten-mile-wide strip bisecting the country. From the perspective of U.S. war-making capabilities, the canal dramatically eased the problem of naval deployment between the Atlantic and Pacific theaters. Consequently, as noted earlier, defense of the canal became the overriding U.S. policy objective in the Caribbean area. Other Caribbean initiatives by the United States, including the acquisition of Puerto Rico and the virtual acquisition of Cuba (and hence Guantánamo) as a result of the Spanish-American War, solidified the U.S. control of the Caribbean and the approaches to it.

President Wilson purchased the Virgin Islands in 1916, justifying their acquisition as necessary for defense of the Panama Canal. The same motive caused Washington to be increasingly concerned that chronic political instability might tempt Europeans to reintroduce military forces into the Caribbean basin. Any foreign military presence, regardless of the use for which it was intended initially, potentially threatened the canal. To avoid such threats the United States assumed the role of Caribbean police officer. Between 1900 and 1933 U.S. armed forces intervened in Panama, Cuba, Nicaragua, Mexico, Haiti, and the Dominican Republic. Far from apoligizing for these interventions, Washington explicitly stated its right to carry them out by the so-called Roosevelt Corollary to the Monroe Doctrine. (Theodore Roosevelt contended that, for all practical purposes, the United States could do whatever it believed necessary under the Monroe Doctrine.)

United States economic interests in the Caribbean basin also grew substantially during the first half of the twentieth century. U.S. corporations invested billions of dollars in Cuban sugar, Mexican petroleum, and Central American bananas. Protection of these investments became an important policy objective, and an influential school of thought about U.S.-Latin American relations maintains that economic factors were more important than political considerations as causes of Washington's Caribbean military adventures.[10]

In any case, all Latin Americans gave high priority to discouraging the

United States from intervening militarily south of the Rio Grande. During the 1930s, Washington gradually abandoned the doctrine of unilateral military intervention in Latin America, replacing it with the so-called Good Neighbor policies of President Franklin Roosevelt.[11] In return, the Latins threw their support behind the European and Asian policies of their northern neighbor.

Venezuela's location on South America's northern coast, and its importance as a source of petroleum for New England and the Middle Atlantic states, caused Washington to treat Caracas as essentially part of its Caribbean basin preserve. (Venezuela's neighbor Colombia has also sometimes been so treated.) The rest of South America was perceived by Washington policymakers as a special sphere of influence, although one of less strategic importance. Except in Brazil, the South American investments of U.S. corporations were less extensive than in the Caribbean area, and the continent's southern and western nations were far from the Panama Canal.

In South America, as in the Caribbean basin, the United States largely had things its own way between 1900 and 1960. During World War I, Latin American governments either declared war on the Central Powers or maintained a pro-Allied neutrality. In World War II they declared war on the Axis powers, and between 1947 and 1960 they sided with Washington against Moscow. Economically, most Latin American countries remained eager to supply raw materials for the United States. They also encouraged foreign investment. By 1960, Latin America accounted for $8.1 billion, or 26 percent, of all U.S. foreign investment.[12] Also, large numbers of Latin Americans, especially military officers, were attending United States universities and professional and military schools. Until late in the Eisenhower administration, virtually all Latin America remained essentially Washington's special preserve.

Brazil, dramatically different from its Spanish-speaking neighbors, long considered itself joined with the United States in a unique partnership. This perception figured significantly in the decision of President Getulio Vargas to send a Brazilian division to Italy during World War II.[13] On the other hand, Washington generally took the Brazilians for granted. Along with the other Latin Americans, they received periodic pats on the head as long as they did not ally with an extrahemispheric power or threaten hemispheric peace.

Latent anti-Yankee feelings, never far below the surface, were expressed more openly and with greater frequency after 1960. The Roosevelt Corollary had neither been forgotten nor forgiven; the area's terms of trade with the United States had shifted so that ever larger quantities of Latin raw materials were needed to purchase U.S. manufactured goods; and Latin resentment had increased against the continual repatriation of profits by U.S. investors. In 1961 Fidel Castro nationalized, without compensation, all U.S. investment in Cuba. Subsequently, after Castro repulsed the half-hearted, CIA-sponsored Bay of Pigs invasion and declared himself a Marxist-Leninist, many Latin Americans felt freer to express their grievances. With Castro's support, various disaffected locals joined in guerrilla warfare that sought to duplicate the Cuban revolution in selected Caribbean and South American countries (see Chapter 13 on "Revolutionary Warfare.") For the first time in more than half a century, the United States faced an important political, economic, and military challenge in the Western Hemisphere.

After the Bay of Pigs fiasco (1961), the United States began responding differently and with greater skill to Castro and his Soviet allies. The widely publicized "Alliance for Progress" launched by the Kennedy administration was intended to diffuse Latin American economic grievances. President Kennedy's success in the 1962 Cuban Missile Crisis discredited Soviet military power while building confidence in U.S. leadership. (The 1965 Dominican Republic intervention also demonstrated U.S. resolve but awakened old fears associated with the Roosevelt Corollary.)[14] U.S. support for various Latin American governments' efforts to innoculate the hemisphere against guerrilla warfare paid large dividends in 1967, when U.S.-trained Bolivian jungle troops located and destroyed Che Guevara's guerrilla band.

Despite important successes, Washington's Latin American policies between 1961 and 1969 did not restore U.S. influence in the Western Hemisphere to its pre-Castro level. U.S. lack of success in Vietnam diminished Washington's prestige and reduced the credibility of its armed forces. Also, U.S. preoccupation with Vietnam guaranteed that the Alliance for Progress would not receive funding sufficient to achieve its ambitious objectives. For many Latins, U.S. sacrifice of Alliance support on behalf of an Asian war laid to rest the notion that the Western Hemisphere peoples were bound together in a special relationship.[15] The Vietnam fighting also suggested that it had become extremely expensive for the industrialized United States to intervene militarily in the developing Southern Hemisphere. Thus while antipathy toward communism remained pervasive in Latin America, there was a widespread perception that, because of the North Vietnamese victory, Latin Americans were in a better bargaining position than ever before with their northern neighbor.

Contemporary Patterns of Hemispheric Interaction: The Emergence of Brazil. Since 1970, Washington's presence in South America has become secondary to issues surrounding the emerging intracontinental balance of power. This balance exhibits three basic characteristics. First, Brazil has come to dwarf any other single South American country in terms of population, economic muscle, and global political influence. This Portuguese-speaking giant presently encompasses half of South America's population, 49 percent of its gross domestic product, and 35 percent of its troops under arms.[16]

A related, but equally basic, consideration of the South American balance is that Argentina, once considered the continent's most promising country, has fallen far behind Brazil in most empirical measures of national power. Concurrently, the Spanish-speaking buffer states separating Brazil and Argentina have gravitated toward the former. Along Brazil's northern and western frontiers, also, increasing activity characterizes Brazil's relations with Peru, Ecuador, Colombia, Venezuela, and Guyana.

Brazil's development has transformed the balance of power throughout the Southern Cone,* historically an area of intense Brazilian-Argentine rivalry. At the end of the colonial era, Buenos Aires controlled territories currently comprising Bolivia, Paraguay, Uruguay, and part of southern Brazil. During the struggle for independence, these areas—assisted by Brazil—resisted efforts by Buenos Aires to incorporate them into the new Argentine nation. Nevertheless, Buenos Aires historically has considered Bolivia, Paraguay, and Uruguay as special spheres of influence.[17] Since 1950, however, continued internal political strife and accompanying economic stagnation have made Argentina increasingly less able to project power beyond its frontiers. The century-old parity between Argentina and Brazil has given way to growing Brazilian superiority.

Uruguay and Paraguay have almost become Brazilian dependencies. In the former, Brazilian police advisers played a central role during the early 1970s in destroying the Tupamaro guerillas. At the height of Tupamaro terrorism the possibility was strong that forces sympathetic to the guerrillas might elect Uruguay's president. Brasília made the unacceptability of this contingency quite clear when its powerful Third Army undertook large-scale maneuvers along the Uruguayan border immediately prior to the balloting. Elements favoring cooperation with Brazil made an unexpectedly strong showing and retained control of the presidency. In 1975, Brazil and Uruguay signed a comprehensive "Treaty of Friendship, Cooperation, and Commerce." Finally, continuing purchases by Brazilians of land on the Uruguayan side of their mutual border is taken by Montevideo and Buenos Aires as having important geopolitical implications.[18]

Brazilian economic dynamism over the past decades, when contrasted to lackluster Argentine performance, has exacerbated the most divisive issue between South America's two most important powers—economic development of the La Plata River Basin. Brazil strengthened ties with Paraguay in 1956, soon after General Juan Perón's ouster ended a decade of close cooperation between the Argentine strongman and his Paraguayan counterpart, General Alfredo Stroessner. The 1956 Brazilian-Paraguayan economic treaty established a duty-free zone for trade between the two countries at Paranagua. Within the year the treaty was followed by agreement to construct a rail link between Paraguay's capital of Asunción and Brazil. A complementary paved highway was also planned. General Stroessner continued expanding Brazilian-Paraguayan economic ties during 1958, specifically by granting Brazilian companies the right to search for oil throughout 4 million hectares of the Chaco. In short, Brazilian-Paraguayan interaction between 1956 and 1958 shifted Asunción away from the Argentine economic orbit.[19]

* The term *Southern Cone* refers to Argentina, Bolivia, Chile, Paraguay, Uruguay, and—in some contexts—southern Brazil.

In 1969, following a decade of relative diplomatic inactivity, Brazil, Argentina, Paraguay, and Bolivia signed a pact calling for joint development of the La Plata River basin. Differences in Argentina's and Brazil's understanding of the document quickly surfaced. Buenos Aires claimed that all signatories were committed not to undertake La Plata River development projects, especially those influencing the flow of rivers passing through another country, without approval from the concerned country. Brazil nevertheless entered into bilateral agreements with Paraguay and Bolivia resulting in the construction of major hydroelectric projects at Sete Quedas and Itaipú.[20] Even the recall of Argentina's ambassador could not shake Brasília from its position that the La Plata River Pact required only that all signatories be informed of Brazilian plans and intentions.

In addition to frustrations associated with perceived Brazilian high-handedness at Itaipú, Argentine-Brazilian relations have been strained by the latter's unwillingness to stem the flow of Brazilian settlers into once-vacant southern frontier areas, some of which encompass Paraguayan territory. Within Brazil itself, many formerly unoccupied areas along the southern frontier have been successfully colonized, a sharp contrast to affairs on the Argentine side of the Brazilian-Argentine border. (On the Brazilian side of this border population densities are more than twice as great as on the Argentine side.) Argentine apprehensions about frontier colonization, as well as about hydroelectric development, are strongly geopolitical. Buenos Aires views each as fresh evidence of Brasília's growing political and economic influence in the La Plata River basin.[21]

West of the La Plata River basin lies Bolivia, the weakest and most vulnerable state on Brazil's southern or southwestern frontiers. Policy-makers in La Paz, the Bolivian capital, generally project unconcern about the possibility of a Brazilian takeover. They point to the writings of General Golbery, the Brazilian military's leading geopolitician. Golbery's widely circulated thesis characterizes Brazil as a territorially satisfied power, not seeking a "way to the Pacific."[22]

General Golbery also stated, however, that Brazil can never be indifferent to security problems on its frontiers or anywhere else in South America. This declaration took on special significance for Bolivia during 1970–71, when Brasialia openly sided with the conservative Banzer forces against the left-wing military government of General Juan J. Torres. The extent of Brazilian aid to Banzer is debatable, but there is no question that it contributed to Torres's overthrow.* Subsequent Brazilian support for Banzer has made it difficult, if not impossible, for Bolivian leftists to attract enough support to

---

* Brazil's desire to have ideologically compatible governments on its frontiers—an ideological security zone—has been stated by various participants in and supporters of the 1964 revolution. In *Geopolítica do Brasil* (Rio de Janeiro: Olympia, 1967), p. 175, General Golbery himself argues that Brasília cannot be indifferent to "security problems on her frontier or anywhere on the continent." Cf. Peter S. Smith, "Bolivian Oil and Brazilian Economic Nationalism," *Journal of Inter-American Studies and World Affairs* 13 (April 1971): 173–75.

seriously challenge the ruling conservatives. Brazil therefore retains important influence in determining what type of political regime is viable in Bolivia.

Brazil's economic presence in Bolivia equals or surpasses its political influence. Economically, Brasília hopes—as a first priority—to mobilize Bolivia's suspected, but as yet largely unproved, energy reserves for Brazilian industrialization. In addition to cooperation in exploring for petroleum, the sale to Brazil of Bolivian natural gas, Brazilian assistance in developing rail links between the two states, and a number of other projects involving Brazilian help in Bolivian development are indicators of the importance of these ties.

Brazilian economic influence in Bolivia was formalized and expanded in August 1977, when the two countries signed a "Treaty of Cooperation, Friendship, and Commerce."[23] While the occasion prompted President Geisel to proclaim that Brazil and Bolivia were now linked in a "special relationship," some Bolivians speculated that they were becoming the appendage of a new imperial power.

Charges of Brazilian imperialist design in Bolivia have not been confined to economic matters. Some Bolivaians speculate that Brasília plans to annex eastern Bolivia, specifically the province of Santa Cruz, and that eventually Brazil hopes for a Pacific frontier. Although these fears of Brazilian territorial expansion may be unwarranted, successful Brazilian colonization along the Bolivian frontier has oriented populations on both sides of the international boundary toward Portuguese-speaking South America. A sizable element in Santa Cruz has long lobbied for greater autonomy from La Paz, and some extremists openly discuss the economic advantages of independence or of an "Outer Mongolia" type relationship with Brazil.[24] Santa Cruz separatism, while currently the source of only moderate tension, remains a problem whose intensification could alter international boundaries in South America and lead to confrontation between Brazil and its Hispanic neighbors.

To the north, the sparsely populated Amazon basin long served as a buffer between Brazil and its northern neighbors—Peru, Colombia, Venezuela, and Guyana. Brazil's Amazon basin encompasses 40 percent of its total land area, but contains only about 3 percent of the national population. But Brazil has begun to emphasize Amazon development, aimed both at exploiting the basin's resources and at its geopolitical importance.[25]

The initial thrust of Brazil's Amazon development was to link the tropical north to southern population and industrial centers. New roads were built, air routes increased, and pioneers settled in scattered jungle communities close to major transportation arteries and on the frontiers. The army staff moved its Amazon Command from the coastal city of Belém to Manaus, a thousand miles inland. Increased emphasis was given to uncovering minerals in the Amazon basin and to attracting foreign investment in logging, agriculture, and manufacturing. Although the pace of development slowed in 1974, following the dramatic rise in petroleum prices and consequent economic troubles, there continues to be a growing Brazilian presence in the Amazon basin.[26]

The northern and western South American countries also look upon their Amazon regions as resource frontiers. During the middle 1960s President Fernando Belaúnde of Peru reactivated long-dormant plans to connect Lima and the Peruvian Amazon by road. More ambitiously, Belaúnde proposed that the Spanish-speaking countries join in building a highway along the eastern slope of the Andes, from Chile to Venezuela. This would stimulate trade among the Andean countries, facilitate the movement of their nationals into and throughout the Amazon, and provide a much needed symbol of cooperation. In principle the governments of Chile, Bolivia, Peru, Ecuador, Colombia, and Venezuela supported the idea of an eastern slope highway. The large investment required, however, made others reluctant to join Peru in its construction.[27] Financial considerations also proved central in the Peruvian army's decision to abandon the entire project following the overthrow of President Belaúnde. Welfare and redistributive expenditures seemed safer and more palatable politically than investing in projects with uncertain and long-run payoffs.

Colombia, too, periodically attempts measures to tie its Amazon periphery to its Andean heartland. The jungle city of Villavicencio is one of Bogotá's more successful efforts. Venezuela has also sought to integrate its Amazonian frontier with its more developed regions. It has linked its Brazilian border town of Santa Elena with the rest of the country by road, but here again its presence along the frontier is overshadowed by Brazilian dynamism.

Brazil's growing power and relative success in opening up the Amazon basin has, not surprisingly, created uneasiness. The vast jungle barrier that shielded Peru, Colombia, Venezuela, and Guyana from effective Brazilian power has been breached, and before the end of the century will provide little protection. Accompanying its economic drive, Brazil has also been increasingly active diplomatically. The Brazilian foreign ministry began negotiating cooperative bilateral treaties with its Amazonian neighbors during the middle 1970s. In late 1977, President Ernesto Geisel invited delegations from all neighboring countries bordering on the Amazon to Brasília for the purpose of working out agreement on an Amazonian common market. Suspicion that Brazil's plan for "physical integration" of the entire Amazon basin would guarantee its hegemony over the area blocked agreement on a formal pact.[28]

More recently, Brazil's diplomatic initiatives have been visible in the Guianas. Brazil continues to retain a geopolitical interest in maintaining the status quo in the Guyana-Venezuela border dispute. In the same context, Brasilia has intervened diplomatically in Suriname to ward off what has appeared to be a move toward Cuba, following a period of domestic turmoil in that country since the early 1980s.

U.S. Relations with Central America. As Brazil's rise to regional power has altered political and security perceptions in South America, the longstanding dominance of the United States is being challenged north of Panama. While increasing political turbulence in the Caribbean and in Central America has not yet seriously injured U.S. security interests, the whole Caribbean basin is obviously receiving renewed U.S. attention, in our effort to deal with social and economic problems and increased Cuban and Soviet activity in support of new "revolutionary" governments.

Mexico. Although U.S.-Mexican relations continue to dominate Mexican foreign policy and although Mexico continues to be closely tied to the U.S. economically, the recent discovery and initial exploitation by Mexico of vast new oil deposits has increased its importance and independence in hemispheric affairs as well as in the world in general. It has also created a new area of interaction between Mexico and the United States, adding oil and gas to the list of matters requiring bilateral accommodation. The Mexicans so far have guarded the advantage the new oil has given them, linking U.S. access to oil at least in part to bilateral progress in such other areas as access to U.S. markets, investment, trade, and migration policies. Moreover, Mexico has avoided selling all its exportable oil to the United States, contracting throughout Latin American and in Europe and Asia as well. Mexican gas is coming to the United States, but in much smaller amounts than the United States wants and at a relatively high price. Finally, Mexico must now pay increasing attention to its neighbors in Central America, a region that has become a battleground of conflicting foreign and domestic interests.

Nicaragua. During the late 1970s, Central America experienced a series of important political events that focused attention on the region. As noted in Chapter 13, the Somoza family in Nicaragua was toppled and replaced by a coalition of mostly leftist forces, dominated by the Sandinista guerillas. The new government has received substantial Cuban support in rebuilding the Nicaraguan economy, as it undoubtedly received training and arms during the revolution. The U.S. government, which contributed to the downfall of Somoza by withdrawing military and diplomatic support, has been publicly vilified as the longstanding ally of the old regime. In response, the United States has sought to strengthen the hand of moderate elements and, by offering aid, to afford the new government an economic and political alternative to reliance on Cuban and other leftist support. Nicaragua's increased support for the leftist guerrillas in El Salvador during the early 1980s proved a major obstacle to improved relations between the United States and Nicaragua. Whether accommodation between the United States and revolutionary Nicaragua can be reached remains to be seen.

Guatemala and El Salvador. Despite the fact that the United States finally turned on the Somoza regime, more than forty years of U.S. support for the family's rule ensured that the revolution's success would be widely seen in Latin America as a reversal by the United States and as a demonstration of its impotence in its own backyard. Nowhere were the lessons of Nicaragua studied more assiduously than in neighboring Guatemala and El Salvador.

Both had become bitterly divided countries during the course of the 1970s—in Guatemala's case the violence stretched back to 1954. Extremist factions on both the left and right have sought to destroy the middle ground in both countries and to impose their own rule. Thousands have been killed in each country, with no end to the bloodshed in sight as the decade of the 1980s began. For the United States, these developments seem increasingly likely to confront it

with a choice between closer identification with repressive regimes, which would be a reversal of a decade of halting attempts to improve the U.S. image in the hemisphere, or watching regimes turn leftward, if not "Communist." The spectre of "another Cuba" in Central America and the Caribbean was a powerful image in American politics, and after Afghanistan it would be all the harder for Washington to resist harsh responses to radical movements.[29]

Cuba. While neighbors all around—not only Guatemala and El Salvador but also Honduras, Panama and Mexico—were anxiously focused on Central American developments, other challenges to U.S. interests were afoot in the Caribbean. The decades-old economic and diplomatic tensions between the United States and Cuba were again by 1983 a major issue in Latin America. Soviet combat troops in Cuba, Cubans in Africa, emergence of another Cuban admirer in the form of Maurice Bishop's Grenada, and major disagreement among Cuba and Peru, Venezuela, Costa Rica, and the United States over tens of thousands of Cubans who sought asylum abroad as political refugees—all these were issues by 1983. Clearly, Cuba was perceived in Latin America and in the United States in quite contradictory ways; on the one hand, as a supporter of revolutionary governments and movements in and around the Caribbean and, on the other, as a country ever more a Soviet dependent and surrogate, beset by domestic economic ills that made it ill-suited to be any kind of model for emerging nationalistic movements in the region.

Cuba notwithstanding, during most of the 1970s, the traditional military and strategic dominance of the United States in the Caribbean was largely unchanged from the situation prevailing after the Cuban Missile Crisis of 1962, when the United States successfully fended off Soviet efforts to turn Cuba into a strategic missile launching platform. Subsequently, the United States reinforced its claim to undisputed strategic primacy in the region by the intervention (technically under the auspices of the Organization of American States [OAS]) in the Dominican Republic, as noted. American forces remained in place in Panama under the new Panama Canal treaties (1978). The Caribbean bastions of Puerto Rico and Guantánamo continued to provide a substantial U.S. military presence in the area. Nonetheless, it was increasingly clear by 1980 that such a presence and presumed U.S. dominance of the area would not preclude turmoil there, and that the United States would face increasing national security problems in the Caribbean area in the decade ahead.

Extrahemispheric Relations. Reducing involvement with, and dependency on, the United States is a prime goal throughout Latin America. To this end, several basic kinds of relationship involving countries outside the Western Hemisphere are pivotal. Unrivaled in importance is the search for technology and the attracting of associated foreign investment from Western Europe and Japan. As a counterpart, Latin Americans demand that Western Europe and Japan open their domestic markets to Latin goods and stabilize the prices paid for such commodities as coffee, sugar, iron, and bauxite. Similar considerations guide Latin America's dealings with Eastern Europe and the Soviet Union, although here an additional pattern emerges: playing the Western and Communist worlds off against each other in order to obtain the best possible terms. Another, third, basic pattern of extrahemispheric relations involves the links with other developing countries.

Despite deep-seated differences, Spanish- and Portuguese-speaking South Americans belong economically to the developing "South" or Third World. South Americans, while often among the most wealthy and industrially developed peoples of the Third World, are in comparison with north temperate nations more dependent on economic trends over which they have little control. Capital importers rather than exporters, borrowers rather than creators of the technology on which their modernization depends, and militarily very weak, South Americans share these traits with most Third World lands. In succeeding paragraphs we will examine some aspects of each of these three basic sets of relationships.

The search for technology, foreign investments, and financial credits from diversified sources is the cornerstone of Latin American economic policies. During the 1970s, by rationalizing their economic policies, Latin America's nations sought primarily to reduce the gap between themselves and the industrialized nations and to decrease their dependence on the United States. The changing economic realities of the 1980s forced most of these countries to take a much more pragmatic, if not economically and politically painful, approach to economic policies. At present, the primary goal for most Latin American nations is survival; with a $300 billion debt to the West, they must struggle even to keep afloat.

The optimistic forecasts for Latin America's economic performance have soured somewhat. The pattern of transformation from "economic miracle" to financial disaster varies from country to country, but the basic symptoms are ubiquitous. Energy price fluctuations, falling commodity prices, and a worldwide economic slow-down combined with a knack for overspending, mismanaging expenditures, and borrowing to cover the ever-growing gap between national income and spending have led to a troubled economic situation. Latin American economics are characterized by massive debts, intolerable debt-service ratios, negative growth rates, three-digit inflation and towering under/unemployment. Although the outlook is bleak, the experience has reinforced the Latin American desire for economic independence. The experience has also taught the necessity of building a strong production base incorporating the most advanced western technologies obtainable. To this extent, Western European, Japanese, and even communist-bloc influence in Latin America has grown as a challenge to U.S. economic preeminence.

As a result of the most recent economic crises, Latin Americans have become more subdued in their calls for commodity price stabilization schemes. The example of OPEC's ineffectiveness in holding up world oil prices in the face of a glutted market demonstrated the tenuous usefulness of even major commodity cartels. Following the oil price drop, Mexico, Venezuela, and Ecuador suffered a recession made all the more frustrating by earlier expectations of windfall oil wealth.

Like most of the developing world, Latin Americans assume that industrialization holds the key to higher living standards and increased international status. The North therefore must be made to accept finished goods, rather than raw material, for its technology. This entails opening Japanese and Western European markets to Brazilian automobiles, Argentine leather goods, Venezuelan petrochemicals, Colombian textiles, and other Latin American manufactures.[30] The reluctance of Western Europeans and Japanese to move in this direction, already a serious problem, is a growing source of friction between Latin America and the North.

Latin American economic relations with Eastern Europe and the Soviet Union are far less important than with Western Europe and Japan. In most respects, the technology available from the Communist world is inferior to that available in the West. Also, until recently, the Communist states have not been major purchasers of typical Latin American exports. Accordingly, relations with Eastern Europe and the Soviet Union (except for Cuba) have thus far expanded slowly from the almost nonexistent level of the middle 1960s.[31]

Despite unease with communism and the lack of a trading tradition with Eastern Europe and the Soviet Union, Latin America is likely to expand relations with the Second World during the closing decades of this century. Despite the increase of leftist insurgency, particularly in Central America, and residual difficulties with radical movements in South America, economic pragmatism has lessened Latin American reservations about trade with the Soviet bloc. Eastern European countries such as Czechoslovakia, East Germany, and Hungary are willing and able to export manufactured goods and technology. They are also showing increased interest in purchasing limited quantities of Latin American products. The same is true of the Soviets, to which recent significant purchases of Argentina's grains by the Soviet Union can attest. Overall, Soviet Eastern European trade with Latin America remains on a modest scale, but the fact that it exists at all provides the Latins with potential alternatives to their historically most important trading partners, the North Atlantic countries and Japan.

Latin American relations with Africa, Asia, and the Middle East—the other developing nations—have crystallized along several dimensions during the past decade. Economically, Brazil and some Spanish-speaking countries have begun selling manufactured goods and limited development technology to Africa and the Middle East (although not to Asia). In turn, Brazil especially has become heavily reliant on Nigerian and Middle Eastern oil.[32] Trade between Latin America and the Third World will expand slowly during the coming decades, but except for Brazilian dependence on imported petroleum, these economic relationships will remain secondary. Politically, Third World ties could become an important lever in Latin American efforts to pry economic concessions from the industrial North. All Latin americans participated as Southern members during the mid 1970s in the North-South dialogues; Mexico, in particular, became a principal spokesman for the Southern bloc. Far from seeing themselves in special relationships with the United States, the Latin Americans' self-image has increasingly become that of the most advanced component in the South. In this role, Latin Americans can be expected to champion greater equity in the New International Economic Order discussed in Chapter 14.[33] As the recent economic crisis attests, there is a wide gap between rhetoric and reality; despite Latin American sensitivities to the contrary, in their hour of need they turned to the United States for assistance they could not have obtained elsewhere.

Since greater equity could involve lowering of living standards in the North Atlantic, ties to the Third World could generate increasing conflict between Latin America and the developed countries. Of all the developing areas, however, Latin America is the only one mostly settled by Europeans. In general, with the exception of some Indian dialects, the languages of Latin America are European, and Latin Americans share the Iberian cultural heritage. This position of being part of the Third World economically and being Northern culturally causes many Latin Americans to believe they can function as a bridge between North and South. Some Asians, Africans, or Middle Easterners, however, seem unwilling to concede such a role to the Latins. Although Latin American ties with the Third World are becoming important, it will be some years before they yield major, tangible benefits to either side.

Military Issues. Although Latin America is not nearly as militarized a region as, say, Southern Africa, Indochina, or the Middle East, conventional military force is no stranger to the area. The recent war in the South Atlantic and the violent upheavals still occurring in Central America attest to a trend toward conflict resolution by force. Military confrontations are by no means new to Latin America. However, the growing levels of manpower and sophistication among belligerents cast doubts on previous predictions of a conflict-free regional evolution into prosperity.

The United States, as discussed earlier, prefers that Latin America remain peaceful and stable. It remains a paradox of U.S. policy that the United States will pay attention only to regions in crisis. Publically and officially, the United States has tended to neglect, if not ignore, Latin America in times of relative peace. In the nineteenth century, when several major Latin American conflicts over territorial disputes occurred, the United States was not in a position to influence events significantly. Once Washington gained undisputed military and economic preeminence in the hemisphere, its power was used to discourage Latin American nations from resorting to force in disputes among themselves. A major exception occurred during the middle 1930s, when Paraguay and Bolivia battled over the Chaco and its potentially wealthy petroleum deposits. Paraguay's victory marked the last successful use of arms to transfer territory from one Latin American country to another. The recent Falklands/Malvinas War marked the resurgence of Latin American willingness to resort to conventional military force to settle territorial disputes.

In 1947, at the height of Washington's influence in the Western Hemisphere, the United States and Latin America joined in a formal military alliance, the Rio de Janeiro Treaty of Reciprocal Assistance, popularly known as the Rio Pact. Articles 6 and 7 of the pact commit all signatories to respect existing international boundaries. Thus, in 1969, when El Salvadoran troops occupied areas of Honduras, allegedly to protect El Salvador's nationals who had settled on the Honduran side of the frontier, the status quo ante-bellum clause of the Rio Pact provided procedures and principles for settling the conflict.[34] With this one brief exception, the U.S. and Latin America joint commitment to the doctrine of nonforceable transfer of territory has significantly lowered the probability of intraregional war during recent times. Again, the South Atlantic conflict proved to be an exception to the applicability of the Rio Pact.

Four general problems in Latin America currently involve military considerations. First, although much less pressing than during the 1960s, challenges to internal order persist, including guerrilla warfare. The Castro revolution of 1959 demonstrated that small, efficiently organized and politically directed forces could employ irregular warfare to defeat established armed forces and create the opportunity for total societal reorganization. Washington and most Latin American governments assign high priority to preventing another guerrilla movement from repeating the Cuban experience. Consequently, the United States transferred its most modern antiinsurgency hardware and training to South America during the 1960s.[35] As noted in Chapter 12, success followed. Regular military forces in Venezuela, Bolivia, and Peru first contained, and then destroyed, significant rural insurgencies. Frustrated in the countryside, guerrilla leaders turned to the cities. Brazil and Uruguay wiped out the urban guerrillas even more thoroughly and rapidly than had been the case with their rural counterparts. By the latter 1970s, governments in Latin America seemed more secure against irregular violence than ever before. By the early 1980s, however, a resurgence of urban guerrilla activity was evident, particularly in Peru, where *Sendero Luminoso* violence has reached critical levels.

Despite success against the guerrillas, Latin American military leaders have not discounted the possibility that irregular warfare might again appear. Persistent rural and urban poverty provide an environment capable of generating antigovernment violence. As late as 1978, the Argentinian insurgents remained a force to be reckoned with, and in countries where antiguerrilla units were disbanded or weakened, such as Venezuela, there is evidence that insurgents are reorganizing. Moreover, Cuba's involvement in Africa and its hand in Central American turbulence have strengthened the impression that Castro is only waiting for the right moment to again fan the flames of guerrilla warfare in Latin America.

Border disputes and conflicting territorial ambitions form a second set of military issues of key importance in Latin America. While these were of minor significance during most of the twentieth century, reduced local preoccupation with insurgency and diminished U.S. influence have allowed such once-dormant issues to take on new life in recent years. As already noted, tensions between Peru and Chile have persisted since the latter's territorial conquests in the War of the Pacific. Bolivia, forced to surrender its outlet to the sea in the same conflict, has continually pressed Chile and Peru for a Pacific port.[36] Brazilian successes in acquiring economic concessions and political influence in Paraguay and Uruguay have created apprehension in Argentina. Some Argentine nationalists cite these Brazilian moves, and developments such as the growing ties between the Brazilian and Uruguayan militaries, as justification for their hope to create a Southern Cone military alliance (to comprise Argentina, Chile, Uruguay, Paraguay, and Bolivia) and for their acquisition of nuclear weapons.[37] Recent flareups between Argentina and Chile over the Beagle Channel dispute serve as reminders of the facility with which territorial disputes can increase the chances of conflict.

In northern South America, Colombia and Venezuela remain at odds over the location of their boundary in the potentially oil-rich Gulf of Venezuela. There have also been Venezuela-Guyana border incidents that signal another potentially troublesome intraregional territorial dispute. These various rivalries among South American states have caused comparative conventional warfare capabilities to reemerge as an important focus of military concern. Andean Pact countries, apprehensive about the economic consequences of large arms purchases and conscious of growing Brazilian power, signed the symbolic Declaration of Ayacucho in 1975.[38] Although the declaration proclaimed the intention of its signatories not to become involved in an arms race among themselves, it has not been followed up by any substantive arms limitation treaty.

The third basic military issue concerns globally oriented missions for which Latin militaries might prepare themselves. Because of Brazilian participation in World War II, the idea of integrating some Brazilian troops into NATO European defenses has occasionally been raised. More realistically, however, Western strategists invariably plan force deployments considering South American armies and air forces as available only to defend their national territory. Between 1945 and 1960 no credible military threat to Latin America existed so the equipment and training of the region's armed forces were not matters of great concern in Washington (or in Western Europe). When guerrilla warfare became a problem, as discussed above, the United States supplied modern counterinsurgency technology; but, other than that, Latin Americans

Table 20.1 Principal Regional Forces in Latin America

Country/Service	Regular Forces	Reserves	Main Armament	Other
Argentina (pop. 28,000,000				
Army	125,000	250,000	395 tks. 725 AFV 340 arty.	
Navy	36,000		3 atk. subs. 1 acft. carrier 8 destroyers 28 cbt. acft.	
Air Force	19,500		97 cbt. acft.	
Paramilitary	43,000			
Brazil (pop. 125,000,000)				
Army	182,750	1,115,000	625 tks. 780 AFV 1348 arty.	
Navy	47,300		8 atk. subs. 1 acft. carrier 12 destroyers 13 cbt. hel.	
Air Force	42,800		227 cbt. acft.	
Paramilitary	185,000			
Cuba (pop. 9,900,000)				
Army	100,000	190,000	660 tks. 400 AFV some arty.	
Navy	11,500		3 atk. subs. 26 maj. surf. ships	
Air Force	16,000		189 cbt. acft.	
Paramilitary	168,500			
Mexico (pop. 71,500,000				
Army	95,000	250,000	40 tks. 120 AFV some arty.	
Navy	20,000			10 maj surf. ships 11 cbt. acft.
Air Force	4,500			14 cbt. acft.

Country/Service	Regular Forces	Reserves	Main Armament	Other
Peru				
(pop.				
18,300,000)				
Army	75,000			485 tks.
				315 AFV
				90 arty.
Navy	20,500			10 atk. subs.
				14 maj. surf.
				ships
				12 cbt. acft.
Air Force	40,000			114 cbt. acft.
Paramilitary	25,000			
Venezuela				
(pop.				
17,000,000)				
Army	27,000			115 tks.
				some AFV
				some arty.
Navy	9,000			3 atk. subs.
				11 maj. surf.
				ships
				6 cbt. acft.
Air Force	4,800			87 cbt. acft.
Paramilitary	20,000			

Source: See table 18.2.
For abbreviations, see table 17.1

generally received only obsolescent equipment and training from the United States, useful only in defending their homelands against similarly armed neighbors.[39]

Defending Latin America against outside attack, even given the remoteness of such an eventuality, gave rise to institutions and arrangements known collectively as the Inter-American Defense System. The system's authority, the Inter-American Defense Board, has always been headed by a U.S. general officer. U.S. disinterest, and Latin American concern about Yankee intervention, have kept the Inter-American Defense Board weak. It persists, however, as a mechanism through which Rio Pact members could cooperate militarily if they were so inclined. The Falklands/Malvinas War demonstrated all too clearly the weakness of the Inter-American Defense Board.

The School of the Americas in Panama, an important U.S. training center since the early 1960s, has graduated thousands of Latin Americans from its rigorous courses in counterinsurgency, infantry tactics, and many other fields. At sea, the annual UNITAS exercise in the South Atlantic has facilitated naval cooperation between the United States and Latin America. Hundreds of Latin American officers also have attended U.S. military service schools, and U.S. military training missions have operated in many Latin American countries during much of this century. Washington has hoped that these efforts would yield Latin American support for the United States in the cold war, as well as in the case of aggression against a Western Hemisphere nation.

But, short of a highly improbable Soviet direct attack on Latin America, even given the Rio Pact, it is highly unlikely that Brazil or its Spanish-speaking neighbors would enter into a conflict involving NATO and the Warsaw Pact. Rather than preparing to defend against the Soviet Union or to fight in Europe, Latin American armies appear to believe that their most important extracontinental mission is to make it unattractive for the United States to interfere militarily in the South. In this context, Latin Americans cast a nervous glance at growing U.S. dependence on their raw materials even as they welcome the increased export earnings.

In speculating about extrahemispheric roles for the Latin American military, Cuba's African involvement stands out as unexpected and dramatic.[40] Brazil contemplated involvement in Portugal's African territories during the early 1970s, but abandoned the idea as beyond its logistic, military, and economic capabilities. Yet Cuba, far smaller, more vulnerable, and less industrialized than Brazil, has managed to maintain a significant military presence in Angola and Ethiopia; of course, it could do so only because of extensive Soviet funding, supplies, and support personnel. The Angolan and Ethiopian interventions occurred because of a unique confluence of Castro's self-image as a major twentieth-century revolutionary and of Soviet interest in an African presence and a position along the petroleum lifeline of NATO. Reported demonstrations by unhappy Cubans against the departure of troops from Havana in 1977 suggest opposition within Cuba to its African adventures. In any case, it seems unlikely that Cuba will serve as a model of extrahemispheric troop deployment of other Latin American nations.

Acquisition of weapons and training, the fourth military issue, is greatly affected by Latin expectations of guerrilla activity, relations with neighboring states, and anticipated extrahemispheric missions. Military training and hardware for Latin America has come from the North since Spain conquered and occupied the New World. Growing sophistication of weapons in the second half of the nineteenth century further increased the Latin American military's dependency on Europe and the United States. The consequences of failing to acquire the new technology appeared self-evident after the War of the Pacific in which Chile's European-trained and -supplied military forces defeated larger but less modernized Peruvian and Bolivian forces. Subsequently, until World War II, Europe dominated the South American arms trade. Between 1945 and 1970 U.S. training and equipment predominated. Initially Washington supplied surplus conventional arms from the Second World War and Korea, but during the 1960s the emphasis shifted to counterinsurgency related items.[41]

In the early 1970s, as most Latin American militaries began replacing their antiquated conventional equipment, Washington reduced foreign military grants and sales to the region. Additionally, Congress prohibited the sale of advanced conventional weapons to Latin American forces irrespective of the nations' concerns about the continental military balance. In contrast, the French, British, Germans, Italians, and Soviets actively merchandised their most advanced aircraft, tanks, and destroyers. The acquisition of Soviet-made tanks and aircraft by Peru broke the "Western" monopoly on military sales to South America. During the last two decades, most Latin American countries have received progressively less U.S. military training and equipment. As table 20.2 illustrates, U.S. military sales to Latin America declined from 3.7 percent of total worldwide sales in 1960–69 to 1.7 percent in 1973–82. For the same two periods, military assistance deliveries declined from 2.4 percent of the worldwide total to 0.7 percent.

Latin American dependence on Northern arms suppliers implies that sophisticated weapons can be employed in Latin America for any length of time only with the acquiescence of these suppliers. Confronting this fact in the past decade or so, Brazil and Argentina, the region's most industrially advanced states, have accelerated their already substantial efforts to develop a domestic arms industry.[42] Until recently, Argentina's greater technological sophistication gave it an advantage in such undertakings, and historically it could rely on superior equipment and training to offset Brazil's larger numbers. By 1970, however, the qualitative differences between the Brazilian and Argentine militaries had narrowed dramatically. Rapidly growing Brazilian industries have begun to outperform their Argentine counterparts in defense-related production.

Recognizing the growing strength of Brazil, Argentine military leaders argued increasingly that only by acquiring nuclear weapons could their country maintain a military force capable of discouraging Brazilian adventurism. Argentine interest in nuclear energy had begun in 1950, when President Juan Perón created the National Atomic Energy Commission.[43] In 1958, it operated South America's first research reactor, and ten years later it built the region's first, and by 1980 only, chemical reprocessing plant. In 1968, Argentina began construction of the Atucha I nuclear power facility, which it put into operation in 1974. Atucha I uses German natural uranium technology rather than the more common enriched uranium process favored by the United States. In addition to thus freeing itself from stringent U.S. controls, Argentina acquired a technology that lends itself to the production of weapons-grade plutonium, which can be chemically separated from spent fuel.

Brazilian analysts estimated in 1970 that Argentina had a two-year lead in nuclear energy technology. The military potential of Atucha I, and the prospect of falling even further behind Argentina in this area, caused alarm throughout Brazil. Thus, in 1975 Brazil signed an agreement with West Germany which would satisfy Brazilian projected demand for atomic energy through 1990 and provide the technological base for manufacturing nuclear weapons. Involving the largest projected transfer ever made of nuclear tech-

Table 20.2 Flow of Military Equipment from the United States to Latin America (in millions of dollars)

Country	U.S. Military Sales Deliveries to Latin American Countries, 1960–82		U.S. Military Assistance[a] Deliveries to Latin American Countries, 1960–82	
	1960–69	1973–82	1960–69	1973–82
Argentina	57.7	88.4	—	0.13
Bolivia	.5	1.0	120.8	15.9
Brazil	61.9	173.4	12.3	0.53
Chile	18.6	138.4	48.4	0.8
Colombia	2.6	42.8	58.9	0.4
Dominican Republic	.9	4.1	9.3	2.4
Ecuador	2.7	59.3	17.9	—
El Salvador	.8	21.4	—	46.3
Guatemala	2.0	21.2	9.6	3.7
Honduras	.2	11.7	—	1.1
Mexico	7.9	83.6	—	—
Peru	16.4	127.6	50.3	—
Uruguay	1.5	14.7	17.3	3.2
Venezuela	71.9	158.0	—	—
Worldwide	6,650.6	55,530.7	14,676.3	10,501.8
Total for Latin America	245.6	945.6	344.8	74.5
Latin America as % of Worldwide Total	3.7	1.7	2.4	0.7

[a]Note that these are grants rather than sales, as is the case in the columns on the left. The totals of military transfers are formed by adding the left and right columns.
Source: U.S., Bureau of the Census, *Statistical Abstract of the United States, 1977,* 98th ed. (Washington, D.C.: U.S. Government Printing Office, 1977), p. 362; and U.S. Dept. of Defense, *Foreign Military Sales, Foreign Military Construction Sales, and Military Assistance Facts.* (Washington, D.C.: Data Management Division, 1983), pp. 7–12.

nology and equipment to a developing country, the agreement significantly advanced Brazil's ambition of becoming a world power.[44]

Brazil and Argentina, each probably capable of producing nuclear weapons during the 1980s if it so chooses, eventually must decide whether to do so and how to integrate this capability in their foreign and defense policies. They have three basic options: the Canadian, the Indian, and the Israeli. The Canadian option focuses exclusively on the peaceful use of atomic energy, although it includes the possibility of selling nuclear technology to others. The Indian options involves building and testing nuclear explosive devices (and probably weapons), using possession as a lever in dealing with neighbors. The Israeli option, in contrast, is intended to keep one's adversaries guessing as to whether or not an operational bomb exists. While Brazil and Argentina are not bound by the Latin American nuclear nonproliferation treaty, neither country could gain much by touching off a nuclear weapons race. There is room for hope, therefore, that both will opt for the Canadian approach, or at worst the Israeli one.

Further Challenges to U.S. National Security. It is clear that in the 1980s the United States can neither ignore nor take for granted its Southern neighbors. The various currents running in Latin America require the United States to define clearly its position on hemispheric matters and to work vigorously, in concert with others if possible, to shape the future. Among the key national security challenges that the United States must address is the growing political turbulence in the Carribean basin. In Central America, the conflict is increasingly polarized and complex. The situation in El Salvador is bad and getting worse. The violent and extreme polarization of the belligerents has made the likelihood of a settlement remote. There is little chance of a military victory by either side, and any political solution—either by election or negotiation—would take time to enact and would provide no guarantee of success. Cuban/Nicaraguan support is a key to the Salvadorean conflict. Any overly optimistic prediction of an easy or immediate settlement runs the risk of being simplistic and ultimately unsuccessful.

While attention is focused primarily on El Salvador and Nicaragua, a key to U.S. policy in the region and a major source of continued difficulty will be Guatemala. As is the case elsewhere in Central America, Guatemala's political and insurgency problems are complex, deeply rooted, and easily exploited. Ironically, U.S. leverage in Guatemala, as demonstrated by the coup that overthrew General Rios Montt, is disappointingly weak.

Besides the Cubans and internal political strains, the insular states of the basin also suffer from economic stagnation or decline. Jamaica's electoral decision in 1980 to reject doctrinaire socialism as the path to economic development opens the way for Western, especially U.S., capital and technology to reverse the dismal decline of that particular economy and to provide an example to other Caribbean states whose economies and political lives are also suffering from an overdose of *etatism* or Marxism.

Although the United States temporized in the late 1970s in handling these acute problems in the Carribean basin, the Reagan administration has taken a much firmer role in the region. In fact, from 1980 to 1983, the dynamics of the regional conflicts changed dramatically: Cuban and Nicaraguan support for the Salvadorean rebels increased; Guatemala went through two violent regime changes; Honduras acquired a democratically elected government; U.S. support for anti-Sandinista Nicaraguan rebels grew; Mexico, Colombia, Panama, and Venezuela formed the so-called Contadora group, which began an initiative aimed at seeking a peaceful resolution to the region's conflicts; and Mexico experienced a severe economic crisis with wide-ranging political ramifications. For the United States, the challenge will be to work with regional powers to bring political stability and economic viability to the Caribbean region.

In South America, too, the United States has largely been on the defensive in the decade of the 1970s. The combination of human rights preachments, arms sales restrictions, and restraints on nuclear technology transfers, which made up the largest part of U.S. policy toward the area in the latter 1970s, have created widespread resentment. U.S. support of Great Britain during the

Falklands/Malvinas War of 1982 did nothing to improve our image in Latin America. Reversing this situation and re-creating or strengthening economic, political, and military ties—on the basis of equality—with the South American states is essential.

Hemispheric defense in the 1940s or 1950s sense is neither needed nor desired. But cooperation in military matters, including intelligence and arms supply, between the principal South American states—particularly Brazil— and the United States is highly desirable. A peaceful Southern flank, secure from the meddling of the U.S.S.R. or its proxies, remains a fundamental condition of U.S. national security.

DISCUSSION QUESTIONS

1. Historically, what terms have been used to describe the relation(s) between the United States and Latin America? How relevant are they today?

2. At least until World War II, U.S. influence in Latin America was greatest in the Caribbean basin area. Why? How did this relate to security questions of that time? And now?

3. Castro's success in Cuba tended to disrupt the traditional relationship patterns in Latin America. How did this alter perceived security interests? How did the United States respond in terms of its security interests?

4. How is Brazil's emergence as a regional power viewed by its South American neighbors, both as it affects each directly and as it affects other South American nations? Cite examples.

5. Brazil's economic and geographic preponderance in South America directly affects Latin American development plans, both overall and those of individual countries. Examine the La Plata River basin and Amazon basin development from Brazilian and other Latin American perspectives.

6. What types of relationship is Latin America developing with countries outside the Western Hemisphere?

7. What general problems in Latin America involve military considerations? How do these problems affect existing security arrangements with the United States?

8. What role do nuclear capabilities in Latin America play in Latin American countries' relationships with one another? Discuss especially the Brazilian-Argentine relationship in these terms.

9. What are the severe internal problems that constrain emergent Brazil's influence beyond its borders? What effects do they have?

10. What possible alternatives to Brazilian dominance might its neighbors explore to counterbalance Brazil? How realistic are these alternatives?

RECOMMENDED READING

Bemis, Samuel F. *The Latin American Policy of the United States.* New York: Harcourt, Brace and World, 1943.

Collier, David, ed. *The New Authoritarianism in Latin America.* Princeton, N.J.: Princeton University Press, 1979.

Cotler, Julio, and Fagen, Richard R., eds. *Latin America and the United States*. Stanford: Stanford University Press, 1974.

Crist, Raymond E., and Nissly, Charles M. *East from the Andes*. Gainesville: University of Florida Press, 1973.

de Janvry, Alain. *The Agrarian Question and Reformism in Latin America*. Baltimore: Johns Hopkins University Press, 1981.

Hunter, John M., and Foley, James W. *Economic Problems of Latin America*. Boston: Houghton Mifflin, 1975.

Lowenthal, Abraham F. *The Dominican Intervention*. Cambridge, Mass.: Harvard University Press, 1972.

Mecham, J. Lloyd. *The United States and Inter-American Security, 1889–1960*. Austin: University of Texas Press, 1962.

Palmer, Thomas. *The Search for a Latin American Policy*. Gainesville: University of Florida Press, 1957.

Rockefeller, Nelson A. *The Rockefeller Report on the Americas*. New York: Quadrangle Books, 1969.

Roett, Riordan. *Brazil in the Seventies*. Washington, D.C.: American Enterprise Institute for Public Policy Research, 1976.

Theberge, James D. *The Soviet Presence in Latin America*. New York: Crane, Russak, 1974.

Wood, Bryce. *The Making of the Good Neighbor Policy*. New York: Columbia University Press, 1961.

APPROACHES TO NATIONAL SECURITY FOR THE 1980s

Since much of national security deals with uncertain knowledge about the present, that uncertainty can only increase as we look ahead into the decade of the 1980s. Yet thinking about how we should tackle the future is a crucial task. The decisions the United States makes today will create its ability or inability to deal with events ten to fifteen years from now; this is particularly true in the area of weapons systems. Yet all too often the future is overwhelmed by the present and the need to deal with its problems. The future has no constituency. In Part 5 we attempt, on the basis of the analyses in the preceding four parts, to weigh the different approaches the United States might take to ensuring its security in the 1980s.

America must adjust to an emerging world order that may not be in agreement with U.S. values or expectations. The global distribution of power seems to be moving toward an increasingly multipolar system, and American ability to influence or shape that evolution appears to be declining. This evolution is accompanied by the frustrations of emerging nations and an increase of conflict and violence as new regimes struggle for control of their internal and external environments. In these circumstances, the United States needs to rally both allies and nonallies to share their insights and to shoulder their part of the task of ensuring peace. Alliances and international peace-keeping arrangements, the topics of Chapters 21 and 22, are two alternative, but not mutually exclusive, means of sharing the tasks of promoting global order. Arms control and disarmament represent still another, separate (but occasionally overlapping) multilateral or sometimes bilateral approach to ensuring national and international security; it is the subject of Chapter 23.

A turbulent world may appear increasingly hostile to—or unmanageable by—the United States. Whether or not this is the case, it is necessary also to focus attention on unilateral means for dealing with our problems. Setting national priorities, the topic of Chapter 24, essentially looks at what the United States needs to do itself, as well as in concert with others, if it is to meet the requirements for security in a more hostile world.

21

ALLIANCES

The numerous American alliances, treaties of guarantee, memberships in regional organizations, and military base agreements around the world constitute a complex alliance structure that cumulatively is a response to the various perceived threats to U.S. foreign policy objectives that have arisen since World War II. In 1947 the United States signed the Rio Pact, breaking a 150-year tradition of nonentanglement. The NATO alliance was concluded in 1949 as a direct result of the growing Soviet threat in Europe. With the outbreak of the Korean War (1950), the United States began adding Asian allies. In relatively quick order the following alliances were formed: U.S.-Japan (1951), U.S.-Philippines (1951), Australia–New Zealand–U.S. (ANZUS, 1951), U.S.-Korea (1953), Southeast Asia Treaty Organization (SEATO, 1954), and U.S.–Republic of China (1954), followed by limited participation in the Central Treaty Organization (CENTO, 1956). Further bilateral defense treaties were signed with Iran, Pakistan, and Turkey in 1959. The United States added military base rights agreements with Spain and Thailand. In support of these alliances, the United States has dispersed military aid of billions of dollars to some sixty countries around the world, and has deployed hundreds of thousands of U.S. service members overseas.

Yet by the early 1970s the entire U.S. worldwide commitment was being questioned. How much national security did the United States gain from its multiple commitments? How were our alliances changing? Were our alliances and commitments actually counterproductive, leading to involvements that eroded our national strength and reduced our security? These have not been easy questions to answer.

It should be recognized at the outset that neither scholars nor statesmen have a fully adequate understanding of why nations join or maintain alliances; under what circumstances alliances of nations act; and the effects of alliance behavior on other nations and alliances and on the structures and processes of the international system. There is no single study that adequately addresses these problems. The purpose of this chapter is to survey some current ideas about the causes and uses of alliances and to review U.S. alliance behavior in the post–World War II era. Finally, we will consider the current nature and value of U.S. alliances and their prospects for the future.

Why Alliances?. An alliance is a contract that, like all other contracts, bestows rights and advantages but also places obligations and restrictions on the contracting parties. Unlike contracts in domestic law, however, nations have no higher authority to appeal to when there is a breach of contract. The primary consideration of national leaders contemplating an alliance is that the benefits of the prospective alliance outweigh the loss of flexibility incurred in becoming dependent upon acts of omission or commission by other nations in the alliance. In this regard, Hans Morgenthau writes, "A nation will shun alliances if it believes that it is strong enough to hold its own unaided or that the burden of commitment resulting from an alliance is likely to outweigh the advantages to be expected."[1]

Faced with an international system best described as "semiorganized anarchy," nations seek various forms of cooperative behavior designed to generate strength and reduce risk. They pursue their national security in a selective manner in an attempt to produce the type and degree of international order that best insures their own interests. Since power tends to be the common denominator in international politics, "the question as to whose values or ends will prevail . . . is determined finally by the relative power positions of the [opposing] parties."[2]

Three motives for alliances spring from this focus on power. First, a nation may join or create an alliance in order to aggregate the capabilities necessary to achieve a foreign policy goal (i.e., a nation's own means are insufficient for its ends). Second, a nation may join an alliance to reduce the costs of securing its objective (i.e., a nation, seeking multiple objectives, may not want to commit all or an undue part of its capabilities to any one specific end). Regarding these two motives, a nation will tend to judge cautiously in measuring the capabilities of nations that oppose their goals, acting to acquire more capabilities than are objectively necessary. Third, a nation may enter into an alliance or entente to secure favorable treatment in the future. In short, nations selectively join alliances to gain coldly calculated advantages in the pursuit of present and future national goals.[3]

Chapter 2 treated the concept of power as a function of a nation's capabilities and its willingness to use them; concluding that power is the ability to influence other political actors so as to shape the structure and processes within the international system in a manner favorable to a particular nation. The increased power of an alliance over that of its individual member nations can of course be used for a variety of specific purposes, including deterrence or actual war-making. Robert Randle stresses this latter purpose.

War (and also the threat of war) is a major incentive for alliance foundations, because war poses more starkly the threat to the single nation's existence, inducing its policy makers to seek the cooperation of other states that feel threatened so that they may share resources for prosecuting the war against the common enemy. The pervasive and fundamental purpose of wartime alliances is the security of the component states or factions; survival of each partner is the key motivation.[4]

Robert Osgood notes that alliances may, in addition to increasing power, serve the functions of preserving the internal security of members, restraining allies, or creating a degree of international order.[5] (With regard to the function of creating a degree of international order, it may be that stabilizing economic relations through alliances—securing access to oil and raw materials, for instance—will become a pattern in the future.)

Preserving an ally's internal security by providing it material and moral support legitimized by the alliance may be a key goal, especially if the alliance involves nations with relatively unstable regimes; of course, such a purpose can backfire badly if the government is toppled.

Using the formal and informal ties of the alliance to restrain allies' behavior is common; it is practiced by both the larger, more powerful actors and the weaker, subordinate actors in an alliance. In this respect, the access the alliance provides to an ally's internal political processes and institutions may be important to other members of the alliance.

The buttressing of a particular aspect of international order and the strengthening of the consistency of behavior among its members may be a critical function of an alliance (the Soviet intervention in Czechoslovakia in 1968 is an extreme example). Predictable, regulated patterns of interactions based on the alliance structures reduce sources of friction and conflict. Furthermore, alliances usually provide some form of institution which facilitates contacts and communication among its members. Clearly, alliances are complex phenomena that do many things and that may encompass many differing objectives of their members.

Alliance Theories. There is no single theory about alliance formation or behavior encompassing all the relevant variables in a manageable and coherent manner. Among the more recent theoretical approaches to alliance behavior are economic theories of alliances and game theory.* Economic theories of alliance behavior stem from welfare economics in their focus on the distribution of costs and benefits generated by an alliance. Undoubtedly, a cost-benefit approach to alliances has some policy relevance for the decision-maker.[6] Unfortunately, though, beyond the obvious lessons of the need for

---

*Economic theories of alliances associate alliance benefits with national costs. Usually, large members of an alliance pay most of the costs (troops and equipment), while small nations receive most of the benefits (deterrence and defense). See Mancur Olson, Jr., and Richard A. Beer, *Alliances: Latent War Communities in the Contemporary World* (New York: Holt, Rinehart & Winston, 1970), pp. 120–40. Game theories of alliances are concerned with the distribution of maximum benefits to a minimum winning coalition (alliance). Since national capabilities are difficult to quantify with any precision, nations usually seek a safe margin in the distribution of capabilities rather than in some marginal or minimum distribution. See William H. Riker, *The Theory of Political Coalitions* (New Haven: Yale University Press, 1962).

establishing priorities and acceptable trade-offs, strictly economic theories provide little insight or guidance. Game theories appear to have still less policy relevance in their present stage of development and will not be discussed here. This section examines two of the more traditional theories: balance of power theories and compatibility theories.

Balance of Power Theories. Balance of power is a central concept in international politics and has long been related to the study of alliances and coalitions. Historically, diplomats have both applauded and condemned the balance of power. Machiavelli, Talleyrand, Metternich, and Churchill called for the maintenance of the balance of power for national survival and world peace. On the other hand, Woodrow Wilson demanded the end of balance-of-power politics and its associated evils, instead calling for collective security in a world of democratic nations. A similar enthusiasm seized many politicians after World War II.

Balance of power, like alliance, is a vague and ambiguous concept. Ernst Haas has identified at least eight definitions or uses for the term *balance of power*. Inis Claude, in his critique of balance of power, states, "The trouble with the balance of power is not that it has no meaning, but that it has too many."[7] While Claude presents an analysis of all these multiple meanings, he finds that they can be reduced to essentially three. He first discusses *balance of power as a situation*—that is, if two nations or alliances have equal strength, there is a balance between them. If one of these nations or alliances suddenly increases its military capability, and others do not move similarly, then an imbalance occurs. For definitional clarity, it is better to say that there has been a change in the distribution of capability rather than a change in the balance of power.

Claude's second meaning is *balance of power as a policy*. This involves a nation's goals and is concerned with the policy of prudence which "involves recognizing and acting upon the principle that unbalanced power is dangerous."[8] A nation or alliance, on discovering that the balance of power is shifting adversely, thereby increasing risk and uncertainty, must attempt to restore the balance by finding new allies, building new armaments, or weakening the opposing coalition. In this context, historians have often discussed British policy toward the continental European powers as a policy of balance of power designed to prevent the dominance of any one nation or alliance. British attempts to "play the balancer" included changing alliances, always aligning to confront the strongest aggressive power. In fact, few nations seek a real equilibrium; rather, a preponderance on their side, however slight, is usually the goal. Another policy alternative, in a situation where a nation faces the beginnings of an adverse disequilibrium, is to engage in a preemptive war before the disequilibrium becomes too threatening.

The final meaning that Claude discusses is *balance of power as a system*. This concept delineates a system of states and the political and military relationships among them, a specific type or structure of the international system, such as existed in Europe from 1648 to the late 1790s and from 1815 to about 1900.[9]

Claude prefers this latter meaning of balance of power, arguing that "the decision to reserve balance of power for the particular meaning 'system' is admittedly arbitrary, but some arbitrary limitation of use is absolutely essential."[10] This usage of the term describes a system in which states seek, individually or jointly, to maintain their independence and sovereignty in an international environment of high risk and high uncertainty by continually adjusting the power relationships among them. The political processes available to states to accomplish this within a balance of power system are many, including diplomacy, propaganda, economic cooperation and sanction, military threats, alliances, and war.

We should note, however, that the balance of power system to which Claude refers is only one of four general types of international systems. These various systems can be described by two dimensions.[11] The first dimension involves the distribution of capabilities of the various nations in the system: one can move along a continuum from a low distribution of capabilities (i.e., two large nations or two large alliances containing most of the economic and military capability in the international system) to a high distribution of capabilities (i.e., many nations having generally similar, even equal, capabilities). A singularly low distribution yields a unique international system, examples of which would be the Roman Empire, various early Chinese dynasties, or a "World Government." The second dimension involves the distribution of attitudes in the international system. The term *attitudes* describes the relationships among nations in terms of their values and goals (revisionist or status quo) and their expectation of others' behavior. If most nations agree on certain common and limited foreign policy goals and on procedures of nonviolent conflict resolution, there exists an attitude of consensus and legitimacy in the policy interactions among them. On the other hand, divergence in national values and goals and disagreement over the means and ends of foreign policy lead to conflict and uncertainty among nations. In our context, a low distribution of attitudes means a relatively high degree of consensus and shared values and a widespread acceptance of the legitimacy of the "rules of the game" in international politics. A high distribution of attitudes is associated with low consensus and conflict over the rules of the game and the ultimate distribution of values in the system.

Figure 21.1 demonstrates how these two dimensions describe the four possible structures of the international system.

There are many historical and current examples of international systems which illustrate the four structures found in the diagram's quadrants. In quadrant 4, one finds the balance of power system as described earlier by Claude. A good example of this system is the period of the Concert of Europe from the Congress of Vienna (1815) until the end of Bismarck's era (1890). Most wars in this period were conducted to maintain an equilibrium in the distribution of power by preventing an adversary from acquiring too much power

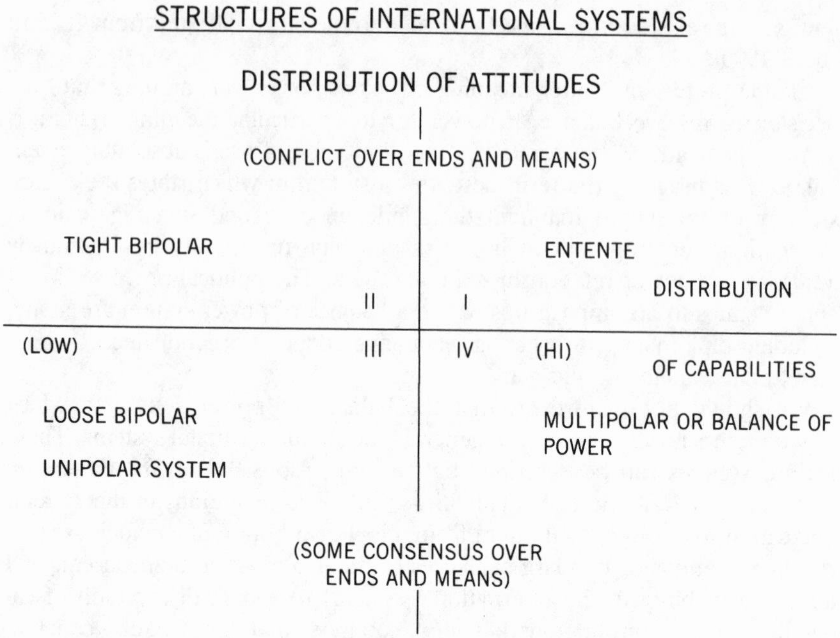

STRUCTURES OF INTERNATIONAL SYSTEMS

DISTRIBUTION OF ATTITUDES

|
(CONFLICT OVER ENDS AND MEANS)

TIGHT BIPOLAR		ENTENTE
		DISTRIBUTION
	II	I
(LOW)	III	IV (HI)
		OF CAPABILITIES
LOOSE BIPOLAR		MULTIPOLAR OR BALANCE OF POWER
UNIPOLAR SYSTEM		

(SOME CONSENSUS OVER
ENDS AND MEANS)
|

FIG. 21.1

or by consolidating power through the conquest and acquisition of smaller states. Most nations during this period demonstrated a high degree of flexibility in the conduct of their diplomacy, changing alliance partners to meet changing circumstances. Wars were characterized by relatively low levels of hostility and intensity, and only a small number of nations in the international system became involved in any specific conflict.

The movement away from a balance of power system usually starts with some nation or nations violating the accepted rules of the game. Many historians would argue that Germany altered the rules after the Franco-Prussian War (1870) by annexing Alsace-Lorraine, generating a continuing major conflict with France which was not settled until the Treaty of Versailles in 1919. The European political structure slowly evolved from a balance of power system (quadrant 4) to a tight bipolar system (quadrant 2) during the period 1890–1907. Capabilities were divided between two major alliance systems, the Triple Entente (Britain, France, and Russia) against the Triple Alliance (Austria-Hungary, Italy, and Germany). By 1914, European statecraft had lost its flexibility in an essentially bipolar world.

A tight bipolar system tends to be a relatively inflexible system, usually described as a zero-sum situation; that is, as any unaligned nation joins one of the major alliances its capability becomes a gain for one alliance at the expense of the other. The same condition exists if one nation leaves one alliance and joins the other. Europe's political structure from the 1890s until 1914, and the world's from 1948 until the early 1960s, can be classified as tight bipolar systems. In both instances, the bulk of the military and economic capabilities in the international system was divided between two mutually hostile camps.

National and alliance behavior in a tight bipolar system is designed to prevent the "other side" from securing additional allies or a predominance of military capability. The opposing alliances must continually react to any changes in the distribution of capabilities in the system. Finally, since by definition there is a broad gap in the attitudes between alliances, a high degree of conflict and hostility is inherent in the system. War in tight bipolar systems is not so much a technique of statecraft as a matter of national survival. Wars in a tight bipolar system become long, large, and costly affairs due to the vital nature of the outcome. As a result of the inflexibility of this type of system, a small confrontation between two nations can easily trigger war. This occurred in August 1914, and the world watched in apprehension for a similar escalation during the Cuban Missile Crisis in 1962.

If ideology becomes less important, or several competing centers of ideology develop, the structure of the system may move away from the quadrants representing high conflict in attitudes toward more consensus. This is particularly true if issues develop that tend to overshadow ideology, such as the need to avoid thermonuclear war or the realization that economic cooperation is increasingly essential for everybody. To some degree, for these reasons the international structure moved from tight bipolar to loose bipolar (i.e., from quadrant 2 to 3) with respect to East-West relationships during the 1960s and 1970s. As capabilities become more widespread or as certain forms of capability appear to become less useable (such as nuclear weapons) or are replaced by other capabilities (such as possession of vital resources), there is a tendency to move from loose bipolar to balance of power (i.e., from quadrant 3 to quadrant 4). This tendency is accelerated as new actors enter the system, each demanding an increased share of goods and power. We have also seen some movement in this direction over the last two decades, but Kissinger was perhaps premature in 1972 when he declared in several speeches that a new pentagonal balance of power existed, comprising the United States, the U.S.S.R., Japan, the P.R.C., and Western Europe. Increased Soviet adventurism in Angola, Ethiopia, and Afghanistan in the latter 1970s has halted the movement away from loose bipolar toward balance of power and may even, in the 1980s, change the direction back toward a tighter bipolar international system.

The future structure of the international system over the next few decades might be viewed within the context of the quadrant representation. Nuclear weapons will prevent a broad distribution of military capabilities across the system, excluding major nuclear proliferation. Although perhaps further weakening in its impact, ideology will continue to divide the world. Resource shortages, interdependence, and other problems whose solution exceeds the capabilities of any limited alliance will tend to limit excessive polarity. Continued nationalism and increasing numbers of significant international actors will insure interest in coalitions. Out of this mix will emerge the international system in which the United States and other nations will have to address their foreign policies.

Compatibility Theories. A second set of theories used in the analysis of alliance behavior is focused on the similarity of attributes and motivations which brings nations into an alliance or is instrumental in maintaining an alliance structure. Specifically, these approaches are called *attributes theory* when describing similar characteristics of nations and *community of interest theory* when specifying similar motivations and interests shared by nations.

Attributes theory is based on the premise that similar attributes (such as geographic proximity, common experiences, cultural and ideological similarity, and comparability of government, size, and level of economic development) forge a strong predisposition to foreign policy cooperation. For example, according to this theory, two large, developed, democratic nations should be expected to exhibit cooperative behavior that could be made explicit by an alliance. In the period from 1950 to the latter 1970s, the large, developed, democratic nations indeed did exhibit strong cooperative behavior (e.g., political, economic, and defense cooperation between the United States and Japan, and between the United States and Western Europe). Yet, similarity of attributes clearly is not a sufficient condition for an alliance. National interests are more important than attributes in bringing and holding nations in alliances. For example, even with Anglo-American similarities and general cooperation, at the turn of the century the British still felt that it was in their own interest to oppose American involvement in the Western Pacific. The United States had a like attitude about British activities in Latin America. General de Gaulle's mistreatment of France's NATO allies further suggests the weakness of attributes theory.

A more interesting and useful approach to the analysis of alliances is community of interest theory. Here an alliance is considered a consequence of a number of shared national interests and goals between two or more nations that desire to distribute the costs and risks of achieving their various goals, be they deterrence, order, defense, internal security, or aggression. A good example is the alliance between the United States, Great Britain, and the Soviet Union which came about when (and lasted only as long as) they had a common interest in defeating Nazi Germany. One can postulate that the greater the divergence in national attributes the less chance for continued alliance cohesion. One can also postulate that the fewer the shared interests and goals, the less chance for continuing alliance success.

The Anglo-American "special relationship" is based on both common attributes and multiple shared interests. Expectations of cooperative behavior between the parties are high and uncertainty is low. In such a case, an alliance that formally stipulates common policies and measures is not really necessary, for there tends to be a common approach on both the means and ends of foreign policy. This is not to imply that there is no conflict between nations with a high community of interests and similar attributes, only that conflict is managed and resolved in such cases by compromise rather than by force. Ultimately there may evolve a feeling of a "security community" where the joint expectation of use of force between them is very low, leading to high certainty in their relations.[12] Certainly, the U.S.-Canadian relationship fits this description, as well as the U.S.-British relationship. These three nations share relationships existing beyond the written agreements of the North Atlantic Treaty.

Analyzing the extent and intensity of the community of interests between states provides a key to judging the strength and durability of any consequent alliance between them. A number of American alliances entered into during the tight bipolar era of the 1950s, for example, are based on shared interests that have for some time appeared relatively weak and limited. In most such cases, the United States promised to support a state, usually a member of the Third World, with an alliance buttressed by military aid to combat a Communist threat. Allies were often ready to cooperate for such inducements since military capabilities have both internal as well as external uses. Over the longer run, there was not only limited community of interests but little in the way of common attributes as well. This meant that, by the 1970s, there was good reason to reevaluate the basis of several longstanding American commitments. The Vietnam era in particular made Americans reconsider the extensive commitments their nation had made. Objections to being "policeman of the world" and worry about "overextension" became commonplace.

As East-West tension grew toward the end of the 1970s, however, the community of interest within the West and among the West, China, and certain vulnerable Third World states—interest, that is, in checking Soviet expansionism—again came to the fore. One of the Carter administration's first responses to the Soviet invasion of Afghanistan at the end of 1979 was, for example, a reaffirmation of U.S.-Pakistan alliance commitments, which had languished for more than a decade.

U.S. Alliances: Selective Security. The traditional American approach to alliances was simple avoidance. Yet by the end of the nineteenth century isolationism was being undercut as U.S. involvement in international politics began to match its international power. Initially reluctant to become involved in World War I, the United States finally intervened as a consequence of a number of factors: recognition that a German victory would unfavorably alter the equilibrium of world power, skillful British propaganda reinforced by the similarity of British-American attributes and common interests, and unrestricted German submarine warfare. After victory, however, expressing disgust with postwar intrigue and the consequent resurgence of alliances in a new balance of power system, America again withdrew into partial isolation, declaring it would not be further drawn into European politics.

This resolve was tested less than two decades later when Pearl Harbor thrust an ill-equipped America into World War II. At the end of the war the

United States made a curious compromise with the realities of the international system. U.S. decision-makers recognized the political reality that America must take an active part in rebuilding and regulating the international system; yet, they rejected the notion that large military forces or coalitions were necessary to support that American role of worldwide involvement and leadership. Abrupt demobilization in 1945–46 left but one widely scattered American army division in all of Europe.

To maintain peace, the American political architects pushed the construction of the United Nations with the expectation that the wartime allies on the Security Council would collectively manage conflict. In less than a decade, however, the vision of collective security had become the reality of selective security arrangements as the United States made alliances with, and security commitments to, dozens of nations around the world. Rather than reflecting an "anticommunist crusade," as sometimes erroneously charged, these arrangements arose out of a variety of causes, as the earlier discussion of alliances would suggest. As the structure of the international system has changed, and as U.S. interests and those of its allies have been modified, the value and cost to the United States of its alliances have also inevitably been altered.

The Inter-American Alliance. The first postwar American alliance was established by the Rio Pact (the Inter-American Defense Treaty), signed in 1947, which created the Organization of American States (OAS). The political relations of the United States with the Latin American nations had long followed an erratic, and often hostile, path. The "pan-American system" had included some significant internal conflicts. By the end of World War II, it was becoming clear that America's major concern in the future would be Europe, not Latin America. America's position of global dominance highlighted the traditional problem of the Western Hemisphere—an economic and military giant amongst far less powerful neighbors. Even though the tensions of what was to become the cold war were already rapidly growing, the threat of Soviet or communist influence in the Western Hemisphere was not generally perceived as important. To the extent that influence from outside the hemisphere was a concern of the signatories, the Rio Pact reflected not so much the evolving conflict with the Soviet Union as the experience with the Axis powers during World War II.[13]

The Rio Pact did not spring from the emerging tight bipolar structure, nor did it represent (despite a century or more of rhetoric about "American republics") commonality of attributes, but rather, complementary interests. The United States was concerned with preserving order and the status quo in the region against challenges from both within and without. Although there was disagreement among the Latin American nations, especially Argentina, they too were concerned with protecting the status quo.[14] They were equally concerned with institutionalizing their special relationship with the United States and forcing it, if they could, to devote more of its attention to them.

Of course, restraining the United States from armed intervention in their countries, as had occurred several times in this century, was also one of their interests.

Still in force, the Rio Pact signatories agree that "an act of aggression against one American State is an act of aggression against all the other American States." The pact also stipulates that a variety of forms of aggression (such as subversion) from any source affecting the "territory or sovereignty or political independence" of the American states will cause the signatories to consult and to act as they deem necessary. Thus, the pact is a regional collective security agreement designed to protect the American nations against all aggressors (internal or external to the hemisphere). Although later used to legitimize anticommunist actions such as the American intervention in the Dominican Republic in 1965, the alliance formed at Rio was not created as an anticommunist or antidictatorial alliance. It was created to regularize the relations among the American nations on a peaceful basis and to preserve the status quo as represented by the regimes of those nations. By the late 1970s the purposes of the OAS were unclear. In La Paz, Bolivia, Secretary of State Cyrus Vance suggested in 1979 that "a prime task before us is to reexamine and redefine the role and function of this organization and how it should relate to the problem of today's world."[15]

NATO. The most important alliance the U.S. joined, NATO, was fundamentally different. By the latter 1940s, the structure of the international system, at least with regard to Europe, was strongly bipolar; only the United States and the Soviet Union had sufficient capabilities to play significant political-military roles. Their attempts to organize Europe so that it would satisfy their vital interests clashed strongly even before World War II ended. Furthermore, ideological differences between the two nations, muted during the war in the pursuit of coalition strength, regained their earlier importance by the war's end.

Faced with growing Soviet intransigence in central and Eastern Europe, and Soviet threats directed against Western and Southern Europe as well, the United States felt compelled to respond. It had attempted in two wars to maintain an equilibrium in Europe; it could not afford to withdraw when this equilibrium was again threatened. America's first response was against growing communist insurgency and pressure in Greece and Turkey. The consequent Truman Doctrine (1947) stated that the United States could survive only in a world where aggression and totalitarianism were not allowed to expand against the institutions of free nations nor to undermine international peace. Within the year, the United States acted to bolster its words, sending military assistance and military advisers to Greece and Turkey.

The Truman Doctrine, a classic response to a disequilibrium of power in a tight bipolar world, was the opening move in what came to be known as the policy of "containment." It was the goal of this policy to confine the power of the Soviet Union to its existing boundaries, thereby ultimately creating pressures and tensions within the Soviet leadership elites, thereby forcing them to accept the status quo. In pursuit of the policy, the American military presence in the Mediterranean area and in Europe was designed to deter and to defend against Soviet expansionism, allowing the southern and Western Europeans to recover from the physical and economic devastation of the war. Recognizing that the Western European nations were essential actors in building and maintaining an equilibrium of power and that economic and social recovery were vital to European security, the United States also formulated the Marshall Plan, a massive economic aid program to restore Europe to economic vitality.

As hostility between the Western powers and the Soviet bloc increased, it became clear to the West that a security arrangement going beyond economic cooperation and assurances of common interests was necessary. The Soviet supported coup in Czechoslovakia (1948) and the Berlin Blockade (1948–49) convinced Americans and Europeans alike that a military alliance was necessary. These Soviet actions, reminiscent of the Nazi seizure of Czechoslovakia a decade earlier, provoked the return of American power to Europe. The Truman Doctrine, initially intended to be limited in scope, was extended to the entirety of Western and southern Europe. Accordingly, in 1949, the common interests and goals of the United States and Western European nations (with the exception of West Germany, which joined in 1955) were formalized in NATO. This was a collective defense pact, providing that an attack on one was an attack on all.

The new alliance's strategic policy stressed deterrence of Soviet aggression by alliance forces on the ground, supported by U.S. strategic nuclear weapons. NATO also provided for a joint command structure with joint planning and forces-in-being. This was a major change from previous American alliance policy. NATO represented America's first peacetime military alliance; as such, it was rooted in the concept of deterrence as opposed to defense against an actual attack.

The build-up of conventional forces in Europe was slow. Initial unwillingness on both sides of the Atlantic to return to large expensive military forces, and belief that America's dominant nuclear power was sufficient for deterrence, meant that NATO conventional forces were starved. However, the North Korean invasion of South Korea in 1950, believed to have been instigated by the Soviet Union, changed attitudes in NATO. Stress was placed on quickly developing a substantial conventional force in Europe capable of repelling a Soviet invasion, which many believed the Korean invasion portended. NATO strategy began to emphasize defense as well as deterrence.

NATO success and the extent and duration of cooperation in it have been unprecedented. With the passage of the years, however, American and European goals, which were virtually identical in the beginning, inevitably began to diverge. Americans wanted European security, but they also wanted to avoid serious conflict, especially with the Soviet Union. A guarantee of European security, with its emphasis on nuclear deterrence, is in tension with

Table 21.1 Principal Regional Forces in the Warsaw Pact and NATO Countries

Country/Service	Regular Force	Reserves	Main Armament	Other
U.S.S.R. (pop. 269,650,000				
Army	1,825,000	up to 25,000,000	50,000 tks. 62,000 AFV 20,000 arty.	Strategic forces: ICBM: 1398 IR/MRBM:606 SLBM: 989 acft.: 809
Navy	450,000		204 atk. subs. 69 msl. subs. 290 maj. cts. ships 755 cbt. acft.	
Air Force	475,000		4,480 cbt. acft.	
Paramilitary	560,000			
All Other Warsaw Pact Countries[a] (pop. 110,200,000)				
Army	792,000	695,000	13,060 tks. 20,825 AFV 4,066 arty.	
Navy	53,000	70,000	6 atk. subs. 300 maj. cbt. ships	
Air Force	269,000	125,000	2,251 cbt. acft.	
Unified Reserves		1,048,000 (all services)		
Paramilitary	524,000			
United States (pop. 230,049,000)				
Army	790,800	614,300	12,130 tks. 20,000 AFV 5,459 arty.	Nuclear forces: ICBM: 1052 SLBM: 520 Bombers:316 SRBM: 108
Navy	553,000	87,900	90 atk. sub. 204 maj. surf. ships 1,350 cbt. acft.	
Marines	192,000	37,000	576 tks. 985 AFV 368 arty. 441 cbt. acft.	
Air Force	581,000	160,000	3,650 cbt. acft.	
Paramilitary (Coast Guard, Civil Air Patrol	104,000	11,600		

Table 21.1 *(cont.)*

Country/Service	Regular Force	Reserves	Main Armament	Other
All Other NATO Countries[b] (pop. 395,711,000)				
Army	2,208,000	2,556,000	17,400 tks. 33,100 AFV 10,100 arty	Nuclear forces SLBM: 144 IRBM: 18 SRBM: 42
Navy	396,000	455,000	150 atk. sub. 370 maj. surf. ships 300 cbt. acft.	
Air Force	564,000	307,000	3,900 cbt. acft.	
Paramilitary	450,000			
United Reserves		2,045,000		

[a]Bulgaria, Czechoslovakia, East Germany, Hungary, Poland, and Romania.
[b]Belgium, Canada, Denmark, France, Great Britain, Greece, Italy, Netherlands, Norway, Portugal, Spain, Turkey, and West Germany.
Source: International Institute for Strategic Studies, *The Military Balance, 1982–1983* (London: IISS, 1982).
For Abbreviations, see table 17.1.

the avoidance of confrontation with the Soviets. When the United States possessed a nuclear monopoly or even nuclear predominance the problem was not so acute. But as the Soviets developed strategic weapons that threatened to destroy the United States if a nuclear war occurred, the American commitment to Europe became considerably more "expensive" and the credibility of the American deterrent became more doubtful.

As Soviet strategic nuclear strength grew inexorably in the course of the 1970s, to the point where it was at least equal to that of the Americans by the decade's end, question of American credibility in defending the national interests of its allies became central. In the 1950s the United States had already demonstrated that it would not defend the vital interests of the Europeans outside of Europe, as shown by the Suez Crisis in 1956. Britain and France were dependent on Middle Eastern oil; the Suez Canal was their lifeline. They intervened after Egyptian President Nasser nationalized the canal, but the United States refused to support their action; instead, we sided with the Soviet Union in insisting that British and French (and Israeli) forces be withdrawn. At the end of the 1970s, the question was, Would the United States risk New York for Paris or Bonn? Henry Kissinger's speech at an unofficial conference on NATO in the autumn of 1979 is instructive. "Our European allies should not keep asking us to multiply strategic assurances that we cannot possibly mean or if we do mean, we should not want to execute because if we execute, we risk the destruction of civilization. Our strategic dilemma is not solved by verbal reassurances; it requires redesigning our forces and doctrine."[16]

Theater nuclear forces have represented another source of intraalliance problems. Efforts in the early 1960s to build European multilateral nuclear force (MLF) came to nothing, and the failed attempts only decreased the members' mutual trust. Through skillful use of a consultative group, formed after the MLF collapsed, called the Nuclear Planning Group, the Americans managed to contain allied nervousness and resentment over U.S. control of theater nuclear forces (TNF). The Europeans are, for the most part, anxious to cooperate in order to have TNF on the ground, both because the forces add to deterrence and also because they link, or "couple," the conventional defenses along the East-West frontier with the American strategic forces. In order to serve these two roles, TNF must themselves be credible, hence TNF modernization has been a recurring issue. Despite Soviet cajoling and threats, the allies reaffirmed their 1979 decision to modernize those forces in the early 1980s, indicating that the commonality of interest within the alliance remained strong.

The strategy of flexible response has also generated alliance problems. Since flexible response is a strategy that includes the option of meeting a Soviet conventional attack, at least initially, by fighting a large scale conventional defense in Europe, it is viewed with great distaste by the Western European countries in whose territories the war would be conducted.[17] Besides, increasing the capability for conventional defense, which Americans emphasize as needed for the strategy, implies less than full readiness to use the strategic nuclear weapons, thus causing declining trust in nuclear deterrence. To most Europeans, deterrence of any attack is the only possible strategy that will guarantee national security and survival on acceptable terms.

The resulting tension over divergent goals and military strategy has had varying effects on the NATO members. The smaller NATO nations have generally let their larger neighbors take the lead and pay the costs. The French have developed and deployed their own strategic weapons, the *force de frappe*, and have withdrawn their forces from the military command of NATO, diminishing the capabilities of a concerted flexible defense in Europe. The Greeks and Turks, locked in their perennial dispute over Cyprus, have decreased their cooperation with NATO, generating doubts concerning NATO southern defense posture. Increasingly, the initiatives and the burdens have shifted to the Germans and the Americans, with the British also bearing a considerable share.

Finally, one could make the ironic observation that NATO has perhaps been too successful for its own longevity. It has been largely responsible for the feeling throughout the West that a Soviet attack is most unlikely, simultaneously creating pressure—at times, almost irresistible pressure—to reduce defenses. In the early and mid 1970s NATO faced considerable difficulty in maintaining the defenses created three decades before. The changed international system and the evolving interests of the members had altered much of what had underpinned the alliance. By the latter 1970s recognition of a mounting Soviet military threat had, however, grown to a point where President Carter was able to secure allied agreement to an across-the-board *real* annual increase in defense spending of 3 percent—an agreement not fulfilled.

Theoretically, it ought not be a serious problem to persuade the Allies to increase their military expenditures, for the Western Europeans should be able to provide adequately for their own defense. Even without the United States in the balance, they have a population and economic base roughly equal to that of the East. With the United States in the equation and taking into account the much greater share of GNP devoted to the military in the East, NATO personnel and defense spending levels are roughly the same as those of the Warsaw Pact. But for a variety of reasons (much lower military personnel costs in the East, lack of standardization in the West, inadequate use of reserve forces in the West, and the lower ratio of support to combat troops in the East, among others), the Warsaw Pact enjoys a very large margin of conventional force superiority in Europe.

When the United States had nuclear predominance over the U.S.S.R., it could plausibly threaten to escalate to nuclear weapons if Soviet conventional attacks were to succeed in overrunning the inadequate conventional defenses of the West. Since such a threatened "first use" of nuclear weapons is no longer credible, the whole doctrine of Western European defense, which tightly couples conventional, tactical nuclear, and strategic nuclear forces, is undermined. Kissinger expressed the same idea in 1979. "NATO is reaching a point where the strategic assumptions on which it has been operating, the force structures that it has been generating, and the joint policies it has been developing will be inadequate for the 1980s."[18]

To restore rationality and credibility, two things are required: first, to build conventional defenses in Western Europe which have a high probability of withstanding a Soviet thrust and, second, to discard the first use policy for nuclear weapons, recognizing that the only sensible purpose for nuclear arms is to deter their use by others. On this latter point, rather than depending on linkage of conventional and nuclear forces as has been NATO strategy, the West should be

reducing or eliminating the probabilities that certain types of events would . . . lead to strategic nuclear exchanges . . . reducing implicit reliance on nuclear weapons in the minds of leaders on both sides and reducing explicit reliance on these weapons as codified in strategy, doctrine, war plans, standing operating procedures, tactics, and force structure.[19]

The key to thus revising the NATO grand strategy in line with the reality of the 1980s is the building of adequate conventional forces. Inasmuch as the NATO nations together have three times the GNP and four times the population of the U.S.S.R., such a task ought to be manageable. As Secretary of Defense McNamara argued in an earlier era, when the United States was trying to wean its European allies away from the notion of total reliance on American nuclear weapons, "Surely an Alliance with the wealth, talent, and experience that we possess can find a better way than extreme reliance on nuclear weapons to meet our common threat. We do not believe that if the formula, $e = mc^2$, had not been discovered, we should all be Communist slaves."[20]

Fortunately, there are a number of ways to increase NATO conventional defenses without crippling costs. Some of these options are: further use of precision-guided munitions, increased combat-to-support troop ratios by extending the use of civilians in support functions, and—most important—much greater use of reservists to fill out divisions in times of emergency. Expert analyses of such measures suggest that adding less than 10 percent to existing defense burdens could provide the needed strengths.[21] Of course, none of the NATO nations—especially the Europeans—will want to undergo the additional sacrifices; but the sooner the necessary revisions in strategy and structure are made, the greater the chances of Western survival.

Other American Alliances. The initial success of NATO and the Truman Doctrine became a rationale and blueprint for additional foreign policy acts along the periphery of the communist world.[22] Reacting quickly to aggression in Korea in 1950, America (under the leadership of Truman and Acheson) extended the concept of containment to the Far East. As the United States fought in Korea, its leaders moved to sign up additional allies to reinforce the containment policy, particularly after the P.R.C. intervened in the conflict. In 1951, bilateral mutual security pacts were quickly concluded with Japan and the Philippines, and a multilateral pact with Australia and New Zealand (the ANZUS Treaty) was signed. The actual military potential of these allies was small, but alliances in a nuclear, bipolar world were designed as much to serve political as military objectives. One major value of these allies to the United States was their strategic location; from bases in these countries the United States was able to project its military capability to the front doors of the P.R.C. and the Soviet Union. Of course, these alliances also had an important ideological dimension, defining who was friend and who was foe.

There were other important elements to the alliances. The Philippines was internally unstable due to the Huk rebellion and needed support against that insurgency more than against any external threat. Australia and New Zealand wanted American assurance against a possible revival of Japanese expansion, and the American pact with Japan in part had the purpose of providing that assurance.[23] Again, this was a case of alliances shaped by an international environment perceived somewhat differently than in Europe; the alliances proceeded from a set of complementary interests, only one of which was a vaguely defined as "containment of communism."

With allies in Europe and the Far East, the Eisenhower administration proceeded to complete the circle of containment by adding new allies in southern and Southeast Asia and in the Middle East. This coincided with the

"New Look" in American national security policy, which was to contain communism through massive retaliation—the reliance on deterrence of aggression rather than a fighting defense of local areas. To be effective, this policy required establishing allies and a credible commitment to them and then convincing the adversary that any aggression would be met by a nuclear attack in its homeland. There were two major problems with the credibility of this policy. First, it was sometimes difficult, if not impossible, to make a believable commitment due to the divergent interests of the United States and its many allies. Second, as the Soviets acquired their own nuclear weapons, the likelihood that the United States would willingly suffer major destruction for a minor interest (or minor ally) was small. However, there was a certain momentum in the Eisenhower administration's plans to encircle the Soviets and Communist Chinese (who were viewed as a single adversary) with alliances.

In 1954 the United States formally guaranteed the security of the Republic of China—in effect also guaranteeing that Taiwan would not attack the P.R.C. and drag American into another war. America had not fully supported the Nationalist government prior to its defeat in 1949 because a huge effort was envisaged and, prior to the Korean War, Asia was seen as a secondary theater to Europe.[24]

Precipitated by the Korean War, the U.S. commitments in Asia grew rapidly. SEATO was founded in 1954 to include the United States, Britain, France, Australia, New Zealand, Pakistan, Thailand, and the Philippines. In a separate protocol, the signatories extended their protection to South Vietnam, Laos, and Cambodia, none of whom were members of the organization. The treaty pledged the members to act only to meet the danger of an armed attack, each nation in accordance with its constitutional processes. The United States, in an addendum, specified that as far as it was concerned, this applied only to communist aggression.[25] Unlike the Rio Pact and the NATO treaty, there was no article stipulating that an attack on one was an attack on all.

Futher complicating the SEATO alliance were the divergent goals and interests of SEATO members. For example, Pakistan had little in common with the Philippines or France. Pakistan's principal adversary was India, not some ill-defined "communist aggressor." It had joined the alliance, in fact, primarily to receive support in its struggle with India. For the United States, the purpose of SEATO was to provide the political framework for building local security forces.[26] Yet America's concern for subversion in the area was not equally shared by the other members. Whether SEATO, as a collective defense arrangement or a means of political cooperation, was well conceived is questionable. Beset almost continuously by major political differences among its members, it languished for twenty years and was disbanded in 1977.

CENTO was founded in 1955. Organized by the British in the area of their prewar influence, it was initially called the Baghdad Pact and included Great Britain, Iran, Iraq, Pakistan, and Turkey. (After the Iraqi revolution of 1958, Iraq withdrew and the alliance became CENTO.) American participation was limited to an advisory role on the Military Council (1956). With Turkey as a member of both CENTO and NATO, the circle of containment around the Sino-Soviet bloc appeared complete. As with SEATO, however, CENTO suffered from a lack of common interests among the participants. A rising sense of Arab nationalism, memories of British colonial rule, and the Suez Crisis (1956) largely vitiated the alliance before it began. Although CENTO continues in name, American presence is felt in the Middle East as a consequence of bilateral, not multilateral, ties.

The United States has a number of commitments not contained in formal treaties or alliances. For example, during the Berlin Crisis in 1962, the Congress passed a resolution reaffirming American access rights to West Berlin and the determination to use force, if necessary, to defend the city. The Tonkin Gulf Resolution, later retracted, affirmed American determination to defend Vietnam. Moreover, there are a number of purely executive agreements concerning defense and security arrangements, such as a 1962 agreement with Thailand. Finally, there are unilateral policy declarations and communiqués (e.g., the Monroe Doctrine and various undertakings concerning Israel) that can be interpreted to bind the United States to foreign areas and nations. All these various ties relate to specific security interests of the United States as those interests have been perceived by American decision-makers at the time. Specific interests call for specific responses, and changing situations require altered commitments.

Alliances in the Nuclear Age. Some have suggested that alliance systems are largely irrelevant to the contemporary nuclear world. They argue that since total war means global destruction, nuclear force between major nations or alliances cannot be an element of statecraft except in its deterrent form. It is further contended that military capability is now based on the quantity and quality of a state's nuclear weapons and not on the incremental addition of an ally's capabilities. There is little additional strategic nuclear capability that can be acquired by a superpower through any alliance.

Although overstated, these points raise pertinent questions about the solidarity and value of American alliances. The first question concerns the credibility of the American commitment when facing a nuclear armed adversary. Through the 1970s there appeared to be sufficient belief in the military capability of the United States and credibility among its allies and adversaries to provide deterrence.

By the decade's end, however, concern about American strength and, even more so, its will had begun to erode this confidence. The passage of the War Powers Act in 1973, placing strong brakes on the president's ability to commit military forces, strongly reinforced this sense of disquiet. The question was one not of motive but of reliability; according to one European the problem with depending on the Americans is that one never knows when they will turn around and stab themselves in the back. Historically, of course, one cannot conclude with certainty that America's allies have not been attacked by the Soviet Union *because* they were allies, for not enough is known about Soviet intentions. It seems safe to conclude, though, that the Soviets were sufficiently worried about American strength and will—at least through the 1970s—to be deterred, had they been inclined to attack.

As to the question of whether or not the United States continues to gain from alliances, the answer is affirmative; alliances are still useful for protecting vital territory, concerting ground defenses, acquiring bases, providing psychological support, and other purposes. There is a final aspect of alliances which should not be overlooked. Kissinger has suggested that alliances, as opposed to other forms of guarantee, make a constellation of power credible, obligatory, and legitimate.[27] Alliances provide a *legitimate* framework for performing selectively the many functions and preserving the many interests discussed above.

By the end of the 1960s the United States found itself in a quite different world from the tight bipolar, alliance-building world of the preceding two decades. The complexity of issues and the limitations on U.S. resources forced a substantial revision of U.S. foreign policy priorities. The so-called Nixon Doctrine was an attempt in 1969 to reorder these priorities with the explicit recognition that America could neither be strong everywhere nor committed everywhere. In the president's words concerning the extent of America's involvements in behalf of other states:

The United States will keep all of its treaty commitments. . . . We shall provide a shield if a nuclear power threatens the freedom of a nation allied with us or of a nation whose survival we consider vital to our security. . . . In cases involving other types of aggression we shall furnish military and economic assistance when requested in accordance with our treaty commitments. But we shall look to the nation directly threatened to assume the primary responsibility of providing the manpower for its defense.[28]

Throughout the 1970s, in accordance with this doctrine, U.S. policy sought to create regional centers of power where American arms, but not American military personnel, would help others pursue their security interests when those interests were compatible with U.S. security interests. As we shall see in later chapters, events in Iran in 1979 and 1980 and in Israel in 1982 called into question the extent to which the United States could and should continue to rely on allies armed with American weapons to protect vital U.S. security interests.

DISCUSSION QUESTIONS

1. Why do nations form alliances?
2. What are the functions of alliances?
3. What is the effect of alliances on nation-state behavior and on the structure of the international system?
4. What is meant by a "balance of power"?

5. What are the four types of international systems? What are the characteristics of each type of international system? Which type of international system is more stable? Why?

6. How do the attribute theory and community of interest theory contribute to our understanding of alliances?

7. Have U.S. alliances been counterproductive, leading to U.S. involvements that eroded our national strength and reduced our sense of security? Explain.

8. Why did the U.S. sign the Rio Treaty? Were the reasons for signing the Rio Treaty the same reasons for joining NATO? Explain. What are the differences between U.S. commitments under the Rio Treaty and NATO?

9. What factors have enhanced and inhibited the credibility of NATO?

10. What is meant by the statement, "NATO has been too successful"? Do you agree? Why?

11. What basic changes in American foreign policy occurred in 1947? What was the rationale for adopting the policy of containment?

12. What were the differences between U.S. commitment to NATO and SEATO? Why was NATO a more credible alliance?

13. How has the possession of nuclear weapons influenced traditional alliance theory and behavior?

14. How do the alliances in which the U.S. is a member contribute to American national security?

RECOMMENDED READING

Bundy, McGeorge; Kennan, George F.; McNamara, Robert; and Smith, Gerald. "Nuclear Weapons and the Atlantic Alliance." *Foreign Affairs* 60, no. 4 (spring 1982).

Claude, Inis L., Jr. *Power and International Relations*. New York: Random House, 1962.

Deutsch, Karl; Burrell, Sidney A.; Kann, Robert A.; et al. *Political Community in the North Atlantic Area*. Princeton: Princeton University Press, 1957.

Gulick, Edward V. *Europe's Classical Balance of Power*. Ithaca: Cornell University Press, 1955.

Hopkins, Raymond F., and Mansbach, Richard W. *Structure and Process in International Politics*. New York: Harper & Row, 1973.

Kissinger, Henry A. *Nuclear Weapons and Foreign Policy*. New York: Harper & Brothers, 1957.

Meyers, Kenneth, ed. *NATO: The Next Thirty Years*. Boulder, Colo.: Westview Press, 1980.

Randle, Robert F. *The Origins of Peace*. New York: Free Press, 1973.

Riker, William H. *The Theory of Political Coalitions*. New Haven: Yale University Press, 1962.

Slater, Jerome. *The OAS and United States Foreign Policy*. Columbus: Ohio State University Press, 1967.

22

INTERNATIONAL FORCES AND PEACE-KEEPING

Preceding chapters have set forth some of the international political and economic realities that challenge the national security interests of the United States. Among the approaches available to meeting those challenges are support for international forces and peace-keeping efforts as alternatives to alliance or independent state action. Although only modestly effective in the post–World War II era, such approaches have proven to be of critical value in some situations. The challenge for American national security policy-makers is to adapt these multilateral approaches in ways that directly enhance the security interests of the United States, yet that are perceived and accepted by others as legitimately contributing to a stable and just international order.

Peace-keeping, in the international context, is "the preventing, containment, moderation and termination of hostilities between and within states, through the medium of peaceful third party intervention, organized and directed internationally, using multinational forces of soldiers, police and civilians to restore and maintain peace."[1]* As it has evolved in the post–World War II environment, however, peace-keeping has been considerably more ambiguous and confusing than any simple definition might suggest. The general notion of international peace-keeping is implied in the preamble to the charter of the United Nations wherein the member states pledge their common strength "to maintain international peace and security, and to ensure, by the acceptance of principles and the institution of methods, that armed force shall not be used, save in the common interest." But nowhere in the charter is the term *peace-keeping*, as such, to be found; this in part accounts for much of the contention regarding the proper role of peace-keeping forces which has been prevalent since the drafting of the charter.

Beyond this vague reference in the preamble, the charter deals with the idea of international peace-keeping either under chapter 6, entitled "Pacific

---

* This is the definition used by the International Peace Academy in its study of international control of violence.

Settlement of Disputes," or under chapter 7, entitled "Action with Respect to Threats to the Peace, Breaches of the Peace, and Acts of Aggression," or both.[2] There is an important distinction between chapters 6 and 7 of the charter, as they relate to peace-keeping, going to the very nature of peace-keeping operations. Chapter 6 provides in a general way for noncoercive means of dispute and conflict settlement based on the consent of the parties involved, including such techniques as "negotiation, enquiry, mediation, conciliation, arbitration, judicial settlement, resort to regional agencies or arrangements, or other peaceful means." Chapter 7, on the other hand, invokes various coercive means of enforcing the peace, to include, for example, economic sanctions or the use of international military forces.[3] It appears that the framers of the charter viewed chapter 7 as providing the means for containing a dispute while the provisions of chapter 6 were to aid the ultimate resolution of the conflict. The failure of the charter to provide for or define clearly the nature of international peace-keeping, however, has resulted in conflicting views as to whether such operations are properly coercive or noncoercive techniques of maintaining international peace and security.

Success in international peace-keeping efforts has usually been achieved through peaceful intervention rather than the use of force. Additionally, the maintenance of an objective and even-handed posture toward the parties to a dispute has permitted each party to rely confidently upon the international force to keep the peace, thereby facilitating the ultimate settlement of the conflict.

Although only marginally successful to date in contributing to the goal of a world free from the "scourge of war," international peace-keeping efforts have contributed to the containment of conflict. Very importantly, too, international peace-keeping efforts have served to prevent direct confrontation between the superpowers in areas of conflict where their respective national interests have clashed. As an alternative to individual state or alliance intervention, international peace-keeping forces have enabled disputing parties to limit the use of violence and to seek alternatives to conflict resolution.

Peace-keeping, whatever its effectiveness on a regional or issue-by-issue basis, derives from the international community's concern over the threat of war, and especially over the threat of superpower confrontation, Accordingly, the success and shortcomings of post–World War II international peace-keeping efforts reflect the realities of the international system. Each peace-keeping operation, therefore, must be evaluated in light of the realities of superpower relationships at the time and the relative importance of the national security interests involved. Except for the UN action in Korea, international peace-keeping efforts would never have been attempted had it not been for a fundamental consensus among the permanent members of the UN Security Council—especially the United States and the Soviet Union—that an international effort was an acceptable means for safeguarding the national security interests of those involved.

The UN Charter and Collective Security. Despite the charter's lack of clarity on the legal authority for the UN peace-keeping function, it seems clear that peace-keeping, at least initially, was envisaged by the international community as part of, or somehow deriving from, the concept of *collective security*. Collective security means that the collective strength of the member states would be used to maintain or restore international peace, with or without the consent of the parties to a conflict. Frustrated by the defects in international peace-keeping machinery under the League of Nations, yet encouraged by the cooperation of the Allies during World War II, the founders of the United Nations set forth in considerable detail in the UN charter the mechanism for enforcing peace through collective security. While the Council of the League of Nations was authorized merely to *recommend* international military action to restore or maintain the peace, chapter 7 of the UN charter was designed to provide an effective "set of teeth" to realize the concept of collective security. Article 42 of the charter empowers the Security Council to "take such action by air, sea, or land forces as may be necessary to maintain or restore international peace and security."[4] Article 43 calls upon member states to provide armed forces, assistance, facilities, and rights of passage for UN forces. Air, sea or land forces, as necessary, are to be used by the UN for such missions as demonstrations, blockades, and other operations.

To enable the United Nations "to take urgent military measures," members are required to "hold immediately available national air force contingents for combined international enforcement action." To supervise the negotiation of required arrangements as well as to provide "for the strategic direction of any armed forces placed at the disposal of the Security Council, a Military Staff Committee is to be established, to consist of the Chiefs of Staff of the permanent members of the Security Council or their representatives."[5]

Clearly, the concept of collective security—and, therefore, peace-keeping—presumed the existence of an effective Security Council. Charged with primary responsibility in matters affecting international peace and security, the Security Council could exercise its authority under chapter 7 only if there existed a certain minimal level of consensus among the permanent members of that body. The validity of this underlying presumption was soon challenged by the realities of the postwar environment.

The Demise of Collective Security. As reflected in Chapter 1 of this book, the international political system of the postwar era has inhibited the realization of collective security efforts as envisaged in the UN charter. Without the cooperation of the permanent, veto-empowered members of the Security Council, especially the U.S. and U.S.S.R., a standby UN peace-keeping force has proved impossible to create. Thus a central aspect of the UN peace-keeping system has never materialized. Those peace-keeping efforts that have been launched under UN auspices were organized and directed on an ad hoc basis. Aptly described, the UN, "condemned to live between two giants in international politics and to be used and abused by each according to the service it renders the national interest,"[6] has been forced to bend with the winds of political reality as a price for its existence.

As the fortunes of the UN have ebbed and flowed, so has support for its peace-keeping operations. Without the convergence of superpower interests (or at least passive tolerance by one of the other's interests), any peace-keeping initiative is doomed from the outset. It is this convergence of interests that allows initiating resolutions to pass and guarantees the financial and logistical support necessary to enforce any final dispute settlement. Without this initial consensus among the superpowers, the peace-keeping effort will be stillborn. Should the consensus dissolve at an intermediate stage, both the effort and the hope for an international settlement through the United Nations will wither.

The collective security system, designed to maintain international peace by the imposition of the collective strength of the members of the UN community, failed to become a reality primarily because the major powers could not agree on an acceptable status quo. The fundamental prerequisite for collective security, namely, that nations subscribing to a status quo be willing and able to muster decisive strength for collective military action, has been absent. Further, the clash of national interests and ideologies has precluded the development of that sense of trust among the "enforcers" which is the essential precondition to the enforcement of the collective will. If a collective security approach is seen as furthering an adversary's interests at the expense of one's own interests, the prospects for developing an international consensus, and especially a great power consensus, are remote. It is clear that "the chief practical obstacle to collective security is the political problem deriving from the conflict of independent foreign policies."[7]

Great power cooperation, partially achieved during World War II and acknowledged as necessary for effective UN peace-keeping efforts, dissipated quickly during the cold war period. It quickly became apparent that reality did not echo the optimistic words of the charter. The Security Council veto, an implicit recognition of the fragility of any consensus, was frequently and routinely employed by the Soviet Union. For the United Nations, reality was to be molded "by national and ideological forces in conflict and armed with increasingly destructive weapons; by processes of technological revolution; by change and growth in the underdeveloped countries that was at times convulsive; and by old fashioned nationalism—all those coexisting with the optimistic aspirations and ideals about the future of world order."[8]

From the beginning, UN structural elements such as the Military Staff Committee have existed more in name than in fact. Fundamental conflicts over its composition, authority and responsibilities thwarted any progress toward an institutionalized UN force. As correctly noted by a Russian member of the committee in 1946, "the whole question of armed forces being made available to the Security Council . . . is not only, and not so much, a technical question as a political one."[9] A viable solution to the political impasse was beyond reach then and appears to remain so today.

An initial source of conflict was the fundamentally different view on the use of international forces held by the Soviet Union and the other permanent members of the United Nations. The United States, reflecting its dominance within the fledging organization, advocated a sizable mobile force—with strength, responsiveness and operational flexibility, once committed. The Soviets, manifesting their understandable fears that the Americans viewed the United Nations as another component of their "containment" policy, demanded a less potent force with more stringent controls on its potential use. The period that had begun with a high faith in collective cooperation witnessed a creeping erosion of trust and effectiveness. A stalemate developed, with the United States attempting to exploit its leverage and the Soviet Union, as the leader of the permanent minority, reacting with suspicion to every initiative.

The paralysis of the Security Council forced Western governments to seek alternative security methods, ones lying within the confines of the charter in letter if not in spirit. One such effort, the development of alliance, or collective self-defense, agreements, was based upon the explicit understanding that "nothing in the present Charter shall impair the inherent right of individual or collective self-defense."[10] These pacts, the first of which were the Inter-American Treaty of Mutual Assistance (1947) and the North Atlantic Treaty (1949), were seen by the Soviets as links in an American chain of encirclement, and did little to promote cooperation within the Security Council. As competitive East-West alliance building developed, the hoped for global alliance for peace through the United Nations progressively became a maze of traditional political-military and economic arrangements which thwarted the overall objectives of the international organization, at least as those objectives were initially conceived.

Faced with a Security Council impasse in collective security matters, a second initiative, promoted vigorously by the United States, was the expansion of the role of the General Assembly in international security affairs. This thrust was epitomized by the Uniting for Peace Resolution passed in 1950, which formalized the assembly's right to intervene in matters affecting "international peace and security" when the Security Council was deadlocked.[11] Correctly perceived by the U.S.S.R. as an attempt to bypass the Soviet veto, it further fanned the fires of East-West antagonism.

By the early 1950s the prospects for effective collective security had dimmed, and the mechanisms of chapter 7 of the charter existed largely as an idealistic goal. The lines of the cold war were clearly drawn, and ideological positions were irrevocably hardened, or so it seemed. UN involvement in the Korean War was not collective security but merely a shadow of it, manipulated by the Unied States and permitted by the Soviet Union's ill-timed boycott of the Security Council. The interlocking defensive alliances, contrary to common belief and semantic usage, tended to supplant the global quest for collective security with regional efforts. In essence, NATO and the Warsaw Pact embodied both a recognition that collective security on a global basis was dead and a guarantee against its resurrection.

Yet even this recognition of the ultimate impotence of the UN represented a milestone in the evolution of peace-keeping. It opened the way for a search for ways in which the United Nations could aid in preventing and containing war despite its inability to enforce peace. From that search, peace-keeping developed more clearly as a chapter 6, rather than a chapter 7, activity—that is, as a noncoercive process based on the consent of the parties to a dispute in contrast to the imposition, by force if necessary, of a collective will on those parties. Former Secretary-General U Thant described this process of evolution.

There has been a tacit transition from the concept of collective security, as set out in Chapter VII of the United Nations Charter, to a more realistic idea of peacekeeping. The idea that conventional military methods—or, to put it bluntly, war—can be used by or on behalf of the United Nations to counter aggression and secure the peace, seems now to be rather impractical.[12]

Earlier, peace-keeping by the UN had been invoked "only in later, more acute stages of conflict, where the range of possible actions [had] become gravely restricted." As a result, the United Nations often found itself in a no-win situation, one in which it was asked "to do what no one else can or will, usually after reason has fled."[13] Perhaps in a period of genuine strategic nuclear parity there will be a greater willingness by the superpowers to let the United Nations play a larger role earlier in managing Third World conflicts, thus detaching themselves from such crises tensions. Moreover, in an era of real parity a greater tendency could develop for each to acquiesce in, rather than forestall, peace-keeping operations supported by the other side. With a mutually augmented stake in stability, each superpower might view peace-keeping operations with greater enthusiasm. The record to date, however, is not encouraging. The prospects for strengthened international institutions depend in large part, then, on the Soviet Union's readiness to become essentially a status quo power. Therein lies the rub!

History attests to the fact that "the role of the United Nations in peace-keeping is valid only when it is formulated in accordance with existing realities."[14] Events of the 1970s transformed the international political environment. It is conceivable that in the 1980s the world is entering a new phase, one which, in theory, may be conducive to more effective use of international peace-keeping efforts. Conversely, the Soviet acquisition of great nuclear and conventional military strength and the dispersion of power taking place in the international system may tempt the U.S.S.R. to use its muscles unilaterally in ways not possible when it was weaker. In short, it remains to be seen if the theoretical potential for peace-keeping in fact will be employed in light of the realities of the 1980s.

Evolution of International Peace-Keeping Efforts. The evolution of peace-keeping can be viewed, then, in two—or potentially three—relatively distinct periods. The first of these phases was initiated by the demise of collective security efforts in the late 1940s and extended for about a decade and a half until the mid 1960s. Crises within the United Nations during 1964–65, in large part arising out of peace-keeping problems in the Congo, ushered in the second, less activist phase, one extending to the present. Against the background of renewed superpower competition and post détente concerns about confrontation, a third phase may have begun.[15]

The first period witnessed a cautious probing and expansion of the consensual limits of the peace-keeping concept. With the death of Stalin in 1953, Soviet intransigence and open hostility were slowly replaced by the reach for peaceful coexistence. Despite this limited and essentially superficial warming of the cold war, there was little genuine understanding between the United States and the U.S.S.R. Amidst the periodic crises and "trips to the brink" that occurred during those years, however, there were indications that both superpowers recognized at least limited utility in pacific settlement by international means. Within this context of a changing and increasingly complex world and under the guidance of activist secretaries-general, the UN peace-keeping role gradually evolved toward selective involvement in international crises.

The early postwar years witnessed a sporadic yet continuing growth in the acceptability and, consequently, the employment of peace-keeping missions. The first UN peace-keeping effort was established by the General Assembly (after the Soviet Union vetoed Security Council action) to "investigate," "report," and provide "mediation assistance" in Greece from 1947 to 1954; this was the UN Special Committee on the Balkans (UNSCOB).[16] This initial UN operation was followed in 1948 by a truce supervision group (UNTSO), established by the Security Council to report on the observance of ceasefires and armistice agreements between Israel and the neighboring Arab states.

From 1949 to 1951, a United Nations observer force monitored implementation of the agreements under which Indonesia acquired its independence from the Netherlands. This observer-type mission was also assigned, with varying degrees of effectiveness, to the UN Commission for India and Pakistan (UNCIP), which became in 1949 a military observer group (UNMOGIP), to assist in maintaining the truce in Kashmir—a mission that still continues.

In 1956, the role of peace-keeping forces expanded from observer-type missions to actual interposition of armed contingents between belligerents. The UN Emergency Force (UNEF), created under the General Assembly's earlier Uniting for Peace Resolution with joint U.S.-U.S.S.R. acquiescence, served as a buffer between Egyptian and Israeli forces in the Gaza Strip and the Sinai. Involving more than six thousand troops from nineteen countries, the UNEF mandate was renewed until May 18, 1967, when, in a decision that remains controversial, the secretary-general acted upon the request of President Nasser and withdrew the buffer force.

Table 22.1 United Nations Peace-Keeping Forces in Existence in 1978

Organization	Commander	Manpower (accurate on)	Contributors	Activities
UNTSO (UN Truce Supervisory Organization) *HQ:* Jerusalem	Col. W. Callaghan (Eire)	294 military, incl observers detailed to other forces (Feb. 5, 1979)	Argentina, Australia, Austria, Belgium, Canada, Chile, Denmark, Eire, Finland, France, Italy, Netherlands, New Zealand, Sweden, U.S., U.S.S.R.	Set up to assist application of 1948 truces and 1949 armistices between Israel and Arabs; now co-ordinates its observers, mostly detailed to UNEF, UNDOF and UNIFIL
UNMOGIP (UN Military Observer Group in India and Pakistan) *HQ:* Rawalpindi	Brig. Gen. Stig Waldenström (Sweden)	50	Australia, Belgium, Canada, Chile, Denmark, Finland, Italy, Norway, Sweden, Uruguay	Supervises 1949 cease-fire line in Kashmir, investigating and adjudicating any violations
UNFICYP (UN Peace-Keeping Force in Cyprus) *HQ:* Nicosia	Maj.-Gen J. J. Quinn (Eire)	2,482, incl 34 civilian police (Nov. 30, 1978)	Australia (20), Austria (312), Britain (817), Canada (515), Denmark (360), Eire (6), Finland (11), Sweden (44)	Took over task of separating the Cypriot communities in 1964. Since 1974 supervises de facto partition line to prevent recurrence of fighting

(cont.)

UNEF (UN Emergency Force) *HQ:* Ismailai	Maj.-Gen. Rais Abin (Indonesia)	4,178, excl units assigned to UNDOF and 120 observers from UNTSO (Oct. 16, 1978)	Australia (66), Canada (840), Finland (637), Ghana (595), Indonesia (509), Poland (917), Sweden (634)	Set up to supervise 1973 Egyptian- Israeli cease-fire. Now mans Sinai disengagement zone; inspects limited armaments and forces zones on either side under 1975 disengagement agreement
UNDOF (UN Disengagement Observer Force) *HQ:* Damascus	Maj.-Gen. Hannes Philipp (Austria)	1,195, excl 88 observers from UNTSO (Nov. 24, 1978)	Austria (535), Canada (169), Iran (390), Poland (101)	Set up under 1974 disengagement agreement between Syria and Israel. Supervises cease-fire in Golan Heights, mans disengagement zone, inspects limited armaments and forces zones
UNIFIL (UN Interim Force in Lebanon) *HQ:* Naqoura	Maj.-Gen. E. A. Erskine (Ghana)	5,931, excl 36 observers from UNTSO (Sept. 13, 1978)	Canada (117), Eire (661), Fiji (500), France (1,181), Iran (559), Nepal (642), Nigeria (673), Norway (924), Senegal (634)	Set up in 1978 to verify Israeli withdrawal from south Lebanon, then establish an area or operation in which to supervise end of hostilities, ensure peace and restore Lebanese sovereignty

Source: International Institute for Strategic Studies, *Strategic Survey, 1978* (London: IISS, 1979).

The UN organization in the Congo (ONUC) was the largest and most complex of the UN peace-keeping operations. From July 1960 to June 1964, ONUC assumed a full array of internal "law and order" missions normally performed by the civilian institutions of a nation. With Belgium's withdrawal from the Congo, the UN secretary-general, under a compromise Security Council resolution, was given broad power to assist the Republic of the Congo in restoring order, preventing intertribal conflict, and protecting life. This mandate was eventually broadened to include authorization for the UN force to employ coercion to restore peace and prevent the secession of Katanga province. This unprecedented role for UN forces not only demonstrated a new potential for international efforts but, more importantly, precipitated a UN constitutional crisis that in turn nearly bankrupted the organization when two permanent members (the U.S.S.R. and France) challenged the legality of the General Assembly resolutions authorizing the undertaking and refused to contribute to expenses. The ONUC case demonstrates that although an initial consensus for UN action may be present, intermediate stages of a crisis may dissolve whatever agreement once ruled. When members could not agree on a continuing mandate for ONUC, particularly on the political goals of force employment and the targets of force application, ONUC lost wide support and therefore, in large part, its effectiveness.

In retrospect, ONUC illustrates the most serious shortcomings of UN peace-keeping efforts. This exercise in international peace-keeping not only high-lighted the political difficulties of maintaining a consensus among the Security Council permanent members, but also demonstrated the administrative and logistical inadequacies of the UN in fielding and maintaining a large heter-ogeneous, multinational force in which national loyalties, languages, proce-dures, armaments, communications equipment, diets, etc., are far from com-patible. The problems of command and control of subordinate elements in such situations are magnified, and the frustrations of dealing with conflicting military and political objectives verge on the unbearable.[17]

It has been noted that the Security Council or the General Assembly "authorized a new peacekeeping operation on the average of once every year and a half" between 1956 and 1968 and "between 200,000 and 250,000 soldiers served under the UN flag."[18] In addition to those operations previously noted, other international commitments included the UN Observer Group in Leb-anon (UNOGIL), dispatched in 1958 to limit the infiltration that was re-portedly directed into Lebanon from Syria. The UN Temporary Executive Authority (UNTEA), consisting largely of a Pakistani security force, was sent to West New Guinea in 1961 to administer the territory until a transfer of sovereignty from the Netherlands to Indonesia could be effected, which was accomplished in 1963. UNTEA, as ONUC (though on a considerably smaller scale), illustrates the use of a peace-keeping force under the United Nations to enhance local stability and promote the cause of international peace by substituting for or assisting indigenous security efforts.

The goal of the UN Observation Mission in Yemen (UNYOM), deployed in 1963, was to observe and verify the disengagement of Egyptian and Saudi-backed Yemeni forces. That particular mission was probably the least successful because the disputants failed to support the accompanying political provisions and because UNYOM was wholly inadequate in size and strength.[19] As with all UN efforts, such forces are effective only if their impartiality is beyond question, so that the disputants accept the alternative to direct military confrontation and expansion of the conflict.

In 1964, with the possibility of major communal warfare between the majority Greek and minority Turkish population growing, a United Nations Force in Cyprus (UNFICYP) was deployed. The Security Council tasked UNFICYP with a law and order mission as a way to create more favorable conditions for the resolution of the longstanding conflict. This force, initially numbering nearly seven thousand, remains in existence as the 1980s begin. Its composition of British, Canadian, Swedish, Danish, Austrian, Finnish, Irish, and Australian troops is representative of the multinational nature of UN peace-keeping forces. The law and order function of the force today is performed by the UN civilian police force in Cyprus (UNCIVPOL), a non-military component of UNFICYP. "Even though the potential for renewed violence remains a constant, the central fact is that UNFICYP has calmed the Cypriot communal war and staved off a Greco-Turkish international war. It has been a positive example of what a peacekeeping force is supposed to be and of how it should operate."[20]

We should note that while the UNFICYP law and order mission is being accomplished relatively successfully, the underlying conflict festers. Moreover, the UNFICYP mandate was interpreted and implemented in such a way as to preclude the force's opposition to the Turkish invasion of Cyprus in 1974. Whatever the limitations of UNFICYP, however, its continued existence and operation throughout the period of high tensions in Cyprus in both the 1960s and the 1970s bear witness to the general observation that such an international force may be necessary for extended, if not indefinite, periods of time.[21]

After the mid 1960s and the UN internal crisis arising out of the ONUC operation, a second phase in peace-keeping operations began. New initiatives were in scarce supply until the 1973 Arab-Israeli War, when a new UNEF (usually called UNEF II) was organized to fulfill the earlier UN role of separating the disputants and of precluding direct superpower involvement. Significantly, for the first time in the recent history of international peace-keeping efforts, a UN forces organization was a direct result of a joint U.S.-U.S.S.R. initiative. UNEF II has been cited as an example of what is realistically possible when superpower interests coincide in the Security Council.[22]

The initial Security Council mandate for UNEF II attempted to impose guidelines that would strengthen the forces' role, while preventing the disputants from precipitating a withdrawal based on a unilateral decision, as happened in 1967. It was specified that the force could act in self-defense "to include resistance to attempts by forceful means to prevent UNEF from discharging its duties under the Security Council mandate." Moreover, a single disputant's legal right to demand the withdrawal of the force was not expressly stated.[23]

In view of the imminent possibility that events in the Middle East in 1973 might draw U.S. and U.S.S.R. military forces into direct conflict, UNEF II presented an alternative that "demonstrates the progress that has been made and the skills and techniques that have come from experience."[24] Although small, UNEF II, consisting of military contingents from Poland, Canada, Sweden, Finland, Ghana, Indonesia, and Australia, has the capability to act effectively and rapidly for the United Nations in a crisis situation. However, it is important to note that such a force cannot resolve the underlying conflict that precipitated international involvement. UNEF II, as with similar UN efforts, strives to maintain an atmosphere within which a lasting peace can be developed.

Lengthy reliance upon a buffer, however, may well stifle peace initiatives and thereby inhibit the overall UN goal to promote pacific settlements of disputes. As has been observed, "military action in support of law enforcement, even of a purely policing nature, stiffens rather than overcomes resistance. It certainly does not remove the structural causes, the roots of the conflict, which remain and are nurtured for a later day when history will repeat itself."[25] UNEF II did, however, help establish an environment for peaceful negotiations. Under the provisions of the U.S.-sponsored Camp David accords, UNEF II was withdrawn from the Sinai in July 1979 and its observer functions assumed by UNTSO. It is also important to note the inclusion in UNEF II for the first time of a contingent from an Eastern bloc nation, Poland, widening the participatory base and perhaps the political legitimacy of collective action.[26]

Peace-keeping efforts under the United Nations have not been adopted in every belligerent situation since World War II. The Vietnam conflict, the Biafran civil war in Nigeria, the various conflicts in Zaire (formerly the Congo) and the hostilities between Ethiopia and Somalia, to name but a few, did not give rise to UN forces. The political realities of the international environment and the attitudes of the superpowers determine in the final analysis if—and to what extent—the United Nations will become involved in a given conflict.

The record of the UN Interim Force in Lebanon (UNIFIL) provides useful insight into the kind of difficulties that confront UN peace-keeping forces in general. UNIFIL was mandated in 1978 to (1) confirm the withdrawal of Israeli forces from southern Lebanon, (2) restore international peace and security, and (3) assist the Lebanese government to reestablish its authority in the occupied area. Each of these tasks requires the cooperation of all parties to the conflict. The extent to which UNIFIL was able to fulfill these tasks directly reflects the level of cooperation shown by those parties. Repeated incursions by the Israeli defense force into southern Lebanon, recurring terrorist attacks on Israel by Lebanon-based PLO guerrillas, and harassment of UN forces by breakaway Lebanese forces made the UNIFIL task extremely difficult. The situation was further exacerbated by the fact that, upon leaving Lebanon, the

Israelis relinquished control of their command posts to the Israeli-backed Christian forces of Major Sa'ad Haddad rather than to the UN forces. As PLO attacks on Israel continued, the Israeli army moved back into Lebanon in June 1982, advancing as far north as Beirut. There was little the UN forces could do besides stand by and let the Israelis pass. The Multinational Peacekeeping Force in Beirut, which was not initiated by the UN but rather by bilateral agreements between the Lebanese governments and the force's member nations, is having greater success. Such forces may be more effective in controlling this kind of situation in the future as they are more flexible and do not have to answer to the UN Security Council. However, it should be noted that this force has had to extend its presence longer than was originally thought necessary.

Recent involvement by the United Nations in local conflict situations, such as in Lebanon, reflects in part a change in membership of the UN. Beginning with the 1955 package admission of sixteen nations and stimulated by the increase in newly independent states during the early 1960s, the membership rolls of the United Nations have progressively grown, particularly with small, nonaligned states. Such nations, opposed on principle to unilateral foreign intervention by the major powers, have supported regional and international efforts at conflict management, including peace-keeping initiatives.

During the 1960s and 1970s progressive improvement of Soviet bilateral relations with Austria, India, Yugoslavia, and the Nordic states further increased the number of countries for which political nonalignment was feasible. From this group of states have come the troop commitments, the administrative talent, and the managerial resources upon which the UN peace-keeping operations have increasingly depended. Additionally, the UN secretariat has played a more active role and has developed increased operational and technical capabilities by which to control peace-keeping operations. Also, attempts have been made to standardize selected operational procedures and logistical categories in order to improve the responsiveness of international forces in local conflict situations.

Of special note has been the customary exclusion of permanent Security Council members from direct participation in peace-keeping operations. Seen as a technique for disengaging great power involvement in operational matters, this exclusion has been actively promoted by the nonaligned nations and the secretariat. It has also enjoyed the acquiescence of the superpowers. By 1960 it was tacitly understood that the operational control of peace-keeping missions, once approved, was the domain of the United Nations and not that of the superpowers themselves. Of course, it became equally well understood that either of the superpowers, by withdrawing logistical or financial support, could hamstring any operation.

The effort to launch a UN Transition Assistance Group (UNTAG) in connection with decolonization of Namibia reveals the political difficulties of collective action even when consensus exists. First proposed by five Western members of the Security Council in 1978, UNTAG formed part of a comprehensive package designed to resolve the problem of South-West Africa. The 8,500-troop military and civilian peace-keeping force would maintain a ceasefire between South African forces and Namibian guerrillas and monitor the initial national assembly elections. With the concurrence of both parties as well as the Soviet Union and the "Front Line" African nations, prospects for force deployment were bright in early 1979. However, South Africa's initial acquiescence evaporated with disagreements over the specific disposition of guerrilla bases in Namibia, and it proceeded with its military operations, including forays into Angola. Clearly, South Africa will not bow to new demands and to possible sanctions evoked by the UN Council unless it perceives that its vital economic and security interests will be better protected by the UN policy package than by its own unilateral actions.[28]

Prerequisites for International Peace-Keeping. Both in principle and in practice, peace-keeping has evolved as an exercise in impartiality and avoidance of coercion by the collective agent, notwithstanding the exception of the Congo operation. Peace-keeping does not require and, in fact, discourages the identification of specific wrongdoing or the assessment of guilt. Instead, peace-keeping focuses upon establishing and maintaining an atmosphere between contending parties which is conducive to the resolution of the conflict. Rather than siding with either of the parties to the conflict, international peace-keeping efforts endeavor to mitigate tension and inhibit violence through a cooperative and/or buffering effort.

In a sense, then, a peace-keeping force is the agent not only of the international community but of the individual disputants as well. In this context, peace-keeping efforts are practical only when the disputants agree to the intervention of an international force and to its composition and roles. The point is not what the United Nations may be legally empowered to do but what it may realistically do, given the nature of the international political environment. The ends as well as the means of the peace-keeping force must be circumscribed. Experience has shown, as in ONUC and UNIFIL, that precise operational parameters are frequently the source of disagreement, even after the peace-keeping efforts have commenced. Inevitably, such forces are greatly constrained not only by the UN mandate under which they operate but by the limits placed upon their elements by both the host country or countries and the participating states.

Indeed, international peace-keeping efforts are influenced by many of the same factors that determine the effectiveness of the United Nations itself. The general determinants of the ability of the UN to act in given situations include the interests, attitudes, and policies of the great powers, the spheres of influence prevailing in the overall system, the ability of small powers to influence the United Nations, underlying attitudes toward the objectives or roles of the UN, and the physical capabilities that the organization can muster to accomplish the objectives of the participating members.[29]

Since it has no standing military capability, the UN depends on its members for their contribution in personnel and supplies to bring a peace-keeping force into reality. Further dependence rests on the fact that it is primarily the great powers who possess the capability to transport forces and supply them for extended periods. Frequently, the success of UN efforts has turned on the timeliness with which a force could be transported and committed.

Although the timely deployment of UNEF II and UNIFIL may reflect favorably on international peace-keeping efforts, problems limiting the effectiveness of support for UN missions remain, especially in light of the disposition of these forces today. Problems include insufficient provision for administrative coordination, insufficient capability for planning a large-scale military mission, and lack of immediately available transportation, equipment, and logistic personnel to assemble and support a UN force. Coupled with these support problems are the complexities of coordinating the activities of a heterogeneous force. Procedural differences are compounded by the diversity in languages. The lack of standardized equipment and supplies seriously limits the ability of commanders to accomplish their missions.[30]

Also, UN military contingents must be trained in peace-keeping procedures and activities that differ substantially from normal military operations. Disagreement between the United States and the Soviet Union on the funding and training of international forces provided an incentive for the establishment of the International Peace Academy (IPA) in 1970. Funded through fees and grants, the IPA is not an organ of the United Nations and therefore avoids some of the consequences of political divergences. Functioning as a professional institution, it offers programs to officers and civilian officials on conflict resolution and peace-keeping operations. Training of military units, however, remains a national responsibility. Some nations have initiated peace-keeping seminars or courses at national military schools, and the Nordic nations have gone so far as to conduct unit training programs in peace-keeping.[31]

The lack of trained contingents obviously hampers the swift and effective employment of UN peace-keeping efforts. As part of a UN reform package, the Carter administration in March 1978 renewed an earlier U.S. proposal for the establishment by member nations of "earmarked" contingents, which would be trained in peace-keeping functions and which would thereby constitute a UN "reserve" force. In addition to the four Nordic countries, Chile, France, the Netherlands, and Italy have responded positively with the earmarking of trained contingents.[32]

As the UN community has gained experience with international peace-keeping efforts, certain basic principles, appropriately referred to as "peace-keeping doctrine,"[33] have been developed and applied. Enunciated by Secretary-General Dag Hammarskjold as early as 1958, these basic principles represent the rules that both constrain international efforts and enable member states to judge international peace-keeping efforts as a means to limit conflict. These principles maintain that: (1) the governments concerned must expressly consent to the stationing of UN units in their territory; (2) the UN alone shall decide the composition of the force to be deployed, with due consideration by the United Nations for the desires of the host country or countries; (3) major powers will not provide contingents of the UN force; (4) the UN force must be assured of freedom of movement within the zone of operations; (5) UN personnel must maintain strict impartiality and cannot be a party to the conflict; (6) though it may use force in self-defense, a UN force is an instrument for conciliation and shall not engage in combat activities.[34] Although these principles are subject to modification on a case-by-case basis, they have generally served as useful guidelines for UN peace-keeping forces. The challenge, then, for the UN community is to employ effective international peace-keeping efforts despite these limitations on force composition, scope, and roles.

For the foreseeable future, most of the familiar peace-keeping problems and constraints will remain. The issue of funding is unresolved, as is the question of the General Assembly's power to authorize peace-keeping operations. The ability of the United Nations to mount peace-keeping efforts has been curtailed and is likely to suffer further from a dearth of joint training, inadequate planning capacity, and often weak political support. Discussion of reviving the long-dormant Military Staff Committee or of even evaluating the readiness of prospective earmarked contingents rests in limbo. In principle, the positions of the superpowers on peace-keeping remain polar opposites. Politics is still the essence of peace-keeping and, as such, the reason for its problems.

Peace-Keeping and U.S. Security in the 1980s. The United Nations—and peace-keeping as one of its key functions—may be on the threshold of a new phase, driven by changing patterns of international politics. The replacement of political bipolarity by a multipolar world, the disengagement of American troops from Southeast Asia, the growing schism between the U.S.S.R. and the P.R.C., the Soviet-American strategic weapons parity, the dynamics of changing superpower relations—each, by altering the realities of the international environment, inevitably alters the perceptions of the possibility and utility of peace-keeping. It is—arguably—conceivable that in this new context commonalities of purpose and perception may serve to make peace-keeping forces an attractive alternative to independent state action.

In the early days of the United Nations, limitations on membership guaranteed Western, largely American, domination of leadership positions within the organization. Today that is no longer the case. Nations possessing less than one-tenth of the world's population can theoretically command a two-thirds majority in the General Assembly. Moreover, by comprising a "blocking third," the nonaligned nations theoretically could forestall both American and Soviet initiatives. The growth of the Afro-Asian blocks, combined with the unpopularity of a variety of American stands, has shaken traditional U.S. strength within the General Assembly. In turn, the United States has moved closer to the long-held Soviet view of relegating the General Assembly to a residual role in international security matters. The Soviet Union, on the other hand, has abandoned some of its traditional animosity toward the United Nations now that it no longer seems to be a ready tool for use by the United States to circumvent Soviet influence.

Multipolarity has had other consequences as well. For the superpowers, or at least the United States, there has come the realization that many regions of the world are less susceptible to superpower leverage. It is possible that the increased diffusion of power will make international peace-keeping less desirable to emerging regional powers, who may perceive greater advantage in unilateral action. Another possibility is the development of regional peace-keeping forces as proposed, for example, in the Organization of African Unity (OAU) summit meeting in July 1979. Working through the United Nations, rather than bypassing it, may well be the key for the superpowers in maintaining some leverage over affairs in those regions. Increasingly aware that disputes between Third World nations could escalate until they impinge upon their own respective security, the United States and the Soviet Union could well look upon future peace-keeping efforts with greater interest and tolerance.

While it seems plausible, at least in a theoretical sense, that an increasingly dangerous international environment would stimulate greater interest in international peace-keeping efforts, it remains to be seen to what extent states will be ready to subordinate their national interests to the broader interests of international order. The dispute, beginning in November 1979, between Iran and the United States over the Iranian seizure of diplomatic hostages may provide an indicator. Despite having unanimously condemned Iran's actions in taking the hostages, the Security Council was incapable of taking any action under chapters 6 or 7 of the charter to promote the settlement of a dispute that clearly endangered "international peace and security."[35]

Setting aside the issue of whether the international political order has changed sufficiently to allow greater employment of peace-keeping efforts, the question should be raised, What security benefits would accrue to the United States if peace-keeping were more actively pursued? Surely there are advantages to the sharing of burdens and risks that the multilateral character of peace-keeping implies. Beyond that generalization, American national security can be seen as a function of both protection against direct attack and development of an international environment that minimizes external threats to our political and economic system. The latter implies "blunting and converting to acceptable and tolerable forms the thrusts . . . of revolution and change."[36] Increased support of the concept of peace-keeping could conceivably contribute to that goal.

Although difficult to envision in the milieu of heightened superpower tensions in 1983, a reinvigoration of détente and a partial reconciliation of superpower interests might serve as a potential contribution to peace-keeping. In effect, those factors that have made peace-keeping more desirable could be reinforced, in circular fashion, by the positive feedback of actual peace-keeping initiatives. As expressions of a willingness to cooperate in the quest for stability, such operations could establish a wider basis for cooperative relationships—if, that is, stability becomes a Soviet goal. With local conflicts isolated, the dangers of superpower confrontation and accidental war might be diminished and levels of tension accordingly reduced. Indeed, it might even prove desirable under certain conditions to use UN forces for militarily sensitive inspection missions generated by any future Soviet-American arms control agreements. As a corollary benefit from a possible reduction of superpower involvement in local conflict, the Western alliance system, which we assume to be the foundation of realistic deterrence, would be spared the discord sometimes sown by past unilateral American actions.

As noted in Chapter 12, during the coming decade insurgencies, border disputes, racially based civil wars, or neoimperialist ventures by Third World nations are likely to be at least as common as in the past. While posing clear dangers to world peace, such disorders and revolutionary changes within the world are still sought by some nations. The 1980s are likely to witness the development of new and unique types of threats to international peace and security—threats particularly appropriate for peace-keeping initiatives. As an example, given the possibility of world raw material shortages, the next decade may bring conflict over competing yet long quiescent territorial claims. If perceived as critical to undersea oil exploration or to seabed mining operations, formerly obscure islands or archipelagos could become sources of controversy. Already, in recent years, disputes over fishing rights in territorial waters have increased. Similar problems could well occur in defining the dimensions of seabed ownership and in resolving the complexities of seabed exploitation. The existence of a viable international peace-keeping machinery might discourage small-scale adventurism, whatever its basis.

Peace-keeping could serve to increase the legitimacy of U.S. policies as perceived by the nonaligned world. Channels for indirect American influence could be maintained, but the negative connotations and external pressures might be blunted if viewed within a framework considered by other nations to be responsive to the international community and largely free of American domination. Through advocacy of peace-keeping operations, the United States might economize in the use of its own military resources, a matter of continuing importance as they become increasingly constrained by conflicting domestic priorities.

The United States, however, cannot rely on peace-keeping forces as a surrogate for the protection of vital interests. Moreover, a revitalization of international peace-keeping operations could well entail a variety of costs or dangers to the United States. We have witnessed instances—for example, ONUC—when peace-keeping ventures, due to unforeseen events, exacerbated rather than smoothed superpower relations. If UN capabilities were developed and strengthened, the United States could well find its interests opposed by some future peace-keeping operations.

Current U.S. policy calls for the enhancement of UN peace-keeping capabilities. In addition to the proposal for earmarked national contingents, U.S. reform measures include the use of U.S. military airlift capability, the provision of U.S. technical expertise and equipment, and the establishment of a $100 million Special Peace-keeping Fund. These measures have been fully supported by the Secretary-General and by the Special Political Committee on Peace-keeping Operations.[37]

A singular source of uncertainty is the question of the future role of the People's Republic of China within the United Nations itself. In assessing, for example, the impact of the P.R.C. upon the resolution of longstanding U.S.-U.S.S.R. differences over the specific peace-keeping responsibilities of the Security Council and the General Assembly, the Department of State noted that "the presence of the People's Republic of China in the Security Council will obviously effect the [outcome], but it is too early at this stage to know whether the Chinese presence will facilitate, or constitute an additional serious barrier to, a solution."[38] To date, at least, the P.R.C. as a permanent member of the Security Council has not been obstructionist in international peace-keeping efforts under the United Nations, though it has not been willing to assist in financing such operations. Given the P.R.C. association with the Third World and growing P.R.C. involvement in world affairs, there is no question of its ultimate impact on the issue of global security in general and of peace-keeping in particular.

Considerations such as these condition any assessment of the future of international peace-keeping efforts in terms-of either American or Soviet interests. While greater selective support of UN initiatives by the superpowers may be a desirable policy as the Third World majority in the General Assembly seeks to influence UN actions, it remains uncertain where and when international peace-keeping forces can best be employed. Although any major augmentation of UN peace-keeping capabilities or authorizations by the superpowers appears unrealistic, the relative success of UNFICYP, UNEF II, and UNIFIL suggest that it may be premature to pen the obituary for international peace-keeping efforts.

Finally, whatever may be the prospects for superpower support of international peace-keeping efforts, it must be recognized that military action on an international scale seldom occurs in isolation. Even the Soviet invasion of Afghanistan in December 1979 led to a flurry of international efforts directed at resolving the conflict. Yet, barring major structural changes, the international system dictates that states will utilize national military forces when it seems politically necessary and when vital interests are at stake. For its part, the United States has supported, and will no doubt continue to support, international peace-keeping efforts congruent with American interests worldwide. In an age when nuclear weapons may actually have weakened restraints on lower levels of violence and created the potential for escalation to nuclear warfare, international peace-keeping forces could well assume an increasingly important role in serving U.S. security interests.

DISCUSSION QUESTIONS

1. What is meant by "peace-keeping"? How does international peace-keeping differ from independent state actions in keeping the peace?

2. What factors influence the effectiveness of an international peace-keeping effort? By what criteria is the effectiveness of an international peace-keeping operation evaluated?

3. What has been the major contribution of international peace-keeping efforts under the United Nations? Has the United Nations "kept the peace," or merely contained conflict?

4. What are the constraints on the use of international peace-keeping efforts?

5. How have the successes and shortcomings of international peace-keeping efforts to date reflected the realities of the international political systems?

6. How has the nature of superpower relations influenced the ability of the United Nations to keep the peace?

7. How does the United Nations Charter provide for international peace-keeping operations? What is the difference between the approaches of chapter 6 and chapter 7 to peace-keeping?

8. What are the realities of international politics which have inhibited the realization of a collective security system? How have international peace-keeping efforts under the United Nations differed from the designs of a collective security system?

9. What was the Uniting for Peace Resolution? How has it enhanced the role of the United Nations in international peace-keeping?

10. What types of international peacekeeping mission have been assigned to UN peace-keeping forces? Give illustrations.

11. What are the prerequisites for effective international peace-keeping?

12. What are the potential conflict areas for the use of international peace-keeping forces?

13. What are the advantages and disadvantages for U.S. national security interests in the use of international peace-keeping forces to contain conflict?

14. In what respect is the topic of international forces and peace-keeping a challenge to American national security in the 1980s?

RECOMMENDED READING

Bloomfield, Lincoln P. *The United Nations and U.S. Foreign Policy: A Look at the National Interest.* New York: Alfred A. Knopf, 1969.

————, and Leiss, Amelia C. *Controlling Small Wars: A Strategy for the 1970s.* New York: Alfred A. Knopf, 1969.

Claude, Inis L., Jr. *Swords into Plowshares.* New York: Random House, 1971.

Fabian, Larry L. *Soldiers without Enemies: Preparing the United States for Peace-keeping.* Washington, D.C.: Brookings Institution, 1971.

Horn, Carl von. *Soldiering for Peace.* New York: David McKay, 1967.

Moskos, Charles C., Jr. *Peace Soldiers: The Sociology of a United Nations Military Force.* Chicago: University of Chicago Press, 1976.

Stoessinger, John G. *The United Nations and the Superpowers: United States-Soviet Interaction at the United Nations.* New York: Random House, 1970.

Young, Oran. "The United Nations and the International System." *International Organization* 20 (August 1968): 904.

23

CONFLICT AND ARMS CONTROL

Sources of Conflict. From the beginning of recorded time, people have been involved in conflict with one another. Although the human race has progressed in many ways since the cave dweller's use of clubs, history makes it painfully clear that people have not yet found a solution to the problem of conflict in society. Yet the highly advanced state of technology of destruction available to some of today's nation-states makes the control of conflict a necessity.

Three basic schools of thought have developed in the various attempts to discover the causes of conflict and war, namely, those that find the causes in (1) human nature, (2) the characteristics of various types of nation-states, and (3) the structure of the international system. In a major theoretical analysis of the causes of war, *Man, The State, and War*, Kenneth Waltz refers to these three views of the cause of war as different "images" of international relations.[1] If conflict is to be controlled, these images must be manipulated: human nature must be altered through social policy, or the characteristics of the nation-state must change to emphasize cooperation over violence in resolving differences, or the international system must provide the means and incentive for cooperative interactions and for constraining violence. As discussed in Chapter 1, significant changes in the post–World War II environment have indeed occurred and continue to transform the arena in which conflict occurs; thus far, however, the changes have been insufficient to provide adequate conflict control.

Human Nature. Consider first the active troublemaker, Homo Sapiens. The human-nature-is-to-blame school of thought emphasizes the existence of various characteristics of human nature which cause conflict. Malthus observed that while human institutions in society could be the cause "of much mischief to mankind; . . . yet they are mere feathers that float on the surface, in comparison with those deeper seated causes of impurity that corrupt . . . the whole stream of human life." Spinoza considered the passions inherent in humans as the force that drew them into conflict. While Spinoza asserted

514

that reason could moderate passions on occasion, he concluded that passion would generally rule in the internal conflict between the two. Freud believed that conflicts between people are resolved by resorting to violence, "the same [as in] the animal kingdom, from which man cannot claim exclusion." Konrad Lorenz, the noted expert on animal behavior, also asserts that humans have an inherent aggressive instinct, like all animals. Lorenz's theories on aggressiveness in human nature and its moderation or exacerbation by the social environment are, however, essentially based on animal data, rather than on empirical human evidence. Extrapolation from the behavior of tropical fish and geese to that of humans is fraught with risk.[2]

Common to many of the writers of this school of thought is the concept that society's institutions are sometimes capable of holding the aggressive tendencies of human nature in check and at least temporarily overcoming its intrinsic evil. A contrary view is taken by another branch of this school, which emphasizes the role that society and its institutions play in perverting human nature which they consider good or essentially neutral prior to exposure to the bias of the social environment. Rousseau is perhaps the most noted exponent of this view of human beings as inherently noble creatures whom society corrupts. Mark May[3] provides a more recent statement of this type of learned behavior view, emphasizing the perverse role of the social environment. By far the most influential exponent of this view of society's crucial role has been Karl Marx; for him the nature of social organization, whether capitalist or socialist, was decisive in determining whether people would pursue war or peace.

The prescription for lessening the incidence of conflict arising from the human nature school calls for the development and education of humanity in a direction that emphasizes cooperation as a means to resolve problems. A variant of this approach focuses on the development of a social environment that elicits cooperative behavior and attenuates the aggressive tendencies of human nature.

The Nature of the Nation-State. A second school holds that the values dominant in a certain type of nation-state affect its structure and behavior, producing bellicose actions in international relations. Lenin's view of the imperialistic activities of capitalist states is an example.[4] Lenin believed that the capitalistic states' struggle for markets, resources, and profits inevitably leads them to dominate and exploit the underdeveloped areas of the world. As the potential colonial territory of the world diminished, Lenin foresaw an increased level of competition that would ultimately result in violent conflict between the capitalist nation-states and the end of the capitalist system.

Various other arguments concerning the nature of states have been contributed by more liberal thinkers. Thomas Paine, for example, described war as the work of the unrepresentative governments of nation-states; since the interest of the people lies in peace, governments that make war do not express the true interests of the people through government policy. A democratic form of government is most conducive to peace, he asserted, since the people have more control over policy. Woodrow Wilson expanded this line of thought to advocate an era in which the same moral standards would apply to the actions of nation-states as apply to peoples' individual actions. To achieve this situation, nation-states must become democratic, for democracies are by definition peaceful. While Wilson admitted that the condition of peace would still be based on force when the democratic international community was realized, that force would not be the force employed by individual nation-states but one based on the consent of the governed and the organized public opinion of the world community—referred to by Wilson as "the organized major force of mankind."[5]

Ideologically motivated states are not, of course, necessarily peaceful. An ideology is both a set "of beliefs that give meaning to life" and "an explicit or implicit program of action."[6] The program of action component can constitute a threat to those nations of differing ideologies whose own programs of action may seek interests that will bring the ideologies into conflict. Nazism, as exemplified in the German Reich, was a threat to every other ideology. Even Christian ideology has generated war. Charlemagne and the Crusaders resolved threats to the soul by spreading their Christian faith by fire and sword. The conviction that one's own side is infallibly and unquestionably righteous can overpower the survival instinct itself and remove all reason and restraint from conflict. During the Crusades, the slogan "God wills it!" was used to rationalize and legitimize a vast array of destructive acts completely antithetical to Christianity.

Whatever the ideology or motivation of particular states, the nation-state is the actor that represents and executes both creative and destructive tendencies of its members. It provides a definition and an embodiment of the legal, cultural, and behavioral values of its members. The sentiment of identification with a nation-state is nationalism, perhaps the single most important form of ideology in the twentieth century. A democratic nation-state is able to strengthen its citizens' identification with it by defining them as sovereign and the state merely as an agent, thus spreading power and responsibility. Indeed, the emergence of the nation-state and of the nationalism it evokes has tended to broaden involvement in war to include total populations.

The political mobilization of the masses in Asia and Africa accompanying the human revolution cited in Chapter 1 has significantly increased the number of nation-state actors in the international environment. The 50 nation-states that constituted the founding members of the United Nations in 1945 represented most of the non-Axis sovereign states of the world at that time. Thirty-five years later, the number of sovereignties had roughly tripled, with about 150 belonging to the United Nations. The growth in the number of states has exacerbated the problem of conflict control, for even the smaller, newly formed states (which may have limited ambitions and claims) make decisions and take independent actions that significantly affect other nation-states possessing extended interests of their own.

The Structure of the International System. Those theoreticians who believe the causes of conflict lie in the nature of the international system assert that war is inevitable due to the lack of any authority above the nation-state which can dampen inevitable conflicts and adjust varying interests to permit resolution of differences short of violence. Even if a nation-state attempts to be just, others will not accept its *bona fides*, for its perception of the situation is bound to be affected by self-interest. In this view, international anarchy is thus the major cause of war. It is difficult to rebut the central concept behind this formulation of the problem; yet the existing international system is hardly structureless. Collective security and international peace-keeping arrangements, alliances, international law, and various forms of transnational institutions all act expressly to contain, manage, or diffuse tension and conflict.

Perhaps the most useful way to approach these three explanations of the sources of conflict is to note that they are in essence three different levels of analysis. While one or another may have greater explanatory power in a given instance, all are likely to bear on the case. A comprehensive understanding of conflict is not likely to be gained by limiting one's attention to any single analytical level.

CONFLICT CONTROL

Up to this point, conflicting interests among nation-states have dominated our consideration of national security. Yet shared interests also exist, even between generally antagonistic states, and national security objectives can often be attained by exploiting common interests. The very sophistication of U.S. and Soviet nuclear arsenals and the numerous crises that the two superpowers have survived without using them, for instance, argue that a shared interest in avoiding nuclear war exists. Neither side has seen fit to attack the other with nuclear weapons despite the routine incompatibility of their foreign policy objectives and the ideological antipathy between their political cultures.

In order for adversaries to benefit mutually from shared interests, explicit or implicit bargaining between them must occur. In the parlance of game theory, a *positive sum* (or cooperative) *game* exists in such cases, and appropriate behavior can result in net gains for both parties. For instance, two powers embroiled in an arms race may jointly agree to equitable, quantitative limits or qualitative restraints on forces or weapons, thereby saving both parties the costs of the competition without lessening security. Among the fields where such shared interests may be present are war termination, arms control, and disarmament. *War termination* is here defined as the mechanism whereby two or more nations in conflict end overt hostilities and establish a mutually acceptable disposition of the values under contention. By *arms control* we mean arrangements whereby two or more nations agree to moderate arms increases, freeze them at present levels, or decrease them according to some scheduled quantitative and/or qualitative terms. *Disarmament* means the arrangement, often similar mechanically to arms control agreements, designed to eliminate all or certain classes of armaments. These bargaining processes are subsumed under the general rubric of *conflict control.*

Conflict control not only presupposes shared interests among nation-states, but it also involves a three-tiered process of negotiation. First, each negotiating government must develop a range of acceptable outcomes. Later, further bargaining at this level may modify goals and acceptable outcomes. Second, an overlapping range of outcomes must emerge between negotiating governments. Again, bargaining involving trade-offs and concessions will generally be required in order to forge commonly acceptable outcomes. Finally, each negotiating government must mobilize support in its own constituency for modified goals and outcomes.[7] The inability of the Carter administration to secure Senate approval of the SALT II Treaty during the 1979–80 period indicates the importance of this often neglected third tier.

War Termination. Before examining the more sophisticated forms of conflict control, we will briefly investigate its minimal form—termination of an existing conflict. In simpler times states often waged war in order to attain relatively well defined objectives, such as the placement of a Bourbon on the throne of Spain, the expulsion of the Moors from Europe, or the right to peddle opium to the Chinese. In such cases it was not difficult for the participants to recognize that victory had been realized; the objectives either had or had not been attained.

Moreover, the question of conflict termination was often trivial. The Vandals clearly knew when their conflict with Rome had ceased; that termination coincided with the physical occupation of the city. In conflicts not involving the destruction of a major civilization, termination of conflict was often signaled symbolically, as in the surrender of a sword—indicating that the defeated power had accepted the altered state of affairs.

In the nuclear age, however, traditional notions of victory are no longer so clear. If a nation suffering reverses possesses nuclear weapons, it may not surrender when its national survival is threatened. Inflicting further damage on such a battered, nuclear-armed adversary may result only in a Pyrrhic victory when conflict jumps to the nuclear level. As a general proposition, in instances of limited war the difficulties of knowing an opponent's intentions coupled with the push-button efficiency of modern strategic weaponry inevitably produces the dangerous possibility of escalation if at least one opponent is nuclear-armed.

If nations fear that general war could well result from accident, miscalculation, or escalation during limited war, then early war termination becomes an important end in itself. With the heavy penalties of general war, nuclear powers can no longer afford to resolve the question of who the victor is prior to terminating conflict. War prompted by accident or miscalculation needs to be quickly identified as such and brought to an end. In short, under a variety of conditions, early war termination should be an explicit objective of national security policy, and national decision-makers should have means and strategies to bring about conflict termination.

The Process of War Termination. To begin the process of terminating conflict, each belligerent government must agree within itself that certain kinds of negotiated peace are preferable to a continued military quest for the political objectives at stake. Since governments—even in totalitarian states— are not monolithic, establishment of an acceptable war termination condition may itself require protracted and frequently bitter negotiation among key domestic political interests—the administration or regime, the professional military, internal or external political oppositions, and, in democratic states, legislatures and political elites. Vietnam is only the most recent example of the difficulty and complexity of achieving even an internal political consensus on the conditions for peace. France encountered similar difficulties in Algeria in the late 1950s, as did Great Britain in South Africa at the turn of the century.

Quite apart from the fact that war itself, especially when protracted, intensifies already existing political rivalries, achievement of an agreed war termination objective is also inhibited by varying degrees of individual optimism and pessimism; by divergent assessments of the probability of military success or failure if the war continues; and by institutional interests, which are often broader than the war and will persist after it is over. Given such cross-cutting interests, development of a consensus on the conditions for peace, even in the face of the continuing costs of war, is no small achievement.[8]

Presuming that each belligerent government can agree on a range of out-comes acceptable to its key elements—that is, to decide that certain kinds of negotiated peace are preferable to continuing the quest for military victory— then a second dimension of bargaining emerges: negotiation between governments, where representatives of the two attempt to secure conditions under which they will cease to fight. We say "attempt" because despite modifications each has made to its original political goals there may be no "overlap" between one side's minimum acceptable gain and the other's maximum acceptable loss. Of course, negotiating nations rarely select their own "worst case" as an initial bargaining position, so several rounds of proposals and some time may be necessary to reveal the presence or absence of overlap.

Negotiations between governments may take several forms. They may be sporadic, punctuated by renewed fighting. They may take place under conditions of military disengagement or truce. They may involve less substance than propaganda, and, in such a case, scrambling for a stronger military position from which to bargain may characterize the negotiations. They may also involve third parties, such as allies, mediators, or international organizations. In particular, each side's assessment of the other's position is unlikely to coincide with the other party's own estimates, given the lack of any absolute standard by which military costs can reliably be compared with political benefits.[9] Finally, one side may suspect that the other is using the talks solely as a respite during which it can build up its capabilities to an overwhelming superiority.

Consensus within and between belligerent governments is but part of the problem of conflict termination. Another dimension occurs between each government and its constituency. Citizens who do not actively fight also care. They may be engaged in some form of war-supporting activity ranging from riveting aircraft wings to rolling bandages. Families must cope with the death, maiming, or disappearance of close relatives.

If the war is of long duration or if it strains the economy of the country, consumer goods may be in short supply and the public disgruntled. Unless the war is short or places an insignificant burden on the economy, most governments will actively seek to involve their publics in its prosecution, generally through appeals to patriotism. Often, propaganda stressing the innate barbarity or treachery of the enemy will be employed, and the nation's objectives in the conflict, wrapped in the flag and crowned with polemics, will appear as dominant themes in the communications media.

All this may work until the government is forced to abandon its original objectives for something less. The parents whose grief for a fallen son was partially overcome by devotion to the "cause" may not want to settle for the lesser outcome. As public opinion has been manipulated in one direction, it must now be led in another. While public opinion in many polities tends to be little valued in initially determining foreign policy, in those systems where the executive is in any way accountable to the populace it is a factor in the survivability of the government. In those nations in which public opinion is important or in which there is an independent legislative body with influence on foreign policy, any modification of initial goals must be accompanied by a major effort to maintain public and legislative support.

War Termination and National Security Policy. More than just procedure must be considered in analyzing the role of war termination in national security policy. If we accept the proposition that war termination should be an important element of a nuclear power's security policy, then the means to affect it must be made available. Conscious direction must be imposed upon defense strategy, targeting plans, force structure, and development of weaponry in order to provide national leaders with the means to terminate hostilities that are short of total nuclear war.

Defense strategy must develop responses appropriate to the intensity and type of attack received. If escalation is required to remedy an adverse battlefield situation, it should be conducted with an eye to the inferences that the opponent will draw. Explicit messages to one's adversary should clarify the intent of the escalating act. In short, the strategy of a nuclear power must acknowledge war termination as a goal and seek to limit escalation possibilities consistent with the political objectives at stake.

Targeting plans must permit a range of appropriate responses to a spectrum of possible attack scenarios. Again, the objective should be in part to assist war termination by preventing or minimizing escalation in nuclear war. The capability to respond in kind to any level of provocation minimizes the likelihood of escalation should conflict occur. An important question in targeting concerns the desirability of attacking an enemy's command, control, and communications (C^3) centers. The greater a nation's commitment to terminating the conflict, the less desirable the enemy's political centers as targets, for their elimination precludes the negotiating process from even beginning. Moreover, such elimination could lead to a spasm reaction culminating in nuclear holocaust. Logically, then, preservation of the opponent's C^3 should be a criterion in preparing targeting plans designed to assist war termination.

War termination also affects the related areas of force structure and weaponry. To minimize the risk of escalation or accidental launching, tight control must be exercised over strategic forces. C^3 systems for these strategic forces should be highly protected, reliable, redundant, and responsive. Moreover, a capability must exist to communicate quickly and reliably with the opposing leadership, as the present U.S.-U.S.S.R. hot line is designed to to do.

To summarize, the nuclear age has changed the previously held antecedent relation of military victory to war termination. Nuclear powers must now be prepared to terminate conventional, limited, or accidental war prior to reaching levels of violence encompassing massive destruction. National security policy requires weapons systems, targeting plans, and C^3 systems that facilitate the termination of conflict should war erupt.

Arms Control and Disarmament. Broadly defined, arms control and disarmament can be characterized as "cooperative or multilateral approach(es) to armament policy."[10] At this general level, the two forms of conflict control share some common attributes, most importantly the supposition that, given shared interests, nations' security objectives can be achieved by cooperative action with one another—perhaps *only* so achieved. Historically, disarmament and arms control have tended to be discussed together, inasmuch as both represent attempts to grapple with the same types of threat to peace and as they would meet many of the same difficulties in implementation. Arms control and disarmament represent fundamentally different approaches to conflict control, however, and it is essential to examine these differences.

Disarmament. Disarmament and its ultimate expression, general and complete disarmament (GCD), are predicated on the renunciation of war and on the idea that arms are the cause of war. While most disarmament proposals have not suggested the abolition of all arms, they have sought to eliminate major items of contemporary strategic weaponry (for example, capital ships or nuclear warheads) under the presumption that, by so doing, not only the means but also the prime motive for major war would disappear. This view subsumes a host of unverified (and often unverifiable) propositions about the causes of war and basic human nature. Among the conditions that would have to obtain if complete disarmament were to prevent war are:

1. People are basically peace loving (or their political institutions make them so); and this characteristic is reflected in the nations in which they live.
2. The major cause of war is the fear that nations have of each other's intentions and capabilities.
3. Levels of arms are the principal indicators by which nations gauge each other's intentions and capabilities.

Implicit in these conditions is the idea that there is, or can be, a distribution of lands, resources, and other values among nations such that no nation is, or would be, sufficiently dissatisfied to attempt to alter the status quo by force.

With the nuclear nations now numbering five (or six, if India is included) and with several other large states and a few small ones technologically within reach of developing a nuclear capability, the prospects for nuclear disarmament appear particularly dim. While it is true that immense stratification exists among the nuclear powers, such that the United States and the Soviet Union each enjoy a clear preponderance of capability over China, France, and Britain, neither superpower could afford to ignore the three "mininuclear powers"—even if they could themselves manage the incredible feat of coming to a verifiable, enforceable agreement to dismantle entirely their own nuclear arsenals. The advantage to be gained from cheating—i.e., surreptitiously retaining a few weapons—would be so great that any nuclear disarmament scheme necessarily presupposes high trust among the nuclear-armed states. Lacking that, and with many megatons of explosive power available and waiting for Armageddon, it has seemed futile to the major nations to discard large naval vessels or tanks or heavy machine guns in the interests of world peace. In short, GCD, as shown by the scant attention paid to it since the mid 1960s, seems to have been overtaken by history.

Arms Control. Arms control does not depend on the assumption that eliminating weapons or armed forces will eliminate war. Rather, arms control aims to reduce the likelihood of armed conflict; its severity and violence, should it occur; and/or the economic burden of military programs.[11] Arms control does not presuppose that any particular weapon will be eliminated or even necessarily reduced in number. Since stability of the arms balance is a prime concern, if stability requires that a certain weapons system be deployed in strength, then the logic of arms control would even encourage such deployment.

Primacy of conflict avoidance and the stability that promotes such avoidance could even lead to ignoring in the short run the objectives of reducing severity of violence or economic costs. Thus, increased military expenditures would be justified if they lower the probability of war through creating a more stable arms balance. Similarly, measures that would reduce the scope of violence during conflict—such as an ABM system protecting population centers—might actually undercut stability and thereby increase the peacetime risk of war; hence, they should be avoided.

Arms control rests on the fundamental assumption that the probability of war is in part a function of the kinds and sizes of opposing military forces. During a crisis, for instance, the probability of war is greater if one side has much larger or qualitatively superior forces, while the probability of war is lower if opposing forces are approximately equivalent in size and quality. Quantitative or qualitative disparities create destabilizing situations, since the stronger side will be tempted to exploit its advantages politically or perhaps even attack, while the weaker side, in expectation of attack and in order to minimize its losses, will be tempted to launch preemptive attacks. Even if the stronger side is inclined towards restraint, perception that its weaker opponent might seek to preempt it becomes a persuasive argument for taking the military initiative. Thus reciprocal expectations of attack under military imbalance start a vicious cycle of calculations culminating in war. Arms control seeks to minimize such a spiraling cycle of expectations, in part by reducing the vulnerability of strategic forces to preemptive attack, so that each nation has little to gain from attacking first but retains confidence in its deterrent and retaliatory capabilities.

Arms control also seeks to reduce the probability of accidents or miscalculations that may precipitate conflict, either through unilateral means or by specific forms of cooperation between the adversaries. Unilateral measures include designing safety devices and procedures in weapons systems to guard against accidental or unauthorized use and against theft by terrorists. The West institutes such measures with nuclear weapons, and it is usually supposed that the U.S.S.R. takes comparable steps. Bilateral cooperative measures have also been adopted, illustrated by the 1972 U.S.-Soviet Incidents at Sea Agreement, the 1971 Accidents Measures Agreement, and the Hot Line Agreement of 1971, all of which establish safeguard procedures and cooperative expectations intended to prevent escalation if accidents or miscalculations do occur.

History of Arms Control and Disarmament. The history of disarmament from the First Hague Conference of 1899 until the advent of the nuclear age is largely a tale of deep and ineffectual idealism. Most of the measures advanced during that half century centered around the limitation or partial reduction of the tools of war. Chronologically, the more important events were:

- The Hague Conferences, 1899 and 1907
- Washington Naval Agreement, 1922
- Geneva Protocol, 1925
- Geneva Disarmament Conference, 1927

In general, these agreements were declaratory in nature; that is, they expressed consensus on certain lofty principles but failed to include effective mechanisms to insure or verify performance or to resolve disputes. Ratification difficulties also frequently frustrated many agreements from ever taking effect.

Reviewing these agreements and their history leads one to several conclusions pertinent for contemporary arms control efforts. First, self-interest and security are apparently stronger influences on the way nations approach arms reductions and limitations than are altruism and a desire for peace. Second, criteria of parity or equivalence of armaments are central in bilateral negotiations and give rise to heated differences; in negotiations involving several principal participants, the problem of security is compounded by the number of ways each computes its potential adversaries, singly and in combination. Finally, no two nations' military establishments are sufficiently similar in either equipment or organization, so that asymmetries in formations and hardware greatly complicate the problem of establishing any parity of forces.

The atomic bomb detonation over Hiroshima in August 1945 abruptly created a new agenda for arms control. The enormous destructive power of atomic weapons dictated that any major effort to reduce or limit national armaments would necessarily have to begin with these weapons. The first attempt to grapple with this problem was the Baruch plan presented to the United Nations in 1946. This U.S. proposal called for UN takeover of the means of constructing atomic weaponry and destruction of existing stockpiles. The plan also assumed, however, that the United States would retain its nuclear monopoly until the transition to UN control was completed; other nations, by contrast, would have to subject themselves in the meantime to intrusions by the international agency controlling atomic energy.[12] Not surprisingly, the Soviet Union refused to submit to such an enduring position of military inferiority and rejected the Baruch plan. This issue of parity was to plague subsequent arms control efforts until the end of the 1960s, when the two superpowers commenced serious arms control talks as virtual equals in nuclear strength.

On the procedural level, the issue of verification divided the United States and the Soviet Union early on. Until 1955 the United States rigidly insisted upon direct inspection of an adversary's facilities as a *sine qua non* of any serious arms control agreement. On the other hand, the Soviets viewed inspection as a form of espionage and refused to agree to any inspection formula. As disarmament discussions between East and West shifted to less ambitious arms control measures, American proposals turned to more limited verification procedures. One such was President Eisenhower's Open Skies Proposal of 1955. Its objective was to reduce the risk of surprise attack through exchanges of military information and a broad verification system of reconnaissance flights and ground inspections. Quite predictably, given their penchant for secrecy and efforts to redress the military balance, the Soviets rejected the proposal.[13] Yet a precedent had been set that shifted the focus of negotiations toward less comprehensive agreements. Progress began on the banning of nuclear weapons testing, culminating in the Limited Test Ban Treaty of 1963, an agreement that could be monitored without direct inspection inside a nation's borders by the use of seismic and other instruments.

Over the next decade a series of limited accords began to evolve from Soviet-American negotiations.

- Antarctica Treaty (signed by 12 nations, 1959)
- Washington-Moscow Hot Line (installed, 1963; modernized, 1971)
- Outer Space Treaty (UN Resolution, 1963; ratified by 76 of 89 signatories, 1980)
- Nonproliferation Treaty (opened for signature, 1968)
- Seabed Treaty (opened for signature, 1972; ratified by 66 of 87 signatories, 1980)
- Accidental War Agreement (U.S. and USSR, 1971)
- Biological Warfare Convention (opened for signature, 1972; signed by 111 nations, 1980)

Yet by the early 1970s no major progress had evolved in the most important area of arms control—efforts to limit the competition in strategic weaponry in order to reduce the probability or destructiveness of nuclear war.

The SALT Negotiations. By the late 1960s the two superpowers were moving toward substantive negotiations on controlling the nuclear arms race. Significant changes during the decade in the strategic and technological environments paved the way. First, as suggested above, the concerted Soviet military build-up after 1963 led to rough parity by the end of the decade in second-strike capabilities between the Soviet Union and the United States. From a clear position of strategic inferiority at the time of the Cuban Missile Crisis, the Soviet Union had made impressive progress in deploying a large-scale ICBM force capable of surviving any U.S. first-strike. It had also deployed a modest SLBM force to strengthen further its second-strike capability. Finally, a small Soviet ABM system had appeared in the mid 1960s, prompting a U.S. reassessment of Soviet technological capabilities. Doubt concerning the stability of the balance of terror emerged in American minds as the effects of the Soviet deployment of a large-scale ABM system were contemplated.

American recognition of a new strategic context was signaled in January 1969 when President Nixon announced his "sufficiency" doctrine, in effect acknowledging the existence of nuclear parity between the superpowers. The stage was set on which the United States and Soviet Union could bargain as equals in the arms control arena.

In the technological dimension, developments appeared that broke the stalemated debate over verification procedures. Satellite reconnaissance capabilities, coupled with extraterritorial sensing systems, allowed a reasonable degree of verification to proceed without requiring on-site inspections. Verification by national technical means (NTM) was now feasible, and many arms control initiatives would subsequently be less hindered by verification difficulties. Additionally, technological advances increased the potential for destabilizing influences on the strategic balance. Thus the possibly destabilizing effect of full-scale deployment of ABM population defenses was an impetus, at least on the American side, for negotiating an arms control agreement.

Arms control must always be analyzed in light of a nation's overall foreign policy, both toward its adversaries and toward its allies. Not only do developments arising out of negotiations impact upon foreign policy objectives, but those objectives also limit the range of options available to a country negotiating an arms control accord. The history of the strategic arms limitation talks (SALT I), from the American perspective, is replete with illustrations of this relationship. During the Nixon and Ford administrations SALT was widely viewed as the centerpiece of the superpower relationship. This preeminence of SALT tended to overshadow other foreign policy considerations (except some NATO-related concerns) that might have deflected the superpowers from détente and pursuit of arms control agreements. Whether future SALT agreements will be that much detached from other policy objectives is highly doubtful.

Within the United States, the primary impetus for specific strategic arms control proposals came from the White House, i.e., from President Nixon and Assistant for National Security Affairs Henry Kissinger; but there was a wide and deep public consensus behind the administration urging such talks.[14] Inside the bureaucracy there were both ardent advocates, in such entities as the Arms Control and Disarmament Agency (ACDA), and worried skeptics, such as the JCS.

ACDA had been established by act of Congress in 1961 in order to provide a continuing policy emphasis on arms control and disarmament. Institutionally, ACDA serves as the principal proponent of arms control within the American government, although its effectiveness in this role is constrained or enhanced by the president's attitudes and bureaucratic preferences. During ACDA's early years, its director also acted as chief arms control negotiator. Perhaps inevitably, though, as arms control issues have assumed greater public and policy prominence, the task of conducting negotiations has shifted to special envoys appointed directly by the president who are in some measure, at least, independent of ACDA.

The acquiescence, if not enthusiastic support, of the JCS to any arms control agreement is vital to ensure its public and congressional acceptance. Since JCS rejection of any tentative agreement would place the president in a difficult internal position, the JCS is in a position to require a strong initial U.S. position or to seek other intragovernmental compromise. The Johnson and Nixon administrations offer contrasting examples of how to deal with the necessity for JCS support. In 1968, the interagency group that sought to hammer out a bargaining position for the Johnson administration's ill-fated efforts at arms control formulated its position with JCS approval in mind. JCS acquiescence required that an ABM system not be banned nor strict limitations be placed on its deployment. Second, no ban on MIRV deployment could be included. On the other hand, the JCS agreed to moderate some of its positions, including (for the first time) acceptance of provisions that could not be verified with complete reliability as it had previously demanded.[15] In contrast, the Nixon administration largely negotiated concessions with the Soviet Union, with only limited bureaucratic participation, and then attempted to bring the bureaucracy—including the JCS—around to the new position. In SALT I, a particularly difficult concession for the JCS to accept was permitting the Soviet Union to have a numerical advantage in SLBMs. Its acquiescence was gained by an understanding that the administration would accelerate development of the Trident submarine in order to begin deployment in 1978.[16]

While every administration must negotiate arms control agreements with an eye toward obtaining Senate approval, Congress has been increasingly assertive and influential in recent years. In the case of SALT I, public support for limiting the competition in strategic arms was so high that senatorial concerns about the specifics of the agreements were readily met. The ABM treaty portion of the overall accord, for instance, was ratified by a Senate vote of 88 to 2! Still, it is noteworthy that at the same time, in the so-called Jackson Resolution (after Senator Henry Jackson), the Congress insisted that numerical parity must be a feature of future SALT agreements. In the case of SALT II, as will be discussed below, the executive's task of acquiring legislative approval escalated greatly.

When, after considerable fencing, the United States and Soviet Union agreed to initiate the SALT I negotiations in Helsinki on November 17, 1969, the climate was favorable. Concerned about military costs, strategic instability, and domestic political problems in attempting to deploy a full-scale ABM system for population defense, the Nixon administration sought from the start to limit ABM systems. Given the traditional Soviet military emphasis on defense, the administration expected that any ABM accord would be difficult to negotiate. However, for reasons that are not fully clear, but probably including Soviet fear that American technological capability would produce a superior U.S. system, the Soviet Union was ready for ABM limitations. While specific agreement on how to limit ABMs remained to be resolved, an important convergence of Soviet and American positions had nonetheless been quickly reached.[17]

Convergence on other aspects of the agenda, especially in limitations on offensive weaponry, proved to be much more difficult. For political, strategic, and technological reasons the superpower positions were far apart. In order to illustrate the process of compromise required to obtain agreement, two issues of SALT I negotiations will be briefly examined: numerical equality in offensive delivery vehicles and the definition of strategic delivery systems.

One of the most important positions of the United States in early SALT negotiations was its demand for numerical equality of strategic delivery vehicles (SDVs). In the foreign policy realm, Nixon's doctrine of sufficiency held that American military forces must not only deter direct attack, but—

in a broader political sense—they must foreclose the possibility of Soviet coercion of the West resulting from an apparent imbalance of forces. As noted earlier, until tested, power is what people perceive it to be; and any imbalance of numerical forces might be perceived by the Soviet Union, and by American allies, as an indication of weakness and lack of resolve on the part of the United States to defend its worldwide interests.

In the technological sphere, there was a very real U.S. concern about the Soviet capability to develop MIRVs for its powerful SS-9 ICBMs, which were several times as powerful as their American counterparts. The Soviet Union already held a numerical advantage in ICBMs. Increasing accuracy of MIRVs, coupled with greater numbers of ICBMs and the substantial payload of the SS-9, inspired fears in the United States that its Minuteman force would be vulnerable to surprise attack. Thus the strategic balance would be upset, and dangerous instabilities would result.

Because of these considerations the initial negotiating position of the Nixon administration emphasized that the superpowers would maintain numerical equality of strategic delivery vehicles.[18] However, Soviet political perceptions, growing strategic threat to the U.S.S.R. from the P.R.C., and Soviet sense of technological inferiority dictated rejection by the Soviet Union of any proposal that would require reducing its numbers of ICBMs to the lower American level. Hence, the first negotiating impasse of SALT centered on the principle of numerical equality of strategic delivery vehicles.

A second impasse developed over the definition of "strategic" weaponry. The Soviet Union has consistently sought to define strategic weaponry as those systems capable of striking an opponent's homeland. From the Soviet strategic point of view such a definition is certainly understandable. Yet American acceptance of such a definition would incorporate under the SALT negotiations those nuclear delivery systems designed to support NATO, such as the FB-111. These so-called forward-based systems (FBS) are vital elements of American alliance policy. They serve as evidence of American guarantees to defend Western Europe, and any unilateral American effort to discuss FBS in SALT would seriously undermine NATO unity and cast doubt upon American security commitments. European concerns about a superpower "condominium" resulting from SALT negotiations mandated American rejection of the Soviet definition of strategic weaponry. Instead the U.S. insisted upon a criterion of intercontinental range with which to define strategic weapons systems.

With such basic disagreement on offensive weaponry, movement toward an agreement required hard bargaining by both parties. Compromise did not occur via the normal negotiating process but instead through direct communications, which had begun in January 1971, between Kissinger and Soviet Ambassador Anatoly Dobrynin. In an agreement announced in May 1971 the Soviet Union deferred including FBS in SALT I negotiations and accepted American insistence on simultaneously negotiating limits on offensive and defensive weapons (a position that the Soviet Union had resisted up to that point, instead insisting on completion of an ABM treaty prior to discussing offensive limitations). In return, the United States dropped its demand for numerical equality in SDVs, thus conceding to the Soviets a numerical advantage in ICBM launchers.[19]

Many other compromises were required during the course of the protracted negotiations. A key provision was agreement in the spring of 1972 on the number of ABM sites authorized each country (two) and Soviet willingness to limit total numbers of SLBMs in return for a numerical advantage in both submarines and launching tubes.

Results of SALT I. On May 26, 1972, some thirty months of negotiations culminated in three separate agreed documents: an ABM treaty, the Interim Agreement on Strategic Offensive Arms, and the Protocol to the Interim Agreement.[20]

The ABM treaty limits each signatory to deploying a total of 200 ABMs in two equal fields, one around the national capital and another at least 1,300 kilometers distant from the first. Other provisions of the treaty limit the ABM testing establishments each nation may maintain and prohibit the development and deployment of multiple launchers, mobile ABM systems, ABM stockpiling, transfer of such missiles to other nations, and upgrading of antiaircraft systems to ABM mode. Modernization and routine replacement of ABM equipment are permitted. (A 1974 protocol reduces each side to only one field of 100 ABMs.)

The Interim Agreement on Strategic Offensive Arms froze for five years certain aspects of offensive weapons competition. The agreement deals only with ICBMs and SLBMs; numbers of warheads and other systems, such as manned bombers and tactical nuclear weapons, are not included. The agreement limits land-based ICBMs to the number in existence or under construction on or before July 1, 1972. SLBMs are limited to the number operational or under construction as of the date the agreement was signed. Both parties can nonetheless increase their total SLBM launchers by replacing pre-1964 ICBMs with SLBMs on a one-for-one basis; this is the "freedom to mix" principle. The replacement of pre-1964 ICBMs with modern land-based missiles is prohibited. The net effect is to encourage the replacement of obsolete land-based missiles with less vulnerable SLBMs. Like the ABM treaty, the agreement relies on NTMs, such as national satellite surveillance and extraterritorial sensing systems, for verification. These numerical limits on offensive weaponry are summarized in table 23.1.

The third basic understanding is the Protocol to the Interim Agreement, which translates certain provisions of the latter document into concrete figures, setting numerical ceilings of 710 SLBMs on 44 modern submarines for the United States and 950 SLBMs on 62 modern submarines for the Soviets. Since these figures represented more missiles and submarines than either nation had at the time of signing, increases to the allowable maximum levels were provided for by the freedom to mix principle.

Table 23.1 Summary of Offensive Weapon Agreements, Salt I

	ICBM/SLBM (no old ICBM retirement)	ICBM/SLBM (old ICBM retirement)
U.S.	1054/656	1000/710
U.S.S.R.	1618/740	1408/950

Source: U.S. Arms Control and Disarmament Agency, *Arms Control, 1979,* Jan. 30, 1980.

Along with the three SALT documents, Brezhnev and Nixon signed an agreement on "Basic Principles of Relations" between the two countries. Among these principles were the conduct of relations on the basis of peaceful coexistence, the avoidance of confrontations and nuclear war, and renunciation of efforts to obtain "unilateral advantage" over each other. Détente was in full flower.

SALT II. Recognizing the interim character of the portion of the SALT I treaty which limited offensive arms and caught up in the euphoria following the ratification process, the Nixon administration quickly sought a follow-up agreement. Negotiations began in Vienna in November 1972. The first aim on the American side was that SALT II must provide for numerical equality of strategic systems between the United States and the U.S.S.R. as stipulated in the Jackson Resolution. The second goal was that the agreement should maintain and, if possible, enhance the stability of the strategic balance, thereby reducing the likelihood of nuclear war. In addition, any agreement should contribute to improving U.S.-Soviet relations, as well as reduce tension and control the military competition between the U.S. and the Soviet Union."[21] Third—and importantly, in view of some concern about Soviet compliance with the terms of SALT I—any new agreement would have to be sufficiently verifiable that it would be a "source of confidence and not uncertainty."

By November 1974 the negotiations had produced basic agreement on the elements of a SALT II pact. These were codified in the so-called Vladivostock Accord, signed by President Ford and President Brezhnev as a preliminary agreement, to last until 1985 or until subsumed in a comprehensive treaty. The Vladivostock Accord called for the indefinite extension of the ABM treaty and limited each side to 2,400 strategic nuclear delivery vehicles (ICBM launchers, SLBM launchers, and heavy bombers)—of which 1,300 could be MIRVed. The accord also banned construction of new ICBM launchers and conversion of existing launchers from light to heavy ICBMs; it also limited the deployment of new types of offensive weapons.

Continuing disagreement over whether or not the new Soviet Backfire bomber would be counted as a heavy bomber, and therefore against the 2,400 ceiling, and over how to deal with cruise missiles, as well as a number of lesser issues, precluded moving at that time beyond the accord to a comprehensive SALT II treaty.

When the new Carter administration took office in January 1977, completing a new strategic arms treaty ranked high in its list of priorities. Rather than building on the Vladivostock Accord, however, which was the Soviet preference, the new administration decided to try for "deep cuts" in the numbers permitted and to bring the negotiations into the glare of public examination, in accordance with President Carter's electoral pledge to open diplomacy. Both departures encountered strong Soviet opposition and the talks promptly collapsed.

After reconsideration, the U.S. leaders returned to the Vladivostock framework and negotiations resumed. These culminated in June 1979 when President Carter and President Brezhnev signed the SALT II Treaty, ending nearly seven years of effort. The basic treaty terms are as follows.

- An equal aggregate limit on the number of strategic nuclear delivery vehicles: ICBM and SLBM launchers, heavy bombers, and air-to-surface ballistic missiles (ASBMs). Initially, this ceiling would be 2,400 as agreed at Vladivostok. The ceiling will be lowered to 2,250 in 1981.
- An equal aggregate limit of 1,320 on the total number of launchers of MIRVed ballistic missiles and heavy bombers equipped for long-range cruise missiles
- A limit of 1,200 on the total number of launchers of MIRVed ballistic missiles
- A limit of 820 on launchers of MIRVed ICBMs
- A ban on construction of additional fixed ICBM launchers and on any increase in the number of fixed heavy ICBM launchers
- A ban on flight-testing or deployment of new types of ICBMs, with an exception of one new type of ICBM
- A ban on increasing the numbers of warheads on existing types of ICBMs, and limits of 10 warheads on the one new type of ICBM, 14 warheads on SLBMs, and 10 warheads on ASBMs
- A provision limiting the number of long-range cruise missiles per bomber to an average of 28; and the number of long-range cruise missiles per existing heavy bomber to 20
- Ceilings on the launch-weight and throw-weight of strategic ballistic missiles
- A ban on the production, testing, and deployment of the Soviet SS-16 missile, including a ban on the production of that missile's unique components
- A ban on rapid reload ICBM systems
- A ban on certain types of strategic offensive systems which are technologically feasible, but which have not yet been deployed, including such systems as long-range ballistic missiles on surface ships, ballistic missile launchers on the seabeds, fractional orbit bombardment systems (FOBS), and mobile launchers of heavy ICBMs or heavy SLBMs
- Provisions for advance notification of simultaneous multiple ICBM test launches

- An agreed data base for systems included in various SALT-limited categories

In an additional protocol, SALT II also

places temporary limits on those systems not yet ready for long-term resolution and will remain in force through December 31, 1981. In the Protocol, the sides have agreed to ban deployment of mobile ICBM launchers and flight-testing of ICBMs from such launchers. Development of such systems, short of flight-testing, is permitted. (The Treaty permits the deployment of mobile ICBM launchers after the Protocol expires.)

Additionally, the Protocol bans deployment, but not testing, of cruise missiles capable of ranges in excess of 600 kilometers on ground-based and sea-based launchers. The Protocol does not limit deployment of such systems after its expiration in 1981. Finally, the Protocol includes a ban on flight-testing and deployment of air-to-surface ballistic missiles.[22]

The third element of the SALT II agreement, the Joint Statement of Principles, established a basis for the next stage of negotiations. The following three goals were selected for the next round of talks.

1. Further reductions in the number of strategic offensive arms
2. Further qualitative limitations on strategic offensive arms
3. Resolution of the issues addressed in the protocol

The treaty was promptly sent to the Senate for ratification. Hearings before the Foreign Relations Committee lasted until November 9, 1979, when the committee reported it favorably to the full Senate. Yet the prospects for Senate approval were far less promising than those SALT I had faced. Détente had withered in the face of the increasing evidence of the Soviet arms build-up described in Chapter 16. Soviet adventurism, including the use of Cuban proxies, in Africa and the Middle East had undercut presumptions that the Soviet Union was interested in international stability and made a mockery of the "Basic Principles of Relations" established at the time of SALT I. Evidence of the presence of a Soviet brigade in Cuba and 1979 invasion of Afghanistan further decisively turned public and congressional opinion against compromise with the U.S.S.R.

Despite administration claims that

without SALT II, the Soviets could have by 1985 one-third more strategic nuclear delivery vehicles than they will be permitted under the agreement . . . many hundreds more MIRVed ballistic missile launchers . . . as many more heavy missiles as they wanted . . . three times as many warheads (on each Soviet SS18) . . . all the Backfire bombers they wanted . . . as many new types of ICBMs as their engineers could dream of . . . [23]

Senate leaders feared defeat of the treaty and deferred voting on it. Finally, in January 1980, citing Soviet agression in Afghanistan as the proximate cause, President Carter withdrew the treaty from Senate consideration. For all intents and purposes SALT II was dead.

START. Nonratification of SALT II inaugurated the longest hiatus in strategic arms control negotiations since the beginning of the SALT process in 1969. Several factors contributed to the pause: Soviet anger at the United States' failure to ratify SALT II; changes in leadership in both nations; and a lengthy process for reexamination by the new administration, whose leadership under Reagan included several of the most outspoken critics of successive SALT agreements and the methods by which they had been reached. Nor were the incentives to resume negotiation increased by worsening U.S.-Soviet atmospherics and a concomitant increase in overall superpower tension.

Nevertheless, by 1982, political pressure on the Reagan administration to resume active strategic arms control efforts had become irresistible and threatened to undermine congressional support for the broad rearmament program sought by the administration. The prospect of such a rearmament may also have influenced the new Soviet leader, General Secretary Andropov. Accordingly, on June 29, 1982, the United States and the U.S.S.R. resumed arms limitation negotiations under the new rubric of Strategic Arms Reduction Talks (START). These negotiations continue at this writing, but thus far with little promise of agreement. For its part, the United States seeks deep reductions in ballistic missile warheads and special limitations on heavy Soviet ICBMs. In contrast, the U.S.S.R. has been unwilling to depart significantly from the SALT II framework and views U.S. efforts to limit heavy ICBMs (in which Soviet capabilities are disproportionately invested) as an attempt to gain unilateral advantage. Such disagreements have only been the more refractory in a continuing atmosphere of U.S.-Soviet antagonism. Their resolution has been further complicated by a concurrent negotiating impasse over intermediate nuclear forces (INF).

INF. As noted in Chapter 12, the United States until recently retained a very significant advantage in theater nuclear capabilities—ground- and air-delivered nuclear weapons deployed in Western Europe in support of NATO. Although typically less powerful than strategic nuclear weapons, such systems nevertheless have special importance as a direct counter to Soviet conventional preponderance and as a visible guarantor of the U.S. nuclear commitment to European security.

By the late 1970s, however, both functions were increasingly in jeopardy, due in part to the growing obsolescence of deployed U.S. systems and in part to a significant expansion of Soviet theater nuclear capabilities. NATO was especially concerned about Soviet fielding of the SS-20, a mobile MIRVed intermediate-range ballistic missile capable of attacking targets throughout Europe from bases in the U.S.S.R. By March 1983, the U.S.S.R. had deployed over 350 SS-20s. Together with several hundred older SS-4 and SS-5 missiles, these deployments gave the Soviets clear superiority in so-called Euro-strategic systems and threatened to undermine the deterrent utility of the NATO nuclear posture—a posture largely concentrated in short-range, "battlefield" weapons.

NATO concern over these developments culminated in December 1979 in a Nuclear Planning Group decision to modernize the U.S. theater nuclear posture by replacing 108 existing PERSHING Is with Pershing IIs and by deploying 464 new ground-launched cruise missiles (GLCMs) at bases throughout Western Europe and Great Britain. At the same time, largely to meet European domestic political requirements, modernization was made conditional on concurrent efforts by the United States to negotiate intermediate nuclear force reductions with the Soviet Union.

Negotiations in accordance with this "dual-track" decision opened in Geneva in November 1981 and continue at this writing. As with START, progress to date has been slow. Also as with START, the slow pace has reflected both substantive disagreements and poor atmospherics—with the additional complication of rising popular opposition in Europe to nuclear weapons generally and the planned INF deployments in particular. Indeed, no arms control process more clearly illustrates the multiple levels of interacting negotiations that characterize arms control efforts in democratic states than INF. Operating simultaneously are bilateral negotiations among the United States and its NATO partners, as well as domestic political negotiations within each of the western nations.

Together, these complications make it exceedingly unlikely that an agreement will be reached before U.S. INF deployments begin in December 1983. So far, movement in the negotiations has been limited to (1) a U.S. offer to modify its original insistence on Soviet dismantling of all SS-4s, SS-5s, and SS-20s in return for U.S. nondeployment of Pershing IIs and GLCMS—a proposal rejected out of hand by the U.S.S.R.—and (2) Soviet modification of its original proposal that NATO and the U.S.S.R. both reduce to 300 intermediate-range systems (including aircraft and both French and British national nuclear systems) to a willingness to consider limiting warheads instead of just missiles. Neither modification goes very far toward closing the substantial gap between the two sides' positions.

Conventional Arms Control Talks. Much of the importance of the NATO nuclear modernization effort, and thus of the dual-track decision of 1979, reflects the imbalance in NATO and Warsaw Pact conventional forces that has existed since the close of World War II. In 1973, Mutual and Balanced Force Reduction (MBFR) negotiations were launched in Vienna to attempt to deal directly with this imbalance (the Western view) and stabilize the balance at reduced levels (the Soviet view). In addition to countries in the so-called guidelines area—West and East Germany, Czechoslovakia, Poland, and the Benelux nations—the principal participants include the United States, Great Britain, Canada, and the Soviet Union. The Western nations have carefully kept in step in the negotiating process, but doing so has been time consuming. On the Eastern side, the Soviet voice has been clearly dominant; but the development of its negotiating positions has also been slow, perhaps because the Soviets believe fissures will develop within the West if the bargaining is

sufficiently hard and protracted. In any case, after nearly ten years of continuous negotiations, there is little evidence that agreement is possible.

The core of the Western MBFR position has been that reductions in ground
and air forces on both sides should reach a common ceiling, reflecting the
significantly larger Eastern forces existing in the reduction area than Western—according to the West. By contrast, the Soviet Union took the position
that both side's forces should be reduced by equal amounts, thus—in Western
eyes—maintaining Eastern force superiority. After lengthy bargaining, the
Soviet Union has accepted the principle of a common ceiling on forces, but
the acquiescence has not succeeded in moving the negotiations forward, for
the two sides cannot agree on the size of the other's initial forces. Disagreement has continued on other aspects of the talks as well, such as on the
Western demand that force limitations be collective in nature, rather than on
a country-by-country basis. Associated measures, dealing with such matters
as verification, have similarly developed into impasses.[24]

Since it is only in central Europe that major East-West military units are
in nose-to-nose confrontation, balanced and verifiable arms reduction measures there would seem desirable if, that is, enhancing stability and reducing
the risks of war were priority concerns on both sides. The fact that the
U.S.S.R. has substantially increased its forces in the area during the MBFR
talks and that it has proven so intransigent, even about data on force sizes,
suggests to many observers in the West that parity as a condition of military
stability is not a Soviet priority and that a MBFR agreement is not achievable.
(In addition to the already noted possibility that the U.S.S.R. may see the
MBFR talks as a chance to divide the NATO allies, Western observers suggest
that Soviet reluctance to reduce may be due to (1) Soviet belief that the
present numbers of U.S.S.R. troops in Eastern Europe are necessary to keep
its allies in line, and (2) its hope that it can use its force superiority someday—
when American strength or will flags—to intimidate Western Europe, if not
to assault it.)

Other Arms Control Measures. Despite continuing disagreements on foreign
policy and defense matters, not only between East and West but throughout
the international community, the postwar period has been marked by a high
level of disarmament and arms control activity. Particularly since the early
1960s, bilateral and multilateral agendas have prominently featured these
topics and a multitude of conferences to deal with them. The UN has a
Disarmament Commission (though moribund from 1965 to 1979), which periodically holds special sessions on disarmament, as was the case in 1978.
Additionally, there is an autonomous forty-member Committee on Disarmament meeting regularly in Geneva, linked to the UN and consisting of the
nuclear weapons states and thirty-five others active in disarmament matters.
Many of the U.S.-U.S.S.R. bilateral negotiations of arms control measures
have moved to these UN or UN-linked forums as it became feasible to
multilateralize discussions. The effort to ban radiological weapons is an ex-

ample of a U.S.-U.S.S.R. joint initiative that has been sent to the Committee on Disarmament for further multilateral negotiation.

Nuclear weapons testing is one of the more important areas of arms control, because testing constraints tend to limit improvements in the existing nuclear-armed states' arsenals as well as inhibit the proliferation of nuclear weapons capabilities of other states. In 1963 an agreement called the Limited Test Ban Treaty (LTBT) was reached to prohibit nuclear explosions in the atmosphere, outer space, and under water. In 1974 the Threshold Test Ban Treaty (TTBT) wa signed, setting a nuclear threshold of 150 KT, a yield above which tests could not be conducted, even underground. The related Treaty on Underground Nuclear Explosions for Peaceful Purposes (the so-called PNE Treaty) was signed in 1976 with the same 150 kiloton (KT) limit. Thus far, however, a comprehensive test ban (CTB) has proven elusive, despite years of effort. The three powers concerned (United States, U.S.S.R. and Great Britain) have varying differences over the issues involved in setting such a fundamental brake on the nuclear arms race, but verification is the principal hurdle. The familiar Soviet opposition to effective on-site inspection is the heart of the problem.[25]

Another agreement, dealing with the same proliferation issue but developed along different lines, is the 1968 Non-Proliferation Treaty (NPT). Designed to halt the spread of nuclear weapons, the NPT prohibits the nuclear powers from transferring nuclear weapons and explosive devices to any nation and, reciprocally, binds the other, non-weapons parties to the treaty not to accept such weapons or undertake to manufacture them on their own. To verify that they are not diverting nuclear materials to the manufacture of weapons or other explosive devices, the non-weapons parties also agreed to accept international inspection and safeguards on all nuclear materials and facilities under their control. By the end of 1982 this landmark treaty had been ratified by 111 countries—but a number of important potential proliferaters were missing from the list: Argentina, Brazil, India, Israel, Pakistan, and South Africa.[26]

One example of successful multilateral disarmament activity has occurred in recent years (indeed, the only one since the Biological Warfare Convention of 1972). The multilateral Convention on the Prohibition of Military or Any Other Hostile Use of Environmental Modification Techniques (ENMOD Convention) was initiated by the United States and the U.S.S.R. and entered into force in 1978. Following on the success of the multilateral Outer Space Treaty (banning weapons of mass destruction in outer space), the United States and the U.S.S.R. have been conducting negotiations aimed at prohibiting antisatellite weapons. By the end of 1982 these talks were in suspense.

During the late 1970s, U.S. and Soviet arms control discussions increasingly tended to bog down. In some cases a particular negotiation was doomed from the start, such as the Carter administration's attempt to reach agreements with the Soviets on limiting conventional arms transfers (CAT). Since arms transfers are a key foreign policy instrument, there was never a serious prospect that the two superpowers could agree on the use of the tool without agreeing on the policies behind such use. Indeed, the United States could not even get its Western allies to agree to its CAT position, and the whole enterprise foundered. U.S.-U.S.S.R. talks on Indian Ocean demilitarization, through which President Carter hoped to stabilize and limit superpower force deployments in the Indian Ocean, produced a similar impasse for similar reasons. Neither set of negotiations uncovered sufficient consensus to suggest their early rebirth.

Other negotiations, both bilateral and multilateral, have been suspended or abandoned as détente withered and the Soviet arms build-up became apparent. As the decade of the 1980s opened, the bloom was off arms control and disarmament.

Arms Control in the 1980s. Viewed correctly as a means to provide national security, rather than as a moral exercise or an expression of political accommodation, arms control will depend in the future upon the superpowers' perceptions of the strength of their shared interests and the value of explicit cooperation. As implied in the discussion in earlier chapters about the Soviet attitude toward cooperation and conflict and its military doctrine, the U.S.S.R. may not be interested in equitable arms control arrangements in the 1980s when it is likely to have, at least through mid decade, strategic military predominance. The fact that the P.R.C. will be increasing its strategic nuclear arsenal and is likely to strengthen its political, economic, and military cooperation with the West over the decade will further incline Soviet leaders to resist any U.S. effort to offset through arms control the strategic arms gains it so expensively acquired in the course of the 1960s and 1970s.

On the American side, too, the barriers to progress in controlling the competition in strategic arms will be formidable. The most important fact is that the Soviet arms build-up, some nineteen or twenty years in duration by 1983,

has had dramatic effects on Western public and elite perceptions of the political and military implications of U.S.-Soviet arms negotiations. Although these Soviet military efforts raise certain specific security concerns, their perhaps more important effects are diffuse and political in character. The Soviet Union's continued willingness to allocate a relatively large percentage of its relatively scarce resources to military forces which already—to a Western eye—appear excessive for defensive purposes, has raised the most serious questions about Soviet ambitions.[27]

A second important element that will continue to affect the American approach to arms control in the 1980s is the West's dependence from the 1950s to the 1970s on U.S. strategic and tactical nuclear superiority to offset Soviet conventional superiority in Europe and thus to maintain an overall deterrent balance. Unable to ensure a stable conventional arms balance in Europe through an equitable MBFR agreement and facing the likelihood of Soviet tactical nuclear superiority in that theater, the U.S. should logically insist on a measure of superiority in, not on mere parity of, strategic forces.

The view that being "number one" is essential has been revived as an article of faith in many American circles. In practice, such a demand is probably not feasible, so that other means to the overall goal of a more stable strategic balance at each level of possible confrontation will have to be sought by the United States and its allies.

The means to deal with the parity-superiority problem available to the United States (and its Western partners) include a major alliance build-up of conventional forces, particularly in Europe, an increase in tactical nuclear weapons, and a substantial strengthening of U.S. strategic forces. Many analysts believe that it is only in the face of such unilateral U.S. and Western actions that the Soviets, with the momentum in the arms race moving against them, will accept arms control measures that are truly stabilizing. Ironically, this argument goes, a build-up is required before a scale-down can occur, and there is some evidence to sustain the concept.

Whether or not it will be possible to successfully conclude START and INF negotiations in the mid 1980s is doubtful. As technology multiplies the types and sophistication level of weapons, making verification ever more difficult and compounding the complexity of the needed bargaining trade-offs, the difficulty of successfully concluding a new agreement mounts. Faced with such technical difficulties, the two sides will have to be driven by strong political and economic imperatives if they are to succeed in major arms control advances.

Yet on the Soviet side, as suggested earlier, there will be reluctance to trade off potential gains from the arms build-up of the two prior decades. Moreover, the new generation of Soviet leaders may be particularly reluctant to pursue advantage or loath to appear accommodating. On the American side, there is widespread conviction that the SALT I and II treaties were cynically used by the Soviets to lull the United States into slowing its strategic arms programs while the U.S.S.R. pressed its drive for superiority. Additionally, under the umbrella of détente, of which SALT was the centerpiece, the Soviets are perceived to have waged an unrelenting campaign to overturn local balances or regimes in such places as Africa and the Middle East.

Still, arms control is such an important and potentially valuable means to limit the dangers of conflict in a nuclear era that it will not disappear from the international agenda. If progress is to be made and not mere lip service paid, however, it will probably be necessary to lower expectations and be more realistic about what is possible. As one veteran negotiator and analyst has observed, it must be recognized that

agreements that result from arms negotiations are not stepping stones to peace; at best, they can accomplish specific things in the context of continuing international political conflict. . . . If negotiated arms limitations are to have a future, they need to return to the more limited concept which originally characterized arms control. In this heterogeneous world of sovereign nations, there are real conflicts—over land, over economic rights, over religious and political values. And there are real villains in this world as well—individuals dedicated to the aggrandizement of themselves, their friends, their nations, even at the expense of others, and even at grave risk of war. Weapons are not the cause of these conflicts, they are their reflection. Discussions about weapons cannot solve these conflicts; they can—and even then only at certain times—contain their effects.

In another sense, given the rhetoric of confrontation which now characterizes U.S.-Soviet exchanges, even this modest agenda may appear naive. An acceptance of a return to more tense U.S.-Soviet relations, however, need not include the abandonment of efforts to contain the military competition at its most dangerous points. Given the extraordinary uncertainties of nuclear war and the unprecedented potential of nuclear weapons for destruction, containing the effects of political conflict, reducing the risk of war—even if only modestly—could be a crucial accomplishment.[28]

DISCUSSION QUESTIONS

1. Why do nations go to war? Are there major reasons and minor reasons? Which of the alternative explanations in the text do you subscribe to? Do you have others to suggest?

2. Have the ideological and technological revolution increased or decreased the prospects for conflict?

3. Define *conflict control* and explain the importance of shared interests for this concept.

4. What considerations for targeting plans, force structure, and weapons development must be made if war termination becomes an important element of defense strategy?

5. What is the fundamental difference between arms control and disarmament as approaches to conflict control?

6. The context surrounding negotiations is important for analysis of the arms control bargaining process. What important changes in the strategic and technological dimensions of this context allowed SALT I to commence in the late 1960s?

7. Which principal bureaucratic actors in the American government are involved in the arms control process? What perspectives are they likely to bring to bear in the intragovernmental bargaining process?

8. How does the American commitment to NATO affect formulation of U.S. negotiating positions in SALT?

9. What advances in technology will tend to frustrate the SALT process in the 1980s? Are there arms control devices that can cap technological advances tending to undermine the stability of the military balance?

10. Why have the MBFR talks proven so difficult and unproductive? Do the same reasons hold for the CAT talks?

RECOMMENDED READING

Blechman, Barry M. "Do Negotiated Arms Limitations Have a Future?" *Foreign Affairs*, fall 1980, p. 104.

Brennan, Donald G., ed. *Arms Control, Disarmament, and National Security*. New York: George Braziller, 1961.

Brodie, Bernard. "On the Objectives of Arms Control." *International Security* (summer 1976).

Frank, Jerome D. *Sanity and Survival: Psychological Aspects of War and Peace.* New York: Random House, 1967.

Halperin, Morton H. "War Termination as a Problem in Civil-Military Relations." *Annals*, November 1970, pp. 86–95.

Hobson, John. *Imperialism.* London: Allen J. Unwin, 1916.

Kelleher, Catherine. "The Present as Prologue." *International Security* (spring 1981).

Lenin, V. I. *Imperialism.* New York: International Publishers, 1939.

Lorenz, Konrad. *On Aggression.* New York: Harcourt Brace, 1966.

Malthus, Thomas. *An Essay on the Principle of Population.* New York: Macmillan, 1895.

May, Mark A. *A Social Psychology of War and Peace.* New Haven: Yale University Press, 1943.

Smith, Gerard. *Doubletalk: The Story of SALT I.* Garden City, N.Y.: Doubleday, 1980.

Tourtellot, Arthur, ed. *Selections for Today.* New York: Cuell, Sloan & Pearce, 1945.

Waltz, Kenneth N. *Man, the State, and War.* New York: Columbia University Press, 1959.

24

NATIONAL SECURITY PRIORITIES IN THE 1980s

One conclusion emerges clearly from the preceding chapters. The complexity of domestic and international politics in the emerging world order is matched only by the magnitude of the national security challenges likely to confront the United States in the 1980s. Wrapped around these difficulties is a veil of uncertainty regarding the proper role of the United States in the international security environment now taking shape. There is a growing awareness in many circles of the precariousness of the American geopolitical position, an awareness reflecting reservations about American political will and sense of direction as well as American military and economic power.[1] Few doubt that this country retains legitimate security interests and objectives in the world. Precisely what those interests and objectives should be will be the subject of continuing debate.[2]

Trends in the International Political System. The most important characteristic of the emerging international security environment is at the same time the least amenable to manipulation by any single nation—the changing structure of power and influence in the world. The international political system is in a state of flux. It is beyond bipolarity in a number of respects, even taking into account the literal inappropriateness of that term during the bitterest days of the original cold war, when the world was mostly divided between the camps of the Soviet-led East and the American-led West.[3] The increasing tension between the industrialized nations of the "North" and the poorer developing countries of the "South" has further complicated the state of contemporary international politics. Indeed, some believe that the North-South cleavage is becoming of greater significance for the resolution of global security concerns than either the East-West or the intrabloc differences that still exist.[4]

It is also clear that power has diffused in the international political system. What is not so apparent is the actual extent of that diffusion, or what it means for the ability of one nation to influence another nation on issues of vital concern to both of them. The world remains essentially *bipolar* if one thinks in terms of the strategic nuclear balance, or even of aggregate military capabilities.[5] No other country's strategic arsenal or total military establishment is likely to approach that of either of the superpowers in size and sophistication for many years.

In terms of diplomatic power, the world has assumed a largely *tripolar* cast, though in some circumstances it is multipolar in character. The People's Republic of China commands the respect, and is accorded the status, of a major power on most geopolitical questions, for reasons that have been discussed in Chapter 17 and elsewhere.*

On the economic dimension, the situation is even more complicated. Here the world can properly be considered to have truly a *multipolar* structure. As explained in Chapter 22, Japan and the European community (and, perhaps, Germany and one or two other countries in the EEC considered alone) are major industrial powers, even if the energy lifeline on which their productivity depends is in the hands of an unstable, and potentially hostile, "resource power center," i.e., OPEC. The continued rise of regional power centers, such as Brazil, Nigeria, India, and Vietnam, only makes matters more complex.†

The confusing distribution of effective power in world politics does not imply a corresponding increase in the number of actual or potential threats to the security of the United States, or to that of any other nation. It does, however, increase the complexity of the environment within which the United States and all countries must attempt to secure themselves. The changed and diffuse distribution of power also adds to the uncertainties with which national security policy-makers in every country must deal, and reduces the ability of any single country to manage the problems confronting it in a purely national context. Nations are not yet truly interdependent, but solely national solutions to national problems are no longer feasible in many instances.[6]

Occasional claims to the contrary notwithstanding, peace remains as elusive as ever in our increasingly small and better-armed world. It is true that most nations—even the most belligerent of them—have been at peace most of the time. Over the past 150 years, for example, more than half of the countries in the international political system have not gone to war.[7] Some conflicts of

---

*The notion that China can be considered a major power was explicit in the original Nixon Doctrine and has been reflected in other analyses of the U.S. decision to normalize relations with the P.R.C. See James E. Dornan, Jr., "The Nixon Doctrine and the Primacy of Detente," *Intercollegiate Review* 9 (spring 1974); and Richard Burt, "Chinese Card: How to Play It," *New York Times,* December 20, 1978.

†It is by no means certain that the greater complexity attending a further diffusion of power on any dimension will necessarily increase the likelihood of conflict in the international system. For classic contending views on this subject, see Karl W. Deutsch and J. David Singer, "Multipolar Power Systems and International Stability," *World Politics* 16 (April 1964); Richard Rosecrance, "Bipolarity, Multipolarity, and the Future," *Journal of Conflict Resolution* 10 (September 1966); and Kenneth Waltz, "International Structure, National Force, and the Balance of World Power," *Journal of International Affairs* 21 (1967).

interest in certain parts of the world, however, simply may not be amenable to peaceful resolution.* Moreover, major powers are prone to intervene, overtly or covertly, in the affairs and conflicts of other countries. Conflicts that might once have escaped the attention of outside powers now seem to draw them into the vortex.

The historical basic conflicts of interest between the United States and either the Soviet Union or the P.R.C. are unlikely to be resolved in the foreseeable future. Each communist state may wish to improve its relations with the United States (and other Western countries as well), in part because of its rivalry with the other communist state, in part because each wishes to have access to American (and Western) technology, skills, and markets to further the modernization of its own economy. It would be a grievous error, however, to mistake conciliatory tactical gestures on the part of either communist nation for a fundamental strategic reorientation in its long-term attitude toward the United States. Realistic détente, including a certain degree of accommodation on all sides, is certainly possible. The Soviet Union and the P.R.C., however, will undoubtedly continue to attempt to extend their influence at the expense of the United States and its allies.

Further, there is a fundamental incompatibility between levels of success in American pursuit of cordial relationships with the Soviet Union and the P.R.C., on the one hand, and the maintenance of the U.S.-centered system of political-military alliances, on the other. Those alliances are predicated on the presumed existence of security threats from those powers or their proxies, as well as on the belief in allied capitals that the United States gives precedence to the interests of its allies over its bilateral relations with either Moscow or Beijing. Better relations (short-term or not) between the United States and either communist power necessarily undermine those perceptions, thereby reducing both the cohesion of the U.S. alliance system and this country's prospects for dealing successfully with the U.S.S.R. and the P.R.C.[8]

As explained in Chapter 2, there are many general constraints on the actual or threatened use of force to settle disputes or to pursue national policy objectives. An increasing number of reservations have surfaced about the legitimacy of the use of force in international affairs, at least within many Western democracies. (Authoritarian regimes do not seem to be inhibited to the same degree.) The proliferation of ever more sophisticated weapons systems throughout the world means that, in the future, the costs of coercion may well exceed the anticipated benefits of success. Prudence counsels against undue reliance on military force, for success has never been a certainty for even the strongest of nations—as the United States learned in the morass of Indochina.† The possibility of escalation, intentional or otherwise, to the deployment of nuclear weapons under certain circumstances also serves to constrain the use of force to resolve controversies.[9]

---

*The Middle East and southern Africa are particularly striking examples of this phenomenon.
†The British and Russian experiences in the Boer and Russo-Finnish wars, respectively, suggest how expensive even a hard-won "success" may be to the "victor."

Yet in an important sense Mao Zedong was right—power does grow out of the barrel of a gun. Even the effective use of diplomatic pressure or economic leverage often reflects the ability to employ military force, either independently or in concert with other nations, if the other means fail. Since the military balance of power is relative and dynamic, every nation's status and influence change in accordance with shifts in its position in that balance. Military power retains political utility—something certain countries seem to understand with greater clarity than others—and a military establishment that is both capable and credible remains the cornerstone of national security.*

Each of these considerations is relevant to the position of the United States in the emerging international security environment. The prevalence of conflict and the enduring centrality of military power in world politics suggest the existence of a number of challenges, some longstanding and others new, to American security interests. The ineffectual character of the United Nations on questions affecting the security of the major powers, plus the continued dependence of American allies on the United States for their own security, place the principal burden for the maintenance of both American interests and a stable world balance on the power of the United States.

That burden will not be borne easily. The United States must reckon with a number of specific limits on its ability to safeguard American national security and exercise influence in world affairs. Militarily, the United States confronts a Soviet Union that has achieved at least parity in strategic nuclear weapons. Indeed, in the opinion of many respected analysts, the Soviets are on the verge of achieving some form of strategic superiority over the United States.[10] The Soviet army is the most powerful in the world, and the blue-water naval capabilities of the U.S.S.R. are impressive and growing, even discounting Soviet possession of the world's largest submarine force.

The burden will be heavy in another sphere as well—the American economy has already shown signs of considerable strain. Inflation and unemployment at home are matched by the country's balance-of-trade difficulties and the weakness of the American dollar. In political terms, many observers at home and abroad have reservations about the extent to which popular support for a more activist foreign policy will be sustained in times of stress. There are even more fundamental reservations about the ability of the American policy-making process to come to terms with the difficulties with which the country must deal. In the diplomatic sphere, doubts about the reliability of American security commitments persist, reinforced by a lack of strategic consistency and direction which all too often seems to characterize the formulation and implementation of contemporary American national security policy.

This is not to say that Moscow's own diplomacy has gone unchallenged. Afghan rebels and Polish strikers have defied the monolithic rule of the Soviet

---

*The Soviet Leadership, for example, seems to understand this point far better than some American and other Western leaders. See Edward N. Luttwak, *The Grand Strategy of the Soviet Union* (New York: St. Martin's Press, 1983).

Union and reinforced the conclusion that the Sino-Soviet split was not a "great aberration." The Kremlin's reaction to defiant allies has been the antithesis of the U.S. response to communist-inspired insurrections in friendly states. While Washington was telling the nation "directly threatened to assume the primary responsibility of providing the manpower for its defense,"[11] the Soviets have been advancing the "Brezhnev Doctrine of limited sovereignty"[12] to the effect that the Red Army would be used to assist communist nations threatened by antirevolutionary forces—a threat that may yet be carried out in Poland.

U.S. liabilities aside, the assets available to the United States to meet these challenges are considerable. The United States is clearly a superpower with a strategic nuclear arsenal matched only by that of the Soviet Union. It possesses one of the largest and most sophisticated military establishments in the world. It has an unparalleled degree of "global reach"—the ability to project conventional forces abroad—centered on its long-range airlift, carrier task forces, and amphibious capability. The United States has the largest GNP in the world, one of the highest standards of living of any industrialized country, and one of the world's most productive and diversified economies. In political terms, by 1980 the United States had recovered surprisingly well from much of the domestic dissent that ravaged the country during the Vietnam War. As the decade of the 1980s began, an increasing number of Americans appeared willing to support a more assertive U.S. foreign and national security policy than was the case only a few years before. The resurgence of support was explained in part by the accumulation of evidence concerning a continuous growth in Soviet military power over the years.[13] Finally, the majority of U.S. alliances remain intact, and most U.S. allies are willing to stand by them, if only for lack of better alternatives.

A nation's position in the world, of course, cannot be ascertained merely by producing a balance sheet of its assets and liabilities, as if a nation were simply a corporation writ large. *Trends* are also important. A nation whose relative power is perceived to be increasing will tend to be more assertive, to project a more positive image abroad, and to have greater influence on the course of international affairs than one whose relative power is seen to be declining, *even if their absolute capabilities are essentially equivalent.**

In fact, despite limited improvement in the U.S. position after 1975, its influence is less favorable on the trends basis than a simple comparison of American assets and liabilities would suggest. U.S. ability to shape world affairs has weakened since the onset of the cold war, or even since the Cuban Missile Crisis of 1962. The intervening years have seen the passing of American strategic superiority and American economic preeminence, both of which contributed to the maintenance of American geopolitical paramountcy and

---

*This reflects differential degrees of (1) political will on the part of the various national elites, (2) domestic support for assertive foreign policies, and (3) perceptions abroad of both of the above.

the stability of the post–World War II international order.[14] A comparison of U.S. *relative* power and influence now and at the time of the Cuban Missile Crisis suggests the extent to which the U.S. position has deteriorated since 1962. Options open to this country then are closed to it now, and—of greatest significance—there has been a reduction in its prospects for success should such a confrontation involving similar interests recur at some point in the future.[15] President Carter's relatively weak foreign and national security policies may have been "realistic," in the sense that they corresponded to the world in which the United States found itself in the late 1970s.

Soviet perceptions of the evolving world order may reflect reality to a greater degree than those preferred by many Americans. An examination of the diplomatic record indicates that the most notable Western successes generally occurred in the 1950s and 1960s, when the relative power positions of the two superpowers were most favorable to the United States, whereas many of the most significant communist political gains have been made in more recent times. The so-called Nixon Doctrine and its related successors in many ways reflected this shift. Many of the formal Soviet-American or East-West accords reached since the United States began its disengagement from Vietnam also have implicitly acknowledged the shifting balance of power. The first SALT Treaty (SALT I) in 1972 certified Soviet strategic nuclear parity with the United States in general terms, and conceded to the U.S.S.R. an advantage in both land-based (ICBM) and sea-based (SLBM) intercontinental ballistic missiles. In practice, détente reflected American willingness to restrain itself and Soviet willingness to capitalize on Western self-restraint, the carefully prepared prose of the joint Soviet-American Declaration of Basic Principles notwithstanding. The Helsinki Treaty (1975) legitimized the postwar division of Europe and, thus, in a sense, Soviet hegemony in Eastern Europe. It also gave the Soviet Union and its Eastern European satellites access to badly needed Western technology and credits in exchange for the *hope* that there would be liberalization of political practices within the communist countries themselves. Even the U.S. decision to abrogate its defense treaty and to break diplomatic relations with Taiwan in order to recognize the P.R.C. has been construed by many as a signal of the failure of thirty years of American policy in Asia.[16*]

Learning from the Past. The question at this point is how the United States should manage a situation that has deteriorated but is not yet irretrievable. The first step we would suggest is for Americans to learn from their past experience what they as a nation can or cannot do and what key factors ought to be taken into account when setting American national security priorities for the 1980s.

---

*Supporters of the U.S. decision argue that the United States is simply rectifying a longstanding error by recognizing the government of one-quarter of the world's population. As noted earlier, however, the two positions are not necessarily incompatible.

Among the central problems the nation has experienced is the continuing lack of a clear sense of direction and priority in American national security policy. Simply put, the United States is entering an increasingly challenging era bereft of a coherent grand strategy, despite the past efforts of various governmental and academic tailors to clothe American strategy in more fitting attire. Many would hold that the absence of a comprehensive strategy has been a principal source of many of this country's difficulties in recent years. American policy from the doctrine of containment onward has been largely defensive and reactive, thereby conceding the strategic initiative to the U.S.S.R., the P.R.C., and other regional powers that chose to challenge American interests or U.S. allies.[17]

An appropriate, preferred role for America in the global community has yet to be persuasively defined. A clear definition of legitimate and defensible U.S. national security interests is both needed and difficult to formulate. Moreover, American military power is inadequately linked to American political purpose. Despite changes in the military balance, U.S. commitments remain virtually unchanged, projecting an image of overextension that weakens the credibility of U.S. response.

Second, it is apparent that the U.S. national security process is far from being the coherent and integrated whole that one might wish it to be. In part, this both reflects and contributes to the lack of a clear sense of direction in American policy. But it is also a function of inadequate public attention and understanding, jousting by interest groups, interservice rivalries, and even division of authority within the federal government itself. In terms of the American national security process, it seems that the nation has a "checks and balances" system that checks more readily than it balances and that all too often permits policy to be guided by concerns other than those directly related to American national interests. De Tocqueville's judgment of the "democratic dilemma" applies to our situation where internal problems inhibit the formulation and implementation of U.S. national security policy.[18]

Third, as explained earlier (see especially Chapter 3), public support is clearly essential for the success of any national security policy. Yet public opinion is also an unreliable guide to the selection and implementation of any such policy. The American mood toward foreign affairs remains unstable at best, alternating between extremes of optimism and pessimism and overreacting to events.[19] The postwar domestic consensus on foreign policy was melted in the crucible of Vietnam, and has yet to be reforged. As Vietnam recedes in the public memory, public confidence is returning and with it a greater willingness to see the United States again act like a major power. That self-confidence is still fragile, however, and may not survive a major test of will and endurance in any situation that the American public does not clearly perceive to challenge the nation's vital interests. Public confidence is neither built nor maintained by policies of realpolitik. If a clearly good cause does not exist and if victory is neither pursued nor attainable, public support for a policy will quickly erode. The constraints this vacillation imposes upon the U.S. leadership are formidable.

Fourth, it appears that the United States may be unprepared to respond to most of the kinds of military challenge likely to confront it. The United States apparently can devastate its enemies if nuclear deterrence fails or can conduct brief interventions, as in the Dominican Republic in 1965. Yet its military capability between those extremes is not at all clear, as seen in the contexts of El Salvador and Chad in 1983.

There is, first of all, unclarity about the proper role of strategic and tactical nuclear weapons in an era of strategic nuclear parity between the superpowers. An effective nuclear strategy, as indicated in Chapter 11, must have both strategic purpose and strategic policies consonant with that purpose. Both seem lacking in an American nuclear strategy whose assumptions may have been valid in an era of U.S. nuclear superiority but which have less currency today in the altered strategic environment. Certainly, the threat of murder-suicide implicit in the notion of mutual assured destruction (MAD) is by itself an inadequate basis for credible deterrence.

Below the strategic nuclear level, differences continue over the employment of tactical nuclear weapons for limited war-fighting and for deterrence of threats of a lesser degree than a direct attack on the United States. As noted in Chapters 2 and 11, one school argues that, except for deterrence and prestige value, nuclear weapons are and should be unusable.[20] Advocates of this position assume there is no firebreak between smaller short-range (*tactical*) nuclear weapons and larger, long-range (*strategic*) nuclear weapons; any use will escalate rapidly to massive strategic exchange to no one's advantage. Recall that the other school argues that the United States must be prepared to fight with nuclear weapons, that Soviet tactical doctrine and training emphasize the offensive use of nuclear weapons, that Soviet armored vehicles are designed to provide protection from the effects of nuclear weapons, and that U.S. conventional forces should, but do not, have similar capabilities to serve as a deterrent and for fighting on a nuclear battlefield should deterrence fail.[21] Refusal to recognize the logic of the latter school appears dangerous unless one believes in the ultimate success of negotiations with the Soviets concerning reductions in theater nuclear forces. In the mid 1980s, such success does not appear likely.[22]

During the 1950s, when the policy of massive retaliation emphasized the war-winning use of nuclear weapons, the armed forces embraced the notion of a nuclear battlefield. In the 1960s, when national policy shifted to flexible response, emphasizing conventional forces, so did the training of U.S. armed forces; there was a significant and abrupt deemphasis in training for a nuclear battlefield. U.S. military doctrine was revised and tactical organization changed to reflect the planning assumption that future wars would begin, and might for some considerable time remain, conventional. As the 1960s progressed, however, attention to mid-intensity conventional warfare increasingly declined in favor of such topics as counterinsurgency operations, special operations, and guerrilla warfare.

With the withdrawal of U.S. forces from Vietnam and the deemphasis on counterinsurgency signaled by the Nixon Doctrine, the armed forces redirected their attention to the Soviet threat in general and European security in particular. At the strategic level, efforts to revitalize the extended nuclear deterrent in conditions of strategic parity[23] resulted in the successive adjustments to strategic nuclear targeting policy described in Chapter 11. Below the strategic level, however, U.S. war-fighting doctrine continued for some time to exhibit the functional separation of conventional from nuclear operations characteristic of the late 1960s. Thus, for example, army tactical doctrine promulgated in the mid 1970s was largely silent on the subject of tactical nuclear employment, concentrating instead on the increased conventional lethalities exhibited in the 1973 Mideast war.

By the late 1970s, however, the growing Soviet capability to conduct battlefield nuclear operations could no longer be ignored. Examination of Soviet ground force equipment and exercises documented impressive efforts to improve survivability and combat effectiveness in a nuclear and/or chemical environment. Evidence also accumulated of Soviet development of the more diverse and discriminate weapons and delivery systems required to support battlefield nuclear operations.

Accordingly, as part of a general shift in U.S. tactical doctrine toward more fluid ground operations, the army at the beginning of the 1980s undertook a serious effort to "reintegrate" nuclear and chemical with conventional operations. This effort coincided with a long-overdue NATO commitment to modernize its increasingly obsolescent theater nuclear posture.

By 1983, however, both the army's new AirLand Battle Doctrine and the NATO nuclear force modernization effort were under political fire. For its part, the AirLand Battle Doctrine was assailed at home for its presumed reliance on improved high-technology weaponry and abroad for its emphasis on offensive maneuver and integrated nuclear-conventional operations. Concurrently, the NATO nuclear force modernization effort—and in particular, the deployment of new Pershing II and cruise missiles—provoked an upsurge of antinuclear sentiment, intensified by careless U.S. rhetoric about nuclear war-fighting and further fueled by intense Soviet propaganda efforts.

Together, these controversies have reopened the same questions of deterrence vice defense and reliance on nuclear vice conventional capabilities that so divided NATO in the early 1960s and that flexible response successfully resolved only by virtue of its inherent ambiguity. Today that comforting ambiguity stands increasingly exposed and, with it, growing differences in U.S. and European threat perceptions, security interests, and risk assessments.

Nor are these differences limited to European security. Disparity between ends and means is equally apparent in other potential theaters of conventional operations (southwest Asia, the Middle East, and northeast Asia). Essentially, the U.S. is attempting to maintain its present interests with relatively fewer general purpose forces than in the past, despite an increasing Soviet capability to project Soviet power into the Middle East and elsewhere.* The decline in American naval and strategic mobility forces is especially worrisome. The inadequacy of U.S. general purpose forces to deal with simultaneous threats in Europe and Asia, despite this country's longstanding commitment to those regions and the possibility that a war in Europe would be matched by one in Asia—or in the Middle East—at the same time underscores the magnitude of the U.S. problem.†

The inadequacy of U.S. national security policy also becomes apparent when compared with the requirements of low intensity conflict. The intractability of such conflicts was made apparent in the course of the Indochina conflict, which revealed the enormous obstacles confronting any effort to manage such protracted, limited conflicts. The conclusions reached in Chapter 12 need to be reiterated: the localization of such conflicts will be difficult to achieve, reciprocity for any U.S. self-imposed restraint in the conduct of a war is unlikely to be forthcoming, and "success" in such conflicts—however that might be defined—will be exceedingly difficult either to measure or to attain.

The maxim that "a democratic state goes to war at its peril" applies with particular force to the potential involvement of the United States in revolutionary war situations. The American experience in Vietnam suggests that any strategy predicated on the ability of U.S. forces to be the principal counter to such challenges will fail. There are some wars the United States can prevent by deterring a potential aggressor; there are other wars the United States can fight and win, if it must; but there are also wars that we cannot win, and so must not fight.‡ The knowledge that the United States has few viable options to meet the challenges of low-intensity conflict situations, other than provision of weapons and advice coupled with diplomatic initiatives, cannot be comforting to American decision-makers or to American allies, especially in the Third World.

The development of sound concepts to meet the varying kinds of challenge cited is of course only one of the essential elements of any national security policy. The effectiveness of the American military institution itself is of at

*The growth in Soviet naval power and ability to employ Cuban armed forces as de facto Soviet proxies in Africa are illustrative of this trend. See Steven F. Kime, "A Soviet Navy for the Nuclear Age," National Security Affairs Issue Paper No. 86 (Washington, D.C.: National Defense University Press, April 1980), pp. 16–20.
†The possibility that the U.S. would have to wage a two-front war against the U.S.S.R. is acknowledged by the Defense Department. See U.S., Senate, Committee on Armed Services, *Hearings, Department of Defense Authorization for Appropriations for Fiscal Year 1978,* 95th Cong., 1st sess., 1977, Part. 1, p. 109. See also William W. Kaufman, "Defense Policy," in *Setting National Priorities: Agenda for the 1980s,* ed. Joseph A. Peckman (Washington, D.C.: Brookings Institution, 1980), pp. 309–12.
‡The Nixon Doctrine acknowledged this point but apparently assumed that the admission would not adversely affect U.S. alliance relationships. Unfortunately, what constitutes a reduced risk for the U.S. means a reduction in the perceptions of the reliability of U.S. security guarantees to its allies.

least equal importance. The fundamental question concerning the American military establishment today is the sustainability of the all-volunteer force (AVF) concept.[24] It is generally recognized that the active components of the armed services in the late 1970s were barely able to attract sufficient numbers of reasonably qualified volunteers. What is not so well known is that the Selected Reserve had done even worse and that the Individual Ready Reserves (IRR) were by 1980 on the verge of disappearing, for all practical purposes. An inadequate reserve structure and the absence of a standby draft mechanism have hampered mobilization, although the Draft Registration Law of 1980 reflects a marginal improvement. Increasing personnel costs compound this "people problem," which is likely to become increasingly severe as the pool of available prime personnel declines in the mid 1980s and early 1990s. Barring significant changes, such as a return to the draft, a corresponding decline in the aggregate capabilities of the armed forces seems likely.

In sum, as the U.S. applies lessons of the past to priorities of the future it needs to reckon on the continuation of major threats to its vital interests, including those from the U.S.S.R. and, to a lesser degree, the P.R.C. Meeting these challenges will require establishing a clear, consistent sense of direction with the requisite public and congressional support behind it. Included therein is the necessity to develop appropriate military policies and forces to meet the entire range of possible challenges—which, in turn, will entail a greater defense effort and higher military troop levels. The past, particularly the recent past, teaches that the future will be both dangerous and difficult to manage.

Setting National Priorities. The foregoing considerations both define the boundaries within which U.S. national security priorities for the 1980s must be set, and emphasize the importance of acting promptly on those priorities once they are determined. The basic question to be addressed is how the United States can define its role, manage its relationships with allies and adversaries alike, and structure its forces and policies in order to optimize its prospects for success in the global arena.

The precise content of a new American grand strategy must take account of many factors whose consideration lies beyond the scope of this chapter. Whatever shape that strategy finally assumes, however, it should incorporate three basic principles:

1. The United States should not adopt a defensive posture that concedes the strategic political initiative to other countries, especially to the U.S.S.R. or the P.R.C. Such a concession allows other nations to determine when and where American interests will be challenged and American commitments activated. This places the United States at a disadvantage at the outset and increases the risk of strategic failure.
2. The essential Soviet-American strategic nuclear balance must not be permitted to shift further in favor of the U.S.S.R. Indeed, the relative Amer-

ican strategic nuclear position should be improved, even if that entails an indefinite postponement of SALT negotiations with the Soviet Union. Unless a stable—and not unfavorable—strategic nuclear balance is maintained, regional military balances and American credibility abroad will be equally difficult to sustain.

3. Whatever strategy is adopted must be backed by a domestic political consensus. America's global interests entail global responsibilities, the maintenance of which is exceedingly difficult to justify to much of the American electorate and many of their representatives. Responding to this situation may entail a narrower definition of U.S. interests, a more modest set of policy objectives, and a more conservative approach to national security issues than might be preferred in many circles. There is a distinction, however, between a *preferred* strategy and one that is at least minimally acceptable to the public. Domestic political realities argue for the latter course of action.

Although the precise nature of an optimal, practical strategy for the 1980s is obscure, it is clear that two frequently advanced strategic approaches are not among the viable alternatives. One is a *neo-isolationist* role, involving a modern variant of the "Fortress America" concept.* The other approach is *collective security*, which seeks security in some form of world government (or in its closest contemporary analogue, the United Nations).† The real choices are activist ones, involving a complex mix of measures to deal with the Soviet Union and the P.R.C., supported to some degree—hopefully, to a high degree—by Western Europe and Japan; further, the real choices will include policies to protect American interests in the Third World, especially in energy producing regions.

One basic element of any viable strategy appears clear. Barring some totally unforeseen change in the policies of the Soviet Union and the P.R.C., the United States must base its strategy on a viable Western security community in which economic competition is not permitted to undermine the more important political-military relationships among its principal members.[25] Within this community, Japan and the nations of Western Europe must assume more extensive and, in the near future, more expensive regional security roles.

The broad political-military policies of the principal Western countries must be more carefully coordinated than in the past. The United States must give greater attention to the legitimate regional interests of its allies, while the latter should recognize that U.S. military support entails an obligation on

---

*Even the most ardent advocates of the neo-isolationist position rarely argue that the U.S. should, or even can, truly isolate itself in the modern world. See Robert Tucker, *A New Isolationism: Threat or Promise?* (New York: Universe Books, 1972), for an appraisal of this approach.

†There is, of course, a distinction between collective security and world government as alternatives to the balance of power mechanism. See Inis L. Claude, Jr., *Power and International Relations* (New York: Random House, 1962).

their part to assist the United States in areas of central concern to this country. Unity and reciprocity, then, must be the hallmarks of a revitalized Western security community, the creation of which makes possible successful undertakings on a wide range of issues.

A related point is that the United States must bring its military forces into line with its commitments and develop realistic doctrines for their employment. Existing American capabilities are incompatible with declared U.S. commitments, and American strategic doctrine is singularly inappropriate in the present geopolitical environment. Unilateral reduction in U.S. commitments (as in the termination of the U.S. defense treaty with Taiwan), is a form of corrective action but one that might undermine U.S. influence and credibility. If present commitments are to be maintained, however, then U.S. military strength must be increased and both active and reserve components must be upgraded. We must also make choices regarding the relative emphasis to be placed on our strategic nuclear forces, tactical nuclear capabilities, and general purpose forces as well, differentiating among them on the basis of specific regional requirements. Trade-offs must also be made concerning the relative utility of naval and air general purpose forces on the one hand, and ground general purpose forces on the other, between the greater flexibility afforded by the former and the greater credibility of the U.S. commitment overseas indicated by the latter.[26] However, given the threat of low-intensity conflict for the future, ground forces will require greater flexibility than heretofore.[27]

Indications from the Reagan administration are encouraging to the extent that they reflect a heightened awareness of the need for revitalized conventional forces. Statements from Secretary of Defense Weinberger suggest a growing emphasis upon the full range of conventional forces, especially those earmarked for use outside the European theater.[28] Quantitative, and even qualitative, improvements in the current force structure are only part of the answer, however.

U.S. general purpose forces must also economize on personnel. This may imply placing greater emphasis on the materiel-intensive navy and air force, and less on the troop-intensive army and Marine Corps, than might be optimal and has been the case in the past. Careful reconsideration must also be made of the way in which general purpose ground forces are to be deployed overseas. *Some* forward basing of army and/or Marine Corps formations is politically and militarily essential. It is by no means certain that very large ground combat forces should be so deployed, at least in Europe, or even that the United States *can* forward deploy them in sufficient strength to wage a nonnuclear war there successfully.[29]

In this context of force adequacy, a searching examination must be made of the long-term viability of the AVF concept. It is becoming increasingly clear that there are few real alternatives open to the United States. If even 1983 force levels are to be maintained—especially within the context of the "Total Force" concept, which relies on rapid mobilization of the Reserve components—the options are limited to: (1) much higher levels of military compensation; (2) greater numbers of women in the armed services on an unrestricted duty basis; or (3) some version of a draft.

In all the services, recruiting and retaining quality personnel in both the active and the reserve forces had become critical problems by 1980. Given a series of "pay caps" in the late 1970s and the persistence of the "Vietnam Syndrome," those who had real income options seldom joined and remained in the armed services, and morale in military units was low indeed. From 1980 to 1983, however, there was a significant change in the personnel situations of all the services. Both recruitment and retention of young people with high school diplomas and who scored higher on military vocational tests increased, and morale in the armed forces improved markedly. What measurable factors caused such a change? First, military pay increases were high—14.1 percent in 1981 alone. Second, the American economy slid into a deep decline, with extraordinary inflation and double-digit recession. In brief, the cost of living (including costs of college tuition) soared and jobs became scarce; military service, a relatively high-paying "job," became attractive for America's youth. Smarter, better motivated young people found themselves serving with others of similar quality—and unit moral increased. Nevertheless, upper-middle-class Americans were still missing from the military ranks in early 1984.

What of the future? Four factors, taken together, make the outlook for the AVF appear dim. First, most 1983 projections of the U.S. economy indicate growth, relatively low inflation, and declining unemployment. Second, Congress has already begun cutting the Reagan Five-Year Defense Program. Rather than the 10 percent rate the administration wants, Congress is thinking more in terms of 4 percent growth.[30] Already, for FY 1984, Congress has capped the military pay increase at 4 percent.[31] Third, demographic projections indicate a decline in the prime military manpower pool in the mid 1980s and early 1990s.[32] The number of eighteen-year-old males will decline. Fourth, although the Vietnam Syndrome, which manifested itself partially in American antimilitarism and neutral attitudes on military service, may be passing, some observers see a danger of similar attitudes toward military service growing from the nuclear freeze and peace movements in America.

Given a high probability that some or all these factors will become operative, an alternative to the AVF should be studied seriously and planned for future implementation. There are several alternatives; however, given the increasing strategic importance of the reserves for the low-intensity conflict environment of the future, a "reserves-only draft" appears optimal. Reserve duty involves only an initial period of training, followed by a requirement to report for paid training at a nearby reserve unit only one weekend per month. In addition to supporting strategic requirements, such a draft could have additional benefits: (1) test the willingness of America's youth to serve; (2) send a signal of national security commitment to potential U.S. adversaries; and (3) send a signal to America's allies (almost all of whom have draft systems) of a renewed willingness of Americans to stand behind the nation's national security commitments.[33]

From the suggestions concerning improvements in current force structures and levels of readiness, however, one should not draw the inference that American national security can be enhanced solely through efforts aimed at augmenting forces-in-being. As noted in Chapter 23, there is a clear relationship between our national security and arms control. Nonetheless, there is a further link between the objective of arms control and the forces that a nation has on hand. Simply stated, the attainment of arms control measures is dependent to some degree on the maintenance of adequate force levels; one cannot negotiate effectively from a position of military inferiority. Statements from the Reagan administration reflect an appreciation of the relationship between force levels and arms control. In his annual report to the Congress for FY 1984, Secretary of Defense Weinberger addressed this point.

What is true, however, is that arms control negotiations must reflect the balance of power, including the forthcoming power obtainable from weapons under development. To the extent that we do make progress in modernizing our forces, the Soviet Union has a stronger incentive to negotiate in good faith, and we thus have a better opportunity to reach agreement on the control of arms.[34]

In setting priorities for the years ahead we must recognize that revitalizing America's military strength is the necessary prelude to effective arms control.

Nontraditional Security Considerations. In the increasingly interdependent world of the 1980s four other areas of challenge bear on national security and warrant brief attention: international economics, refugees, nuclear proliferation, and terrorism.

International Economics. There can no longer be any question—if indeed there ever was—that the broad framework of U.S. national security policy must be built upon the bedrock of a healthy economy. In addition to the obvious defense budget link between the state of the economy and the means to protect national security is Henry Kissinger's point that ''if we do not solve the problem of recession in the industrial democracies, no government is going to have enough public support to conduct long-range foreign policy.''[35]

Growing interdependence and the continued importance of the U.S. economy in the global economic system dictate that U.S. policy in this arena be driven, in the first instance, by policies aimed at revitalizing the American economy. High unemployment and interest rates have become the persistent symptoms of more fundamental ailments—declining American productivity and decreasing savings rates. Some reduction in governmental overregulation and overspending and the formulation of adequate incentives for investment spending are needed to encourage the modernization of aging American plants and to provide a long-term stimulus toward higher levels of productivity. If our domestic economic policies fail to address this crucial issue, other actions taken on the international level will serve merely as cosmetic solutions for symptoms of a more serious ailment.

As noted earlier, the overvaluing of the dollar abroad during the early 1980s cannot go unchecked without profoundly adverse domestic and international repercussions. More, however, is required here than the ad hoc intervention of the government to adjust the dollar temporarily. Restoration of a healthy international trading and financial system, as well as measures to strengthen American productivity, are also needed.

By the end of 1983 the first signs of world recovery from the simultaneous recessions in the industrial democracies, which marked the early 1980s, were beginning to appear. But the continued shakiness of world trade (with protectionism widespread and still gathering strength) and the problems of managing unprecedented levels of international debt threatened to stall or reverse the recovery. Particularly vulnerable were the weak economies of the LDCs, whose export markets were slow to revive and whose foreign debts were often so large that even paying the interest on them was beyond their means. Yet internal and regional stability in many vital areas of the Third World depends on the maintenance or improvement of inadequate living standards.

Whether the United States and its industrial allies can concert their domestic and international economic policies sufficiently to sustain their own recoveries, revive world trade, and succor the LDCs remains an open—but key—question. The lessons of interdependence, that the health of each depends on the health of all, do not come naturally to nation-states, particularly to ones such as the United States, which have traditionally been mostly self-sufficient.

Beyond the immediate problems of economic recovery, which may linger for some years, American policy-makers must wrestle with such persistent problems as East-West trade and technology transfer. Not only is there likely to be continuing divergent views within the United States on this matter, but it also tends to divide the West. If these disagreements cannot be managed, allied political and military cooperation will suffer. Similarly, unless compromises and acceptable trade-offs can be achieved in North-South economic relations, American interests can be severely damaged.

Refugees. A second nontraditional challenge will likely derive from the magnitude and complexity of the mounting worldwide refugee problem, which can prove to be one of the most significant and difficult issues of the next decade.[36] While reports concerning Soviet-American relations, Third World turmoil, and problems of energy and inflation dominated the front pages of the world's newspapers during the 1970s, the largely unnoticed mass movement across international borders of large portions of the world's population continued. In 1980 it was estimated that "in recent years, more than 15 million people worldwide have fled their homes as refugees—of war, civil unrest, persecution and hunger."[37] The U.S. general public has been largely unaware of refugee movements taking place outside North America, and uninformed of the potential implications of the overall problem for U.S. national security.

By 1980 the plight of the Vietnamese Boat People and the sudden exodus of over one hundred thousand Cuban citizens to southern Florida had served to focus American attention on refugee issues. And, for a time, the United States accepted Vietnamese and Cuban refugees en masse. Then, limiting measures were enacted in the 1980 Refugees Act. These are but sensational examples of a worldwide problem, however, about which there has been considerable rhetoric but little concrete action in seeking solutions. From Kampuchea, Afghanistan, Ethiopia, and many other countries, refugees totaling in the millions have fled their homes. From 1978 to 1980 more than 1.2 million refugees fled to Somalia from southern and eastern Ethiopia, increasing Somalia's population by at least 25 percent.[38] For Somalia, a nation classified as one of the world's poorest countries, the financial strain caused by this exodus would be unbearable without international assistance.

The humanitarian concerns associated with the refugee problem are obvious. Undoubtedly, many Americans find it hard to blind themselves to the reality of a vast sea of homeless, starving, and destitute people. In mid 1983, there were still over 162,000 Vietnamese, Cambodians, and Laotians in refugee camps in Southeast Asia, and their living conditions were abysmal. In the first six months of 1983, 16,865 boat people risked piracy, rape, murder, and abduction to arrive in neighboring countries, where they were turned back, forced into refugee camps, or imprisoned.[39] Assistance in alleviating human suffering on a massive scale is not only consistent with concern for human rights, but also important in dealing with the unsettling political tensions that large refugee migrations spawn. In his final year in office, President Carter stated that U.S. foreign policy must strive "to blend commitment to high ideals with a sober calculation of our own national interests."[40] Recognizing the growing international security dimensions of the refugee problem, President Reagan in May 1983 signed into law National Security Decision Directive 93, "which for the first time suggests that almost everyone who has fled Cambodia should be considered as a political refugee, with a right to enter the United States."[41]

Refugee problems raise several national security questions. What should the U.S. response be in the event that the pursuit of refugees across an international border threatens escalation and expansion of a local conflict inimical to American national security interests, e.g., the Soviet Union into Pakistan or Vietnam into Thailand? Should humanitarian or national security considerations be the primary yardstick used to determine the amount of aid provided an asylum country? What will be the domestic consequences of allowing increasing millions of refugees or illegal migrants, for example, to enter the United States from Latin American areas, especially when they are unwilling or unable to identify with U.S. values, traditions, and customs?

Nuclear Proliferation. A third nontraditional area of challenge to U.S.

"NO, SON. THAT'S NOT LAND"

Reprinted with permission of Ranan R. Lurie from his book, *Lurie's Worlds, 1970–1980*
(Hawaii: University Press of Hawaii, and King Features Syndicate, Inc., 1980).

security interests derives from the problems of nuclear proliferation. The
dangers that could result from possession and irresponsible use of nuclear
devices by terrorists or by any number of countries—primarily in the developing world—are obvious. As signatory to and leader in the Nuclear Non-
Proliferation Treaty (NPT) of 1968, the United States has adopted less than
coherent and far-sighted policies on nuclear proliferation. As a result, the
nation risks finding itself overtaken by events, with inadequate planning for
reasonably predictable challenges in the next decade. In several key areas,
policy weaknesses were evident in 1983.

First, there was a lack of consistency and focus in U.S. policy on proliferation. The U.S. response to India's violation of a key NPT provision prohibiting diversion of nuclear materials for military purposes provides an example. By May 1974 India had diverted enough materials from its Canadian-
supplied research center to test a nuclear device. Canada had signed the NPT;
India had not. The nuclear detonation by India clearly violated a fundamental
nonproliferation goal of the United States. Initially, the United States attempted a combination of diplomatic pressure and threat to cut off Indian
nuclear fuel supplies; it then lapsed into passive acquiescence. In 1980, when
India threatened to seek nuclear fuel supplies elsewhere, the United States—
after an internal battle—delivered the requested enriched uranium. The lesson

to be learned by other nations appeared to be that they could not be confident about the type or timing of U.S. actions toward violators of fuel cycle accords.

There has also been inadequate attention to incentives to persuade other nations to follow a U.S. lead in nonproliferation. Only potential violators were addressed; only negative incentives proposed. For various reasons, the United States has not proven to be a reliable supplier of nuclear materials and services to nations observing their NPT obligations. Moreover, American policy has failed to recognize that nonnuclear arms aid or other assistance can help meet the genuine security fears of states that might otherwise seek recourse to nuclear weapons.

New developments in the field of nuclear weapons technology had by 1980 changed some of the assumptions under which U.S. proliferation policy operated in the 1970s. Exclusive possession of scientific knowledge concerning weapons technology no longer provides the political opportunity to prevent proliferation. Most nations now have the knowledge or ready access to it. Second, developing fuel technology has shortened the time required for weapons development to a matter of months. Finally, weapons made in the 1980s do *not* have to be tested. They can be built quickly and stored surreptitiously, with a high degree of confidence that they can be detonated when needed. These changes, along with the shortcomings of existing policy, indicate a need for revising not only the thrust but also the scope of U.S. proliferation policy for the 1980s.

Guidelines for a realistic reappraisal of U.S. proliferation policy are several. Long-term planning is necessary. Planners must consider the most realistic, eventual future scenario—a world proliferated by dozens of nuclear-armed states. Having already developed the "worst case," our planning for any lesser case should be much more manageable.[42] Contingency options for both active and passive military actions against proliferators who threaten U.S. security directly should be developed. Active options would include better intelligence acquisition and planning for the use of surgical strikes on nuclear facilities and delivery systems; passive options would include construction of thin anti-ballistic missile shields, civil defense efforts, and increased border and coastal surveillance. Incentives should be reviewed, with consideration of possible offers of positive incentives to potential victims of nuclear weapons. For example, the United States might enter security pacts, agreeing to retaliate against specified nations acquiring nuclear weapons, or agreement violators would know that their neighbors probably would be the immediate recipients of U.S. manufactured long-range delivery systems, Nike-Hercules missiles, or atomic demolition munitions.

Terrorism. A final set of nontraditional challenges to U.S. security derives from the threat of terrorism at the international, national, and even local levels. Although this threat is increasing, there are few realistic policies or programs on the horizon for its containment. One reason for the growth of this frightening phenomenon is that "very few people in the civilized world—governments, parliaments, journalists and the public generally—take terrorism seriously enough.''[43] Mass hostage situations have become commonplace, only highlighted by seizure in 1979 of American Embassy officials by Iranian militants. Key political figures are murdered or taken hostage, business executives are murdered or kidnapped, planes are hijacked; far worse, the specter of threats, blackmail, or mass murder by terrorists armed with nuclear devices in a nuclear proliferating world haunts those who contemplate the trends.[44] The problem appears intractable as the world observes national leaders, their protestations notwithstanding, negotiating in apparent helplessness with those operating clearly outside the rule of existing international and domestic legal systems.

Some analysts fear that the necessities of programs effective against terrorism will create a "democratic dilemma." Thus, the principles of constitutional democracy appear to guarantee individual rights that protect terrorists as well as their actual or intended victims. Putting the same point differently, if the nations that are constitutional democracies—or even the United Nations, which is founded upon similar principles—were to adopt forceful measures to interdict terrorist activities, they would have to abandon the fundamental principles of individual liberty and thus be transformed to the likeness of the repressive governments they abhor.[45] Yet tougher and better coordinated action against terrorism must be pursued, lest democratic values be lost through violence and anarchism.

The "justice" of the goals of various terrorist organizations is widely debated. Since the causes of terrorism are many and varied and there is little agreement about them, no consensus exists on precise solutions to the problem. Many government agencies in many nations, including the United States, have offices charged with the responsibility for developing policies designed to deal with terrorism. Many studies, books, and articles dealing with various aspects of terrorism have been published privately. Yet effective solutions clearly are not at hand.

In the United States, federal, state, and local government officials and the public alike should be led to understand that terrorism is no longer just another marginal problem, and they should be provided the rationale behind and both short- and long-term policy proposals for dealing with it. In the short run, repression may be the only answer, requiring special legislation and powers of investigation and prosecution for terrorist activities. At the international level, similar grants of extraordinary authority for some form of international investigatory and law enforcement authority may be essential. In order to gain international cooperation, the vast majority of national governments and certainly the permanent members of the U.N. Security Council must be persuaded that terrorism is an imminent threat and that they share a fundamental security interest in meeting it.

For the democratic nations of the world, the long-term answer to terrorism probably rests in reintroducing elements of stability in their social systems which have been weakened over recent decades. The vast majority of the world's known terrorists are university-educated males, ages twenty-two to twenty-five, from middle to upper class, urban families; these are mostly individuals whose personal views have been shaped by the philosophies of the extreme left or right, which advocate violence and abhor the very foundations of constitutional democracy.[46]

Setting U.S. national security priorities to cope with these various nontraditional challenges of the 1980s is a monumental task requiring the best of intellect, determination, experience, political skills, and selfless service. National security goals, interests, objectives and policies must be supported by action programs that require sacrifices to sustain them. The competition for attention and resources to serve alternative goals, interests, and objectives is likely to be more severe in the 1980s than heretofore. Acquiring the support of the American public and its representatives requires a carefully considered, sustained, and straightforward approach by the nation's leadership.

Conclusion: Making America's Choices. The central theses of this chapter can be stated directly. The world is increasingly complex; the balance of power therein is changing; and security is increasingly uncertain, even for a major power such as the United States. The U.S. role in world affairs must be reappraised in light of this country's reduced position in the emerging international security environment relative to that which existed in the pre-Vietnam era. Unfortunately, many U.S. policies at the turn of the decade of the 1980s were little more than attempts to rationalize an American retrenchment. There are significant constraints on the formulation and implementation of a comprehensive U.S. national security policy appropriate to meeting the demands being placed on this country in the evolving situation. On balance, however, a hard, realistic, "power politics" game played by a militarily preeminent United States within a strong Western security community offers this country the best prospects for success. History is littered with the wreckage of nations and empires that attempted to ignore the ancient lessons of power in world politics. The Reagan administration appears to know those lessons. It remains to be seen, however, if the Congress or the American public are prepared to sacrifice scarce American resources to develop requisite capabilities.

Finally, it should be recognized that only this country can safeguard American interests and underwrite American security. The United Nations is relatively impotent on all important issues. America's allies remain dependent on the United States for their own security. No other nation will defend American interests or act in concert with this country if there is a sense of apprehension concerning American power, political will, and sense of direction.

America's choices are not simply a matter of aligning with one set of nations or another. The alternatives concern whether or not the American people have the will to permit the United States to be and act as a major power— or are content to rationalize and to accept the dominance of others. A hesitant America, disengaging from its commitments and uncertain as to its role, will inspire disillusion among its allies and confidence on the part of its adversaries. A strong, self-confident America will help create the conditions for its own security, and that of its allies and friends.

DISCUSSION QUESTIONS

1. What are the principal characteristics of the emerging international security environment? Which is most important? Why?

2. Discuss the geopolitical implications of different degrees of "polarity" in the international political system for U.S. national security in the 1980s.

3. What is the utility of collective security today? What role does a collective security organization play in the affairs of a major power? What can be done to increase its relevance to American national security concerns?

4. What is the geopolitical position of the United States today relative to that of the U.S.S.R.? How has American power and influence changed since the beginning of the original cold war? Why have those changes occurred?

5. What are the principal lessons of the past that can be derived from an inspection of the U.S. conduct of its national security policy since the end of World War II? What do those lessons suggest about the ability of the United States to manage its security affairs in the next decade?

6. How well does American doctrine deal with the employment of strategic and tactical nuclear weapons? What can, or should, be done to upgrade U.S. nuclear weapons doctrine?

7. How would you appraise the present status and future prospects of the AVF? What would either the retention or the rejection of the AVF concept mean for the future direction of American national security policy?

8. What is the single greatest national security need of the United States today? Why is it important for the future conduct of U.S. national security policy? What principles should be incorporated in it, and why?

9. What is the optimal political role of the United States in the emerging world order? What are the principle alternatives to it?

10. What is the current role of military power in world politics? How has that role changed since 1945? Is military power likely to have greater, less, or the same political utility in the 1980s as at present? Why?

RECOMMENDED READING

Aron, Raymond. *The Imperial Republic: The United States and the World, 1945–1973.* Translated by Frank Jellinek. Englewood Cliffs, N.J.: Prentice-Hall, 1974.

Baldwin, David A., ed. *America in an Interdependent World.* Hanover, N.H.: University Press of New England, 1976.

Brodie, Bernard. *Escalation and the Nuclear Option.* Princeton: Princeton University Press, 1966.

Brown, Harold. *Thinking about National Security.* Boulder, Colo: Westview Press, 1983.

Brzezinski, Zbigniew. *Power and Principle.* New York: Farrar, Straus & Giroux, 1983.

Cole, Paul M., and Taylor, William J., Jr., eds. *The Nuclear Freeze Debate: Arms Control Issues for the 1980s.* Boulder, Colo.: Westview Press, 1983.

Collins, John M., and Cordesman, Anthony. *Imbalance of Power.* San Rafael, Calif.: Presidio, 1978.

Council on Foreign Relations. *America and the World, 1982.* New York: CFR, 1983.

Hoffmann, Stanley. *Primacy or World Order.* New York: McGraw Hill, 1978.

Komer, Robert W. "Maritime Strategy versus Coalition Defense." *Foreign Affairs* 60, no. 5 (summer 1982).

Luttwak, Edward N. *The Grand Strategy of the Soviet Union.* New York: St. Martin's Press, 1983.

Moulton, Harland B. *From Superiority to Parity.* Westport, Conn.: Greenwood, 1973.

Peckman, Joseph A., ed. *Setting National Priorities: Agenda for the 1980s.* Washington, D.C.: Brookings Institution, 1980.

Sabrosky, Alan Ned. "The United States in Asia: A Forward Strategy in the Pacific Basin." In *United States National Security Policy in the Decade Ahead.* Edited by James E. Dornan, Jr. New York: Crane, Russak, 1978.

Singer, J. David, and Small, Melvin. *The Wages of War.* New York: John Wiley, 1972.

Spero, Joan Edelman. *The Politics of International Economic Relations.* New York: St. Martin's, 1977.

Summers, Harry G. *On Strategy: The Vietnam War in Context.* Carlisle, Penn.: Strategic Studies Institute, U.S. Army War College, 1981.

Taylor, William J., Jr., and Kupperman, Robert H., eds. *Strategic Requirements for the Army to the Year 2000.* Lexington, Mass.: Lexington Books, 1984.

Taylor, William J., Jr., and Maaranen, Steven A., eds. *The Future of Conflict in the 1980s.* Lexington, Mass.: D. C. Heath, 1982.

Taylor, William J., Jr.; Maaranen, Steven A.; and Gong, Gerrit W., eds. *Strategic Responses to Conflict in the 1980s.* Lexington, Mass.: Lexington Books, 1984.

Taylor, William J., Jr.; Olson, Eric T.; and Schrader, Richard, eds. *Defense Manpower Planning: Issues for the 1980s.* New York: Pergamon, 1981.

Watts, William, and Free, Lloyd A. "Nationalism, Not Isolationism." *Foreign Policy,* no. 24 (fall 1976).

Whetten, Lawrence L., ed. *The Political Implications of Soviet Military Power.* New York: Crane, Russak, 1977.

NOTES

CHAPTER 1

1. Helmut Schmidt, "The 1977 Alastair Buchan Memorial Lecture," October 28, 1977, reprinted in *Survival* (London: International Institute for Strategic Studies, January-February 1978).

2. For a more thorough expression of Professor Hoffman's categorization, see his *State of War* (New York: Frederick A. Praeger, 1965), pp. 3–21.

3. Hans J. Morgenthau, *Politics among Nations,* 5th ed. (New York: Alfred A. Knopf, 1973).

4. Morton A. Kaplan, "Variants on Six Models of the International System," in *International Politics and Foreign Policy,* ed. James N. Rosenau (New York: Free Press, 1969), pp. 291–303.

5. Still one of the best surveys of the field is James E. Dougherty and Robert L. Pfaltzgraff, Jr., *Contending Theories of International Relations* (Philadelphia: J. B. Lippincott, 1971).

6. J. David Singer, "The Level of Analysis Problem in International Relations," in *International Politics,* ed. Rosenau, pp. 21–22.

7. John Foster Dulles, *War or Peace* (New York: Macmillan 1950), pp. 72–73.

8. See Henry A. Kissinger, *American Foreign Policy,* 3d ed. (New York: W. W. Norton, 1977), pp. 416–17.

9. Wolfram F. Hanrieder, "The International System: Bipolar or Multibloc?" in *The International Political System: Introduction & Readings,* ed. Romano Romani (New York: John Wiley & Sons, 1972), pp. 188–89.

10. K. J. Holsti, *International Politics: A Framework for Analysis,* 2d ed. (Englewood Cliffs, N.J.: Prentice-Hall, 1972), pp. 155–56.

11. Harold Sprout and Margaret Sprout, *Foundations of National Power,* 2d ed. (New York: D. Van Nostrand Co., 1951), pp. 108–11.

12. Clifford German, "A Tentative Evaluation of World Power," *Journal of Conflict Resolution* 4, no. 1 (March 1960): 138–44.

13. Ray S. Cline, *World Power Assessment, 1977* (Boulder, Colo.: Westview Press, 1977).

14. Klaus Knorr, *Military Power and Potential* (Lexington, Mass.: D. C. Heath, 1970), p. 143.

15. Holsti, *International Politics,* pp. 160–61.

16. These assumptions on power politics are variations of and suggested by those expressed in Charles O. Lerche, Jr., and Abdul A. Said, *Concepts of International Politics,* 2d ed. (Englewood Cliffs, N.J.: Prentice-Hall, 1970), pp. 109–10.

17. Hans Kelsen, "The Essence of International Law," in *The Relevance of International Law,* ed. Karl Deutsch and Stanley Hoffman (Garden City, N.Y.: Doubleday, 1971), p. 118.

18. George F. Kennan, *The Cloud of Danger: Current Realities of American Foreign Policy* (Boston: Little, Brown, 1977), p. 29.

19. Klaus Knorr, *On the Uses of Military Power in the Nuclear Age* (Princeton: Princeton University Press, 1966), p. 33.

20. Helga Haftendorn, "The Proliferation of Conventional Arms," Adelphi Papers, no. 133 (London: Institute for International and Strategic Studies, spring 1977), p. 34.

21. Daniel Bell, "The Future World Disorder," *Foreign Policy* 27 (summer 1977): 132–33.

22. Arthur S. Banks, ed., *Political Handbook of the World: 1977* (New York: McGraw-Hill, 1977), p. 497.

23. Lord Ritchie Calder, "The Doctor's Dilemma," *Center Magazine* 4, no. 5 (September-October 1971): 72.

24. Daniel J. Boorstin, *The Americans: The Democratic Experience* (New York: Random House, 1973), p. 598.

25. Lerche and Said, *Concepts of International Politics,* p. 137.

26. Samuel P. Huntington, "Transnational Organizations in World Politics," *World Politics* 25, no. 3 (April 1973):338–39.

CHAPTER 2

1. K. J. Holsti, *International Politics: A Framework for Analysis,* 2d ed. (Englewood Cliffs, N.J.: Prentice-Hall, 1972), p. 77.

2. Henry Bienen, *The Military and Modernization* (New York: Aldine Atherton, 1971), pp. 11–14.

3. See Bernard Brodie, *Strategy in the Missile Age* (Princeton: Princeton University Press, 1959), pp. 319–21.

4. Holsti, *International Politics,* p. 305.

5. See Thomas C. Schelling, *Arms and Influence* (New Haven: Yale University Press, 1966), pp. 69–86.

6. See J. I. Coffey, *Strategic Power and National Security* (Pittsburgh: University of Pittsburgh Press, 1971), pp. 72–73.

7. See David C. Gompert et al., *Nuclear Weapons and World Politics: Alternatives for the Future* (New York: McGraw-Hill, 1977), pp. 83–88.

8. Klaus Knorr, *On the Uses of Military Power in the Nuclear Age* (Princeton: Princeton University Press, 1966), pp. 67–68.

9. See Stanley Hoffman, *Gulliver's Troubles, or the Setting of American Foreign Policy* (New York: McGraw-Hill, 1968), pp. 418–21, and Hanson W. Baldwin, *Strategy for Tomorrow* (New York: Harper & Row, 1970), pp. 237–46. However, rearmament was again an issue of political debate in Japan in 1978.

10. See Hans J. Morgenthau, *Politics among Nations,* 5th ed. (New York: Alfred A. Knopf, 1973), pp. 532–40.

11. See the International Institute for Strategic Studies, *The Military Balance: 1979–1980* (London: IISS, 1980), pp. 11–12, and *U.S., Department of Defense Annual Report, Fiscal Year 1980* (Washington, D.C.: U.S. Government Printing Office, 1979), pp. 32–34.

12. See Chap. 22.

13. Knorr, *Military Power in the Nuclear Age,* p. 49.

14. See, for example, James R. Schlesinger et al., *Defending America* (New York: Basic Books, 1977), pp. 18–20, 35, passim.

15. *Webster's Third New International Dictionary of the English Language,* 2d ed., unabridged, p. 711.

16. Jerome D. Frank, *Sanity and Survival: Psychological Aspects of War and Peace* (New York: Random House, 1967), p. 139.

17. See Morton H. Halperin, *Defense Strategies for the Seventies* (Boston: Little, Brown, 1971), pp. 104–7.

18. Ibid., p. 109.

19. See André Beaufre, *Introduction to Strategy* (New York: Frederick A. Praeger, 1965), pp. 85–86.

20. For detailed presentation and analysis of "firebreaks," see Herman Kahn, *On Escalation: Metaphors and Scenarios* (New York: Praeger, 1965), and Klaus Knorr and Thornton Read, eds., *Limited Strategic War* (New York: Praeger, 1962), especially chaps. 1, 2, 3, and 8.

21. Adapted from Edward L. Warner III, "Escalation and Limitation in Warfare," in *American Defense Policy,* ed. Richard G. Head and Ervin J. Rokke, 3d ed. (Baltimore: Johns Hopkins University Press, 1973), p. 185.

22. See Alain C. Enthoven, "U.S. Forces in Europe: How Many? Doing What?" *Foreign Affairs* 53, no. 3 (April 1975): 512–32.

23. For the United States, even the world wars were "limited" in the sense that not all material resources were mobilized. See Henry A. Kissinger, "The Problems of Limited War," in *The Use of Force,* ed. Robert J. Art and Kenneth N. Waltz (Boston: Little, Brown, 1971), p. 102.

24. See Beaufre, *Introduction to Strategy,* p. 85.

25. For a detailed discussion of Soviet strategy, written by a marshal in the Soviet armed forces, see V. D. Sokolovskiy, *Soviet Military Strategy* (New York: Crane, Russak, 1975).

26. Kissinger, *Limited War,* p. 104.

27. See Samuel P. Huntington, *The Common Defense* (New York: Columbia University Press, 1961), pp. 342–43.

28. For the quotation on Vietnam, see W. Scott Thompson and Donaldson D. Frizzel, eds., *The Lessons of Vietnam* (New York: Crane, Russak, 1977), p. 279. For a discussion of limited war, see Robert E. Osgood, "The Reappraisal of Limited War," in Head and Rokke, *American Defense Policy*, pp. 168–69.

29. From St. Luke 14: 31–32.

30. See Barry M. Blechman and Stephen S. Kaplan, *The Use of the Armed Forces as a Political Instrument* (Washington, D.C.: Defense Advanced Research Projects Agency, 1976), pp. 3–5.

31. Ibid., p. 14.

32. Hans J. Morgenthau, *Politics among Nations,* 5th ed. (New York: Alfred A. Knopf, 1973), p. 80.

33. Blechman and Kaplan, *Armed Forces as a Political Instrument,* p. 18.

34. See Louis A. Dunn, *Controlling the Bomb: Nuclear Proliferation in the 1980s* (New Haven: Yale University Press, 1982).

35. See John Newhouse, *U.S. Troops in Europe: Issues, Costs, and Choices* (Washington, D.C.: Brookings Institution, 1971), p. 45.

36. See Bernard Brodie, "The Development of Nuclear Strategy," *International Security* 2, no. 4 (spring 1978): 76. Brodie suggests that all who refuse to envision the difference between use of tactical and strategic nuclear warfare are wrong.

CHAPTER 3

1. Gabriel A. Almond, *The American People and Foreign Policy,* 2d ed. (New York: Frederick A. Praeger, 1977), p. 54.

2. Alexis de Tocqueville, *Democracy in America* (New York: Alfred A. Knopf, 1945), vol. 1, pp. 234–35.

3. Walter Lippmann, quoted in Melvin Small, "Public Opinion," in *Encyclopedia of American Foreign Policy,* ed. Alexander DeConde (New York: Charles Scribner's Sons, 1978), vol. 3, pp. 844–45.

4. See Charles O. Lerche, Jr., *Foreign Policy of the American People,* 3d ed. (Englewood Cliffs, N.J.: Prentice-Hall, 1967), pp. 120–22. See also Daniel Yankelovich, "Farewell to 'President Knows Best,' " in *America and the World,* ed. Council on Foreign Relations (New York: Pergamon Press, 1978), pp. 670–93.

5. See, for instance, Gene E. Rainey, *Patterns of American Foreign Policy* (Boston: Allyn & Bacon, 1975), pp. 81–82.

6. Charles O. Lerche, Jr., and Abdul A. Said, *Concepts of International Politics,* 3d ed. (Englewood Cliffs, N.J.; Prentice-Hall, 1979), pp. 23–24.

7. See Ralph B. Levering, *The Public and American Foreign Policy, 1918–1978* (New York: William Morrow, 1978), p. 94.

8. Lyndon Johnson, reported in "An Interview with Eric Sevareid," *TV Guide,* March 14, 1970, pp. 6–7.

9. Arthur M. Schlesinger, Jr., *The Crisis of Confidence* (Boston: Houghton Mifflin, 1969), p. 135.

10. Ralph B. Levering, *The Public and American Foreign Policy,* pp. 134–37.

11. Ibid.

12. For details on one example of erosion—foreign aid—see the *Congressional Quarterly Weekly Report* 24 (May 15, 1976): 1163–64.

13. Lewis Burwell, quoted in R. W. Van Alstyne, *The Rising American Empire* (New York: Oxford University Press, 1960), p. 15.

14. Louis L. Snyder, ed., *The Imperialism Reader* (Princeton, N.J.: D. Van Nostrand, 1962), p. 20.

15. Thomas Jefferson, quoted in R. W. Van Alstyne, *The Rising American Empire,* p. 87.

16. See Frederick H. Hartmann, *The New Age of American Foreign Policy* (New York: Macmillan, 1970), p. 30.

17. Selig Adler, *The Uncertain Giant: American Foreign Policy between the Wars* (New York: Macmillan, 1965), pp. 87–92.

18. See Carl Becker, *The Declaration of Independence: A Study in the History of Political Ideas* (New York: Alfred A. Knopf, 1942), pp. 76–78.

19. Thomas Hobbes, *Leviathan* (New York: Collier Books, 1962), p. 100.

20. Ibid., p. 101.

21. See Robert' E. Osgood, *Limited War: The Challenge to American Strategy* (Chicago: University of Chicago Press, 1957), p. 38.

22. See Hans J. Morgenthau, *Politics among Nations*, 5th ed. (New York: Alfred A. Knopf, 1973), pp. 33–34.

23. Frederick H. Hartmann, *The Relations of Nations*, 4th ed. (New York: Macmillan, 1973), pp. 101–2; and Kenneth W. Thompson, *American Diplomacy and Emergent Patterns* (New York: New York University Press, 1962), pp. 45–46.

24. See Hartmann, *The Relations of Nations*, p. 102.

25. See Harry R. Davis and Robert C. Good, *Reinhold Niebuhr on Politics* (New York: Charles Scribner's Sons, 1960), pp. 308–13.

26. See Frederick Merk, *Manifest Destiny and Mission in American History* (New York: Alfred A. Knopf, 1963), p. 261.

27. Albert Gallatin, quoted in ibid., pp. 262–63.

28. See Lerche, *Foreign Policy*, pp. 110–11.

29. See Davis and Good, *Reinhold Niebuhr*, p. 140.

30. Karl von Clausewitz, *On War* (Princeton: Princeton University Press, 1976), p. 87.

31. Lerche, *Foreign Policy*, p. 117.

32. See Osgood, *Limited War*, p. 31.

33. Robert W. Tucker, *The Just War: A Study in Contemporary American Doctrine*, 2d ed. (Baltimore: Johns Hopkins University Press, 1979), p. 11.

34. See also Michael Walzer, *Just and Unjust Wars* (New York: Basic Books, 1977), pp. 76–78.

35. Harry S. Truman, quoted in ibid., p. 15.

36. Daniel J. Boorstin, *The Americans: The Colonial Experience* (New York: Random House, 1958), p. 356.

37. George Washington, quoted in ibid., p. 368.

38. James Gerhardt, *The Draft and Public Policy* (Columbus: Ohio State University Press, 1971), pp. 83–122.

39. Resolution, Continental Congress, quoted in Samuel P. Huntington, *The Soldier and the State* (Cambridge, Mass.: Belknap Press, 1957), p. 144.

40. George F. Kennan, *American Diplomacy, 1900–1950* (Chicago: University of Chicago Press, 1951), pp. 65–66.

41. President McKinley, quoted in Samuel Flagg Bemis, *A Diplomatic History of the United States* (New York: Henry Holt, 1955), p. 472.

42. Stanley Hoffmann, *Gulliver's Troubles, or the Setting of American Foreign Policy* (New York: McGraw-Hill, 1968), pp. 236–37.

43. See Almond, *The American People and Foreign Policy*, pp. 30–31, 48–50.

44. See ibid., p. 51.

45. The phrase, as well as the analysis that follows, is Rob Paarlberg's. See his "Forgetting about the Unthinkable," *Foreign Policy*, no. 10 (spring 1973), pp. 132–40.

46. Office of Civil Defense, Office of the Secretary of the Army, *Civil Defense and the Public: An Overview of Public Attitude Studies*, Research Report no. 17 (October 1971), pp. 31–32.

47. Ibid.

CHAPTER 4

1. Walter Lippman, *U.S. Foreign Policy: Shield of the Republic* (Boston: Little, Brown, 1943), p. 51.

2. Henry Kissinger, *American Foreign Policy* (New York: W. W. Norton, 1974), p. 13.

3. Samuel P. Huntington, *The Common Defense* (New York: Columbia University Press, 1961), pp. 3–4.

4. Henry T. Nash, *American Foreign Policy: Response to a Sense of Threat* (Homewood, Ill.: Dorsey Press, 1973), p. 19.

5. Huntington, *The Common Defense,* p. 35.

6. Nash, *American Foreign Policy*, p. 19.

7. George Kennan, "The Sources of Soviet Conduct," *Foreign Affairs* 25, no. 4 (July 1947): 575–76.

8. Walter Millis, ed., *The Forrestal Diaries* (New York: Viking Press, 1951), p. 350.

9. Huntington *The Common Defense*, p. 41.

10. Ibid., p. 42.

11. Ibid., p. 43.

12. Chief of Staff, *Final Report*, United States Army, February 7, 1948, pp. 11–12.

13. G. A. Lincoln, *Military Establishment Appropriations*, 1948, pp. 11–12.

14. Huntington, *The Common Defense*, p. 45.

15. Ibid., p. 47.

16. President Harry S. Truman, Address delivered to a joint session of Congress, March 12, 1947, reprinted in Joseph M. Jones, *The Fifteen Weeks* (New York: Harcourt, Brace & World, 1955), p. 272.

17. Nash, *American Foreign Policy*, p. 25.

18. Ibid., p. 29.

19. Warner Schilling, Paul Hammond, and Glenn Snyder, *Strategy, Politics, and the Defense Budget* (New York: Columbia University Press, 1962), p. 292.

20. Paul H. Nitze, "The Need for a National Strategy," Address delivered at Army War College, Carlisle Barracks, Pa., August 27, 1958.

21. Huntington, *The Common Defense*, p. 54.

22. For a discussion of U.S. perceptions of communist intentions, see Morton Halperin, *Limited War in the Nuclear Age* (New York: Wiley, 1963), chap. 3.

23. Huntington, *The Common Defense*, p. 54.

24. Ibid., p. 56.

25. Ibid., pp. 73–74.

26. Jerome Kahan, *Security in the Nuclear Age* (Washington, D.C.: Brookings Institution, 1975), p. 28.

27. *New York Times*, January 13, 1954, p. 2.

28. John Foster Dulles, "The Evolution of Foreign Policy," *Department of State Bulletin* 30 (January 25, 1954): 108.

29. Huntington, *The Common Defense*, p. 88.

30. Ibid., p. 92.

31. Ibid., pp. 96–97.

32. Morton Halperin, *Defense Strategies for the Seventies* (Boston: Little, Brown, 1971), p. 46.

33. Huntington, *The Common Defense*, p. 105.

34. John Foster Dulles, "Challenge and Response in U.S. Policy," *Foreign Affairs* 36, no. 1 (October 1951): 31.

35. Maxwell D. Taylor, *The Uncertain Trumpet* (New York: Harper, 1959), pp. 82–83.

36. William W. Kaufmann, *The McNamara Strategy* (New York: Harper & Row, 1964), p. 29.

37. Alain C. Enthoven and K. Wayne Smith, *How Much is Enough?* (New York: Harper & Row, 1971), p. 21.

38. U.S., Congress, House, Committee on Armed Services, *Hearings on Military Posture*, 85th Cong., 2d sess., 1962, p. 3162.

39. Kaufmann, *The McNamara Strategy*, pp. 53–54.

40. Ibid., p. 71.

41. Edward R. Fried, Alice M. Rivlin, Charles L. Schultze, and Nancy H. Teeters, *Setting National Priorities: The 1974 Budget* (Washington, D.C.: Brookings Institute, 1973), p. 292.

42. U.S. *Department of Defense Annual Report, Fiscal Year 1975* (Washington, D.C.: U.S. Government Printing Office), p. 22.

43. Halperin, *Defense Strategies for the Seventies,* p. 52.

44. Alton H. Quanback and Barry M. Blechman, *Strategic Forces: Issues for the Mid-Seventies* (Washington, D.C.: Brookings Institution, 1973), pp. 6–7.

45. Ibid., p. 9.

46. Halperin, *Defense Strategies for the Seventies*, p. 126.

47. Ibid.

48. Ibid., p. 127.

49. Bernard Brodie, "Technology, Politics, and Strategy," Adelphi Papers, no. 55 (London: International Institute for Strategic Studies, March 1969), p. 22.

CHAPTER 5

1. Alexander Hamilton, *The Federalist No. 74*, Great Books of the Western World, ed. Robert M. Hutchins, vol. 43 (Chicago: Encyclopaedia Britannica, 1952), p. 21.

2. Arthur M. Schlesinger, Jr. *The Imperial Presidency* (Boston: Houghton Mifflin, 1973), p. 3.

3. Edwin S. Corwin, *The President: Office and Powers, 1787–1957* (New York: New York University Press, 1957), p. 171.

4. Schlesinger, *The Imperial Presidency*, p. 291.

5. Robert A. Diamond and Patricia Ann O'Connor, eds., *Guide to Congress* (Washington, D.C.: Congressional Quarterly, 1976), p. 279.

6. Clinton Rossiter, *The American Presidency*, (New York: New American Library, 1960), pp. 14–40.

7. Keith C. Clark and Laurence J. Legere, eds., *The President and the Management of National Security* (New York: Frederick A. Praeger, 1969), p. 19.

8. George Reedy, quoted in Doris Kearns, *Lyndon Johnson and the American Dream* (New York: New American Library, 1977), p. 339.

9. Richard E. Neustadt, "Approaches to Staffing the Presidency," in *The Presidential Advisory System*, ed. Thomas E. Cronin and Sanford D. Greenberg, (New York: Harper & Row, 1969), p. 15.

10. Ibid., p. 19.

11. Discussion of the Hoover staffing arrangements is from Henry T. Nash, *American Foreign Policy: Response to a Sense of Threat* (Homewood, Ill.: Dorsey Press, 1973), p. 113. Data on the Carter administration are contained in Susan Fraker and Eleanor Clife, "White House Green," *Newsweek*, May 23, 1977, p. 19. Comments on the proliferation of presidential assistants are derived from Harold Seidman, *Politics, Position, and Power: The Dynamics of Federal Organization* (New York: Oxford University Press, 1970), p. 213.

12. Seidman, *Politics, Position, and Power*, p. 165.

13. Ibid., p. 91.

14. For a discussion of presidential *modus operandi*, see Andrew J. Goodpaster, "Four Presidents and the Conduct of National Security Affairs: Impressions and Highlights," *Journal of International Relations* 2 (spring 1977): 27–29.

15. Dwight D. Eisenhower, "The Central Role of the President in the Conduct of Security Affairs," in *Issues of National Security in the 1970s*, ed. Amos Jordan (New York: Frederick A. Praeger, 1967), p. 214.

16. John F. Kennedy, quoted in Clark and Legere, *The President and the Management of National Security*, p. 70.

17. For detailed views of the Johnson presidency, see Kearns, *Lyndon Johnson*.

18. Ibid., p. 294.

19. Henry A. Kissinger, *The White House Years* (Boston: Little, Brown, 1979), p. 30.

20. For a detailed discussion of the functions and organizational culture of the Department of State, see Nash, *American Foreign Policy*, pp. 65–99.

21. Kissinger, *The White House Years*, pp. 26–31.

22. Nash, *American Foreign Policy*, pp. 71–72. See also Roger Hilsman, *The Politics of Policy Making in Defense and Foreign Affairs* (New York: Harper & Row, 1971), pp. 47–48.

23. J. M. Destler, *Presidents, Bureaucrats, and Foreign Policy* (Princeton: Princeton University Press, 1972), pp. 156–60.

24. Nash, *American Foreign Policy*, p. 91.

25. Ibid., p. 74.

26. Alain C. Enthoven and K. Wayne Smith, *How Much is Enough?* (New York: Harper & Row, 1971), p. 3.

27. Lawrence J. Korb, *The Joint Chiefs of Staff: The First Twenty-five Years* (Bloomington: Indiana University Press, 1976), pp. 7–14.

28. The flavor of this criticism is captured in Ronald Reagan's remarks contained in "Yes or No on the Panama Treaties," *National Review*, February 17, 1978, pp. 210–17.

29. Matthew B. Ridgeway, "My Battles in War and Peace," *Saturday Evening Post*, January 21, 1956, p. 46.

30. Samuel P. Huntington, *The Common Defense* (New York: Columbia University Press, 1961), p. 146.

31. Henry Stimson, quoted in Miles Copeland, *Without Cloak or Dagger* (New York: Simon & Schuster, 1974), p. 36.

32. Nash, *American Foreign Policy*, pp. 146–49. See also Marjorie Hunter, "Carter Won't Oppose CIA Cost Disclosure," *New York Times*, April 28, 1977, p. 17.

33. Theodore C. Sorensen, *Decision Making in the White House* (New York: Columbia University Press, 1963), pp. 29–30.

34. For a detailed discussion of the origins of legislative central clearance, see Richard E. Neustadt, "Presidency and Legislation: The Growth of Central Clearance," *American Political Science Review* 48, no. 1 (September 1954): 641–71.

35. Richard E. Neustadt, *Presidential Power* (New York: New American Library, 1960), p. 42.

36. Ibid., pp. 53, 47.

37. Ibid., pp. 54–63.

38. Kearns, *Lyndon Johnson*, pp. 258–59.

39. Jules Witcover, "The Mayaguez Decision: Three Days of Crisis for President Ford," *Washington Post*, May 17, 1975, p. 1.

40. Sorensen, *Kennedy*, pp. 296–97.

41. Graham Allison, *Essence of Decision: Explaining the Cuban Missile Crisis* (Boston: Little, Brown, 1971), pp. 141–42.

CHAPTER 6

1. Haass, Richard "Congressional Power: Implications for American Security Policy," Adelphi Papers, no. 153 (London: International Institute for Strategic Studies, summer 1979), p. 2.

2. Abshire, David, *Foreign Policy Matters: Presidents vs. Congress*, Sage Policy Papers, no. 66 (Washington, D.C.: Center for Strategic and International Studies, 1979), p. 10.

3. Charles B. Brownson, ed., *Congressional Staff Directory* (Mount Vernon, Va.: Congressional Staff Directory, 1980).

4. Haass, "Congressional Power," p. 3.

5. Abshire, *Foreign Policy Matters*, p. 11.

6. Theodore Roosevelt, *An Autobiography: Theodore Roosevelt* (New York: Charles Scribner's Sons, 1923), pp. 552–53.

7. *Time*, February 11, 1980, p. 23.

8. Haass, "Congressional Power," p. 7.

9. Ibid., p. 32.

10. Samuel P. Huntington, *The Common Defense* (New York: Columbia University Press, 1961), pp. 131–38.

11. Bruce E. Cain, John A. Ferejohn, and Morris P. Fiorina, *The Roots of Legislator Popularity in Great Britain and the United States*, (St. Louis: Center for the Study of American Business, Washington University, January 1980).

12. Ernest W. Lefever, *TV and National Defense*, (Boston: Institute for American Strategy Press, 1974).

13. Abshire, *Foreign Policy Matters*, p. 47.

14. Lee D. Hamilton and Michael H. Van Dusen, "Making the Separation of Powers Work," *Foreign Affairs* 57, no. 1 (fall 1978):22.

15. Haass, "Congressional Power," p. 6.

16. Ibid., p. 14.

17. Abshire, *Foreign Policy Matters*, p. 53.

18. R. A. Bernstein and W. W. Anthony, "ABM Issue in the Senate, 1968–70: The Importance of Ideology," *American Political Science Review* 68 (September 1974): 1198–1206.

19. Les Aspin, "The Defense Budget and Foreign Policy: The Role of Congress," in *Arms, Defense Policy, and Arms Control*, ed. Franklin A. Long and George W. Rathjens (New York: W. W. Norton, 1976), p. 165.

20. "Crises on Cyprus: 1975," U.S., Congress, Senate, *Staff Report to the Committee on the Judiciary* 94th Cong., 1st sess. (Washington, D.C.: U.S. Government Printing Office, July 20, 1975), p. 57.

21. Public Law 93–448, p. 2.

22. Public Law 93–148, pp. 1–4.

23. Haass, "Congressional Power," p. 21.

24. Ibid., p. 20.

25. John R. Johanner, "Study and Recommend: Statutory Reporting Requirements as a Technique of Legislative Initiative in Congress: A Research Note," *Western Political Quarterly*, December 1976, p. 590.

26. The Congressional Budget Office (CBO) has made great strides in sharpening the debate concerning the allocation of budget dollars across federal programs. The long tenure of its first director, Dr. Alice Rivlin (1974–83), was undoubtedly helpful in crystalizing the CBO role in national security affairs. In the 1983 debate over the defense budget and its relationship to the federal deficit, a CBO study, *Defense Spending and the Economy* (Washington, D.C.: U.S. Government Printing Office, 1983), made a major contribution.

27. Haass, "Congressional Power," p. 8.

28. Ibid., p. 8.

29. Abshire, *Foreign Policy Matters*, p. 63.

30. Edward J. Lawrence, "The Changing Role of Congress in Defense Policy-making," *Journal of Conflict Resolution* 20, no. 2 (June 1976): 236.

31. Dennis Farney, "A Bureaucracy Grows in Congress as Panels and Staffs Mushroom," *Wall Street Journal*, December 18, 1979, p. 1.

32. Haass, "Congressional Power," p. 32.

33. Abshire, *Foreign Policy Matters*, p. 68.

CHAPTER 7

1. Tyrus G. Fain, ed., *The Intelligence Community*, Public Document Series (New York: R. R. Bowker, 1977), p. 973. This volume encompasses that body of official reports, hearings, and studies released by the government from 1970 to 1976 concerning the U.S. foreign intelligence establishment.

2. Ibid., p. 248.

3. See Alexander Hamilton, *The Federalist No. 75*, Great Books of the Western World, ed. Robert M. Hutchins, vol. 43 (Chicago: Encyclopedia Britannica, 1952).

4. See John Jay, *The Federalist No. 64*, Great Books of the Western World, ed. Robert M. Hutchins, vol. 43 (Chicago: Encyclopedia Britannica, 1952).

5. See the remarks of Gerald R. Ford, "Statement by the President," in *Report to the President by the Commission on CIA Activities within the United States* (Washington, D.C.: U.S. Government Printing Office, 1975), p. 273. President Carter's concern for preservation of the information-reporting capability is reflected in remarks quoted in James T. Wooten, "Carter Says

Foreign Sources are Questioning their Safety in Providing Secrets after CIA Reports," *New York Times,* February 25, 1977, p. A-9. President Reagan's views appear in the *Weekly Compilation of Presidential Documents* 17, no. 49 (December 7, 1981): 1335–36. See also the remarks of Sen. Frank Church, former chairman of the Senate Foreign Relations Committee, in U.S., Congress, Senate, Select Committee to Study Governmental Operations with Respect to Intelligence Activities, *Final Report,* 94th Cong., 2d sess., 1976, S. Rept. 94–755, bk. 1, *Foreign and Military Intelligence,* p. 563. (Hereafter cited as the Church Committee's *Final Report.*)

6. The applicable directives are described in U.S., Congress, Senate, Select Committee to Study Governmental Operations with Respect to Intelligence Activities, *Alleged Assassination Plots Involving Foreign Leaders,* 94th Cong., 1st sess., 1975, S. Rept. 94–465. (Hereafter cited as the Church Committee's *Interim Report.*)

7. A similar intelligence production model, and real-world deviations from it, are also described in the Church Committee's *Final Report,* p. 18.

8. Fain, *The Intelligence Community,* p. 319.

9. Ibid., p. 347.

10. Prominent examples are Victor Marchetti and John D. Marks, *The CIA and the Cult of Intelligence* (New York: Alfred A. Knopf, 1974); Philip Agee, *Inside the Company: CIA Diary* (New York: Stonehill, 1975); and L. Fletcher Prouty, *The Secret Team* (Englewood Cliffs, N.J.: Prentice-Hall, 1973).

11. An excellent example is Nelson Blackstock, *COINTELPRO: The FBI's Secret War on Political Freedom* (New York: Random House, 1975).

12. Ray S. Cline, for instance, has provided insightful and knowledgeable commentary in "Policy without Intelligence," *Foreign Policy,* no. 17 (winter 1974/75), pp. 121–35, and in *Secrets, Spies, and Scholars: Blueprint of the Essential CIA* (Washington, D.C.: Acropolis, 1976).

13. Fain, *The Intelligence Community,* p. 409.

14. Marchetti and Marks, *The CIA and the Cult of Intelligence,* pp. 229–37.

15. "Brutal Intelligence," *New Republic,* December 6, 1975, p. 5.

16. Agee, *Inside the Company,* pp. 561–92.

17. See, for example, Harry Rositzke, "America's Secret Operations: A Perspective," *Foreign Affairs* 53, no. 2 (January 1975): 334; William J. Barnds, "Intelligence and Foreign Policy: Dilemmas of Democracy," *Foreign Affairs* 47, no. 2 (January 1969): 285; Nicholas DeB. Katzenbach, "Foreign Policy, Public Opinion, and Secrecy," *Foreign Affairs* 52, no. 1 (October 1973): p. 15.

18. See, for example, Morton Halperin, "CIA, Denying What's Not in Writing," *New Republic,* October 4, 1975, pp. 11–12.

19. Church Committee's *Final Report,* pp. 423–74.

20. U.S., Congress, Senate, Select Committee on Intelligence, 95th Cong., 1st sess., 1977, S. Rept. 95–217.

21. Ibid., p. 1.

22. Text of the proposed charter was printed in full in the *Congressional Record,* February 10, 1978, p. E-533.

23. S. Rept. 95–217, pp. 6–7.

24. The citation for the act is Foreign Intelligence Surveillance Act of 1978 (50 U.S.C.). Carter's remarks are printed in the *Weekly Compilation of Presidential Documents* 14, no. 43 (October 30, 1978): 1853–54. For a rare discussion of how the act has been implemented, see Leslie Maitland, "A Closed Court's One-Issue Caseload," *New York Times,* Oct. 14, 1982.

25. White House press release, January 24, 1978, "Remarks of the President upon Signing of the Intelligence Executive Order," referring to Executive Order 12036, "United States Intelligence Activities," January 24, 1978.

26. 277 U.S. 438 (1928).

27. *Katz* v. *United States,* 389 U.S. 347 (1967), and *Berger* v. *New York,* 388 U.S. 41 (1967). See also Justice Stewart's opinion in *Giordano* v. *United States,* 395 U.S. 314 (1967).

28. See *United States* v. *United States District Court*, 407 U.S. 297 (1972), and *United States* v. *Butenko*, 494 F.2d 593 (3d Cir., en banc, 1974), cert. den. 419 U.S. 881 (1974).

29. *Berlin Democratic Club* v. *Brown*, 410 F. Supp. 144 (1976). Description of this case can also be found in bk. 3 of the Church Committee's *Final Report*, pp. 818–21.

30. The commission's investigative charter is published with its final report, *Report to the President by the Commission on CIA Activities within the United States* (Washington, D.C.: U.S. Government Printing Office, 1975). Perspective on the commission's effort is provided in William Colby and Peter Forbath, *Honorable Men: My Life in the CIA* (New York: Simon & Schuster, 1978). Colby, then director of Central Intelligence, describes the narrowly drawn investigative charter as an intentionally conservative response to criticism of the CIA (p. 226).

31. U.S., President, Executive Order 11905, "United States Foreign Intelligence Activities," *Federal Register* 41, no. 34 (February 19, 1976): 7701.

32. See U.S., Congress, Senate, Select Committee on Intelligence, *Hearings on the Nomination of Admiral Stansfield Turner to be Director of Central Intelligence*, 9th Cong., 1st sess., February 22–23, 1977, p. 4.

33. Fain, *The Intelligence Community*, p. 87.

34. Ibid., p. 92.

35. See U.S., Congress, House, Subcommittee on Evaluation of the Permanent Select Committee on Intelligence, *Staff Report, Iran: Evaluation of U.S. Intelligence Performance Prior to November 1978*, January 1979. Intelligence performance in Iran and elsewhere is also discussed in Robert F. Ellsworth and Kenneth L. Adelman, "Foolish Intelligence," *Foreign Policy*, no. 36, (fall 1979), p. 147.

36. This excerpt from the report of the commission is reprinted in Fain, *The Intelligence Community*, p. 96.

37. Ibid., p. 253.

38. Ibid., p. 46.

CHAPTER 8

1. Forrest Pogue, *Command Decisions*, p. 381, cited in Urs Schwarz, *American Strategy: A New Perspective* (New York: Doubleday, 1966), p. 48.

2. Gerhard Loewenberg, "The Remaking of the German Party System," in *European Politics: A Reader*, ed. Mattei Dugan and Richard Rose (Boston: Little, Brown, 1971), pp. 259–80.

3. John C. Ries, *The Management of Defense* (Baltimore: Johns Hopkins Press, 1964), pp. 26–30.

4. Walter Millis, *Arms and the State* (New York: Twentieth Century Fund, 1958), pp. 124–32.

5. See Cordell Hull, *The Memoirs of Cordell Hull*, 2 vols. (New York: Macmillan, 1948), 2:1625–1713.

6. Public Law 253, 80th Cong., 1st sess., approved July 26, 1947, 61 *Stat.* 495. This section draws largely on Lawrence J. Korb, *The Joint Chiefs of Staff: The First Twenty-five Years* (Bloomington: Indiana University Press, 1976), pp. 15–21.

7. Public Law 253, 61 *Stat.* 44.

8. Millis, *Arms and the State*, p. 214.

9. Samuel P. Huntington, *The Common Defense* (New York: Columbia University Press, 1961), p. 35.

10. See Burton M. Sapin and Richard C. Snyder, *The Role of the Military in American Foreign Policy*, (New York: Doubleday, 1954).

11. Lawrence M. Martin, "The American Decision to Rearm Germany," in *American Civil Military Decisions*, ed. Harold Stein (Birmingham: University of Alabama Press, 1963), pp. 652–60.

12. Huntington, *The Common Defense*, p. 54.

13. A good discussion of the many issues involved in the MacArthur case can be found in Millis, *Arms and the State*, pp. 259–332.

14. Message JCS95977, JCS to UNCFE, July 10, 1951.

15. See Huntington, *The Common Defense*, pp. 282–83, and U.S., *Department of Defense Annual Report, Fiscal Year 1979* (Washington, D.C.: U.S. Government Printing Office, 1978), p. 366. (Hereafter cited as *DOD Report, FY 79.*)

16. Huntington, *The Common Defense*, p. 380.

17. For a good discussion of the many postwar problems of interservice rivalry, see Ries, *The Management of Defense*, pp. 129–92. For a discussion of why defense issues frequently are resolved by political bargaining, see Huntington, *The Common Defense*, pp. 123–96.

18. An illuminating discussion of the intricacies of the joint staffing process may be found in Lawrence B. Tatum, "The Joint Chiefs of Staff and Defense Policy Formulation," *Air University Review*, May–June 1966, pp. 40–45; July–August 1966, pp. 11–20; reprinted in Mark D. Smith III and Claude J. Johns, eds. *American Defense Policy*, (Baltimore: Johns Hopkins Press, 1968), pp. 377–92.

19. Quoted in Millis, *Arms and the State*, p. 348.

20. Adam Yarmolinsky, *The Military Establishment* (New York: Perennial Library, 1973), pp. 175–76.

21. Ibid., pp. 138–40.

22. See, for example, Maxwell Taylor, *Swords and Plowshares* (New York: W. W. Norton, 1972), p. 249; or Yarmolinsky, *The Military Establishment*, pp. 37–40.

23. Lannon Walker, "Our Foreign Affairs Machinery: Time for an Overhaul," *Foreign Affairs* 27, no. 2 (January 1969): 311–15.

24. See, for example, David Halberstam, *The Best and the Brightest* (New York: Random House, 1972).

25. For the best analysis of the army's management of its civil disturbance control mission during the period 1962–73, see James R. Gardner, "The Regular Army and Domestic Disorder, 1963–1973: An Analysis of Role Perceptions, Restraint, and Policy," Ph.D. dissertation, Princeton University, 1977.

26. U.S., Congress, Senate, Subcommittee on Constitutional Rights, Committee on the Judiciary, *Hearings*, 88th Cong., 1st sess., Feb. 23, 1971.

27. See, for example, Bruce Russett, *What Price Vigilance?* (New Haven: Yale University Press, 1970); pp. 56–90.

28. See Yarmolinsky, *The Military Establishment*, chap. 4.

29. U.S., Congress, Senate, Department of Defense Appropriations, *Hearings*, 1974, pt. 1, p. 17.

30. See, for example, "Senate Ratings Reveal Conservative Leanings," *Washington Post*, December 18, 1978, p. A-8; "The 70s: Decade of Second Thoughts," *Public Opinion* 3, no. 1 (December 1979-January 1980): 22, 32–34, 37; and "Confidence Rollercoaster," *Public Opinion* 2, no. 5 (October-November 1979): 30–32.

31. Korb, *The Joint Chiefs of Staff*, pp. 103–11.

32. Ibid., pp. 111–21; Arnold Kanter, *Defense Politics: A Budgetary Perspective* (Chicago: University of Chicago Press, 1975), p. 55f.

33. Korb, *The Joint Chiefs of Staff*, p. 121.

34. Ibid., pp. 121–28; Lawrence J. Korb, "The Budget Process in the Department of Defense, 1947–1977," *Public Administration Review* 37, no. 4 (July-August 1977): 334–346. For a discussion of the difference in style between McNamara and Laird, see James M. Roherty, "The Office of the Secretary of Defense: The Laird and McNamara Styles," in *The New Civil-Military Relations*, ed. John P. Lovell and Phillip S. Kronenberg (New Brunswick, N.J.: Transaction Books, 1974), pp. 299–54.

35. Lawrence J. Korb, "The Civil-Military Balance at the Policymaking Level in the Carter Administration: An Assessment," in *Final Report*, Senior Conference, United States Military Academy, June 14–16, 1979, pp. 147–56.

36. George C. Wilson, "Joint Chiefs of Staff Break with Carter on Budget Planning for Defense Needs," *Washington Post*, May 30, 1980, p. A-1.

37. For the B-1 bombers, see "Senate Panel Approves Aircraft Carrier Funds", *New York Times*, May 11, 1978, p. A-18; and Brooks Jackson, *New York Times Supplementary Material*, August 28, 1978, pp. 1–4; for the neutron bomb, see Richard Burt, "Pressure from Congress

Mounts to Reverse Ban on Neutron Bomb", *New York Times*, April 6, 1978, p. 1; for increases in defense spending, see Charles Mohr, "Nunn Links His Support for Pact to Arms Budget Rise," *New York Times*, July 26, 1979, p. A-5.

38. Data on active force and dependents are from *Selected Manpower Statistics*, Department of Defense, OASD (Comptroller) May 1977, and U.S., *Department of Defense Annual Report, Fiscal Year 1981*; data on defense contractors is from U.S., Department of Commerce, Bureau of Census, *Statistical Abstract of the United States*, 1979.

39. For a balanced perspective on the "military-industrial complex," see Benjamin Franklin Cooling, "The Military-Industrial Complex: Update on an Old American Issue," in *The Military in America: From the Colonial Era to the Present*, ed. Peter Karsten (New York: Free Press, 1980), pp. 317–29.

40. Douglas MacAuthur, Address delivered at West Point, May 12, 1962.

41. Matthew Ridgeway's "Farewell Letter" to Secretary of Defense Charles E. Wilson, June 27, 1955.

42. Millis makes one of the most comprehensive analyses of these changes in the second part of his book with Harvey C. Mansfield and Harold Stein, *Arms and the State*. See also William Fox, "Representativeness and Efficiency: Dual Problem of Civil-Military Relations," *Political Science Quarterly* 76 (September 1961): 354–66. For a short summary and critique of the fusionist theory, see Huntington, *The Common Defense*, p. 350–54.

43. John F. Kennedy, Commencement address, delivered at West Point, June 1962.

44. Robert Lovett, Address delivered at West Point, May 1964. For an elaboration of this point, see William J. Taylor, Jr. "Military Professionals in Changing Times," *Public Administration Review* 37, no. 6 (November-December 1977): 633–41.

45. Maxwell D. Taylor, Address delivered at West Point, February 18, 1969.

46. See Amos A. Jordan and William J. Taylor, Jr., "The Military Man in Academia," *Annals* 406 (March 1973): 129–45.

47. See Samuel P. Huntington, *The Soldier and the State* (Cambridge; Mass.: Belknap Press, 1957). In the literature on American civil-military politics, this book is a landmark. Written from a conservative perspective, Huntington's book is one of the most comprehensive analytical critiques of the fusionist doctrine. Its polar opposite is Morris Janowitz's *The Professional Soldier* (New York: Free Press, 1960), an important book that advanced the thesis that external sociological and political forces made fusionism inevitable in the American military. See also Arthur D. Larson, "Military Professionalism and Civil Control: A Comparative Analysis of Two Interpretations," *Journal of Military and Political Sociology* 2, no. 1 (spring 1974): 57–72, for an incisive critique of Huntington's and Janowitz's analyses.

48. Huntington, *The Soldier and the State*, p. 163.

49. See Taylor, "Military Professionals in Changing Times"; Korb, "The Civil-Military Balance at the Policymaking Level in the Carter Administration," Paper prepared for the Annual Meeting of the Peace Science Society, April 27–28, 1978, Columbia, South Carolina; Korb, *The Joint Chiefs of Staff*; George Wilson, "The Decline of America's Military Chiefs," *Washington Post*, Sunday ed., June 25, 1978, p. D-1; and Bernard Weintraub, "Naming of General Jones Reflects Shift from Combat Veterans to Management Experts," *New York Times*, July 5, 1978, p. A-13.

50. For evidence that the military's administrative functions are beginning to dominate the instrumental-operational priorities, see William J. Gregor, "The Leader as Subordinate: The Politics and Performance of Unit Commanders in the U.S. Army," Ph.D. dissertation, Yale University, 1980: and Richard A. Gabriel and Paul C. Savage, *Crisis in Command: Mismanagement in the Army* (New York: Hill & Wang, 1978).

51. For a discussion of the military's evolving ethics, see Sam C. Sarkesian, "Professional Problems and Adaptations," in *The Limits of Military Intervention*, ed. Ellen P. Stern (Beverly Hills, Calif: Sage, 1977), pp. 301–23; William L. Hauser, *America's Army in Crisis* (Baltimore: Johns Hopkins University Press, 1973); and Charles C. Moskos, Jr., "The All-Volunteer Military: Calling, Profession, or Occupation," *Parameters* 7, no. 1 (1977): 2–10.

52. Edward N. Luttwak, "A Critical View of the U.S. Military Establishment," *Forbes*, May 26, 1980, p. 38.

53. Morris Janowitz, "Toward a Redefinition of Military Strategy in International Relations," *World Politics* 26 (July 1974). 495, fn. 44.

54. Maxwell Taylor, in a letter to Col. William J. Taylor, Jr., Dept. of Social Sciences, U.S. Military Academy, West Point, N.Y., February 11, 1981.

55. John G. Kester, "The Future of the Joint Chiefs of Staff," *AEI Foreign Policy and Defense Review* 2, no. 1 (1980): 23.

56. Jeffrey Record, "The Fortunes of War," *Harper's*, April 1980, p. 19.

57. Kester, "The Future of the Joint Chiefs of Staff," p. 11.

58. Henry A. Kissinger, *The White House Years* (Boston: Little, Brown, 1979), p. 398.

CHAPTER 9

1. Charles L. Schultze et al., *Setting National Priorities: The 1972 Budget* (Washington, D.C.: Brookings Institution, 1971), pp. 12–13.

2. "National Security Amendments of 1949," *United States Statutes at Large*, 81st Cong., 1st sess., vol. 63, I, p. 81.

3. Lawrence J. Korb, "The Secretary of Defense and the Joint Chiefs of Staff in the Nixon Administration: The Method and the Men," in *The New Civil-Military Relations*, ed. John P. Lovell and Philip S. Kronenberg (New Brunswick, N.J.: Transaction Books, 1974), p. 258.

4. Lawrence J. Korb, *The Joint Chiefs of Staff: The First Twenty-five Years* (Bloomington: Indiana University Press, 1976), p. 129.

5. Alain C. Enthoven and K. Wayne Smith, *How Much Is Enough?* (New York: Harper & Row, 1971), p. 14.

6. Among the most important of these were Arthur Smithies, *The Budgetary Process of the United States* (New York: McGraw-Hill, 1955); Maxwell Taylor, *The Uncertain Trumpet*; (New York: Harper & Bros., 1960); and a series of articles for the Rand Corp. by David Novick, Charles Hitch, and Roland McKean.

7. Enthoven and Smith, *How Much Is Enough?* p. 66.

8. Harvey Sopolsky, *The Polaris System Development* (Cambridge, Mass.: Harvard University Press, 1973), pp. 53–54.

9. Aaron Wildavsky, *The Politics of the Budgetary Process* (Boston: Little, Brown, 1964), pp. 147–67.

10. U.S., Senate, Subcommittee on National Security and International Operations, *Hearings on Planning-Programming-Budgeting*, 91st Cong., 1st sess., Pt. 1 (Washington, D.C.: U.S. Government Printing Office, 1969), p. 16.

11. For a more complete discussion of these points, see Neil M. Singer, *Public Microeconomics* (Boston: Little, Brown, 1976), pp. 295–300.

12. OMB Bulletin 77–9, "Zero-Base Budgeting," April 19, 1977, p. 1.

13. U.S., Department of Defense, *Annual Report, Fiscal Year 1978*, January 17, 1977, pp. C2, C9.

14. Ibid., p. 7.

15. Lawrence J. Korb, "The Price of Preparedness: The FY 1978–1982 Defense Program," *AEI Defense Review* 1, no. 3, (1977): 18–19.

16. Graham T. Allison, "Military Capabilities and American Foreign Policy," *Annals* 407 (March 1973): 32.

CHAPTER 10

1. Samuel P. Huntington, *The Common Defense* (New York: Columbia University Press, 1961), p. 1.

2. Roger Hilsman, *The Politics of Policy Making in Defense and Foreign Affairs* (New York: Harper & Row, 1971), pp. 118–22. Hilsman uses three circles; the concept has been modified to five here.

3. Morton H. Halperin, *Bureaucratic Politics and Foreign Policy* (Washington, D.C.: Brookings Institution, 1974), p. 193.

4. *Washington Star*, December 17, 1979, p. A-2.

5. Russell Watson, "A Talk with Zbig," *Newsweek*, May 9, 1977, p. 58.

6. Bernard Gwertzman, "Carter Looks to New Arms Talks with Russians within 3 Months," *New York Times*, January 27, 1977, p. 1.

7. Watson, "A Talk with Zbig," p. 58.

8. Gwertzman, "Carter Looks to New Arms Talks," p. 7.

9. Office of the Federal Register, *United States Government Manual*, National Archives and Records Service, General Services Administration, 1977, p. 181.

10. Graham T. Allison et al., *Adequacy of Current Organization: Defense and Arms Control*, Commission on the Organization of the Government for the Conduct of Foreign Policy, vol. 4 (Washington, D.C.: U.S. Government Printing Office, 1975), p. 3.

11. Alain C. Enthoven and K. Wayne Smith, *How Much Is Enough?* (New York: Harper & Row, 1971), p. 5.

12. Halperin, *Bureaucratic Politics and Foreign Policy*, p. 51.

13. Kelly Orr, "U.S. Navy in Distress," *U.S. News and World Report*, March 6, 1978, pp. 24–26.

14. Bernard Weintraub, "Brown Seeks to Cut Involvement of Navy in Non-nuclear War," *New York Times*, January 27, 1978, p. A-8; see also "Navy Protests Limitation of Its Long-Term Mission," *New York Times*, March 14, 1978, p. 3.

15. Bernard Weintraub, "House Panel Would Raise Navy Shipbuilding Budget," *New York Times*, March 10, 1978, p. A-13.

16. For a complete description of the analytic model see Graham Allison, *The Essence of Decision: Explaining the Cuban Missile Crisis* (Boston: Little, Brown, 1971). The quote is on p. 162.

17. See Marver H. Bernstein, *The Job of the Federal Executive* (Washington, D.C.: Brookings Institution, 1958), for an excellent treatment of multiple roles of executives.

18. See Allison, *The Essence of Decision*, pp. 164–77, and Halperin, *Bureaucratic Politics and Foreign Policy*, pp. 16–25, for further explanation of this concept.

19. Harry S. Truman, *Memoirs*, vol. 2, *Years on Trial and Hope, 1946–1952* (Garden City, N.Y.: Doubleday, 1956), p. 33.

20. Henry T. Nash, *American Foreign Policy: Response to a Sense of Threat* (Homewood, Ill.: Dorsey Press, 1973), p. 126.

21. "Report Cites Risks: Carter's Korea Troop Withdrawal Faulted," *Congressional Quarterly Weekly Report*, February 25, 1978, pp. 542–44.

22. Hilsman, *The Politics of Policy Making*, pp. 123–24.

23. Marriner S. Eccles, *Beckoning Frontiers* (New York: Alfred A. Knopf, 1951), p. 336.

24. Thomas E. Cronin, *The State of the Presidency*, 2d ed. (Boston: Little, Brown, 1980), p. 274.

25. Richard E. Neustadt, "White House and White Hall," *Public Interest*, winter 1966, p. 64.

26. Henry A. Kissinger, *The White House Years* (Boston: Little, Brown, 1979), pp. 18–19.

27. Halperin, *Bureaucratic Politics and Foreign Policy*, p. 279.

28. For a detailed analysis of the Cuban Missile Crisis, see Allison, *Essence of Decision*.

29. Robert E. Hunter, *Presidential Control of Foreign Policy: Management or Mishap?* CSIS Washington Papers no. 91 (New York: Frederick A. Praeger, 1982).

30. "Schultz No Longer Perceived as Driving Force in Foreign Policy," *Washington Post*, August 15, 1893, pp. 1–2.

31. Amos A. Jordan, "Secretary of State/National Security Advisor: The Push for Power," *Los Angeles Times*, December 31, 1981.

CHAPTER 11

1. U.S, *Department of Defense Annual Report, Fiscal Year 1981* (Washington, D.C.: U.S. Government Printing Office, 1980), p. 68. (Hereafter cited as *DOD Report, FY 81*.)

2. Ibid., p. 69.

3. Alain C. Enthoven and K. Wayne Smith, *How Much Is Enough?* (New York: Harper & Row, 1971), p. 207. See also *DOD Report, FY 81*, p. 79.

4. Colin S. Gray, "Nuclear Strategy: The Case for A Theory of Victory," *International Security* 4, no. 3 (summer 1979): 58-65.

5. Ibid., pp. 76-87.

6. Albert Wohlstetter, "The Delicate Balance of Terror," *Foreign Affairs* 37, no. 2 (January 1959). 216.

7. Defense analysts recognize this explicitly. See, for example, Fritz W. Ermarth, "Contrasts in American and Soviet Strategic Thought," *International Security*, vol. 3, no. 4 (fall 1978).

8. *Annual Report to the Congress, Caspar W. Weinberger, Secretary of Defense, Fiscal year 1984.* (Washington, D.C.: U.S. Government Printing Office, 1984), pp. 3, 320.

9. For a more detailed explanation of allied warning systems, see John M. Collins, *American and Soviet Military Trends since the Cuban Missile Crisis* (Washington, D.C.: Center for Strategic and International Studies, 1978), pp. 130-32.

10. *DOD Report, FY 84*, p. 228.

11. Collins, *American and Soviet Military Trends*, p. 102.

12. *Department of Defense Annual Report, FY 81* (Washington, D.C.: U.S. Government Printing Office, 1980), p. 139. FEMA FY 1984 budget information is available from FEMA public offices, Washington, D.C. For Brown quote, see *Annual Report to the Congress,* Harold Brown, *Secretary of Defense, Fiscal Year 1981* (Washington, D.C.: U.S. Government Printing Office, 1981), p. 139.

13. Perry R. Nuhn, "WWMCCS and the Computer that Can," *Parameters* 10, no. 3 (September 1980). 16-21.

14. *DOD Report, FY 81*, pp. 140-44.

15. William R. Van Cleave, "Soviet Doctrine and Strategy: A Developing American View," in *The Future of Soviet Military Power*, ed. Lawrence L. Whetten (New York: Crane, Russak, 1976), pp. 50-51.

16. Joint Chiefs of Staff, *Department of Defense Dictionary of Military and Associated Terms* (Washington, D.C.: U.S. Government Printing Office, June 1979), p. 217.

17. Steven Canby, "The Alliance and Europe, Part IV: Military Doctrine and Technology," Adelphi Papers, no. 109 (London: International Institute for Strategic Studies, winter 1974/75), p. 2.

18. For a depiction of the adverse trends in the balance since 1966, see *DOD Report, FY 81*, p. 75.

19. International Institute for Strategic Studies, *The Military Balance, 1979-1980* (London: IISS, 1980), pp. 114-17.

20. For a detailed development of this position, see Joseph I. Coffey, *Strategy Power and National Security* (Pittsburgh: University of Pittsburgh Press, 1971), pp. 12-18.

21. U.S., *Department of Defense Annual Report, Fiscal Year 1975* (Washington, D.C.: U.S. Government Printing Office, 1974), pp. 35-37.

22. Herman Kahn, *On Escalation: Metaphors and Scenarios,* Hudson Institute Papers (New York: Praeger, 1965), pp. 194-95, 299.

23. Thomas C. Schelling, *Arms and Influence* (New Haven: Yale University Press, 1966), p. 183.

24. Robert Jervis, *Perception and Misperception in International Politics* (Princeton: Princeton University Press), pp. 62-77, and Jerome Kahan, *Security in the Nuclear Age* (Washington, D.C.: Brookings Institution, 1975), p. 204.

25. Kahan, *Security in the Nuclear Age,* p. 254.

26. *DOD Report, FY 81*, p. 65.

27. André Beaufre, *Deterrence and Strategy,* trans. R. H. Barry (New York: Praeger, 1966), pp. 25-26.

28. For an interesting historical example of the bureaucratic strife between agencies trying to get control of a single function, see Michael H. Armacost, *The Politics of Weapons Innovation: The Thor-Jupiter Controversy* (New York: Columbia University Press, 1969).

29. John A. Lauder, "Lessons of the Strategic Bombing Survey," *Orbis* 18, no. 3 (fall 1974): 775-77.

30. *Los Angeles Times,* September 10, 1980, p. 1.

31. Harold Brown, quoted in ibid.

32. *New York Times,* August 21, 1980, p. A-9.

33. Frank Church, quoted in the *Washington Post,* September 17, 1980, p. 8.

34. Richard Burt, "U.S. Moving toward Vast Revision of Its Strategy on Nuclear War," *New York Times,* November 30, 1978, p. A-1; Bernard Weintraub, "Pentagon Seeking Shift in Nuclear Deterrent Policy," *New York Times,* January 5, 1979, p. A-5; Richard Burt, "Carter Shifts U.S. Strategy for Deterring Nuclear War," *New York Times,* February 10, 1979; Elmo Zumwalt, Jr., and Worth H. Bagley, "Old, 'New' Nuclear Strategy," *Journal of Commerce,* September 3, 1980, p. 4.

35. William W. Kaufmann, "Defense Policy," in *Setting National Priorities: Agenda for the 1980s,* ed. Joseph A. Peckman (Washington, D.C.: Brookings Institution, 1980), pp. 295–96.

36. Herman Kahn, "U.S. Strategic Security in the 1980s," Hudson Institute Perspective Series (Croton-on-Hudson, N. Y., August, 1980), pp. 2, 15, 31; Gray, "Nuclear Strategy," p. 220.

37. Leon Sloss, "Carter's Nuclear Policy: It's Evolutionary, Not Revolutionary, and Aims to Strengthen Deterrence," *Los Angeles Times,* August 31, 1980, p. 3.

38. "The New Nuclear Strategy and Its Perils," *New York Times,* August 21, 1980, p. A-26.

39. See *President's Commission on Strategic Forces,* April 6, 1983.

40. See Steven V. Roberts, "If the MX Is Near, Politics of '84 Can't Be Far Away," *Washington Post,* May 27, 1983, p. A14.

41. See Lou Cannon, "Three Options under Study for Improving Arms Control Counsel," *Washington Post,* May 30, 1983, p. A3.

CHAPTER 12

1. Thomas C. Schelling, *Arms and Influence* (New Haven: Yale University Press, 1966), p. 95.

2. For a discussion of vital interests and their subjective nature, see Bernard Brodie, *War and Politics* (New York: Macmillan, 1973), pp. 341–74.

3. Henry A. Kissinger, *A World Restored* (New York: Universal Library, 1964), p. 8.

4. Robert Endicott Osgood, *Limited War: The Challenge to American Strategy* (Chicago: University of Chicago Press, 1957), chap. 2. A concise description of American "national style" and its impact on the use of force by the United States is provided in John Spanier, *American Foreign Policy since World War II,* 8th ed. (New York: Holt, Rinehart & Winton, 1980), pp. 4–11. See also Henry Kissinger's comments in *The White House Years* (Boston: Little, Brown, 1979), pp. 63–64.

5. Geoffrey Blainey, *The Causes of War* (New York: Free Press, 1973), pp. 196–97.

6. Ibid., pp. 193–94.

7. Alan Morehead, *The Russian Revolution* (New York: Harper & Bros., 1958), p. 51.

8. An incisive analysis of the difficulties nations face in limiting their wartime objectives once the battle is joined is contained in Fred C. Iklé, *Every War Must End* (New York: Columbia University Press, 1971), pp. 84–105.

9. Dwight D. Eisenhower, quoted in Samuel P. Huntington, *The Common Defense* (New York: Columbia University Press, 1961), p. 80.

10. Bernard Brodie, *Strategy in the Missile Age* (Princeton: Princeton University Press, 1959), pp. 316–21. See also Morton H. Halperin, "The Korean War," in *American Defence Policy,* ed. John E. Endicott and Roy W. Stafford, Jr., 4th ed. (Baltimore: Johns Hopkins University Press, 1977), pp. 191–200.

11. This analysis is particularly well developed by Thomas Schelling, *Arms and Influence,* pp. 18–24.

12. For a comparison of U.S. and Soviet strategic views, see Fritz W. Ermarth, "Contrasts in American and Soviet Strategic Thought," *International Security* 3, no. 4 (fall 1978); 138–55.

13. "The New Nuclear Strategy and Its Perils," *New York Times,* August 21, 1980, p. A-26.

14. International Institute for Strategic Studies, *The Military Balance, 1979–1980* (London: IISS, 1980), pp. 108–13.

15. International Institute for Strategic Studies, *The Military Balance*, p. 111.

16. Roger Facer, "The Alliance and Europe, Part III: Weapons Procurement in Europe—Capabilities and Choices," Adelphi Papers, no. 108 (London: International Institute for Strategic Studies, 1975), and D. Keynes, "The Alliance and Europe, Part VI: The European Programme Group," Adelphi Papers, no. 129 (London: International Institute for Strategic Studies, 1977). See also Stanley Sloan and Robert Bell, *NATO Standardization: Political, Economic, and Military Issues for Congress* (Washington, D.C.: U.S. Government Printing Office, 1977), and U.S., Congress, House, Subcommittee of the Committee on Government Operations, *Hearings*, "Problems in the Standardization and Interoperability of NATO Military Equipment," 95th Cong., 1st sess., Pts. 1 and 2 (Washington, D.C.: U.S. Government Printing Office, 1977).

17. For Pearl Harbor, see Warren A. Samouce, "Political Warning and Military Planning," *Military Review* 53, no. 4 (April 1973): 17–24.

18. "War Signals Misjudged, U.S. Officials Concede," *New York Times*, October 10, 1973, p. 18, and *Newsweek*, November 5, 1973, p. 54.

19. See Michael Pillsbury, "Future Sino-American Security Ties: The View from Tokyo, Moscow, and Peking," *International Security* 1, no. 4 (spring 1977): 124–42, and Jonathan Pollack, "The Implications of Sino-American Normalization," *International Security* 3, no. 4 (spring 1979): 37–57.

20. Wolfgang Heisenberg, "The Alliance and Europe, Part I: Crisis Stability in Europe and Theater Nuclear Weapons," Adelphi Papers, no. 96 (London: International Institute for Strategic Studies, 1973), p. 1.

21. Morton H. Halperin, *Limited War in the Nuclear Age* (New York: John Wiley & Sons, 1963), p. 60.

22. Jeffrey Record and Thomas Anderson, *U.S. Nuclear Weapons in Europe* (Washington, D.C.: Brookings Institution, 1974), pp. 37–44. See also International Institute for Strategic Studies, *The Military Balance*, pp. 114–19. Trends in this area have become a major concern to some Western analysts; see, for example, Stewart Menaul, "The Shifting Theater Nuclear Balance in Europe," *Strategic Review*, fall 1978, 34–45.

23. For example, see Record and Anderson, *Nuclear Weapons in Europe*, pp. 45–70; Colin Gray, "Theater Nuclear Weapons," *World Politics* 28 (January 1976): 300–314; William R. Van Cleave and S. T. Cohen, *Tactical Nuclear Weapons; An Examination of the Issues* (New York: Crane, Russak, 1978), pp. 14–15, 20–21; J. J. Martin, "Nuclear Weapons in NATO's Deterrent Strategy," *Orbis*, winter 1979, pp. 875–79; and Uwe Neilich, "Theatre Nuclear Forces in Europe," *Washington Quarterly* 3 (winter 1980): 100–125.

24. "Small Atomic Arms Are Urged for NATO," *New York Times*, January 27, 1974, p. 2; Colin Gray, "Mini-Nukes and Strategy," *International Journal*, spring 1974, pp. 235–38. See also Van Cleave and Cohen, *Tactical Nuclear Weapons*, pp. 30–40.

25. Record and Anderson, *Nuclear Weapons in Europe*, pp. 41–44. Soviet rationale is examined by Ermarth, "American and Soviet Strategic Thought," pp. 148–49.

26. Heisenberg, "Crisis Stability in Europe," p. 8. See also Secretary General's Consultative Group, *Effects of the Possible Use of Nuclear Weapons and the Security and Economic Implications for States of the Acquisition and Further Development of These Weapons* (New York: United Nations Publications, 1968), pp. 15–19.

27. Record and Anderson, *Nuclear Weapons in Europe*, pp. 43–44. See also Pipes, "The Soviet Union," pp. 26–31.

28. Thomas C. Schelling, *A Strategy of Conflict* (New York: Oxford University Press, 1960), chap. 3 and app. A.

29. Heisenberg, "Crisis Stability in Europe," p. 9. See also Halperin, *Limited War*, pp. 656–66.

30. Halperin, *Limited War*, p. 67. See also Record and Anderson, *Nuclear Weapons in Europe*, p. 242.

31. Van Cleave and Cohen, *Tactical Nuclear Weapons*, pp. 79–83, and Heisenberg, "Crisis Stability in Europe," pp. 3–9.

32. For commentaries on Vietnam as a limited war, see Osgood, *Limited War Revisited*, pp. 33–52, and Brodie, *War and Politics,* pp. 113–222.

33. "Egyptian Says Kissinger Warned: Peace Is 'Not around the Corner,' " *New York Times,* December 5, 1973, p. 18.

34. Henry A. Kissinger, press conference, January 24, 1973 (Washington, D.C.: Department of State, Office of Media Services, 1973).

CHAPTER 13

1. Robert Kupperman, *Low-Intensity Conflict* (Washington, D.C.: Robert H. Kupperman Associates, 1983), p. 21.

2. William J. Taylor, Jr., "Pyschological Operations in the Spectrum of Conflict in the 1980s," in *The Future of Conflict in the 1980s,* ed. William J. Taylor, Jr., and Steven Maaranen (Lexington, Mass.: Lexington Books, 1982), p. 113.

3. Peter Vannemann and Martin James, "Soviet Thrust into the Horn of Africa," *Strategic Review* (spring 1978), p. 34.

4. William J. Taylor, Jr., and James J. Townsend, "Proxy Warfare to the Year 2000," in *Strategic Requirements for the Army to the Year 2000,* ed. William J. Taylor, Jr., and Robert Kupperman (Lexington, Mass.: Lexington Books, 1984).

5. For more information on this vulnerability, see Amory Lovins and L. Hunter Lovins, *Brittle Power* (Andover, Mass: Brick House Publishing, 1982).

6. Kupperman, *Low Intensity Conflict,* pp. 33–41.

7. Executive Summary, *Strategic Requirements for the Army to the Year 2000.* (Washington, D.C.: Center for Strategic and International Studies, 1982), pp. 13–14.

8. Interview with General John A. Wickham, Jr., *Army Times,* July 25, 1983.

9. For an exhaustive treatment of one aspect of political violence, see Robert B. Asprey, *War in the Shadows,* 2 vols. (Garden City, N.Y.: Doubleday, 1975); see also Walter Laqueur, *Guerrilla* (Boston: Little, Brown, 1976).

10. Nikita Khrushchev, Speech delivered January 6, 1961, quoted in *Documents on International Affairs, 1961* (London: Oxford University Press, 1965), pp. 259–73.

11. Mao Tse-tung, "Why Is It that Red Political Power Can Exist in China?" and, "The Struggle in the Chingkand Mountains," in *Selected Military Writings of Mao Tse-tung* (Peking: Foreign Languages Press, 1963), pp. 9–18, 19–50.

12. Mao Tse-tung, "Problems of Strategy in China's Revolutionary War," in ibid., pp. 75–150.

13. Karl von Clausewitz, *On War,* ed. and trans. Michael Howard and Peter Paret (Princeton: Princeton University Press, 1976), p. 596.

14. Chalmers A. Johnson, *Peasant Nationalism and Communist Power* (Stanford: Stanford University Press, 1962).

15. Guenther Lewy, *America in Vietnam* (New York: Oxford University Press, 1978), p. 272.

16. Ibid., pp. 208–10.

17. Barry Rubin, *Paved with Good Intentions: The American Experience and Iran* (New York: Oxford University Press, 1980), p. 334.

18. Jack Davis, "Political Violence in Latin America," Adelphi Papers, no. 85 (London: International Institute for Strategic Studies, February 1972).

19. Carlos Marighella, "The Mini-Manual of the Urban Guerrilla," in Robert Moss, "Urban Guerrilla Warfare," Adelphi Papers, no. 79 (London: International Institute for Strategic Studies, August 1971), p. 40.

20. Tom Hayden, *Rebellion and Repression* (Cleveland: Meridian, 1969), pp. 14, 16.

21. Examples of revolutions that have withered through lack of endurance are legion, but for a few, conveniently treated, see Geoffrey Fairbairn, *Revolutionary Guerrilla Warfare* (Baltimore: Penguin, 1974).

22. Nathan Leites and Charles World, Jr., *Rebellion and Authority* (Chicago: Markham, 1970), p. 150.

23. Leites and World, *Rebellion and Authority.*

CHAPTER 14

1. U.S, President, *Economic Report of the President* (Washington, D.C.: U.S. Government Printing Office, 1983), p. 282.

2. U.S., *Department of Defense Annual Report, Fiscal Year 1978* (Washington, D.C.: U.S. Government Printing Office, 1977), p. 26.

3. Compiled from import-export data from Bureau of the Census.

4. Klaus Knorr and Frank N. Trager, eds., *Economic Issues and National Security* (Lawrence, Kan.: Regent Press of Kansas, 1977), p. 6.

5. Franklin R. Root, *International Trade and Investment* (Cincinnati: South-Western, 1978), pp. 17–21.

6. *Economic Report of the President*, p. 318.

7. Graham Bannock, R. E. Baxter, and Ray Rees, eds., *The Penguin Dictionary of Economics* (London: Penguin, 1978).

8. Robert W. Tucker, *The Inequality of Nations* (New York: Basic Books, 1977), pp. 47–51.

9. See, for example, Felix Kessler, "West Germany Resists U.S. Plans to Increase Outlays and Aid Growth," *Wall Street Journal,* February 9, 1977, p. 1; and R. Janssen and R. Levine, "London Summit Strengthens Willingness of West to Continue Fighting Inflation," *Wall Street Journal,* May 9, 1977, p. 2.

10. Knorr and Trager, *Economic Issues,* pp. 246–50.

11. Mordechai E. Kreinin, *International Economics: A Policy Approach* (New York: Harcourt Brace Jovanovich, 1979), p. 3.

12. "EMS Lives: Europe's Antidote to the Dollar Makes Fine Debut," *Financial Times World Business Weekly,* March 19, 1979.

13. *World Development Report, 1980* (Washington, D.C.: World Bank, August 1980).

14. A. Bryan, A. A. Jordan, and M. Moodie, *Facing the International Energy Problem* (New York: Praeger, 1979).

15. Knorr and Trager, *Economic Issues,* p. 13.

16. See Clark A. Murdock, "Economic Factors as Objects of National Security," in ibid., pp. 67–98.

17. Kessler, "West Germany Resists," p. 1, and Janssen and Levine, "London Summit," p. 2.

18. See James E. Dougherty and Diane K. Pfaltzgraff, *Eurocommunism and the Atlantic Alliance* (Cambridge, Mass.: Institute for Foreign Policy Analysis, January 1977).

19. Knorr and Trager, *Economics Issues,* pp. 1–14.

20. Daniel Bell, "The Future World Disorder," *Foreign Policy,* no. 22 (summer 1977), p. 115.

21. Ibid., p. 116.

22. *Washington Post,* September 25, 1983, p. H1.

23. Thibault de Saint Phalle, ed., *The International Financial Crisis: An Opportunity for Constructive Action* (Washington, D.C.: Center for Strategic and International Studies, 1983).

24. Karl P. Sauvant and Hajo Hasenpflug, *The New International Economic Order: Confrontation or Cooperation between North and South?* (Boulder, Colo.: Westview Press, 1977), pp. 3–6.

25. Irving Louis Horowitz, *Three Worlds of Development: The Theory and Practice of International Stratification* (New York: Oxford University Press, 1966), p. 24.

26. Ibid., pp. 44–46.

27. Bell, "The Future World Disorder," p. 115.

28. Ibid., p. 126.

29. For examples of the varying viewpoints of the developed and developing nations in the North-South dialogue, see J. Amuzegar, "The North-South Dialogue: From Conflict to Compromise," *Foreign Affairs* 54, no. 3 (April 1976); and N. H. Neff, "The New Economic Order: Bad Economics, Worse Politics," *Foreign Policy,* no. 24 (fall 1976).

30. Roger D. Hansen, "North-South Policy: What Is the Problem?" *Foreign Affairs* 58, no. 5 (summer 1980): 1110.

31. See Klaus Knorr, "International Economic Leverage and Its Uses," in Knorr and Trager, *Economic Issues,* pp. 99–126.

32. Paula Stern, "Economic Leverage on the U.S.S.R.," *Executive,* Cornell University, 1979, pp. 35–37.

33. "Soviet Invasion of Afghanistan," Department of State Bulletin Current Policy no. 123 (Washington, D.C.: Bureau of Public Affairs, U.S. Department of State, January 4, 1980).

34. "U.S. Sanctions Against Russia: A Flop," *U.S. News and World Report,* June 16, 1980, pp. 33–34.

35. "The Kama River Source," *Wall Street Journal,* February 8, 1980, p. 1.

CHAPTER 15

1. Richard G. Head, "Technology and the Military Balance," *Foreign Affairs* 56, no. 3 (April 1978): 553.

2. *Random House Dictionary of the English Language,* unabridged, s.v. "science."

3. Charles J. Hitch and Roland N. McKean, *The Economics of Defense in the Nuclear Age* (Santa Monica, Calif.: Rand Corp., 1960), p. 246.

4. Ibid., pp. 245–46.

5. Ibid., p. 243.

6. Stefan J. Possony and J. E. Pournelle, *The Strategy of Technology* (Cambridge, Mass.: Dunellen Press, 1970), p. xxvi.

7. U.S., *Department of Defense Annual Report, Fiscal Year 1979* (Washington, D.C.: U.S. Government Printing Office, 1978), p. 15.

8. Possony and Pournelle, *Strategy of Technology,* p. 62.

9. Aerospace Industries Association of America, *International R&D Trends and Policies* (Washington, D.C.: AIAA, 1972), p. 8.

10. Aerospace Industries Association of America, *The National Technology Program* (Washington, D.C.: AIAA, December 1972), p. 6.

11. Arthur F. Burns, "The Defense Sector: Its Economic and Social Impact," in *The Military and American Society,* ed. Martin B. Hickman (Beverly Hills, Calif.: Glencoe Press, 1971), p. 61.

12. U.S., Congress, Senate, Committee on Armed Services, *Hearings, Department of Defense Authorization for Appropriations for Fiscal Year 1979, Statement of Undersecretary of Defense for Research and Engineering William J. Perry,* 95th Cong., 2d sess., February 28, 1978, p. 5509.

13. U.S., Congress, House, Committee on Foreign Affairs, Subcommittee on National Security Policy and Scientific Developments, *Hearings, Strategy and Science: Toward a National Security Policy for the 1970s,* 91st Cong., 1st sess. (Washington, D.C.: U.S. Government Printing Office, 1969), p. vi (hereafter cited as *Hearings toward a National Security Policy*); Possony and Pournelle, *Strategy of Technology,* p. 9.

14. For a theoretical treatment of this point, see Klaus Knorr, *Military Power and Potential* (Lexington, Mass.: D. C. Heath, 1970), pp. 73–90.

15. For details of this campaign, see Arnold L. Horelick and Myron Rush, *Strategic Power and Soviet Foreign Policy* (Chicago: University of Chicage Press, 1965), pp. 58–70, passim.

16. Frederick Seitz and Rodney W. Nichols, *Research and Development and the Prospects for International Security* (New York: Crane, Russak, 1973), p. 44.

17. AIAA, *International R&D Trends and Policies,* pp. 8–9.

18. Ibid., p. 9.

19. Ibid., p. 25.

20. Possony and Pournelle, *Strategy of Technology,* p. 2.

21. U.S., Congress, House, Committee on Armed Services, *Statement by the Director of Defense Research and Engineering, Dr. John S. Foster, Jr., on the Fiscal Year 1973 RD&E Program,* 92nd Cong., 2d sess., February 29, 1972, mimeographed, pp. 1–2.

22. *United States Government Manual, 1976–1977* (Washington, D.C.: Office of the Federal Register, National Archives and Records Service, General Services Administration, 1976), pp. 98–99.

23. Statement by Herman Kahn in *Hearings toward a National Security Policy,* p. 100.

24. Jack N. Merritt and Pierre M. Sprey, "Negative Marginal Returns in Weapons Acquisition"

in *American Defense Policy,* ed. Richard G. Head and Ervin J. Rokke, 3d ed. (Baltimore: Johns Hopkins University Press, 1973), p. 494.

25. Seitz and Nichols, *Research and Development,* pp. 12–13.

26. Possony and Pournelle, *Strategy of Technology,* p. 4.

27. Adam Yarmolinsky, "The President, the Congress, and Arms Control," in *The Military-Industrial Complex: A Reassessment,* ed. Sam C. Sarkesian (Beverly Hills, Calif.: Sage, 1972), pp. 278–79.

28. Ibid., p. 293. For a thorough treatment of the problem of congressional self-interest, see Bruce M. Russett, *What Price Vigilance?* (New Haven: Yale University Press, 1970), pp. 72–90.

29. Burns, "The Defense Sector," p. 60.

30. Merritt and Sprey, "Negative Marginal Returns," p. 486.

31. Drew Middleton, *New York Times,* April 19, 1974, p. C-20.

32. See, for examples of such problems, Richard Burt, "New Weapons Technologies: Debate and Directions," Adelphi Papers, no. 126 (London: International Institute for Strategic Studies, 1976), pp. 10–13.

33. Merritt and Sprey, "Negative Marginal Returns," p. 491. For a series of contrasting views, see Adelphi Papers, nos. 144 and 145 (London: International Institute for Strategic Studies, 1978).

34. Merritt and Sprey, "Negative Marginal Returns," p. 494.

35. For examples, see both William Proxmire, *Report from Wasteland* (New York: Praeger, 1970), chap. 10, and Sidney Lens, *The Military-Industrial Complex* (Philadelphia: Pilgrim Press, 1970), pp. 79–99.

CHAPTER 16

1. The term *superpower* orginated in William T. R. Fox, *The Superpowers: The United States, Britain, and the Soviet Union—Their Responsibility for Peace* (New York: Harcourt Brace, 1944). The "conventional wisdom" of a multipolar world is neatly rebutted in Kenneth Walth, *Theory of International Politics* (Reading, Mass.: Addison-Wesley, 1979), pp. 129–93. An analysis of order in anarchical systems can be found in Hedley Bull, *Anarchical Society* (New York: Columbia University Press, 1977).

2. Marshall Shulman, quoted in Helmut Sonnenfeldt, "Russia, America, and Detente," *Foreign Affairs* 56, no. 2 (January 1978): 275.

3. The Soviet perspective on U.S.-Soviet relations and national security can be found in N. Sivachev and N. Yakovlev, *Russia and the United States* (Chicago: University of Chicago Press, 1979), and Helmut Sonnennfeldt and William Hyland, "Soviet Perspectives on Security," Adelphi Papers, no. 150 (London: International Institute for Strategic Studies, spring 1979). For an analysis of the domestic determinants of Soviet policy, see Robert Byrnes, ed., *After Brezhnev: Sources of Soviet Conduct in the 1980s* (Bloomington: University of Indiana Press, 1983).

4. A selected bibliography of works on the cold war can be found in Toby Trister, "Traditionalists, Revisionists, and the Cold War," in *Caging the Bear: Containment and the Cold War,* ed. Charles Gati (New York: Bobbs Merrill, 1974), pp. 211–22.

5. George Kennan, "The Sources of Soviet Conduct," *Foreign Affairs* 25, no.4 (July 1947, reprinted in Gati, *Caging the Bear.*

6. Walter Lippmann, *U.S. Foreign Policy: Shield of the Republic* (Boston: Little, Brown, 1943), pp. 1–10.

7. Samuel Huntington, *The Common Defense* (New York: Columbia University Press, 1961), pp. 35–37.

8. Harry S. Truman, Address delivered to joint session of Congress, March 12, 1947, quoted in U.S., Congress, *Congressional Record,* 80th Cong., 1st sess., 1947, 93, pt. 2, p. 1981; and Kennan, *Sources of Soviet Conduct.*

9. Adam Ulam, *Expansion and Coexistence: Soviet Foreign Policy, 1917–1973,* rev. ed. (New York: Praeger, 1974), pp. 543–44.

10. For a complete record of the crisis, see Theodore C. Sorensen, *Kennedy* (New York: Harper & Row, 1965), pp. 667–719.

11. Urs Schwarz, *Confrontation and Intervention in the Modern World* (Dobbs Ferry, N.Y.: Oceana Press, 1970), p. 59.

12. V. V. Kuznetsov, quoted in Schwartz, *Foreign Policy of the U.S.S.R.*, p. 60, and John Newhouse, *Cold Dawn: The Story of SALT* (New York: Holt, Rinehart, & Winston, 1973), p. 68.

13. Herbert Dinerstein, "The Soviet Outlook," in *America and the World*, ed. Robert Osgood et al. (Baltimore: Johns Hopkins Press, 1970), pp. 82–83.

14. The conceptual framework behind détente (on the U.S. side) can be found in Henry Kissinger, "Detente with the Soviet Union: The Reality of Competition and the Imperative of Cooperation," *Department of State Bulletin* (Washington, D.C.: U.S. Government Printing Office, October 14, 1974), pp. 505–19. Cf. Theordore Draper, "Appeasement and Detente," *Commentary*, February 1976; Pierre Hassner, "Western European Perceptions of the U.S.S.R.," *Daedalus*, winter 1979, p. 115.

15. Kissinger, *Detente with the Soviet Union*, p. 509.

16. Leonid Brezhnev, quoted in *Current Soviet Policies VII: The Documentary Record of the Twenty-fifth Congress of the Communist Party of the Soviet Union* (Columbus, Ohio: American Association for the Advancement of Slavic Studies, 1976), pp. 13–14.

17. Dimitri Simes, "Detente, Russian-Style," *Foreign Policy*, no. 32 (fall 1978), p. 51.

18. For a concise account of this crisis, see Scott Sagan, "Lessons of the Yom Kippur Alert," *Foreign Policy*, no. 36 (fall 1979).

19. See Donald Zagoria, "Into the Breach: New Soviet Alliances in the Third World," *Foreign Affairs* 57, no. 4 (spring 1979): 733–35. Cf. Robert Legvold, "The Super Rivals: Conflict in the Third World," in the same issue.

20. On aid to the Baluchis, see Drew Middleton, "Moscow's Goal in Afghanistan: Encircle Iran?" *New York Times*, April 6, 1980, p. 16. See also, Selig Harrison, "Nightmare in Baluchistan," *Foreign Policy*, no. 32 (fall 1978), pp. 136–60.

21. These tactics are described in Kenneth Adelman, "Fear, Seduction, and Growing Soviet Strength," *Orbis*, winter 1978.

22. Edward Luttwak, "After Afghanistan, What?" *Commentary* 69, no. 4 (April 1980): 40–48.

23. "World Communist Solidarity with the Afghan Revolution," *Novoye Vremya* (Moscow), no. 3 (January 1980), p. 10. The original Brezhnev Doctrine was summarized by the Soviet leader himself at the Polish Party Congress in November 1968 when he said:

When the internal and external forces hostile to socialism seek to turn back the development of any Socialist country to restore the capitalist order, when a threat emerges to the cause of socialism in that country, a threat to the security of the Socialist Commmonwealth as a whole, this is no longer a matter only for the people of the country in question, but it is also a common problem, which is a matter of concern for all Socialist countries.

It goes without saying that such an action as military aid to a fraternal country to thwart the threat to the Socialist order is an extraordinary, enforced (that is, last resort) measure. It can be caused only by the direct actions of the enemies of socialism inside the country and beyond its boundaries—actions which create a threat to the common interests of the Socialist camp.

24. The material on the Afghan invasion is adapted from Joseph Collins, "The Soviet Invasion of Afghanistan: Methods, Motives, and Ramifications," *Naval War College Review* 33, no. 6 (November-December 1980). For a penetrating analysis of the fear and bluster behind the Soviet view of the correlation of forces, see Vernon Aspaturian, "Soviet Global Power and the Correlation of Forces," *Problems of Communism*, May 1980, pp. 1–18.

25. Richard Pipes, "Why the Soviet Union Thinks It Could Fight and Win a Nuclear War," *Commentary* 64, no. 1 (July 1977). Cf. Raymond Garthoff, "Mutual Deterrence and Strategic Arms Limitation in Soviet Policy," *International Security*, summer 1978.

26. For an explanation of Minuteman vulnerability and its alleged political consequences, see interview with Henry Kissinger, "Kissinger's Critique," pt. 1, *Economist*, February 1979, pp. 17–22. A balanced examination of this and other Soviet threats can be found in Grayson Kirk and Nils Wessell, eds. *The Soviet Threat: Myths and Realities* (New York: Academy of Political Science, 1978).

27. Daniel Gouré and Gordon McCormick, "Soviet Strategic Defense: The Neglected Dimension of the U.S.-Soviet Balance," *Comparative Strategy*, spring 1980, pp. 103–27.

28. For an explanation of "fear and seduction," see "Growing Soviet Strength." For Soviet economic relations with Europe, see Fritz Stern, "Germany in a Semi-Gaullist Europe," *Foreign Affairs* 58, no. 4 (spring 1980), pp. 877–86, which contains a description of European problems related to East-West détente. See also Hassner, "Western European Perceptions."

29. International Institute for Strategic Studies, *The Military Balance, 1979–1980* (London: IISS, 1980), p. 112.

30. For a description of NATO efforts to redress the imbalances, see U.S., *Department of Defense Annual Report, Fiscal Year 1981* (Washington, D.C.: U.S. Government Printing Office, 1980). (Hereafter cited as *DOD Report, FY 81.*)

31. Amoretta Hoeber and Joseph Douglass, Jr., "The Neglected Threat of Chemical Warfare," *International Security*, summer 1978, p. 56.

32. For an analysis of this metaphor, see Adam Garfinkel, *"Finlandization": A Map to a Metaphor*, Foreign Policy Research Institute Monograph 24 (Philadelphia: FPRI, 1978), pp. 1–56. For an analysis of other structural options that might develop if Western Europe were separated from the United States, see Warner Schilling et al., *American Arms and a Changing Europe: Dilemmas of Deterrence and Disarmament* (New York: Colombia University Press, 1973), pp. 123–95.

33. Zbigniew Brzezinski, "Peace and Power," *Encounter*, November 1968, pp. 3–13.

34. Constraints on Soviet naval power are summarized in John Collins, *U.S.-Soviet Military Balance: Concepts and Capabilities, 1960–1980* (New York: McGraw-Hill, 1980), pp. 239–66.

35. Material on Soviet intelligence, except where otherwise noted, comes from ibid., pp. 77–81; U.S., Congress, Senate, Select Committee on Intelligence, *Report on Foreign and Military Intelligence*, 94th Cong., 2d sess., 1976, pp. 557–62; and G. Skilling and D. Griffiths, eds., *Interest Groups in Soviet Politics* (Princeton: Princeton University Press, 1973).

36. See D. Shipler, "A Palestinian Guerilla Describes Taking Combat Training in Soviet Union," *New York Times*, October 31, 1980, p. 1.

37. Seweryn Bialer, *Stalin's Successors: Leadership, Stability, and Change in the Soviet Union* (New York: Cambridge University Press, 1980), p. 263.

38. Byrnes, *After Brezhnev*, p. 93.

39. CIA, *Problems and Prospects*, p. 5.

40. Luttwak, "After Afghanistan," pp. 45–46.

41. See Nigerian General Obasanjo's commentary, quoted in U.S., Congress, House, Committee on International Relations, *United States-Soviet Relations, 1978*, 95th Cong., 1st sess., p. 25.

42. Richard Burt, "New Nuclear Strategy: An Inevitable Shift" *New York Times*, August 7, 1980, p. 3. See also the *Washington Post* during September–December 1983 period for presidential candidate statements on defense and foreign policy.

43. *DOD Report, FY 1981*, pp. 65–66.

44. A balanced analysis of SALT II can be found in Foreign Policy Association, *SALT II: Toward Security of Danger* (New York: FPA, June 1979). For a rigorous examination of Soviet performance under SALT I, see David Sullivan, *Soviet SALT Deception* (Boston: Coalition for Peace through Strength, 1979). An analysis of future arms control options can be found in Leslie Gelb, "The Future of Arms Control: A Glass Half Full," *Foreign Policy*, no. 36 (fall 1979), pp. 21–32. See also Richard Burt's article, "A Glass Half Empty," in the same issue, and Barry Blechman's "Do Negotiated Arms Limitations Have a Future?" *Foreign Affairs* 59, no. 1 (fall 1980): 119–25.

CHAPTER 17

1. Leslie H. Brown, "American Security Policy in Asia," Adelphi Papers, no. 132 (London: International Institute for Strategic Studies, spring 1977).

2. Richard H. Solomon, "American Defense Planning and Asian Security: Policy Choices for a Time of Transition," in Solomon, ed., *Asian Security in the 1980s: Problems and Policies for a Time of Transition* (Santa Monica, Calif.: Rand Corp., November 1979), pp. 9–11.

3. Ibid., p. 2.

4. Noel Gayler, "Security Implications of the Soviet Military Presence in Asia," in Solomon, ed., *Asian Security*, p. 67.

5. William G. Hyland, "The Sino-Soviet Conflict: A Search for New Security Strategies," in ibid., pp. 39–53.

6. Ibid.

7. Goh Keng Swee, "Vietnam and Big-Power Rivalry," in Solomon, *Asian Security*, pp. 148–52.

8. Solomon, "American Defense Planning," pp. 27–28.

9. Ibid., pp. 30–31.

10. Ibid., pp. 26–27.

11. Paul F. Langer, "Changing Japanese Security Perspectives," in Solomon, *Asian Security*, pp. 83–87.

12. Saburo Okita, "Japan, China, and the United States," *Foreign Affairs* 57, no. 5 (summer 1979): 1098.

13. Isaac Shapiro, "The Risen Sun," *Foreign Policy*, no. 41 (winter 1980/81), p. 73.

14. Richard L. Sneider, "Prospects For Korean Security," in Solomon, *Asian Security,* pp. 110–12.

15. Ibid., p. 131.

16. Ibid., p. 115.

17. Edwin K. Snyder, A. James Gregor, and Maria Hsia Chang, "The Taiwan Relations Act and the Defense of the Republic of China" (Berkeley: Institute of International Studies, University of Southern California, 1980).

18. Ibid., pp. 63–81.

19. Ibid.

20. Ibid., pp. 81–100.

21. Leslie H. Gelb, "U.S. Defense Policy, Technology Transfers, and Asian Security," in Solomon, *Asian Security,* pp. 266–68.

22. Guy J. Pauker, "The Security Implications of Regional Energy and Natural Resource Exploitation," in ibid., pp. 216–19.

23. Snyder et al., "Taiwan Relations Act," p. 102.

24. Ibid., pp. 2–3.

25. Swee, "Vietnam and Big-Power Rivalry," pp. 148–68.

CHAPTER 18

1. For a comprehensive discussion of U.S. interests in the Middle East before the 1967 war, see George Lenczowski, ed., *United States Interests in the Middle East* (Washington, D.C.: American Enterprise Institute for Public Policy Research, 1968), pp. 14–76.

2. James Schlesinger, "The Strategic Vortex," *Washington Quarterly*, winter 1980, pp. 177–84.

3. Lenczowski, *United States Interests*, pp. 39–40.

4. British Petroleum Co., Ltd., *BP Statistical Review of the World Oil Industry, 1974* (London: BP, 1974), p. 21.

5. R. D. McLaurin, Mohammed Mughisuddin, and Abraham R. Wagner, *Foreign Policy Making in the Middle East* (New York: Praeger, 1977), p. 11; *Petroleum Intelligence Weekly*, April 25, 1983, p. 6.

6. James A. Bill and Robert W. Stookey, *Politics and Petroleum: The Middle East and the United States* (Brunswick, Ohio: King's Court Communications, 1975), pp. 123–24.

7. Ibid., p. 128.

8. Amos A. Jordan, "Energy and National Security: Sizing Up the Risks," *Washington Quarterly* 3, no. 3 (summer 1980), 154–63.

9. R. J. Sontag and J. S. Beddie, eds., *Nazi-Soviet Relations, 1939–1941* (Washington, D.C.: U.S. Government Printing Office, 1948), p. 259.

10. Tareq Y. Ismael, *The Middle East in World Politics* (Syracuse: Syracuse University Press, 1974), pp. 124–27.

11. Perhaps the best treatment of the conflict between competition and détente in the Middle

East is Lawrence L. Whetten, *The Canal War: Four-Power Conflict in the Middle East* (Cambridge, Mass.: MIT Press, 1974), pp. 331–40.

12. For a detailed discussion of the issue, see William B. Quandt, *Decade of Decisions: American Policy toward the Arab-Israeli Conflict, 1967–1976* (Berkeley and Los Angeles: University of California Press, 1977), pp. 9–12.

13. Ibid., pp. 15–24.

14. Whetten, *The Canal War*, pp. 137, 165, 203–5, 289.

15. Letter to Gerald Ford, May 1975, quoted in *The Middle East: U.S. Policy, Israel, Oil, and the Arabs* (Washington, D.C.: Congressional Quarterly, 1977), p. 96.

16. W. Seth Carus, "The Military Balance of Power in the Middle East," *Current History*, no. 74 (January 1978), pp. 29–30.

17. A comprehensive treatment of such problems can be found in Majid Khadduri, *Political Trends in the Arab World* (Baltimore: Johns Hopkins Press, 1970). Iran and Turkey faced the same difficulties but to a lesser extent.

18. The classic treatment of this subject is Malcolm Kerr, *The Arab Cold War*, 3d ed. (London: Oxford University Press, 1971).

19. Sidney H. Zebel, *Balfour: A Political Biography* (Cambridge: At the University Press, 1973), p. 238.

20. Janet L. Abu-Lughod, "The Demographic Transformation of Palestine," in *The Transformation of Palestine*, ed. Ebrahim Abu-Lughod (Evanston, Ill.: Northwestern University Press, 1971), pp. 141–53.

21. Ann Mosely Lesch, "The Palestine Arab Nationalist Movement under the Mandate," in *The Politics of Palestinian Nationalism*, ed. William B. Quandt (Berkeley and Los Angeles: University of California Press, 1973), pp. 33–40. See also David Hirst, *The Gun and the Olive Branch: The Roots of Violence in the Middle East* (New York: Harcourt Brace Jovanovich, 1977), pp. 97–106.

22. For a detailed discussion of the UN partition plan and the role of the United States in getting it passed, see Khouri, *Dilemma*, pp. 43–67. For its immediate effects in Palestine, see William B. Quandt, "The Eclipse of Palestinian Nationalism, 1947–1967," in Quandt, *Politics of Palestinian Nationalism*, pp. 45–48.

23. Khouri, *Dilemma*, pp. 72, 77.

24. Ibid., pp. 187–89.

25. David A. Deese and Joseph S. Nye, eds. *Energy and Security* (Cambridge, Mass.: Ballinger, 1981), pp. 88–91.

26. International Institute for Strategic Studies, "The Middle East," in *Strategic Survey, 1979* (London: IISS, 1979), p. 73.

27. Shahram Chubin and Sepehr Zabin, *The Foreign Relations of Iran* (Berkeley and Los Angeles: University of California Press, 1974), pp. 178–81. See also McLaurin et al., *Foreign Policy Making*, pp. 130–39, and Rouhollah K. Ramazani, *The Persian Gulf: Iran's Role* (Charlottesville: University Press of Virginia, 1972), pp. 45–68.

28. See Amos A. Jordan, "Saudi Pillar on Firmer Soil," *Washington Star*, February 18, 1979, p. D-1.

29. Claudia Wright, "Implications of the Iran-Iraq War," *Foreign Affairs* 59, no. 2 (winter 1980/81): 275–303.

30. Craig R. Whitney, "Soviet Union and Turkey Sign Nonaggression, Trade, and Cultural Pacts," *New York Times*, June 24, 1978, p. 3.

31. McLaurin et al., *Foreign Policy Making*, pp. 20–25.

32. Alvin J. Cottrell and R. M. Burrell, "Soviet-U.S. Naval Competition in the Indian Ocean," *Orbis*, no. 18 (winter 1975).

33. Whetten, *The Canal War*, pp. 59–60.

34. Robert O. Freedman, *Soviet Policy toward the Middle East since 1970* (New York: Praeger, 1975), pp. 172–79.

35. Bill and Stooley, *Politics and Petroleum*, p. 123.

36. Jimmy Carter, State of the Union address, January 1980.

CHAPTER 19

1. For a coherent analysis of Zaire's massive internal problems, see Crawford Young, "Zaire: The Unending Crisis," *Foreign Affairs* 57, no. 1 (fall 1978): 169–85.

2. For an elaboration of the U.S. interests in Africa discussed in this chapter, see U.S., Congress, House, Committee on Foreign Affairs, Subcommittee on Africa, *Hearings, U.S. Interests in Africa, Prepared Statement of Hon. Joseph J. Sisco, President, American University*, 96th Cong., 1st sess. (Washington, D.C.: U.S. Government Printing Office, 1980), pp. 7–10.

3. Anthony Lake, Director of Policy Planning Staff, U.S. Department of State, in a speech for the Christian A. Herter Lecture, Johns Hopkins University, October 27, 1977 (Washington, D.C.: Bureau of Public Affairs, Department of State, 1977).

4. U.S., Congress, *U.S. Interests in Africa, Prepared Statement of Hon. C. Fred Bersten, Assistant Secretary of the Treasury for International Affairs*, pp. 249–255.

5. Philip L. Christenson, "Some Economic Facts of Life," *AEI Foreign Policy and Defense Review* 1, no. 1 (*Options for U.S. Policy toward Africa*), ed. Helen Kitchen (1979). (Hereafter cited as *AEI FPDR.*)

6. For an excellent discussion of the military coup as an African political institution, see Aristide Zolberg, "The Structure of Political Conflict in the New States of Tropical Africa," *American Political Science Review* 62, no. 1 (March 1968): pp. 70–87; Claude E. Welch, Jr., ed., *The Soldier and the State in Africa* (Evanston, Ill.: Northwestern University Press, 1970); and Henry Bienen, *Armies and Parties in Africa* (New York: Africana, 1978).

7. Abdul A. Said, *The African Phenomenon* (Boston: Allyn & Bacon, 1968), pp. 120–22.

8. A concise background to the three southern African crises is John Marcum's chapter, "Southern Africa after the Collapse of Portuguese Rule," in *Africa: From Mystery to Maze*, ed. Helen Kitchen (Lexington, Mass.: D. C. Heath, 1976).

9. See Gerard Chaliand, "The Horn of Africa's Dilemma," *Foreign Policy*, no. 30 (spring 1978).

10. Kofi A. Busia, *Africa in Search of Identity* (New York: Frederick A. Praeger, 1967), p. 111. For a more extensive discussion of corruption and military coups in Africa, see Joseph S. Nye, "Corruption and Political Development: A Cost-Benefit Analysis," *American Political Science Review* 61, no. 2 (June 1967): 417–27, and Aaron S. Klieman, "Confined to Barracks: Emergencies and the Military in Developing Societies," *Comparative Politics* 12, no. 2 (January 1980): 143–63.

11. This section summarizes material in Henry A. Kissinger, Speech delivered before the Opportunities Industrializations Centers (Washington, D.C.: Bureau of Public Affairs, Department of State, August 31, 1976); see also David B. Bolen, "Trade and Investment: Another Dimension of U.S.-Africa Relations," *Department of State Bulletin* 75, no. 1951 (Washington, D.C.: U.S. Government Printing Office, 1976), pp. 616–22.

12. The state of African agriculture is more fully elaborated in Kissinger, OIC speech, and Bolen, "Trade and Investment."

13. Bolen, "Trade and Investment," pp. 616–22.

14. Zdenek Cervenka, "The Organization of African Unity in 1976," in *Africa Contemporary Record: Annual Survey and Documents, 1976–1977*, ed. Colin Legum (New York: Africana, 1977), p. A-74. See also Joseph Margolis, "Dissension and Resolution," *Africa Report*, September-October 1979, pp. 52–55.

15. David Ottaway, "Africa: U.S. Policy Eclipse," *Foreign Affairs* 58, no. 3 (*America and the World*) (1979): 653–54.

16. Cervenka, "African Unity," p. A-70.

17. Colin Legum, "The African Crisis," *Foreign Affairs* 57, no. 3 (*America and the World*) (1978): 646–50.

18. Murray Marder and Michael Getler, "Kissinger Says U.S. Must Stop Soviets in Angola: Says African War Not like Vietnam," *Washington Post*, December 13, 1975, p. A-1.

19. Joseph Kraft, "African Reward," *Washington Post*, April 2, 1978, p. C-7.

20. Lake, Herter speech.

21. Ernest W. Lefever, *Spear and Scepter* (Washington, D.C.: Brookings Institution, 1970), p. 14.

22. Chester Crocker, "Why the Debate on Soviet Policy Misses the Point," *AEI FPDR,* pp. 52–53.

23. For the quagmire theory, see Arthur M. Schlesinger, Jr., "Russians and Cubans in Africa," *Wall Street Journal,* May 2, 1978, reprinted in *AEI FPDR,* pp. 31–33. For the economic determinism theory, see Robert M. Price, "Flaws in the Strategic Paradigm," excerpted from *U.S. Foreign Policy in Sub-Saharan Africa: National Interest and Global Strategy, AEI FPDR,* p. 38.

24. Among those who perceive a serious threat to U.S. security in Soviet African policy are Lt. Gen. Daniel O. Graham, U.S. Army (ret.), Chester Crocker, Bayard Rustin, and Carl Gershman. See their articles on the subject in *AEI FPDR* for a more complete elaboration of this viewpoint.

25. Kevin Klose, "The State of Detente," *Washington Post,* March 26, 1978, p. A-19.

26. Schlesinger, *AEI FPDR,* pp. 31–33.

27. Shirley Washington, "Toward a New Relationship," *Africa Report,* March-April 1980, pp. 17–22.

28. Bruce Larkin, "China and the Third World," *Current History* 69, no. 408 (September 1975): 75.

29. "The Cubans in Africa," *Newsweek,* March 13, 1978, p. 36. Arthur Schlesinger takes the opposite view. He sees a growing Cuban domestic crisis due to its African involvement; see his article in *AEI FPDR,* p. 33.

30. Legum, "The African Crisis," pp. 638–39.

31. John F. Burns, "South Africa Modifying Apartheid without Weakening White Power," *New York Times,* April 6, 1978, p. 1.

CHAPTER 20

1. Arthur P. Whitaker, *The Western Hemisphere Idea* (Ithaca: Cornell University Press, 1954).

2. James Monroe, Annual message delivered to the Congress, December 2, 1833.

3. Article 5f, Charter of the Organization of American States.

4. Donald M. Dozer, "The Contemporary Significance of the Monroe Doctrine," in *Latin America Politics, Economics, and Hemispheric Security,* ed. Norman A. Bailey (New York: Frederick A. Praeger, 1965).

5. Margaret Daly Hayes, "Security to the South: U.S. Interests in Latin America," *International Security* 5, no. 1 (summer 1980): 133.

6. A further discussion of U.S. involvement appears in James Petras and Morris Morley, "On the U.S. and the Overthrow of Allende: A Reply to Professor Sigmund's Criticism," *Latin American Research Review* 13, no. 1 (1978), pp. 205–24.

7. David Ronfeldt, Richard Nehring, and Arturo Gandara, *Mexico's Petroleum and U.S. Policy Implications for the 1980s* (Santa Monica, Calif.: Rand Corp., June 1980), p. 8.

8. Nelson A. Rockefeller, *The Rockefeller Report on the Americas* (New York: Quadrangle Books, 1969). A strikingly different view appears in Gregory F. Treverton, "Latin America in World Politics: The Next Decade," Adelphi Papers, no. 137 (London: International Institute for Strategic Studies, 1977).

9. Among the best works on U.S.–Latin American relations between 1850 and 1950 are Samuel Flagg Bemis, *The Latin American Policy of the United States* (New York: Harcourt, Brace and World, 1943); J. Lloyd Mecham, *The United States and Inter–American Security, 1889–1960* (Austin: University of Texas Press, 1962); Thomas Palmer, *The Search for a Latin American Policy* (Gainesville: University of Florida Press, 1957); and Ann Van Wynen Thomas and A. J. Thomas, *Non-Intervention: The Law and Its Import in the Americas* (Dallas: Southern Methodist University Press, 1956).

10. For example, see Anibal Quijano Obregon, "Imperialism and International Relations," in *Latin America and the United States,* ed. Julio Cotler and Richard R. Fagen (Stanford: Stanford University Press, 1974), pp. 67–91; and C. Wright Mills, *Listen Yankee* (New York: Ballantine Books, 1960).

11. An excellent account is Bryce Wood, *The Making of the Good Neighbor Policy* (New York: Columbia University Press, 1961).

12. John M. Hunter and James W. Foley, *Economic Problems of Latin America* (Boston: Houghton Mifflin, 1975), p. 204.

13. See Frank D. McCann, *The Brazilian American Alliance* (Princeton: Princeton University Press, 1974).

14. See Abraham F. Lowenthal, *The Dominican Intervention* (Cambridge, Mass.: Harvard University Press, 1972).

15. Lawrence Harrison, "Waking from the Pan-American Dream," *Foreign Policy*, no. 5 (winter 1971–72).

16. U.S., Department of State Publication no. 7756, Bureau of Public Affairs (Washington, D.C.: U.S. Government Printing Office, October 1977).

17. Olive Holmes, "Peron's 'Greater Argentina' and the United States," *Foreign Policy Reports*, no. 24 (December 1, 1946), pp. 158–71. Cf. the same author's "Argentina and the Dream of Southern Union," in *Political, Economic, and Social Problems of the Latin American Nations of Southern South America* (Austin: University of Texas, Institute of Latin American Studies, 1949), pp. 43–57.

18. *Caretas* (Lima, Peru), October 7, 1971. Cf. Foreign Policy Research Institute, *Brazil's Future Role in International Politics*, mimeographed (Philadelphia, 1973), pp. 323–24.

19. *Hispanic American Report* 9, no. 10 (November 1956): 500; vol. 10, no. 9 (October 1957): 491; and vol. 11, no. 2 (March 1958): 109.

20. A detailed discussion of the Itaipú conflict appears in *Correio Brasiliense* (Brasília, Brazil), July 11, 1973. Cf. Almeida Salles, "A fabula do o lobo e o cordeiro," *Folha de Sao Paulo* (Sao Paulo, Brazil), June 3, 1971.

21. Instituto Argentino de Estudios Estrategicos y de Relaciones Internacionales, "Argentina y Brazil: Estudio comparativo de algunas de sus aspectos fundamentales," *Estrategia* (Buenos Aires, January-February 1970), p. 74.

22. Gen. Golbery do Couto e Silva, *Geopolitica do Brasil* (Rio de Janeiro: Olympio, 1967), p. 174.

23. Smith, "Bolivian Oil."

24. Embaixada do Brasil, *Boletim especial,* July 5, 1977.

25. Martin Katzman, "The Geopolitical Significance of Brazilian Frontier Expansion" (Paper delivered at a meeting of the Latin American Studies Association, Houston, Texas, November 1977), pp. 12–13.

26. Miguel Ozorio de Almeida, "Amazonica: O problema da urbanizacao em areas pioneras," *Revista Brasileira de politica internacional* 14, no. 55–56 (September-December 1971), pp. 30–44.

27. Raymond E. Crist and Charles M. Nissly, *East from the Andes* (Gainesville: University of Florida Press, 1973), p. 116.

28. *Journal do Brasil* (Rio de Janeiro, Brazil), November 30, 1977.

29. International Institute for Strategic Studies, *Strategic Survey, 1979* (London: IISS, 1979), pp. 108–12.

30. United Nations Economic Commission for Latin America, "Center and Periphery: New Basis for Negotiation," *Economic Survey for Latin America, 1973* (New York: United Nations, 1975), pp. 1–12.

31. James D. Theberge, *The Soviet Presence in Latin America* (New York: Crane, Russak, 1974), pp. 12–16.

32. "The Brazilian Gamble: Why Bankers Bet on Brazil's Technocrats," *Business Week,* December 5, 1977, pp. 72–81.

33. United Nations, "Center and Periphery," pp. 7–12.

34. Norman J. Padelford, George A. Lincoln, and Lee D. Olvey, *The Dynamics of International Politics,* 3d ed. (New York: Macmillan, 1976), pp. 477–78.

35. John Saxe-Fernandez, "From Counterinsurgency to Counterintelligence," in Colter and Fagen, *Latin America and the United States,* pp. 347–60.

36. Norman D. Arbaiza, *Mars Moves South* (Jericho, N.Y.: Exposition Press, 1974), pp. 17–19.

37. Osiris Guillerno Villegas, *Politicas y estrategias para el desarrollo y la seguridad nacional* (Buenos Aires: Editorial Pleamar, 1969), chap. 10.

38. Interview with a high official in the Venezuelan Institute for Foreign Commerce, March 30, 1978.

39. This is confirmed by taking inventory of the weapons possessed by the Latin American states, International Institute for Strategic Studies, *The Military Balance, 1974–1979* (London: IISS, 1979), pp. 70–77.

40. Robert D. Bond, "Venezuela's Role in International Affairs," in *Contemporary Venezuela and Its Role in International Relations,* ed. Robert D. Bond (New York: New York University Press, 1977), pp. 248–56. Cf. *Veja* (Rio de Janeiro), January 14, 1976.

41. U.S. Arms Control and Disarmament Agency, *World Military Expenditures and Arms Trade, 1963–1973* (Washington, D.C.: U.S. ACDA, 1975). Cf. John Samuel Fitch, "The Political Consequences of U.S. Military Assistance to Latin America," paper, University of Florida, January 1977.

42. Larry Rohter, "Brazil Stepping up Arms Output," *New York Times,* December 18, 1977.

43. Cilt Waisman, "Incentives for Nuclear Proliferation: The Case of Argentina," in *Nuclear Proliferation and the Near Nuclear Countries,* ed. Onkar Marivah and Ann Schuby (Cambridge, Mass.: Ballinger, 1975), chap. 12.

44. Normal Gall, "Atoms for Brazil, Dangers for All," *Foreign Policy,* no. 23 (summer 1976), pp. 155–201.

CHAPTER 21

1. Hans J. Morgenthau, *Politics among Nations: The Struggle for Power and Peace,* 5th ed. (New York: Alfred A. Knopf, 1973), p. 181.

2. Norman J. Padelford and George A. Lincoln, *The Dynamics of International Politics,* 2d ed. (New York: Macmillan, 1967), p. 5.

3. This discussion of alliance motives is adapted from Raymond F. Hopkins and Richard W. Mansbach, *Structure and Process in International Politics* (New York: Harper & Row, 1973), pp. 306–8.

4. Robert F. Randle, *The Origins of Peace* (New York: Free Press, 1973), p. 117.

5. Robert Endicott Osgood, *Alliances and American Foreign Policy* (Baltimore: Johns Hopkins Press, 1968), pp. 21–22.

6. See Philip M. Burgess and James A. Robinson, "Alliances and the Theory of Collective Action: A Simulation of Coalition Processes," in *International Politics and Foreign Policy,* rev. ed., James N. Rosenau (New York: Free Press, 1969).

7. Ernst B. Haas, "Balance of Power: Prescription, Concept, or Propaganda?" in *A Multi-Method Introduction to International Politics,* ed. William D. Coplin and Charles W. Kegley, Jr. (Chicago: Markham, 1975); Inis L. Claude, Jr., *Power and International Relations* (New York: Random House, 1962), p. 13.

8. Ibid., pp. 17–20.

9. An excellent discussion of the European balance of power system is Edward V. Gulick, *Europe's Classical Balance of Power* (Ithaca: Cornell University Press, 1955).

10. Claude, *Power and International Relations,* p. 41.

11. These two dimensions are from Hopkins and Mansbach, *Structure and Process,* pp. 84–93.

12. See Karl Deutsch et al., *Political Community in the North Atlantic Area* (Princeton: Princeton University Press, 1957).

13. Osgood, *Alliances and American Foreign Policy,* p. 38.

14. Jerome Slater, *The OAS and United States Foreign Policy* (Columbus: Ohio State University Press, 1967), p. 33.

15. For the original intent of the OAS, see ibid., p. 36; Cyrus Vance, quoted in Hopkins and Mansbach, *Structure and Process,* p. 326.

16. Henry A. Kissinger, "The Future of NATO," *Washington Quarterly* 2, no. 4 (autumn 1979): 7.

17. For a brief but useful discussion of the military doctrine of flexible response, see Richard Hart Sinnreich, "NATO's Doctrinal Dilemma," *Orbis* 19 (summer 1975): 461–77; see also

Robert Kennedy, "NATO Defense Posture in an Environment of Strategic Parity and Precision Weaponry," in *Strategies, Alliances, and Military Power: Changing Roles*, ed. James A. Kuhlman (Leiden, Neth.: A. W. Sijthoff, 1977), pp. 297–317.

18. Kissinger, "The Future of NATO," p. 4.

19. Howard Roberts, "Retaliation in Kind: A Rational and Feasible Strategy for NATO," paper, Princeton University, March 20, 1979.

20. Robert McNamara, Commencement address delivered at the University of Michigan, Ann Arbor, Michigan, June 16, 1962.

21. For an example, see Steven Canby, *NATO Military Policy: Obtaining Conventional Comparability with the Warsaw Pact*, R-1088/ARPA (Santa Monica, Calif.: Rand Corp., 1973).

22. Osgood, *Alliances and American Foreign Policy*, pp. 78–79.

23. Ibid., p. 76.

24. Ibid., p. 77.

25. *U.S. Military Commitments Abroad* (Washington, D.C.: Congressional Quarterly, September 1969).

26. Osgood, *Alliances and American Foreign Policy*, p. 80.

27. Henry A. Kissinger, *Nuclear Weapons and Foreign Policy* (New York: Harper & Bros., 1957), pp. 237–38.

28. Richard M. Nixon, "U.S. Foreign Policy for the 1970s," *A Report to the Congress*, February 25, 1971 (Washington, D.C.: U.S. Government Printing Office, 1971), pp. 12–14.

CHAPTER 22

1. Indar Jit Rikhye, Michael Karbottle, and Ejorn Egge, *The Thin Blue Line: International Peacekeeping and Its Future* (New Haven: Yale University Press, 1974), p. 11.

2. The history and theory that underpin chaps. 6 and 7 of the charter are cogently described in Inis L. Claude, Jr., *Swords into Plowshares* (New York: Random House, 1971), pp. 215–84.

3. Noncoercive techniques are cited in charter of the United Nations, article 33; various coercive means are cited in ibid., article 42.

4. Ibid., article 42.

5. For urgent military measures, see ibid., article 45; for negotiations, see ibid., article 47.

6. John G. Stoessinger, *The United Nations and the Superpowers: United States–Soviet Interaction at the United Nations* (New York: Random House, 1970), p. 192.

7. Kenneth W. Thompson, "The Concept of Collective Security," in *Discord and Harmony: Readings in International Politics,* ed. Ivo D. Duchacek (New York: Holt, Rinehart & Winston, 1972), p. 356.

8. Lincoln P. Bloomfield, *The United Nations and U.S. Foreign Policy: A Look at the National Interest* (New York: Alfred A. Knopf, 1969), p. 4.

9. Leland M. Goodrich and Anne P. Simons, "The Rise and Fall of the Military Staff Committee," in *From Collective Security to Preventive Diplomacy,* ed. Joel Larus (New York: John Wiley & Sons, 1965), p. 224.

10. Charter of the United Nations, chapter 7, article 51.

11. United Nations General Assembly Resolution 377A (V), November 3, 1950.

12. Secretary-General U Thant, Address delivered to the Harvard Alumni Association, Cambridge, Mass., June 13, 1963, quoted in William Bishop, Jr., *International Law,* 3d ed. (Boston: Little, Brown, 1971), p. 260.

13. Lincoln P. Bloomfield and Amelia C. Leiss, *Controlling Small Wars: A Strategy for the 1970s* (New York: Alfred A. Knopf, 1969), p. 410.

14. Bloomfield, *The United Nations and U.S. Foreign Policy,* p. 10.

15. A useful discussion of recent UN peace-keeping activities is contained in International Institute for Strategic Studies, *Strategic Survey, 1978* (London: IISS, 1979), pp. 17–22.

16. For a synopsis of United Nations peace-keeping missions since 1945, see Larry L. Fabian, *Soldiers without Enemies: Preparing the United States for Peacekeeping* (Washington, D.C.: Brookings Institution, 1971), pp. 261–65.

17. For a firsthand account of the complexities of ONUC, see Carl von Horn, *Soldiering for Peace* (New York: David McKay, 1967).

18. Fabian, *Soldiers without Enemies,* p. 79.

19. Rikhye et al., *The Thin Blue Line,* pp. 133–38.

20. Charles C. Moskos, Jr., *Peace Soldiers: The Sociology of a United Nations Military Force* (Chicago: University of Chicago Press, 1976), p. 45.

21. Ibid., pp. 140–47; James O. C. Jonah, "Importance of UN Peacekeeping Operations Emphasized," *UN Chronicle* 16, no. 5 (July 1979): 80–81.

22. Rikhye et al., *The Thin Blue Line,* p. 315.

23. Ibid., pp. 62–65, 317–18.

24. Ibid., p. 309.

25. Ibid., p. 12.

26. "Council Decides Not to Extend UNEF Mandate," *UN Chronicle* 16, no. 6 (July-October 1979): 24; Jonah, "UN Peacekeeping Operations," pp. 81–82.

27. Jonah, "UN Peacekeeping Operations," pp. 81–82; "Council Calls on Israel to End Incursions into Lebanon," *UN Chronicle* 16, no. 5 (July 1979): 5–8.

28. "Secretary-General Reports to Council on Namibia Issue," *UN Chronicle* 16, no. 3 (March 1979): 18–19; "Security Council to be Asked to Impose Mandatory Sanctions on South Africa," *UN Chronicle* 17, no. 1 (January 1980): 20–21; and Kenneth Adelman, "Western Policy in Southern Africa," *Current History* 78, no. 455 (March 1980): 124–26.

29. Oran Young, "The United Nations and the International System," *International Organization* 20 (August 1968): 904.

30. For support problems, see Edward H. Bowman and James L. Fanning, "Logistics: Experience and Requirements," in *International Military Forces: The Question of Peacekeeping in an Armed and Disarming World,* ed. Lincoln P. Bloomfield (Little, Brown, 1964), p. 162. For coordination problems, see von Horn, *Soldiering for Peace.*

31. See U.S., Congress, House, Committee on Foreign Affairs, Subcommittee on International Organizations, *Hearings, U.S. Participation in the UN and UN Reform,* 96th Cong., 1st sess., June 14, 1979, pt. 2, pp. 38–46.

32. Ibid. See also U.S., Congress, Senate, Committee on Foreign Relations, *Hearings, UN Reform,* 96th Cong., 1st sess., October 26, 1979, pp. 7–14.

33. Moskos, *Peace Soldiers,* p. 25.

34. UN Document, A/3943, October 9, 1958, quoted in ibid., p. 25.

35. See, for example, Bernard D. Nossiter, "Iran Is the Target but UN Can Only Fire Words," *New York Times,* December 2, 1979, sec. 6, p. 1.

36. Bloomfield, *The United Nations and U.S. Foreign Policy,* p. 30.

37. An excellent discussion of U.S. interests is provided in Frederic S. Pearson et al., "The Carter Foreign Policy and the Use of International Organizations: The Limits of Policy Innovation," *World Affairs* 142, no. 2 (fall 1979). For the recent U.S. government policy toward the UN and toward strengthening UN peace-keeping capabilities, see U.S., Congress, Senate, Report to the Committee on Foreign Relations, *Proposals for United Nations Reforms,* 95th Cong., 2d sess., March 1978). For the UN response to U.S. proposals, see United Nations, General Assembly, *Special Committee on Peace-keeping Operations, Comprehensive Review of the Whole Question of Peace-Keeping Operations in All Their Aspects: Report of the Secretary General,* UNGA, 34th sess., August 27, 1979.

38. U.S., Department of State, *Department of State Bulletin* 66 (Washington, D.C.: U.S. Government Printing Office, March 13, 1972): 405.

CHAPTER 23

1. Kenneth N. Waltz, *Man, the State, and War* (New York: Columbia University Press, 1959), p. 12.

2. Thomas Malthus, *An Essay on the Principle of Population* (New York: Macmillan, 1895), pp. 47–48; Benedict de Spinoza, "Political Treatise," chap. i, sec. 5, in *The Chief Works of Benedict de Spinoza,* trans. R.H.M. Elwes, 2 vols. (New York: Dover, 1951); Sigmund Freud,

in his 1932 letter to Albert Einstein, see Freud, "On War," reprinted in *War: Studies from Psychology, Sociology and Anthropology*, ed. Leon Bramson and George W. Goethals (New York: Basic Books, 1964), p. 72; Konrad Lorenz, *On Aggression* (New York: Harcourt Brace, 1966), esp. chaps. 7 and 13.

3. See Mark A. May, *A Social Psychology of War and Peace* (New Haven: Yale University Press, 1943).

4. See V. I. Lenin, *Imperialism: The Highest Stage of Capitalism* (New York: International, 1939). See also John Hobson, *Imperialism* (London: Allen J. Unwin, 1916).

5. See Arthur Tourtellot, ed., *Woodrow Wilson: Selections for Today* (New York: Duell, Sloan & Pearce, 1945), p. 131.

6. Jerome D. Frank, *Sanity and Survival: Psychological Aspects of War and Peace* (New York: Random House, 1967), p. 109.

7. This discussion of conflict termination leans heavily on Richard Hart Sinnereich, "An Approach to Adversary Negotiations . . .," unpublished monograph, mimeographed, United States Military Academy, West Point, N.Y.

8. The idea that the military must continually reassess the relative benefits of conflict is an oft-ignored premise from Clausewitz. See Michael Howard's excellent appraisal of *On War* in which he re-examines important elements of Clausewitz that have been largely overlooked; Michael Howard, *Clausewitz* (Oxford: Oxford University Press, 1983).

9. Paul Kecskemeti, "Political Rationality in Ending War," *Annals*, November 1970, pp. 105–15.

10. Donald G. Brennan, ed. *Arms Control, Disarmament, and National Security* (New York: George Braziller, 1961), p. 30.

11. U.S. Arms Control and Disarmament Agency, *Arms Control Report* (Washington, D.C.: U.S. ACDA, 1976), p. 3.

12. Trevor N. Dupuy and Gay M. Hammerman, eds. *A Documentary History of Arms Control and Disarmament* (Dunn Loring, Va.: T. N. Dupuy Associates, 1973), pp. 301–8.

13. Ibid., pp. 379–81.

14. Henry Kissinger, *The White House Years* (Little, Brown, 1979), pp. 130–38.

15. John Newhouse, *Cold Dawn: The Story of SALT* (New York: Holt, Rinehart & Winston, 1973), pp. 41–43.

16. Ibid., p. 24.

17. Ibid., p. 246.

18. Ibid., p. 176.

19. Ibid., pp. 176–80.

20. A concise description of the SALT negotiations is found in U.S. Arms Control and Disarmament Agency, *Arms Control, 1979*, Publication 104 (Washington, D.C.: U.S. ACDA, 1980).

21. Ibid., p. 6.

22. Ibid.

23. Ibid.

24. Ibid., pp. 47–49.

25. J. Martenson, "A Review of Progress in Disarmament: 1975–1980," *International Atomic Energy Agency Bulletin* 22, no. 3-4 (August 1980): 87.

26. B. Goldschmidt, "The Negotiation of the Non-Proliferation Treaty," *International Atomic Energy Agency Bulletin* 22, no. 3-4 (August 1980): 73.

27. Barry M. Blechman, "Do Negotiated Arms Limitations Have a Future?" *Foreign Affairs* 59, no. 1 (fall 1980): 104.

28. Ibid., pp. 119, 125.

CHAPTER 24

1. See, for example, James R. Schlesinger, "U.S. National Security Challenges for the 1980s," in *The Future of Conflict in the 1980s*, ed. William J. Taylor, Jr., and Steven A. Maaranen (Lexington, Mass.: Lexington Books, 1983), pp. 11–18.

2. See, for example, Stanley Hoffman, *Primacy or World Order* (New York: McGraw-Hill, 1978); David A. Baldwin, ed., *America in an Interdependent World* (Hanover, N.H.: University Press of New England, 1976); Richard Rosecrance, ed., *America as an Ordinary Country* (Ithaca: Cornell University Press, 1976); and William J. Taylor, Jr., *The Future of Conflict: U.S. Interests.* CSIS Washington Paper no. 91 (New York: Frederick A. Praeger, 1982).

3. For an informative discussion of bipolarity in the international system, see Joseph L. Nogee, "Polarity: An Ambiguous Concept," *Orbis* 18 (winter 1975).

4. For relevant treatments, see Joan Edelman Spero, *The Politics of International Economic Relations* (New York: St. Martin's, 1977), esp. chaps. 5–9; and C. Fred Bergsten and Lawrence B. Krause, eds., *World Politics and International Economics* (Washington, D.C.: Brookings Institution, 1975).

5. See, for example, the data in International Institute for Strategic Studies, *The Military Balance, 1982–83* (London: IISS, 1982); and Ray S. Cline, *World Power Trends and U.S. Foreign Policy for the 1980s* (Boulder, Colo.: Westview Press, 1980).

6. For differing views on this question, see Robert Tucker, *Inequality of Nations* (New York: Basic Books, 1977); and Edward L. Morse, *Modernization and the Transformation of International Relations* (New York: Free Press, 1976).

7. See J. David Singer and Melvin Small, *The Wages of War* (New York: John Wiley, 1972).

8. For a comprehensive discussion of what this would entail plus some applications to the U.S. position, see John Collins, *Grand Strategy* (Annapolis: Naval Institute Press, 1973).

9. See Bernard Brodie, *Escalation and the Nuclear Option* (Princeton: Princeton University Press, 1966).

10. R. J. Rummel, *Peace Endangered: The Reality of Detente* (Beverly Hills, Calif.: Sage, 1976), provides an especially impressive analysis of this prospect.

11. See *United States Foreign Policy, 1969–1970: A Report of the Secretary of State* (Washington, D.C.: U.S. Department of State, 1971), pp. 35–37.

12. Henry Kissinger, *The White House Years* (Boston: Little, Brown, 1979), p. 166.

13. William Watts and Lloyd A. Free, "Nationalism, Not Isolationism," *Foreign Policy,* no. 24 (fall 1976); and Daniel Yankelovich, "Cautious Internationalism: A Changing Mood toward U.S. Foreign Policy," *Public Opinion* 1 (March-April 1978).

14. Raymond Aron, *The Imperial Republic: The United States and the World, 1945–1973,* trans. Frank Jellinek (Englewood Cliffs, N.J.: Prentice-Hall, 1974).

15. See John Collins and Anthony Cordesman, *Imbalance of Power* (San Rafael, Calif.: Presidio Press, 1978); and Harland B. Moulton, *From Superiority to Parity* (Westport, Conn.: Greenwood Press, 1973).

16. See Alan Ned Sabrosky, "America and the Asian Power Game," *Seapower,* January-February 1979.

17. Edward N. Luttwak, *The Grand Strategy of the Soviet Union* (New York: St. Martin's Press, 1983), p. 29.

18. The classic statement of this dilemma appears in Alexis de Tocqueville, *Democracy in America,* ed. J. P. Mayer and trans. George Lawrence (Garden City, N.Y.: Doubleday, 1969), pp. 228–29.

19. See the discussion of American "moodiness" in Gabriel A. Almond, *The American People and Foreign Policy* (New York: Praeger, 1960), pp. 53–68. For an analysis of the current dichotomy in American mood that shuns intervention in prolonged conflicts and, simultaneously, seeks to flex American muscle in "quick and dirty" operations, see Philip Geyelin, "A Desert Doesn't Look like a Quagmire," *Washington Post,* August 14, 1983, p. C8.

20. See David C. Gompert et al., *Nuclear Weapons and World Politics: Alternatives for the Future* (New York: McGraw-Hill, 1977), pp. 83–88.

21. For data pertaining to Soviet emphasis given to warfare in a nuclear environment, see Maj. John P. Rose, "The Battlefield Threat: Soviet Concepts, Doctrine and Strategy," *Air Defense Magazine,* July-September 1978; Leon Gouré, Foy D. Kohler, and Mose L. Harvey, *The Role of Nuclear Forces in Current Soviet Strategy* (Miami: Center for Advanced International Studies, University of Miami, 1974); William R. Van Cleave, "Soviet Doctrine and Strategy: A Developing American View," in *The Future of Soviet Military Power,* ed. Lawrence L. Whetten (New York: Crane, Russak, 1976); and Joseph D. Douglass, Jr., *The Soviet Theater Nuclear*

Offensive (Colorado Springs, Colo.: U. S. Air Force Academy, n.d.).

22. See International Institute for Strategic Studies, *Strategic Survey, 1979* (London: IISS, 1980), p. 116.

23. See Herman Kahn, "U.S. Strategic Security in the 1980s," *Hudson Institute Perspective Series,* HPS Paper no. 3 (Croton-on-Hudson, N.Y.: August 1980), p. 1.

24. For recent discussions of the AVF, see William J. Taylor, Jr., et al., eds., *Defense Manpower Planning: Issues for the 1980s* (New York: Pergamon Press, 1981); and Andrew J. Goodpaster et al., *Toward a Consensus on Military Service,* Report of the Atlantic Council's Working Group on Military Service (New York: Pergamon Press, 1982).

25. A variant on this appears in Ray S. Cline, "A New Grand Strategy for the United States,"· *Comparative Strategy* 1 (1978).

26. See the discussion of the greater flexibility inherent in naval forces in James D. Hessman, "A Bipartisan Recommendation for Naval Supremacy," *Seapower,* June 1978, p. 22.

27. See Robert H. Kupperman and William J. Taylor, Jr., eds., *Strategic Requirements for the Army to the Year 2000* (Boulder, Colo.: Westview Press, 1984).

28. Drew Middleton, "Pentagon Likes Budget Proposal, but Questions Specifics," *New York Times,* March 13, 1981, p. A-14.

29. See Melvin R. Laird and Lawrence J. Korb, "The Problem of Military Readiness," *American Enterprise Institute Special Analyses* (Washington, D.C.: 1980), p. 25.

30. See George C. Wilson, "Pentagon Regroups for the Leaner Years," *Washington Post,* August 14, 1983, p. A12.

31. Ibid.

32. See Robert B. Pirie, Jr., "An Overview: Military Manpower into the 1980s," in *Defense Manpower Planning,* ed. Taylor, et al., p. xv. See also Richard V. L. Cooper, "The All-Volunteer Force: Status and Prospects of the Forces," in *Military Service,* ed. Goodpaster et al., p. 79.

33. See William J. Taylor, Jr., and Paul R. Ingholt, "Manpower Issues for the 1990s," in *Strategic Requirements,* ed. Kupperman and Taylor, chap. 8.

34. Caspar W. Weinberger, *Annual Report to the Congress, Fiscal Year 1984* (Washington, D.C.: U.S Government Printing Office, 1983), p. 58.

35. Henry A. Kissinger, *Trialogue* 33 (April 1983): 17.

36. For a detailed description of refugee issues, see Michael S. Teitelbaum, "Immigrants and Refugees," *Foreign Affairs* 59 (fall 1980): 21–59.

37. Secretary of State Edmund Muskie, "The United States and World Refugees," Department of State Bulletin Current Policy no. 231 (Washington, D.C.: Bureau of Public Affairs, U.S. Department of State, October 6, 1980).

38. "Somali Relief: US Policy," *Gist* (Washington, D.C.: U.S. Department of State, Bureau of Public Affairs, August 1980).

39. See William Shawcross, "When Governments Burn out while Refugees Suffer," *Washington Post,* August 14,1983, p. C1.

40. Jimmy Carter, "U.S. Interests and Ideals," Department of State Bulletin Current Policy no. 180 (Washington, D.C.: Bureau of Public Affairs, U.S. Department of State, May 9, 1980).

41. Shawcross, "Refugees," p. C5.

42. For an excellent analysis of nuclear proliferation and U.S. policy implications, see Rodney W. Jones, "Nuclear Weapons Proliferation and Future Conflict," in *The Future of Conflict,* ed. Taylor and Maaranen, pp. 81–107.

43. Paul Johnson, "The Seven Deadly Sins of Terrorism," *NATO Review* 28, no. 5 (October 1980): 29.

44. See Robert W. Kupperman and Darrell Trent, *Terrorism: Threat, Reality, Response* (Stanford, Calif.: Hoover Institution Press, 1979).

45. See Johnson, "Terrorism," p. 33; see also Edward F. Mickolus, "Negotiating for Hostages: A Policy Dilemma," in *Contemporary Terrorism: Selected Readings,* ed. John D. Elliot and Leslie K. Gibson (Gaithersburg, Md.: International Association of Chiefs of Police, 1978), pp. 214–20.

46. See Charles A. Russell and Bowman H. Miller, 'Profile of a Terrorist," *Terrorism, An International Journal* 1, no. 1 (1977).

INDEX